NOLO *Your Legal Companion*

"In Nolo you can trust." —**THE NEW YORK TIMES**

Whether you have a simple question or a complex problem, turn to us at:

NOLO.COM

Your all-in-one legal resource

Need quick information about wills, patents, adoptions, starting a business—or anything else that's affected by the law? **Nolo.com** is packed with free articles, legal updates, resources and a complete catalog of our books and software.

NOLO NOW

Make your legal documents online

Creating a legal document has never been easier or more cost-effective! Featuring Nolo's Online Will, as well as online forms for LLC formation, incorporation, divorce, name change—and many more! Check it out at **http://nolonow.nolo.com**.

NOLO'S LAWYER DIRECTORY

Meet your new attorney

If you want advice from a qualified attorney, turn to Nolo's Lawyer Directory—the only directory that lets you see hundreds of in-depth attorney profiles so you can pick the one that's right for you. Find it at **http://lawyers.nolo.com**.

ALWAYS UP TO DATE

Sign up for **NOLO'S LEGAL UPDATER**

Old law is bad law. We'll email you when we publish an updated edition of this book—sign up for this free service at nolo.com/legalupdater.

Find the latest updates at NOLO.COM

Recognizing that the law can change even before you use this book, we post legal updates during the life of this edition at **nolo.com/updates**.

Is this edition the newest? **ASK US!**

To make sure that this is the most recent edition available, just give us a call at **800-728-3555**.

(Please note that we cannot offer legal advice.)

Please note

We believe accurate, plain-English legal information should help you solve many of your own legal problems. But this text is not a substitute for personalized advice from a knowledgeable lawyer. If you want the help of a trained professional—and we'll always point out situations in which we think that's a good idea—consult an attorney licensed to practice in your state.

9th edition

Chapter 13 Bankruptcy

Keep Your Property & Repay Debts Over Time

by Attorney Stephen Elias & Robin Leonard

Ninth Edition	MAY 2008
Editor	LISA GUERIN
Proofreading	ROBERT WELLS
Index	JEAN MANN
Printing	CONSOLIDATED PRINTERS, INC.

Elias, Stephen.
  Chapter 13 bankruptcy : keep your property & repay debts over time / by
Stephen Elias & Robin Leonard. -- 9th ed.
      p. cm.
  Includes index.
  ISBN-13: 978-1-4133-0855-6 (pbk.)
  ISBN-10: 1-4133-0855-4 (pbk.)
  1. Bankruptcy--United States--Popular works. I. Leonard, Robin. II. Title.
KF1524.85.L46 2008
346.7307'8--dc22

                                                            2007047030

Quantity sales: For information on bulk purchases or corporate premium sales, please
contact the Special Sales Department. For academic sales or textbook adoptions, ask for
Academic Sales. 800-955-4775, Nolo, 950 Parker Street, Berkeley, CA 94710.

Acknowledgments

Robin Leonard gratefully acknowledges the following people.

Barbara McEntyre, a bankruptcy attorney in San Rafael, California. Barbara is a smart, competent, and extraordinarily ethical lawyer. Barbara was incredibly generous and gracious in sharing her time and knowledge with me, including meticulously reading the manuscript and sending me detailed comments. I am honored to be able to call her a friend.

Joan and Bob Leonard. Mom and Dad let me live in their house for nearly a month, 3,000 miles from my own home, away from telephone calls, meetings, and the stress of day-to-day work life so I could actually write this book.

Mary Randolph, Senior Legal Editor at Nolo. Mary is the perfect editor. Her ability to take a good, but disorganized submission and turn it into a great and easy-to-use guide made writing the second, third, and fourth drafts pleasurable.

Steve Elias would like to thank:

Lisa Guerin for her unparalleled editing skills.

The Nolo production and marketing staff for their creative skills and hard work in producing and distributing this book.

The National Association of Consumer Bankruptcy Attorneys for their wonderful conferences that helped me understand how Chapter 13 works under the new bankruptcy laws.

Table of Contents

Part I: Is Chapter 13 Right for You?

Part II: Filing for Chapter 13 Bankruptcy

Part III: Making Your Plan Work

Glossary

Appendixes

C Charts 453

Index

Is Chapter 13 Right for You?

How Chapter 13 Works

Chances are good that you've picked up this book because your debts have become overwhelming. Maybe you are facing foreclosure on your home, repossession of your car, or constant letters and phone calls from debt collectors. Or perhaps, you've realized that your debts have grown far beyond your ability to repay them, and you're wondering if there's anything you can do to get back in control of your finances.

Chapter 13 bankruptcy could be the best way to resolve your debt problems. When you file for Chapter 13, you agree to repay all or a portion of your debts over time, under the supervision of the bankruptcy court. Chapter 13 allows you to keep your property while using your income to repay some or all of your debts. In contrast, Chapter 7 bankruptcy allows you to immediately wipe out many debts, but in exchange, you must give up any property you own that isn't protected by state or federal exemption laws. (You'll find more information on Chapter 7, including how to decide whether Chapter 7 or Chapter 13 bankruptcy is the better remedy for your debt problems, in "Is Chapter 13 Right for You?" below.)

This book explains every step in the Chapter 13 process, including who can use Chapter 13, how to file the necessary papers, and how to come up with a workable repayment plan. To help you get started, this chapter provides an overview of Chapter 13 bankruptcy—how it works and what it will do for you. It also explains other types of bankruptcy relief and options for dealing with your debts outside of bankruptcy.

An Overview of Chapter 13 Bankruptcy

Chapter 13 can be a good solution for people who need time to pay off certain debts and who have enough income to meet the Chapter 13 requirements. In Chapter 13, you get to keep all of your property, regardless of its value. However, you will have to pay your unsecured debtors (those to whom you owe credit card debts, medical debts, and most court judgments, for example) the value of the property you would lose if you filed for Chapter 7 bankruptcy.

If you are facing foreclosure on your home, Chapter 13 provides a powerful remedy. You can keep your home by proposing a feasible repayment plan that includes your missed payments, as long as you stay current on your mortgage. And that's not all: Legislation pending in Congress may even allow the bankruptcy judge to modify your loan to make your current payments more affordable. To find out whether this legislation has become law, check out Nolo's Bankruptcy Blog: Select "Blogs" from our home page, www.nolo.com.

Here is a brief overview of the Chapter 13 bankruptcy process, from start to finish.

Costs

Everyone who files for Chapter 13 bankruptcy has to pay the filing fee of $274, due either when you file your initial bankruptcy paperwork or in four equal installments (with the court's permission). You'll also have to pay a fee—typically about $100 total—to the credit counseling agency where you receive your mandatory prefiling credit counseling and postfiling budget counseling. If you decide to hire a lawyer to help you with your case, you can expect to pay an additional $2,500 or more. You won't have to come up with the entire lawyer's fee all at once, but you will probably have to make a sizable initial payment (maybe $750–$1,000) and pay the rest off over the course of your plan.

If you decide to handle your own case (as an increasing number of people do), you most likely will need to pay for some assistance or information. This will typically consist of one or more of the following:

- one or more self-help law books on Chapter 13 bankruptcy, including this one (roughly $30–$50 a pop)
- consultation with a lawyer (roughly $100–$200 an hour), and
- clerical assistance (help completing your forms) from a bankruptcy petition preparer (roughly $125–$250).

Filing Your Papers

To begin a Chapter 13 bankruptcy, you fill out a packet of forms in which you disclose your property, debts, and economic transactions during the several years before you file. If you are familiar with Chapter 7 bankruptcy, the official forms for Chapter 13 are pretty much the same.

In addition, you must prepare or produce:

- A form (Form 22C: *Chapter 13 Statement of Current Monthly Income and Calculation of Commitment Period and Disposable Income*) that determines whether your income is more or less than the median income in your state. This calculation determines how long your repayment plan must last. If your income is more than the median, your plan must last five years; if your income is less, you can propose a three-year plan. If your income is more than the median, you must also use this form to calculate how much disposable income you will have available to commit to your plan over the five-year period.

- Your Chapter 13 repayment plan, showing how you propose to pay your mandatory debts (child support, tax arrearages, and so on) and some or all of your other debts over the three- to five-year period. (See Ch. 8 for help creating a repayment plan that the court will approve.)

- A certificate showing you have participated in a credit counseling program during the 180-day period before filing for bankruptcy (this requirement is explained in Ch. 9). If the credit counseling agency comes up with a proposed repayment plan that would allow you to pay your debts outside of bankruptcy, you must submit this as well.

- Pay stubs received from your employer during the 60-day period before you file, along with an accompanying court form.

- Proof that you've filed your federal and state income tax returns for the previous four years.

- A copy of your most recent IRS income tax return (or a transcript of that return).

Chs. 7 through 9 take you through the form preparation and filing process, step by step.

The Repayment Plan

When you file for Chapter 13, you must submit a repayment plan. This plan must demonstrate that you can pay your mandatory debts, and perhaps repay all or a portion of your other debts, over the three- or five-year repayment period.

Reducing Your Secured Debts

Chapter 13 allows you to reduce the amount you owe on certain secured debts to the value of the collateral. For instance, if you owe $20,000 on a car that is worth only $15,000, you can reduce the debt to $15,000 and pay off that amount in equal installments over the life of your Chapter 13 repayment plan. This remedy, called a "cramdown," makes it easier to keep some kinds of collateral and still propose a plan that the judge will confirm.

Currently, you can't use Chapter 13 to cram down mortgages or other liens on your home. Legislation pending in Congress to combat the subprime loan crisis may change this law and authorize bankruptcy judges to apply cramdown rules to mortgages. To find out the current state of the law, check our bankruptcy blog at www.nolo.com (select "Blogs").

Even under the current law, you can sometimes get rid of liens on your home using Chapter 13. This might be an option if the current value of your home is less than or equal to what you owe on your first mortgage, leaving no equity to secure second and third mortgages. In this situation, you can use Chapter 13 to "strip off" the other mortgages and reclassify these obligations as unsecured debts that need not be paid off in full in your Chapter 13 bankruptcy. For more information on cramdowns, see Ch. 7 (disclosing liens in your bankruptcy forms) and Ch. 8 (reclassifying a debt or a portion of it as unsecured).

Which Debts Must Be Repaid

Chapter 13 requires you to pay some of your debts in full—and as much of your remaining debts as you can—from the income you have available. Generally, you will have to be able to show, at the beginning of your case, that you are likely to have enough income to remain current on debts that secure collateral you want to keep (for example, a mortgage or car note) while paying off your back taxes, back child support owed to a child or ex-spouse, and any mortgage and secured debt arrearages you owe. And, as explained in Ch. 3, your plan also has to allow for total payments to your unsecured creditors that are at least equal to the value of your nonexempt property—the property you would lose in a Chapter 7 bankruptcy.

Of course, if you are willing to sell your home or give back your car, you can minimize the amount of debt you have to repay—and you don't have to pay back all of the back child support you owe during your Chapter 13 repayment period if the support is owed to a government agency rather than your ex-spouse or child.

> **EXAMPLE:** Ken owes $27,000 in back child support. His ex-wife assigned this debt to the local government agency that enforces child support orders when she went on public assistance. Ken doesn't earn much income, and he would not be able to propose a confirmable Chapter 13 plan if he had to pay back the entire child support debt. Because he now owes the debt to a government agency rather than to his ex, however, he doesn't have to repay it all over the life of his plan. The remainder of the debt won't be discharged when his Chapter 13 case is over; he will continue to owe whatever he can't pay back after his bankruptcy case ends.

Length of the Repayment Period

You must propose a repayment plan that lasts for either three or five years, depending on your income. As you'll learn in Ch. 4, the bankruptcy law now imposes a number of requirements on filers whose average monthly income in the six months before they file for bankruptcy is more than the median income in their state. Among other things, these filers must propose a five-year repayment plan.

Filers whose average monthly income for the six-month period is less than the median have the choice of filing for either Chapter 7 or Chapter 13 bankruptcy (as long as they meet the other eligibility requirements and they don't have enough excess actual income to fund a Chapter 13 plan). If they use Chapter 13, these filers may propose a three-year repayment plan, and may use their actual expenses to calculate how much disposable income they will have to devote to that plan.

Filers whose income is more than the median must propose a five-year repayment plan, and must use standard amounts set by the IRS—rather than their actual expenses—to calculate their disposable income. As a result, higher-income filers may have to devote more of their money, for a longer period of time, to repaying their debts.

To learn more about how to calculate your average monthly income, find out whether you are above or below your state's median, and figure out which expenses to use in calculating your disposable income, see Ch. 4.

Coming Up With a Plan the Judge Will Approve

You can't proceed with a Chapter 13 bankruptcy unless a bankruptcy judge approves (confirms) your plan. As mentioned, some creditors are entitled to receive 100% of what you owe them, while others may receive a much smaller percentage or even nothing at all if you won't have any disposable income left over after the mandatory debts are paid. For example, a Chapter 13 plan must propose that any child support you owe to a spouse or child (as opposed to a government agency) will be paid in full over the life of your plan; otherwise, the judge will not confirm it. On the other hand, the judge can confirm a plan that doesn't repay any portion of your credit card debts if you won't have any disposable income left after paying your child support obligations, whether you owe them to your former spouse or to the government.

> **TIP**
> **You may have more—or less—disposable income than you think.** Chapter 13 requires you to commit your "projected disposable income" to repaying your debts over the life of your plan. Some courts calculate your projected disposable income by subtracting your allowable expenses from your average income during the six months before you filed for bankruptcy, which may not give an accurate picture of your current income and expenses. Other courts look at your current income and expenses at the time you file, if those figures more accurately reflect your finances going forward. For more information on calculating your disposable income, see Ch. 5.

The Automatic Stay

When you file for Chapter 13 bankruptcy, the bankruptcy court automatically issues an order preventing most creditors (with some exceptions) from taking action to collect a debt against you or your property. So, for example, if a foreclosure sale of your home or a vehicle repossession is in the works, the stay stops the sale or repossession dead in its tracks. (However, the automatic stay doesn't apply if you've had two previous bankruptcy cases dismissed in the past year.) The automatic stay is discussed in more detail in Ch. 2.

The Meeting of Creditors

Once you file your papers, the court will schedule a meeting of creditors within 20 to 40 days after your filing date—and send notice of this meeting to you and the creditors listed in your bankruptcy papers. You (and your spouse if you have filed jointly) are required to attend. You'll need to bring two forms of identification—a picture ID and proof of your Social Security number.

The creditors' meeting is conducted by the Chapter 13 bankruptcy trustee for your court. No judge is present, and the meeting is held outside of court, often in the nearest federal building. Although the bankruptcy trustee is not a judge, you still have a duty to cooperate with the trustee.

A typical creditors' meeting lasts less than 15 minutes. The trustee will briefly go over any questions raised by the information you entered in the forms. The trustee is likely to be most interested in the fairness and legality of your proposed repayment plan, and your ability to make the payments you have proposed. (See Ch. 8 for more on Chapter 13 plans.) The trustee has a vested interest in helping you successfully navigate the Chapter 13 process because the trustee gets paid a percentage of all payments doled out under your plan.

The trustee will also make sure you have filed your tax returns for the previous four years. If not, the trustee will continue the creditors' meeting to give you a chance to file these returns. Ultimately, you will not be allowed to proceed with a Chapter 13 bankruptcy unless and until you bring your tax filings up to date.

When the trustee is finished asking questions, any creditors who show up will have a chance to question you. Secured creditors will likely attend, especially if they have any objections to the plan you have proposed as part of your Chapter 13 filing. They may claim, for example, that your plan isn't feasible, that you're giving yourself too much time to pay your arrears on your car note or mortgage (if any), or that your plan proposes to pay less on a secured debt than the replacement value of the collateral.

An unsecured creditor who is scheduled to receive very little under your plan might show up, too, if that creditor thinks you should cut your living expenses and thereby increase your disposable income (the amount from which unsecured creditors are paid). This is more likely to happen if you are using your actual expenses to compute your disposable income (as filers whose income is less than the state median are allowed to do) instead of standard expense figures set by the IRS.

Come to the meeting prepared to negotiate with disgruntled creditors. If you agree to make changes to accommodate their objections, you must submit a modified plan. While the trustee won't use the creditors' meeting to rule on any objections raised by the creditors, the trustee may raise these objections on behalf of the creditors later, at your confirmation hearing before the judge.

The Confirmation Hearing

Chapter 13 bankruptcy requires at least one appearance before a bankruptcy judge. (In some districts, the judge comes into the courtroom only if the trustee or a creditor objects to your plan, and you want the judge to rule on the objection.) At this "confirmation hearing," which will be held shortly after the creditors' meeting, the judge either confirms (approves of) your proposed plan or sends you back to the drawing board for various reasons—usually because your plan doesn't meet Chapter 13 requirements. (For example, a judge might reject your plan because you don't have enough income to pay off your priority creditors and stay current on your secured debts, such as a car note or mortgage.)

You are entitled to amend your proposed plan until you get it right or the judge decides that it's hopeless. Each amendment requires a new confirmation hearing and appropriate written notice to your creditors. (For more information on the confirmation hearing and how to amend your plan and serve your creditors, see Ch. 10.) Once your plan is confirmed, it will govern your payments for the three- to five-year repayment period.

Possible Additional Court Appearances

If your plan is drafted correctly from the beginning, your confirmation hearing will probably be the only time you have to appear before the bankruptcy judge.

However, you may need to make one or more additional appearances in court to:

- confirm your repayment plan if you later amend it
- value an asset, if your plan proposes to pay less for a car or other property than the creditor thinks it's worth (this might happen if you try to "cram down" the debt to the item's current value)
- respond to requests by a creditor or the trustee to dismiss your case or amend your plan
- respond to a creditor who opposes your right to discharge a particular debt (perhaps claiming that you incurred the debt through fraud)
- discharge a type of debt that can be discharged only if the judge decides that it should be (for example, to discharge a student loan because of hardship)
- eliminate a lien on your property that will survive your Chapter 13 bankruptcy unless the judge removes it, or
- reaffirm a debt that would otherwise not survive your bankruptcy.

Many of these procedures are covered in Ch. 11.

SEE AN EXPERT

You'll need to talk to a lawyer. For the best possible outcome, you will probably find it necessary to hire an attorney if any of these court appearances are required. While some judges and trustees may be helpful, we're sorry to say that many will make every attempt to make your life difficult—and bully you into hiring a lawyer—if you try to go it alone. See Ch. 15 for information on finding and working with a bankruptcy lawyer.

Making Your Payments Under the Plan

You are required to make your first payment under your proposed repayment plan within 30 days after you file for bankruptcy. If the bankruptcy court ultimately confirms your plan, your payment will be distributed to your creditors in accordance with the plan's terms. If your Chapter 13 bankruptcy never gets off the ground, the trustee will return the money to you, less administrative expenses.

Once your plan is confirmed, you will make payments, usually monthly, to the bankruptcy trustee, an official appointed by the bankruptcy court to oversee your case. The trustee will usually require you to agree to an order that takes the payments directly out of your bank account or paycheck. The trustee uses your monthly payments to pay the creditors in accordance with the payment order contained in your plan. The trustee also collects a statutory fee (roughly 8% to 10% of the amount you will pay under your plan).

If you can show that you have a history of regular income spread out in uneven payments over the year— for example, quarterly royalty payments or predictable seasonal income fluctuations (for instance, if you do construction work in a location that has severe winters)—your plan may provide for payments when you typically earn income, rather than every month.

If Something Goes Wrong

Three to five years is a long time. What happens if you can't make a payment or it becomes apparent— perhaps because of a change in your income or life circumstances—that you won't be able to complete your plan? If you miss only a payment or two, you can usually arrange with the trustee to make up the difference. If you lose your income stream, however, and you definitely won't be able to complete the plan, you can convert your bankruptcy to Chapter 7 (if that makes sense) or perhaps obtain a "hardship" Chapter 13 discharge from the court. In many cases, Chapter 13 bankruptcies that don't work out are dismissed entirely.

If your case is dismissed, you'll owe your creditors the balances on your debts from before you filed your Chapter 13 case, less the payments you made, plus the interest that accrued while your Chapter 13 case was open. See Ch. 13 for more on what happens if you are unable to complete your plan.

Personal Financial Management Counseling

Before you make your last plan payment, you'll have to complete a personal financial management counseling course (called budget counseling)—and file an official form certifying that you did so—in order to get your discharge. This counseling covers basic budgeting, managing your money, and using credit responsibly. See Ch. 10 for more on this requirement.

After You Complete Your Plan

Once you complete your plan, certify that you've remained current on your child support or alimony obligations, and file proof that you've completed your personal financial management counseling, your remaining debts will be discharged, if they are the type of debts that can be discharged in Chapter 13. (See "Which Debts Are Discharged in Chapter 13 Bankruptcy," below, for more information.) For instance, if you have $40,000 in credit card debt, and you pay off $10,000 through your repayment plan, the remaining $30,000 will be discharged once you complete the plan. However, you will still owe whatever is left of the debts that you can't, by law, discharge in Chapter 13. Debts that you can't discharge include domestic support obligations and student loans (unless you can show that repaying the loan would cause undue hardship); most types of debts—including credit card debts—are discharged.

> **EXAMPLE:** Karen owes $60,000 in credit card debts, $60,000 in student loans, and $2,000 in alimony. Karen pays off the alimony in full (as required by law) and 10% of her credit card debts and student loans. The remainder of the credit card debts will be discharged, but she will still owe the rest of her student loan debt ($54,000) unless she can convince the judge to order it discharged because of undue hardship.

Which Debts Are Discharged in Chapter 13 Bankruptcy

Not all debts are discharged in Chapter 13 bankruptcy. Of course, if you will repay all of your unsecured debts in full over the life of your plan, no discharge is necessary. But if your plan provides for less than full repayment of your unsecured debts, whatever you still owe may or may not be discharged.

Debts That Are Discharged

As a general rule, whatever you still owe on most credit card debts, medical bills, and lawyer bills is discharged, as are most court judgments and loans. Also, under the new bankruptcy law, debts you owe to an ex-spouse arising from a divorce or separation agreement that are not for support are discharged in Chapter 13 (but not in Chapter 7), as are debts incurred for the purpose of paying taxes.

Debts That Are Not Discharged

Debts that survive a Chapter 13 bankruptcy (unless you pay them in full during the life of your plan) include:
- debts that you don't list in your bankruptcy forms
- court-imposed fines and restitution
- back child support and alimony
- student loans (with rare exceptions)
- recent back taxes
- taxes for years in which you did not file a return, and
- debts you owe because of a civil judgment arising out of your willful or malicious acts, or for personal injuries or death caused by your drunk driving.

Debts That Are Not Discharged If the Creditor Successfully Objects

Some types of debts will survive your bankruptcy only if the creditor files a motion in court to prove that the debt shouldn't be discharged. For example, if a creditor successfully objects to a debt arising from your fraudulent actions or recent credit card charges for luxuries, those debts will be waiting for you after your bankruptcy, unless you managed to pay them all off during your repayment plan.

Is Chapter 13 Right for You?

Some of you won't have a choice between Chapter 7 and Chapter 13 bankruptcy—if you want to file for bankruptcy, you will have to use Chapter 13 and repay some of your debt. (See Ch. 4 to find out whether you'll be limited to Chapter 13.) Likewise, if you don't have a steady income, your only bankruptcy choice is Chapter 7. Many people who have a choice decide to file under Chapter 7, but there are some situations when Chapter 13 will be the better option.

Upper Income Filers Must Use Chapter 13

If your average monthly income during the six months before you file for bankruptcy is higher than the median income for your state, you may not be able to use Chapter 7. If your average income is more than the median, you cannot file for Chapter 7 bankruptcy if your disposable income would allow you to pay your unsecured creditors at least $10,950 over a five-year period (about $182 a month). (See Ch. 4 for more on this "means" test.)

Reasons to Choose Chapter 7

Most people who have a choice traditionally have opted to file for Chapter 7 bankruptcy because it is relatively fast, effective, easy to file, and doesn't require payments over time. It also doesn't require you to be current in your income tax filings. In the typical situation, a case is opened and closed within three to four months, and the filer emerges debt free except for a mortgage, car payments, and certain types of debts that survive bankruptcy (such as student loans, recent taxes, and back child support).

If you have any secured debts, such as a mortgage or car note, Chapter 7 allows you to keep the collateral as long as you are current on your payments. However, if your equity in the collateral substantially exceeds the exemption available to you for that type of property, the trustee can sell the property, pay off the loan, pay you your exemption (if any), and pay the rest to your unsecured creditor. If you are behind on your payments, the creditor can come into the bankruptcy court and ask the judge for permission to repossess the car (or other personal property) or foreclose on your mortgage. As a general rule, however, most Chapter 7 filers are able to keep all their property, either because they don't own much to begin with or because any equity they own is protected by an exemption.

Recent changes in the bankruptcy law have put a few obstacles in the way of Chapter 7 filers. Nevertheless, assuming you qualify, you likely will find it easier —and more effective—to file for Chapter 7 than to keep up with a long-term payment plan under Chapter 13. And if you do file for Chapter 13 and don't keep up with your repayment plan, you will likely get no benefit from having engaged in the Chapter 13 process if you

later convert to a Chapter 7 (unless the court lets you off the hook early for hardship reasons).

> **EXAMPLE:** Frank files for Chapter 13 bankruptcy. His five-year plan includes current payments on his mortgage, repayment of part of his $50,000 credit card debt, and payment in full of a $2,000 back child support debt. Frank remains current on his plan for three years, and then loses his job. In that three-year period, Frank, through the Chapter 13 trustee, paid off $12,000 worth of the credit card debt as well as the child support debt.
>
> If Frank converts his case to Chapter 7, he can discharge all of the remaining credit card debt. But had Frank filed Chapter 7 from the beginning, he could also have discharged the $12,000 that he already paid to the credit card companies under his Chapter 13 plan. If Frank decides to skip Chapter 7 and negotiate a repayment schedule for the remaining $38,000, Frank will at least have made a $12,000 dent in the original $50,000 debt by filing for Chapter 13.

The moral of the story is that you should file for Chapter 7 in the first place if:

- you are eligible to use Chapter 7
- you have significant doubts about your ability to complete a Chapter 13 repayment plan, and
- none of the pressing reasons to use Chapter 13 is present in your case (see below).

Reasons to Choose Chapter 13

Although Chapter 7 is easier and doesn't require repayment, there are many good reasons why people who qualify for both types of bankruptcy choose Chapter 13 instead. Generally, Chapter 13 bankruptcy might make sense if you will have adequate, steady income to fund your plan for the appropriate period of time, and are in any of the following situations:

- You are facing foreclosure on your home or your car is being repossessed, and you want to keep your property. Using Chapter 13, you can make up the missed payments over time and reinstate the original agreement. You generally cannot do this in Chapter 7 bankruptcy—instead, you'll ultimately lose the property.

- You have more than one mortgage and are facing foreclosure because you can't make all the payments. If your home's value is less than or equal to what you owe on your first mortgage, you can use Chapter 13 to change the additional mortgages into unsecured debts—which don't have to be repaid in full—and lower the amount of your monthly payments.
- Your car is reliable and you want to keep it, but it's worth far less than you owe. You can take advantage of Chapter 13 bankruptcy's cramdown option (for cars purchased more than 2½ years before filing for bankruptcy) to keep the car by repaying its replacement value in equal payments over the life of your plan, rather than the full amount you owe on the contract (see Ch. 8).
- You have a codebtor who will be protected under your Chapter 13 plan but would not be protected if you used Chapter 7 (see Ch. 2).
- You have a tax obligation, student loan, or other debt that cannot be discharged in bankruptcy, but can be paid off over time in a Chapter 13 plan.
- You owe debts that can be discharged in a Chapter 13 bankruptcy but not in a Chapter 7 bankruptcy. For instance, debts incurred to pay taxes can't be discharged in Chapter 7 but can be discharged in Chapter 13.
- You want to use the Chapter 13 forum to sue one or more harassing creditors for violating state and federal antiharassment laws. For more information on these laws, see *Solve Your Money Troubles*, by Robin Leonard and John Lamb (Nolo).
- You have a sincere desire to repay your debts, but you need the protection of the bankruptcy court to do so.

Alternatives to Bankruptcy

By now, you should have a pretty good idea of what filing a Chapter 13 bankruptcy will involve—and what you can hope to get out of it. Before you decide whether a Chapter 13—or Chapter 7—bankruptcy is the right solution for your debt problems, however, you should consider some basic options outside of the bankruptcy system. Although bankruptcy is the only sensible remedy for some people with debt problems, an alternative course of action makes better sense for others. This section explores some of your other options.

Do Nothing

Surprisingly, the best approach for some people who are deeply in debt is to take no action at all. You can't be thrown in jail for not paying your debts (with the exception of child support), and your creditors can't collect money from you that you just don't have.

Creditors Must Sue to Collect

Except for taxing agencies and student loan creditors, creditors must sue you in court and get a money judgment before they can go after your income and property. The big exception to this general rule is that a creditor can take collateral—repossess a car or furniture, for example—when you default on a debt that's secured by that collateral.

Under the typical security agreement (a contract involving collateral), the creditor can repossess the property without first going to court. But the creditor will not be able to go after your other property and income for any "deficiency" (the difference between what you owe and what the repossessed property fetches at auction) without first going to court for a money judgment.

To secure a money judgment, a creditor must have you personally served with a summons and complaint. In most states, you will have 30 days to file a response in the court where you are being sued. If you don't respond, the creditor can obtain a default judgment and seek to collect it from your income and property. If you do respond—and you are entitled to do so even if you think you owe the debt—the process will typically be set back several months until the court can schedule a trial where you can be heard. In most courts, you respond by filing a single document in which you deny everything in the creditor's complaint (or, in some courts, admit or deny each of the allegations in the complaint).

Much of Your Property Is Protected

Even if creditors get a money judgment against you, they can't take away such essentials as:

- basic clothing
- ordinary household furnishings
- personal effects
- food
- Social Security or SSI payments necessary for your support
- unemployment benefits
- public assistance
- bank accounts with direct deposits from government benefit programs, and
- 75% of your wages (but more can be taken to pay child support judgments).

The state exemptions described in Ch. 4 (and listed in Appendix A) apply whether or not you file for bankruptcy. Even creditors who get a money judgment against you can't take these protected items. (However, neither the federal bankruptcy exemptions nor the California system 2 exemptions apply if a creditor sues you: Those are bankruptcy-only exemptions.)

When You Are Judgment Proof

Judgments are good only if the person who has it—the judgment creditor—can seize income or property from the debtor. If there is nothing to collect, the debtor is said to be "judgment proof." For example, if your only income is from Social Security (which can be seized only by the IRS) and all your property is exempt under your state's exemption laws, your judgment creditor can't take your income. Your life will continue as before, although one or more of your creditors may get pushy from time to time. While money judgments last a long time and can be renewed, this won't make any difference unless your fortunes change for the better. If that happens, you might reconsider bankruptcy at that time.

If your creditors know that their chances of collecting a judgment from you any time soon are slim, they probably won't sue you in the first place. Instead, they'll simply write off your debt and treat it as a deductible business loss for income tax purposes. After some years have passed (usually between four and ten), the debt will become legally uncollectible, under state laws known as statutes of limitation.

These statutes of limitation won't help you if the creditor sues or renews its judgment within the time limit, but most won't. Lawsuits typically cost thousands of dollars in legal fees. If a creditor decides, on the basis of your economic profile, not to go to court at the present time, it is unlikely to seek a judgment down the line to extend its claims. In short, because creditors are reluctant to throw good money after bad, your poor economic circumstances might shield you from trouble.

CAUTION

Don't restart the clock. The statute of limitations can be renewed if you revive an old debt by, for example, admitting that you owe it or making a payment. As soon as you acknowledge a debt, the clock starts all over again. Savvy creditors are aware of this loophole and may try to trick you into admitting the debt so they can sue to collect it. Sometimes, it might be a good idea to try to repay a debt, particularly one to a local merchant with whom you wish to continue doing business. But unless you are planning to make good on the debt or try to negotiate a new payment schedule, you should avoid any admissions.

Stopping Bill Collector Harassment

Many people are moved to file for bankruptcy to stop their creditors from making harassing telephone calls and writing threatening letters. As explained above and in Ch. 2, the automatic stay stops most collection efforts as soon as you file for bankruptcy. However, you don't have to start a bankruptcy case to get annoying creditors off your back. Federal law forbids collection agencies from threatening you, lying about what they can do to you, or invading your privacy. And many state laws prevent original creditors from taking similar actions.

Under federal law, you can legally force collection agencies to stop phoning or writing you by simply demanding that they stop, even if you owe them a bundle and can't pay a cent. (This law is the federal Fair Debt Collections Practices Act, 15 U.S.C. §§ 1692 and following.) For more information, see *Solve Your Money Troubles*, by Robin Leonard and John Lamb (Nolo). Here's a sample letter asking a creditor to stop contacting the debtor.

Sample Letter Telling Collection Agency to Stop Contacting You

Sasnak Collection Service
49 Pirate Place
Topeka, Kansas 69000

November 11, 2008

Attn: Marc Mist

Re: Lee Anne Ito
    Account No. 88-90-92

Dear Mr. Mist:

For the past three months, I have received several phone calls and letters from you concerning an overdue Rich's Department Store account.

This is my formal notice to you under 15 U.S.C. § 1692c(c) to cease all further communications with me except for the reasons specifically set forth in the federal law.

This letter is not meant in any way to be an acknowledgment that I owe this money.

Very truly yours,

Lee Anne Ito

Lee Anne Ito

SEE AN EXPERT

Your debt collector may be putting money in your pocket. The Fair Debt Collection Practices Act places a number of restrictions on debt collector activity. The remedies provided by the act include damages and attorneys fees. More and more attorneys are interested in using these remedies, because they can earn some money without taking it out of their client's recovery. If you are suffering debt collection abuses, consider consulting with a bankruptcy attorney to find out if this type of lawsuit might be worth your while. For more information on the Act and its remedies, see *Solve Your Money Troubles*, by Robin Leonard and John Lamb (Nolo).

Negotiate With Your Creditors

If you have some income, or you have assets you're willing to sell, you may be a lot better off negotiating with your creditors than filing for bankruptcy. Negotiation may buy you some time to get back on your feet, or you and your creditors may agree to settle your debts for less than what you owe.

Creditors hate it when debtors don't pay their debts. They don't like the hassle of instituting collection proceedings, or the fact that these proceedings tend to turn debt-owing customers into former customers. To avoid the collection process and keep customers, creditors sometimes will reduce the debtor's expected payments, extend the time to pay, drop their demands for late fees, and make similar adjustments. They're most likely to be lenient if they believe you are making an honest effort to deal with your debt problems.

TIP

More lenders are offering foreclosure "work outs." As the number of foreclosures has skyrocketed, lenders are increasingly willing to help homeowners keep their homes. These processes, called foreclosure work outs, might include:

- renegotiating the terms of the mortgage so that the arrearage is paid at the end of the mortgage term, either over additional time or as a balloon payment
- renegotiating the interest rate to lower the payments or keep them at the same level (if the interest rate is adjustable and will soon go up), or
- using a deed in lieu of foreclosure, where the debtor gives back the house in return for the lender's agreement not to foreclose and not to go after any additional money the debtor owes on the mortgage.

As soon as you realize that you're going to have trouble paying a bill, write to the creditor. Explain the problem—whether it's an accident, job layoff, divorce, emergency expense for your child, unexpected tax bill, or something else. Mention any developments that point to an improving financial condition, such as job prospects. Also, consider sending a token payment every month (the more the better, of course). This tells the creditor that you are serious about making good on the debt but just can't afford to pay it off right now.

Token payments make a big difference, especially to local creditors. And if you want to keep that credit or business relationship, paying even a small amount might help. On the other hand, if it's been a long time since you've made any payments, you might want to hold off on your token payment until you've checked on the "statute of limitations" for that debt (the state time limit after which the debt goes away if no court action has been filed to collect it). Your payment might have the unfortunate effect of starting up a new limitations period.

Your success in getting creditors to give you time to pay will depend on the types of debts you have, how far behind you are, and the creditors' policies toward debts that are in arrears.

If you are not yet behind on your bills, be aware that a number of creditors have a ridiculous policy that requires you to default—and in some cases, become at least 90 days past due—before they will negotiate better repayment terms. If any creditor makes this a condition of negotiating, find out from the creditor how you can keep the default out of your credit report.

In addition, increasing numbers of creditors simply refuse to negotiate with debtors. Despite the fact that creditors get at least something when they negotiate settlements, many ignore debtors' pleas for help, continue to make telephone calls demanding payment (unless you assert your right under federal law to not receive the calls—see "Stopping Bill Collector Harassment," above), and leave debtors with few options other than to file for bankruptcy. Historically, nearly one-third of the people who filed for bankruptcy stated that the final straw was the unreasonableness of their creditors or the collection agencies hired by their creditors.

You might be wondering whether you should tell your creditors that you are thinking about filing for bankruptcy. After all, shouldn't they be willing to negotiate for a lesser amount—that you can pay—if you can get rid of the debt entirely? Unfortunately, experience shows that this tactic often backfires. Some creditors will call you every day demanding to know who your attorney is. When you tell them you don't have an attorney, they may well take the opportunity to berate you for not paying your debts and warn you to call them when you do get an attorney. In short, mentioning the "B" word is more likely to cause you grief than it is to produce a good result.

Get Outside Help to Design a Repayment Plan

Prior to the new bankruptcy law, the combination of high consumer debt and easy access to information (especially on the Internet) led to an explosion in the number of credit and debt counseling agencies. Some provided limited services, such as budgeting and debt repayment, while others offered a range of services, from debt counseling to financial planning. Now, however, the advent of new requirements for credit-counseling agencies under the new bankruptcy law, coupled with an aggressive auditing policy adopted by the IRS toward "nonprofit" counseling agencies, has significantly changed the credit-counseling landscape.

Credit and Debt Counseling

Before you choose a credit counselor or debt management plan off the Web, be aware that while some of these agencies are legitimate, others are not. How can you tell the difference? The key will be whether the agency has been approved by the Office of the U.S. Trustee to provide credit counseling to bankruptcy filers.

Prior to the new law, Money Management International and its family of Consumer Credit Counseling Services agencies had a good track record of providing consumers nationwide with financial education and credit counseling. Counseling is available by telephone (888-845-5669), on the Internet (www. moneymanagement.org), and in person at one of its more than 130 local branch offices. In addition to the U.S. Trustee requirements, guidelines for these credit-counseling services are provided by the National Foundation for Credit Counseling (NFCC)™ (at www. nfcc.org), the trade organization that created the Consumer Credit Counseling Services (CCCS) network.

Credit Counseling Under the New Bankruptcy Law

The new bankruptcy law requires debtors to complete a credit-counseling course before filing for bankruptcy. To implement this law, Congress has set out a number of requirements for credit-counseling agencies and has designated the Office of the U.S. Trustee to approve and supervise credit-counseling agencies. It's much safer to choose an agency that has been approved by the Office of the U.S. Trustee than an unapproved agency. You can find a list of approved agencies at the U.S. Trustee's website, www.usdoj.gov/ust.

How Debt Management Works

To use a credit counseling agency to help you pay your debts, you must have some steady income. A counselor will contact your creditors to let them know that you've sought assistance and need more time to pay. Based on your income and debts, the counselor, with your creditors, will decide how much you must pay and for how long. You must then make one payment each month to the counseling agency, which in turn will pay your creditors. The agency will ask the creditors to return a small percentage of the money received to the agency office, in order to fund its work. This arrangement is generally referred to as a "debt management program."

Some creditors will make overtures to help you when you're participating in a debt management program such as reducing interest, waiving minimum payments, and forgiving late charges. But many creditors will not make interest concessions, such as waiving a portion of the accumulated interest to help you repay the principal portion of the debt. More likely, you'll get the late fees dropped and the opportunity to reinstate your credit if you successfully complete the program.

Pros and Cons of Debt Management

Participating in a credit counseling agency's debt management program is a little bit like filing for Chapter 13 bankruptcy. But working with a credit or debt counseling agency has one big advantage: No bankruptcy will appear on your credit record.

On the other hand, a debt management program has two disadvantages when compared to Chapter 13 bankruptcy. First, if you miss a plan payment, Chapter 13 will often provide a way for you to make it up and continue to protect you from creditors who would otherwise start collection actions. A debt management program has no such protection, so any one creditor can pull the plug on your plan. Also, a debt management program plan usually requires you to pay your unsecured debts in full, over time. In Chapter 13, you often are required to pay only a small fraction of your nonpriority unsecured debts (such as credit card and medical debts).

Critics of credit counseling agencies point out that the counselors tilt toward signing people up for a repayment plan when they would be better off filing for bankruptcy. This way, the agency gets a commission from the creditors that isn't available in cases that end up in bankruptcy. Under the new bankruptcy law, credit counseling agencies approved by the Office of the U.S. Trustee must follow a number of requirements intended to inform you of your rights and protect against undue influence by creditors. These new rules should prevent you from being ripped off. (See the U.S. Trustee's website at www.usdoj.gov/ust for more on these requirements.)

The Automatic Stay

One of the most powerful features of bankruptcy is the automatic stay: a court order that goes into effect as soon as you file, protecting you from certain actions by your creditors. The automatic stay stops most debt collectors dead in their tracks and keeps them at bay for the rest of your case. Once you file, all collection activity (with some exceptions, explained below) must go through the bankruptcy court—and most creditors cannot take any further collection actions against you while the bankruptcy is pending.

This chapter explains how the automatic stay applies to typical debt collection efforts, including a couple of situations in which you might not get the protection of the automatic stay. It also explains how the automatic stay protects your codebtors from collection activities. And, it covers how the automatic stay workers in eviction proceedings—vital information for any renter who files for bankruptcy.

TIP

You don't need bankruptcy to stop your creditors from harassing you. Many people begin thinking about bankruptcy when their creditors start phoning them at home and on the job. Federal law prohibits debt collectors from doing this once you tell the creditor, in writing, that you don't want to be called. And if you orally tell debt collectors that you refuse to pay, it is illegal for them to contact you except to send one last letter making a final demand for payment before filing a lawsuit. While just telling the creditor to stop usually works, you may have to send a written follow-up letter. (You can find a sample letter in Ch. 1.)

How Long the Stay Lasts

The automatic stay is "automatic" because you don't have to ask the court to issue it, and the court doesn't have to take any special action to make it effective—once you file, the stay is in place, automatically, by operation of law. The stay prohibits creditors and collection agencies from taking any action to collect most kinds of debts you owe them—unless the law or the bankruptcy court says they can. In some circumstances, the creditor can file an action in court to have the stay lifted (called a

"Motion to Lift Stay"). In others, the creditor can simply begin collection proceedings without seeking advance permission from the court.

The stay will remain in effect until:
- the court confirms your Chapter 13 plan (see Ch. 10) or
- your case is dismissed.

The stay ends when the court confirms your Chapter 13 plan because it is no longer necessary. Once the plan is confirmed, it governs all creditor and debtor behavior as to the debts included in the plan. The confirmation is a federal court order (just like the automatic stay), and any attempt by a creditor to collect a debt covered by the plan is a violation of that order.

How the Stay Affects Common Collection Actions

Most common types of creditor collection actions are stopped dead by the stay—including harassing calls by debt collectors, reporting debts to credit reporting bureaus, threatening letters by attorneys, and lawsuits to collect payment for credit card and health care bills.

Home Foreclosures

Many people file for Chapter 13 bankruptcy to prevent their home from being taken in a foreclosure. While the automatic stay will temporarily prevent a foreclosure no matter which type of bankruptcy is filed, the creditor will be able to have the stay lifted—and proceed with the foreclosure—in a Chapter 7 bankruptcy, but the forfeiture can be permanently stopped in a Chapter 13 bankruptcy.

> **EXAMPLE:** Angel owns his home. He has been faithfully making his monthly mortgage payment of $900 for eight years, and has incurred $50,000 worth of credit card debt. In May, 2007, Angel's job at a local telecommunications company is outsourced as part of a monster layoff. He obtains another job at a much lower salary and slowly but surely falls two months behind on his mortgage payments. His lender sends him a three-month notice of intent to foreclose on the mortgage.
>
> Angel visits a bankruptcy lawyer, who explains that he can file for Chapter 7 bankruptcy to wipe

out the credit card debt, but unless he can get current on his mortgage, the lender will probably be able to get permission from the bankruptcy court to proceed with the foreclosure. On the other hand, if Angel files for Chapter 13 bankruptcy, he can not only stop the foreclosure from proceeding, but also buy some time to pay off the arrearage as part of his Chapter 13 plan.

As is true of just about everything related to bankruptcy, there is an exception to this wonderful remedy. The automatic stay won't stop a foreclosure in a Chapter 13 bankruptcy if you filed another bankruptcy case within the previous two years and the court, in that proceeding, lifted the stay and allowed the lender to proceed with the foreclosure. In other words, the law won't allow you to prevent a foreclosure by filing serial bankruptcies.

EXAMPLE: Julie falls three months behind on her mortgage and receives a notice of intent to foreclose from her lender. Julie stops making any further payments and tries to sell her home to recover her remaining equity, but the market has slowed, and she can't find a buyer. Julie files for Chapter 7 bankruptcy to prevent her home being sold at auction (the procedure frequently used in nonjudicial foreclosures). The auction is postponed because of the automatic stay, but the creditor moves to have the stay lifted. The judge grants the motion two months after Julie filed for bankruptcy. The lender sets a new date for the auction.

Julie now files for Chapter 13 bankruptcy, intending to keep her home by paying the arrearage over the life of the plan. Because Julie filed her Chapter 7 bankruptcy within the previous two years, and the stay was lifted in that case, however, the stay will not apply in her Chapter 13 case. The lender will be allowed to proceed with the rescheduled auction.

Even if you are in Julie's position, you may still be able to keep your home. As mentioned, the automatic stay in Chapter 13 cases lasts only until the court confirms the plan filed by the debtor. Once the plan is confirmed, it governs the behavior of debtor and creditor alike. For example, if Julie continues with her

Chapter 13 case, and the court confirms a plan that provides for repayment of the arrearage, the lender will have to abide by the plan and allow her to catch up on her payments.

If your home is sold or auctioned off before your plan is confirmed or the stay ends, you won't be able to get it back. Courts generally will not undo this type of transaction because it would be unfair to the buyer.

Vehicle Repossessions

Vehicle repossessions work in much the same way as foreclosures except that there is typically no advance repossession notice. If you fall behind on your car note and really don't want your car repossessed, you can file for Chapter 13 bankruptcy and schedule to repay your arrearage as part of your plan. If you file your bankruptcy petition before the repossession, the automatic stay will protect your car up until the time the judge confirms a plan that proposes to pay the arrearage. You'll have to include "adequate protection" payments in your proposed plan to cover the depreciation that occurs between the date you file for bankruptcy and the date your plan is finally confirmed. Typically, this means paying the same amount that you would otherwise pay monthly on your car loan.

Even if your car is repossessed before you file, if the judge confirms a repayment plan that provides for payment of the arrearage and the amount you owe monthly on the note, you will be able to get your car back.

Often, a car is worth much less than the debtor owes on it. Unlike homes, cars almost always depreciate in value. This means you may owe more than your car is worth. If you're in this situation, it may not be a bad idea to let the repossession go forward, especially if you bought the car fairly recently.

However, if you bought the car at least 2½ years ago, Chapter 13 gives you an alternative: You can reduce the amount you owe to the replacement value of the car (taking its age and condition into account), plus interest at a relatively low rate. This is called a "cramdown." Even if you can't make your payments under your current car note, your monthly bill might be much more affordable once the loan has been crammed down.

Credit Card Debts, Medical Debts, and Attorney Fees

Anyone trying to collect credit card debts, medical debts, attorney fees, debts arising from breach of contract, or legal judgments against you (other than child support and alimony) must cease all collection activities after you file your bankruptcy case. They cannot:

- file a lawsuit or proceed with a pending lawsuit against you
- record liens against your property
- report the debt to a credit reporting bureau, or
- seize your property or income, such as money in a bank account or your paycheck.

Public Benefits

Government entities that are seeking to collect over-payments of public benefits such as SSI, Medicaid, or Temporary Assistance to Needy Families (welfare) benefits cannot reduce or terminate your benefits to get that money back while your bankruptcy is pending. If, however, you become ineligible for benefits, including Medicare benefits, bankruptcy doesn't prevent the agency from denying or terminating your benefits on that ground.

Criminal Proceedings

If a case against you can be broken down into criminal and debt components, only the criminal component will be allowed to continue—the debt component will be put on hold while your bankruptcy is pending. For example, if you were convicted of writing a bad check and have been sentenced to community service and ordered to pay a fine, your obligation to do community service will not be stopped by the automatic stay (but your obligation to pay the fine will).

IRS Liens and Levies

As explained in "When the Stay Doesn't Apply," below, certain tax proceedings are not affected by the automatic stay. The automatic stay does, however, stop the IRS from issuing a lien or seizing (levying against) any of your property or income.

Utilities

Companies providing you with utilities (such as gas, heating oil, electricity, telephone service, and water) may not discontinue service because you file for bankruptcy. However, they can shut off your service 20 days after you file if you don't provide them with a deposit or other means to assure future payment.

How the Stay Affects Actions Against Codebtors

Many people file for Chapter 13 bankruptcy to protect their codebtors from liability. For example, if your parent cosigns a loan and you file for bankruptcy, you certainly don't want the creditor to enforce the debt against your parent. With rare exceptions, the automatic stay also protects your codebtors unless the court lifts the stay. The court will lift the stay only if:

- your codebtor received the item or services for which the debt was taken (for instance, the car obtained by the loan in question)
- your repayment plan will not pay the debt
- the creditor's interest would be irreparably harmed if the stay were allowed to continue, or
- the debt is a tax debt.

If your Chapter 13 case is closed, dismissed, or converted to Chapter 7 or 11, your codebtor loses the protection of the automatic stay. Also, the stay does not protect a codebtor whose liability for the debt arose in the ordinary course of the codebtor's business.

When the Stay Doesn't Apply

The stay doesn't put a stop to every type of collection action, nor does it apply in every situation. Congress has determined that certain debts or proceedings are sufficiently important to "trump" the automatic stay. In these situations, collection actions can continue just as if you had never filed for bankruptcy. And even in circumstances when the stay would otherwise apply, you can lose the protection of the stay through your own actions.

Actions Not Stopped by the Stay

The automatic stay does not prohibit the following types of actions from proceeding.

Divorce and Child Support

Almost all proceedings related to divorce or parenting continue as before—they are not affected by the automatic stay. These include actions to:

- set and collect current child support and alimony
- collect back child support and alimony from property that is not in the bankruptcy estate (for instance, postfiling income that isn't included in your plan)
- determine child custody and visitation
- establish paternity in a lawsuit
- modify child support and alimony
- protect a spouse or child from domestic violence
- withhold income to collect child support
- report overdue support to credit bureaus
- intercept tax refunds to pay back child support, and
- withhold, suspend, or restrict drivers' and professional licenses as leverage to collect child support.

Tax Proceedings

The IRS can continue certain actions, such as conducting a tax audit, issuing a tax deficiency notice, demanding a tax return, issuing a tax assessment, demanding payment of an assessment, or pursuing a codebtor for taxes owed.

Pension Loans

The stay doesn't prevent withholding from a debtor's income to repay a loan from an ERISA-qualified pension (this includes most job-related pensions and individual retirement plans).

How You Can Lose the Protection of the Stay

Even if the stay would otherwise apply, you can lose its protection through your own actions. The stay won't protect you from collection efforts if you had a previous bankruptcy case that was pending but dismissed within a year of your current bankruptcy filing.

Under the new bankruptcy law, the automatic stay will last only 30 days if you had one prior bankruptcy case pending but dismissed within the year before you file. You can ask the court to extend the stay, but you have to file a motion. And if you had two cases pending but dismissed within the last year, the automatic stay will never kick in at all (unless the court orders it). There are two lessons here for debtors:

- don't let your case be dismissed (a dismissed case counts as a pending case), and
- if your case is dismissed and you want to file again within the year, you should talk to an attorney.

One Dismissal in the Past Year

With a couple of exceptions, if you had a bankruptcy case dismissed during the previous year for any reason, voluntarily or involuntarily, the court will presume that your new filing is in bad faith, and the stay will terminate 30 days after your new case is filed. You, the trustee, the U.S. Trustee, or the creditor can ask the court to continue the stay beyond the 30-day period, but the court will do this only if you (or whoever else makes the request) can show that your current case was not filed in bad faith.

The motion to extend the stay must be scheduled for hearing within the 30-day period after you file for bankruptcy, and must give creditors adequate notice under local motion rules of why the stay should be extended. This means the motion must:

- be filed within several days after you file for bankruptcy (unless you obtain an "Order Shortening Time" from the judge, a simple procedure)
- be served on all creditors to whom you want the stay to apply, and
- provide specific reasons why your filing was not in bad faith and the stay should be extended.

When deciding whether to extend the stay beyond 30 days, the court will look at a number of factors to decide whether your current filing is in good faith. Here are some of the factors that will work against you:

- More than one prior bankruptcy case was filed by (or against) you in the past year.
- Your prior case was dismissed because you failed to file required documents on time (for instance, you didn't give the trustee your most recent tax

return at least seven days before the first meeting of creditors) or amend the petition on a timely basis when required to do so. If you failed to file these documents inadvertently or because of a careless error, that won't help you with the judge—unless you used an attorney in the prior case. Judges are more willing to give debtors the benefit of the doubt here if their attorney was responsible for the mistake.

- The prior case was dismissed while a creditor's request for relief from the stay was pending.
- Your circumstances haven't changed since your previous case was dismissed.

Two Dismissals in the Past Year

If you had more than two cases dismissed during the previous year, no stay will apply in your current case unless you convince the court, within 30 days of your filing, that your current case was not filed in bad faith and that a stay should therefore be granted. The court will look at the factors outlined above to decide whether you have overcome the presumption of bad faith.

Evictions

In the past, many people filed for bankruptcy to stop the sheriff from enforcing a judgment for possession (an eviction order). While landlords could come into court and ask the judge to lift the automatic stay and let the eviction proceed, many landlords didn't know they had this right—and many others didn't have the wherewithal to hire an attorney (or the confidence to handle their own case). In other words, filing for bankruptcy often stopped court-ordered evictions dead in their tracks for the duration of the bankruptcy.

Today, things are a bit different. The new bankruptcy law gives landlords the right to evict a tenant, despite the automatic stay, if:

- the landlord obtained a judgment for possession before the tenant filed for bankruptcy (if the judgment was for failing to pay rent, there is a possible exception to this rule—see below), or
- the landlord is evicting the tenant for endangering the property or the illegal use of controlled substances on the property.

If the landlord does not already have a judgment when you file, and he or she wants to evict you for reasons other than endangering the property or using controlled substances (for example, the eviction is based on your failure to pay rent or violation of another lease provision), the automatic stay prevents the landlord from beginning or continuing with eviction proceedings. However, the landlord can always ask the judge to lift the stay—and courts tend to grant these requests.

If the Landlord Already Has a Judgment

If your landlord already has a judgment of possession against you when you file for bankruptcy, the automatic stay won't help you (with the possible exception described below). The landlord may proceed with the eviction just as if you never filed for bankruptcy.

If the eviction order is based on your failure to pay rent, you may be able to have the automatic stay reinstated. However, this exception applies only if your state's law allows you to stay in your rental unit and "cure" (pay back) the rent delinquency after the landlord has a judgment for possession. Here's what you'll have to do to take advantage of this exception:

Step 1: As part of your bankruptcy petition, you must file a certification (a statement under oath) that your state's laws allow you to cure the rent delinquency after the judgment is obtained, and to continue living in your rental unit. Very few states allow this. To find out whether yours is one of them, ask the sheriff or someone at legal aid (if you have legal aid in your area). In addition, when you file your bankruptcy petition, you must deposit with the court clerk the amount of rent that will become due during the 30-day period after you file.

Once you have filed your petition containing the certification and deposited the rent, you are protected from eviction for 30 days unless the landlord success-fully objects to your initial certification before the 30-day period ends. If the landlord objects to your certification, the court must hold a hearing on the objection within ten days, so theoretically you could have less than 30 days of protection if the landlord files and serves the objection immediately.

Step 2: To keep the stay in effect longer, you must, before the 30-day period runs out, file and serve a

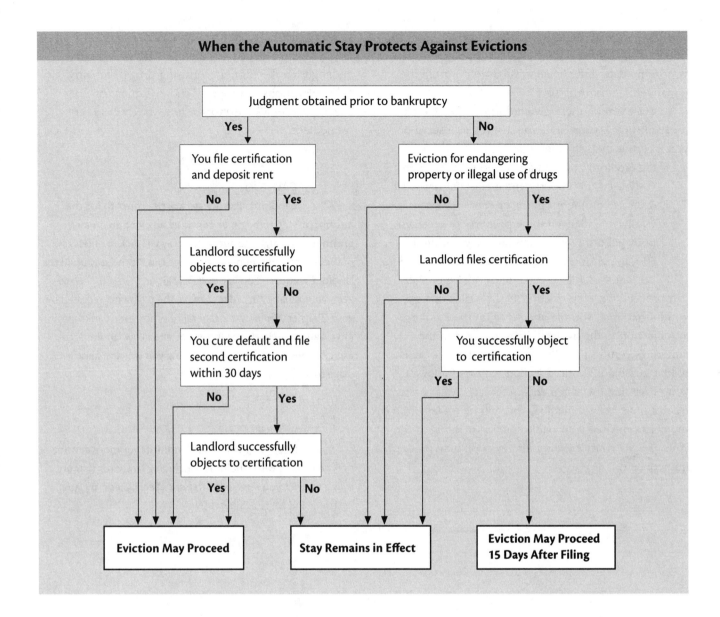

When the Automatic Stay Protects Against Evictions

second certification showing that you have fully cured the default in the manner provided by your state's law. However, if the landlord successfully objects to this second certification, the stay will no longer be in effect and the landlord may proceed with the eviction. As in Step 1, the court must hold a hearing within ten days if the landlord objects.

 SEE AN EXPERT

If you really want to keep your apartment, talk to a lawyer. As you can see, these new rules are somewhat complicated. If you don't interpret your state's law properly, file the necessary paperwork on time, and successfully argue your

side if the landlord objects, you could find yourself put out of your home. A good lawyer can tell you whether it's worth fighting an eviction—and, if so, what tactics to use.

Endangering the Property or Using Controlled Substances

Under the new bankruptcy law, an eviction action will not be stayed by your bankruptcy filing if your landlord wants you out because you endangered the property or engaged in the "illegal use of controlled substances" on the property. And your landlord doesn't have to have a judgment in hand when you file for bankruptcy:

The landlord may start an eviction action against you or continue with a pending eviction action even after your filing date if the eviction is based on property endangerment or drug use.

To evict you on these grounds after you have filed for bankruptcy, your landlord must file and serve on you a certification showing that:

- the landlord has filed an eviction action against you based on property endangerment or illegal drug use on the property, or
- you have endangered the property or engaged in illegal drug use on the property during the 30-day period prior to the landlord's certification.

If your landlord files this certification, he or she can proceed with the eviction 15 days later unless, within that time, you file and serve on the landlord an objection to the truth of the statements in the landlord's certification. If you do that, the court must hold a hearing on your objection within ten days. If you prove that the statements in the certification aren't true or have been remedied, you will be protected from the eviction while your bankruptcy is pending. If the court denies your objection, the eviction may proceed immediately.

As a practical matter, you will have a very difficult time proving a negative—that is, that you weren't endangering the property or using drugs. Similarly, once allegations of property endangerment or drug use are made, it's hard to see how they would be "remedied."

CAUTION

Landlords can always ask the court to lift the automatic stay to begin or continue an eviction on any grounds. Although the automatic stay will kick in unless one of these exceptions applies, the judge can lift the stay upon the landlord's request. You can certainly argue that you need to keep your tenancy in order to make the payments required by your Chapter 13 plan. As a general rule, however, bankruptcy judges are more likely to lift the stay and allow landlords to exercise their property rights, figuring you will find another place to live.

RESOURCE

Need help with your landlord? For more information on dealing with landlords—including landlords that are trying to evict you—see *Every Tenant's Legal Guide*, by Janet Portman and Marcia Stewart (Nolo).

Are You Eligible to Use Chapter 13?

Before you can decide whether you should file for Chapter 13, you need to figure out whether you are legally eligible to do so. Not everyone can use Chapter 13: To qualify, you must meet certain eligibility requirements, and you must be able to propose a legally confirmable repayment plan. This chapter explains these requirements.

Prior Bankruptcy Discharges May Postpone Your Chapter 13 Discharge

You can't get a Chapter 13 discharge if you received a discharge in a previous Chapter 13 case in the last two years, or a discharge in a Chapter 7 case filed within the last four years. You aren't barred from filing for Chapter 13 bankruptcy in these circumstances, but you can't get a discharge until the requisite time has passed. For instance, you can file for Chapter 13 bankruptcy the moment you receive a Chapter 7 discharge (to handle liens that survived your Chapter 7 case or debts that weren't discharged in that case), but you won't get your Chapter 13 discharge until four years have passed since you filed the earlier Chapter 7 case. (Filing for Chapter 13 after filing for Chapter 7 is known colloquially as a "Chapter 20 bankruptcy.")

Business Entities Can't File for Chapter 13 Bankruptcy

To file a Chapter 13 bankruptcy case, you must be an individual (or a husband and wife filing jointly). If you own your own business as a sole proprietor or partner, you can include all business debts on which you have personal liability. You have to file your case in your name, however, not in the name of the business, because a business entity cannot file for Chapter 13 bankruptcy. On your bankruptcy papers, you will need to list all fictitious business names or dba ("doing business as") names that you've used as a sole proprietor or partnership.

If you operate your business as a sole proprietorship or as a partnership with your spouse or someone else, you, or you and your partner, are personally liable for the debts of the business. For bankruptcy purposes, you and your business (or your share of a partnership) are one and the same. You can include all of the business debts in your Chapter 13 bankruptcy case. There is one exception: Stockbrokers and commodity brokers cannot file a Chapter 13 bankruptcy case, even for personal (nonbusiness) debts.

You cannot file for Chapter 13 bankruptcy on behalf of a corporation, limited liability company (LLC), or partnership as such. If you want to file a reorganization bankruptcy in that situation, you must file a business Chapter 11 bankruptcy, which is beyond the scope of this book.

Your Debts Must Not Be Too High

You do not qualify for Chapter 13 bankruptcy if your secured debts exceed $1,010,650 or your unsecured debts are more than $336,900. For example, if you owe two million dollars on your home, you can't file for Chapter 13 bankruptcy. The same would be true if you owed $100,000 on a student loan (unsecured), $100,000 on credit card debt (unsecured), and $150,000 on a court judgment due to injuries resulting from your negligent driving (unsecured). If you need help figuring out which of your debts are secured and which are unsecured, see "Classifying Your Debts" in Ch. 4.

You have to include only debts that are both liquidated and uncontingent. A debt is liquidated if you know the exact dollar amount you owe; a debt is uncontingent if you owe it regardless of what happens in the future. For example, you don't have to include a debt that someone says you owe because you caused them property damage or personal injury, unless you have already settled the claim (or lost a lawsuit) for a set amount of money. Until that happens, you don't know how much you owe—and, if the person decides not to sue you, you might not owe anything at all.

You Must Be Current on Your Income Tax Filings

Within several months after you file for bankruptcy, you will have to prove that you filed federal and state income tax returns for the four prior tax years. You can prove this by submitting the returns themselves or transcripts of the returns obtained from the IRS. You have to give the returns or transcripts to the trustee (the court official handling your case on behalf of the court) no later than the date set for your first meeting of creditors (about a month after you file). The trustee can keep the creditors' meeting open for up to 120 days to give you time to file the returns, and the court can give you an additional 30 days. Ultimately, if you don't produce your returns or transcripts of the returns or transcripts for those four preceding years, the trustee will ask the court to dismiss your Chapter 13 case.

In addition to getting current on your tax returns, you have to produce your most recent federal tax return for the trustee no later than seven days before the first date set for the meeting of creditors. You can obtain a transcript of your returns from the IRS within two weeks. To arrange for this, call 800-829-1040 or submit IRS Form 4506T, *Request for Transcript of Tax Return* (you can find a copy at www.irs.gov).

During the course of your plan, you must remain current on your tax filings and must provide the trustee—and any creditor who requests it—with a copy. Failure to do so can result in your bankruptcy case being dismissed.

You Must Keep Making Your Child Support and Alimony Payments

Even if you owe back child support or alimony, you must meet your current support obligations during the course of your plan. If you don't keep up with your payments, your bankruptcy can be dismissed.

You Must File Annual Income and Expense Reports

You are required to file annual income and expense reports in order to keep your Chapter 13 case alive. Failure to file these reports can result in your case being dismissed.

Your Proposed Repayment Plan Must Pay All Required Debts

Certain debts must be paid in full in a Chapter 13 plan. If your current monthly income, less reasonable living expenses, won't allow you to pay off those debts within the required plan period (three years for people whose incomes are less than the state median and five years

for people whose incomes are more), then the court will not confirm your plan. Ch. 5 explains the process you must use to determine whether you can propose a confirmable Chapter 13 plan over the appropriate time period.

In addition to your required debts, you must also pay a commission to the trustee, equal to about 10% of the total payments you make under your plan. For example, if you owe $50,000 in back taxes that would have to be paid in your Chapter 13 plan, you must have enough income to pay at least $10,000 a year for five years, plus interest, toward that debt. You would also have to come up with another $1,000 each year for the trustee. And, you would have to be able to show that you could pay your living expenses while making these payments. If the judge doesn't think you'll have enough income to cover all of your obligations, your plan won't be approved.

This section gives a very quick overview of the debts that have to be paid in full in Chapter 13, as this requirement often disqualifies would-be Chapter 13 filers.

Debts That Must Be Paid in Chapter 13

Here are the types of debts that must be paid in full over the course of your Chapter 13 plan. Even if you qualify for a three-year plan (because your income is less than your state's median), you may wish to ask the court to allow a five-year plan if you will need that much time to pay your mandatory debts.

Priority Debts

Priority debts are unsecured debts (that is, debts for which you haven't pledged collateral and for which the creditor has not filed a lien against you) that are considered sufficiently important to jump to the head of the bankruptcy repayment line. The general rule is that priority debts must be paid in full over the course of a Chapter 13 case. The most common priority debts that knock people out of Chapter 13 are back taxes and child support arrearages. (However, child support arrearages don't have to be paid in full if you owe the debt to a government agency rather than to your child or former spouse.) See "Classifying Your Debts" in Ch. 4 for a full list of priority debts.

Secured Debts That Will Outlive Your Plan

Your plan must provide that you will keep current on secured debts that will last longer than your repayment plan (such as mortgages). You must also pay off any arrearages you owe during the life of the plan, unless you are willing to surrender the collateral.

Other Secured Debts

All other secured debts must be paid in full under the plan. Typical of such debts are tax liens on your property, promissory notes securing personal property collateral, and judgment liens that can't be removed for one reason or another.

Quick Calculation: Can You Repay Required Debts in Chapter 13?

To determine whether you could pay these mandatory debts over a five-year period, you must find out whether you will have enough income left over each month after paying your reasonable living expenses. (Remember, even though your income may be low enough to make you eligible for a three-year plan, you may propose a five-year plan if it will take you that long to pay off your mandatory debts.) Here's a quick way to figure out whether you can make these required payments:

Step 1: Compute your household's gross income over the past six months, divide it by six, and then multiply it by 60 to come up with your total income for five years. (For help calculating your average monthly income, see Ch. 1.)

Step 2: Compute your actual monthly living expenses, including monthly installment payments on your car and other property necessary for your family's welfare, and multiply by 60.

Step 3: Deduct your expenses computed in Step 2 from your income computed in Step 1.

Step 4: Add up all of your priority debts, secured debt arrearages for property you plan to keep, and secured debts, as described in "Debts That Must Be Paid in Chapter 13," above.

Step 5: Subtract your total mandatory debts, as calculated in Step 4, from the total amount of income you will have left over after paying expenses, as calculated in Step 3.

If this amount is a positive number, it means you may have enough income to pay your mandatory debts. If the amount is negative, you may have to make some adjustments, such as giving up property on which you are making payments or lowering your expenses, to propose a confirmable Chapter 13 plan. Remember, however, that your expenses must appear to be reasonable to the court. If your expenses look too low, the court may reject your plan as unreasonable.

 CROSS-REFERENCE
See Ch. 5 for detailed instructions on calculating income, expenses, and repayment obligations. The quick test above is intended to give you a rough idea of which debts have to be paid in full and whether you might be able to pay them, but the actual math is much more complicated (especially if your income exceeds the median income in your state for a household of your size). Ch. 5 takes you step by step through the required income and expense computations and helps you figure out whether you can propose a confirmable Chapter 13 plan.

Your Proposed Payments Must Equal the Value of Your Nonexempt Assets

Many people choose Chapter 13 rather than Chapter 7 because they want to hang on to valuable nonexempt property—that is, property that they would have to surrender to the trustee so it could be sold to raise money for their creditors if they filed for Chapter 7. If you are one of them, here is some bad news: Your plan must propose payments to your nonpriority, unsecured creditors (those to whom you owe credit card debts, medical bills, lawsuit judgments, and so on) that are at least equal to the value of your nonexempt property. This requirement won't affect your ability to file for Chapter 13 bankruptcy unless you have a lot of valuable nonexempt property.

The purpose of this requirement is to protect your creditors. If you were to file for Chapter 7, you would have to turn over your nonexempt property to be sold, and the assets would be distributed to your creditors. By requiring you to pay at least this much to your nonpriority, unsecured creditors over the life of your

Chapter 13 plan, the law ensures that these creditors won't be any worse off than they would have been if you had filed for Chapter 7.

What Is Exempt Property?

Each state has laws that determine which items of property are exempt from creditors, and in what amounts. These items cannot be seized to repay a debt or taken and sold by the bankruptcy trustee in a Chapter 7 case. Property that is not exempt may be taken by creditors or by the trustee in Chapter 7. If you file for Chapter 13 bankruptcy, the trustee won't take your nonexempt property, but your repayment plan must provide that your creditors will be paid at least the total value of that property over the course of your plan. Each state's exemptions are different, and the exemptions that apply to you depend on how long you have lived in the state where you currently reside. Many states exempt "personal effects" (things such as electric shavers, hair dryers, and toothbrushes), ordinary household furniture, clothing, and health aids without regard to their value. Other kinds of property are often exempt only up to a limit. For example, in many states, furniture or a car is exempt to several thousand dollars. Any equity that exceeds the limit isn't exempt. (Equity is the market value of the property minus what you still owe on it, if anything.)

Typically, the following items are exempt:
- part of the equity in motor vehicles (the amount varies from state to state)
- reasonably necessary clothing (no fur coats)
- reasonably necessary household goods and furnishings
- household appliances
- jewelry, to a few hundred dollars
- personal effects
- life insurance (cash or loan value or proceeds, in an amount that varies from state to state)
- part of the equity in a residence (the amount varies from state to state)
- pensions
- public benefits
- tools of a trade or profession, to a certain value, and
- unpaid earned wages.

For detailed information on exemptions, see Ch. 5.

To know for sure whether you have nonexempt property that might interfere with your ability to propose a confirmable Chapter 13 plan, you'll need to skip to Ch. 5 and read the discussion of exemptions. Then, go to the exemption lists in Appendix A and compare your property (or the value of your property) with the state or federal exemptions available to you. If you do have nonexempt property, you'll have to revisit your income and expense figures (from "Quick Calculation: Can You Repay Required Debts in Chapter 13?" above) and figure out whether you'll have enough income left over, after subtracting expenses and the amount you'll have to pay for your mandatory debts, to make payments to your other creditors that at least equal the value of your nonexempt property.

EXAMPLE 1: Jane and John are considering filing for Chapter 13 bankruptcy. John owes $15,000 in back alimony and child support to his ex-wife and child. Jane owes $20,000 in back taxes. To propose a confirmable Chapter 13 plan, Jane and John must be able to pay at least $35,000—the total of their mandatory debts—over five years. Their average monthly income is $5,000 and their monthly expenses are $4,000, leaving $1,000 a month extra. They divide $35,000 by 60 to figure out how much they'll have to pay on their mandatory debts each month. Because they have $1,000 left over each month and their monthly debt payments will be only $583, Jane and John will be able to pay off their mandatory debts. Plus the trustee's 10% commission (another $58 per month). But what about their nonexempt property?

One of the reasons Jane and John decided to file Chapter 13 was that Jane owns a share of a family summer cabin that has been passed down through the generations. Her share is worth approximately $15,000. Because Jane's share of the cabin is not exempt, Jane and John will have to pay their nonpriority, unsecured creditors at least $15,000 over five years, or $250 a month. This means they'll have to come up with $583 for their mandatory debt, plus $250 for their nonexempt property, plus the trustee's 10% commission (about $83) each month, for a grand total of $916. Because they have extra income of $1,000 a month, they should still be able to propose a confirmable plan.

EXAMPLE 2: Suppose now that Jane and John have only $600 in extra income each month. They can still file a confirmable plan, but only if they are willing and able to earn more income, cut their expenses, or sell Jane's share of the cabin before they file and devote the proceeds to paying off their nonpriority, unsecured creditors through their Chapter 13 plan.

You Must Participate in an Approved Personal Financial Management Course

Although you don't have to take a personal financial management course prior to filing for Chapter 13 bankruptcy, you must complete such a program before the court will discharge your debts. The agencies providing this service must be approved by the Office of the U.S. Trustee, which imposes specific curriculum requirements that are intended to require about two hours of your time. Typically, the agency where you get your prefiling credit counseling will also offer this personal financial management course. For more information about the requirements for these agencies and how to find one, visit the Office of the U.S. Trustee's website at www.usdoj.gov (select "Credit Counseling & Debtor Education" from the home page).

Do You Have to Use Chapter 13?

n October 2005, a massive change took place in the bankruptcy field. Believing that too many people were taking advantage of Chapter 7 bankruptcy to wipe out their debts, Congress passed the Bankruptcy Abuse Prevention and Consumer Protection Act of 2005 (BAPCPA). The stated purpose of this law is to force people who could afford to repay some of their debt to file for bankruptcy under Chapter 13 instead of under Chapter 7. To further this purpose, the BAPCPA makes it harder and more expensive to file under Chapter 7.

Because of the changes wrought by the new bankruptcy law, some debtors no longer have the option to use Chapter 7: If they want to file for bankruptcy, they have to use Chapter 13. However, most people will still have a choice. This chapter will help you figure out whether you have to use Chapter 13, or whether Chapter 7 is still an option for you.

CAUTION

Don't skip this chapter, even if you know you will use Chapter 13. Even if you have already decided to file for Chapter 13 on the basis of information you can trust, make sure to read the instructions for Parts I, II, and III under "The Means Test," below. This information will help you compute your current monthly income and compare that figure to your state's median income. You will need this information to figure out the requirements of your repayment plan in Ch. 5.

Can You Pass the Means Test?

There are two income tests that determine whether you are eligible for Chapter 7 bankruptcy:

- the means test, which compares your average monthly income for the six months before you file for bankruptcy to the median income in your state, and
- the "abuse under all the circumstances" test, which looks at your actual income and your actual expenses to determine whether you have enough money coming in to repay some of your debts.

If you fail the means test, you are presumed to be abusing the bankruptcy laws and will be forced into a Chapter 13 bankruptcy unless you can prove that the law shouldn't be applied to you for some reason. If you fail the "abuse under all the circumstances" test, the Office of the U.S. Trustee—the government agency responsible for policing the bankruptcy system—has the burden of proving your ineligibility for Chapter 7. The only way to know for certain whether your income is too high under either of these tests is to complete a form that all Chapter 7 debtors must complete as part of their bankruptcy, Form 22A: *Chapter 7 Statement of Current Monthly Income and Means-Test Calculation.*

RESOURCE

Prefer to let your computer crunch the numbers? Rather than completing the means test form by hand, you can use an online calculator to run the numbers for you. You'll find an excellent online calculator—as well as many other bankruptcy resources—at www.legalconsumer.com. Just enter your zip code, click the means test link, and away you go.

In the first part of the form, you determine whether your average income (for the previous six months) is more or less than the median income for your state for your household size.

If your income is less than your state's median income. If you earn less than your state's median, you pass the means test and won't be presumed ineligible to use Chapter 7. But, as mentioned above, you might face another hurdle if you file under Chapter 7. If the U.S. Trustee believes that your actual income less your actual expenses leaves you with enough money to repay a reasonable portion of your debt, it will ask the court to find that allowing you to use Chapter 7 would be an abuse of the process. If the court agrees, you'll have to use Chapter 13.

Whether you choose or are required to use Chapter 13, you will have two advantages if your income is less than the state median: You may propose a three-year (rather than a five-year) repayment plan, and you may use your actual expenses—not amounts approved by the IRS—to calculate how much disposable income you will have left to devote to your plan.

If your income is more than your state's median income. If you earn more than the state median, you must take the rest of the means test—by completing the second part of Form 22A—to find out whether you'll have the option of using Chapter 7 or will have to use

Chapter 13. The purpose of this part of the form is to find out whether you would have enough income left over, after subtracting the amounts allowed by the IRS for certain expenses, to pay a portion of your unsecured debts (credit card debts, medical bills, and the like) over a five-year period.

TIP

Business debtors can skip the means test. If your debts are primarily due to your business, you may choose between a Chapter 7 and Chapter 13 bankruptcy, regardless of the outcome of the means test. You are considered a business debtor if more than half of the total value of your debts comes from your business.

The Means Test

SKIP AHEAD

Those who initially filed for Chapter 7 bankruptcy can skip ahead. If you are using Chapter 13 because you initially filed under Chapter 7 and have already taken and flunked the means test, or if the Court has converted your case to Chapter 13, skip to "Forced Conversion to Chapter 13," below.

Remove Form 22A from Appendix B and fill it in, following the instructions below. If you later decide to file under Chapter 13, you can use a lot of the work you do here to complete a similar form (Form 22C: *Statement of Current Monthly Income and Calculation of Commitment Period and Disposable Income*) that you must submit with your Chapter 13 documents.

Part I. Exclusion for Disabled Veterans and Non-Consumer Debts

Line 1a. If all of the facts in the Veteran's Declaration are true of your situation, you can choose between Chapter 7 and Chapter 13 bankruptcy. If you know that you want to file for Chapter 13, however, you still have to calculate your "current monthly income" and compare it to your state's median income. This comparison will determine how long your Chapter 13 plan must last and how much of your disposable income you will have to commit to your plan.

To qualify for the veterans' exclusion, you must have a disability rating of at least 30%, and more than half of your debt must have been incurred while you were either on active duty or performing homeland defense activity.

Line 1B. If the majority of your debts comes from running a business, check the box. Those who have primarily nonconsumer (that is, business) debts don't have to take the means test, and are free to choose between Chapter 7 and Chapter 13 bankruptcy. If the majority of your debts are personal, you have to take the means test to see whether you will have a choice of bankruptcy chapters.

Part II. Calculation of Monthly Income for § 707(b)(7) Exclusion

Line 2a. If you are unmarried, check this box and follow the instructions (complete only Lines 3 through 11 in column A).

Line 2b. If you are married but filing separately because you have separate households, check this box and complete only Lines 3 through 11 in column A. If you check this box, you are declaring, under penalty of perjury, that you are legally separated under the laws of your state or that you are living separately for reasons other than to qualify for Chapter 7 bankruptcy.

Line 2c. If you are married but filing separately for reasons other than those stated in Section 2c, check this box and complete Lines 3 through 11 in columns A and B.

Line 2d. If you are married and filing jointly, check this box and complete Lines 3 through 11 in columns A and B.

CAUTION

Use the right figures. All figures you enter in Lines 3 through 11 must be monthly averages of your actual income during the six months before you file for bankruptcy. The six-month period ends on the last day of the month before the month in which you file your bankruptcy. For instance, if you file on September 9, the six-month period ends on August 31. If you have earned the same amount for each of those six months (for example, because you've held the same job and worked the same hours during that period), then use your monthly income. If your earnings vary, add them up for the six-month period, then divide the total by six to get a monthly average.

Line 3. Enter your average monthly earnings over the last six months for gross wages, salary, tips, bonuses, overtime, and commissions. ("Gross" means before any taxes, Social Security, or other amounts are withheld.)

Line 4. If you operate a business, profession, or farm, you'll need to compute your average monthly expenses for the six-month period and subtract them from your income for that period. The lowest figure you can enter is zero—in other words, you can't enter a loss.

Line 5. Enter your average monthly rental income for the six-month period (if you have any), and deduct ordinary and necessary operating expenses for that same period.

Line 6. Enter your average monthly income from interest, dividends, and royalties over the last six months.

Line 7. Here's where you include your average monthly pension and retirement income. Don't include Social Security retirement benefits.

Line 8. Enter the monthly average of any amounts regularly contributed by someone else to your household expenses. If you are filing separately but your spouse's income is included in column B, don't include any contributions that your spouse makes to your household—his or her income is already being taken into account.

Line 9. Your average monthly unemployment compensation goes here. If you want, you can argue that unemployment compensation should be excluded under the general Social Security exclusion (see *In re Munger,* 370 B.R. 21 (D. Mass. 2007) and *In re Sorrell,* 359 B.R. 167 (S.D. Ohio 2007)) and omit it from columns A and B. However, you'll need to enter the amount you receive in the boxes supplied for this purpose.

Line 10. Insert the average monthly amount you received from any other source. Do not include money or benefits received under the SSI, SSA, or TANF programs. These are Social Security benefits, which are excluded from your current monthly income computation.

Line 11. Compute the subtotals for columns A and B (if used). Remember, these subtotals should reflect an average monthly figure for all of the items you entered in Lines 3 through 10.

Line 12. Add the subtotals for Lines A and B together. This is what the new bankruptcy law calls your "current monthly income." Because it's a six-month average, it might not match your actual monthly income at the time you file, especially if you've had a job loss or become unable to work in the last six months.

Part III. Application of § 707(b)(7) Exclusion

This is where the rubber meets the road: In this Part, you must compare the current monthly income figure you calculated in Part II with the median family income for your state. If your income is more than the median, you'll have to continue filling in the form to figure out whether you are barred from using Chapter 7. If your income is equal to or less than the median, you can skip the rest of the form and file for Chapter 7, if you wish.

Line 13. Convert your monthly figure on Line 12 to an annual figure by multiplying it by 12. This is your current annual income.

Line 14. Enter the median income for your state and household size. Note that your household might be larger than your actual family. For instance, you may have a relative or friend who is living with you as part of your household; if so, include the friend as a household member. The basic test for a household member is whether his or her income and expenses are intermingled with yours; he or she does not have to be your dependent for tax or other government purposes. (See *In re Ellinger,* 370 B.R. 905 (D. Minn. 2007).) The most recent state median income figures as of the date this book is published are in Appendix C. To make sure that you are using the most current figures, however, you should visit the U.S. Trustee's website, www.usdoj.gov/ust, and click "Means Testing Information." Scroll down a bit for the link to the state median income figures.

Line 15. Do the math. If your "current monthly income" exceeds the state median, check the bottom box on Line 15 and continue to Part IV to find out whether you can choose between Chapter 7 and Chapter 13.

If your income is equal to or less than the median, check the top box on Line 15. This means that you aren't banned from using Chapter 7. You don't need to proceed with the form any further. If you decide to proceed under Chapter 13, having an income that doesn't exceed the state median income offers you two big advantages: You can propose a three-year (rather than a five-year) plan, and you can calculate the income you must commit to the plan using your actual expenses rather than expense figures set by the IRS, which are often lower.

TIP

Consider postponing your filing if you want to qualify for Chapter 7. If you conclude, on the basis of your "current monthly income," that you'll have to complete the rest of the forms, think about whether your income will decrease in the next few months. If you recently lost a high-paying job or had a sudden decrease in commissions or royalties, for example, your average income over the past six months might look pretty substantial. But in a few months, when you average in your lower earnings, it will come down quite a bit—perhaps to even to less than the state median. If so, and if Chapter 7 would provide you a better remedy than Chapter 13, you might want to delay your bankruptcy filing.

Part IV. Calculation of Current Monthly Income for § 707(b)(2)

Much of the work you do here will be applicable to Form 22C (described in Ch. 5) if you decide to proceed under Chapter 13.

With a couple of exceptions, the values you will be entering in the form are fairly straightforward. The purpose of the means test is to find out whether you have enough income to pay some of your unsecured, nonpriority debts over a five-year period. (See "Classifying Your Debts," below, for help figuring out which debts fall into this category.)

Line 16. Enter the total from Line 12.

Line 17. If you checked the box on Line 2c (married, not filing jointly, and not making the declaration in item 2b), you can subtract the amount of your spouse's income (as listed in Line 11, column B) that was not regularly contributed to your household expenses or those of your dependents. For example, if Line 11, column B shows that your nonfiling spouse has a monthly income of $2,000, but your spouse contributes only $400 a month to your household, you can enter $1,600 here.

Line 18. Subtract the amount on Line 17 from the amount on Line 16. Enter the total here.

SKIP AHEAD

If you know you will use Chapter 13. If you have already decided to file for Chapter 13 bankruptcy, you can skip the rest of this chapter and continue on to Ch. 5. If you still want to know whether you have a choice between a Chapter 7 and Chapter 13 bankruptcy, continue completing this form.

Part V. Calculation of Deductions From Income

In this Part, you will figure out which expenses you can deduct from your current monthly income. After you subtract all allowed expenses, you will be left with your monthly disposable income—the amount you would have left over, in theory, to pay into a Chapter 13 plan for the benefit of your nonpriority, unsecured creditors.

Subpart A: Deductions Under Standards of the Internal Revenue Service (IRS)

If you have to complete this part of the form—that is, if your current monthly income exceeds the state median income—you are not allowed to subtract all of your actual expenses. Instead, you must calculate some of your expenses according to standards set by the IRS. (The IRS uses these standards to decide how much a delinquent taxpayer should have to give the agency each month to repay back taxes on an installment plan.)

If you eventually decide to file under Chapter 13, you will have to use these same expenses to determine the amount of disposable income you must devote to your plan. (See Ch. 5 for more information.)

Line 19A. Enter the total IRS National Standards for Food, Clothing, and Other Items for your family size and income level. This is the amount the IRS believes you should get to spend for food, clothing, household supplies, personal care, and miscellaneous other items. You can get these figures from www.usdoj.gov/ust. Click "Means Testing Information," then scroll down to find the right link. You also can get these figures from your court clerk.

Line 19B. Enter the amount you are allowed to claim for health expenses from the IRS National Standards for

Out-of-Pocket Health Care. You can find these figures at www.usdoj.gov/ust. Click "Means Testing Information," then scroll down to the appropriate link. As you'll see, you can claim more for household members who are at least 65 years old, which is reflected on the form. You'll also see that the total amount you can claim is quite small; if you spend more than you're allowed to claim here, you can claim it on Line 31.

Line 20A. Enter the amount of the IRS Housing and Utilities Expense Standards, nonmortgage expenses for your county and family size. Get these figures from www.usdoj.gov/ust. Click "Means Testing Information," then scroll down to the IRS Housing and Utilities Expense Standards section and enter your state in the drop-down menu. Find the figures for your county and family size, then enter the figure that appears under the heading "Non-Mortgage."

Line 20B. On Line a, enter the amount of the IRS Housing and Utility Expense Standards, Mortgage/Rent expenses for your county and family size. These figures appear on the U.S. Trustee's website, on the same chart as nonmortgage expenses—follow the instructions for Line 20A, above.

On Line b, enter the average monthly payment for any debts secured by your home, including a mortgage, home equity loan, taxes, and insurance. The average monthly payment is the total of all amounts contractually due to each secured creditor in the five years after you file for bankruptcy, divided by 60.

On Line c, subtract Line b from Line a. This may turn out to be a negative figure—if so, enter a zero in the right-hand column. Later in the means test, you'll be able to add your average monthly payment back in as an expense.

Line 21. If your actual rental or mortgage expense is higher than that allowed by the IRS, you can claim an adjustment here. For instance if the IRS mortgage/rental expense for a family of two is $550, you pay an actual rent of $900, and that amount is average for the area in which you live, enter the additional $350 here and explain why you should be able to subtract it (that you couldn't possibly find housing in your area for less, for example).

Line 22A. You are entitled to claim an expense here whether or not you actually have a car. First, indicate the number of cars for which you pay operating expenses or for which somebody else contributes the operating expenses as part of the amount entered on Line 8. If you don't have a car, enter the amount listed under "Public Transportation" from the IRS Local Transportation Expense Standards. You can find these at www.usdoj.gov/ust; click "Means Testing Information," then scroll down to the appropriate link and choose your region. If you indicated that you have one or two cars, enter the amount listed for your region (and sometimes, your city) under "Operating Costs" in the same chart.

Line 22B. If you have a car and also use public transportation, you may claim a public transportation expense here. You can find the correct amount by following the instructions for Line 22A, above.

Line 23. These are your expenses for owning or leasing a car.

> ⓘ **CAUTION**
>
> **If you aren't making payments, you might face a challenge.** A dispute exists over whether you can claim this expense if you aren't paying for or leasing a car. Some U.S. Trustees (and courts) insist that you can't claim the expense. (See, for example, *In re Bennett*, 371 B.R. 440 (C.D. Cal. 2007) and *In re Cole*, 371 B.R. 454 (W.D. Wash. 2007).) However, the National Association for Consumer Bankruptcy Attorneys has filed briefs arguing that you should be able to, because old cars wear out, and you will need to lease or buy a new car sometime during the next five years. (See, for example, *In re Armistrong*, 370 B.R.323 (E.D. Wash. 2007).)If you aren't making payments on a car and you claim this expense, be aware that the trustee in your case may challenge you if the amount determines whether you pass or fail the means test.

On Line 23a, enter the IRS Local Transportation Standards for ownership of a first car. This amount is actually a national figure; currently, it is $478. To make sure you are using the most up-to-date numbers, check the website of the U.S. Trustee, www.usdoj.gov/ust. Click "Means Testing Information," then scroll down to the Local Transportation Expense Standards drop-down menu and choose your region. The ownership figure is near the bottom of the page.

On Line 23b, enter your average monthly payment (over the next five years) for all debts secured by your first car. For example, assume you have three years left to pay on the car and the monthly payment is $350. The total amount you will owe in the next five years is $12,600 (36 months times $350). If you spread that amount over the next five years—by dividing the total by 60, the number of months in five years—you'll see that your average monthly payment is $210.

On Line 23c, subtract Line b from Line a and enter the result in the column on the right. Later on, if necessary, you will be able to deduct your car payments to figure out whether you have enough disposable income to fund a Chapter 13 plan.

Line 24. Complete this only if you have a second car (and you checked the second car box in Line 23). Follow the instructions for Line 23 to enter the required figures for your second car.

Line 25. Enter the total average monthly expense that you actually incur for all taxes *other than real estate or sales taxes*. Examples of taxes that you should enter here are income taxes, self-employment taxes, Social Security taxes, and Medicare taxes. In some cases, these taxes will show up on your wage stub. You'll need to convert the period covered by your wage stub to a monthly figure. Once you have figured out how much you pay each month for each type of tax, add them all together and enter them in the column on the right.

Converting Taxes to a Monthly Figure

If you are paid weekly, biweekly, or twice a month, you will have to convert the tax amounts on your pay stubs to a monthly amount. And, if you pay quarterly taxes (estimated income taxes, for example), you'll need to convert that figure as well. Here's how to do it:

- Weekly taxes: multiply by 4.3 to get a monthly amount.
- Biweekly taxes: divide by 2 to get a weekly amount, then multiply by 4.3.
- Bimonthly taxes: divide by 2.
- Quarterly taxes: divide by 3.

Line 26. Enter all of your mandatory payroll deductions here, other than those entered in Line 25. Use the conversion rules set out above to arrive at average monthly deductions. Make sure you deduct only mandatory deductions (such as required retirement contributions, union dues, and uniform costs). Contributions to a 401(k) should not be included, for example, because they are voluntary.

Line 27. Enter any monthly payments you make for term life insurance. Do not enter payments for any other type of insurance, such as credit insurance, car insurance, renters insurance, insurance on the lives of your dependents, or whole life insurance on your own life. (Whole life insurance is the type that allows you to borrow against the policy.)

Line 28. Enter the amount of any payments you make pursuant to a court order. Child support and alimony are the most common examples, but you may also have to pay to satisfy a court money judgment or a criminal fine. Do not include court-ordered payments toward a child support or alimony arrearage; only the payments you need to make to stay current should be entered here.

Line 29. Enter the total monthly amount that you pay for education required by your employer to keep your job, and the total monthly amount you pay for the education of a physically or mentally challenged dependent child for whom no public education providing similar services is available. Included in this amount would be the actual costs of after-school enrichment educational services for a physically or mentally challenged child, and the actual educational expenses you are paying in support of an individual educational plan.

Line 30. Enter the average monthly cost of child care. If your employment (and therefore, your need for child care) is seasonal, add up your child care costs for the year and divide the total by 12. Do not equate education with child care. For instance, child care for a child who is of public education school age should cover only the hours before and after school.

Line 31. Enter the average monthly amount you pay for out-of-pocket health care expenses, but only to the extent it exceeds the amount you were allowed to claim on Line 19B. Do not include health care expenses that are reimbursed by insurance or provided by an HMO or by Medicaid. Also, don't include premiums you pay for health insurance; you claim these on Line 34.

Line 32. Enter the average monthly expenses you pay for any communication devices that are necessary for the health and welfare of you or your dependents. Examples provided by the form are cell phones, pagers, call waiting, caller identification, and special long distance or Internet services. Virtually all of these devices arguably are necessary for the health and welfare of your family. However, some expenses might not be allowed (for example, a cell phone you use for your business, or broadband Internet service). When in doubt, list the expense.

Line 33. Add the expenses you entered in Lines 19 through 32 and put the total in the column at the right.

Note: If your average monthly income, as calculated on Line 18, less the expenses totaled on Line 33, is less than $110, you can file for Chapter 7 if you desire. Remember, however, that you can still be forced out of Chapter 7 if the U.S. Trustee successfully argues that your actual income, less your actual expenses, would produce enough disposable income to pay off a significant portion of your unsecured debts over a five-year period. Just what percentage of your unsecured debts would have to be paid off to warrant pushing you into Chapter 13 varies from court to court, but 20% is a pretty good working minimum.

Subpart B: Additional Expense Deductions

The expenses in this Subpart are allowed by the Bankruptcy Code, in addition to the IRS expenses. However, you can't list an expense twice; if you already claimed it in Subpart A, or on Lines 4 or 5 in Section II (business expenses), don't list it again here.

Line 34. Here, list your reasonably necessary monthly expenses for health insurance, disability insurance, and health savings accounts (HSAs) on the lines provided. The form was revised in January 2008 to clarify that you can list a "reasonable" expense here whether you actually pay that amount each month or not. If, however, you pay less than the reasonable amount you list, you must indicate how much you actually spend each month on the additional line provided. If the U.S. Trustee or one of your creditors later wants to challenge your expense claims—for example, to argue that you really have more disposable income than the form indicates—they can use this information.

Line 35. Anything you spend to care for a member of your household or immediate family because of his or her age, illness, or disability can be deducted here. If your contributions are episodic—a wheelchair here, a vacation with a companion there—estimate your average monthly expense and enter it here.

> **CAUTION**
> **Your response here could affect eligibility for government benefits.** Expenses you list here could render the person you are assisting ineligible for Social Security or other government benefits. For example, if you state that you are spending $500 a month for the care of a relative, and that relative is receiving SSI, your relative might receive a lower benefit amount each month, to reflect your contribution. On the other hand, if you are making such expenditures, you are required to disclose them here. If you find yourself in this predicament, talk to a lawyer.

Line 36. The average monthly expense of security systems and any other method of protecting your family should be entered here.

Line 37. If your actual home energy costs exceed the figure you entered on Line 20A, enter the extra money you spend here. As the form indicates, you may need to prove this extra expense to the trustee. Whether you need to prove this extra expense will depend on the results of this means test. If the amount you enter here is the deciding factor in determining that you don't have enough disposable income to fund a Chapter 13 plan, proof will definitely be required.

Line 38. This item is for money you spend on your children's education. If your average monthly expense is $137.50 or more, put $137.50 in this blank; that's the maximum you can deduct. Remember not to list an amount twice; if you already listed an expense on Line 29 or 30, for example, don't repeat it here.

Line 39. Here, you can list the amount by which your actual expenses for food and clothing exceed the IRS allowance for these items as entered in item 19. However, you cannot list more than 5% over the IRS allowance.

Line 40. If you have been making charitable contributions to an organization before your bankruptcy filing date, you can enter them here as long as the group is organized and operated exclusively for religious, charitable, scientific, literary, or educational purposes; to foster national or international amateur sports competition (but only if no part of its activities involve the provision of athletic facilities or equipment); or for the prevention of cruelty to children or animals. The organization can't be disqualified from tax exemption status because of its political activities.

Line 41. Enter the total of Lines 34 through 40 in the column on the right.

Note: If you subtract the amounts on Line 41 and 33 from the amount on Line 18 and the total is less than $110, you won't be prohibited from using Chapter 7 on the basis of the means test. Remember, however, that the U.S. Trustee can still challenge your Chapter 7 filing if your actual income less your actual expenses would give you enough disposable income to fund a Chapter 13 plan.

Subpart C: Deductions for Debt Payment

Here, you deduct average monthly payments you will have to make over the next five years. Once you've completed this section, you can put all the numbers together to figure out whether you pass the means test.

Line 42. List the average monthly payment you will have to make over the next five years to creditors that hold a secured interest in your property (for example, the mortgage holder on your house or the creditor that holds your car note). As explained in the instructions for Line 23, you can calculate this amount by figuring out the total amount you will owe over the next five years, then dividing that total by 60. You can include your contractual mortgage payments even if you will be surrendering your home—and, therefore, won't actually be making those payments. (See *In re Randle*, 358 B.R. 360 (N.D. Ill. 2006) and *In re Hayes*, 376 B.R. 55 (D. Mass 2007).)

Line 43. Here, list the average monthly payment you would have to make to pay off any past amounts due to creditors on property that you must keep for your support or support of your dependents. That would typically include a car, your home, and any property you need for your employment. (Come up with the monthly figure by dividing the total amount you would have to pay by 60.)

Line 44. List the average monthly amount you will have to pay for priority claims over the next five years. (See "Classifying Your Debts," below, for a list of priority claims.) Typical priority claims include back

taxes and back child and spousal support. Divide the total by 60 to arrive at the monthly average. Don't include payments you've already listed on the form, such as current child support obligations. This line is only for debts you owe at the time of filing.

Line 45. Here, you must calculate the fee that the trustee would charge if you ended up in Chapter 13 bankruptcy. The fee depends on how much you would be paying, through the trustee, to your secured and unsecured creditors. It's impossible to come up with a figure at this point in the form, so leave it blank for now. If you don't pass the means test with this line left blank, come back here when you've complete Part VI and follow these instructions to come up with a figure:

- Add Lines 42, 43, and 44.
- Divide the total on Line 54 by 60 (to calculate the average monthly payment you would have to make to pay down 25% of your unsecured debt over five years).
- Add this number to the total of Lines 42, 43, and 44, and put the result on Line 45a. This is the average amount you would have to pay into a Chapter 13 plan to cover your secured debts, arrearages on those debts, priority debts, and 25% of your unsecured debts.
- On Line 45b, enter the multiplier percentage from the U.S. Trustee's website for your state and district. Go to www.usdoj.gov/ust, click "Means Testing Information," scroll down to the section called "Administrative Expenses Multipliers" and click "Schedules," then select your state and district to get the percentage.
- Multiply Line 45a by Line 45b and enter the result in the column on the right.

Line 46. Add Lines 42 through 45, and enter the total in the column on the right.

Subpart D: Total Deductions From Income

Line 47. Enter the total of Lines 33, 41, and 46 in the column at the right. This is the total amount you can subtract from your current monthly expenses to arrive at your disposable income.

Part VI. Determination of § 707(b)(2) Presumption

This is where you find out whether you received a passing grade on the means test.

Line 48. Enter the amount from Line 18 in the column at the right.

Line 49. Enter the amount from Line 47 in the column at the right

Line 50. Subtract Line 49 from Line 48 and enter the result in the column at the right.

Line 51. Multiply the total from Line 50 by 60 (to find out how much disposable income you will have over the next five years, according to these figures). Enter the result in the column at the right.

Line 52. Here you must check one of three boxes. If the amount on Line 51 is less than $6,575 ($110 a month over five years), check the top box. This means that you don't have enough money left over to make a Chapter 13 plan feasible, so you have the choice of filing for Chapter 7. If the total on Line 51 is more than $10,950 ($182.50 over five years), you have enough income to make a Chapter 13 plan feasible, and you probably won't be allowed to use Chapter 7. If your total is at least $6,575 but no more than $10,950, you will have to do a few more calculations to figure out where you fall. Proceed to Line 53.

Line 53. Enter the total of your nonpriority, unsecured debts. See "Classifying Your Debts," below, for help figuring out which of your debts qualify.

Line 54. Multiply the amount on Line 53 by 0.25 and enter the result in the box on the right. This amount represents 25% of your total nonpriority, unsecured debt.

Line 55. Here, you determine whether the income you have left over (listed on Line 51) is sufficient to pay 25% of your unsecured, nonpriority debt (listed on Line 54). If Line 51 is less than Line 54, you have passed the means test and may choose to file for Chapter 7 bankruptcy. (Remember, however, that you might still face a challenge if your actual income less your actual expenses would leave you with enough money to fund a Chapter 13 repayment plan.)

If Line 51 is greater than Line 54, you have failed the means test. If you fail the means test, you can complete Part VII, in which you list additional expenses that were somehow not included in the earlier parts of the form. Those expenses would be taken into account by the U.S. Trustee if you file a Chapter 7 case, as long as they don't duplicate expenses you already listed and are reasonably necessary for the support of you and your family.

 TIP
Make sure not to understate your expenses. If you want to use Chapter 7 but have failed the means test, go back over the form and carefully examine the expenses you listed for categories that aren't mandated by the IRS. People often underestimate their actual expenses. If you underestimated one or more expenses, or left an expense out that is provided for in the form, make the adjustments and see whether you can get a passing grade. Because this form is so complex, we recommend that you go through it at least twice before arriving at your final figures.

Classifying Your Debts

To complete the means test, you need to know how to categorize each of your debts. As explained above, you have to calculate what you owe on your priority debts and your secured debts for the next five years, and you have to add up all of your nonpriority, unsecured debts to figure out what portion of them you could repay in a Chapter 13 plan. This section will help you determine which debts are which. The classifications you make here will also help you draft your repayment plan and complete your bankruptcy forms.

Secured Debts

A debt is "secured" if you stand to lose a particular piece of property when you don't make your payments to the creditor. Most secured debts are created when you sign loan papers giving a creditor a security interest in your property—such as a home loan or car loan. But a debt might also be secured if a creditor has filed a lien (a legal claim against your property that must be paid before the property can be sold). Here is a list of common secured debts and liens:

- **Mortgages.** Called deeds of trust in some states, these are loans to buy or refinance a house or other real estate. If you fail to pay, the lender can foreclose on your house.
- **Home equity loans (second mortgages).** If you fail to pay, the lender (typically a bank or finance company) can foreclose on your house.
- **Loans for cars, boats, tractors, motorcycles, or RVs.** If you fail to pay, the lender can repossess the vehicle.

- **Store charges with a security agreement.** Almost all store purchases on credit cards are unsecured. Some stores, notably Sears and J.C. Penney, however, claim to retain a security interest in all hard goods (durable goods) purchased, or they make customers sign security agreements when they use their store charge card.
- **Personal loans from banks, credit unions, or finance companies.** Often, you must pledge valuable personal property, such as a paid-off motor vehicle, as collateral for these loans. The property can be repossessed if you don't make the payments.
- **Judicial liens.** A judicial lien can be imposed on your property only after somebody sues you and wins a money judgment against you. In most states, the judgment creditor then must record (file) the judgment with the county or state. The recorded judgment creates a lien on your real estate and, in some states, on some of your personal property as well.
- **Statutory liens.** Some liens are automatic, by law. For example, in most states, when you hire someone to work on your house, the worker and the supplier of materials automatically gets a mechanic's lien (sometimes called a materialman's or contractor's lien) on the house if you don't pay.
- **Tax liens.** If you owe money to the IRS or another taxing authority, the debt is secured if the agency has recorded a lien against your property. (See "Tax Debts," below, for more information.)

Priority Debts

Priority debts are unsecured debts that are considered sufficiently important to jump to the head of the bankruptcy repayment line. Priority debts that may come up in consumer bankruptcies include:

- wages, salaries, and commissions owed by an employer
- contributions to employee benefit plans
- money owed to certain farmers and fishermen
- up to $2,425 in deposits made for the purchase, lease, or rental of property or services for personal, family, or household use, that were not delivered or provided
- alimony, maintenance, or support

- claim for death or personal injury the debtor caused while intoxicated
- nondischargeable taxes (see "Tax Debts," below), and
- customs, duties, and penalties you owe to the federal, state, or local government.

Nonpriority, Unsecured Debts

Not surprisingly, nonpriority, unsecured debts are all debts that are neither secured nor priority. Debts in this category include:

- credit and charge card purchases and cash advances
- department store credit card purchases, unless the store retains a security interest in the items you buy or requires you to sign a security agreement
- gasoline company credit card purchases
- back rent
- medical bills
- certain tax debts (see "Tax Debts," below)
- student loans
- utility bills
- loans from friends or relatives, unless you signed a promissory note secured by some property you own
- money judgments for breach of contract or negligence
- health club dues
- lawyers' bills (unless there's a lien on your property to secure payment)
- church or synagogue dues, and
- union dues.

Tax Debts

A tax debt can be secured, priority, or unsecured. If a taxing agency has placed a lien on your property, the debt is secured. If the tax debt is not dischargeable in bankruptcy, the debt is priority. And if the tax debt can be discharged, it is unsecured. The chart below will help you figure out what category particular tax debts fall into.

Classifying Your Tax Debt	
If...	**Your tax debt is...**
All of the following are true: • the tax year for which you owe taxes ended more than three years before the date you plan to file your bankruptcy case • you properly filed your tax return (if the IRS filed a Substitute for Return for you, it doesn't count unless you agreed and signed the substitute return for the year in question at least two years before filing for bankruptcy) • the IRS has not assessed the taxes against you within 240 days before you plan to file your bankruptcy case, and • the IRS has not recorded a Notice of Federal Tax Lien with your county land records office.	**Dischargeable,** meaning you can completely eliminate your income tax debt, and the interest and penalties associated with it.
The IRS has recorded a Notice of Federal Tax Lien.	**Secured,** meaning you may be able to discharge your personal liability in bankruptcy, but the lien remains. If you don't pay off the entire debt during your case, the IRS can seize property you owned before filing to cover the rest. Practically speaking, the IRS looks to collect from real estate and retirement plans.
Your tax debt is not dischargeable or secured.	**Priority,** which means that it must be paid in full in your Chapter 13 plan.
Both of the following are true: • your tax debt is not dischargeable or secured, and • the IRS has recorded a Notice of Federal Tax Lien, but your property won't cover what you owe the IRS.	**Undersecured** (if you have no seizable assets) or partially undersecured (if you have some). The undersecured portion is dischargeable if the first three conditions listed above for dischargeable taxes are met.

Forced Conversion to Chapter 13

If you already filed for Chapter 7 and flunked the means test, the U.S. Trustee, the trustee, or a creditor will have filed a motion under 11 U.S.C. § 707(b)(2) to have the court declare your filing "abusive." If the court agrees, it will give you the choice of having your case dismissed or converted to Chapter 13. If you consent to the conversion, the court will order it.

To remain in Chapter 13, you will have to file a confirmable plan within 15 days of the conversion, start making payments on the plan within 15 days after that, and otherwise comply with the eligibility requirements unique to Chapter 13 (see Ch. 3 for more on these requirements).

CAUTION

You may not be eligible for either type of bankruptcy. It's entirely possible to be kicked out of Chapter 7 because your income is too high, then be unable to come up with a Chapter 13 repayment plan that's acceptable to the judge. In other words, there may be no bankruptcy remedy for you. For instance, you may get tossed out of Chapter 7 because your current monthly income was too high when you filed. If, however, you don't have a steady income by the time you convert to Chapter 13, your plan won't be confirmed. If you find yourself in this situation, talk to a lawyer right away.

Can You Propose a Plan the Judge Will Approve?

Before you are allowed to proceed with your Chapter 13 bankruptcy, the judge must approve your repayment plan. As explained briefly in Ch. 3, your plan will be approved only if it shows that you will have enough steady income to:

- pay certain types of debts—including most priority debts and some secured debts—in full over the life of your plan, and
- pay your nonpriority, unsecured creditors at least the value of your nonexempt property.

The plan must also show that all of your "disposable income" (as defined by the bankruptcy laws) will be used to repay your remaining debts for the duration of your plan.

How long your plan must last and how much money you must devote to it depends on whether your current monthly income, which you calculated in Ch. 4, is more or less than your state's median income. If your current monthly income is less than the median income for your state, you can propose a three-year plan, and you may use your actual expenses to calculate your disposable income.

If your current monthly income is more than the median income for your state, your plan must last five years, and you must use expense amounts set by the IRS (which might differ from your actual expenses) to calculate your disposable income. In essence, this means that you will probably have to devote more money to your plan for a longer period of time.

CROSS-REFERENCE

If you haven't calculated your current monthly income, go back to Ch. 4. Ch. 4 explains how to come up with this figure and compare it to your state's median. You'll need to know your current monthly income—and whether it is more or less than your state's median—to figure out whether you can come up with a confirmable repayment plan.

This chapter will help you decide whether you can propose a repayment plan that meets the legal requirements. If you decide to go ahead with a Chapter 13 bankruptcy, you can use your rough calculations from this chapter when you actually draft your repayment plan in Ch. 8.

SEE AN EXPERT

Talk to a lawyer if you can't make the numbers work. This chapter will help you determine whether you can come up with a plan the judge will approve, if you decide to file for Chapter 13. If you can't, there is no reason to do the work required to actually draft a plan unless you first consult with a bankruptcy attorney. An attorney may be able to provide a different slant on the numbers you provide in the form and the choices you make when completing this chapter.

If Your Current Monthly Income Is Less Than Your State's Median Income

If your current monthly income is less than your state's median income, you can propose a plan that lasts for three years or less. However, the court can authorize a plan lasting up to five years, if necessary. You might need a five-year plan if it will take you that long to pay off a priority debt (such as child support or alimony you owe directly to your child or former spouse).

SKIP AHEAD

This section is only for those whose current monthly income is less than their state's median income. If your income—as calculated in Ch. 4—is equal to or more than the state median, skip ahead to "If Your Current Monthly Income Is More Than Your State's Median Income," below.

Step 1: Calculate Your Base Income

Your base income is the amount you will use throughout this section to determine whether you have sufficient disposable income to fund a Chapter 13 plan. Your base income is simply your current monthly income (your average gross income over the six-month period before you filed for bankruptcy, as calculated in Ch. 4) less any child support payments, foster care payments, or disability payments you receive for a dependent child, as long as those amounts are necessary for the child's care.

1. Current Monthly Income: _____

2. Dependent Child Payments: – _____

3. Base Income:: = _____

Step 2: Subtract Your Expenses

When determining your disposable income, you can subtract only those expenses that are reasonably necessary for you and your dependents, and any child support or alimony obligation that first arose after you filed your bankruptcy petition.

The best way to calculate these expenses is to use one of the official bankruptcy forms—Schedule J: *Current Expenditures of Individual Debtor(s)*— as a starting point, then add certain other expenses allowed by the bankruptcy code. Incidentally, the work you do here will be useful if you continue on to file for bankruptcy, because you will have to file a Schedule J with the court. (A sample Schedule J appears in Ch. 7.)

Use Schedule J to Determine Reasonably Necessary Expenses

Tear out the blank version of Schedule J from the appendix. If you and your spouse have separated but are filing jointly, you can each complete a separate Schedule J and combine your expenses at the end of this procedure.

For each listed item, fill in your monthly expenses for you and any dependents. Remember to include payments you make for your dependents' expenses in your figures only if those expenses are reasonable and necessary for the dependents' support.

If you make some payments biweekly, quarterly, semiannually, or annually, prorate them to show your monthly payment.

1. Rent or home mortgage payment. If your rent or mortgage payment is unusually high for your area, the court might suggest that you move in order to bring this expense down, if alternate housing is easily available. If you are facing foreclosure and will be surrendering your home in your Chapter 13 bankruptcy, what amount should you put for your rent or home mortgage payment? You can either hunt around the neighborhood where you plan to live and list an average rental amount or you can use the IRS figure for average rentals in your area. (You can find them at www.usdoj.gov/ust; click "Means Testing Information," then scroll down to "Local Housing and Utilities Expense Standards" and choose your state.) At the bottom of your expense form, indicate that you are using an artificial expense standard for your rent.

What's a Reasonable Expense?

When it comes to expenses, what is considered reasonable varies from debtor to debtor, court to court, and even region to region. In general, expenses for luxury items or services (such as a gardener) will not be allowed. If an expense seems particularly high, the court will look to see whether you can achieve the same goal by spending less; the court will let you live adequately, but not high on the hog. For example, if you are making payments of $550 per month on a Cadillac, the court may only allow $300 per month toward a less expensive car, freeing up another $250 per month of disposable income.

Courts also tend not to allow any voluntary payments to retirement plans, unless the debtor is approaching retirement age or is financially challenged. (See *In re Behlke*, 358 F.3d 429 (6th Cir. Ohio 2004).) Your best approach when completing Schedule J is to enter your actual expenses. If you want to know whether your expenses will later be considered reasonable, compare them with the cost of living schedules published by the federal government and collected for your convenience by the U.S. Trustee's Office at www.usdoj.gov/ust. These are the same expenses as you used in Ch. 4 if you completed the means test there. If you didn't, click the "Means Testing" link on the right side of the U.S. Trustee's website and check out the following categories:

- National Standards for Allowable Living Expenses (for food, clothing, household supplies, personal care, and miscellaneous)
- Local Standards: Housing and Utilities, and
- Local Standards: Transportation Expenses.

You can also find out the applicable IRS standards for your area by taking the free, online means test at www.legalconsumer.com.

2. Utilities. List your monthly utility expenses. Be sure to take a monthly average of gas, heating fuel, and electricity if your bills vary month to month. Also under the utility category, put expenses for satellite TV, cellular telephone, pager, caller identification, and special long distance and Internet subscriptions necessary for the welfare of you or your dependents (use an attachment if necessary to list all your utility expenses). Some courts might refuse high phone bills (for example, if you call a parent or child in a distant city every day). A court might also question the expense of full-service cable or satellite TV, so you may have to adjust your plan to keep the basic service but drop the premium channels.

3. Home Maintenance. If your estimates of maintenance and upkeep are high, you may have to provide the court with documentation for past years' expenses. Obviously, the court will want you to maintain your home's condition, but will want you to do so in a reasonably inexpensive manner.

4. Food. To determine whether or not your figure is reasonable, the court will most likely compare it to the federal cost of living figure for your area. (See "What's a Reasonable Expense?" above.) If your expenses are higher than average, be ready to explain them—for example, because a family member needs a special diet. If the expenses are high because you eat out a lot, be prepared to explain why.

5. Clothing. You are not expected to wear only second-hand clothing, especially if your employment requires a high-end dress standard. But extravagant or frequent purchases may not be allowed. A court might also suggest that you buy used clothing for your still-growing children. To get an idea of how much you spend now, total up the clothing purchases for which you have receipts, credit card statements, or an entry in your checkbook, and arrive at a monthly average.

6. Laundry and dry cleaning. Enter your expenses here. Especially if you have to dress up for work, the court will allow you to spend some money on dry cleaning every month.

7. Medical and dental expenses. The court will want you to maintain your medical insurance coverage, so it will allow medical insurance for you and your dependents as an expense. Don't list payments you're making on bills from medical providers and hospitals for services that you've already received. The court

will probably want you to pay those through your Chapter 13 plan—that is, out of your disposable income. The court might let you include 100% of the bill as part of your monthly expenses if you need ongoing medical care and the provider won't continue to provide it unless you pay your bill in full—if you are in this situation, you can include the expense on this worksheet. The court may also reject expenses for mental health therapy and instead suggest that you visit a free or low-cost county mental health facility, if you qualify.

8. Transportation. The court will let you pay a reasonable amount to get to and from work and provide necessary transportation for your children. The court will allow expenses for vehicle insurance, maintenance, and registration. The IRS figures for a reasonable operating and public transportation expense vary from $200 to $400, depending on where you live and whether you have one or two cars. As mentioned on the form, you shouldn't put your car payments on this line: They come later.

9. Recreation, clubs and entertainment, newspapers, magazines, etc. Many debtors are tempted to leave this line blank because they think it will look bad for them to incur expenses for recreation. For now, don't worry what it will look like. Just list your actual expenses. Later on, if you lack adequate disposable income, you might need to tighten your belt, and recreation may be one category where you can cut back.

10. Charitable contributions. You can include donations to charity, in an amount up to 15% of your income for the year in which you make them. You can subtract charitable contributions even if you are paying your nonpriority, unsecured creditors only 1% of what you owe them. (*In re Tony and Martha Petty*, Case No. 4:05-BK-26362 (E.D. Ark. 2006).)

11. Insurance. The court generally will let you maintain your disability or life insurance, especially if your health is compromised and you may need to use the disability insurance, or if you have young children or other dependents who would need the life insurance money if you died. If you have a whole life insurance policy, you may be told to convert it to a term policy, which has much lower premiums.

12. Taxes. List the monthly average of all taxes that are deducted from your wages or that you pay as a self-employed person or independent contractor.

13. Installment payments. Don't list your installment payments here—you will include them elsewhere in your repayment plan.

14. Alimony, maintenance, and support paid to others. List your current support obligations only. Don't list any back support you owe.

15. Payments for support of additional dependents not living at your home. Your expenses listed so far have included expenses for your dependents living at home. You also are permitted to claim expenses for the support of other dependents not living at home, including your children. These expenses include child care, clothes, books, an occasional movie, and the like.

16. Regular expenses from operation of business, profession, or farm. If you run a business, enter all expenses that are necessary for the continuation, preservation, and operation of the business. This would include monthly payments on business assets as well as any expenses you would include on your IRS Schedule C. You can include expenses only if you own the business as a sole proprietor or as a partner with your spouse. If you file for Chapter 13 bankruptcy, you will have to attach a detailed statement of your expenses anyway, so you might as well do it here. Anyone with a financial background, such as a banker, accountant, bookkeeper, or tax preparer, can help you draft an expense statement.

17. Other. List any additional expenses here, except payments you are making on back income taxes and on unsecured installment debts such as student loans, credit card accounts, and personal loans: These debts must be paid out of your disposable income through your Chapter 13 plan. Be ready to explain why the expenses you list here are reasonable. Other expenses not already listed might include:

- Educational expenses for your children. Courts are reluctant to let you send your children to private school if it means your creditors won't be paid. You may be able to convince the court of the need for private school, however, if the public schools in your area are quite bad or dangerous, you want your children to receive religious education, or your child has special educational needs. If your child is in college, a court may not let you deduct tuition at an expensive private university, but may let you count the payments for a state college.

- Your or your spouse's educational expenses. If either you or your spouse is currently in school, list your expenses here. The court may reject a portion of these expenses if you or your spouse could be working and increasing the family's income.

- Miscellaneous personal expenses. Often, these are the expenses that your creditors, the trustee, and the court scrutinize the most. Some courts do not think you should be allowed to spend anything for entertainment, to participate in any hobbies that cost money, or to buy gifts for friends or relatives. As with all expenses, the key to getting these expenses approved is their reasonableness. You can't include in your budget money to see Broadway shows, go sailing once a week, keep a subscription to an expensive journal, or renew your country club membership. You can probably budget to go out to or rent an occasional movie, go bowling, get a daily newspaper, keep your membership at the local Y, and take care of your pet.

Once you have completed the form, add up all of the expenses you have listed. Subtract these expenses from your base income, as calculated above.

1. Base Income (from Step 1): _____
2. Schedule J Expenses: − _____
3. Total: = _____

If you still have a positive number—that is, if it looks like you will have some money left over after paying the expenses listed on Schedule J—you may be able to propose a confirmable Chapter 13 plan. If the number is negative, you won't have anything left to put toward a repayment plan. If you find yourself in this situation, revisit your expenses. Some of them may not be reasonable.

Step 3: Subtract Your Installment Payments

Here is where you figure out the monthly average of any installment payments you are making on property that is collateral for a secured debt. These are typically car and home furniture payments, but you may also be making payments on other valuable objects, such as jewelry and electronic equipment.

Add up all of the installment payments you are contractually obligated to make, then subtract that amount from what you had left at the end of Step 2.

1. Base Income Less Expenses
   (from Step 2): _____
2. Installment Payments: – _____
3. Total: = _____

If you still have money left over after subtracting your expenses and your installment payments from your base income, you may be able to propose a confirmable Chapter 13 plan. If your total is zero (or less), revisit your installment payments. If you are paying $600 a month for a Corvette and you could get by with a more economical car or with no car at all, make the adjustment here so that you will have some income left over. (Incidentally, the IRS national standard for a reasonable monthly car payment is $478.)

Reducing Your Secured Debt Payments

In your Chapter 13 case, you might be entitled to reduce the amount you owe on a debt securing personal property—such as a car note—and thereby reduce the amount of your monthly installment payments. This strategy is called a "cramdown," and you may be able to use it to reduce the amount you owe to the value of the property.

You can't cram down or modify voluntary liens on your home (for example, a first, second, or even third mortgage). However, if your home is worth no more than you owe on your first mortgage, that means your second mortgage (and your third, if you have one) is no longer secured by your home. In this situation, you may be able to "strip off" the second mortgage and treat it as unsecured debt in your Chapter 13 plan. This procedure allows you to greatly reduce the amount you have to pay each month to stay current on your home.

For example, assume you pay $1,500 on your first mortgage, $750 on your second mortgage, and $400 on a third mortgage (such as a home equity loan). If your home is worth $200,000 and you still owe that much on your first mortgage, you can strip off the second and third mortgages. This would reduce your monthly payment from $2,650 to $1,500.

Step 4: Subtract Your Priority Debts

As mentioned in Ch. 3, you must pay certain debts in full over the life of your plan—three years, unless the court authorizes a longer time. Among the debts that have to be paid in full are priority debts. (You can find a list of priority debts in Ch. 4, "Classifying Your Debts.")

If you owe any priority debts, divide the total amount you owe by 36 to determine how much you would have to pay each month in order to pay off these debts in three years. Subtract this amount from what's left of your base income after subtracting expenses and installment payments, in Step 3, above.

1. Remaining Income
   (from Step 3, above): _____
2. Monthly Priority Debt
   Payments: – _____
3. Total: = _____

If you have a positive number, move on to the next section. If the number is negative, you still might propose a confirmable plan under the following conditions:

- If one of the priority debts was child support or alimony that was assigned to a government agency (rather than money you owe directly to your child or ex-spouse), you don't have to pay the full amount in your plan. However, you do have to include the debt in your plan and commit all of your disposable income to a plan for five years rather than three years, unless it won't take you that long to pay the child support debt in full.
- As mentioned, if you could pay off all of your priority debts over a five-year period rather than a three-year period, you can ask the court to allow a five-year plan as part of your confirmation hearing.

Step 5: Subtract Secured Debt Arrearages

One of the main reasons people file Chapter 13 is to deal with arrearages—amounts past due—on their home or car note, to prevent a foreclosure or repossession. Chapter 13 allows you to keep your home or car while paying off the arrearages under your plan. If you owe an arrearage and your plan shows that you are keeping the collateral (your home, car, or the like), you'll have to pay 100% of the arrearage and stay current on the main debt.

Add up all arrearages on debts securing collateral you want to keep. If you will be proposing a three-year plan, divide the total by 36 to get the amount you would have to pay each month. For a five-year plan, divide the total by 60 to arrive at a monthly amount. Subtract this total monthly payment from your remaining income, from Step 4, above.

1. Remaining Income
   (from Step 4, above):   _____

2. Monthly Secured Debt
   Arrearage Payments: – _____

3. Total: = _____

If the number is positive, proceed to Step 5 below. If the number is negative, even over a five-year repayment period, you won't be able to present a confirmable plan.

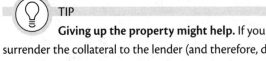

TIP

Giving up the property might help. If you surrender the collateral to the lender (and therefore, don't have to pay the full past due amount), you might have some income left over. This means you may be able to come up with a confirmable plan yet.

Step 6: Debts Secured by a Lien

In most cases, if you have a lien on your property other than a purchase money lien (such as a car note or mortgage), you'll have to pay the lien off in full in your plan. For example, if the IRS has recorded a lien against your property for back taxes, or a contractor has placed a mechanic's lien on your property for work that you didn't pay for, your plan will not be confirmed unless it provides for payment of these liens in full.

TIP

Different rules apply to judgment liens. If there is a lien on your property because you lost a lawsuit and owe someone money as a result, you might be able to remove the lien in a separate proceeding called "lien avoidance." If you use lien avoidance to remove a lien, you won't have to pay it under your plan. See Ch. 11 for information on lien avoidance.

Add up all liens on your property (other than judgment liens and liens created when you obtained loans to purchase the property). Divide the total by 36 for a three-year plan (or by 60 if you are proposing a five-year plan) to obtain the monthly amount you will have to pay. Then, subtract this total from your remaining income from Step 5, above.

1. Remaining Income
   (from Step 5):   _____

2. Monthly Lien Payment: – _____

3. Total Disposable Income: = _____

If you still have money left over, you can move on to Step 7. If your total disposable income is zero or less, your plan won't be confirmed.

Your Chapter 13 Trustee Will Get a Cut

Your Chapter 13 trustee is entitled to roughly 10% of all payments you make under the plan, as a fee. It's hard to compute what that figure will be at this point; the total trustee's cut may vary depending on whether your mortgage (if you have one) and other secured debts will be paid under the plan or directly to the creditor. For example, assume your mortgage payment is $2,000 a month, and you want to use Chapter 13 to cure an arrearage of $5,000. If you make your mortgage payment directly to the creditor, you will owe the trustee only $500 (10% of the arrearage). However, if you also make your mortgage payment to the trustee as part of the plan, the trustee will be entitled to another $7,200 over the life of a three-year plan. Although some courts permit debtors to make mortgage payments directly to a creditor (see *In re Lopez*, 372 B.R. 40 (9th Cir. B.A.P. 2007)), others require debtors to make these payments through the plan, so the trustee gets paid more (see *In re Breeding*, 366 B.R. 21 (E.D. Ark. 2007)).

To get a rough figure, multiply the amount you came up with in Step 6 by 0.1 (10%), then subtract that amount from your total disposable income. If the 10% knocks you out of contention, don't give up. You can take a closer look at some of your other expenses to get yourself back in the running.

Step 7: Compare Your Disposable Income to the Value of Your Nonexempt Property

As explained in Ch. 3, if you own property that does not qualify for an exemption under the exemption laws applicable to your case, you will have to pay your nonpriority, unsecured creditors at least the value of that nonexempt property. For example, if you have $15,000 in a savings account and the exemptions you are using allow you to exempt only $10,000, your Chapter 13 plan would have to include payments to your nonpriority, unsecured creditors of at least $5,000 over a three-year period, or $139 a month.

If you don't know whether you have nonexempt property, skip to "Understanding Property Exemptions," below, for information on which exemptions you can use and how to apply them to your specific property items. If you have nonexempt property, add up the value of that property. Then subtract the total value from your disposable income, as calculated in Step 6.

1. Disposable Income
   (from Step 6):   _____

2. Value of Nonexempt
   Property (Monthly):   − _____

3. Total: = _____

As long as your total is not a negative number, you may be able to propose a confirmable plan. This means you will have enough money to pay your nonpriority, unsecured creditors. If your total is zero, this means you will have *exactly* enough money to meet your plan obligations, not a penny more or less.

If all of your property is exempt, and the disposable income you calculated in Step 6 was zero, it means that your unsecured creditors won't get paid a cent. This is what is called a zero-percent plan. Prior to the new bankruptcy law (October 2005), many courts wouldn't confirm a plan that paid the unsecured creditors less than a particular percentage (anywhere from 20% to 80%, depending on the court). But under the new law, as long as your expenses are reasonable—that is, the court can't find any expense you are paying that should go to your creditors—there is no legal reason why a zero-percent plan won't be confirmed.

If Your Current Monthly Income Is More Than Your State's Median Income

If your current monthly income is more than your state's median income, you are required to use Form 22C, *Chapter 13 Statement of Current Monthly Income and Calculation of Commitment Period and Disposable Income*, to compute your disposable income. You'll find instructions for completing that form below, including a completed sample. If you later decide to file for Chapter 13 bankruptcy, you will have to complete this form, and use the information to draft your plan in Ch. 8, so your work here won't go to waste.

Step 1: Use Form 22C to Calculate Your Disposable Income

In Ch. 4, you may have completed Form 22A to find out whether you are required to use Chapter 13 or whether you have a choice between Chapter 13 and Chapter 7. If you completed that form, be aware that Lines 19–47 of Form 22A are the same as Lines 24–52 of Form 22C. If you completed Form 22A, you can start Form 22C by transferring the amount you entered in Line 47 of Form 22A to Line 52 of Form 22C, then starting with our instructions below for Line 53.

Otherwise, start computing your disposable income with Line 24. You'll find a completed sample Form 22C at the end of this section; a blank copy is in Appendix B.

Line 24A. Enter the total IRS National Standards for Food, Clothing, and Other Items for your family size and income level. This is the amount the IRS believes you should get to spend for food, clothes, household supplies, personal care, and miscellaneous other items. You can get these figures from www.usdoj.gov/ust. Click "Means Testing Information," then scroll down to find the right link.

Line 24B. Enter the amount you are allowed to claim for health expenses from the IRS National Standards for Out-of-Pocket Health Care. You can find these figures at www.usdoj.gov/ust. Click "Means Testing Information," then scroll down to the appropriate link. As you'll see, you can claim more for household members who are at least 65 years old, which is reflected on the form. You'll also see that the total amount you can claim is quite small; if you spend more than you're allowed to claim here, you can claim it on Line 36.

Line 25A. Enter the amount of the IRS Housing and Utilities Expense Standards, nonmortgage expenses for your county and family size. Get these figures from www.usdoj.gov/ust. Click "Means Testing Information," then scroll down to the IRS Housing and Utilities Expense Standards section and enter your state in the drop-down menu. Find the figures for your county and family size, then enter the figure that appears under the heading "Non-Mortgage."

Line 25B. On Line a, enter the amount of the IRS Housing and Utility Expense Standards, Mortgage/Rent expenses for your county and family size. These figures appear on the U.S. Trustee's website, on the same chart as nonmortgage expenses—follow the instructions for Line 20A, above.

On Line b, enter the average monthly payment for any debts secured by your home, including a mortgage, home equity loan, taxes, and insurance. The average monthly payment is the total of all amounts contractually due to each secured creditor in the five years after you file for bankruptcy, divided by 60. Even if you are planning to move, you should still enter your mortgage payment here. If your mortgage payment is higher than the IRS allowance for housing in the area where you live, the court might calculate your disposable income using the IRS allowance. (See *In re Meek,* 370 B.R. 294 (D. Idaho 2007).)

On Line c, subtract Line b from Line a. This may turn out to be a negative figure—if so, enter a zero in the right-hand column. Later in the means test, you'll be able to add your average monthly payment back in as an expense.

Line 26. If your actual rental or mortgage expense is higher than that allowed by the IRS, you can claim an adjustment here. For instance if the IRS mortgage/rental expense for a family of two is $550, you pay an actual rent of $900, and that amount is average for the area in which you live, enter the additional $350 here and explain why you should be able to subtract it (that you couldn't possibly find housing in your area for less, for example).

Line 27A. You are entitled to claim an expense here whether or not you actually have a car. First, indicate the number of cars for which you pay operating expenses or for which somebody else contributes the operating expenses as part of the amount entered on Line 7. If you don't have a car, enter the amount listed under "Public Transportation" from the IRS Local Transportation Expense Standards. You can find these at www.usdoj.gov/ust; click "Means Testing Information," then scroll down to the appropriate link and choose your region. If you indicated that you have one or two cars, enter the amount listed for your region (and sometimes, your city) under "Operating Costs" in the same chart.

Line 27B. If you have a car and also use public transportation, you may claim a public transportation expense here. You can find the correct amount by following the instructions for Line 27A, above.

Line 28. These are your expenses for owning or leasing a car.

CAUTION

If you aren't making payments, you might face a challenge. A dispute exists over whether you can claim this expense if you aren't paying for or leasing a car. Some U.S. Trustees insist that you can't claim the expense. (See, for example, *In re Bennett,* 371 B.R. 400 (C.D. Cal. 2007) and *In re Cole,* 371 B.R. 454 (W.D. Wash. 2007).) However, the National Association for Consumer Bankruptcy Attorneys has filed briefs arguing that you should be able to, because old cars wear out, and you will need to lease or buy a new car sometime during the next five years. (See *In re Armstrong,* 370 B.R. 323 (E.D. Wash. 2007).) If you aren't making payments on a car and you claim this expense, be aware that the trustee in your case may challenge you if the amount determines whether you pass or fail the means test.

On Line 28a, enter the IRS Local Transportation Standards for ownership of a first car. This amount is actually a national figure; currently, it is $478. To make sure you are using the most up-to-date numbers, check the website of the U.S. Trustee, www.usdoj.gov/ust. Click "Means Testing Information," then scroll down to the Local Transportation Expense Standards drop-down menu and choose your region. The ownership figure is near the bottom of the page.

On Line 28b, enter your average monthly payment (over the next five years) for all debts secured by your first car. For example, assume you have three years left to pay on the car and the monthly payment is $350.

The total amount you will owe in the next five years is $12,600 (36 months times $350). If you spread that amount over the next five years—by dividing the total by 60, the number of months in five years—you'll see that your average monthly payment is $210.

On Line 28c, subtract Line b from Line a and enter the result in the column on the right. Later on, if necessary, you will be able to deduct your car payments to figure out whether you have enough disposable income to fund a Chapter 13 plan.

Line 29. Complete this only if you have a second car (and you checked the second car box in Line 23). Follow the instructions for Line 23 to enter the required figures for your second car.

Line 30. Enter the total average monthly expense that you actually incur for all taxes *other than real estate or sales taxes*. Examples of taxes that you should enter here are income taxes, self-employment taxes, Social Security taxes, and Medicare taxes. In some cases, these taxes will show up on your wage stub. You'll need to convert the period covered by your wage stub to a monthly figure. Once you have figured out how much you pay each month for each type of tax, add them all together and enter them in the column on the right.

Converting Taxes to a Monthly Figure

If you are paid weekly, biweekly, or twice a month, you will have to convert the tax amounts on your pay stubs to a monthly amount. And, if you pay quarterly taxes (estimated income taxes, for example), you'll need to convert that figure as well. Here's how to do it:

- Weekly taxes: multiply by 4.3 to get a monthly amount.
- Biweekly taxes: divide by 2 to get a weekly amount, then multiply by 4.3.
- Bimonthly taxes: divide by 2.
- Quarterly taxes: divide by 3.

Line 31. Enter all of your mandatory payroll deductions here, other than those entered in Line 25. Use the conversion rules set out above to arrive at average monthly deductions. Make sure you deduct only mandatory deductions (such as required retirement contributions, union dues, and uniform costs). Contributions to a 401(k) should not be included, for example, because they are voluntary.

Line 32. Enter any monthly payments you make for term life insurance. Do not enter payments for any other type of insurance, such as credit insurance, car insurance, renters insurance, insurance on the lives of your dependents, or whole life insurance on your own life. (Whole life insurance is the type that allows you to borrow against the policy.)

Line 33. Enter the amount of any payments you make pursuant to a court order. Child support and alimony are the most common examples, but you may also have to pay to satisfy a court money judgment or a criminal fine. Do not include court-ordered payments toward a child support or alimony arrearage; only the payments you need to make to stay current should be entered here.

Line 34. Enter the total monthly amount that you pay for education required by your employer to keep your job, and the total monthly amount you pay for the education of a physically or mentally challenged dependent child for whom no public education providing similar services is available. Included in this amount would be the actual costs of after-school enrichment educational services for a physically or mentally challenged child, and the actual educational expenses you are paying in support of an individual educational plan.

Line 35. Enter the average monthly cost of child care. If your employment (and therefore, your need for child care) is seasonal, add up your child care costs for the year and divide the total by 12. Do not equate education with child care. For instance, child care for a child who is of public education school age should cover only the hours before and after school.

Line 36. Enter the average monthly amount you pay for out-of-pocket health care expenses, but only to the extent it exceeds the amount you were allowed to claim on Line 24B. Do not include health care expenses that are reimbursed by insurance or provided by an HMO or Medicaid. Also, don't include premiums you pay for health insurance; you can claim these on Line 39.

Line 37. Enter the average monthly expenses you pay for any communication devices that are necessary for the health and welfare of you or your dependents. Examples provided by the form are cell phones, pagers, call waiting, caller identification, and special long distance or Internet services. Virtually all of these devices arguably are necessary for the health and welfare of your family. However, some expenses might not be allowed (for example, a cell phone you use for your business, or broadband Internet service). When in doubt, list the expense.

Line 38. Add the expenses you entered in Lines 24 through 37 and put the total in the column at the right.

Subpart B: Additional Living Expense Deductions

The expenses in this Subpart are allowed by the Bankruptcy Code, in addition to the IRS expenses. However, you can't list an expense twice; if you already claimed it in Subpart A, don't list it again here.

Line 39. Here, list your reasonably necessary monthly expenses for health insurance, disability insurance, and health savings accounts (HSAs) on the lines provided. The form was revised in January 2008 to clarify that you can list a "reasonable" expense here whether you actually pay that amount each month or not. If, however, you pay less than the reasonable amount you list, you must indicate how much you actually spend each month on the additional line provided. If the U.S. Trustee or one of your creditors later wants to challenge your expense claims—for example, to argue that you really have more disposable income than the form indicates—they can use this information.

Line 40. Anything you spend to care for a member of your household or immediate family because of his or her age, illness, or disability can be deducted here. If your contributions are episodic—a wheelchair here, a vacation with a companion there—estimate your average monthly expense and enter it here.

> **CAUTION**
> **Your response here could affect eligibility for government benefits.** Expenses you list here could render the person you are assisting ineligible for Social Security or other government benefits. For example, if you state that you are spending $500 a month for the care of a relative, and that relative is receiving SSI, your relative might receive a lower benefit amount each month, to reflect your contribution. On the other hand, if you are making such expenditures, you are required to disclose them here. If you find yourself in this predicament, talk to a lawyer.

Line 41. The average monthly expense of security systems and any other method of protecting your family should be entered here.

Line 42. If your actual home energy costs exceed the figure you entered on Line 25A, enter the extra money you spend here. As the form indicates, you may need to prove this extra expense to the trustee.

Line 43. This item is for money you spend on your children's education. If your average monthly expense is $137.50 or more, put $137.50 in this blank; that's the maximum you can deduct. Remember not to list an amount twice; if you already listed an expense on Line 34 or 35, for example, don't repeat it here.

Line 44. Here, you can list the amount by which your actual expenses for food and clothing exceed the IRS allowance for these items as entered in item 24. However, you cannot list more than 5% over the IRS allowance.

Line 45. Although this line appears to allow a deduction for charitable contributions, at least one court has barred such deductions except in very limited circumstances. (*In re Diagostino*, No 06-10384 (Bankr. N.D. N.Y., August 2006).) Congress is considering legislation to clarify that these deductions should be allowed, and several Republican lawmakers have urged the attorney general to instruct the U.S. Trustees not to challenge charitable contributions. If you believe this issue might come up in your case, talk to an attorney.

Line 46. Enter the total of Lines 39 through 45 in the column on the right.

Subpart C: Deductions for Debt Payment

Here, you deduct average contractually due monthly payments you will have to make over the next five years.

Line 47. List the average monthly payment you will have to make over the next five years to creditors that hold a secured interest in your property (for example, the mortgage holder on your house, or the creditor that holds your car note). Calculate this amount by figuring out the total amount you will owe over the next five years, then dividing that total by 60. Even if you are planning to move, you should still enter your mortgage payment here. If your mortgage payment is higher than the IRS allowance for housing in the area where you live, the court might calculate your disposable income using the IRS allowance. (See *In re Meek*, 370 B.R. 294 (D. Idaho 2007).)

Line 48. Here, list the average monthly payment you would have to make to pay off any back amounts due to creditors on property that you must keep for your support or support of your dependents. That would typically include a car, your home, and any property you need for your employment. (Come up with the monthly figure by dividing the total amount you would have to pay by 60.)

Line 49. List the average monthly amount you will have to pay for priority claims over the next five years. (See "Classifying Your Debts," in Ch. 4, for a list of priority claims.) Typical priority claims include back taxes and back child and spousal support. Divide the total by 60 to arrive at the monthly average. Don't include payments you've already listed on the form, such as current child support obligations. This line is only for debts you owe at the time of filing.

Line 50. Calculate the fee the trustee will charge if you file Chapter 13 bankruptcy. That fee will depend on how much you would be paying, through the trustee, to your secured and unsecured creditors. It's impossible to come up with a figure at this point in the form, so leave it blank for now.

Line 51. Add Lines 47 through 50, and enter the total in the column on the right.

Subpart D: Total Deductions From Income

Line 52: Enter the total of items 38, 46, and 51 in the column at the right. This is the total amount you can subtract from your current monthly income to arrive at your disposable income.

Part V: Determination of Disposable Income Under § 1325(b)(2)

Here is where you subtract your expenses from your income to arrive at your total disposable income.

Line 53. Enter your current monthly income, as calculated in Ch. 4.

Line 54. Enter the monthly average of any child support payments, foster care payments, or disability payments for a dependent child, that:
- are necessary to spend on the child, and
- you included in Line 7 when computing your current monthly income, in Ch. 4.

Line 55. Enter the monthly average of:
- all contributions or wage deductions made to qualified retirement plans, as specified in Section 541(b)(7) (these include virtually all defined-benefit pension plans arising from employment), and
- all repayments of loans from retirements plans, as specified in Section 362(b)(19) (employment pension plans and 401(k)s).

Line 56. Bring down the total expenses from Line 52.

Line 57. Special circumstances are situations that give rise to unexpected expenses that don't qualify as "additional expense claims" on Line 60. The new law lists a serious medical condition (such as cancer, Alzheimer's disease, or Parkinson's disease) or a call to active duty in the armed forces as examples of special circumstances. It's not enough just to show that special circumstances exist: You must also show that they justify additional expenses or adjustments to your current monthly income "for which there is no reasonable alternative." And, you must be able to document the expenses. If you believe that something in your life—that is not already provided for in this form—will eat up part of your disposable income, list the expense here and line up your documentation.

Line 58. Add Lines 54, 55, 56, and 57, and enter the total.

Line 59. Subtract Line 57 from Line 53 and enter the result. This is your first calculation of disposable income, but you're not through yet. Now return to Line 50 and enter the amount on Line 58 on Line 50a. On Line 50b, multiply the amount on Line 50a by the correct multiplier, which can be found on the U.S. Trustee's website (www.usdoj.gov/ust). Enter the result on Line 50c. Then, subtract Line 50c from Line 58.

Line 60. If you have additional expenses that you couldn't include anywhere else on the form, you can enter them here, provided they really are necessary for the health and welfare of you and your family. The court will look at these expenses with special scrutiny. If you include additional expenses here, subtract them from the total on Line 58, less the amount on Line 50c, for a final disposable income figure.

To find out whether you have enough disposable income to get a Chapter 13 plan confirmed, divide the total of any secured debts that weren't included in Line 47 by 60, to figure out how much you'd have to pay each month to pay off these liens in five years. Subtract the result from your disposable income. If this results in a negative figure, then you can't propose a

B22C (Official Form 22C) (Chapter 13) (01/08)

In re **Carrie Anne Edwards**
_____
Debtor(s)

Case Number: _____
(If known)

According to the calculations required by this statement:

☐ **The applicable commitment period is 3 years.**

■ **The applicable commitment period is 5 years.**

■ **Disposable income is determined under § 1325(b)(3).**

☐ **Disposable income is not determined under § 1325(b)(3).**

(Check the boxes as directed in Lines 17 and 23 of this statement.)

CHAPTER 13 STATEMENT OF CURRENT MONTHLY INCOME
AND CALCULATION OF COMMITMENT PERIOD AND DISPOSABLE INCOME

In addition to Schedules I and J, this statement must be completed by every individual chapter 13 debtor, whether or not filing jointly. Joint debtors may complete one statement only.

	Part I. REPORT OF INCOME		
1	**Marital/filing status.** Check the box that applies and complete the balance of this part of this statement as directed. a. ■ Unmarried. **Complete only Column A ("Debtor's Income") for Lines 2-10.** b. ☐ Married. **Complete both Column A ("Debtor's Income") and Column B ("Spouse's Income") for Lines 2-10.**		
	All figures must reflect average monthly income received from all sources, derived during the six calendar months prior to filing the bankruptcy case, ending on the last day of the month before the filing. If the amount of monthly income varied during the six months, you must divide the six-month total by six, and enter the result on the appropriate line.	**Column A** Debtor's Income	**Column B** Spouse's Income
2	**Gross wages, salary, tips, bonuses, overtime, commissions.**	$ 5,060.00	$
3	**Income from the operation of a business, profession, or farm.** Subtract Line b from Line a and enter the difference in the appropriate column(s) of Line 3. If you operate more than one business, profession or farm, enter aggregate numbers and provide details on an attachment. Do not enter a number less than zero. **Do not include any part of the business expenses entered on Line b as a deduction in Part IV.**		

		Debtor	Spouse		
	a.	Gross receipts	$ 0.00	$	
	b.	Ordinary and necessary business expenses	$ 0.00	$	
	c.	Business income	Subtract Line b from Line a		$ 0.00	$

| 4 | **Rents and other real property income.** Subtract Line b from Line a and enter the difference in the appropriate column(s) of Line 4. Do not enter a number less than zero. **Do not include any part of the operating expenses entered on Line b as a deduction in Part IV.** | | |

		Debtor	Spouse		
	a.	Gross receipts	$ 0.00	$	
	b.	Ordinary and necessary operating expenses	$ 0.00	$	
	c.	Rent and other real property income	Subtract Line b from Line a		$ 0.00	$

5	**Interest, dividends, and royalties.**	$ 1,500.00	$
6	**Pension and retirement income.**	$ 0.00	$
7	**Any amounts paid by another person or entity, on a regular basis, for the household expenses of the debtor or the debtor's dependents, including child support paid for that purpose.** Do not include alimony or separate maintenance payments or amounts paid by the debtor's spouse.	$ 1,000.00	$
8	**Unemployment compensation.** Enter the amount in the appropriate column(s) of Line 8. However, if you contend that unemployment compensation received by you or your spouse was a benefit under the Social Security Act, do not list the amount of such compensation in Column A or B, but instead state the amount in the space below:		

	Unemployment compensation claimed to be a benefit under the Social Security Act	Debtor $ 0.00	Spouse $	$ 0.00	$

B22C (Official Form 22C) (Chapter 13) (01/08)   2

			Debtor	Spouse		
9	**Income from all other sources.** Specify source and amount. If necessary, list additional sources on a separate page. Total and enter on Line 9. **Do not include alimony or separate maintenance payments paid by your spouse, but include all other payments of alimony or separate maintenance. Do not include** any benefits received under the Social Security Act or payments received as a victim of a war crime, crime against humanity, or as a victim of international or domestic terrorism.					
		a.	$	$		
		b.	$	$	$ 0.00	$
10	**Subtotal.** Add Lines 2 thru 9 in Column A, and, if Column B is completed, add Lines 2 through 9 in Column B. Enter the total(s).				$ 7,560.00	$
11	**Total.** If Column B has been completed, add Line 10, Column A to Line 10, Column B, and enter the total. If Column B has not been completed, enter the amount from Line 10, Column A.				$ 7,560.00	

Part II. CALCULATION OF § 1325(b)(4) COMMITMENT PERIOD

12	Enter the amount from Line 11		$ 7,560.00
13	**Marital Adjustment.** If you are married, but are not filing jointly with your spouse, AND if you contend that calculation of the commitment period under § 1325(b)(4) does not require inclusion of the income of your spouse, enter on Line 13 the amount of the income listed in Line 10, Column B that was NOT paid on a regular basis for the household expenses of you or your dependents and specify, in the lines below, the basis for excluding this income (such as payment of the spouse's tax liability or the spouse's support of persons other than the debtor or the debtor's dependents) and the amount of income devoted to each purpose. If necessary, list additional adjustments on a separate page. If the conditions for entering this adjustment do not apply, enter zero. a. $ b. $ c. $ Total and enter on Line 13		$ 0.00
14	**Subtract Line 13 from Line 12 and enter the result.**		$ 7,560.00
15	**Annualized current monthly income for § 1325(b)(4).** Multiply the amount from Line 14 by the number 12 and enter the result.		$ 90,720.00
16	**Applicable median family income.** Enter the median family income for applicable state and household size. (This information is available by family size at www.usdoj.gov/ust/ or from the clerk of the bankruptcy court.) a. Enter debtor's state of residence: **CA** b. Enter debtor's household size: **3**		$ 64,766.00
17	**Application of § 1325(b)(4).** Check the applicable box and proceed as directed. ☐ **The amount on Line 15 is less than the amount on Line 16.** Check the box for "The applicable commitment period is 3 years" at the top of page 1 of this statement and continue with this statement. ■ **The amount on Line 15 is not less than the amount on Line 16.** Check the box for "The applicable commitment period is 5 years" at the top of page 1 of this statement and continue with this statement.		

Part III. APPLICATION OF § 1325(b)(3) FOR DETERMINING DISPOSABLE INCOME

18	Enter the amount from Line 11.		$ 7,560.00
19	**Marital Adjustment.** If you are married, but are not filing jointly with your spouse, enter on Line 19 the total of any income listed in Line 10, Column B that was NOT paid on a regular basis for the household expenses of the debtor or the debtor's dependents. Specify in the lines below the basis for excluding the Column B income(such as payment of the spouse's tax liability or the spouse's support of persons other than the debtor or the debtor's dependents) and the amount of income devoted to each purpose. If necessary, list additional adjustments on a separate page. If the conditions for entering this adjustment do not apply, enter zero. a. $ b. $ c. $ Total and enter on Line 19.		$ 0.00
20	**Current monthly income for § 1325(b)(3).** Subtract Line 19 from Line 18 and enter the result.		$ 7,560.00

B22C (Official Form 22C) (Chapter 13) (01/08)   3

21	**Annualized current monthly income for § 1325(b)(3).** Multiply the amount from Line 20 by the number 12 and enter the result.	$ 90,720.00
22	**Applicable median family income.** Enter the amount from Line 16.	$ 64,766.00
23	**Application of § 1325(b)(3).** Check the applicable box and proceed as directed. ■ **The amount on Line 21 is more than the amount on Line 22.** Check the box for "Disposable income is determined under § 1325(b)(3)" at the top of page 1 of this statement and complete the remaining parts of this statement. ☐ **The amount on Line 21 is not more than the amount on Line 22.** Check the box for "Disposable income is not determined under § 1325(b)(3)" at the top of page 1 of this statement and complete Part VII of this statement. **Do not complete Parts IV, V, or VI.**	

Part IV. CALCULATION OF DEDUCTIONS FROM INCOME

Subpart A: Deductions under Standards of the Internal Revenue Service (IRS)

24A	**National Standards: food, apparel and services, housekeeping supplies, personal care, and miscellaneous.** Enter in Line 24A the "Total" amount from IRS National Standards for Allowable Living Expenses for the applicable household size. (This information is available at www.usdoj.gov/ust/ or from the clerk of the bankruptcy court.)	$ 1,123.00

24B	**National Standards: health care.** Enter in Line a1 below the amount from IRS National Standards for Out-of-Pocket Health Care for persons under 65 years of age, and in Line a2 the IRS National Standards for Out-of-Pocket Health Care for persons 65 years of age or older. (This information is available at www.usdoj.gov/ust/ or from the clerk of the bankruptcy court.) Enter in Line b1 the number of members of your household who are under 65 years of age, and enter in Line b2 the number of members of your household who are 65 years of age or older. (The total number of household members must be the same as the number stated in Line 14b.) Multiply Line a1 by Line b1 to obtain a total amount for household members under 65, and enter the result in Line c1. Multiply Line a2 by Line b2 to obtain a total amount for household members 65 and older, and enter the result in Line c2. Add Lines c1 and c2 to obtain a total health care amount, and enter the result in Line 24B.	

Household members under 65 years of age			Household members 65 years of age or older		
a1.	Allowance per member	54	a2.	Allowance per member	144
b1.	Number of members	3	b2.	Number of members	0
c1.	Subtotal	162.00	c2.	Subtotal	0.00

$ 162.00

25A	**Local Standards: housing and utilities; non-mortgage expenses.** Enter the amount of the IRS Housing and Utilities Standards; non-mortgage expenses for the applicable county and household size. (This information is available at www.usdoj.gov/ust/ or from the clerk of the bankruptcy court).	$ 523.00

25B	**Local Standards: housing and utilities; mortgage/rent expense.** Enter, in Line a below, the amount of the IRS Housing and Utilities Standards; mortgage/rent expense for your county and household size (this information is available at www.usdoj.gov/ust/ or from the clerk of the bankruptcy court); enter on Line b the total of the Average Monthly Payments for any debts secured by your home, as stated in Line 47; subtract Line b from Line a and enter the result in Line 25B. **Do not enter an amount less than zero.**	

a.	IRS Housing and Utilities Standards; mortgage/rent Expense	$ 820.00	
b.	Average Monthly Payment for any debts secured by your home, if any, as stated in Line 47	$ 1,565.10	
c.	Net mortgage/rental expense	Subtract Line b from Line a.	$ 0.00

26	**Local Standards: housing and utilities; adjustment.** If you contend that the process set out in Lines 25A and 25B does not accurately compute the allowance to which you are entitled under the IRS Housing and Utilities Standards, enter any additional amount to which you contend you are entitled, and state the basis for your contention in the space below:	$ 0.00

B22C (Official Form 22C) (Chapter 13) (01/08) 4

27A	**Local Standards: transportation; vehicle operation/public transportation expense.** You are entitled to an expense allowance in this category regardless of whether you pay the expenses of operating a vehicle and regardless of whether you use public transportation. Check the number of vehicles for which you pay the operating expenses or for which the operating expenses are included as a contribution to your household expenses in Line 7. ☐ 0 ■ 1 ☐ 2 or more. If you checked 0, enter on Line 27A the "Public Transportation" amount from IRS Local Standards: Transportation. If you checked 1 or 2 or more, enter on Line 27A the "Operating Costs" amount from IRS Local Standards: Transportation for the applicable number of vehicles in the applicable Metropolitan Statistical Area or Census Region. (These amounts are available at www.usdoj.gov/ust/ or from the clerk of the bankruptcy court.)	$	194.00
27B	**Local Standards: transportation; additional public transportation expense.** If you pay the operating expenses for a vehicle and also use public transportation, and you contend that you are entitled to an additional deduction for your public transportation expenses, enter on Line 27B the "Public Transportation" amount from the IRS Local Standards: Transportation. (This amount is available at www.usdoj.gov/ust/ or from the clerk of the bankruptcy court.)	$	0.00
28	**Local Standards: transportation ownership/lease expense; Vehicle 1.** Check the number of vehicles for which you claim an ownership/lease expense. (You may not claim an ownership/lease expense for more than two vehicles.) ■ 1 ☐ 2 or more. Enter, in Line a below, the "Ownership Costs" for "One Car" from the IRS Local Standards: Transportation (available at www.usdoj.gov/ust/ or from the clerk of the bankruptcy court); enter in Line b the total of the Average Monthly Payments for any debts secured by Vehicle 1, as stated in Line 47; subtract Line b from Line a and enter the result in Line 28. **Do not enter an amount less than zero.**	$	78.00
	a. IRS Transportation Standards, Ownership Costs	$ 478.00	
	b. Average Monthly Payment for any debts secured by Vehicle 1, as stated in Line 47	$ 400.00	
	c. Net ownership/lease expense for Vehicle 1	Subtract Line b from Line a.	
29	**Local Standards: transportation ownership/lease expense; Vehicle 2.** Complete this Line only if you checked the "2 or more" Box in Line 28. Enter, in Line a below, the "Ownership Costs" for "One Car" from the IRS Local Standards: Transportation (available at www.usdoj.gov/ust/ or from the clerk of the bankruptcy court); enter in Line b the total of the Average Monthly Payments for any debts secured by Vehicle 2, as stated in Line 47; subtract Line b from Line a and enter the result in Line 29. **Do not enter an amount less than zero.**	$	0.00
	a. IRS Transportation Standards, Ownership Costs	$ 0.00	
	b. Average Monthly Payment for any debts secured by Vehicle 2, as stated in Line 47	$ 0.00	
	c. Net ownership/lease expense for Vehicle 2	Subtract Line b from Line a.	
30	**Other Necessary Expenses: taxes.** Enter the total average monthly expense that you actually incur for all federal, state, and local taxes, other than real estate and sales taxes, such as income taxes, self employment taxes, social security taxes, and Medicare taxes. **Do not include real estate or sales taxes.**	$	1,013.71
31	**Other Necessary Expenses: mandatory deductions for employment.** Enter the total average monthly payroll deductions that are required for your employment, such as mandatory retirement contributions, union dues, and uniform costs. **Do not include discretionary amounts, such as voluntary 401(k) contributions.**	$	0.00
32	**Other Necessary Expenses: life insurance.** Enter total average monthly premiums that you actually pay for term life insurance for yourself. **Do not include premiums for insurance on your dependents, for whole life or for any other form of insurance.**	$	0.00
33	**Other Necessary Expenses: court-ordered payments.** Enter the total monthly amount that you are required to pay pursuant to the order of a court or administrative agency, such as spousal or child support payments. **Do not include payments on past due obligations included in line 49.**	$	0.00
34	**Other Necessary Expenses: education for employment or for a physically or mentally challenged child.** Enter the total average monthly amount that you actually expend for education that is a condition of employment and for education that is required for a physically or mentally challenged dependent child for whom no public education providing similar services is available.	$	0.00
35	**Other Necessary Expenses: childcare.** Enter the total average monthly amount that you actually expend on childcare - such as baby-sitting, day care, nursery and preschool. **Do not include other educational payments.**	$	300.00

B22C (Official Form 22C) (Chapter 13) (01/08)   5

36	**Other Necessary Expenses: health care.** Enter the average monthly amount that you actually expend on health care that is required for the health and welfare of yourself or your dependents, that is not reimbursed by insurance or paid by a health savings account, and that is in excess of the amount entered in Line 24B. **Do not include payments for health insurance or health savings accounts listed in Line 39.**	$	138.00
37	**Other Necessary Expenses: telecommunication services.** Enter the total average monthly amount that you actually pay for telecommunication services other than your basic home telephone and cell phone service - such as pagers, call waiting, caller id, special long distance, or internet service-to the extent necessary for your health and welfare or that of your dependents. **Do not include any amount previously deducted.**	$	175.00
38	**Total Expenses Allowed under IRS Standards.** Enter the total of Lines 24 through 37.	$	3,706.71

Subpart B: Additional Living Expense Deductions
Note: Do not include any expenses that you have listed in Lines 24-37

39	**Health Insurance, Disability Insurance, and Health Savings Account Expenses.** List the monthly expenses in the categories set out in lines a-c below that are reasonably necessary for yourself, your spouse, or your dependents..		
	a. Health Insurance $ 100.00		
	b. Disability Insurance $ 0.00		
	c. Health Savings Account $ 0.00		
	Total and enter on Line 39	$	100.00
	If you do not actually expend this total amount, state your actual total average monthly expenditures in the space below: $_____		
40	**Continued contributions to the care of household or family members.** Enter the total average actual monthly expenses that you will continue to pay for the reasonable and necessary care and support of an elderly, chronically ill, or disabled member of your household or member of your immediate family who is unable to pay for such expenses. **Do not include payments listed in Line 34.**	$	0.00
41	**Protection against family violence.** Enter the total average reasonably necessary monthly expenses that you actually incur to maintain the safety of your family under the Family Violence Prevention and Services Act or other applicable federal law. The nature of these expenses is required to be kept confidential by the court.	$	0.00
42	**Home energy costs.** Enter the total average monthly amount, in excess of the allowance specified by IRS Local Standards for Housing and Utilities, that you actually expend for home energy costs. **You must provide your case trustee with documentation of your actual expenses, and you must demonstrate that the additional amount claimed is reasonable and necessary.**	$	0.00
43	**Education expenses for dependent children under 18.** Enter the total average monthly expenses that you actually incur, not to exceed $137.50 per child, for attendance at a private or public elementary or secondary school by your dependent children less than 18 years of age. **You must provide your case trustee with documentation of your actual expenses, and you must explain why the amount claimed is reasonable and necessary and not already accounted for in the IRS Standards.**	$	0.00
44	**Additional food and clothing expense.** Enter the total average monthly amount by which your food and clothing expenses exceed the combined allowances for food and clothing (apparel and services) in the IRS National Standards, not to exceed 5% of those combined allowances. (This information is available at www.usdoj.gov/ust/ or from the clerk of the bankruptcy court.) **You must demonstrate that the additional amount claimed is reasonable and necessary.**	$	41.00
45	**Charitable contributions.** Enter the amount reasonably necessary for you to expend each month on charitable contributions in the form of cash or financial instruments to a charitable organization as defined in 26 U.S.C. § 170(c)(1)-(2). **Do not include any amount in excess of 15% of your gross monthly income.**	$	0.00
46	**Total Additional Expense Deductions under § 707(b).** Enter the total of Lines 39 through 45.	$	141.00

B22C (Official Form 22C) (Chapter 13) (01/08)   6

	Subpart C: Deductions for Debt Payment					

47 Future payments on secured claims. For each of your debts that is secured by an interest in property that you own, list the name of creditor, identify the property securing the debt, state the Average Monthly Payment, and check whether the payment includes taxes or insurance. The Average Monthly Payment is the total of all amounts scheduled as contractually due to each Secured Creditor in the 60 months following the filing of the bankruptcy case, divided by 60. If necessary, list additional entries on a separate page. Enter the total of the Average Monthly Payments on Line 47.

	Name of Creditor	Property Securing the Debt	Average Monthly Payment	Does payment include taxes or insurance	
a.	GMAC	2003 Buick LeSabre fully loaded in good condition (replacement value from nada.com)	$ 400.00	☐yes ☐no	
b.	Grand Junction Mortgage	Residence Location: 3045 Berwick St, Lakeport CA	$ 1,465.10	☐yes ☐no	
c.	Lending Tree	Residence Location: 3045 Berwick St, Lakeport CA	$ 100.00	☐yes ☐no	
			Total: Add Lines		$ 1,965.10

48 Other payments on secured claims. If any of debts listed in Line 47 are secured by your primary residence, a motor vehicle, or other property necessary for your support or the support of your dependents, you may include in your deduction 1/60th of any amount (the "cure amount") that you must pay the creditor in addition to the payments listed in Line 47, in order to maintain possession of the property. The cure amount would include any sums in default that must be paid in order to avoid repossession or foreclosure. List and total any such amounts in the following chart. If necessary, list additional entries on a separate page.

	Name of Creditor	Property Securing the Debt	1/60th of the Cure Amount	
a.	Grand Junction Mortgage	Residence Location: 3045 Berwick St, Lakeport CA	$ 53.84	
			Total: Add Lines	$ 53.84

49 Payments on prepetition priority claims. Enter the total amount, divided by 60, of all priority claims, such as priority tax, child support and alimony claims, for which you were liable at the time of your bankruptcy filing. **Do not include current obligations, such as those set out in Line 33.** | $ 91.67

50 Chapter 13 administrative expenses. Multiply the amount in Line a by the amount in Line b, and enter the resulting administrative expense.

a.	Projected average monthly Chapter 13 plan payment.	$ 1,587.00
b.	Current multiplier for your district as determined under schedules issued by the Executive Office for United States Trustees. (This information is available at www.usdoj.gov/ust/ or from the clerk of the bankruptcy court.)	x 9.80
c.	Average monthly administrative expense of Chapter 13 case	Total: Multiply Lines a and b	$ 155.53

51 Total Deductions for Debt Payment. Enter the total of Lines 47 through 50. | $ 2,266.14

Subpart D: Total Deductions from Income	
52 Total of all deductions from income. Enter the total of Lines 38, 46, and 51. | $ 6,113.85

Part V. DETERMINATION OF DISPOSABLE INCOME UNDER § 1325(b)(2)	

53 Total current monthly income. Enter the amount from Line 20. | $ 7,560.00

54 Support income. Enter the monthly average of any child support payments, foster care payments, or disability payments for a dependent child, reported in Part I, that you received in accordance with applicable nonbankruptcy law, to the extent reasonably necessary to be expended for such child. | $ 0.00

55 Qualified retirement deductions. Enter the monthly total of (a) all amounts withheld by your employer from wages as contributions for qualified retirement plans, as specified in § 541(b)(7) and (b) all required repayments of loans from retirement plans, as specified in § 362(b)(19). | $ 0.00

B22C (Official Form 22C) (Chapter 13) (01/08)   7

56	**Total of all deductions allowed under § 707(b)(2).** Enter the amount from Line 52.	$	6,113.85

57	**Deduction for special circumstances.** If there are special circumstances that justify additional expenses for which there is no reasonable alternative, describe the special circumstances and the resulting expenses in lines a-c below. If necessary, list additional entries on a separate page. Total the expenses and enter the total in Line 57. **You must provide your case trustee with documentation of these expenses and you must provide a detailed explanation of the special circumstances that make such expense necessary and reasonable.**		

	Nature of special circumstances	Amount of Expense	
a.		$	
b.		$	
c.		$	
		Total: Add Lines	$ 0.00

58	**Total adjustments to determine disposable income.** Add the amounts on Lines 54, 55, 56, and 57 and enter the result.	$	6,113.85
59	**Monthly Disposable Income Under § 1325(b)(2).** Subtract Line 58 from Line 53 and enter the result.	$	1,446.15

Part VI. ADDITIONAL EXPENSE CLAIMS

60	**Other Expenses.** List and describe any monthly expenses, not otherwise stated in this form, that are required for the health and welfare of you and your family and that you contend should be an additional deduction from your current monthly income under § 707(b)(2)(A)(ii)(I). If necessary, list additional sources on a separate page. All figures should reflect your average monthly expense for each item. Total the expenses.	

	Expense Description	Monthly Amount
a.		$
b.		$
c.		$
d.		$
	Total: Add Lines a, b, c and d	$

Part VII. VERIFICATION

61	I declare under penalty of perjury that the information provided in this statement is true and correct. *(If this is a joint case, both debtors must sign.)* Date: October 3, 2008 Signature: *Carrie Anne Edwards* **Carrie Anne Edwards** (Debtor)

confirmable plan, given your current expenses and property holdings. If your disposable income is zero or more, then you can propose a confirmable plan, as long as the total is at least equal to the value of your nonexempt property (see below).

Actual or Projected Income?

The disposable income figure you come up with after completing Form 22C may not reflect your actual ability to fund a confirmable Chapter 13 plan. That's because your projected disposable income is based on your average income over the six months before you file, rather than your actual income when you file. And, the extensive deductions that Form 22C allows might make it look like you'll have nothing left to pay into your plan, even though you might not spend that much in the real world.

So what happens when your projected disposable income and your actual disposable income are different? So far, bankruptcy courts have handled this in a variety of ways. For example, courts have held that:

- It doesn't matter what your actual disposable income is; your projected disposable income, as calculated on Form 22C, is all that matters in determining your ability to fund a Chapter 13 plan and how much you must pay into it. (See *In re Puetz*, 370 B.R. 386 (D. Kan. 2006); *In re Guzman*, 345 B.R. 640 (E.D. Wis. 2006).)
- Courts can consider your actual income and expenses—not just your projected disposable income—in deciding whether you can propose a confirmable Chapter 13 plan. (See *In re Jass*, 340 B.R. 411 (D. Utah 2006); *In re Meek*, 370 B.R. 294 (D. Idaho).)
- Only your actual income, as shown in Schedules I and J, determines your ability to fund a Chapter 13 plan, not your projected disposable income. (See *In re Purdy*, 373 B.R. 142 (N.D. Fla. 2007).)
- You may claim the IRS allowed expense amounts in calculating your disposable income on Form 22C, even if you actually spend less. (See *In re Barrett*, 371 B.R. 855 (S.D. Ill. 2007).)

This actual disposable income versus projected disposable income dance is sure to go on for some time. If there's a significant difference between the two figures in your case, talk to a lawyer.

Step 2: Compare Your Disposable Income to the Value of Your Nonexempt Property

As explained in Ch. 3, if you own property that is not exempt under the exemption laws available to you, you will have to pay your nonpriority, unsecured creditors at least the value of that nonexempt property. For example, if you have $15,000 in a savings account and the exemptions you are using allow you to exempt only $10,000, your Chapter 13 plan would have to include payments to your nonpriority, unsecured creditors of at least $5,000 over a five-year period, or $83 a month.

If you don't know whether you have nonexempt property, skip to "Understanding Property Exemptions," below, for information on which exemptions you can use and how to apply them to your property. If you have nonexempt property, add up the value of that property. Then subtract the total value from your disposable income, as calculated by completing Form 22C, in Step 1.

1. Disposable Income (from Step 1): _____
2. Value of Nonexempt Property (Monthly): − _____
3. Total: = _____

As long as your total is not a negative number, you may be able to propose a confirmable plan. This means you will have enough money to pay your nonpriority, unsecured creditors. If your total is zero, this means you will have *exactly* enough money to meet your plan obligations, not a penny more or less.

If all of your property is exempt, and the disposable income you calculated in Step 1 was zero, it means that your unsecured creditors won't get paid a cent. This is what is called a zero-percent plan. Prior to the new bankruptcy law (October 2005), many courts wouldn't confirm a plan that paid the unsecured creditors less than a particular percentage (anywhere from 20% to 80%, depending on the court). But under the new law, as long as your expenses are reasonable—that is, the court can't find any expenses you are paying that should go to your creditors—there is no legal reason why a zero-percent plan won't be confirmed.

Understanding Property Exemptions

This section covers exemptions—the rules that determine how much, if any, your Chapter 13 plan will have to pay to your nonpriority, unsecured creditors.

Your Bankruptcy Estate

Your bankruptcy estate refers to all of your property that is part of your bankruptcy case. Not all property is in your bankruptcy estate—for example, most property you acquire after you file for bankruptcy is not part of the estate, and you need not account to the trustee about what you do with it. If property falls outside of your bankruptcy estate, you don't need to worry about whether or not it's exempt, because the court can't touch it or ask you to pay its value to your creditors.

Several broad categories of property make up your bankruptcy estate:

- **Property you own and possess.** Everything in your possession that you own, whether or not you owe money on it—for example, a car, real estate, clothing, books, television, stereo system, furniture, tools, boat, artworks, or stock certificates—is included in your bankruptcy estate. Property that you have in your possession but belongs to someone else (such as the car your friend stores in your garage or the television you borrowed from your sister) is not part of your bankruptcy estate, because you don't have the right to sell it or give it away.
- **Property you own but don't possess.** You can own something even if you don't have physical possession of it. For instance, you may own a car that someone else is using. Other examples include a deposit held by a stockbroker, a security deposit held by your landlord or a utility company, or a business in which you've invested money.
- **Property you are entitled to receive.** Property that you have a legal right to receive but haven't gotten yet when you file for bankruptcy is included in your bankruptcy estate. Common examples include:
  - wages, royalties, or commissions you have earned but have not yet been paid
  - a tax refund legally due you

  - vacation or termination pay you've earned
  - property you've inherited but not yet received from someone who has died
  - proceeds of an insurance policy, if the death, injury, or other event that gives rise to payment has already occurred, and
  - money owed you for goods or services you've provided (often called "accounts receivable").
- **Community property.** If you live in a community property state, all property either spouse acquires during the marriage is ordinarily considered "community property," owned jointly by both spouses. (The community property states are Arizona, California, Idaho, Louisiana, Nevada, New Mexico, Texas, Washington, and Wisconsin, and—if you have a written community property agreement or trust—Alaska.) Gifts and inheritances to only one spouse are the most common exceptions—these are the separate property of the spouse who receives them. If you're married and file jointly for bankruptcy, all the community property you and your spouse own, as well as all of both of your separate property, is considered part of your bankruptcy estate. If your spouse doesn't file, then your bankruptcy estate consists of all of the community property and all of your separate property—your spouse's separate property isn't included.
- **Marital property in a common law property state.** If you are married and filing jointly, your bankruptcy estate includes all the property you and your spouse own, together and separately. If you are filing alone for bankruptcy in a common law property state (all states other than the community property states listed above), your bankruptcy estate includes:
  - your separate property (property that has only your name on a title certificate or that was purchased, received as a gift, or inherited by you alone), and
  - half of the property that is jointly owned by you and your spouse, unless you own the property as tenants by the entirety.
- **Certain property you receive within 180 days after filing for bankruptcy.** Most property you acquire or become entitled to after you file for bankruptcy isn't included in your bankruptcy estate. But there

are a few exceptions. If you acquire or become entitled to the following items within 180 days after you file, you must notify the trustee:

- an inheritance (but not money "inherited" through a living trust or beneficiary designation form; see *In re Szwyd,* 370 B.R. 882 (1st Cir. B.A.P. 2007) and *In re Kester,* 493 F.3d 1208 (10th Cir. 2007).

- property you receive or have a right to receive from a marital settlement agreement or divorce decree, and

- death benefits or life insurance policy proceeds.

- **Property (revenue) generated by estate property.** This type of property typically consists of the proceeds of contracts—such as those providing for rent, royalties, and commissions—that were in effect at the time of the bankruptcy filing, but which produced earnings after that date. For example, if you are a composer or author and receive royalties each year for a book that was written before you filed for bankruptcy, the trustee may collect those royalties as property of your estate. Proceeds from work you do after your filing date belong to you.

Property That's Not Part of Your Bankruptcy Estate

Property that is not in your bankruptcy estate is not subject to the bankruptcy court's jurisdiction, which means that you don't have to worry about whether or not it's exempt.

The most common examples of property that doesn't fall within your bankruptcy estate are:

- property you buy or receive after your filing date (with the few exceptions described above)

- pensions subject to the federal law known as ERISA (commonly, defined benefit pensions, 401(k)s, and Keogh plans)

- property pledged as collateral for a loan where a licensed lender (pawnbroker) retains possession of the collateral

- property in your possession that belongs to someone else (for instance, property you are storing for someone), and

- wages that are withheld, and employer contributions that are made, for employee benefit and health insurance plans.

Under the new bankruptcy law, funds placed in a qualified tuition program or Coverdell education savings account are also not part of your bankruptcy estate under certain conditions.

Value Your Property

As you'll see below, many exemptions apply only up to a certain dollar value. This means that you need to know what your property is worth in order to figure out whether it's exempt. Under the new bankruptcy law, you must use the property's replacement value: what it would cost to buy that specific property from a retail merchant, considering its age and condition.

It's easy to enter a dollar amount for cash and most investments.

If you own a car, start with the middle *Kelley Blue Book* price. If the car needs repair, reduce the value by what it would cost you to fix the car. You can find the *Kelley Blue Book* at a public library or online at www.kbb.com.

Online, visit eBay (www.ebay.com) to get a fix on the going price for just about anything. Or briefly describe the item in Google (or your search engine of choice) and see what turns up. As long as your valuations are based on the going retail price for the item in question, you should use the lowest value you can find. That means it is more likely to be exempt and not require payments to your nonpriority, unsecured creditors.

If you are filing separately and own something jointly with someone (other than a spouse with whom you would file for bankruptcy), reduce the value of the item to reflect only the portion you own. For example, you and your brother jointly bought a music synthesizer worth $10,000. If your ownership share is 40% and your brother's is 60%, the value of your portion is $4,000.

If you are married and filing separately in a community property state, include the total value of all the community property as well as the value of your separate property.

If you are married, you own the property with your spouse as tenants by the entirety, and you are filing separately, your ownership interest may not be 50% for purposes of computing your exemption. (Talk to a lawyer to find out what percentage of your tenancy by the entirety property you can claim as exempt.)

Applying Exemptions

Bankruptcy is intended to give debtors a fresh start—not to leave them utterly destitute. Exempt property can literally range from "the shirt on your back" to a million-dollar estate, depending on which state's exemptions you use.

State and Federal Exemption Systems

Every state has its own fairly lengthy list of exempt property. (You can find these lists in Appendix A.) In addition, some states offer bankruptcy filers an alternative choice of exemptions—a list of exempt property found in the federal bankruptcy code. States that offer this choice are: Arkansas, Connecticut, Hawaii, Massachusetts, Michigan, Minnesota, New Hampshire, New Jersey, New Mexico, Pennsylvania, Rhode Island, Texas, Vermont, Washington, and Wisconsin. In these states, you must choose between the state exemption system and the federal exemption system; you can't mix and match.

California Note: Although California doesn't make the federal bankruptcy code exemptions available, it also has two separate exemption systems—but both are created by state law. Debtors who use the California exemptions must choose between System 1 (the regular exemptions available to debtors in and out of bankruptcy) and System 2 (available only in bankruptcy and very similar to the federal exemptions).

How Exemptions Work

Under both the federal and state exemption systems, some types of property are exempt regardless of value. For example, in some states, home furnishings, wedding rings, or clothing are exempt without regard to value. In Florida and Texas, homes are exempt regardless of their value or the value of the bankruptcy filer's ownership (equity) in the home.

Other kinds of property are exempt up to a limited value. For instance, cars are often exempt up to a certain amount—typically $2,500 to $3,000. The home equity exemption ranges from thousands of dollars to hundreds of thousands, depending on the state. When there is a dollar limit on an exemption, any equity above the limit is considered nonexempt. (Your equity is the amount you would get to keep if you sold the property.)

Many states offer a "wildcard" exemption—a dollar amount that you can apply to any property, in order to make it (or more of it) exempt. This type of exemption typically runs from a few hundred to several thousand dollars (but more than $20,000 in California's System 2 exemptions).

EXAMPLE: Fred and Susan are married and live in Virginia. They rent rather than own their home. Under the Virginia exemptions, equity in an automobile is limited to $2,000 ($4,000 for couples). Fred and Susan own $12,000 of equity in their cars. Fortunately for Fred and Susan, Virginia allows debtors to use the Virginia homestead exemption as a wildcard for their personal property, if they don't use it for a home. Because Fred and Susan rent, they can use this wildcard for their cars. The homestead exemption is $10,000 for couples. So, by adding $8,000 of the wildcard to their $4,000 car exemption, Fred and Susan can exempt all of their equity in their cars. They can apply the other $2,000 of the wildcard exemption to property that isn't otherwise protected by the Virginia exemptions.

Property Typically Not Exempt

The kinds of property listed below are typically not exempt unless you use a wildcard exemption:
- interests in real estate other than your home
- substantial equity in a newer-model motor vehicle
- expensive musical instruments unrelated to your job or business
- stamp, coin, and other collections
- cash, deposit accounts, stocks, bonds, and other investments
- business assets
- valuable artwork
- expensive clothing and jewelry, or
- antiques.

Domicile Requirements for Exemption Claims

In October 2005, Congress passed domicile requirements that filers have to meet before claiming a state's exemptions. Your domicile is where you are living and plan to continue living for the indefinite future. For most people, their domicile is where they are living, period. But for some people, such as those in the armed forces, their domicile may be in one state and their residence in another (such as when they live on an army base in North Carolina but maintain a home in Tennessee). Here are the domicile rules:

- If you have been living (been domiciled) in your current state for at least two years, you must use that state's exemptions (or the federal exemptions, if they are available)
- If you have been living (been domiciled) in your current state for less than two years, you must use the exemptions of the state where you were domiciled for the better part of the 180-day period immediately prior to the two-year period preceding your filing—unless that state allows only current residents to use its exemptions. In that case, you can use the federal exemptions.
- If you have been domiciled in your current state for fewer than 91 days, you'll need to wait until you have lived there for 91 days to file in that state (and then use whatever exemptions are available to you according to the rules set out above).
- If the state you are filing in makes the federal exemptions available, you can use that exemption list regardless of how long you've been living in the state.
- If these rules deprive you of the right to use any state's exemptions, you can use the federal exemptions. For example, if you were living in another country during the 180-day period prior to the two years before you filed for bankruptcy, you can use the federal exemptions.

A longer domicile requirement applies to homestead exemptions: If you acquired a home in your current state less than 40 months before your filing date, your homestead exemption may be subject to a $136,875 cap regardless of which state's exemption system you use. People convicted of felonies and certain securities violations are also subject to this cap.

Using the Exemptions Appendix

You can find the exemptions for all 50 states in Appendix A. If you are considering filing for bankruptcy in one of the states listed below, you'll also want to look at the federal exemptions, which are listed in the appendix right after Wyoming.

States That Offer the Federal Exemptions

Arkansas	Minnesota	Rhode Island
Connecticut	New Hampshire	Texas
Hawaii	New Jersey	Vermont
Massachusetts	New Mexico	Washington
Michigan	Pennsylvania	Wisconsin

Use Appendix A to find the applicable exemptions for your property, using the domicile rules set out above. Compare the type and value of your property, and the amount of equity you have in the property, with the exemptions.

Remember, if you are filing in a state that offers the federal bankruptcy exemptions, you should also check the federal exemption chart (it comes right after Wyoming). Items that aren't exempt under the state exemptions available to you may be exempt under the federal system, and vice versa. However, you must pick one system or the other to use in your bankruptcy— you can't mix and match.

If you are married and filing jointly, you can double your exemptions unless the chart says that you can't. This will be indicated either at the top of the chart or next to a particular exemption.

If you have been domiciled in California for more than two years when you file, you may choose System 1 (the regular state exemptions) or System 2, a state list that is derived from the federal exemptions but differs in important particulars. If you file in California but haven't been domiciled there for two years, you can't use either California system—you'll have to use the domicile rules set out above to figure out which exemptions you can use.

Federal Nonbankruptcy Exemptions

If you are using the exemptions of a particular state rather than the federal exemptions, you may also exempt property listed in Appendix A under Federal Nonbankruptcy Exemptions. Don't confuse those with the federal bankruptcy exemptions, which may be used only if a state allows it, and only as an alternative to the state exemptions.

Making the Decision

Now you have all of the information you need to decide whether you can—and should—file for Chapter 13 bankruptcy. To help you sort through this information, weigh the pros and cons, and reach a decision, this chapter provides a transcript of a consultation between a debtor and a lawyer.

As you'll see, the debtor, Georgia Cox, is trying to figure out whether to file for bankruptcy under Chapter 7 or Chapter 13. She has decided to consult with a bankruptcy lawyer to help her with her decision. The questions the lawyer asks will help remind you of factors you should consider as you evaluate your own situation.

Lawyer: Good morning. What's your name?

Debtor: Georgia Cox.

Lawyer: Hi, Georgia. How can I help you today?

Debtor: Well, I've run up quite a bit of debt, and I've decided to file for bankruptcy. I know there are different types of bankruptcy, but I think I need to learn more about them. I need some help figuring out what my options are.

Lawyer: Okay, I can help you with that. The two basic types of bankruptcy for individuals are Chapter 7 bankruptcy and Chapter 13 bankruptcy. There are a couple of major differences between them. In a Chapter 13 bankruptcy, you pay off some or all of your debts over time. You don't have to give up any of your property, but you do have to make regular payments to the court for three to five years. In a Chapter 7 bankruptcy, you don't have to pay off your debts, and the whole thing is over in three to six months. But you have to give up any property you own that isn't exempt from being taken by creditors, so it can be sold and the proceeds distributed to your creditors.

In either type of bankruptcy, many of your debts will be discharged—that is, they'll be wiped out and

you won't have to pay them—once the case is over. But you'll still have to pay some debts, like child support and student loans. Also, more types of debts can be wiped out in Chapter 13 than in Chapter 7. But we'll get to that later. Do you understand so far?

Debtor: Yes. I know a little bit about the types of bankruptcy, and I'm leaning toward the one where you pay back some debt. But I'm not sure if that's a good idea.

Lawyer: Okay. Well, let's start by figuring out whether you have a choice. Some people can't file for Chapter 7 bankruptcy under the new bankruptcy law. If both options are available to you, we can talk about which one makes more sense.

Debtor: Okay.

Lawyer: What state do you live in?

Debtor: New Hampshire.

Lawyer: How long have you lived there?

Debtor: Three years.

Lawyer: Have you actually lived there continuously for the last three years, or did you live or maintain a residence somewhere else?

Debtor: I've lived here the whole time. I moved here from Vermont because of a job, but I didn't keep a home in Vermont, and I haven't retained my residence there for voting purposes.

Lawyer: Great. Because you've been living in New Hampshire for more than two years, we'll use that state's exemptions when we look at what property you'd have to give up if you filed for Chapter 7. We'll also use them to figure out how much you would have to pay into your Chapter 13 repayment plan, if you went that route.

If you had lived there for less than two years, or if you still had a residence in Vermont, we would be looking at Vermont's exemptions.

Debtor: Why do the exemptions matter in a Chapter 13 bankruptcy? I thought I could keep all of my property if I use Chapter 13.

Lawyer: Yes, you're right about that. But the law doesn't want your creditors to be worse off because you use Chapter 13. So a Chapter 13 repayment plan has to give your unsecured, nonpriority creditors—those who hold debts that are not secured by collateral and do not have to be repaid in full—at least the value of your nonexempt property. That's what they would have gotten if you filed for Chapter 7, so they're entitled to at least that much if you use Chapter 13.

Debtor: Okay, I guess that's fair.

Lawyer: We'll get to exemptions later. But first, I need to figure out whether you have a choice between Chapter 13 and Chapter 7. Who lives with you as part of your household? That includes not only relatives and dependents but anyone else whose income and expenses are combined with yours to maintain your home.

Debtor: Just me and my two children. One is eight and the other just turned 12.

Lawyer: Okay. And do you operate a business?

Debtor: Actually, I do. What difference does that make?

Lawyer: Well, business debts are treated differently than consumer debts when it comes to deciding your eligibility for filing Chapter 7. Also, Chapter 13 is often the better type of bankruptcy for an ongoing business, since you can keep your business assets and use your business earnings to make your required payments.

Debtor: Okay. I run my own business, selling used electronic equipment.

Lawyer: Have you incorporated your business or is it a partnership?

Debtor: No, just me, a sole proprietor.

Lawyer: And do you have other work? In other words, do you have a regular job and operate your business on the side?

Debtor: No. Just the business.

Lawyer: Is your income pretty steady?

Debtor: Well, my earnings aren't steady from month to month, but my income averages out pretty steady from year to year. And my alimony and child support help stabilize my income over the year.

Lawyer: Looking at your debts as a whole, were more of them due to your business or more due to your personal needs?

Debtor: I would say about 40% were from my business and 60% were personal.

Lawyer: Okay, that means you are considered a consumer debtor and not a business debtor. How much did you earn in the last six months? That's gross earnings less your reasonable business expenses.

Debtor: About $3,000 a month after expenses for the last six months.

Lawyer: You mentioned that you receive child support, too. What other income do you receive, in addition to your business earning?

Debtor: I receive $1,000 a month in alimony from my ex, and $800 a month for child support.

Lawyer: Have those amounts been steady over the last six months?

Debtor: Yes, there haven't been any changes.

Lawyer: So, it looks like your average monthly earnings over the past six months are $3,000 from your business, $1,000 in alimony, and $800 for child support, for a total of $4,800. Does that sound right?

Debtor: Yes.

Lawyer: Under the bankruptcy law, if your income is less than the median annual income for a family of your size in your state, you are eligible to file for Chapter 7 bankruptcy. You don't have to take what people are calling "the means test," which requires you to fill out a lengthy form comparing your income to your expenses. Are you familiar with these rules?

Debtor: I've read a little bit about it, just that people who earn more might not be able to use Chapter 7 any more. Is that what you mean?

Lawyer: Yes, that's it. Also, if your income is less than the median for your state and you decide to file a Chapter 13 bankruptcy, your repayment plan only has to last for three years. If your income is more than the median, your plan would have to last for five years.

Debtor: I didn't know that.

Lawyer: So, let's see how these numbers work out. Your annual income is $57,600. The New Hampshire median income for a household of three people is a little more than $70,722. You earn less than the median, so you can file a Chapter 7 bankruptcy if you so choose. You are not hobbled by the new bankruptcy rules. And if you decide to use Chapter 13, you can repay your debts over three years, instead of five.

Debtor: I guess that's good news, but when it comes right down to it, I wish I earned more, even if that meant I had to take the means test and have a Chapter 13 case last longer. Of course, if I had more money, I guess I wouldn't be talking to you about filing for bankruptcy in the first place.

Lawyer: I see what you mean. But at least you have a choice between Chapter 7 and Chapter 13 bankruptcy. Now, we have to figure out which one is the better choice for you. To do that, I have to ask you some questions about your property and debts. Do you own your home?

Debtor: Yes.

Lawyer: Are you making payments on a mortgage?

Debtor: Yes.

Lawyer: What's your monthly payment?

Debtor: $1,200.

Lawyer: Are you current on your payments?

Debtor: Yes.

Lawyer: What's your home worth?

Debtor: $200,000.

Lawyer: And how much do you owe on it?

Debtor: About $110,000.

Lawyer: That's a total?

Debtor: Yes.

Lawyer: Okay. Under the New Hampshire homestead exemption, you are entitled to protect $100,000 of equity in your home. You have $90,000 of equity, so all of your equity is protected.

Debtor: What's a homestead exemption?

Lawyer: That's an exemption for your home. You are entitled to keep that much equity in your home, even if you file for Chapter 7 bankruptcy. If your equity exceeded the exemption, you might lose the extra equity if you filed for Chapter 7. The trustee could sell your home, pay off the mortgage, pay you your exemption, and still have money left over to distribute among your creditors. But because your equity is protected by the exemption, there wouldn't be anything left for your creditors after you got your exemption amount and the mortgage was paid. That's how exemptions work.

We already discussed how exemptions work in Chapter 13. If you have property that isn't exempt, your repayment plan has to pay at least the value of that property to certain creditors.

Debtor: I read in the paper that the new bankruptcy law makes it harder for people to keep their homes. Will that affect me?

Lawyer: Nope. The new law puts a cap of about $137,000 on the exemption amount for people who bought their home within the 40 months before they filed for bankruptcy. So it only affects people who bought a home more recently, and then only if their state would otherwise allow them to take a higher exemption. For example, if you bought your home in New Hampshire that recently, the New Hampshire homestead is only $100,000, so the cap wouldn't make any difference.

Debtor: So, I don't have to worry about that.

Lawyer: Right. Actually, the new law might also limit your exemption if you used nonexempt property in the last ten years to buy your home in order to cheat your creditors. I guess I should ask how you got the money to pay for your home.

Debtor: I borrowed money from my parents.

Lawyer: Great. Your home equity is covered by your state's homestead exemption and you can keep it if you file for Chapter 7 bankruptcy.

Debtor: What happens to my home if I file for Chapter 13 bankruptcy?

Lawyer: As long as you keep making your mortgage payments and the other payments required by your Chapter 13 plan, there won't be a problem. However, if you fall behind on your payments, your lender could foreclose, just as if you hadn't filed bankruptcy.

Debtor: So I have to keep my mortgage payments current, no matter which type of bankruptcy I file.

Lawyer: That's right. What other debts do you owe?

Debtor: Mainly credit card debts. And one SBA bank loan for my business.

Lawyer: Is the SBA loan secured by any of your property?

Debtor: No, it's just a bank loan.

Lawyer: How much are you paying on that loan?

Debtor: About $300 a month.

Lawyer: And how much credit card debt do you owe?

Debtor: About $20,000.

Lawyer: What were the credit card debts for?

Debtor: About $14,000 for personal expenses and $6,000 for paying off back taxes.

Lawyer: Oh yeah? What period did you owe the taxes for?

Debtor: The last couple of years.

Lawyer: That's interesting. I'll come back to this later, but the bankruptcy law allows you to discharge credit card charges used to pay off taxes in a Chapter 13 bankruptcy but not in a Chapter 7 bankruptcy. So, if there is no other reason to choose one type of bankruptcy over the other, you would be wise to choose Chapter 13.

Lawyer: So, having paid those taxes, are you now current on your taxes for the past four years?

Debtor: Yes.

Lawyer: That's good. You can't file for Chapter 13 unless you have filed your state and federal taxes for the previous four years.

Lawyer: How much was the bank loan for?

Debtor: $40,000

Lawyer: Did anybody cosign on that loan?

Debtor: As matter of fact my mother cosigned that loan.

Lawyer: Hmm. Even if you could get rid of that debt in bankruptcy, your mother would still be on the hook to repay it if you filed under Chapter 7. Even though you wouldn't be responsible for the debt any more, she would be.

But if you file for Chapter 13 bankruptcy, your mother won't have to repay it while your plan is in place, as long as your plan provides for payment of some or all of that debt. So, assuming your plan lasts for three years, your mother won't be on the hook for that period. However, she will still be responsible for any amount you haven't paid when your plan ends. So, again, if there is no other reason to choose one type of bankruptcy instead of the other, it looks like Chapter 13 might be a good choice.

Do you have any other debts?

Debtor: Nothing significant, maybe a total of $2,000 in miscellaneous bills. And, oh, does child support count?

Lawyer: I thought you were receiving child support.

Debtor: I am, but I also owe child support, for a child from a previous marriage. I never paid because my ex never asked, but now he's seeking current support as well as $5,000 in back support.

Lawyer: How much will you owe?

Debtor: Under the court order, $300 a month.

Lawyer: Have you started paying the support?

Debtor: No. I have to start paying it next month.

Lawyer: If you decide to file for Chapter 13, you will have to remain current on your child support payments throughout the life of your plan. If you don't, your case will be dismissed or converted to a Chapter 7 bankruptcy.

Debtor: I understand.

Lawyer: Let's talk later about the back support you owe. When were you divorced?

Debtor: A couple of years ago.

Lawyer: Did you assume any of the debts in the course of your divorce?

Debtor: Yes, I assumed the credit card charges for personal expenses in exchange for my ex-husband's share of our home.

Lawyer: Okay. That gives you another good reason to use Chapter 13. You can get rid of credit card debts you owe as a result of a divorce settlement in Chapter 13, but not in a Chapter 7. So here again, other things being equal, Chapter 13 is a better choice.

Debtor: It sounds like I should probably file for Chapter 13.

Lawyer: So far, I agree. But we're not through yet. Let's talk about your other property. And this is where exemptions will become important. Other than your home, do you have any other property you would want to keep in your bankruptcy?

Debtor: Oh, yes. I have a concert piano and some copyright interests in several books I wrote. Also, I have a car I want to hold on to.

Lawyer: How much is the car worth?

Debtor: About $4,000 according to *Kelley Blue Book*.

Lawyer: Are you making payments on it?

Debtor: Yes.

Lawyer: How much is left on your note?

Debtor: About $8,000.

Lawyer: When did you buy it?

Debtor: Three years ago.

Lawyer: If you file for Chapter 13, you can pay off the value of the car rather than what you still owe on the note. This is called a cramdown, and it's another great reason to file for Chapter 13. And it's a good thing you didn't buy your car more recently: You couldn't use this cramdown procedure if you bought the car within 2½ years of your bankruptcy filing date.

Now let's take a look at the New Hampshire exemptions, to see whether your other property is covered. Remember, exemptions are laws that determine what property you can keep in your bankruptcy. As I read them, the car is covered because you owe more than it's worth, so your creditors wouldn't get anything if it were sold. Because you don't have any equity in the car, you don't need to protect it with an exemption. As for the piano and your copyright interests, there are no state exemptions that specifically cover those items.

Debtor: Does that mean I'll lose my piano?

Lawyer: No. Remember, if you file for Chapter 13, you don't lose any property—you just have to make sure you pay your creditors at least the value of your nonexempt property. And even though New Hampshire doesn't specifically exempt pianos, it has a $3,500 exemption for all your furniture. So depending on

your piano's value, it might be covered by the furniture exemption.

Debtor: I think my piano would sell for about $12,000 and I guess my copyrights are pretty much worthless.

Lawyer: Why do you say your copyright interests are worthless?

Debtor: Well, they belong to three songs I wrote, but I've never had the songs published, so there is no one to sell them to.

Lawyer: Okay, we're only talking about the piano. Looking at the New Hampshire exemptions, in addition to the portion of the piano's value arguably covered by the furniture exemption—$3,500—there are also some wildcard exemptions. This type of exemption can be used to protect any property you choose. New Hampshire's wildcard exemptions will provide an additional $8,000 that you can put toward the piano: That takes into account a $1,000 straight wildcard, plus a $7,000 wildcard that you can use if you don't fully take advantage of certain other exemptions. If you use these wildcards for your piano, only about $500 of its value is not exempt. Your Chapter 13 plan has to pay at least that much to your unsecured creditors, if you decide to go that route. Of course, if you need part of the furniture exemption for other pieces of furniture, that would take away from the exemption available for your piano.

Debtor: Okay.

Lawyer: Here is a copy of the New Hampshire exemptions. Other than the piano, do you have any property that exceeds the exemption limit or that isn't listed in the exemption list?

Debtor: No, the piano is the only problem. But if I use the furniture exemption for my piano, my furniture won't be exempt. It's old furniture I bought at the Goodwill. I have nothing that would be of any value.

Lawyer: Well, that's up to the trustee. If you choose to use the entire furniture exemption for your piano, you might have to place some value on your furniture equal to what it would cost you to replace it.

Debtor: That would probably be about $1,000.

Lawyer: Okay, so you would have about $6,000 worth of nonexempt property. That's under the New Hampshire state exemptions. If your state allows it, you may choose to use a different set of exemptions set out in the bankruptcy code termed the "federal exemptions." As it turns out, New Hampshire does allow use of the federal exemptions. You can choose from the federal exemption list or from the New Hampshire state list, but you can't mix or match.

The federal exemptions protect only $20,000 in your home equity. You have $90,000 equity to protect, so you wouldn't want to choose the federal exemptions.

So, we know you can file for Chapter 7 bankruptcy if you wish. You could keep your home and probably your piano, even though it isn't completely exempt. The cost of collecting and storing the piano, then selling it at auction, would probably be more than $500—the nonexempt portion—which means there wouldn't be anything left after selling it to pay to your unsecured creditors. If you had to use the whole furniture exemption for other pieces of furniture, however, $4,000 of the value of your piano would be nonexempt. If that were the case, the trustee would probably take it and sell it, giving you the exempt amount and paying the rest to your unsecured creditors. Or, you could keep the piano if the trustee were willing to sell it to you for a negotiated price. Because the trustee would probably have to pay about $1,000 to sell it, you might be able to keep it by paying the trustee $3,000. But that's all in a Chapter 7 bankruptcy.

Debtor: It's sounding to me like Chapter 13 is a good idea. But you said I have to make sure I'm eligible. What are the requirements?

Lawyer: Before we get to that, I have a couple of more questions.

Debtor: Okay.

Lawyer: During the previous year, have you made payments on any loans you owe to relatives?

Debtor: Nope.

Lawyer: Good. If you had, the trustee might require the relative to return the money so it could be added to the amount your creditors would get.

Debtor: I wouldn't want that to happen.

Lawyer: Have you sold any property to anyone within the past two years?

Debtor: No.

Lawyer: That also simplifies things. If you had sold some property, and the amount you sold it for was less than what it was worth, the difference in value would be considered nonexempt property. You'd have to add that to the amount you have to pay under your plan. But you didn't sell any property, so this rule doesn't affect you.

Lawyer: Chapter 13 has some limitations on how much debt you can owe. Let's see, you owe a total of $69,000 of unsecured debt (a $40,000 bank loan, $22,000 in credit card debts, $5,000 in child support arrearage, and $2,000 other debts. You owe a total of $118,000 secured debt (your home and car). This means you fall within the eligibility guidelines, which are $1,010,650 for secured debts and $336,900 for unsecured debts.

Debtor: That's good.

Lawyer: Now let's see what debts you would have to pay in your Chapter 13 bankruptcy. Some debts have to be paid in full while others could be paid in part, depending on your income. The debts that would have to be paid in full over the life of your plan would be the $5,000 arrearage for your child support and the $500 for the nonexempt portion of your piano and your furniture, or $5,500 total debt payable in full over the course of your Chapter 13 plan.

Debtor: So how much would that be a month?

Lawyer: Under the new bankruptcy law, people whose average gross income for the preceding six months is less than the state median income—which is your situation—can propose a three-year repayment plan. If your income were higher than the median, you'd have to propose a five-year program.

So, when spreading out $5,500 over three years, you would have to pay at least $153 a month, plus the monthly payment on your car as modified downwards to reflect its value ($111), your current mortgage payment, and other expenses related to Chapter 13 bankruptcy, such as the trustee's fee and your attorney's fee if you use an attorney. If you don't have enough income to pay that after you subtract your living expenses (including your mortgage payment and your car payment) you won't qualify for a three-year Chapter 13 plan.

Debtor: How can I tell whether I have enough income to meet the Chapter 13 requirements?

Lawyer: If you decide to file a Chapter 13 bankruptcy, you have to fill out some forms to determine your income and your expenses. These forms will basically show whether you can afford a Chapter 13 bankruptcy. If you don't have enough income to pay all necessary debts in three years, you can ask the judge to let you propose a five-year plan, so you can pay less each month. If you still won't have enough left, after paying your expenses, to make your payments, you probably won't be able to use Chapter 13.

Debtor: So, do you suggest that I file for Chapter 7? Or should I use Chapter 13?

Lawyer: As long as you have enough income left over to use Chapter 13, that would be an excellent choice for you because:

- It will protect your codebtor—your mother—for the life of the plan.
- It will allow you to keep your car and pay it off at market value rather than reaffirming the current note, which is twice what it's worth.
- Unlike Chapter 7, it will allow you to discharge the credit card debts you assumed in your divorce.
- Unlike Chapter 7, it will allow you to discharge the credit card debts you incurred to pay off your taxes.

- It will allow you to pay off your child support arrearage—that is, the back child support you owe—over the life of your plan without worrying about wage garnishments and bank levies.

There are a couple of other great advantages to Chapter 13 that you might consider. You probably can pay off a healthy portion of your attorney fees over the life of your plan rather than having to pay them before you file, which you would have to do in a Chapter 7 bankruptcy. Also, you can complete your personal financial management course—which is required by the new bankruptcy law—any time before your last payment is due, which is about three years away. If you filed for Chapter 7, you'd have to complete it within the next few months.

Assuming you have enough income to propose a confirmable Chapter 13 plan, I recommend Chapter 13. If you can't propose a confirmable Chapter 13 plan, even over a five-year period, I suggest you hold off on bankruptcy for awhile, given the fact that you'll probably lose your piano in a Chapter 7 bankruptcy unless you can come up with enough money to buy it back from the trustee.

Filing for Chapter 13 Bankruptcy

Complete Your Bankruptcy Forms

This chapter shows you how to complete the Chapter 13 bankruptcy petition as well as all of the schedules and other forms you need for your Chapter 13 case (except for your repayment plan, which is covered in Ch. 8). Once you've completed these forms and drafted your plan, you can file for bankruptcy, using the instructions in Ch. 9.

As you'll see, you have to complete quite a few forms to file for bankruptcy, and some of them request a lot of information. For the most part, however, the process is fairly straightforward. Just take your time and follow the instructions provided below, and you'll do just fine.

> **TIP**
> **If you need help with the paperwork, consider a bankruptcy petition preparer.** Many nonlawyer paralegals do the paperwork for people filing their own Chapter 7 bankruptcies. Called "bankruptcy petition preparers" (BPPs), these nonlawyers usually won't prepare the paperwork for Chapter 13 bankruptcies. Preparing the repayment plan that must be submitted in a Chapter 13 case is considered practicing law, something that nonlawyers aren't legally allowed to do. If, however, you are going to prepare your own plan with the help of this book, you may be able to talk a BPP into preparing your basic Chapter 13 paperwork, which is almost identical to Chapter 7 paperwork except for the plan.

Get Some Information From the Court

Although bankruptcy courts operate similarly throughout the country, every bankruptcy court has its own picky requirements for filing bankruptcy papers. If your papers don't meet these local requirements, the court clerk may reject them. So, before you begin preparing your papers, contact your bankruptcy court to find out its rules.

In urban areas especially, you may get no response to a letter or phone call. You may need to visit the court and get the information in person. Or, the information may be available on the Internet. Almost all bankruptcy courts have websites with this sort of information. To find your court's website, visit www.uscourts.gov/courtlinks. Many court sites have special self-help areas for people handling their own bankruptcies. While these are intended primarily for

Chapter 7 filers, you may be able to pick up some valuable information for your Chapter 13 case, including the fees, local forms, local rules, and court locations.

Here are some of the things you should find out before preparing and filing your papers.

Fees

The total fee to file for Chapter 13 bankruptcy is $274. Fees change, however, so make sure to check with the court. This fee is due upon filing, unless you qualify for a waiver of the fees or obtain court permission to pay in installments. (To make these request, you must complete Form 3A or 3B, as explained below.)

Local Forms

In addition to the official forms that every bankruptcy court uses, your local bankruptcy court may require you to file one or two additional forms that it has developed. For example, different courts have different forms that you must file along with your wage stubs. You can get all local forms from your local bankruptcy court or a local stationery store, or you can download them from your court's website. (Go to www.uscourts. gov/courtlinks for a list of links to local courts.)

Of course, we can't include all local forms in this book or tell you how to fill them out. Most, however, are self-explanatory. If you need help in obtaining or understanding them, see a local bankruptcy lawyer or visit a bankruptcy petition preparer. (See Ch. 15 for information on petition preparers.)

Follow Your Court's Local Rules

Most bankruptcy courts publish local rules that govern the court's procedures. These rules mainly govern hearings conducted by the bankruptcy judge and aren't relevant in routine Chapter 13 bankruptcy cases, which usually involve only filing papers and appearing at a creditors' meeting and confirmation hearing. Still, on occasion, a rule does affect a Chapter 13 bankruptcy. You can get your local rules from the bankruptcy court—in person or on its website—but be prepared to comb through reams of material to find the one or two rules that might apply in your case.

Finding the Right Court

Because bankruptcy is a creature of federal, not state, law, you must file for bankruptcy in a special federal court. There are federal bankruptcy courts all over the country.

The federal court system divides the country into judicial districts. Every state has at least one judicial district; most have more. You can file in any of the following districts:

- the district where you have been living for the greater part of the 180-day period before you file
- the district where you are domiciled—that is, where you maintain your home, even if you have been living elsewhere (such as on a military base) temporarily
- the district where your principal place of business is located (if you are a business debtor), or
- the district where the majority of your business assets are located.

Most readers will be using the first option—and many will probably file in the large city closest to their home. To find a bankruptcy court in your state, check the government listings in your white pages (under "United States, Courts"), call directory assistance, ask your local law librarian, or go to www.legalconsumer.com and enter your zip code.

If you live in a state with more than one district, call the court in the closest city and ask whether that district includes your county or zip code.

EXAMPLE: For the past two months, you've lived in San Luis Obispo, which is in California's central judicial district. Before that you lived in Santa Rosa, in California's northern judicial district. Because you spent more of the past six months in the northern district than in the central, you should file in the bankruptcy court in the northern district. If it's too inconvenient to file there, you could wait another month, when you would qualify to file in the central district court.

Required Forms

Bankruptcy uses official forms prescribed by the federal office of the courts. This section provides a list of forms you'll have to file, as well as information on how to find them.

Required Bankruptcy Forms

These are the standard forms that must be filed in every Chapter 13 bankruptcy:

- ☐ Form 1—Voluntary Petition
- ☐ Form 3A (only if you are paying your filing fee in installments)
- ☐ Form 6, which consists of:
  - ☐ Schedule A—Real Property
  - ☐ Schedule B—Personal Property
  - ☐ Schedule C—Property Claimed as Exempt
  - ☐ Schedule D—Creditors Holding Secured Claims
  - ☐ Schedule E—Creditors Holding Unsecured Priority Claims
  - ☐ Schedule F—Creditors Holding Unsecured Nonpriority Claims
  - ☐ Schedule G—Executory Contracts and Unexpired Leases
  - ☐ Schedule H—Codebtors
  - ☐ Schedule I—Current Income
  - ☐ Schedule J—Current Expenditures
  - ☐ Summary of Schedules A through J
  - ☐ Declaration Concerning Debtor's Schedules
- ☐ Form 7—Statement of Financial Affairs
- ☐ Form 21—Statement of Social Security Number
- ☐ Form 22C—Chapter 13 Statement of Current Monthly Income and Calculation of Commitment Period and Disposable Income
- ☐ Form 201—Notice to Individual Consumer Debtor Under § 342 of the Bankruptcy Code
- ☐ Mailing Matrix
- ☐ Chapter 13 repayment plan (covered in Ch. 8)
- ☐ required local forms, if any.

With the exception of Form 22C, which requires you to do a fair bit of math, the forms addressed in this chapter are very straightforward and easy to complete, as long as you take them one at a time. Also, you probably won't have to spend time on each form, even though all of them are part of your filing package. For instance, if you don't own real estate, you can simply check the "None" box on Schedule A and proceed to Schedule B.

All together, these forms usually are referred to as your "bankruptcy petition," although technically your petition is only Form 1. (In case you're wondering, Forms 2, 4, and 5 aren't used in voluntary Chapter 13 bankruptcy filings.)

Where to Get the Official Forms

Appendix B of this book includes tear-out copies of all of the required bankruptcy forms—other than the Chapter 13 repayment plan (see Ch. 8). You can type the necessary information in the blanks or complete the forms by hand. Other options for forms (other than the Chapter 13 repayment plan) include:

- Get free, fill-in-the-blanks PDF forms from the website of the U.S. Trustee, www.usdoj.gov/ust (click "Data Enabled Form Standard" from the home page). You can enter your information on the computer, but you can't save your entries— you'll have to print them out. And, you'll have to make sure that the forms available on the site are the most current versions: Because bankruptcy forms change fairly often, the forms on this site are often out of date.
- Get free fillable PDF forms from the website of the federal judiciary at www.uscourts.gov/ bkforms/bankruptcy_forms.html#official. This site includes a complete set of forms that you can fill in on the computer, but you can't save your entries. One way around this problem is to use the Foxit PDF reader, which is available free at www.foxitsoftware.com/pdf/rd_intro.php.

Tips for Completing the Forms

Here are some tips that will make filling in your forms easier and the whole bankruptcy process smoother. A sample, completed form accompanies each form's instructions. Refer to it while you fill in your bankruptcy papers.

Make several copies of each form. That way, you can make a draft, changing things as you go until the form is complete and correct. Prepare final forms to file with the court only after you've double-checked your drafts.

If you use the PDF, fill-in-the-blanks forms available from the U.S. Trustee's website, remember that you can't save the information in the forms. It's easiest to do a draft by hand, then complete the form and print it all at once.

Type your final forms. If you are using the Nolo forms or the nonfillable PDF forms available from the federal judiciary website, you could write in your information by hand. However, the trustee handling your case will likely be friendlier if they are typewritten. If you don't own a typewriter, many libraries have typewriters available to the public (for a small rental fee), or you can hire a bankruptcy form preparation service to prepare your forms using the information you provide. (See Ch. 15 for more on these services.)

Be ridiculously thorough. Always err on the side of giving too much information rather than too little. If you leave information out, the bankruptcy trustee may become suspicious of your motives. If you leave creditors off the forms, the debts you owe these creditors won't be discharged—hardly the result you would want. If you intentionally or carelessly fail to list all your property and debts, or fail to accurately describe your recent property transactions, the court, upon a request by the trustee, may rule that you acted with fraudulent intent. It may deny your bankruptcy discharge altogether.

Respond to every question. Even if you think the question is unnecessary, respond to it. For instance, when you are asked to describe your clothing, respond to the question in full even if your clothing is worth little or nothing. Most of the forms have a box to check when your answer is "none." If a question doesn't have a "none" box and the question doesn't apply to you, type in "N/A" for "not applicable." This will let the trustee know that you didn't overlook the question. Occasionally, a question that doesn't apply to you will have a number of blanks. Put "N/A" in only the first blank if it is obvious that this applies to the other blanks as well. If it's not clear, put "N/A" in every blank.

Don't worry about repetition. Sometimes different forms—or different questions on the same form—may ask for the same or overlapping information. Don't worry about providing the same information multiple times—too much information is never a sin in bankruptcy.

Explain uncertainties. If you can't figure out which category on a form to use for a debt or an item of property, list the debt or item in what you think is the appropriate place and briefly note next to your entry that you're uncertain. The important thing is to disclose the information somewhere. The bankruptcy trustee will sort it out, if necessary.

Be scrupulously honest. As part of your official bankruptcy paperwork, you must complete declarations, under penalty of perjury, swearing that you've been truthful. It's important to realize that you could be prosecuted for perjury if it's evident that you deliberately lied. Approximately one out of every 250 bankruptcy cases is audited by a private firm. If yours is one of them, you don't want to have any explaining to do.

Use continuation pages if you run out of room. The space for entering information is sometimes skimpy, especially if you're filing jointly with a spouse. Most of the forms come with preformatted continuation pages that you can use if you need more room. If there is no continuation form, prepare one yourself, using a piece of regular white 8½" by 11" paper. Put "see continuation page" next to the question you're working on and enter the additional information on the continuation page. Label the continuation pages with your name and the form name, and indicate "Continuation Page 1," "Continuation Page 2," and so on. Be sure to attach all continuation pages to their appropriate forms when you file your bankruptcy papers.

Get help if necessary. If your situation is complicated, you're unsure about how to complete a form, or you run into trouble when you go to file your papers, consult a bankruptcy attorney or do some legal research before proceeding. (See Ch. 15.)

Refer to—but don't copy—the sample forms. This chapter includes completed sample Chapter 13 forms for Carrie Anne Edwards, who lives in California. These forms are intended as examples, so you can see what a completed form should look like. However, everyone's bankruptcy situation is different—and obviously, you will owe different debts, own different property, have different bank accounts and Social Security numbers, and otherwise be utterly dissimilar from this fictional gal. DO NOT COPY THESE EXAMPLES, even if you live in California, because they won't fit your precise situation.

For Married Filers

If you are married, you and your spouse will have to decide whether one of you should file alone or whether you should file jointly. To make this decision, you'll first have to make sure that you're married in the eyes of the federal law (a trickier issue than you might think), then consider how filing together or separately will affect your debts and property.

Are You Married?

If you are married to a partner of the opposite sex, and you were married with a valid state license, you are married for purposes of filing a joint petition—and you can skip down to "Should You File Jointly?" below. However, if you were not married with a license and ceremony, or if you are married to a same-sex partner, read on.

Common Law Marriage

Some states allow heterosexual couples to establish "common law" marriages, which the states will recognize as valid marriages even though the couples do not have a state marriage license or certificate. Contrary to popular belief, a common law marriage is not created when two people simply live together for a certain number of years. In order to have a valid common law marriage, the couple must do all of the following:

- live together for a significant period of time (not defined in any state)
- hold themselves out as a married couple—typically this means using the same last name, referring to the other as "my husband" or "my wife," and filing a joint tax return, and
- intend to be married.

Alabama, Colorado, the District of Columbia, Georgia, Idaho, Iowa, Kansas, Montana, New Hampshire (but only for inheritance purposes), Ohio, Oklahoma, Pennsylvania, Rhode Island, South Carolina, Texas, and Utah recognize some form of common law marriage, but the rules for what constitutes a marriage differ from state to state. And, several of these states will only recognize common law marriages that were created before a certain date.

If you live in one of these states and you meet your state's requirements for a common law marriage, you have the option to file jointly, if you wish.

Same-Sex Marriage

If you married your same-sex partner in a country or province that recognizes same-sex marriage, or in Massachusetts after that state began allowing same-sex marriage, it's not clear whether you can file jointly. At least one court has refused to allow a lesbian couple who had married in Canada to file a joint bankruptcy petition, based on a provision of federal law that defines marriage as a union between a man and a woman. If you choose to file jointly with your same-sex spouse, you may well face opposition on these grounds from the trustee or the U.S. Trustee. Consider consulting with a bankruptcy attorney who has some experience with issues facing same-sex couples before you decide how to proceed.

Should You File Jointly?

Unfortunately, there is no simple formula that will tell you whether it's better to file alone or with your spouse. In the end, it will depend on which option allows you to discharge more of your debts and keep more of your property. Here are some of the factors you should consider:

- If you are living in a community property state and most of your debts were incurred, and your property acquired, during marriage, you should probably file jointly. Even if only one spouse files, all community property is considered part of the bankruptcy estate—and any of the property that is nonexempt will determine the amount that nonpriority unsecured creditors will be paid (see Ch. 5 for more information). The same is generally true for debts—that is, all community debts are listed and most will be dealt with in the plan even though only one spouse files.
- If you have recently married, you haven't acquired any valuable assets as a married couple, and one of you has all the debts, it may make sense for that spouse to file for bankruptcy alone (especially if the nonfiling spouse has good credit to protect).

- You may want to file alone if you and your spouse own property as tenants by the entirety, most of the debts are in your own name, and you live in a state that excludes such property from the bankruptcy estate when one spouse files. This is a particularly important consideration if your home would be nonexempt property if both spouses filed—that could push the level of payment to your nonpriority unsecured creditors past the point that you could afford to pay in your repayment plan.
- If the exemption system you are using allows married spouses to double their exemptions, filing jointly may reduce the amount you would have to pay to your nonpriority unsecured creditors.
- If you are still married but separated, you may have to file alone if your spouse won't cooperate. Still, if your debts and property are joint rather than separate, a joint filing would probably be to your best advantage.

 SEE AN EXPERT

If you are uncertain about how to file, see a lawyer. Deciding whether to file jointly or alone can have significant consequences. Because the best choice will depend on your unique situation, we advise you to talk to a bankruptcy lawyer if you are unsure whether or not to file jointly.

Form 1—Voluntary Petition

A completed sample Voluntary Petition and line-by-line instructions follow.

First Page

Court Name. At the top of the first page, fill in the name of the judicial district you're filing in, such as the "Central District of California." If your state has only one district, fill in your state's name. If your state divides its districts into divisions, enter the division after the state name, such as "Northern District of California, Santa Rosa Division."

Name of Debtor. Enter your full name (last name first), as used on your checks, driver's license, and other formal documents. If you are married and filing jointly (see above), put one of your names as the debtor (on the left) and the other formal name as the "joint debtor (spouse)," on the right. If you are married but filing separately, enter "N/A" in the second blank.

All Other Names. The purpose of this box is to make sure that your creditors will know who you are when they receive notice of your bankruptcy filing. If you have been known by any other name in the last eight years, list it here. If you've operated a business as a sole proprietor during the previous six years, include your trade name (fictitious or assumed business name) preceded by "dba" for "doing business as." But don't include minor variations in spelling or form. For instance, if your name is John Lewis Odegard, you don't have to put down that you're sometimes known as J.L. But if you've used the pseudonym J.L. Smith, you should list it. If you're uncertain, list any name that you think you may have used with a creditor. Do the same for your spouse (in the box to the right) if you are filing jointly. If you're filing alone, type "N/A" anywhere in the box to the right.

Soc. Sec./Tax I.D. No. Enter only the last four digits of your Social Security number or taxpayer's I.D. number. Do the same for your spouse (in the box to the right) if you are filing jointly. If you're filing alone, type "N/A" anywhere in the box to the right.

Street Address of Debtor. Enter your current street address. Even if you get all of your mail at a post office box, list the address of your personal residence.

Street Address of Joint Debtor. Enter your spouse's current street address (even if it's the same as yours) if you are filing jointly—again, no post office boxes. If you're filing alone, type "N/A" anywhere in the box.

County of Residence. Enter the county in which you live. Do the same for your spouse if you're filing jointly. Otherwise, type "N/A" in the box. If you are doing business, enter the county where your (or your spouse's) business assets are located, if it's different than your mailing address.

Mailing Address of Debtor. Enter your mailing address if it is different from your street address. If it isn't, put "N/A." Do the same for your spouse (in the box to the right) if you are filing jointly.

Location of Principal Assets of Business Debtor. If you—or your spouse, if you are filing jointly—have been self-employed or operated a business as a sole proprietor

within the last six years, you may be considered a "business debtor." This means you will have to provide additional information on Form 7 (Statement of Affairs). (See the instructions for that form, below.) If your business owns any assets—such as machines or inventory—list their primary location. If they are all located at your home or mailing address, enter that address.

Type of Debtor. Check the first box—"Individual(s)"— even if you have been self-employed or operated a sole proprietorship during the previous six years. If you are filing bankruptcy for a corporation, partnership, or other type of business entity, you shouldn't be filing a Chapter 13 bankruptcy—which is only for individuals.

Nature of Business. See a bankruptcy lawyer if any of these business descriptions apply to you or your spouse. For instance, if you or your spouse own an assisted living facility (11 U.S.C. § 101 (27A)), you would need a lawyer's services, because the law has gotten quite complicated regarding how health care businesses are treated in bankruptcy.

Chapter of Bankruptcy Code Under Which the Petition is Filed. Check "Chapter 13."

Nature of Debts. Check the box for consumer debts if most of your debts are owed personally—not by a business. If, however, the bulk of your debts are due to the operation of a business, check the business debts box. If you are in doubt, check the business debts box.

Filing Fee. If you will attach the entire fee, check the first box. If you plan to ask the court for permission to pay in installments, check the second box.

Chapter 11 Debtors. Leave this section blank.

Statistical/Administrative Information. Here there are a number of boxes. The first set of boxes tells the trustee whether you have nonexempt property. If you did your homework in Ch. 5, you will have a good idea of whether all of your assets can be claimed as exempt, or whether you will have to pay your nonpriority unsecured creditors at least the value of your nonexempt assets—if not more. Check the top or bottom box accordingly. If you haven't a clue yet about your property and exemptions, come back to this question after you've completed Schedules A, B, and C later in this chapter.

Similarly, if you can provide pretty good estimates of the other information requested (estimated number of creditors, assets, and debts), fill in the appropriate box on the form. If not, come back to these questions when you've completed more of your paperwork.

Second Page

Name of Debtor(s). Enter your name and your spouse's, if you are filing jointly.

Prior Bankruptcy Case Filed Within Last 8 Years. If you haven't filed a bankruptcy case within the previous eight years, type "N/A" in the first box. If you—or your spouse, if you're filing jointly—have, enter the requested information. A previous Chapter 7 bankruptcy discharge bars you from filing a Chapter 13 case until four years have passed since you filed in the previous case. A previous Chapter 13 filing bars you from filing a new Chapter 13 case within two years from receiving a discharge in the previous case.

Pending Bankruptcy Case Filed by any Spouse, Partner, or Affiliate of this Debtor. "Affiliate" refers to a related business under a corporate structure. "Partner" refers to a business partnership. Again, you shouldn't use this book if you're filing as a corporation, partnership, or other type of business entity. If your spouse has a bankruptcy case pending anywhere in the country, enter the requested information. Otherwise, type "N/A" in the first box.

Exhibit A. This is solely for people who are filing for Chapter 11 bankruptcy. Leave it blank.

Exhibit B. This is solely for people who are represented by an attorney. If you are representing yourself or using a bankruptcy petition preparer, leave this section blank.

Exhibit C. If you own or have in your possession any property that might cause "imminent and identifiable" harm to public health or safety (for example, real estate that is polluted with toxic substances, or explosive devices such as hand grenades or dynamite), check the "Yes" box, fill in Exhibit C (see Appendix B), and attach Exhibit C to this petition. If you are unsure about whether a particular piece of property fits the bill, err on the side of inclusion.

Exhibit D. With rare exceptions, debtors filing for Chapter 13 bankruptcy are required to participate in debt counseling sessions within 180 days of their bankruptcy filing (see Ch. 9 for more details). Exhibit D gives the court information about your compliance with this requirement. Instructions for completing Exhibit D are set out below. Check the top box in this part of the petition if you are filing individually and have completed Exhibit D; if you are filing jointly and your spouse has completed Exhibit D, check the bottom box.

Information Regarding the Debtor—Venue. Most filers will check the top box. Check the middle box if it is appropriate (it won't be for most users of this book, which is intended for individuals and sole proprietors). Leave the bottom box blank. If it applies to you, see a lawyer.

Certification by a Debtor Who Resides as a Tenant of Residential Property. As explained in Ch. 2, certain evictions are allowed to proceed after you file for bankruptcy, despite the automatic stay. The questions in this section of the petition are intended to figure out whether your landlord has already gotten a judgment for possession (eviction order), and whether you might be able to postpone the eviction. See Ch. 2 for the information you need to complete these boxes, if they apply.

Third Page

Signature(s) of Debtor(s) (Individual/Joint). You—and your spouse, if you are filing jointly—must sign where indicated. If you are filing alone, type "N/A" on the joint debtor signature line. Include your telephone number and the date. You—and your spouse, if you are filing jointly—declare that you are aware that you may file under other sections of the bankruptcy code, and that you still choose to file for Chapter 13 bankruptcy. If you think you want to pursue one of those options, put your Chapter 13 petition aside and either consult a lawyer or find a book that explains your proposed alternative in more detail. For example, check out *The New Bankruptcy: Will It Work for You?*, by Stephen Elias (Nolo).

Signature of Attorney. If you are representing yourself, type "debtor not represented by attorney" in the space for the attorney's signature. If you are represented by a lawyer, fill in the blanks accordingly.

Signature of Non-Attorney Bankruptcy Petition Preparer. If a bankruptcy petition preparer typed your forms, have that person complete this section. Otherwise, type "N/A" on the first line.

B1 (Official Form 1)(1/08)

United States Bankruptcy Court Northern District of California	Voluntary Petition

Name of Debtor (if individual, enter Last, First, Middle): **Edwards, Carrie Anne**	Name of Joint Debtor (Spouse) (Last, First, Middle):
All Other Names used by the Debtor in the last 8 years (include married, maiden, and trade names):	All Other Names used by the Joint Debtor in the last 8 years (include married, maiden, and trade names):

Last four digits of Soc. Sec. or Individual-Taxpayer I.D. (ITIN) No./Complete EIN (if more than one, state all) **xxx-xx-6287**	Last four digits of Soc. Sec. or Individual-Taxpayer I.D. (ITIN) No./Complete EIN (if more than one, state all)

Street Address of Debtor (No. and Street, City, and State): **3045 Berwick St** **Lakeport, CA** ZIP Code **95453**	Street Address of Joint Debtor (No. and Street, City, and State): ZIP Code
County of Residence or of the Principal Place of Business: **Lake**	County of Residence or of the Principal Place of Business:
Mailing Address of Debtor (if different from street address): **PO Box 1437** **Lakeport, CA** ZIP Code **95453**	Mailing Address of Joint Debtor (if different from street address): ZIP Code
Location of Principal Assets of Business Debtor (if different from street address above):	

Type of Debtor
(Form of Organization)
(Check one box)

■ Individual (includes Joint Debtors)
See Exhibit D on page 2 of this form.
☐ Corporation (includes LLC and LLP)
☐ Partnership
☐ Other (If debtor is not one of the above entities, check this box and state type of entity below.)

Nature of Business
(Check one box)

☐ Health Care Business
☐ Single Asset Real Estate as defined in 11 U.S.C. § 101 (51B)
☐ Railroad
☐ Stockbroker
☐ Commodity Broker
☐ Clearing Bank
☐ Other

Tax-Exempt Entity
(Check box, if applicable)

☐ Debtor is a tax-exempt organization under Title 26 of the United States Code (the Internal Revenue Code).

Chapter of Bankruptcy Code Under Which the Petition is Filed (Check one box)

☐ Chapter 7
☐ Chapter 9
☐ Chapter 11
☐ Chapter 12
■ Chapter 13
☐ Chapter 15 Petition for Recognition of a Foreign Main Proceeding
☐ Chapter 15 Petition for Recognition of a Foreign Nonmain Proceeding

Nature of Debts
(Check one box)

■ Debts are primarily consumer debts, defined in 11 U.S.C. § 101(8) as "incurred by an individual primarily for a personal, family, or household purpose."
☐ Debts are primarily business debts.

Filing Fee (Check one box)

■ Full Filing Fee attached

☐ Filing Fee to be paid in installments (applicable to individuals only). Must attach signed application for the court's consideration certifying that the debtor is unable to pay fee except in installments. Rule 1006(b). See Official Form 3A.

☐ Filing Fee waiver requested (applicable to chapter 7 individuals only). Must attach signed application for the court's consideration. See Official Form 3B.

Chapter 11 Debtors

Check one box:
☐ Debtor is a small business debtor as defined in 11 U.S.C. § 101(51D).
☐ Debtor is not a small business debtor as defined in 11 U.S.C. § 101(51D).

Check if:
☐ Debtor's aggregate noncontingent liquidated debts (excluding debts owed to insiders or affiliates) are less than $2,190,000.

Check all applicable boxes:
☐ A plan is being filed with this petition.
☐ Acceptances of the plan were solicited prepetition from one or more classes of creditors, in accordance with 11 U.S.C. § 1126(b).

Statistical/Administrative Information

■ Debtor estimates that funds will be available for distribution to unsecured creditors.

☐ Debtor estimates that, after any exempt property is excluded and administrative expenses paid, there will be no funds available for distribution to unsecured creditors.

THIS SPACE IS FOR COURT USE ONLY

Estimated Number of Creditors

■	☐	☐	☐	☐	☐	☐	☐	☐	☐
1- 49	50- 99	100- 199	200- 999	1,000- 5,000	5,001- 10,000	10,001- 25,000	25,001- 50,000	50,001- 100,000	OVER 100,000

Estimated Assets

☐	☐	■	☐	☐	☐	☐	☐	☐	☐
$0 to $50,000	$50,001 to $100,000	$100,001 to $500,000	$500,001 to $1 million	$1,000,001 to $10 million	$10,000,001 to $50 million	$50,000,001 to $100 million	$100,000,001 to $500 million	$500,000,001 to $1 billion	More than $1 billion

Estimated Liabilities

☐	☐	■	☐	☐	☐	☐	☐	☐	☐
$0 to $50,000	$50,001 to $100,000	$100,001 to $500,000	$500,001 to $1 million	$1,000,001 to $10 million	$10,000,001 to $50 million	$50,000,001 to $100 million	$100,000,001 to $500 million	$500,000,001 to $1 billion	More than $1 billion

B1 (Official Form 1)(1/08)												Page 2

Voluntary Petition

(This page must be completed and filed in every case)

Name of Debtor(s):
Edwards, Carrie Anne

All Prior Bankruptcy Cases Filed Within Last 8 Years (If more than two, attach additional sheet)		
Location Where Filed: **- None -**	Case Number:	Date Filed:
Location Where Filed:	Case Number:	Date Filed:

Pending Bankruptcy Case Filed by any Spouse, Partner, or Affiliate of this Debtor (If more than one, attach additional sheet)		
Name of Debtor: **- None -**	Case Number:	Date Filed:
District:	Relationship:	Judge:

Exhibit A

(To be completed if debtor is required to file periodic reports (e.g., forms 10K and 10Q) with the Securities and Exchange Commission pursuant to Section 13 or 15(d) of the Securities Exchange Act of 1934 and is requesting relief under chapter 11.)

☐ Exhibit A is attached and made a part of this petition.

Exhibit B
(To be completed if debtor is an individual whose debts are primarily consumer debts.)

I, the attorney for the petitioner named in the foregoing petition, declare that I have informed the petitioner that [he or she] may proceed under chapter 7, 11, 12, or 13 of title 11, United States Code, and have explained the relief available under each such chapter. I further certify that I delivered to the debtor the notice required by 11 U.S.C. §342(b).

X_____
   Signature of Attorney for Debtor(s)   (Date)

Exhibit C

Does the debtor own or have possession of any property that poses or is alleged to pose a threat of imminent and identifiable harm to public health or safety?

☐ Yes, and Exhibit C is attached and made a part of this petition.

■ No.

Exhibit D

(To be completed by every individual debtor. If a joint petition is filed, each spouse must complete and attach a separate Exhibit D.)

■ Exhibit D completed and signed by the debtor is attached and made a part of this petition.

If this is a joint petition:

☐ Exhibit D also completed and signed by the joint debtor is attached and made a part of this petition.

Information Regarding the Debtor - Venue
(Check any applicable box)

■ Debtor has been domiciled or has had a residence, principal place of business, or principal assets in this District for 180 days immediately preceding the date of this petition or for a longer part of such 180 days than in any other District.

☐ There is a bankruptcy case concerning debtor's affiliate, general partner, or partnership pending in this District.

☐ Debtor is a debtor in a foreign proceeding and has its principal place of business or principal assets in the United States in this District, or has no principal place of business or assets in the United States but is a defendant in an action or proceeding [in a federal or state court] in this District, or the interests of the parties will be served in regard to the relief sought in this District.

Certification by a Debtor Who Resides as a Tenant of Residential Property
(Check all applicable boxes)

☐ Landlord has a judgment against the debtor for possession of debtor's residence. (If box checked, complete the following.)

_____
(Name of landlord that obtained judgment)

_____
(Address of landlord)

☐ Debtor claims that under applicable nonbankruptcy law, there are circumstances under which the debtor would be permitted to cure the entire monetary default that gave rise to the judgment for possession, after the judgment for possession was entered, and

☐ Debtor has included in this petition the deposit with the court of any rent that would become due during the 30-day period after the filing of the petition.

☐ Debtor certifies that he/she has served the Landlord with this certification. (11 U.S.C. § 362(l)).

B1 (Official Form 1)(1/08)   Page 3

Voluntary Petition

(This page must be completed and filed in every case)

Name of Debtor(s):
Edwards, Carrie Anne

Signatures

Signature(s) of Debtor(s) (Individual/Joint)

I declare under penalty of perjury that the information provided in this petition is true and correct.
[If petitioner is an individual whose debts are primarily consumer debts and has chosen to file under chapter 7] I am aware that I may proceed under chapter 7, 11, 12, or 13 of title 11, United States Code, understand the relief available under each such chapter, and choose to proceed under chapter 7.
[If no attorney represents me and no bankruptcy petition preparer signs the petition] I have obtained and read the notice required by 11 U.S.C. §342(b).

I request relief in accordance with the chapter of title 11, United States Code, specified in this petition.

X _____
Signature of Debtor

X _____
Signature of Joint Debtor

(707) 274 1234
Telephone Number (If not represented by attorney)

_____
Date

Signature of Attorney*

X **Debtor not represented by attorney**
Signature of Attorney for Debtor(s)

_____
Printed Name of Attorney for Debtor(s)

_____
Firm Name

_____
Address

_____
Telephone Number

_____
Date

*In a case in which § 707(b)(4)(D) applies, this signature also constitutes a certification that the attorney has no knowledge after an inquiry that the information in the schedules is incorrect.

Signature of Debtor (Corporation/Partnership)

I declare under penalty of perjury that the information provided in this petition is true and correct, and that I have been authorized to file this petition on behalf of the debtor.

The debtor requests relief in accordance with the chapter of title 11, United States Code, specified in this petition.

X _____
Signature of Authorized Individual

_____
Printed Name of Authorized Individual

_____
Title of Authorized Individual

_____
Date

Signature of a Foreign Representative

I declare under penalty of perjury that the information provided in this petition is true and correct, that I am the foreign representative of a debtor in a foreign proceeding, and that I am authorized to file this petition.

(Check only one box.)

☐ I request relief in accordance with chapter 15 of title 11. United States Code. Certified copies of the documents required by 11 U.S.C. §1515 are attached.

☐ Pursuant to 11 U.S.C. §1511, I request relief in accordance with the chapter of title 11 specified in this petition. A certified copy of the order granting recognition of the foreign main proceeding is attached.

X _____
Signature of Foreign Representative

_____
Printed Name of Foreign Representative

_____
Date

Signature of Non-Attorney Bankruptcy Petition Preparer

I declare under penalty of perjury that: (1) I am a bankruptcy petition preparer as defined in 11 U.S.C. § 110; (2) I prepared this document for compensation and have provided the debtor with a copy of this document and the notices and information required under 11 U.S.C. §§ 110(b), 110(h), and 342(b); and, (3) if rules or guidelines have been promulgated pursuant to 11 U.S.C. § 110(h) setting a maximum fee for services chargeable by bankruptcy petition preparers, I have given the debtor notice of the maximum amount before preparing any document for filing for a debtor or accepting any fee from the debtor, as required in that section. Official Form 19 is attached.

_____
Printed Name and title, if any, of Bankruptcy Petition Preparer

_____
Social-Security number (If the bankrutpcy petition preparer is not an individual, state the Social Security number of the officer, principal, responsible person or partner of the bankruptcy petition preparer.)(Required by 11 U.S.C. § 110.)

_____
Address

X _____

_____
Date

Signature of Bankruptcy Petition Preparer or officer, principal, responsible person,or partner whose Social Security number is provided above.

Names and Social-Security numbers of all other individuals who prepared or assisted in preparing this document unless the bankruptcy petition preparer is not an individual:

If more than one person prepared this document, attach additional sheets conforming to the appropriate official form for each person.

A bankruptcy petition preparer's failure to comply with the provisions of title 11 and the Federal Rules of Bankruptcy Procedure may result in fines or imprisonment or both 11 U.S.C. §110; 18 U.S.C. §156.

Official Form 1, Exhibit D (10/06)

United States Bankruptcy Court
Northern District of California

In re   **Carrie Anne Edwards**   Case No. _____

Debtor(s)   Chapter   **13**

EXHIBIT D - INDIVIDUAL DEBTOR'S STATEMENT OF COMPLIANCE WITH CREDIT COUNSELING REQUIREMENT

Warning: You must be able to check truthfully one of the five statements regarding credit counseling listed below. If you cannot do so, you are not eligible to file a bankruptcy case, and the court can dismiss any case you do file. If that happens, you will lose whatever filing fee you paid, and your creditors will be able to resume collection activities against you. If your case is dismissed and you file another bankruptcy case later, you may be required to pay a second filing fee and you may have to take extra steps to stop creditors' collection activities.

Every individual debtor must file this Exhibit D. If a joint petition is filed, each spouse must complete and file a separate Exhibit D. Check one of the five statements below and attach any documents as directed.

☐ 1. Within the 180 days **before the filing of my bankruptcy case**, I received a briefing from a credit counseling agency approved by the United States trustee or bankruptcy administrator that outlined the opportunities for available credit counseling and assisted me in performing a related budget analysis, and I have a certificate from the agency describing the services provided to me. *Attach a copy of the certificate and a copy of any debt repayment plan developed through the agency.*

■ 2. Within the 180 days **before the filing of my bankruptcy case**, I received a briefing from a credit counseling agency approved by the United States trustee or bankruptcy administrator that outlined the opportunities for available credit counseling and assisted me in performing a related budget analysis, but I do not have a certificate from the agency describing the services provided to me. *You must file a copy of a certificate from the agency describing the services provided to you and a copy of any debt repayment plan developed through the agency no later than 15 days after your bankruptcy case is filed.*

☐ 3. I certify that I requested credit counseling services from an approved agency but was unable to obtain the services during the five days from the time I made my request, and the following exigent circumstances merit a temporary waiver of the credit counseling requirement so I can file my bankruptcy case now. *[Must be accompanied by a motion for determination by the court.][Summarize exigent circumstances here.]* ____

If the court is satisfied with the reasons stated in your motion, it will send you an order approving your request. You must still obtain the credit counseling briefing within the first 30 days after you file your bankruptcy case and promptly file a certificate from the agency that provided the briefing, together with a copy of any debt management plan developed through the agency. Any extension of the 30-day deadline can be granted only for cause and is limited to a maximum of 15 days. A motion for extension must be filed within the 30-day period. Failure to fulfill these requirements may result in dismissal of your case. If the court is not satisfied with your reasons for filing your bankruptcy case without first receiving a credit counseling briefing, your case may be dismissed.

Official Form 1, Exh. D (10/06) - Cont.

☐ 4. I am not required to receive a credit counseling briefing because of: *[Check the applicable statement.] [Must be accompanied by a motion for determination by the court.]*

☐ Incapacity. (Defined in 11 U.S.C. § 109(h)(4) as impaired by reason of mental illness or mental deficiency so as to be incapable of realizing and making rational decisions with respect to financial responsibilities.);

☐ Disability. (Defined in 11 U.S.C. § 109(h)(4) as physically impaired to the extent of being unable, after reasonable effort, to participate in a credit counseling briefing in person, by telephone, or through the Internet.);

☐ Active military duty in a military combat zone.

☐ 5. The United States trustee or bankruptcy administrator has determined that the credit counseling requirement of 11 U.S.C. § 109(h) does not apply in this district.

I certify under penalty of perjury that the information provided above is true and correct.

Signature of Debtor: _Carrie Anne Edwards_
                    Carrie Anne Edwards

Date: _October 3, 2008_

Exhibit D

At the top of the page, fill in the court name, your name(s) as debtor(s), and the case number (if you have it).

The warning (in bold letters) explains that you have to check one of the five statements regarding credit counseling listed in Exhibit D.

Most people will check **box 1,** which means you obtained the certificate of completion from the credit counseling agency and can attach the certificate (and any debt repayment plan developed through the agency) to your petition.

If you have received counseling but haven't got your certificate yet, check **box 2.** To remain in bankruptcy, you'll need to obtain and file your certificate (and debt repayment plan if any) within 15 days after your bankruptcy filing date.

Checking **box 3** indicates that you have requested credit counseling but were unable to obtain the services within five days after your request, and have not yet received counseling. If you check this box, you'll have to explain why you couldn't complete the credit counseling before your filing date. Also, to stay in bankruptcy, you'll have to request that the court grant you an exception because of exigent (emergency) circumstances. Read the bold type for additional information regarding your obligations if you wish to remain in bankruptcy.

Box 4 summarizes the exceptions to the credit counseling requirement and asks you to check the appropriate reason.

Box 5 only applies if the credit counseling requirement doesn't apply in your district. This exception is very rare.

Sign and date this document under penalty of perjury and file it with your petition.

Form 6—Schedules

"Form 6" refers to a series of schedules that provides the trustee and court with a picture of your current financial situation.

CAUTION
Use the correct address for your creditors.
Many of these schedules ask you to provide addresses for the creditors you list. For creditors who have dunned you with written requests or demands for payment, you should provide the address that the creditor listed as a contact address on at least two written communications you received from the creditor within the 90-day period prior to your anticipated filing date. If the creditor has not contacted you within that 90-day period, provide the contact address that the creditor gave in the last two communications it sent to you. If you no longer have the address of your original creditor, use the contact address of the most recent creditors—for instance a collection agency or attorney's office. If a creditor is a minor child, simply put "minor child" and the appropriate address. Don't list the child's name.

Schedule A—Real Property

Here you list all the real estate you own as of the date you'll file the petition. Don't worry about whether a particular piece of property is exempt; you don't have to deal with exemptions until you get to Schedule C.

A completed sample of Schedule A and line-by-line instructions follow. Even if you don't own any real estate, you still must complete the top of this form.

In re. (This means "In the matter of.") Type your name and the name of your spouse, if you're filing jointly. "In re [your name(s)]" will be the name of your bankruptcy case.

Case No. If you made an emergency filing, fill in the case number assigned by the court. Otherwise, leave this blank.

SKIP AHEAD
If you don't own real estate, type "N/A" anywhere in the first column, type "0" in the total box at the bottom of the page, and move on to Schedule B.

Description and Location of Property. For each piece of real property you own, list the type of property—for example, house, farm, or undeveloped lot—and street address. You don't need to include the legal description of the property (the description on the deed).

B6A (Official Form 6A) (12/07)

In re **Carrie Anne Edwards** , Case No. _____

Debtor

SCHEDULE A - REAL PROPERTY

Except as directed below, list all real property in which the debtor has any legal, equitable, or future interest, including all property owned as a cotenant, community property, or in which the debtor has a life estate. Include any property in which the debtor holds rights and powers exercisable for the debtor's own benefit. If the debtor is married, state whether husband, wife, both, or the marital community own the property by placing an "H," "W," "J," or "C" in the column labeled "Husband, Wife, Joint, or Community." If the debtor holds no interest in real property, write "None" under "Description and Location of Property."

Do not include interests in executory contracts and unexpired leases on this schedule. List them in Schedule G - Executory Contracts and Unexpired Leases.

If an entity claims to have a lien or hold a secured interest in any property, state the amount of the secured claim. See Schedule D. If no entity claims to hold a secured interest in the property, write "None" in the column labeled "Amount of Secured Claim." If the debtor is an individual or if a joint petition is filed, state the amount of any exemption claimed in the property only in Schedule C - Property Claimed as Exempt.

Description and Location of Property	Nature of Debtor's Interest in Property	Husband, Wife, Joint, or Community	Current Value of Debtor's Interest in Property, without Deducting any Secured Claim or Exemption	Amount of Secured Claim
Residence **Location: 3045 Berwick St, Lakeport CA**	**Fee Simple**	-	**160,000.00**	**140,000.00**

Sub-Total >	**160,000.00**	(Total of this page)
Total >	**160,000.00**	

0 continuation sheets attached to the Schedule of Real Property

(Report also on Summary of Schedules)

Real Property Defined

Real property—land and things permanently attached to land—includes more than just a house. It can also include unimproved land, vacation cabins, condominiums, duplexes, rental property, business property, mobile home park spaces, agricultural land, airplane hangars, and any other buildings permanently attached to land.

You may own real estate even if you can't walk on it, live on it, or get income from it. This might be true, for example, if:

- you own real estate solely because you are married to a spouse who owns real estate and you live in a community property state, or
- someone else lives on property that you are entitled to receive in the future under a trust agreement.

There's a separate schedule for leases and time shares. If you hold a time-share lease in a vacation cabin or property, lease a boat dock, lease underground portions of real estate for mineral or oil exploration, or otherwise lease or rent real estate of any description, don't list it on Schedule A. All leases and time-shares should be listed on Schedule G. (See the instructions for that schedule below.)

Nature of Debtor's Interest in Property. In this column, you need to provide the legal definition for the interest you (or you and your spouse) have in the real estate. The most common type of interest—outright ownership—is called "fee simple." Even if you still owe money on your mortgage, as long as you have the right to sell the house, leave it to your heirs, and make alterations, your ownership is fee simple. A fee simple interest may be owned by one person or by several people jointly. Normally, when people are listed on a deed as the owners—even if they own the property as joint tenants, tenants in common, or tenants by the entirety—the ownership interest is in fee simple. Other types of real property interests include:

- **Life estate.** This is the right to possess and use property only during your lifetime. You can't sell the property, give it away, or leave it to someone when you die. Instead, when you die, the property passes to whomever was named in the instrument (trust, deed, or will) that created

your life estate. This type of ownership is usually created when the sole owner of a piece of real estate wants his surviving spouse to live on the property for the rest of her life, but then have the property pass to his children. In this situation, the surviving spouse has a life estate. Surviving spouses who are beneficiaries of AB, spousal, or marital bypass trusts have life estates.

- **Future interest.** This is your right to own property sometime in the future. A common future interest is owned by a person who—under the terms of a deed or irrevocable trust—will inherit the property when its current possessor dies. Simply being named in a will or living trust doesn't create a future interest, because the person who signed the deed or trust can easily amend the document to cut you out.
- **Contingent interest.** This ownership interest doesn't come into existence unless one or more conditions are fulfilled. Wills sometimes leave property to people under certain conditions. If the conditions aren't met, the property passes to someone else. For instance, Emma's will leaves her house to John provided that he takes care of her until her death. If John doesn't care for Emma, the house passes to Emma's daughter Jane. Both John and Jane have contingent interests in Emma's home.
- **Lienholder.** If you are the holder of a mortgage, deed of trust, judgment lien, or mechanic's lien on real estate, you have an ownership interest in the real estate.
- **Easement holder.** If you are the holder of a right to travel on or otherwise use property owned by someone else, you have an easement.
- **Power of appointment.** If you have a legal right, given to you in a will or transfer of property, to sell a specified piece of someone's property, that's called a power of appointment and should be listed.
- **Beneficial ownership under a real estate contract.** This is the right to own property by virtue of having signed a binding real estate contract. Even though the buyer doesn't yet own the property, the buyer does have a "beneficial interest"—that is, the right to own the property once the formalities are completed. For example, property buyers

have a beneficial ownership interest in property while the escrow is pending.

If you have trouble figuring out which of these definitions best fits your type of ownership interest, leave the column blank and let the trustee help you sort it out.

Husband, Wife, Joint, or Community. If you're not married, put "N/A." If you are married, indicate whether the real estate is owned:

- by the husband (H)
- by the wife (W)
- jointly by husband and wife as joint tenants, tenants in common, or tenants by the entirety (J), or
- jointly by husband and wife as community property (C).

Current Value of Debtor's Interest in Property Without Deducting any Secured Claim or Exemption. Enter the actual value of your real estate ownership interest.

To value your property, compare it to similar real estate parcels in your neighborhood that have recently sold (comparables). For a modest fee, you can get details on comparables—including neighborhood information, sales history, address, number of bedrooms and baths, square footage, and property tax information—from SmartHomeBuy at www. smarthomebuy.com. Less detailed information (purchase price, sales date, and address) is available free from sites such as www.homevalues.com, www. zillow.com, www.domania.com, www.homeradar.com, and http://list.realestate.yahoo.com/re/homevalues. Simply enter the home's address or zip code. In an era of falling home prices, it is harder to pin a value on real estate than it used to be. For example, if a comparable sold three months ago for $250,000, your home may not be worth that much today (although it can be tough to figure out how to translate this change into dollars and cents).

Don't figure in homestead exemptions or any mortgages or other liens on the property. Just put the actual current value as best you can calculate it. However, you can deduct the costs of sale from the actual value and enter the difference, as long as you explain what you did on the schedule.

If you own the property with someone else who is not joining you in your bankruptcy, list only your ownership share in this column. For example, if you and your brother own a home as joint tenants (each

owns 50%), split the property's current market value in half and list that amount here.

If your interest is intangible—for example, you are a beneficiary of real estate held in trust that won't be distributed for many years—enter an estimate provided by a real estate appraiser or put "don't know" and explain why you can't be more precise.

Mobile Home Note

If you own a mobile home in a park, insert the value of the mobile home in its current location. Many parks are located in desirable areas, and the park itself adds value to the mobile home—even though you may not have any ownership interest in the park itself. For instance, the mobile home itself may not be worth very much if it were situated in a different area, but it could be worth quite a bit more if it's sitting in a fancy park.

Total. Add the amounts in the fourth column and enter the total in the box at the bottom of the page. The form reminds you that you should also enter this total on the Summary of Schedules (see the instructions for completing the Summary, below).

Amount of Secured Claim. List mortgages and other debts secured by the property. If there is no secured claim of any type on the real estate, enter "None." If there is, enter separately the amount of each outstanding mortgage, deed of trust, home equity loan, or lien (judgment lien, mechanic's lien, materialman's lien, tax lien, or the like) that is claimed against the property. If you don't know the balance on your mortgage, deed of trust, or home equity loan, call the lender. To find out the existence and values of liens, visit the land records office in your county and look up the parcel in the records; the clerk can show you how. Or, you can order a title search through a real estate attorney or title insurance company. If you own several pieces of real estate and there is one lien on file against all the real estate, list the full amount of the lien for each separate property item. Don't worry if, taken together, the value of the liens is higher than the value of the property; it's quite common.

How you itemize liens in this schedule won't affect how your property or the liens will be treated in bankruptcy. The idea here is to notify the trustee of all possible liens that may affect your equity in your real estate.

TIP

You might be able to get rid of liens. If you have liens on your property that aren't secured by it, you may be able to strip them off and reduce the amount of your current mortgage expense. For example, if your property is worth $250,000, and you owe $250,000 on your first mortgage, any other liens listed here can be "stripped off" in your Chapter 13 bankruptcy and reclassified as unsecured debt. If your total mortgage payment is $2,500, and $1,750 of that is attributable to your first mortgage, you can reduce your mortgage payment by the remaining $750, which will make a Chapter 13 plan more feasible. This is why it's important to be accurate here about liens arising from second and third mortgages.

If you are simply unable to obtain this information, and you can't afford the help of a lawyer or title insurance company, put "unknown." This will be okay for the purpose of filing your papers, but you may need to get the information later. For example, a question might come up as to whether the equity in your home is protected by your exemption. Suppose your exemption is $10,000 and your equity is $30,000. You would probably have to pay your nonpriority unsecured creditors at least $20,000 in your plan, because your nonexempt property is worth that much. But if there were an unknown lien on the property for $20,000, then you wouldn't have to pay your nonpriority unsecured reditors anything in your plan—as a result of this item of real estate, anyway. So it's to your benefit to get this information any way you can.

Schedule B—Personal Property

Here you must list and evaluate all of your personal property, including property that is security for a debt and property that is exempt.

CAUTION

Be honest and thorough. When listing all of your stuff on a public document like Schedule B, you might feel tempted to cheat a little. Don't give in to the temptation to "forget" any of your assets. Bankruptcy law doesn't give you the right to decide that an asset isn't worth mentioning. Even if, for example, you've decided that your CD collection is worthless given the advent of the iPod, you still have to list it. You can explain on the form why you think it's worthless. If you omit something and get caught, your case can be dismissed—or your discharge revoked—leaving you with no bankruptcy relief for your current debts.

A completed sample of Schedule B and line-by-line instructions follow. If you need more room, use an attached continuation page, or create a continuation page yourself.

In re and Case No. Follow the instructions for Schedule A.

Type of Property. The form lists general categories of personal property. Leave this column as is.

None. If you own no property that fits in a category listed in the first column, enter an "X" in the "None" column. But make sure that you really don't own anything in this category.

Description and Location of Property. List specific items that fall in each general category.

CAUTION

Use the property's replacement value. The new bankruptcy law requires you to use the property's replacement value—what it would cost to purchase the property from a retail vendor, given its age and condition—when estimating what it's worth.

Separately list all items worth $50 or more. Combine small items into larger categories whenever reasonable. For example, you don't need to list every spatula, colander, garlic press, and ice cream scoop; instead, put "kitchen cookware" (unless one of these items exceeds $50). If you list numerous items in one category (as is likely for household goods and furnishings), you may need to attach a continuation sheet.

For each category of property listed, you must describe where it is located. If your personal property is at your residence, just enter "Residence" or your home address in the box. If someone else holds property for you (for example, you loaned your aunt your color TV), put that person's name and address in this column. The idea is to tell the trustee where all your property is located.

B6B (Official Form 6B) (12/07)

In re   **Carrie Anne Edwards**   Case No. _____
                                             Debtor

SCHEDULE B - PERSONAL PROPERTY

Except as directed below, list all personal property of the debtor of whatever kind. If the debtor has no property in one or more of the categories, place an "x" in the appropriate position in the column labeled "None." If additional space is needed in any category, attach a separate sheet properly identified with the case name, case number, and the number of the category. If the debtor is married, state whether husband, wife, both, or the marital community own the property by placing an "H," "W," "J," or "C" in the column labeled "Husband, Wife, Joint, or Community." If the debtor is an individual or a joint petition is filed, state the amount of any exemptions claimed only in Schedule C - Property Claimed as Exempt.

Do not list interests in executory contracts and unexpired leases on this schedule. List them in Schedule G - Executory Contracts and Unexpired Leases.

If the property is being held for the debtor by someone else, state that person's name and address under "Description and Location of Property." If the property is being held for a minor child, simply state the child's initials and the name and address of the child's parent or guardian, such as "A.B., a minor child, by John Doe, guardian." Do not disclose the child's name. See, 11 U.S.C. §112 and Fed. R. Bankr. P. 1007(m).

Type of Property	N O N E	Description and Location of Property	Husband, Wife, Joint, or Community	Current Value of Debtor's Interest in Property, without Deducting any Secured Claim or Exemption
1. Cash on hand		**Cash in wallet**	-	**50.00**
2. Checking, savings or other financial accounts, certificates of deposit, or shares in banks, savings and loan, thrift, building and loan, and homestead associations, or credit unions, brokerage houses, or cooperatives.		**Bank of America Checking Account #12345 Lakeport California** **from wages** **WestAmerica Bank, Lakeport CA Savings Account**	- -	**150.00** **300.00**
3. Security deposits with public utilities, telephone companies, landlords, and others.	X			
4. Household goods and furnishings, including audio, video, and computer equipment.		**All items at replacement value** **Stereo system ($300), washer dryer set (200), refrigerator (400), electric stove (250), misc furniture (couch, 2 chairs) (450) minor appliances (blender, toaster, mixer) (125), vacuum (50), 20 inch tv (75), lawnmower (200), swing set, childrens toys (240), snowblower (160) Location: 3045 Berwick St, Lakeport CA** **2 end tables (500), roll top desk (700), bed and bedding (800), oriental rug (2500)**	- -	**2,450.00** **4,500.00**
5. Books, pictures and other art objects, antiques, stamp, coin, record, tape, compact disc, and other collections or collectibles.		**250 books at used book store prices Location: 3045 Berwick St, Lakeport CA** **stamp collection at stamp dealer price Location: 3045 Berwick St, Lakeport CA**	- -	**1,250.00** **2,500.00**
6. Wearing apparel.		**normal clothing at used clothing store prices Location: 3045 Berwick St, Lakeport CA**	-	**800.00**
7. Furs and jewelry.		**diamond necklace at used jewelry store price (800), watch at flea market price (75) Location: 3045 Berwick St, Lakeport CA**	-	**875.00**

Sub-Total >   **12,875.00**
(Total of this page)

<u> 3 </u> continuation sheets attached to the Schedule of Personal Property

B6B (Official Form 6B) (12/07) - Cont.

In re   **Carrie Anne Edwards**   Case No. _____
                                         Debtor

SCHEDULE B - PERSONAL PROPERTY
(Continuation Sheet)

Type of Property	N O N E	Description and Location of Property	Husband, Wife, Joint, or Community	Current Value of Debtor's Interest in Property, without Deducting any Secured Claim or Exemption
8. Firearms and sports, photographic, and other hobby equipment.		**Mountain bike at used bicycle store price (250), Digital camera priced at ebay (200), sword collection priced at antique store (800) Location: 3045 Berwick St, Lakeport CA**	-	1,250.00
9. Interests in insurance policies. Name insurance company of each policy and itemize surrender or refund value of each.	X			
10. Annuities. Itemize and name each issuer.	X			
11. Interests in an education IRA as defined in 26 U.S.C. § 530(b)(1) or under a qualified State tuition plan as defined in 26 U.S.C. § 529(b)(1). Give particulars. (File separately the record(s) of any such interest(s). 11 U.S.C. § 521(c).)	X			
12. Interests in IRA, ERISA, Keogh, or other pension or profit sharing plans. Give particulars.		**TIAA/CREF (ERISA Qualified Pension), not in bankruptcy estate**	-	0.00
		IRA, Bank of America, Lakeport CA (25,000), not in bankruptcy estate	-	0.00
13. Stock and interests in incorporated and unincorporated businesses. Itemize.		**5,000 shares in BLP Bankruptcy Services, Inc, a close corporation Location of certificates: 3045 Berwick St, Lakeport CA (valued at $.10 a share**	-	500.00
14. Interests in partnerships or joint ventures. Itemize.	X			
15. Government and corporate bonds and other negotiable and nonnegotiable instruments.		**U.S. Savings Bonds, all certificates at Ameritrust, 10 Financial Way, Cleveland Heights OH 41118**	-	2,250.00
		Negotiable promissory note from Jonathan Edwards, Carrie's brother, dated 11/3/XX Location: 3045 Berwick St, Lakeport CA	-	500.00
16. Accounts receivable.	X			
17. Alimony, maintenance, support, and property settlements to which the debtor is or may be entitled. Give particulars.	X			

Sub-Total >   **4,500.00**
(Total of this page)

Sheet __1__ of __3__ continuation sheets attached
to the Schedule of Personal Property

B6B (Official Form 6B) (12/07) - Cont.

In re   **Carrie Anne Edwards**   Case No. _____
_____,
                              Debtor

SCHEDULE B - PERSONAL PROPERTY
(Continuation Sheet)

Type of Property	N O N E	Description and Location of Property	Husband, Wife, Joint, or Community	Current Value of Debtor's Interest in Property, without Deducting any Secured Claim or Exemption
18. Other liquidated debts owed to debtor including tax refunds. Give particulars.		**Wages for 6/1/XX to 8/1/XX from ABC Typing Services**	-	500.00
19. Equitable or future interests, life estates, and rights or powers exercisable for the benefit of the debtor other than those listed in Schedule A - Real Property.	X			
20. Contingent and noncontingent interests in estate of a decedent, death benefit plan, life insurance policy, or trust.	X			
21. Other contingent and unliquidated claims of every nature, including tax refunds, counterclaims of the debtor, and rights to setoff claims. Give estimated value of each.	X			
22. Patents, copyrights, and other intellectual property. Give particulars.		**Copyright in book published by Nolo Press (Independent Paralegal's Handbook)**	-	Unknown
23. Licenses, franchises, and other general intangibles. Give particulars.	X			
24. Customer lists or other compilations containing personally identifiable information (as defined in 11 U.S.C. § 101(41A)) provided to the debtor by individuals in connection with obtaining a product or service from the debtor primarily for personal, family, or household purposes.	X			
25. Automobiles, trucks, trailers, and other vehicles and accessories.		**2003 Buick LeSabre fully loaded in good condition (replacement value from nada.com)**	-	8,000.00
26. Boats, motors, and accessories.	X			
27. Aircraft and accessories.	X			
28. Office equipment, furnishings, and supplies.		**Used computer valued at Ebay price, used in business**	-	800.00
		Copier (used Xerox) no known market for replacement value	-	Unknown
			Sub-Total > (Total of this page)	9,300.00

Sheet __2__ of __3__ continuation sheets attached
to the Schedule of Personal Property

B6B (Official Form 6B) (12/07) - Cont.

In re **Carrie Anne Edwards**   ,   Case No. _____
                                      Debtor

SCHEDULE B - PERSONAL PROPERTY
(Continuation Sheet)

Type of Property	N O N E	Description and Location of Property	Husband, Wife, Joint, or Community	Current Value of Debtor's Interest in Property, without Deducting any Secured Claim or Exemption
29. Machinery, fixtures, equipment, and supplies used in business.	X			
30. Inventory.	X			
31. Animals.	X			
32. Crops - growing or harvested. Give particulars.	X			
33. Farming equipment and implements.	X			
34. Farm supplies, chemicals, and feed.	X			
35. Other personal property of any kind not already listed. Itemize.	X			

Sub-Total >   0.00
(Total of this page)
Total >   26,675.00

Sheet __3__ of __3__ continuation sheets attached
to the Schedule of Personal Property

(Report also on Summary of Schedules)

Here are further instructions for filling in some of the blanks.

Item 1: Include all cash you expect to have on the date you file the petition.

Items 1 and 2: Explain the source of any cash on hand or money in financial accounts—for example, from wages, Social Security payments, or child support. This will help you (and the trustee) decide later whether any of this money qualifies as exempt property.

Item 11: Although an education IRA and a qualified state tuition plan may technically not be part of the bankruptcy estate, list them here anyway. Also, you are required to file any records you have of these interests as an attachment to Schedule B.

Item 12: Although ERISA-qualified pension plans, IRAs, and Keoghs may not be part of your bankruptcy estate, list them here anyway and describe each plan in detail. In the Current Value column, enter the value of the pension, if known.

Item 13: Include stock options.

Item 16: If you are a sole proprietor or independent contractor, you likely will be owed money by one or more of your customers. Specify each such debt by customer name, the reason for the debt, and the date the debt was incurred. These debts belong to your bankruptcy estate and may be used by the trustee to compute payments to your nonpriority, unsecured creditors under your plan unless you are able to claim them as exempt.

Item 17: List all child support or alimony arrears—that is, money that should have been paid to you but hasn't been. Specify the dates the payments were due and missed, such as "$250 monthly child support payments for June, July, August, and September 20xx." Also list any debts owed you from a property settlement incurred in a divorce or dissolution.

Item 18: List all money owed to you and not yet paid, other than child support, alimony, and property settlements. If you've obtained a judgment against someone but haven't been paid, list it here. State the defendant's name, the date of the judgment, the court that issued the judgment, the amount of the judgment, and the kind of case (such as car accident).

Item 19: An "equitable or future interest" means that sooner or later you will get property that is currently owned by someone else. Your expectation is legally recognized and valuable. For instance, if your parents'

trust gives them the right to live in the family home, that's a "life estate." If the trust gives you the home and all personal effects in the home when they die, you have an "equitable interest" in the home while they're alive. "Powers exercisable for the benefit of the debtor" means that a person has been given the power to route property your way, but it hasn't happened by the time you file your bankruptcy petition. In sum, if it looks like property is coming your way eventually, and that property hasn't been listed in Schedule A, list it here.

Item 20: You have a contingent interest in property if, for example, you are named the remainder beneficiary of an irrevocable trust (a trust that can't be undone by the person who created it). It's contingent because you may or may not get anything from the trust—it all depends on whether there's anything left by the time it gets to you. A noncontingent interest means you will get the property sooner or later, for example, under the terms of an insurance policy. Also list here any wills or revocable living trusts that name you as a beneficiary. Even though you don't have an absolute right to inherit under these documents (they can be changed at any time prior to the person's death), the trustee wants to know this information. The inheritance becomes part of your bankruptcy estate if the person dies within the six-month period following your bankruptcy filing date—and can result in your plan being modified to increase payments to your nonpriority unsecured creditors.

Item 21: List all claims that you have against others that might end up in a lawsuit. For instance, if you were recently rear-ended in an automobile accident and are struggling with whiplash, you may have a cause of action against the other driver (and that driver's insurer). If you fail to list this type of claim here, you might not be allowed to pursue it after bankruptcy.

Item 22: This question asks about assets commonly known as intellectual property. State what the patent, copyright, trademark, or the like is for. Give the number assigned by the issuing agency and length of time the patent, copyright, trademark, or other right will last. Keep in mind that both copyright and trademark rights may exist without going through a government agency. If you claim trademark rights through usage, or copyright through the fact that you created the item and reduced it to tangible form, describe them here.

Item 23: List all licenses and franchises, what they cover, the length of time remaining, who they are with, and whether you can transfer them to someone else.

Item 24: Describe customer lists or other compilations containing personally identifiable information that you obtained from people as part of providing them with consumer goods or services.

Items 25-27: Include the make, model, and year of each item.

Item 32: For your crops, list whether they've been harvested, whether they've been sold (and, if so, to whom and for how much), whether you've taken out any loan against them, and whether they are insured.

Husband, Wife, Joint, or Community. If you're not married, put "N/A" at the top of the column.

If you are married and live in a community property state, then property acquired during the marriage is community property and you should put "C" in this column. Gifts and inheritances received by one spouse are separate property, as is property a spouse owned prior to marriage or after separation. Identify this property with an "H" (for husband) or "W" (for wife), as appropriate.

If you live in any state that is not a community property state, write "J" if you own the property jointly with a spouse, and "H" or "W" if a spouse owns that property as an individual.

Current Value of Debtor's Interest in Property, Without Deducting any Secured Claim or Exemption. List the replacement value of the property, without regard to any secured interests or exemptions. For example, if you own a car with a replacement value of $6,000, you still owe $4,000 on the car note, and your state's motor vehicle exemption is $1,200, put down $6,000 for the value of the car.

Total. Add the amounts in this column and put the total in the box at the bottom of the last page. If you used any continuation pages in addition to the preprinted form, remember to attach those pages and include the amounts from those pages in this total.

Schedule C—Property Claimed as Exempt

On this form, you claim all property you think is legally exempt. In the overwhelming majority of bankruptcies filed by individuals, all—or virtually all—of the debtor's property is exempt. If, however, you have any property that is not exempt, you will have to pay the value of that property to your nonpriority, unsecured creditors. (See Ch. 5.)

Give Yourself the Benefit of the Doubt

When you claim exemptions, give yourself the benefit of the doubt—if an exemption seems to cover an item of property, claim it. You may find that you're legally entitled to exempt much of the property you're deeply attached to, such as your home, car, and family heirlooms.

When determining whether your proposed payments to your nonpriority unsecured creditors are sufficient, your trustee and possibly a creditor or two will examine your exemption claims. In close cases, bankruptcy laws require the trustee (and creditors) to honor rather than dishonor your exemption claims. In other words, you're entitled to the benefit of the doubt.

If the trustee or a creditor successfully objects to an exemption claim, you've lost nothing by trying (except that you'll have to modify your plan to increase your payments to your nonpriority unsecured creditors). See Ch. 11 for more on objections to claimed exemptions.

When you work on this form, you'll need to refer frequently to several other documents. Have in front of you:

- your drafts of Schedules A and B
- the list of state or federal bankruptcy exemptions you'll be using, provided in Appendix A, and
- if you're using a state's exemptions, the additional nonbankruptcy federal exemptions, provided in Appendix A.

Set out below is a sample completed Schedule C and line-by-line instructions.

Looking at the sample Schedule C exemptions, you might notice that a particular exemption can apply to more than one category of personal property from Schedule B. That's because the exemption categories are set up by each state, but the property categories are determined by the official form Schedule B. As a result, the property and exemption categories don't necessarily have any relation to each other. For example, the California "tools of the trade" exemption (see Appendix A) could apply to a number of the federal property categories, including category 28 (Office equipment, furnishings, and supplies), category 33 (Farming equipment and implements), category 25 (Automobiles, trucks, trailers and other vehicles and accessories), and category 5 (Books, etc.).

In re and Case No. Follow the instructions for Schedule A.

Debtor elects the exemptions to which the debtor is entitled under. If you're using the federal exemptions, check the top box. Everybody else, check the second box. See Ch. 5 for information on the new residency requirements for using a state's exemptions, and tips on how to choose between the federal and state exemption systems. As explained in Ch. 5, if you are living in a state that offers the federal exemption system, but you haven't been there long enough to meet the two-year residency requirement for the state exemptions, you can choose the federal system (and check the top box on Schedule C).

States That Offer the Federal Exemptions

Arkansas	Minnesota	Rhode Island
Connecticut	New Hampshire	Texas
Hawaii	New Jersey	Vermont
Massachusetts	New Mexico	Washington
Michigan	Pennsylvania	Wisconsin

SEE AN EXPERT

Property out of state. You'll generally choose the exemptions of the state you live in when you file as long as you've lived there for at least two years. If you want to protect your equity in property in a state other than the one you file in, see a lawyer.

Check if debtor claims a homestead exemption that exceeds $136,875. Check this box if:

- the exemptions of the state you are using allow a homestead of more than $136,875
- you have more than $136,875 equity in your home, and

- you acquired your home at least 40 months prior to your bankruptcy filing date.

If you didn't acquire your home at least 40 months before filing, and you didn't purchase it from the proceeds of selling a home in the same state, your homestead exemption may be capped at $136,875 regardless of the exemption available in the state where your home is located. See Ch. 5 for detailed information on the homestead exemption cap.

The following instructions cover one column at a time. But rather than listing all your exempt property in the first column and then completing the second column before moving on to the third column, you might find it easier to list one exempt item and complete all columns for that item before moving on to the next exempt item.

Description of Property. To describe the property you claim as exempt, take these steps:

Step 1: Turn to Ch. 5 to find out which exemptions are available to you and which property to claim as exempt

Step 2: Decide which of the real estate you listed on Schedule A, if any, you want to claim as exempt. Remember that state homestead allowances usually apply only to property you are living in when you file, but you can use a wildcard exemption for any type of property. Use the same description you used in the Description and Location of Property column of Schedule A.

Step 3: Decide which of the personal property you listed on Schedule B you want to claim as exempt. For each item identified, list both the category of property (preprinted in the Types of Property column) and the specific item, from the Description and Location of Property column. Do not include the location of the property. If the exemptions you are using apply to an entire category, such as clothing, simply list "clothing" as the item you are exempting.

Specify Law Providing Each Exemption. You'll find citations to the specific laws that create exemptions in the state and federal exemption lists in Appendix A. Remember to use the rules for choosing your exemptions explained in detail in Ch. 5.

B6C (Official Form 6C) (12/07)

In re   **Carrie Anne Edwards**   ,   Case No. _____

                             Debtor

SCHEDULE C - PROPERTY CLAIMED AS EXEMPT

Debtor claims the exemptions to which debtor is entitled under: ☐ Check if debtor claims a homestead exemption that exceeds
(Check one box) $136,875.
☐ 11 U.S.C. §522(b)(2)
■ 11 U.S.C. §522(b)(3)

Description of Property	Specify Law Providing Each Exemption	Value of Claimed Exemption	Current Value of Property Without Deducting Exemption
Real Property **Residence** **Location: 3045 Berwick St, Lakeport CA**	C.C.P. § 703.140(b)(1)	20,000.00	160,000.00
Cash on Hand **Cash in wallet**	C.C.P. § 703.140(b)(5)	0.00	50.00
Checking, Savings, or Other Financial Accounts, Certificates of Deposit **Bank of America Checking Account #12345** **Lakeport California** **from wages**	C.C.P. § 703.140(b)(5)	0.00	150.00
WestAmerica Bank, Lakeport CA **Savings Account**	C.C.P. § 703.140(b)(5)	0.00	300.00
Household Goods and Furnishings **All items at replacement value** **Stereo system ($300), washer dryer set (200), refrigerator (400), electric stove (250), misc furniture (couch, 2 chairs) (450) minor appliances (blender, toaster, mixer) (125), vacuum (50), 20 inch tv (75), lawnmower (200), swing set, childrens toys (240), snowblower (160)** **Location: 3045 Berwick St, Lakeport CA**	C.C.P. § 703.140(b)(3)	2,450.00	2,450.00
2 end tables (500), roll top desk (700), bed and bedding (800), oriental rug (2500)	C.C.P. § 703.140(b)(5)	1,900.00	4,500.00
Books, Pictures and Other Art Objects; Collectibles **250 books at used book store prices** **Location: 3045 Berwick St, Lakeport CA**	C.C.P. § 703.140(b)(5)	475.00	1,250.00
stamp collection at stamp dealer price **Location: 3045 Berwick St, Lakeport CA**	C.C.P. § 703.140(b)(5)	475.00	2,500.00
Wearing Apparel **normal clothing at used clothing store prices** **Location: 3045 Berwick St, Lakeport CA**	C.C.P. § 703.140(b)(3)	475.00	800.00
Furs and Jewelry **diamond necklace at used jewelry store price (800), watch at flea market price (75)** **Location: 3045 Berwick St, Lakeport CA**	C.C.P. § 703.140(b)(4)	875.00	875.00

___1___   continuation sheets attached to Schedule of Property Claimed as Exempt

B6C (Official Form 6C) (12/07) -- Cont.

In re   **Carrie Anne Edwards**   ,   Case No. _____

                             Debtor

SCHEDULE C - PROPERTY CLAIMED AS EXEMPT
(Continuation Sheet)

Description of Property	Specify Law Providing Each Exemption	Value of Claimed Exemption	Current Value of Property Without Deducting Exemption
Firearms and Sports, Photographic and Other Hobby Equipment Mountain bike at used bicycle store price (250), Digital camera priced at ebay (200), sword collection priced at antique store (800) Location: 3045 Berwick St, Lakeport CA	C.C.P. § 703.140(b)(5)	1,250.00	1,250.00
Stock and Interests in Businesses 5,000 shares in BLP Bankruptcy Services, Inc, a close corporation Location of certificates: 3045 Berwick St, Lakeport CA (valued at $.10 a share	C.C.P. § 703.140(b)(5)	0.00	500.00
Government & Corporate Bonds, Other Negotiable & Non-negotiable Inst. U.S. Savings Bonds, all certificates at Ameritrust, 10 Financial Way, Cleveland Heights OH 41118	C.C.P. § 703.140(b)(5)	750.00	2,250.00
Negotiable promissory note from Jonathan Edwards, Carrie's brother, dated 11/3/XX Location: 3045 Berwick St, Lakeport CA	C.C.P. § 703.140(b)(5)	500.00	500.00
Other Liquidated Debts Owing Debtor Including Tax Refund Wages for 6/1/XX to 8/1/XX from ABC Typing Services	C.C.P. § 703.140(b)(5)	0.00	500.00
Office Equipment, Furnishings and Supplies Used computer valued at Ebay price, used in business	C.C.P. § 703.140(b)(6)	800.00	800.00
	Total:	29,950.00	178,675.00

Sheet __1__ of __1__ continuation sheets attached to the Schedule of Property Claimed as Exempt

You can simplify this process by entering the name of the statutes you are using at the top of the form. The name is noted at the top of the exemption list you use in Appendix A. For example, you might type "All law references are to the Florida Statutes Annotated unless otherwise noted."

For each item of property you are claiming as exempt, enter the citation (number) of the specific law that creates the exemption, as set out on the exemption list. If you are combining part or all of a "wildcard" exemption with a regular exemption, list both citations. If the wildcard and the regular exemption have the same citation, list the citation twice and put "wildcard" next to one of the citations. If you use any reference other than one found in the state statutes you are using, such as a federal nonbankruptcy exemption or a court case, list the entire reference for the exempt item.

Value of Claimed Exemption. Claim the full exemption amount allowed, up to the value of the item. The amount allowed is listed in Appendix A.

Bankruptcy law allows married couples to double all exemptions unless the state expressly prohibits it. That means that each of you can claim the entire amount of each exemption, if you are both filing. If your state's chart in Appendix A doesn't say your state forbids doubling, go ahead and double.

> **EXAMPLE:** South Carolina allows a motor vehicle exemption up to $1,200. There is no language about doubling. This means a husband and wife can double the motor vehicle exemption in South Carolina—that is, a husband and wife using the South Carolina rules may exempt $2,400 worth of motor vehicles. On the other hand, California System 1 allows $2,550 for a motor vehicle but the exemption language states that husband and wife may not double. This means—perhaps surprisingly—that a husband and wife have only a slightly higher motor vehicle exemption California than in South Carolina.

If you are using part or all of a wildcard exemption in addition to a regular exemption, list both amounts. For example, if the regular exemption for an item of furniture is $200, and you plan to exempt it to $500 using $300 from your state's wildcard exemption, list

$200 across from the citation you listed for the regular exemption and $300 across from the citation you listed for the wildcard exemption (or across from the term "wildcard").

> **CAUTION**
> **Don't claim more than you need for any particular item.** For instance, if you're allowed household furniture up to a total amount of $2,000, don't inflate the value of each item of furniture simply to get to $2,000. Use the values as you stated them on Schedule B.

Current Value of Property Without Deducting Exemption. Enter the current (replacement) value of the item you are claiming as exempt. For most items, this information is listed on Schedules A and B. However, if you listed the item as part of a group in Schedule B, list it separately here and assign it a separate replacement value.

Schedule D—Creditors Holding Secured Claims

In this schedule, you list all creditors who hold claims secured by your property. This includes:

- holders of a mortgage or deed of trust on your real estate
- creditors who have won lawsuits against you and recorded judgment liens against your property
- doctors or lawyers to whom you have granted a security interest in the outcome of a lawsuit, so that the collection of their fees would be postponed (the expected court judgment is the collateral)
- contractors who have filed mechanic's or materialman's liens on your real estate
- taxing authorities, such as the IRS, that have obtained tax liens against your property
- creditors with either a purchase-money or nonpurchase-money security agreement (for an explanation of this jargon, see "Nature of Lien" below), and
- all parties who are trying to collect a secured debt, such as collection agencies and attorneys.

Credit Card Debts

Most credit card debts, including cards issued by a bank, gasoline company, or department store, are unsecured and should be listed on Schedule F. Some department stores, however, claim to retain a security interest in all durable goods, such as furniture, appliances, electronics equipment, and jewelry, bought using the store credit card. Also, if you were issued a bank or store credit card as part of a plan to restore your credit, you may have had to post property or cash as collateral for debts incurred on the card. If either of these exceptions apply to you, list the credit card debt on Schedule D.

Line-by-line instructions and a completed sample of Schedule D follow.

In re and Case No. Follow instructions for Schedule A.

☐ **Check this box if debtor has no creditors holding secured claims to report on this Schedule D.** Check the box at the bottom of the schedule's instructions if you have no secured creditors, then skip ahead to Schedule E. Everyone else, keep reading.

Creditor's Name and Mailing Address, Including Zip Code and an Account Number. List all secured creditors, preferably in alphabetical order. For each, fill in the last four digits of the account number, if you know it; the creditor's name; and the complete mailing address, including zip code. As mentioned earlier, the mailing address should be the contact address shown on at least two written communications you received from the creditor during the previous 90 days. Call the creditor to get this information if you don't have it.

If you have more than one secured creditor for a given debt, list the original creditor first, followed by the other creditors. For example, if you've been sued or hounded by a collection agency, list the information for the collection agency after the original creditor.

If, after typing up your final papers, you discover that you've missed a few creditors, don't retype your papers to preserve perfect alphabetical order. Simply add the creditors at the end. Make as many copies of the preprinted continuation page as you need to list them all. Debtors commonly use up to five continuation pages.

If the creditor is a child, list the child's initials and the name and address of the child's parent or guardian. For example, "A.B., a minor child, by John Doe, Guardian, 1111 Alabama Avenue, San Francisco, CA 94732." Don't state the child's name.

Codebtor. Someone who owes money with you probably isn't the first person you think of as your creditor. But if someone else agreed to cosign your loan, lease, or purchase, then creditors can still go after your codebtor, who will then look to you to cough up the money. As long as your Chapter 13 case is pending, however, no creditor may proceed in court against a codebtor—except in the circumstances explained in Ch. 2. If someone else (other than a spouse with whom you are filing jointly) could be legally forced to pay your debt to a listed secured creditor (outside of bankruptcy), enter an "X" in this column and list the codebtor in the creditor column of this schedule. You'll also need to list the codebtor as a creditor in Schedules F and H (explained below).

The most common codebtors are:

- cosigners
- guarantors (people who guarantee payment of a loan)
- ex-spouses with whom you jointly incurred debts before divorcing
- joint owners of real estate or other property
- coparties in a lawsuit
- nonfiling spouses in a community property state (most debts incurred in a community property state by a nonfiling spouse during marriage are considered community debts, making that spouse equally liable with the filing spouse for the debts), and
- nonfiling spouses in states other than community property states, for debts incurred by the filing spouse for basic living necessities such as food, shelter, clothing, and utilities.

Husband, Wife, Joint, or Community. Follow the instructions for Schedule A.

Date Claim Was Incurred, Nature of Lien, and Description and Value of Property. This column calls for a lot of information for each secured debt. If you list two or more creditors on the same secured claim (such as the lender and a collection agency), simply put ditto marks (") in this column for the second creditor. Let's take these one at a time.

B6D (Official Form 6D) (12/07)

In re   **Carrie Anne Edwards** _____ ,   Case No. _____

                                            Debtor

SCHEDULE D - CREDITORS HOLDING SECURED CLAIMS

State the name, mailing address, including zip code, and last four digits of any account number of all entities holding claims secured by property of the debtor as of the date of filing of the petition. The complete account number of any account the debtor has with the creditor is useful to the trustee and the creditor and may be provided if the debtor chooses to do so. List creditors holding all types of secured interests such as judgment liens, garnishments, statutory liens, mortgages, deeds of trust, and other security interests.

List creditors in alphabetical order to the extent practicable. If a minor child is a creditor, the child's initials and the name and address of the child's parent or guardian, such as "A.B., a minor child, by John Doe, guardian." Do not disclose the child's name. See, 11 U.S.C. §112 and Fed. R. Bankr. P. 1007(m). If all secured creditors will not fit on this page, use the continuation sheet provided.

If any entity other than a spouse in a joint case may be jointly liable on a claim, place an "X" in the column labeled "Codebtor" ,include the entity on the appropriate schedule of creditors, and complete Schedule H - Codebtors. If a joint petition is filed, state whether the husband, wife, both of them, or the marital community may be liable on each claim by placing an "H", "W", "J", or "C" in the column labeled "Husband, Wife, Joint, or Community".

If the claim is contingent, place an "X" in the column labeled "Contingent". If the claim is unliquidated, place an "X" in the column labeled "Unliquidated". If the claim is disputed, place an "X" in the column labeled "Disputed". (You may need to place an "X" in more than one of these three columns.)

Total the columns labeled "Amount of Claim Without Deducting Value of Collateral" and "Unsecured Portion, if Any" in the boxes labeled "Total(s)" on the last sheet of the completed schedule. Report the total from the column labeled "Amount of Claim" also on the Summary of Schedules and, if the debtor is an individual with primarily consumer debts, report the total from the column labeled "Unsecured Portion" on the Statistical Summary of Certain Liabilities and Related Data.

☐   Check this box if debtor has no creditors holding secured claims to report on this Schedule D.

CREDITOR'S NAME AND MAILING ADDRESS INCLUDING ZIP CODE, AND ACCOUNT NUMBER (See instructions above.)	CODEBTOR	Husband, Wife, Joint, or Community	DATE CLAIM WAS INCURRED, NATURE OF LIEN, AND DESCRIPTION AND VALUE OF PROPERTY SUBJECT TO LIEN	CONTINGENT	UNLIQUIDATED	DISPUTED	AMOUNT OF CLAIM WITHOUT DEDUCTING VALUE OF COLLATERAL	UNSECURED PORTION, IF ANY
Account No. **444555666777** **GMAC** **PO Box 23567** **Duchesne, UT 84021**		-	November, 2002 **Purchase Money Security** **2003 Buick LeSabre fully loaded in good condition (replacement value from nada.com)** Value $ **8,000.00**			X	**15,000.00**	**7,000.00**
Account No. **64-112-1861** **Grand Junction Mortgage** **3456 Eight St.** **Clearlake, CA 95422**		-	5/2005 **First Mortgage** **Residence** **Location: 3045 Berwick St, Lakeport CA** Value $ **160,000.00**				**135,000.00**	**0.00**
Account No. **55555555555** **Lending Tree** **PO Box 3333** **Palo Alto, CA 94310**		-	12/xx **Second Mortgage** **Residence** **Location: 3045 Berwick St, Lakeport CA** Value $ **160,000.00**				**5,000.00**	**0.00**
Account No. Value $								

0   continuation sheets attached

	Subtotal (Total of this page)	**155,000.00**	**7,000.00**
	Total (Report on Summary of Schedules)	**155,000.00**	**7,000.00**

Date Claim Was Incurred. For most claims, the date the claim was incurred is the date you signed the security agreement. If you didn't sign a security agreement with the creditor, the date is most likely the date a contractor or judgment creditor recorded a lien against your property or the date a taxing authority notified you of a tax liability or assessment of taxes due.

Nature of Lien. What kind of property interest does your secured creditor have? Here are the possible answers:

- **First mortgage.** You took out a loan to buy your house. (This is a specific kind of purchase-money security interest.)

- **Purchase-money security interest.** You took out a loan to purchase the property that secures the loan—for example, a car note. The creditor must have "perfected" the security interest by filing or recording it with the appropriate agency within 20 days. (*Fidelity Financial Services, Inc. v. Fink*, 522 U.S. 211 (1998).) Otherwise, the creditor has no lien and you should list the debt on Schedule F (unsecured debt) instead.

- **Nonpossessory, nonpurchase-money security interest.** You borrowed money for a purpose other than buying the collateral. This includes refinanced home loans, home equity loans, or loans from finance companies.

- **Possessory, nonpurchase-money security interest.** This is what a pawnshop owner has when you pawn your stuff.

- **Judgment lien.** This means someone sued you, won a court judgment, and recorded a lien against your property.

- **Tax lien.** This means a federal, state, or local government agency recorded a lien against your property for unpaid taxes.

- **Child support lien.** This means that another parent or government agency has recorded a lien against your property for unpaid child support.

- **Mechanic's or materialman's lien.** This means someone performed work on your real property or personal property (for example, a car) but didn't get paid, and recorded a lien on that property. Such liens can be an unpleasant surprise if you paid for the work, but your contractor didn't pay a subcontractor who got a lien against your property.

- **Unknown.** If you don't know what kind of lien you are dealing with, put "Don't know nature of lien" after the date. The bankruptcy trustee can help you figure it out later.

Description of Property. Describe each item of real estate and personal property that is collateral for the secured debt listed in the first column. Use the same description you used on Schedule A for real property, or Schedule B for personal property. If a creditor's lien covers several items of property, list all items affected by the lien.

Value of Property. The amount you put here must be consistent with what you put on Schedule A or B. If you put only the total value of a group of items on Schedule B, you must now get more specific. For instance, if a department store has a secured claim against your washing machine, and you listed your "washer/dryer set" on Schedule B, now you must provide the washer's specific replacement value. You may have already done this on the Property Exemption Worksheet. If not, see the instructions for "Current Value" on Schedule B.

Contingent, Unliquidated, Disputed. Indicate whether the creditor's secured claim is contingent, unliquidated, or disputed. Check all categories that apply. If you're uncertain of which to choose, check the one that seems closest. If none applies, leave them blank. Briefly, these terms mean:

- **Contingent.** The claim depends on some event that hasn't yet occurred and may never occur. For example, if you cosigned a secured loan, you won't be liable unless the principal debtor defaults. Your liability as cosigner is contingent upon the default.

- **Unliquidated.** This means that a debt may exist, but the exact amount hasn't been determined. For example, say you've sued someone for injuries you suffered in an auto accident, but the case isn't over. Your lawyer has taken the case under a contingency fee agreement—he'll get a third of the recovery if you win, and nothing if you lose—and has a security interest in the final recovery amount. The debt to the lawyer is unliquidated because you don't know how much, if anything, you'll win.

- **Disputed.** A claim is disputed if you and the creditor do not agree about the existence or amount of the debt. For instance, suppose the IRS says you owe $10,000 and has put a lien on your property, and you say you owe $500. List the full amount of the lien, not the amount you think you owe.

TIP

You're not admitting you owe the debt. You may think you don't really owe a contingent, unliquidated, or disputed debt, or you may not want to "admit" that you owe the debt. By listing a debt here, however, you aren't admitting anything. Instead, you are making sure that, if you owe the debt after all, it will be discharged in your bankruptcy (if it is dischargeable).

Amount of Claim Without Deducting Value of Collateral. For each secured creditor, list the amount it would take to pay off the secured claim, regardless of what the property is worth. The lender can give you this figure. In some cases, the amount of the secured claim may be more than the property's value.

EXAMPLE: Your original loan was for $13,000, plus $7,000 in interest (for $20,000 total). You've made enough payments so that $15,000 will cancel the debt. You would put $15,000 in this column.

If you have more than one creditor for a given secured claim (for example, the lender and a collection agency), list the debt only for the lender and put ditto marks (") for each subsequent creditor.

Subtotal/Total. Total the amounts in the Amount of Claim column for each page. Do not include the amounts represented by the ditto marks if you listed multiple creditors for a single debt. On the final page of Schedule D, which may be the first page or a preprinted continuation page, enter the total of all secured claims.

Unsecured Portion, If Any. If the replacement value of the collateral is equal to or greater than the amount of the claim, enter "0," meaning that the creditor's claim is fully secured. If the replacement value of the collateral is less than the amount of the claim(s) listed, enter the difference here.

EXAMPLE: If the current value of your car is $5,000 but you still owe $6,000 on your car loan, enter $1,000 in this column ($6,000 − $5,000). This is

the amount of the loan that is unsecured by the collateral (your car).

If you list an amount in this column for a creditor, do not list this amount again on Schedule F (where you will list all other creditors with unsecured claims). Otherwise, this unsecured amount will be listed twice.

Schedule E—Creditors Holding Unsecured Priority Claims

Schedule E identifies certain creditors who—with the exception of child support claims assigned to a government agency—are entitled to be paid in full in your Chapter 13 case.

Set out below are a sample completed Schedule E and line-by-line instructions.

In re and Case No. Follow the instructions for Schedule A.

☐ **Check this box if debtor has no creditors holding unsecured priority claims to report on this Schedule E.** As mentioned, except for child support claims owed to a government agency, priority claims must be paid in full in your Chapter 13 plan. The most common examples are unsecured nondischargeable income tax debts and past due alimony or child support owed to an ex-spouse or child. There are several other categories of priority debts, however. Read further to figure out whether or not you can check this box.

These are the categories of priority debts, as listed on Schedule E. Check the appropriate box on the form if you owe a debt in that category.

☐ **Domestic Support Obligations.** Check this box for claims for domestic support that you owe to, or that are recoverable by, a spouse, former spouse, or child; the parent, legal guardian, or responsible relative of such a child; or a governmental unit to whom such a domestic support claim has been assigned.

☐ **Extensions of credit in an involuntary case.** Don't check this box. You are filing a voluntary, not an involuntary, case.

☐ **Wages, salaries, and commissions.** If you own a business and owe a current or former employee wages, vacation pay, or sick leave that was earned within 180 days before you file your petition or within 180 days of the date you ceased your business, check this box. If you owe money to an independent contractor who

B6E (Official Form 6E) (12/07)

In re   **Carrie Anne Edwards** _____,   Case No. _____
                                                         Debtor

SCHEDULE E - CREDITORS HOLDING UNSECURED PRIORITY CLAIMS

A complete list of claims entitled to priority, listed separately by type of priority, is to be set forth on the sheets provided. Only holders of unsecured claims entitled to priority should be listed in this schedule. In the boxes provided on the attached sheets, state the name, mailing address, including zip code, and last four digits of the account number, if any, of all entities holding priority claims against the debtor or the property of the debtor, as of the date of the filing of the petition. Use a separate continuation sheet for each type of priority and label each with the type of priority.

The complete account number of any account the debtor has with the creditor is useful to the trustee and the creditor and may be provided if the debtor chooses to do so. If a minor child is a creditor, state the child's initials and the name and address of the child's parent or guardian, such as "A.B., a minor child, by John Doe, guardian." Do not disclose the child's name. See, 11 U.S.C. §112 and Fed. R. Bankr. P. 1007(m).

If any entity other than a spouse in a joint case may be jointly liable on a claim, place an "X" in the column labeled "Codebtor," include the entity on the appropriate schedule of creditors, and complete Schedule H-Codebtors. If a joint petition is filed, state whether the husband, wife, both of them, or the marital community may be liable on each claim by placing an "H," "W," "J," or "C" in the column labeled "Husband, Wife, Joint, or Community." If the claim is contingent, place an "X" in the column labeled "Contingent." If the claim is unliquidated, place an "X" in the column labeled "Unliquidated." If the claim is disputed, place an "X" in the column labeled "Disputed." (You may need to place an "X" in more than one of these three columns.)

Report the total of claims listed on each sheet in the box labeled "Subtotals" on each sheet. Report the total of all claims listed on this Schedule E in the box labeled "Total" on the last sheet of the completed schedule. Report this total also on the Summary of Schedules.

Report the total of amounts entitled to priority listed on each sheet in the box labeled "Subtotals" on each sheet. Report the total of all amounts entitled to priority listed on this Schedule E in the box labeled "Totals" on the last sheet of the completed schedule. Individual debtors with primarily consumer debts report this total also on the Statistical Summary of Certain Liabilities and Related Data.

Report the total of amounts <u>not</u> entitled to priority listed on each sheet in the box labeled "Subtotals" on each sheet. Report the total of all amounts not entitled to priority listed on this Schedule E in the box labeled "Totals" on the last sheet of the completed schedule. Individual debtors with primarily consumer debts report this total also on the Statistical Summary of Certain Liabilities and Related Data.

☐ Check this box if debtor has no creditors holding unsecured priority claims to report on this Schedule E.

TYPES OF PRIORITY CLAIMS (Check the appropriate box(es) below if claims in that category are listed on the attached sheets)

■ **Domestic support obligations**

Claims for domestic support that are owed to or recoverable by a spouse, former spouse, or child of the debtor, or the parent, legal guardian, or responsible relative of such a child, or a governmental unit to whom such a domestic support claim has been assigned to the extent provided in 11 U.S.C. § 507(a)(1).

☐ **Extensions of credit in an involuntary case**

Claims arising in the ordinary course of the debtor's business or financial affairs after the commencement of the case but before the earlier of the appointment of a trustee or the order for relief. 11 U.S.C. § 507(a)(3).

☐ **Wages, salaries, and commissions**

Wages, salaries, and commissions, including vacation, severance, and sick leave pay owing to employees and commissions owing to qualifying independent sales representatives up to $10,950* per person earned within 180 days immediately preceding the filing of the original petition, or the cessation of business, whichever occurred first, to the extent provided in 11 U.S.C. § 507(a)(4).

☐ **Contributions to employee benefit plans**

Money owed to employee benefit plans for services rendered within 180 days immediately preceding the filing of the original petition, or the cessation of business, whichever occurred first, to the extent provided in 11 U.S.C. § 507(a)(5).

☐ **Certain farmers and fishermen**

Claims of certain farmers and fishermen, up to $5,400* per farmer or fisherman, against the debtor, as provided in 11 U.S.C. § 507(a)(6).

☐ **Deposits by individuals**

Claims of individuals up to $2,425* for deposits for the purchase, lease, or rental of property or services for personal, family, or household use, that were not delivered or provided. 11 U.S.C. § 507(a)(7).

■ **Taxes and certain other debts owed to governmental units**

Taxes, customs duties, and penalties owing to federal, state, and local governmental units as set forth in 11 U.S.C. § 507(a)(8).

☐ **Commitments to maintain the capital of an insured depository institution**

Claims based on commitments to the FDIC, RTC, Director of the Office of Thrift Supervision, Comptroller of the Currency, or Board of Governors of the Federal Reserve System, or their predecessors or successors, to maintain the capital of an insured depository institution. 11 U.S.C. § 507 (a)(9).

☐ **Claims for death or personal injury while debtor was intoxicated**

Claims for death or personal injury resulting from the operation of a motor vehicle or vessel while the debtor was intoxicated from using alcohol, a drug, or another substance. 11 U.S.C. § 507(a)(10).

* Amounts are subject to adjustment on April 1, 2010, and every three years thereafter with respect to cases commenced on or after the date of adjustment.

                                      2_____ continuation sheets attached

B6E (Official Form 6E) (12/07) - Cont.

In re **Carrie Anne Edwards**   ,   Case No. _____
                                           Debtor

SCHEDULE E - CREDITORS HOLDING UNSECURED PRIORITY CLAIMS
(Continuation Sheet)

Domestic Support Obligations

TYPE OF PRIORITY

CREDITOR'S NAME, AND MAILING ADDRESS INCLUDING ZIP CODE, AND ACCOUNT NUMBER (See instructions.)	C O D E B T O R	H W J C	DATE CLAIM WAS INCURRED AND CONSIDERATION FOR CLAIM	C O N T I N G E N T	U N L I Q U I D A T E D	D I S P U T E D	AMOUNT OF CLAIM	AMOUNT NOT ENTITLED TO PRIORITY, IF ANY / AMOUNT ENTITLED TO PRIORITY
Account No. Jon Edwards 900 Grand View Jackson, WY 83001		-	2005 Child support				2,500.00	0.00 2,500.00
Account No.								
Account No.								
Account No.								
Account No.								

Sheet __1__ of __2__ continuation sheets attached to
Schedule of Creditors Holding Unsecured Priority Claims

Subtotal
(Total of this page)

	0.00
2,500.00	2,500.00

B6E (Official Form 6E) (12/07) - Cont.

In re   **Carrie Anne Edwards**   ,   Case No. _____
                          Debtor

SCHEDULE E - CREDITORS HOLDING UNSECURED PRIORITY CLAIMS
(Continuation Sheet)

**Taxes and Certain Other Debts
Owed to Governmental Units**

TYPE OF PRIORITY

CREDITOR'S NAME, AND MAILING ADDRESS INCLUDING ZIP CODE, AND ACCOUNT NUMBER (See instructions.)	CODEBTOR	Husband, Wife, Joint, or Community			DATE CLAIM WAS INCURRED AND CONSIDERATION FOR CLAIM	CONTINGENT	UNLIQUIDATED	DISPUTED	AMOUNT OF CLAIM	AMOUNT NOT ENTITLED TO PRIORITY, IF ANY / AMOUNT ENTITLED TO PRIORITY
		H	W	JC						
Account No.					April 15, 20XX tax liability and interest					0.00
IRS **Columbus, OH 43266**		-							3,000.00	3,000.00
Account No.										
Account No.										
Account No.										
Account No.										

Sheet __2__ of __2__ continuation sheets attached to
Schedule of Creditors Holding Unsecured Priority Claims

Subtotal (Total of this page)	3,000.00	0.00 / 3,000.00
Total (Report on Summary of Schedules)	5,500.00	0.00 / 5,500.00

did work for you, and the money was earned within 180 days before you file your petition or within 180 days of the date you ceased your business, check this box only if, in the 12 months before you file for bankruptcy, this independent contractor earned at least 75% of his or her total independent contractor receipts from you. Only the first $10,950 owed per employee or independent contractor is a priority debt.

☐ **Contributions to employee benefit plans.** Check this box if you own a business and you owe contributions to an employee benefit fund for services rendered by an employee within 180 days before you file your petition, or within 180 days of the date you ceased your business.

☐ **Certain farmers and fishermen.** Check this box only if you operate or operated a grain storage facility and owe a grain producer, or you operate or operated a fish produce or storage facility and owe a U.S. fisherman for fish or fish products. Only the first $5,400 owed per person is a priority debt.

☐ **Deposits by individuals.** If you took money from people who planned to purchase, lease, or rent goods or services from you that you never delivered, you may owe a priority debt. For the debt to qualify as a priority, the goods or services had to have been planned for personal, family, or household use. Only the first $2,425 owed (per person) is a priority debt.

☐ **Taxes and Certain Other Debts Owed to Governmental Units.** Check this box if you owe unsecured back taxes or if you owe any other debts to the government, such as fines imposed for driving under the influence of drugs or alcohol. Not all tax debts are unsecured priority claims. For example, if the IRS has recorded a lien against your real property, and the equity in your property fully covers the amount of your tax debt, your debt is a secured debt. It should be on Schedule D, not on this schedule. And if the debt is dischargeable, it should be listed on Schedule F.

☐ **Commitments to Maintain the Capital of an Insured Depository Institution.** Don't check this box. It is for business bankruptcies.

☐ **Claims for Death or Personal Injury While Debtor Was Intoxicated.** Check this box if there are claims against you for death or personal injury resulting from your operation of a motor vehicle or vessel while intoxicated from using alcohol, a drug, or another substance. This priority doesn't apply to property damage—only to personal injury or death.

If you didn't check any of the priority debt boxes, go back and check the first box, showing you have no unsecured priority claims to report. Then go on to Schedule F.

If you checked any of the priority debt boxes, make as many photocopies of the continuation page as the number of priority debt boxes you checked. You will need to complete a separate sheet for each type of priority debt, as follows:

In re and Case No. Follow the instructions for Schedule A.

Type of Priority. Insert the category for one of the boxes you checked (for example, "Domestic Support Obligations").

Creditor's Name, Mailing Address Including Zip Code, and Account Number. List the name and complete mailing address (including zip code) of each priority creditor, as well as the account number, if you know it. The address should be the one provided by the creditor in two written communications you have received from the creditor within the past 90 days, if possible. You may have more than one priority creditor for a given debt. For example, if you've been sued or hounded by a collection agency, list the collection agency in addition to the original creditor.

If the creditor is a child, list the child's initials and the name and address of the child's parent or guardian. For example, "A.B., a minor child, by John Doe, Guardian, 1111 Alabama Avenue, San Francisco, CA 94732." Don't state the child's name.

Codebtor. If someone else can be legally forced to pay your debt to a priority creditor, enter an "X" in this column and list the codebtor in the creditor column of this schedule. You'll also need to list the codebtor as a creditor in Schedule F and Schedule H. Common codebtors are listed in the instructions for Schedule D.

Husband, Wife, Joint, or Community. Follow the instructions for Schedule A.

Date Claim Was Incurred and Consideration for Claim. State the date you incurred the debt—this may be a specific date or a period of time. Also briefly state what the debt is for. For example, "goods purchased," "hours worked for me," or "deposit for my services."

Contingent, Unliquidated, Disputed. Follow the instructions for Schedule D.

Amount of Claim. For each priority debt other than taxes, put the amount it would take to pay off the debt in full, even if it's more than the priority limit. For taxes, list only the amount that is unsecured and non-dischargeable (and therefore a priority). You should list the secured amount on Schedule D. If the amount isn't determined, write "not yet determined" in this column. If you owe some back child support to a child or ex-spouse and other support to a government agency, state the amounts separately. As mentioned, your plan will have to propose 100% payment of the amount you owe to a child or ex-spouse, but can propose less than 100% payment of support owed to a government agency.

Subtotal/Total. Total the amounts in the Amount of Claim column on each page. If you use continuation pages for additional priority debts, enter the total of all priority debts on the final page.

Amount Entitled to Priority. If the priority claim is larger than the maximum indicated on the first two pages of Schedule E (for example, $10,950 of wages owed to each employee), put the maximum here. If the claim is less than the maximum, put the amount you entered in the Total Amount of Claim column here.

Amount Not Entitled to Priority, If Any. If you owe more than the maximum for any of the priority debts listed on the first two pages of Schedule E, list the excess amount here. For example, the maximum for wages owed to employees is $10,950. If you owe former employees $12,000, you should list $1,050—the amount by which your debt exceeds the maximum—here.

Schedule F—Creditors Holding Unsecured Nonpriority Claims

In this schedule, list all creditors you haven't listed in Schedules D or E. You should include even debts that are or may be nondischargeable, such as a student loan. Even if you believe that you don't owe the debt or you owe only a small amount and intend to pay it off, you must include it here. It's essential that you list every creditor to whom you owe, or possibly owe, money. The only way you can legitimately leave off a creditor is if your balance owed is $0.

> **EXAMPLE:** Peter owes his favorite aunt $8,000. Peter files for bankruptcy and lists the debt, which is discharged when Peter's bankruptcy is over. Peter can voluntarily repay the $8,000 out of wages he earns any time after he files, because the wages he earns after filing are not part of his bankruptcy estate. He cannot use property that belongs to the bankruptcy estate, however, until he receives a discharge. The important thing is, repayment is completely voluntary on Peter's part. Peter's aunt can't sue him in court to enforce payment of the debt.

Inadvertent errors or omissions on this schedule can come back to haunt you. If you don't list a debt you owe to a creditor, it won't be discharged in your Chapter 13 bankruptcy. Also, leaving a creditor off the schedule might raise suspicions that you deliberately concealed information, perhaps to give that creditor preferential treatment in violation of bankruptcy rules.

Below are a sample completed Schedule F and line-by-line instructions. Use as many preprinted continuation pages as you need.

In re and Case No. Follow the instructions for Schedule A.

☐ **Check this box if debtor has no creditors holding unsecured claims to report on this Schedule F.** Check this box if you have no unsecured nonpriority debts. This would be very rare.

Creditor's Name, Mailing Address Including Zip Code, and Account Number. List, preferably in alphabetical order, the name and complete mailing address of each unsecured creditor, as well as the account number (if you know it). If you have more than one unsecured creditor for a given debt, list the original creditor first, followed by the other creditors. For example, for a particular debt, you might have the name, address, and account number for the original creditor, a collection agency run by the original creditor, an independent collection agency, an attorney debt collector, and an attorney who has sued you.

It's best to list all the creditors, because it never hurts to be thorough. But you could omit the intermediate collectors and just list the original creditor and the latest collector or attorney. Or, if you no longer have contact information for the original creditor, listing the latest collector will do.

When you are typing your final papers, if you get to the end and discover that you left a creditor off, don't start all over again in search of perfect alphabetical order. Just add the creditor to the end of the list.

B6F (Official Form 6F) (12/07)

In re **Carrie Anne Edwards**   , Case No. _____
                                              Debtor

SCHEDULE F - CREDITORS HOLDING UNSECURED NONPRIORITY CLAIMS

State the name, mailing address, including zip code, and last four digits of any account number, of all entities holding unsecured claims without priority against the debtor or the property of the debtor, as of the date of filing of the petition. The complete account number of any account the debtor has with the creditor is useful to the trustee and the creditor and may be provided if the debtor chooses to do so. If a minor child is a creditor, state the child's initials and the name and address of the child's parent or guardian, such as "A.B., a minor child, by John Doe, guardian." Do not disclose the child's name. See, 11 U.S.C. §112 and Fed. R. Bankr. P. 1007(m). Do not include claims listed in Schedules D and E. If all creditors will not fit on this page, use the continuation sheet provided.

If any entity other than a spouse in a joint case may be jointly liable on a claim, place an "X" in the column labeled "Codebtor," include the entity on the appropriate schedule of creditors, and complete Schedule H - Codebtors. If a joint petition is filed, state whether the husband, wife, both of them, or the marital community may be liable on each claim by placing an "H," "W," "J," or "C" in the column labeled "Husband, Wife, Joint, or Community."

If the claim is contingent, place an "X" in the column labeled "Contingent." If the claim is unliquidated, place an "X" in the column labeled "Unliquidated." If the claim is disputed, place an "X" in the column labeled "Disputed." (You may need to place an "X" in more than one of these three columns.)

Report the total of all claims listed on this schedule in the box labeled "Total" on the last sheet of the completed schedule. Report this total also on the Summary of Schedules and, if the debtor is an individual with primarily consumer debts, report this total also on the Statistical Summary of Certain Liabilities and Related Data.

☐ Check this box if debtor has no creditors holding unsecured claims to report on this Schedule F.

CREDITOR'S NAME, MAILING ADDRESS INCLUDING ZIP CODE, AND ACCOUNT NUMBER (See instructions above.)	CODEBTOR	H W J C	DATE CLAIM WAS INCURRED AND CONSIDERATION FOR CLAIM. IF CLAIM IS SUBJECT TO SETOFF, SO STATE.	CONTINGENT	UNLIQUIDATED	DISPUTED	AMOUNT OF CLAIM
Account No. **Alan Accountant** **5 Green St.** **Cleveland, OH 44118**	-		**4/xx** **Tax preparation**				500.00
Account No. **41 89-0000-2613-5556** **American Allowance** **PO Box 1** **New York, NY 10001**	-		**1/xx to 4/xx** **credit card charges**				5,600.00
Account No. **Angel of Mercy Hospital** **4444 Elevisior St.** **Belmont, CA 94003**	-		**12/xx** **uninsured surgery and medical treatment**				34,000.00
Account No. **Bob Jones III** **4566 Fifth Ave.** **New York, NY 10020**	-		**5/xx** **Auto accident--negligence claim**				75,000.00

  2   continuation sheets attached

Subtotal (Total of this page) 115,100.00

B6F (Official Form 6F) (12/07) - Cont.

In re   **Carrie Anne Edwards**_____ ,   Case No. _____
                                        Debtor

SCHEDULE F - CREDITORS HOLDING UNSECURED NONPRIORITY CLAIMS
(Continuation Sheet)

CREDITOR'S NAME, MAILING ADDRESS INCLUDING ZIP CODE, AND ACCOUNT NUMBER (See instructions above.)	C O D E B T O R	H W J C	DATE CLAIM WAS INCURRED AND CONSIDERATION FOR CLAIM. IF CLAIM IS SUBJECT TO SETOFF, SO STATE.	C O N T I N G E N T	U N L I Q U I D A T E D	D I S P U T E D	AMOUNT OF CLAIM
Account No. **Bonnie Johnson** **3335 Irving St** **Clearlake, CA 95422**		-	**8/xx** **Personal loan**				5,500.00
Account No. **845061-86-3** **Citibank** **200 East North St** **Columbus, OH 43266**		-	**20xx** **Student loan**				10,000.00
Account No. **4401** **Dr. Dennis Dentist** **45 Superior Way** **Cleveland, OH 44118**		-	**12/xx to 6/xx** **dental work**				1,050.00
Account No. **555671** **Dr. Helen Jones** **443 First St.** **Soledad, CA 94750**		-	**4/xx to 8/xx** **Pediatric Care**				5,000.00
Account No. **Fannie's Furniture** **55544 Grove St.** **Berkeley, CA 94710**	X	-	**12/xx** **used bedroomset**				1,300.00

Sheet no. _**1**_ of _**2**_ sheets attached to Schedule of Creditors Holding Unsecured Nonpriority Claims

Subtotal (Total of this page)   22,850.00

B6F (Official Form 6F) (12/07) - Cont.

In re   **Carrie Anne Edwards**   Case No. _____
                                                        _____ .
                            Debtor

SCHEDULE F - CREDITORS HOLDING UNSECURED NONPRIORITY CLAIMS
(Continuation Sheet)

CREDITOR'S NAME, MAILING ADDRESS INCLUDING ZIP CODE, AND ACCOUNT NUMBER (See instructions above.)	CODEBTOR	H W J C	DATE CLAIM WAS INCURRED AND CONSIDERATION FOR CLAIM. IF CLAIM IS SUBJECT TO SETOFF, SO STATE.	CONTINGENT	UNLIQUIDATED	DISPUTED	AMOUNT OF CLAIM
Account No. **222387941** **Illuminating Co.** **20245 Old Hwy 53** **Clearlake, CA 95422**		-	**3/xx to 7/xx** **electrical work on house**				750.00
Account No. **John White Esq.** **PO Box 401** **Finley, CA 95435**		-	**2/xx to 8/xx** **Legal representation in lawsuit against neighbor for incursion on property**				3,450.00
Account No. **4567-3453-5432-5678** **Loan Shark Collections** **PO Box 666** **Clearlake, CA 95422**		-	**2001-2003** **Misc Living Costs**				56,000.00
Account No. **11210550** **PG&E** **315 North Forbes St.** **Lakeport, CA 95453**		-	**12/xx to 6/xx** **gas and electric service**				1,200.00
Account No. **487310097** **Sears** **PO Box 11** **Chicago, IL 60619**		-	**20xx to 20xx** **Dept store and catalog charges**				3,800.00

Sheet no. __2__ of __2__ sheets attached to Schedule of Creditors Holding Unsecured Nonpriority Claims

Subtotal (Total of this page)	65,200.00
Total (Report on Summary of Schedules)	203,150.00

Creditors That Are Often Overlooked

One debt may involve several different creditors. Remember to include:

- your ex-spouse, if you are still obligated under a divorce decree or settlement agreement to pay joint debts, turn any property over to your ex, or make payments as part of your property division
- anyone who has cosigned a promissory note or loan application you signed
- any holder of a loan or promissory note that you cosigned for someone else
- the original creditor, anybody to whom the debt has been assigned or sold, and any other person (such as a bill collector or attorney) trying to collect the debt, and
- anyone who might sue you in the future because of a car accident, business dispute, or the like.

Codebtor. If someone else can be legally forced to pay your debt to a listed unsecured creditor, enter an "X" in this column and list the codebtor as a creditor in this schedule. Also list the codebtor in Schedule H. The instructions for Schedule D list common codebtors.

Husband, Wife, Joint, or Community. Follow the instructions for Schedule A.

Date Claim Was Incurred and Consideration for Claim. If Claim Is Subject to Setoff, So State. State when the debt was incurred. It may be one date or a period of time. With credit card debts, put the approximate time over which you ran up the charges, unless the unpaid charges were made on one or two specific dates. Then state what the debt was for. You can be general ("clothes" or "household furnishings") or specific ("refrigerator" or "teeth capping").

If you are entitled to a setoff against the debt—that is, the creditor owes you some money, too—list the amount and why you think you are entitled to the setoff. If there is more than one creditor for a single debt, put ditto marks (") in this column for the subsequent creditors.

Contingent, Unliquidated, Disputed. Follow the instructions for Schedule D.

Amount of Claim. List the amount of the debt claimed by the creditor, even if you dispute the amount. That way, it will all be wiped out if it's dischargeable. If there's more than one creditor for a single debt, put the debt amount across from the original creditor and put ditto marks (") across from each subsequent creditor you have listed. Be as precise as possible when stating the amount. If you must approximate, write "approx." after the amount.

Subtotal/Total. Total the amounts in the last column for this page. Do not include the amounts represented by the ditto marks if you listed multiple creditors for a single debt. On the final page (which may be the first page or a preprinted continuation page), enter the total of all unsecured, nonpriority claims. On the first page in the bottom left-hand corner, note the number of continuation pages you are attaching.

Schedule G—Executory Contracts and Unexpired Leases

In this form, you list every executory contract or unexpired lease to which you're a party. "Executory" means the contract is still in force—that is, both parties are still obligated to perform important acts under it. Similarly, "unexpired" means that the contract or lease period hasn't run out—that is, it is still in effect. Common examples of executory contracts and unexpired leases are:

- car leases
- residential leases or rental agreements
- business leases or rental agreements
- service contracts
- business contracts
- time-share contracts or leases
- contracts of sale for real estate
- personal property leases, such as equipment used in a beauty salon
- copyright and patent license agreements
- leases of real estate (surface and underground) for the purpose of harvesting timber, minerals, or oil
- future homeowners' association fee requirements
- agreements for boat docking privileges, and
- insurance contracts.

CAUTION

If you're behind in your payments. If you are not current on payments that were due under a lease or executory contract, the delinquency should also be listed as a debt on Schedule D, E, or F. The sole purpose of this schedule is to identify existing contractual obligations that you still owe or that someone owes you.

Below are a sample completed Schedule G and line-by-line instructions.

In re and Case No. Follow the instructions for Schedule A.

☐ **Check this box if debtor has no executory contracts or unexpired leases.** Check this box if it applies; otherwise, complete the form.

Name and Mailing Address, Including Zip Code, of Other Parties to Lease or Contract. Provide the name and full address (including zip code) of each party—other than yourself—to each lease or contract. These parties are either people who signed agreements or the companies for whom these people work. If you're unsure about whom to list, include the person who signed an agreement, any company whose name appears on the agreement, and anybody who might have an interest in having the contract or lease enforced. If you still aren't sure, put "don't know."

Description of Contract or Lease and Nature of Debtor's Interest. For each lease or contract, give:

- a description of the basic type (for instance, residential lease, commercial lease, car lease, business obligation, or copyright license)
- the date the contract or lease was signed
- the date the contract is to expire (if any)
- a summary of each party's rights and obligations under the lease or contract, and
- the contract number, if the contract is with any government body.

What Happens to Executory Contracts and Unexpired Leases in Chapter 13 Bankruptcy

The trustee has until the confirmation hearing on your plan (see Ch. 10) to decide whether an executory contract or unexpired lease should be assumed (continued in force) as property of the estate or terminated (rejected). As a general matter, most leases and contracts are liabilities and are rejected by the trustee.

If the trustee rejects the contract or lease, you can assume or reject the contract or lease in your Chapter 13 plan. If your plan rejects the lease or contract, you and the other parties to the agreement are cut loose from any obligations, and any money you owe the creditor will be treated as an unsecured debt in your plan, even if the debt arose after your filing date. For example, say you are leasing a car when you file for bankruptcy. You want out of the lease. The car dealer cannot repossess the car until the trustee rejects the lease, or you reject the lease in your plan. During that period, you can use the car without paying for it (although you will have to make "adequate protection" payments equal to your monthly payments, unless you have sufficient equity in the car to cover the value it will lose in depreciation while you're using it; see *In re Singer*, 368 B.R. 435 (E.D. Pa. 2007)). The payments you don't make during this period will be treated as an unsecured debt just as if they were incurred prior to your bankruptcy.

Bankruptcy law has special rules for executory contracts related to intellectual property (copyright, patent, trademark, or trade secret), real estate, and time-share leases. If you are involved in one of these situations, see a lawyer.

B6G (Official Form 6G) (12/07)

In re   **Carrie Anne Edwards**   ,   Case No. _____
                                    Debtor

SCHEDULE G - EXECUTORY CONTRACTS AND UNEXPIRED LEASES

Describe all executory contracts of any nature and all unexpired leases of real or personal property. Include any timeshare interests. State nature of debtor's interest in contract, i.e., "Purchaser", "Agent", etc. State whether debtor is the lessor or lessee of a lease. Provide the names and complete mailing addresses of all other parties to each lease or contract described. If a minor child is a party to one of the leases or contracts, state the child's initials and the name and address of the child's parent or guardian, such as "A.B., a minor child, by John Doe, guardian." Do not disclose the child's name. See, 11 U.S.C. §112 and Fed. R. Bankr. P. 1007(m).

☐ Check this box if debtor has no executory contracts or unexpired leases.

Name and Mailing Address, Including Zip Code, of Other Parties to Lease or Contract	Description of Contract or Lease and Nature of Debtor's Interest. State whether lease is for nonresidential real property. State contract number of any government contract.
Beauty Products Leasing Co. **44332** **Geismar, LA 70734**	**Laser skin treatment machine. Lease for 5 year period that expires on 2010**
Herman Jones **45543 Woodleigh Court** **Smith River, CA 95567**	**Sales contract for debtor's home entered into between debtor and Herman Jones on 2 /1/XX**

   0   continuation sheets attached to Schedule of Executory Contracts and Unexpired Leases

Schedule H—Codebtors

In Schedules D, E, and F, you identified those debts for which you have codebtors—usually, a cosigner, guarantor, ex-spouse, nonfiling spouse in a community property state, nonfiling spouse for a debt for necessities, nonmarital partner, or joint contractor. You must also list those codebtors here. In addition, you must list the name and address of any spouse or former spouse who lived with you in Puerto Rico or in a community property state during the eight-year period immediately preceding your bankruptcy filing. (To remind you, the community property states are Alaska, Arizona, California, Idaho, Louisiana, Nevada, New Mexico, Texas, Washington, and Wisconsin.) If you are married but filing separately, include all names used by your spouse during the eight-year period.

In Chapter 13 bankruptcy, your codebtors will be responsible for whatever portion of the debts are left after you complete your plan. For instance if the debt they cosigned on is $2,000, and you pay 50% of the debt in your Chapter 13 bankruptcy, they will be responsible for the remaining $1,000.

Below are a sample completed Schedule H and line-by-line instructions.

In re and Case No. Follow instructions for Schedule A.

☐ **Check this box if debtor has no codebtors.** Check this box if it applies; otherwise, complete the form.

Name and Address of Codebtor. List the name and complete address (including zip code) of each codebtor. If the codebtor is a nonfiling, current spouse, put all names by which that person was known during the previous eight years.

If the creditor is a child, list the child's initials and the name and address of the child's parent or guardian. For example, "A.B., a minor child, by John Doe, Guardian, 1111 Alabama Avenue, San Francisco, CA 94732." Don't state the child's name.

Name and Address of Creditor. List the name and address of each creditor (as listed on Schedule D, E, or F) to which each codebtor is indebted.

EXAMPLE: Tom Martin cosigned three different loans —with three different banks—for debtor Mabel Green, who is filing for bankruptcy. In the first column, Mabel lists Tom Martin as a codebtor. In the second, Mabel lists each of the three banks.

MARRIED FILERS

If you are married and filing alone. If you live in a community property state, your spouse may be a codebtor for most of the debts you listed in Schedules D, E, and F. This is because, in these states, most debts incurred by one spouse are owed by both spouses. In this event, don't relist all the creditors in the second column. Simply write "all creditors listed in Schedules D, E, and F, except:" and then list any creditors whom you owe alone.

If you lived with a former spouse in a community property state or Puerto Rico in the eight-year period prior to filing, list his or her name and address.

Schedule I—Current Income of Individual Debtor(s)

In this schedule, you calculate your actual current income (not your average monthly income in the six months before you file, which you calculated in Form 22C in Ch. 4).

Directly below are a sample completed Schedule I and line-by-line instructions. If you're married and filing jointly, you must fill in information for both spouses. If you are married but filing alone, fill in the information only for yourself.

In re and Case No. Follow the instructions for Schedule A.

Debtor's Marital Status. Enter your marital status. Your choices are single, married, separated (you aren't living with your spouse and plan never to again), widowed, or divorced. You are divorced only if you have received a final judgment of divorce from a court.

Dependents of Debtor and Spouse. List all people, according to their relationship with you (son, daughter, and so on), for whom you and your spouse provide at least 50% of support. There is no need to list their names. This list may include your children, your spouse's children, your parents, other relatives, and domestic partners. It does not include your spouse.

Employment. Provide the requested employment information. If you have more than one employer, enter "See continuation sheet" just below the box containing the employment information, then complete a continuation sheet. If you are retired, unemployed, or disabled, enter that in the blank for "occupation."

B6H (Official Form 6H) (12/07)

In re   **Carrie Anne Edwards**   ,   Case No. _____

                                     Debtor

SCHEDULE H - CODEBTORS

     Provide the information requested concerning any person or entity, other than a spouse in a joint case, that is also liable on any debts listed by debtor in the schedules of creditors. Include all guarantors and co-signers. If the debtor resides or resided in a community property state, commonwealth, or territory (including Alaska, Arizona, California, Idaho, Louisiana, Nevada, New Mexico, Puerto Rico, Texas, Washington, or Wisconsin) within the eight year period immediately preceding the commencement of the case, identify the name of the debtor's spouse and of any former spouse who resides or resided with the debtor in the community property state, commonwealth, or territory. Include all names used by the nondebtor spouse during the eight years immediately preceding the commencement of this case. If a minor child is a codebtor or a creditor, state the child's initials and the name and address of the child's parent or guardian, such as "A.B., a minor child, by John Doe, guardian." Do not disclose the child's name. See, 11 U.S.C. §112 and Fed. R. Bankr. P. 1007(m).

☐   Check this box if debtor has no codebtors.

NAME AND ADDRESS OF CODEBTOR	NAME AND ADDRESS OF CREDITOR
Bonnie Johnson **3335 Irving St.** **Clearlake, CA 95422**	**Fannie's Furniture** **55544 Grove St.** **Berkeley, CA 94710**

   0   continuation sheets attached to Schedule of Codebtors

Income. Enter your estimated monthly gross income from your current employment, before any payroll deductions are taken. In the second blank, put your estimated monthly overtime pay. Add them together and enter the subtotal in the third blank.

Three Different Income Figures

The bankruptcy law that went into effect in October 2005 produces a number of strange results. One of these is that you will report three different income figures—the "current monthly income" figure in Form 22C, the actual income you report here, and the annual income figures you report in your Statement of Financial Affairs (see below).

Schedule I explicitly states that the income you report there will likely be different from what you report as your current monthly income on Form 22C (See Ch. 5). That's because the income you report on Form 22C is your average gross income for the six months before you file, but the income you report here is the actual net income you expect to be receiving every month going forward. If, for example, you lost your job a couple of months ago and are now working for a far lesser wage, your income will be less than it was on Form 22C.

Courts are divided on whether to use the income you report on Schedule I or on Form 22C to determine how much you have to pay into your Chapter 13 plan. The law seems to say that you must use the figures from Form 22C, but some judges think that it makes no sense to base your plan on income that you might not have anymore, especially because you already have to provide up-to-date figures on Schedule I.

CAUTION
Make sure the numbers add up. As you juggle these income and deduction numbers, remember that you need to use a monthly amount. This means you may need to convert the numbers on your pay stub or other documents if you're paid weekly, every two weeks, or twice a month.

Item 4: Payroll Deductions. In the four blanks, enter the deductions taken from your gross salary. The deductions listed are the most common ones, but you may have others to report. Other possible deductions are state disability taxes, wages withheld or garnished for child support, credit union payments, or perhaps payments on a student loan or a car.

Item 5: Subtotal of Payroll Deductions. Add your payroll deductions and enter the subtotal.

Item 6: Total Net Monthly Take Home Pay. Subtract your payroll deductions subtotal from your income subtotal.

Item 7: Regular income from operation of business or profession or farm. If you are self-employed or operate a sole proprietorship, enter your monthly net income from that source here. If it's been fairly steady for at least one calendar year, divide the amount you entered on your most recent tax return (IRS Schedule C: *Profit or Loss From Business*) by 12 for a monthly amount. If your income hasn't been steady for at least one calendar year, enter the average monthly net income from your business or profession over the past three months. In either case, you must attach a detailed statement of your income and expenses (you can use your IRS Schedule C).

Item 8: Income from real property. Enter your net monthly income from real estate rentals, leases, or licenses (such as mineral exploration, oil, and the like).

Item 9: Interest and dividends. Enter the average estimated monthly interest you receive from bank or security deposits and other investments, such as stocks.

Item 10: Alimony, maintenance or support payments payable to the debtor for the debtor's use or that of dependents listed above. Enter the average monthly amount you receive for your support (alimony, spousal support, or maintenance) or for your children (child support).

Item 11: Social Security or other government assistance. Enter the total monthly amount you receive in Social Security, SSI, public assistance, disability payments, veterans' benefits, unemployment compensation, workers' compensation, or any other government benefit. If you receive food stamps, include their monthly value. Specify the source of the benefits. Although you don't have to report Social Security benefits on Form 22C, you do have to include it here—and some courts may consider it in determining how much you have to pay into your Chapter 13 plan every month.

Item 12: Pension or retirement income. Enter the total monthly amount of all pension, annuity, IRA, Keogh, or other retirement benefits you currently receive.

Item 13: Other monthly income. Specify any other income (such as royalty payments or payments from

B6I (Official Form 6I) (12/07)

In re   __Carrie Anne Edwards_____   Case No. _____
                          Debtor(s)

SCHEDULE I - CURRENT INCOME OF INDIVIDUAL DEBTOR(S)

The column labeled "Spouse" must be completed in all cases filed by joint debtors and by every married debtor, whether or not a joint petition is filed, unless the spouses are separated and a joint petition is not filed. Do not state the name of any minor child. The average monthly income calculated on this form may differ from the current monthly income calculated on Form 22A, 22B, or 22C.

Debtor's Marital Status:	DEPENDENTS OF DEBTOR AND SPOUSE	
Divorced	RELATIONSHIP(S): **daughter** **Son**	AGE(S): **12** **14**

Employment:	DEBTOR	SPOUSE
Occupation	**Retail**	
Name of Employer	**Macy's**	
How long employed	**2 months**	
Address of Employer	**2356 Cleveland Ave. Santa Rosa, CA 95402**	

INCOME: (Estimate of average or projected monthly income at time case filed)	DEBTOR	SPOUSE
1. Monthly gross wages, salary, and commissions (Prorate if not paid monthly)	$ **4,766.67**	$ **N/A**
2. Estimate monthly overtime	$ **0.00**	$ **N/A**
3. SUBTOTAL	$ **4,766.67**	$ **N/A**
4. LESS PAYROLL DEDUCTIONS		
a. Payroll taxes and social security	$ **541.67**	$ **N/A**
b. Insurance	$ **0.00**	$ **N/A**
c. Union dues	$ **0.00**	$ **N/A**
d. Other (Specify): _____	$ **0.00**	$ **N/A**
	$ **0.00**	$ **N/A**
5. SUBTOTAL OF PAYROLL DEDUCTIONS	$ **541.67**	$ **N/A**
6. TOTAL NET MONTHLY TAKE HOME PAY	$ **4,225.00**	$ **N/A**
7. Regular income from operation of business or profession or farm (Attach detailed statement)	$ **0.00**	$ **N/A**
8. Income from real property	$ **0.00**	$ **N/A**
9. Interest and dividends	$ **0.00**	$ **N/A**
10. Alimony, maintenance or support payments payable to the debtor for the debtor's use or that of dependents listed above	$ **500.00**	$ **N/A**
11. Social security or government assistance (Specify): _____	$ **0.00**	$ **N/A**
	$ **0.00**	$ **N/A**
12. Pension or retirement income	$ **0.00**	$ **N/A**
13. Other monthly income (Specify): **royalties from book on bankruptcy**	$ **1,500.00**	$ **N/A**
	$ **0.00**	$ **N/A**
14. SUBTOTAL OF LINES 7 THROUGH 13	$ **2,000.00**	$ **N/A**
15. AVERAGE MONTHLY INCOME (Add amounts shown on lines 6 and 14)	$ **6,225.00**	$ **N/A**
16. COMBINED AVERAGE MONTHLY INCOME: (Combine column totals from line 15)	$ **6,225.00**	

(Report also on Summary of Schedules and, if applicable, on Statistical Summary of Certain Liabilities and Related Data)

17. Describe any increase or decrease in income reasonably anticipated to occur within the year following the filing of this document:

a trust) you receive on a regular basis, and enter the monthly amount here. You may have to divide by three, six, or 12 if you receive the payments quarterly, semiannually, or annually.

Item 14: Subtotal of items 7-13. Add up your additional income (items 7 through 13).

Item 15: Total Monthly Income. Combine items 6 and 14.

Item 16: Total Combined Monthly Income. If you are filing jointly, add your total income to your spouse's total income and enter the result here.

Item 17: Describe any increase or decrease in income reasonably anticipated to occur within the year following the filing of this document. As we have emphasized, courts are split on whether the income figures on this form or on Form 22C will determine your Chapter 13 plan payment. If it appears that your income will increase in the next year, your plan payment might be larger than it would be if it were based on Form 22C (which calculates your income for the previous six months). Nolo's Bankruptcy Blog at http://blogs.nolo. com/bankruptcy will provide updates on this subject as they occur. For the time being, courts in different judicial circuits are reaching different conclusions, a development that most likely means the U.S. Supreme Court will sort it all out in a few years.

Schedule J—Current Expenditures of Individual Debtor(s)

You already completed a modified Schedule J in Ch. 5 if your current monthly income is below your state's median income. However, if your current monthly income is above your state's median income, you completed a different form in Ch. 5—Form 22C. In that event, return to Ch. 5 and complete Schedule J following the instructions there.

$\bigcirc$ **CAUTION**

Be consistent on your forms. Bankruptcy thrives on consistency. If you list certain expenses in Form 22C and list different amounts for the same items in your Schedule J, the bankruptcy trustee will likely want an explanation of the discrepancies. For instance, if you list $500 for charitable contributions in Form 22C and $1,000 for charitable

contributions on your Schedule J, the trustee will want to know which one is correct—and might also take a closer look at your other entries. Before you sign your bankruptcy papers, make sure your entries are consistent—and, needless to say, correct.

Summary of Schedules

This form helps the bankruptcy trustee and judge get a quick look at your bankruptcy filing. Below is a completed Summary and line-by-line instructions.

Court Name. Copy this information from Form 1—Voluntary Petition.

In re and Case No. Follow the instructions for Schedule A.

Name of Schedule. This lists the schedules. Don't add anything.

Attached (Yes/No). You should have completed all of the schedules, so type "Yes" in this column for each schedule, even if you added no information.

No. of Sheets. Enter the number of pages you completed for each schedule. Remember to count continuation pages. Enter the total at the bottom of the column.

Amounts Scheduled. For each column—Assets, Liabilities, and Other—copy the totals from Schedules A, B, D, E, F, I, and J and enter them where indicated. Add up the amounts in the Assets and Liabilities columns and enter their totals at the bottom. (Once you've completed this form, you can go back and fill in the "Statistical/Administrative Information" section on Form 1—Voluntary Petition.)

Statistical Summary of Certain Liabilities. The second page of the summary sheet asks you to list the amounts of particular types of debts, including child support, student loans, and loans from a pension plan. Fill in the requested amounts.

Declaration Concerning Debtor's Schedules

In this form, you are required to swear that everything you have said on your schedules is true and correct. Deliberate lying is a major sin in bankruptcy and could cost you your bankruptcy discharge, a fine of up to $500,000, and up to five years in prison.

Below is a completed Declaration and instructions.

In re and Case No. Follow the instructions for Schedule A.

B6J (Official Form 6J) (12/07)

In re   **Carrie Anne Edwards**_____   Case No. _____
                                    Debtor(s)

SCHEDULE J - CURRENT EXPENDITURES OF INDIVIDUAL DEBTOR(S)

Complete this schedule by estimating the average or projected monthly expenses of the debtor and the debtor's family at time case filed. Prorate any payments made bi-weekly, quarterly, semi-annually, or annually to show monthly rate. The average monthly expenses calculated on this form may differ from the deductions from income allowed on Form 22A or 22C.

☐   Check this box if a joint petition is filed and debtor's spouse maintains a separate household. Complete a separate schedule of expenditures labeled "Spouse."

1. Rent or home mortgage payment (include lot rented for mobile home)		$ 1,565.10
a. Are real estate taxes included?	Yes **X** No ___	
b. Is property insurance included?	Yes **X** No ___	
2. Utilities: a. Electricity and heating fuel		$ 150.00
b. Water and sewer		$ 150.00
c. Telephone		$ 200.00
d. Other **See Detailed Expense Attachment**		$ 130.00
3. Home maintenance (repairs and upkeep)		$ 75.00
4. Food		$ 500.00
5. Clothing		$ 125.00
6. Laundry and dry cleaning		$ 40.00
7. Medical and dental expenses		$ 300.00
8. Transportation (not including car payments)		$ 200.00
9. Recreation, clubs and entertainment, newspapers, magazines, etc.		$ 0.00
10. Charitable contributions		$ 0.00
11. Insurance (not deducted from wages or included in home mortgage payments)		
a. Homeowner's or renter's		$ 0.00
b. Life		$ 0.00
c. Health		$ 200.00
d. Auto		$ 100.00
e. Other		$ 0.00
12. Taxes (not deducted from wages or included in home mortgage payments)		
(Specify) _____		$ 0.00
13. Installment payments: (In chapter 11, 12, and 13 cases, do not list payments to be included in the plan)		
a. Auto		$ 250.00
b. Other **Payment on home equity loan**		$ 100.00
c. Other		$ 0.00
14. Alimony, maintenance, and support paid to others		$ 0.00
15. Payments for support of additional dependents not living at your home		$ 0.00
16. Regular expenses from operation of business, profession, or farm (attach detailed statement)		$ 0.00
17. Other **Child care**		$ 300.00
Other		$ 0.00

18. AVERAGE MONTHLY EXPENSES (Total lines 1-17. Report also on Summary of Schedules and, if applicable, on the Statistical Summary of Certain Liabilities and Related Data.) $ | 4,385.10 |

19. Describe any increase or decrease in expenditures reasonably anticipated to occur within the year following the filing of this document:

_____

20. STATEMENT OF MONTHLY NET INCOME

a.	Average monthly income from Line 15 of Schedule I	$ 6,225.00
b.	Average monthly expenses from Line 18 above	$ 4,385.10
c.	Monthly net income (a. minus b.)	$ 1,839.90

B6 Summary (Official Form 6 - Summary) (12/07)

United States Bankruptcy Court
Northern District of California

In re   **Carrie Anne Edwards** _____.

                                    Debtor

Case No. _____

Chapter_____**13**_____

SUMMARY OF SCHEDULES

Indicate as to each schedule whether that schedule is attached and state the number of pages in each. Report the totals from Schedules A, B, D, E, F, I, and J in the boxes provided. Add the amounts from Schedules A and B to determine the total amount of the debtor's assets. Add the amounts of all claims from Schedules D, E, and F to determine the total amount of the debtor's liabilities. Individual debtors must also complete the "Statistical Summary of Certain Liabilities and Related Data" if they file a case under chapter 7, 11, or 13.

NAME OF SCHEDULE	ATTACHED (YES/NO)	NO. OF SHEETS	ASSETS	LIABILITIES	OTHER
A - Real Property	Yes	1	160,000.00		
B - Personal Property	Yes	4	26,675.00		
C - Property Claimed as Exempt	Yes	2			
D - Creditors Holding Secured Claims	Yes	1		155,000.00	
E - Creditors Holding Unsecured Priority Claims (Total of Claims on Schedule E)	Yes	3		5,500.00	
F - Creditors Holding Unsecured Nonpriority Claims	Yes	3		203,150.00	
G - Executory Contracts and Unexpired Leases	Yes	1			
H - Codebtors	Yes	1			
I - Current Income of Individual Debtor(s)	Yes	1			6,225.00
J - Current Expenditures of Individual Debtor(s)	Yes	2			4,385.10
Total Number of Sheets of ALL Schedules		19			
Total Assets			186,675.00		
Total Liabilities				363,650.00	

Form 6 - Statistical Summary (12/07)

United States Bankruptcy Court
Northern District of California

In re   **Carrie Anne Edwards**   Case No. _____

Debtor

Chapter _____ **13** _____

STATISTICAL SUMMARY OF CERTAIN LIABILITIES AND RELATED DATA (28 U.S.C. § 159)

If you are an individual debtor whose debts are primarily consumer debts, as defined in § 101(8) of the Bankruptcy Code (11 U.S.C.§ 101(8)), filing a case under chapter 7, 11 or 13, you must report all information requested below.

☐ Check this box if you are an individual debtor whose debts are NOT primarily consumer debts. You are not required to report any information here.

This information is for statistical purposes only under 28 U.S.C. § 159.

Summarize the following types of liabilities, as reported in the Schedules, and total them.

Type of Liability	Amount
Domestic Support Obligations (from Schedule E)	2,500.00
Taxes and Certain Other Debts Owed to Governmental Units (from Schedule E)	3,000.00
Claims for Death or Personal Injury While Debtor Was Intoxicated (from Schedule E) (whether disputed or undisputed)	0.00
Student Loan Obligations (from Schedule F)	0.00
Domestic Support, Separation Agreement, and Divorce Decree Obligations Not Reported on Schedule E	0.00
Obligations to Pension or Profit-Sharing, and Other Similar Obligations (from Schedule F)	0.00
TOTAL	5,500.00

State the following:

Average Income (from Schedule I, Line 16)	6,225.00
Average Expenses (from Schedule J, Line 18)	4,385.10
Current Monthly Income (from Form 22A Line 12; OR, Form 22B Line 11; OR, Form 22C Line 20)	7,560.00

State the following:

1. Total from Schedule D, "UNSECURED PORTION, IF ANY" column		7,000.00
2. Total from Schedule E, "AMOUNT ENTITLED TO PRIORITY" column	5,500.00	
3. Total from Schedule E, "AMOUNT NOT ENTITLED TO PRIORITY, IF ANY" column		0.00
4. Total from Schedule F		203,150.00
5. Total of non-priority unsecured debt (sum of 1, 3, and 4)		210,150.00

B6 Declaration (Official Form 6 - Declaration). (12/07)

United States Bankruptcy Court
Northern District of California

In re **Carrie Anne Edwards** _____ Case No. _____

                                          Debtor(s)   Chapter **13** _____

DECLARATION CONCERNING DEBTOR'S SCHEDULES

DECLARATION UNDER PENALTY OF PERJURY BY INDIVIDUAL DEBTOR

      I declare under penalty of perjury that I have read the foregoing summary and schedules, consisting of **21** sheets, and that they are true and correct to the best of my knowledge, information, and belief.

Date ___October 3, 2008___   Signature ___*Carrie Anne Edwards*___

                                              Carrie Anne Edwards
                                              Debtor

Penalty for making a false statement or concealing property: Fine of up to $500,000 or imprisonment for up to 5 years or both.
18 U.S.C. §§ 152 and 3571.

Declaration Under Penalty of Perjury by Individual Debtor. Enter the total number of pages in your schedules (the number on the Summary plus one). Enter the date and sign the form. Be sure that your spouse signs and dates the form if you are filing jointly.

Certification and Signature of Non-Attorney Bankruptcy Petition Preparer. If a BPP typed your forms, have that person complete this section. Otherwise, type "N/A" anywhere in the box.

Declaration Under Penalty of Perjury on Behalf of Corporation or Partnership. Enter "N/A" anywhere in this blank.

Form 7—Statement of Financial Affairs

This form gives information about your recent financial transactions, such as payments to creditors, sales, or other transfers of property and gifts. Under certain circumstances, the trustee may be entitled to take back property that you transferred to others prior to filing for bankruptcy, and sell it for the benefit of your unsecured creditors. This rarely happens in Chapter 13 cases, however, unless your plan proposes to pay your nonpriority, unsecured creditors only a small percentage of what you owe them.

The questions on the form are, for the most part, self-explanatory. Spouses filing jointly combine their answers and complete only one form.

If you have no information for a particular item, check the "None" box. If you fail to answer a question and don't check "None," you will have to amend your papers—that is, file a corrected form—after you file. Add continuation sheets if necessary.

! **CAUTION**

Be honest and complete. Don't give in to the temptation to leave out a transfer or two, assuming that the trustee won't find or go after the property. You must sign this form under penalty of perjury. And, if the trustee or a creditor discovers that you left information out, your bankruptcy will probably be dismissed and you may be prosecuted.

A completed Statement of Financial Affairs and instructions follows.

Court Name. Copy this information from Form 1 —Voluntary Petition.

In re and Case No. Follow the instructions for Schedule A.

1. Income from employment or operation of business. Enter your gross income for this year and for the previous two years. This means the total income before taxes and other payroll deductions or business expenses are removed.

2. Income other than from employment or operation of business. Include interest, dividends, royalties, workers' compensation, other government benefits, and all other money you have received from sources other than your job or business during the last two years. Provide the source of each amount, the dates received, and the reason you received the money so that the trustee can verify it if he or she desires.

Make sure the amounts provided here are consistent with the income disclosed on the IRS return you provide to the trustee. For instance, if you enter $25,000 gross income for the previous year, and you also provide the trustee with a tax return for that year, the tax return should be consistent with the $25,000 figure entered here.

3. Payments to creditors. Here you list payments you've recently made to creditors. There are two kinds of creditors: regular creditors and insiders. An insider— defined on the first page of the Statement of Financial Affairs—is essentially a relative or close business associate. All other creditors are regular creditors.

a. **Individual or joint debtor with primarily consumer debts.** List payments made to a regular creditor that total more than $600, if the payment was made:
   - to repay a loan, installment purchase, or other debt
   - during the 90 days before you file your bankruptcy petition.

   If you have made payments exceeding $600 during that 90-day period to satisfy a domestic support obligation (child support or alimony), identify that payment with an asterisk. Include payments as part of a creditor repayment plan negotiated by an approved budget and credit-counseling agency.

b. **Debtor whose debts are not primarily consumer debts.** If your debts are primarily business debts, list all payments or other transfers made to a creditor within 90 days of filing regarding property that is worth $5,475 or more.

c. All debtors. List all payments or other transfers made to an insider creditor, if the payments or transfers were made within one year before you file your bankruptcy petition. Include alimony and child support payments.

The purpose of these questions is to find out whether you have preferred any creditor over others. If you have paid a regular creditor during the 90 days before you file, or an insider during the year before you file, the value of the payment will be part of your bankruptcy estate and will not be considered exempt. Rather, you will have to pay your unsecured creditors at least the value of the amount you paid to these creditors before you filed for bankruptcy. Exceptions to this rule are payments you made toward a domestic support obligation (child support or alimony) or payments you made under an alternative repayment schedule arranged by an approved nonprofit budget and credit counseling agency.

4. Suits and administrative proceedings, executions, garnishments and attachments.

a. Include all court actions that you are currently involved in or that you were involved in during the year before filing. Court actions include personal injury cases, small claims actions, contract disputes, divorces, paternity actions, support or custody modification actions, and the like. Include:

- **Caption of the suit and case number.** The caption is the case title (such as *Molly Maytag v. Ginny Jones*). The case number is assigned by the court clerk and appears on the first page of any court-filed paper.
- **Nature of the proceeding.** A phrase, or even a one-word description, is sufficient. For example, "suit by debtor for compensation for damages to debtor's car caused by accident," or "divorce."
- **Court and location.** This information is on any summons you received or prepared.
- **Status or disposition.** State whether the case is awaiting trial, is pending a decision, is on appeal, or has ended.

b. If, at any time during the year before you file for bankruptcy, your wages, real estate, or personal property was taken from you under the authority of a court order to pay a debt, enter the requested information. If you don't know the exact date, put "on or about" the approximate date.

5. Repossessions, foreclosures and returns. If, at any time during the year before you file for bankruptcy, a creditor repossessed or foreclosed on property you had bought and were making payments on, or had pledged as collateral for a loan, give the requested information. For instance, if your car, boat, or video equipment was repossessed because you defaulted on your payments, describe it here. Also, if you voluntarily returned property to a creditor because you couldn't keep up the payments, enter that here.

6. Assignments and receiverships.

a. If, at any time during the 120 days (four months) before you file for bankruptcy, you assigned (legally transferred) your right to receive benefits or property to a creditor to pay a debt, list it here. Examples include assigning a percentage of your wages to a creditor for several months or assigning a portion of a personal injury award to an attorney. The assignee is the person to whom the assignment was made, such as the creditor or attorney. The terms of the assignment should be given briefly—for example, "wages assigned to Snorkle's Store to satisfy debt of $500."

b. Identify all of your property that has been in the hands of a court-appointed receiver, custodian, or other official during the year before you file for bankruptcy. If you've made child support payments directly to a court, and the court in turn paid your child's other parent, list those payments here.

7. Gifts. Provide the requested information about gifts you've made in the past year. The bankruptcy court and trustee want this information to make sure you haven't improperly unloaded any property before filing for bankruptcy. List all charitable donations of more than $100 and gifts to family members of more than $200.

You don't have to list gifts to family members that are "ordinary and usual," but there is no easy way to identify such gifts. The best test is whether someone outside of the family might think the gift was unusual under the circumstances. If so, list it. Forgiving a loan is also a gift, as is charging interest substantially below the market rate. Other gifts include giving a car or prepaid trip to a business associate.

B7 (Official Form 7) (12/07)

United States Bankruptcy Court
Northern District of California

In re   **Carrie Anne Edwards**   Case No. _____

                                          Debtor(s)   Chapter   **13** _____

STATEMENT OF FINANCIAL AFFAIRS

This statement is to be completed by every debtor. Spouses filing a joint petition may file a single statement on which the information for both spouses is combined. If the case is filed under chapter 12 or chapter 13, a married debtor must furnish information for both spouses whether or not a joint petition is filed, unless the spouses are separated and a joint petition is not filed. An individual debtor engaged in business as a sole proprietor, partner, family farmer, or self-employed professional, should provide the information requested on this statement concerning all such activities as well as the individual's personal affairs. To indicate payments, transfers and the like to minor children, state the child's initials and the name and address of the child's parent or guardian, such as "A.B., a minor child, by John Doe, guardian." Do not disclose the child's name. See, 11 U.S.C. § 112; Fed. R. Bankr. P. 1007(m).

Questions 1 - 18 are to be completed by all debtors. Debtors that are or have been in business, as defined below, also must complete Questions 19 - 25. **If the answer to an applicable question is "None," mark the box labeled "None."** If additional space is needed for the answer to any question, use and attach a separate sheet properly identified with the case name, case number (if known), and the number of the question.

DEFINITIONS

"In business." A debtor is "in business" for the purpose of this form if the debtor is a corporation or partnership. An individual debtor is "in business" for the purpose of this form if the debtor is or has been, within six years immediately preceding the filing of this bankruptcy case, any of the following: an officer, director, managing executive, or owner of 5 percent or more of the voting or equity securities of a corporation; a partner, other than a limited partner, of a partnership; a sole proprietor or self-employed full-time or part-time. An individual debtor also may be "in business" for the purpose of this form if the debtor engages in a trade, business, or other activity, other than as an employee, to supplement income from the debtor's primary employment.

"Insider." The term "insider" includes but is not limited to: relatives of the debtor; general partners of the debtor and their relatives; corporations of which the debtor is an officer, director, or person in control; officers, directors, and any owner of 5 percent or more of the voting or equity securities of a corporate debtor and their relatives; affiliates of the debtor and insiders of such affiliates; any managing agent of the debtor. 11 U.S.C. § 101.

---

1. Income from employment or operation of business

None
☐

State the gross amount of income the debtor has received from employment, trade, or profession, or from operation of the debtor's business, including part-time activities either as an employee or in independent trade or business, from the beginning of this calendar year to the date this case was commenced. State also the gross amounts received during the **two years** immediately preceding this calendar year. (A debtor that maintains, or has maintained, financial records on the basis of a fiscal rather than a calendar year may report fiscal year income. Identify the beginning and ending dates of the debtor's fiscal year.) If a joint petition is filed, state income for each spouse separately. (Married debtors filing under chapter 12 or chapter 13 must state income of both spouses whether or not a joint petition is filed, unless the spouses are separated and a joint petition is not filed.)

            AMOUNT   SOURCE
            $144,600.00   **2006 ($60,100) (employment at Microsoft as software engineer)**
                                               2007 ($60,100) (employment at Microsoft)

                                               Jan-Mar 2008 (15,400) (employment at Microsoft and Macy's)

2

2. Income other than from employment or operation of business

None ☐ State the amount of income received by the debtor other than from employment, trade, profession, or operation of the debtor's business during the **two years** immediately preceding the commencement of this case. Give particulars. If a joint petition is filed, state income for each spouse separately. (Married debtors filing under chapter 12 or chapter 13 must state income for each spouse whether or not a joint petition is filed, unless the spouses are separated and a joint petition is not filed.)

AMOUNT	SOURCE
$32,000.00	**Mar 07-Mar 08 (18,000 royalties, 12000 child support**
	Mar 06-Mar 07 (15,000 royalities, 12,000 child support)

3. Payments to creditors

None ☐ *Complete a. or b., as appropriate, and c.*

a. *Individual or joint debtor(s) with primarily consumer debts.* List all payments on loans, installment purchases of goods or services, and other debts to any creditor made within **90 days** immediately preceding the commencement of this case unless the aggregate value of all property that constitutes or is affected by such transfer is less than $600. Indicate with an (*) any payments that were made to a creditor on account of a domestic support obligation or as part of an alternative repayment schedule under a plan by an approved nonprofit budgeting and creditor counseling agency. (Married debtors filing under chapter 12 or chapter 13 must include payments by either or both spouses whether or not a joint petition is filed, unless the spouses are separated and a joint petition is not filed.)

NAME AND ADDRESS OF CREDITOR	DATES OF PAYMENTS	AMOUNT PAID	AMOUNT STILL OWING
Loantree **PO Box 305** **Lucerne, CA 95458**	**12/xx**	**$800.00**	**$0.00**

None ■ b. *Debtor whose debts are not primarily consumer debts:* List each payment or other transfer to any creditor made within **90 days** immediately preceding the commencement of the case unless the aggregate value of all property that constitutes or is affected by such transfer is not less than $5,475. If the debtor is an individual, indicate with an asterisk (*) any payments that were made to a creditor on account of a domestic support obligation or as part of an alternative repayment schedule under a plan by an approved nonprofit budgeting and creditor counseling agency. (Married debtors filing under chapter 12 or chapter 13 must include payments by either or both spouses whether or not a joint petition is filed, unless the spouses are separated and a joint petition is not filed.)

NAME AND ADDRESS OF CREDITOR	DATES OF PAYMENTS/ TRANSFERS	AMOUNT PAID OR VALUE OF TRANSFERS	AMOUNT STILL OWING

None ■ c. *All debtors:* List all payments made within **one year** immediately preceding the commencement of this case to or for the benefit of creditors who are or were insiders. (Married debtors filing under chapter 12 or chapter 13 must include payments by either or both spouses whether or not a joint petition is filed, unless the spouses are separated and a joint petition is not filed.)

NAME AND ADDRESS OF CREDITOR AND RELATIONSHIP TO DEBTOR	DATE OF PAYMENT	AMOUNT PAID	AMOUNT STILL OWING

4. Suits and administrative proceedings, executions, garnishments and attachments

None ☐ a. List all suits and administrative proceedings to which the debtor is or was a party within **one year** immediately preceding the filing of this bankruptcy case. (Married debtors filing under chapter 12 or chapter 13 must include information concerning either or both spouses whether or not a joint petition is filed, unless the spouses are separated and a joint petition is not filed.)

CAPTION OF SUIT AND CASE NUMBER	NATURE OF PROCEEDING	COURT OR AGENCY AND LOCATION	STATUS OR DISPOSITION
Bob Jones III v. Carrie Edwards Case # cv34457	**Negligence action for auto accident**	**Lake County Superior Court 255 N. Forbes St. Lakeport, CA 95453**	**Trial pending**

3

None ☐ b. Describe all property that has been attached, garnished or seized under any legal or equitable process within **one year** immediately preceding the commencement of this case. (Married debtors filing under chapter 12 or chapter 13 must include information concerning property of either or both spouses whether or not a joint petition is filed, unless the spouses are separated and a joint petition is not filed.)

NAME AND ADDRESS OF PERSON FOR WHOSE BENEFIT PROPERTY WAS SEIZED	DATE OF SEIZURE	DESCRIPTION AND VALUE OF PROPERTY
JNR Adjustment Co. **PO Box 27070** **Minneapolis, MN 55427**	**4/XX**	**wage garnishment for two months totaling $510 for judgment on debt owed to DVD club.**

5. Repossessions, foreclosures and returns

None ☐ List all property that has been repossessed by a creditor, sold at a foreclosure sale, transferred through a deed in lieu of foreclosure or returned to the seller, within **one year** immediately preceding the commencement of this case. (Married debtors filing under chapter 12 or chapter 13 must include information concerning property of either or both spouses whether or not a joint petition is filed, unless the spouses are separated and a joint petition is not filed.)

NAME AND ADDRESS OF CREDITOR OR SELLER	DATE OF REPOSSESSION, FORECLOSURE SALE, TRANSFER OR RETURN	DESCRIPTION AND VALUE OF PROPERTY
Eskanos & Adler **2325 Clayton Rd.** **Concord, CA 94520**	**4/XX**	**Repossessed furniture worth $800**

6. Assignments and receiverships

None ■ a. Describe any assignment of property for the benefit of creditors made within **120 days** immediately preceding the commencement of this case. (Married debtors filing under chapter 12 or chapter 13 must include any assignment by either or both spouses whether or not a joint petition is filed, unless the spouses are separated and a joint petition is not filed.)

NAME AND ADDRESS OF ASSIGNEE	DATE OF ASSIGNMENT	TERMS OF ASSIGNMENT OR SETTLEMENT

None ■ b. List all property which has been in the hands of a custodian, receiver, or court-appointed official within **one year** immediately preceding the commencement of this case. (Married debtors filing under chapter 12 or chapter 13 must include information concerning property of either or both spouses whether or not a joint petition is filed, unless the spouses are separated and a joint petition is not filed.)

NAME AND ADDRESS OF CUSTODIAN	NAME AND LOCATION OF COURT CASE TITLE & NUMBER	DATE OF ORDER	DESCRIPTION AND VALUE OF PROPERTY

7. Gifts

None ■ List all gifts or charitable contributions made within **one year** immediately preceding the commencement of this case except ordinary and usual gifts to family members aggregating less than $200 in value per individual family member and charitable contributions aggregating less than $100 per recipient. (Married debtors filing under chapter 12 or chapter 13 must include gifts or contributions by either or both spouses whether or not a joint petition is filed, unless the spouses are separated and a joint petition is not filed.)

NAME AND ADDRESS OF PERSON OR ORGANIZATION	RELATIONSHIP TO DEBTOR, IF ANY	DATE OF GIFT	DESCRIPTION AND VALUE OF GIFT

8. Losses

None ■ List all losses from fire, theft, other casualty or gambling within **one year** immediately preceding the commencement of this case **or since the commencement of this case.** (Married debtors filing under chapter 12 or chapter 13 must include losses by either or both spouses whether or not a joint petition is filed, unless the spouses are separated and a joint petition is not filed.)

DESCRIPTION AND VALUE OF PROPERTY	DESCRIPTION OF CIRCUMSTANCES AND, IF LOSS WAS COVERED IN WHOLE OR IN PART BY INSURANCE, GIVE PARTICULARS	DATE OF LOSS

4

9. Payments related to debt counseling or bankruptcy

None ☐ List all payments made or property transferred by or on behalf of the debtor to any persons, including attorneys, for consultation concerning debt consolidation, relief under the bankruptcy law or preparation of the petition in bankruptcy within **one year** immediately preceding the commencement of this case.

NAME AND ADDRESS OF PAYEE	DATE OF PAYMENT, NAME OF PAYOR IF OTHER THAN DEBTOR	AMOUNT OF MONEY OR DESCRIPTION AND VALUE OF PROPERTY
Jim McDonald Esq. **444 State St.** **Ukiah, CA**	**7/xx**	**$100 for bankruptcy telephone advice**

10. Other transfers

None ■ a. List all other property, other than property transferred in the ordinary course of the business or financial affairs of the debtor, transferred either absolutely or as security within **two years** immediately preceding the commencement of this case. (Married debtors filing under chapter 12 or chapter 13 must include transfers by either or both spouses whether or not a joint petition is filed, unless the spouses are separated and a joint petition is not filed.)

NAME AND ADDRESS OF TRANSFEREE, RELATIONSHIP TO DEBTOR	DATE	DESCRIBE PROPERTY TRANSFERRED AND VALUE RECEIVED

None ■ b. List all property transferred by the debtor within **ten years** immediately preceding the commencement of this case to a self-settled trust or similar device of which the debtor is a beneficiary.

NAME OF TRUST OR OTHER DEVICE	DATE(S) OF TRANSFER(S)	AMOUNT OF MONEY OR DESCRIPTION AND VALUE OF PROPERTY OR DEBTOR'S INTEREST IN PROPERTY

11. Closed financial accounts

None ☐ List all financial accounts and instruments held in the name of the debtor or for the benefit of the debtor which were closed, sold, or otherwise transferred within **one year** immediately preceding the commencement of this case. Include checking, savings, or other financial accounts, certificates of deposit, or other instruments; shares and share accounts held in banks, credit unions, pension funds, cooperatives, associations, brokerage houses and other financial institutions. (Married debtors filing under chapter 12 or chapter 13 must include information concerning accounts or instruments held by or for either or both spouses whether or not a joint petition is filed, unless the spouses are separated and a joint petition is not filed.)

NAME AND ADDRESS OF INSTITUTION	TYPE OF ACCOUNT, LAST FOUR DIGITS OF ACCOUNT NUMBER, AND AMOUNT OF FINAL BALANCE	AMOUNT AND DATE OF SALE OR CLOSING
WestAmerica Bank **444 North Main St.** **Lakeport, CA 95453**	**Checking Acct #4444444** **Final balance ($50)**	**July, XX, XXXX**

12. Safe deposit boxes

None ■ List each safe deposit or other box or depository in which the debtor has or had securities, cash, or other valuables within **one year** immediately preceding the commencement of this case. (Married debtors filing under chapter 12 or chapter 13 must include boxes or depositories of either or both spouses whether or not a joint petition is filed, unless the spouses are separated and a joint petition is not filed.)

NAME AND ADDRESS OF BANK OR OTHER DEPOSITORY	NAMES AND ADDRESSES OF THOSE WITH ACCESS TO BOX OR DEPOSITORY	DESCRIPTION OF CONTENTS	DATE OF TRANSFER OR SURRENDER, IF ANY

13. Setoffs

None
■

List all setoffs made by any creditor, including a bank, against a debt or deposit of the debtor within **90 days** preceding the commencement of this case. (Married debtors filing under chapter 12 or chapter 13 must include information concerning either or both spouses whether or not a joint petition is filed, unless the spouses are separated and a joint petition is not filed.)

NAME AND ADDRESS OF CREDITOR	DATE OF SETOFF	AMOUNT OF SETOFF

14. Property held for another person

None
☐

List all property owned by another person that the debtor holds or controls.

NAME AND ADDRESS OF OWNER	DESCRIPTION AND VALUE OF PROPERTY	LOCATION OF PROPERTY
Bonnie Johnson **3335 Irving St** **Clearlake, CA 95422**	**Poodle (Binkie) $300**	**Edwards residence**
Vannie Edwards **4444 Cleveland Ave.** **Pope Valley, CA 94567**	**$50,000 savings account owned by my grandmother. I am on the account as an informal trustee to help her manage her expenses**	**Bank of America, 5555 Cleveland Ave. Pope Valley CA 94567**

15. Prior address of debtor

None
☐

If the debtor has moved within **three years** immediately preceding the commencement of this case, list all premises which the debtor occupied during that period and vacated prior to the commencement of this case. If a joint petition is filed, report also any separate address of either spouse.

ADDRESS	NAME USED	DATES OF OCCUPANCY
21 Scarborough Rd. South **Cleveland Heights OH 41118**	**Carrie Edwards**	**1/1/XX-- 5/1/XX**

16. Spouses and Former Spouses

None
☐

If the debtor resides or resided in a community property state, commonwealth, or territory (including Alaska, Arizona, California, Idaho, Louisiana, Nevada, New Mexico, Puerto Rico, Texas, Washington, or Wisconsin) within **eight years** immediately preceding the commencement of the case, identify the name of the debtor's spouse and of any former spouse who resides or resided with the debtor in the community property state.

NAME
Torrey Edwards

17. Environmental Information.

For the purpose of this question, the following definitions apply:

"Environmental Law" means any federal, state, or local statute or regulation regulating pollution, contamination, releases of hazardous or toxic substances, wastes or material into the air, land, soil, surface water, groundwater, or other medium, including, but not limited to, statutes or regulations regulating the cleanup of these substances, wastes, or material.

"Site" means any location, facility, or property as defined under any Environmental Law, whether or not presently or formerly owned or operated by the debtor, including, but not limited to, disposal sites.

"Hazardous Material" means anything defined as a hazardous waste, hazardous substance, toxic substance, hazardous material, pollutant, or contaminant or similar term under an Environmental Law

6

None ■ a. List the name and address of every site for which the debtor has received notice in writing by a governmental unit that it may be liable or potentially liable under or in violation of an Environmental Law. Indicate the governmental unit, the date of the notice, and, if known, the Environmental Law:

SITE NAME AND ADDRESS	NAME AND ADDRESS OF GOVERNMENTAL UNIT	DATE OF NOTICE	ENVIRONMENTAL LAW

None ■ b. List the name and address of every site for which the debtor provided notice to a governmental unit of a release of Hazardous Material. Indicate the governmental unit to which the notice was sent and the date of the notice.

SITE NAME AND ADDRESS	NAME AND ADDRESS OF GOVERNMENTAL UNIT	DATE OF NOTICE	ENVIRONMENTAL LAW

None ■ c. List all judicial or administrative proceedings, including settlements or orders, under any Environmental Law with respect to which the debtor is or was a party. Indicate the name and address of the governmental unit that is or was a party to the proceeding, and the docket number.

NAME AND ADDRESS OF GOVERNMENTAL UNIT	DOCKET NUMBER	STATUS OR DISPOSITION

18 . Nature, location and name of business

None ■ a. *If the debtor is an individual*, list the names, addresses, taxpayer identification numbers, nature of the businesses, and beginning and ending dates of all businesses in which the debtor was an officer, director, partner, or managing executive of a corporation, partner in a partnership, sole proprietor, or was self-employed in a trade, profession, or other activity either full- or part-time within **six years** immediately preceding the commencement of this case, or in which the debtor owned 5 percent or more of the voting or equity securities within **six years** immediately preceding the commencement of this case.

If the debtor is a partnership, list the names, addresses, taxpayer identification numbers, nature of the businesses, and beginning and ending dates of all businesses in which the debtor was a partner or owned 5 percent or more of the voting or equity securities, within **six years** immediately preceding the commencement of this case.

If the debtor is a corporation, list the names, addresses, taxpayer identification numbers, nature of the businesses, and beginning and ending dates of all businesses in which the debtor was a partner or owned 5 percent or more of the voting or equity securities within **six years** immediately preceding the commencement of this case.

NAME	LAST FOUR DIGITS OF SOCIAL-SECURITY OR OTHER INDIVIDUAL TAXPAYER-I.D. NO. (ITIN)/ COMPLETE EIN	ADDRESS	NATURE OF BUSINESS	BEGINNING AND ENDING DATES

None ■ b. Identify any business listed in response to subdivision a., above, that is "single asset real estate" as defined in 11 U.S.C. § 101.

NAME	ADDRESS

The following questions are to be completed by every debtor that is a corporation or partnership and by any individual debtor who is or has been, within **six years** immediately preceding the commencement of this case, any of the following: an officer, director, managing executive, or owner of more than 5 percent of the voting or equity securities of a corporation; a partner, other than a limited partner, of a partnership, a sole proprietor or self-employed in a trade, profession, or other activity, either full- or part-time.

*(An individual or joint debtor should complete this portion of the statement **only** if the debtor is or has been in business, as defined above, within six years immediately preceding the commencement of this case. A debtor who has not been in business within those six years should go directly to the signature page.)*

19. Books, records and financial statements

None ■ a. List all bookkeepers and accountants who within **two years** immediately preceding the filing of this bankruptcy case kept or supervised the keeping of books of account and records of the debtor.

NAME AND ADDRESS	DATES SERVICES RENDERED

7

None ■   b. List all firms or individuals who within the **two years** immediately preceding the filing of this bankruptcy case have audited the books of account and records, or prepared a financial statement of the debtor.

NAME	ADDRESS	DATES SERVICES RENDERED

None ■   c. List all firms or individuals who at the time of the commencement of this case were in possession of the books of account and records of the debtor. If any of the books of account and records are not available, explain.

NAME	ADDRESS

None ■   d. List all financial institutions, creditors and other parties, including mercantile and trade agencies, to whom a financial statement was issued by the debtor within **two years** immediately preceding the commencement of this case.

NAME AND ADDRESS	DATE ISSUED

20. Inventories

None ■   a. List the dates of the last two inventories taken of your property, the name of the person who supervised the taking of each inventory, and the dollar amount and basis of each inventory.

DATE OF INVENTORY	INVENTORY SUPERVISOR	DOLLAR AMOUNT OF INVENTORY (Specify cost, market or other basis)

None ■   b. List the name and address of the person having possession of the records of each of the two inventories reported in a., above.

DATE OF INVENTORY	NAME AND ADDRESSES OF CUSTODIAN OF INVENTORY RECORDS

21 . Current Partners, Officers, Directors and Shareholders

None ■   a. If the debtor is a partnership, list the nature and percentage of partnership interest of each member of the partnership.

NAME AND ADDRESS	NATURE OF INTEREST	PERCENTAGE OF INTEREST

None ■   b. If the debtor is a corporation, list all officers and directors of the corporation, and each stockholder who directly or indirectly owns, controls, or holds 5 percent or more of the voting or equity securities of the corporation.

NAME AND ADDRESS	TITLE	NATURE AND PERCENTAGE OF STOCK OWNERSHIP

22 . Former partners, officers, directors and shareholders

None ■   a. If the debtor is a partnership, list each member who withdrew from the partnership within **one year** immediately preceding the commencement of this case.

NAME	ADDRESS	DATE OF WITHDRAWAL

None ■   b. If the debtor is a corporation, list all officers, or directors whose relationship with the corporation terminated within **one year** immediately preceding the commencement of this case.

NAME AND ADDRESS	TITLE	DATE OF TERMINATION

8

23 . Withdrawals from a partnership or distributions by a corporation

None
■ If the debtor is a partnership or corporation, list all withdrawals or distributions credited or given to an insider, including compensation in any form, bonuses, loans, stock redemptions, options exercised and any other perquisite during **one year** immediately preceding the commencement of this case.

NAME & ADDRESS OF RECIPIENT, RELATIONSHIP TO DEBTOR	DATE AND PURPOSE OF WITHDRAWAL	AMOUNT OF MONEY OR DESCRIPTION AND VALUE OF PROPERTY

24. Tax Consolidation Group.

None
■ If the debtor is a corporation, list the name and federal taxpayer identification number of the parent corporation of any consolidated group for tax purposes of which the debtor has been a member at any time within **six years** immediately preceding the commencement of the case.

NAME OF PARENT CORPORATION	TAXPAYER IDENTIFICATION NUMBER (EIN)

25. Pension Funds.

None
■ If the debtor is not an individual, list the name and federal taxpayer identification number of any pension fund to which the debtor, as an employer, has been responsible for contributing at any time within **six years** immediately preceding the commencement of the case.

NAME OF PENSION FUND	TAXPAYER IDENTIFICATION NUMBER (EIN)

DECLARATION UNDER PENALTY OF PERJURY BY INDIVIDUAL DEBTOR

I declare under penalty of perjury that I have read the answers contained in the foregoing statement of financial affairs and any attachments thereto and that they are true and correct.

Date _October 3, 2008_   Signature _Carrie Anne Edwards_

Carrie Anne Edwards
Debtor

Penalty for making a false statement: Fine of up to $500,000 or imprisonment for up to 5 years, or both. 18 U.S.C. §§ 152 and 3571

8. Losses. Provide the requested information. If the loss was for an exempt item, most states also exempt the proceeds, up to the exemption limit for the item. (See Appendix A.) If the item was not exempt, the trustee is entitled to the proceeds. In either case, list any proceeds you've received or expect to receive. If you experience a loss after you file, you should promptly amend your papers, as this question applies to losses both before you file and afterwards.

9. Payments related to debt counseling or bankruptcy. If you paid an improperly high fee to an attorney, bankruptcy petition preparer, debt consultant, or debt consolidator, the trustee may try to get some of it back to distribute to your creditors. Be sure to list all payments someone else made on your behalf, as well as payments you made directly.

10. Other transfers.

a. List all real and personal property that you've sold or given to someone else during the two years before you file for bankruptcy. Some examples are selling or abandoning (junking) a car, pledging your house as security (collateral) for a loan, granting an easement on real estate, or trading property. Also, describe any transfer within the past two years to your ex-spouse as part of a marital settlement agreement. If you are filing alone, describe gifts to your current spouse made during that same period.

Don't include any gifts you listed in Item 7. Also, don't list property you've parted with as a regular part of your business or financial affairs. For example, if you operate a mail-order book business, don't list the books you sold during the past year. Similarly, don't put down payments for regular goods and services, such as your phone bill, utilities, or rent. The idea is to disclose transfers of property that might legally belong in your bankruptcy estate.

EXAMPLE 1: Three years before filing for bankruptcy, Jack sold some personal electronic mixing equipment to a friend for a modest sum. This sale wasn't made within the previous two years, so Jack needn't list it here.

EXAMPLE 2: John has accumulated a collection of junked classic cars to resell to restoration hobbyists.

Within the past year, John has sold three of the cars for a total of $20,000. Because this is part of John's regular business, he needn't report the sales here. However, as a sole proprietor, John will be completing questions 18 through 20.

EXAMPLE 3: A year and a half before filing for bankruptcy, Louise, a nurse, sold a vintage Jaguar E-Type for $17,000. Because this isn't part of her business, Louise should list this sale here.

b. List all transfers of your own property you have made in the previous ten years to an irrevocable trust that lists you as a beneficiary. These types of trusts—referred to as self-settled trusts—are commonly used by wealthy people to shield their assets from creditors and by disabled people to preserve their right to receive government benefits. In bankruptcy, however, assets placed in a self-settled trust will be considered nonexempt, which means you will have to pay your unsecured creditors at least the value of those assets. There is an exception that applies to assets placed in certain special needs trusts. (*In re Schultz,* 368 B.R 832 (D. Minn. 2007).) If you are the beneficiary of a self-settled trust, see an attorney before filing for bankruptcy.

11. Closed financial accounts. Provide information for each account in your name or for your benefit that was closed or transferred to someone else during the past year.

12. Safe deposit boxes. Provide information for each safe deposit box you've had within the past year.

13. Setoffs. A setoff is when a creditor, often a bank, uses money in a customer's account to pay a debt owed to the creditor by that customer. Here, list any setoffs your creditors have made during the last 90 days.

14. Property held for another person. Describe all the property you've borrowed from, are storing for, or hold in trust for someone else. Examples include funds in an irrevocable trust held for someone else as beneficiary but controlled by you as trustee, and property you're holding as executor or administrator of an estate. This type of property is not part of your bankruptcy estate. However, you must disclose it so the trustee is aware of it and can ask for more details. (Some people dishonestly describe all of their property as being in trust or otherwise belonging to someone else, hoping to avoid having to give it to the trustee. Disclosures in this part of the Statement of Financial Affairs allow the trustee to explore this possibility.)

A trustee who becomes interested in property you describe here may invoke several court procedures designed to get more information. However, it is unlikely that the trustee will invade your house to seize the property. If you can establish that the property truly belongs to someone else—by producing the trust document, for example—you needn't worry about losing it in your bankruptcy case.

> **EXAMPLE:** You are renting an unfurnished apartment owned by a friend. The friend has left a valuable baby grand piano in your care. If and when you decide to move, you have agreed to place the piano in storage for your friend. Because you don't own the piano but rather are taking care of it for your friend, you would describe it here.

15. Prior address of debtor. If you have moved within the three years before you file for bankruptcy, list all of your residences within those three years.

16. Spouses and Former Spouses. If you lived in a community property state (or Puerto Rico) within eight years prior to filing for bankruptcy, list the name of your spouse and of any former spouses who lived with you in the community property state. To remind you, community property states are Alaska, Arizona, California, Idaho, Louisiana, Nevada, New Mexico, Texas, Washington, and Wisconsin.

17. Environmental Information. Few individuals will have much to say here. It's intended primarily for businesses that do business on polluted premises. Still, read the questions carefully and provide the requested information, if applicable.

18. Nature, location and name of business. Provide all of the information requested on line a if you are in business or have been in business for the previous six years. Note that the definition of business is very broad: It includes not only sole proprietors but anyone self-employed in a trade, profession, or other activity either full or part time or a business in which the debtor owned 5% or more of the voting or equity securities within the six-year period. It is very important that you answer this question completely so that the trustee will

have a good idea of how you earned your money over the past six years and what you did with your business interests (if you are no longer in business).

SKIP AHEAD

If you don't own a business. Only business debtors have to provide responses on lines 19 through 25. If you aren't one, skip to the declaration at the end of the form.

If the majority of your business income for any one business comes from renting, leasing, or otherwise operating a single piece of real property (other than an apartment building with fewer than four units), include your business name and the address of the property on line b.

19. Books, records and financial statements.
a. Identify every person other than yourself—usually a bookkeeper or accountant—who was involved in the accounting of your business during the previous two years. If you were the only person involved in your business's accounting, check "None."

b. If your books weren't audited during the past two years, check "None." Otherwise, fill in the requested information.

c. Usually, you, your bookkeeper, your accountant, an ex-business associate, or possibly an ex-mate will have business records. If any are missing, explain (you'll be better off if the loss of your records was beyond your control).

d. You may have prepared a financial statement if you applied to a bank for a loan or line of credit for your business or in your own name. If you're self-employed and applied for a personal loan to purchase a car or house, you probably submitted a financial statement as evidence of your ability to repay. Such statements include:
  - balance sheets (these compare assets with liabilities)
  - profit and loss statements (these compare income with expenses), and
  - financial statements (these provide an overall financial description of a business).

20. Inventories. If your business doesn't have an inventory because it's a service business, check "None." If your business deals in products, but you were primarily the middle person or original manufacturer, put "no inventory required" or "materials purchased for each order as needed." If you have an inventory, fill in the information requested in items a and b.

21 through 25. These items are intended for filers who are part of a business entity such as a partnership, corporation, or limited liability company. Our book is designed for individuals only, so you should be able to check "None" for each of these items. If you are part of a business entity, consult with a bankruptcy lawyer before filing.

Declaration Under Penalty of Perjury by Individual Debtor. Sign and date this section. If you're filing jointly, be sure your spouse dates and signs it as well.

If completed on behalf of a partnership or corporation. Type "N/A."

Certification and Signature of Non-Attorney Bankruptcy Petition Preparer. If a BPP typed your forms, have that person complete this section. Otherwise, type "N/A" anywhere in the box.

Be sure to insert the number of continuation pages, if any, you attached.

Form 21—Statement of Social Security Number

This schedule requires you to list your full Social Security number. It will be available to your creditors and the trustee but, to protect your privacy, will not be part of your regular bankruptcy case file.

Form 22C—Chapter 13 Statement of Current Monthly Income and Calculation of Commitment Period and Disposable Income

In Ch. 4, you calculated your current monthly income and compared it with your state's median income. If your current monthly income was more than your state's median income, you completed a form labeled 22C (in Ch. 5) to find out whether you could propose a plan that the court would likely confirm. You will file that completed form along with your other paperwork completed in this chapter.

If your income was less than your state's median income, you skipped Form 22C and instead completed a modified Schedule J and deducted those expenses from your current monthly income to see whether you had enough disposable income to propose a confirmable Chapter 13 plan. Now, however, you will need to go back to Ch. 5 and complete the rest of Form 22C in order to file the completed form with your other paperwork. You will find that most of the work you did to complete a modified Schedule J will work with the expenses asked for in 22C. Either way, in Ch. 5 you completed all or most of the necessary work on this form.

Form 201—Notice to Individual Consumer Debtor Under § 342(b) of the Bankruptcy Code

This form, required by the new bankruptcy law, gives you some information about credit counseling and the various types of bankruptcy available. It also warns you sternly of the consequences of lying on your bankruptcy papers, concealing assets, and failing to file the required forms on time.

You can find a blank copy of the form in Appendix B. Sign and date it in the space provided. If a bankruptcy petition preparer assisted you with your paperwork, have that person fill in the requested information.

Mailing Matrix

As part of your bankruptcy filing, you are required to submit a list of all of your creditors, so the court can give them official notice of your bankruptcy. Called the mailing "matrix," this list must be prepared in a specific format prescribed by your local bankruptcy court. Your court may also require you to submit a declaration, or "verification," stating that your list is correct (as ever, be sure to check your court's local rules). In a few courts, the form consists of boxes on a page in which you enter the names and addresses of your creditors. This is an artifact from the time when the trustee used the form to prepare mailing labels.

Now, most courts ask you to submit the list on a computer disk in a particular word processing format, or at least submit a computer printout of the names so that they may be scanned. You should check with the bankruptcy court clerk or the court's local rules to learn the precise format.

Once you understand the format, make a list of all of your creditors, in alphabetical order. You can copy them from Schedules D, E, F, and H. Be sure to include cosigners and joint debtors. If you and your spouse jointly incurred a debt and are filing jointly, however, don't include your spouse. Also include collection agencies, sheriffs, and attorneys who either have sued you or are trying to collect the debt. And, if you're seeking to discharge marital debts you assumed during a divorce, include both your ex-spouse and the creditors. Finally, if you have two or more debts owed to the same creditor at the same address, you can just list one.

> **CAUTION**
>
> **It is very important to be complete when preparing the matrix.** If you leave a creditor off the matrix, that debt may survive your bankruptcy—and you will have to pay it down the line.

Income Deduction Order

Your bankruptcy court might require you to draft and submit an income deduction order with the rest of your Chapter 13 bankruptcy papers. (You can ask the court clerk if you must prepare one when you send your letter requesting local forms and information.)

An income deduction order is an order the bankruptcy court sends to your employer. It requires the employer to automatically deduct your monthly repayment plan amount from your wages and send it to the bankruptcy court.

Below is a sample income deduction order. To complete your own, type up the sample, filling in the information requested in italics. Some courts have their own forms; if yours does, use it. Leave blank any information you don't yet know.

UNITED STATES BANKRUPTCY COURT

_____ [Name of district] _____ DISTRICT OF _____ [Your state] _____

In re _____)
   [Set forth here all names including married,)
   maiden, and trade names used by debtor)
   within last 8 years.])
            Debtor(s)) Case No. _____ [leave this blank] _____
Address _____)
)
_____) Chapter 13
)
Last four digits of Social Security or Individual)
Taxpayer Identification (ITIN) No(s). (if any): _____)
)
Employer's Tax Identification (EIN) No(s). (if any):)
_____)

INCOME DEDUCTION ORDER

TO: [Name of Employer
   Address
   City, State, Zip Code]
   Attention: Payroll Department

  _____ [Name of debtor employed by this employer] _____, (Debtor), whose Social Security number

is ____ [your or your spouse's Social Security number] ____, has filed a Petition under Chapter 13 of the Bankruptcy

Code with this Court, and a proposed plan for paying his/her debts.

  _____ [Name of trustee] _____ has been appointed Standing Chapter 13 Trustee by the U.S.

Trustee and has accepted the appointment.

  Section 1325(b) of the Bankruptcy Code authorizes this Court to order an entity from whom Debtor

receives income to pay all or any part of that income to the Standing Trustee.

  IT IS THEREFORE ORDERED that until you receive further order from this court or from the Standing

Trustee that you withhold from the wages payable to the Debtor, the sum of $____ [monthly plan amount] ____ each

month, beginning with the date of this Order. You are further Ordered to pay the money withheld to the

Standing Trustee, at the address below, in convenient installments at least once a month, the first payment to be

// // // // //

// // // // //

paid within one month from the date below. Each successive monthly installment must be paid to the Standing

Trustee on or before the last day of each month thereafter.

Dated: _____   _____
                                         U.S. Bankruptcy Judge

Order prepared by:
[*Your name*
Your street address
Your city, state, zip
Your telephone number]

Copy mailed to:
[*Trustee's name*]
Standing Chapter 13 Trustee
[*Trustee's street address*
Trustee's city, state, zip
Trustee's telephone number]

[*Name of Employer*
Employer's street address
Employer's city, state, zip
Employer's telephone number]

Drafting Your Plan

Your Chapter 13 plan is the cornerstone of your bankruptcy case. The plan tells the court and your creditors how you intend to repay your debts, including the total amount you will pay each month, how much each creditor will receive under your plan, and how long your plan will last. As we've discussed in earlier chapters, you will pay some of your creditors in full and others only a portion of what you owe them. Some creditors are entitled to be paid before other creditors. All of these details will be in your plan, along with some automatic conditions required by law—commonly termed "boilerplate."

Your repayment plan will control your financial life while your bankruptcy is pending. With a few exceptions, once the court confirms your plan, both you and your creditors are bound by its terms.

This chapter explains how to put together your plan, using the work you did in earlier chapters. For example, the income calculations you did in Ch. 4 determine what expense amounts you can use and how long your plan must last. And the preliminary figures from Ch. 5, in which you calculated your disposable income, determine how much you must pay into your plan.

As you'll see, putting together a Chapter 13 plan can get a bit tricky, mostly because you have to calculate the proper interest rates for your secured and priority debts, and how quickly various types of debts will be repaid under your plan. The order in which some debts will be paid can also be difficult to figure out. The best approach is to do your best and be willing to negotiate with objecting creditors and the trustee, and to amend your plan to accommodate these negotiations. Even skilled Chapter 13 lawyers find it necessary to amend an original plan several times in the course of a Chapter 13 bankruptcy.

SEE AN EXPERT

A lawyer can help you draft an optimal plan. Trying to learn everything there is to know about Chapter 13 repayment plans can be tough, if not impossible for a person stepping up to the plate for the first time. This chapter provides the basic information you need to represent yourself. But especially in the case of repayment plans, you may need the services of an attorney to guarantee the best possible outcome. Keep in mind that attorneys can collect their fee under your

plan and may not require a high retainer to enter your case. See Ch. 15 for more on bankruptcy attorneys.

Chapter 13 Plan Formats

Although the general rules for drafting a repayment plan are the same everywhere, many of the details are determined by individual bankruptcy districts and courts—and these requirements may differ significantly from place to place. Many bankruptcy courts require you to use a particular form or format for your plan. Some of these forms are only a couple of pages long; others run to seven or eight pages. Perhaps oddly, the longer forms tend to be easier to complete. The longer the form is, the more likely it is to include headings and guidance for debtors; the shorter forms tend to assume (sometimes mistakenly) that debtors know what they're doing.

Regardless of your court's requirements, all plans have to include the same basic information. If the trustee opposes your plan because it doesn't comply with every one of your court's rules, the trustee should give you feedback on what you have to do to get your plan confirmed. Then, you'll have some time to file an amended plan. If you are hopelessly in over your head, it's time to hunt for an attorney to help you draft a plan.

Most courts that require a particular format post it on their website for downloading. You can also usually get a copy of the form from the court clerk. You can find links to all court websites at www.uscourts.gov; click "Court Links" at the top of the page. You'll usually find repayment plans under the "forms" link on your court's Web page.

This book can't provide specific instructions for every plan from every court. However, this chapter uses a format based on several model plans used by courts throughout the country. If your court has no required or suggested plan format, you will probably be safe following our sample format.

What You Must Pay

To propose a plan that the judge will confirm, you must show that you will have sufficient income, after deducting allowed expenses, to pay certain debts in full over the life of your plan. Some of these debts must be paid through your Chapter 13 plan—that is, you must pay the trustee, who will then pay the creditor. Others may be paid outside of your plan.

 CROSS-REFERENCE

If you have not read Chs. 1 through 5, do so now. Before you can draft your plan, you need to know the rules for calculating your income and expenses. You also need to know how to classify your debts, which debts you have to repay in Chapter 13, and how to figure out how long your plan will have to last. All of this information is explained in detail in Chs. 1 through 5. To draft your plan, you will have to complete the calculations in those chapters, particularly Ch. 5.

What You Must Pay Through Your Plan

At a minimum, you must pay all of the following debts through your Chapter 13 plan:

- All priority debts other than child support owed to a government agency.
- All secured debts that are contractually due to end within the life of your plan (such as a home equity loan). If the debt is no longer secured when you file, you can strip off the lien and classify the debt as unsecured, then treat it just like your other unsecured debts.
- All other secured debts that aren't contractually due within the life of your plan (for example, a government tax lien on your property).
- Any arrearage necessary to keep your home, car, or other secured property.
- An amount equal to the value of your nonexempt property.
- All administrative expenses, including trustee and lawyer fees.
- All of your remaining disposable income.

If your income is more than the median for your state and household size, your plan must last for five years. If your income is less than the median, your plan may last for only three years. If you are a lower-income filer and you don't have enough income to pay all mandatory debts within the three-year period, you can ask the court to extend your repayment time to five years. If you don't have enough income to pay your

mandatory debts within five years, you can't propose a feasible Chapter 13 plan.

The first six categories of debts that must be repaid through your plan are pretty easy to calculate because they are all set values. You know—or can easily find out—how much you owe on priority and secured debts, as well as any arrearages you owe on secured debts. In Ch. 5, you determine the value of your nonexempt property. You also know how much you're paying a lawyer (if you are using one), and that the trustee is entitled to 10%.

The last category of debt—your disposable income—can be tougher to value. Here are the rules:

- If your current monthly income (as calculated in Ch. 5) is less than your state's median income, calculate your disposable income by subtracting the expenses listed on Schedule J from either your current monthly income shown on Form 22C or the monthly income figure shown on Schedule I.
- If your current monthly income is more than your state's median income, calculate your disposable income by completing Form 22C. The amount shown on Line 58 is your disposable income.

As we've explained in earlier chapters, however, not all courts hew strictly to this last rule. Some courts have ruled that filers whose income is more than the median may calculate their disposable income from their Schedules I (income) and J (expenses) rather than from their Form 22C if necessary to propose a feasible Chapter 13 plan. (See *In re Jass*, 340 B.R. 411 (D. Utah 2006); *In re Hardacre*, 338 B.R. 718 (N.D. Tex. 2006).) Other courts have followed the literal language of the bankruptcy law and used the amount on Line 58 of Form 22C as the debtor's disposable income. (See *In re Barr*, 341 B.R. 181 (M.D. N.C. 2006).) The best practice for higher-income filers is to use the figure you come up with on Line 58 of Form 22C as your disposable income unless your court follows a different practice—or unless you need to use your actual disposable income to propose a feasible plan.

What You Must Pay Either Through or Outside of Your Plan

In addition to making payments through your plan, you will have to make other payments either inside or outside of the plan. For instance, even if you pay your arrearage on a mortgage through the plan, you'll have to continue making your regular monthly mortgage payments. You'll also have to pay your other current expenses.

If you make these payments through your Chapter 13 plan, you will have to pay significantly more over the life of your plan to cover the trustee's fee. The trustee gets 10% on all payments made through the plan, but gets nothing on payments made outside of the plan. If your current monthly mortgage payment is $2,000, the trustee would get 10% of your monthly payment, or $200 a month, if you paid through your plan. This amount is added to what you're already paying into the plan. Over the life of a five-year plan, paying your mortgage this way would require you to pay an extra $120,000! The lesson here is that it makes a huge difference whether you pay through or outside of the plan.

Obviously, you should try to pay outside of the plan if at all possible. Unfortunately, courts are split on whether mortgages must be paid through the plan. One case (*In re Breeding*, 366 B.R. 21 (E.D. Ark. 2007)) has ruled that judges can require debtors to make their regular mortgage payments through the plan. However, a Ninth Circuit Court of Appeal case has authorized mortgage payments outside of the plan. (*In re Lopez*, 372 B.R. 40 (9th Cir. B.A.P. 2007).)

If you are paying an arrearage on a car note through the plan, you may also have to make the current payment through the plan. The same is true of other secured property for which you are using Chapter 13 to make up an arrearage. On the other hand, current payments for rent, utilities, Internet services, telephone, child support, taxes, and the like can—and should—be made outside of the plan.

Repayment of Unsecured Debts: Allowed Claims

Payments of unsecured debts under your Chapter 13 plan will be based on "allowed claims" filed by your creditors. After receiving notice of your bankruptcy, unsecured creditors that want a share of the payments you make under your plan must file a Proof of Claim. Once the creditor files a Proof of Claim, you or the

trustee can object to the claim—you can argue that you don't really owe the claim or that you owe less than the creditor says, for example. (Objections to creditors' claims are covered briefly in Ch. 11.) The court will then decide which claims are allowed; creditors with allowed claims are entitled to share in the money you pay into your plan.

Which Creditors Must File Proofs of Claims

All unsecured creditors—whether you owe them priority or nonpriority debts—must file a Proof of Claim in order to be paid by the trustee. Only secured creditors do not have to file a Proof of Claim

The deadline for filing a Proof of Claim is 90 days after the date set for the first meeting of creditors (Rule 3002). However, the confirmation hearing—at which the judge either confirms your repayment plan or sends you back to the drawing board to make changes—must be held between 20 and 45 days after the first meeting of creditors (or earlier, if the court approves). This means that a creditor could well file a Proof of Claim after your plan is confirmed. Because of this scheduling oddity, you can't assume that your plan must include only those claims for which proofs have been filed.

> **EXAMPLE:** Peter files for Chapter 13 bankruptcy on July 1, 2008. He files his plan at the same time. The confirmation hearing in his case is held 60 days later. By then, some proofs of claim have been filed, but others have not. Peter amends his plan to include only the claims that have been filed at that point. If more claims are filed before the deadline, Peter will have to amend his plan again, and another confirmation hearing will be required.

Dealing With Unfiled Claims

If a creditor doesn't file a Proof of Claim within the deadline and you want that creditor to be paid in your plan, you'll have 30 days after the deadline to file a claim for the creditor. You might want to do this if, for example, the debt cannot be discharged in bankruptcy—by filing a Proof of Claim, you can make sure that at least part of the debt is paid off through your plan, so you won't owe as much when your bankruptcy case is over. Ch. 11 covers filing proofs of claim on behalf of a creditor.

Probably the best approach when drafting your plan is to assume that all of your creditors will file a Proof of Claim in a timely manner. This means your plan should include:

- payment in full to all secured creditors listed in Schedule D (except those with debts contractually lasting longer than your plan, such as a mortgage)
- payment in full to all priority creditors listed in Schedule E (except child support owed to a government agency), and
- payment in part to all the unsecured, nonpriority creditors you listed in Schedule F. Of course, the amount these creditors receive depends solely on your disposable income—they each get a share of the amount of your payment that doesn't go to secured debt arrearages, priority debts, the trustee's fee, and so on. However, you have to list your unsecured creditors in your plan, and we advise that you list all of them, whether or not they have filed a Proof of Claim by the time you submit your plan.

If you intend to object to (that is, claim that you don't owe) any of the debts listed on Schedules D, E, or F, you should indicate that in your plan. If one or more of those creditors doesn't file a timely Proof of Claim, you can either file a Proof of Claim on the creditor's behalf (see Ch. 11) or amend your plan to take those defaults into account.

EXAMPLE: Tony's Schedule E shows that he owes $7,500 in child support, which he must pay in full (because it is a priority debt) if an allowed claim is filed by the deadline. Tony assumes that the creditor will file a Proof of Claim, so his plan provides for payment of the child support debt. If the creditor doesn't file a Proof of Claim, this debt won't be paid under Tony's plan unless he files a Proof of Claim on the creditor's behalf. Because back child support is a nondischargeable debt, Tony will probably want to file the Proof of Claim on the creditor's behalf and take care of the child support through his plan. But if he doesn't file the Proof of Claim, he will amend his plan to route the child support money to his other creditors.

A Model Plan Format

At the end of this chapter, you will find a complete model plan form. The instructions below explain every section of that plan, step by step. This will help you figure out which information to include in each part of the plan, and how to put that information together for the court.

> **CAUTION**
> **Remember to use your court's form.** As explained above, many bankruptcy districts and courts have their own repayment plan forms. If your court has its own form, by all means use it. You should be able to transfer the information and instructions from our model form to your court's form without too much trouble.

Notice

The first section is a notice to creditors, explaining what happens in Chapter 13 bankruptcy. You don't have to add any information here.

Although it's not required by the bankruptcy code, the notice gives creditors some basic information on Chapter 13 bankruptcy and what they can do to preserve their rights. It prevents your creditors from later complaining that they didn't understand what they were supposed to do. The downside of providing this notice is that you may be better off if your creditors aren't alerted to their possible remedies. For that reason, if your court doesn't require a notice of this type, you may wish to eliminate it.

Section a explains that any modifications of liens in the Chapter 13 case will survive the bankruptcy unless the underlying debt is paid off in full or a discharge is granted. Section b is self-explanatory. Section c explains that creditors with secured claims and priority claims will be paid according to the plan unless they file different proofs of claim. Section d explains that secured debtors can file claims at any time and receive payment regardless of the plan, unless the court orders otherwise. All other creditors must file timely claims if they wish to be paid anything.

Notice

This plan is proposed by the above debtor under penalty of perjury. Any creditor can object to this plan being confirmed by written notice filed with the court and served upon the debtor, the trustee, and other parties in interest not less than 8 days before the date set for the meeting of creditors. Absent a timely objection, the court may confirm this plan as drafted. The plan, and payments under the plan, will be subject to all relevant Bankruptcy Code provisions.

With certain exceptions, a confirmed plan holds the debtor and creditors to the treatment provided in the plan—even if the plan modifies rights and duties held by the debtor and creditor. The exceptions are:

a. Each creditor will retain its lien until the earlier of payment of the underlying debt determined under nonbankruptcy law or discharge under Section 1328. If the case under this chapter is dismissed or converted without completion of the plan, the holder of such lien shall retain it to the extent recognized by applicable nonbankruptcy law.

b. Defaults will be cured using the interest rate set forth below in the plan. Any ongoing obligation will be paid according to the terms of the plan.

c. Holders of secured claims and Class 1 claimants will be paid according to the plan after confirmation unless the secured creditor or Class 1 claimant files a proof of claim in a different amount than that provided in the plan.

d. If a secured creditor files a proof of claim, that creditor will be paid according to that creditor's proof of claim, unless the court orders otherwise. Holders of all other claims must timely file proofs of claims, if the code so requires, or they will not be paid any amount. A debtor who confirms a Chapter 13 plan may be eligible thereafter to receive a discharge of debts to the extent specified in 11 U.S.C. Section 1328.

Plan Payments

Here, you indicate how much you will pay each month and what that money will be used for. We've divided this section into parts, as you'll see below.

Plan Payments

The debtor proposes the following Chapter 13 plan and makes the following declarations:

Monthly Amounts Paid to Trustee Under the Plan

The debtor submits the following to the supervision and control of the trustee:

Section A. You won't be able to complete the first blank in Section A until you have completed the rest of your plan and added up all of the amounts you are required to pay. Remember to come back and complete this provision. This section also requires you to make your first monthly plan payment to the trustee within 30 days after you file your petition. Failure to make this payment can get your Chapter 13 case dismissed.

In the second blank, indicate how long your plan will last. Remember, if your income is more than your state's median income, your plan must last for 60 months (five years) unless you can pay 100% of your debt in a shorter period. If your income is less than your state's median income, your plan must last for 36 months (three years) unless you can pay 100% of your debt in a shorter time or you need a longer period to pay off your secured and/or priority debts. (For more information, review Chs. 4 and 5.)

A. Payments by debtor of $_____ per month for _____ months. The monthly payment will begin within 30 days of the date the petition was filed.

Section B. The base plan dollar amount is your disposable income, as calculated in Ch. 5. Because you calculated your disposable income as a monthly amount, you'll have to multiply it by the number of months your plan will last to obtain the base plan amount. Enter this in the first blank.

To complete the second blank, add up all of your unsecured, nonpriority debts. These are the debts you listed on Schedule F (see Ch. 7). Once you have a total, divide it by your base plan amount (your disposable income) to figure out what percentage of these debts will be repaid over the life of your plan. For example, if your total disposable income is $500 a month for three years, or $18,000 total, and your debts in Schedule F total $100,000, the percent of the allowed nonpriority unsecured claims will be 18%.

B. The base plan amount is $_____ , which will pay _____% of the allowed claims of nonpriority unsecured creditors. If that percentage is less than 100%, the debtor will pay the plan payment stated in this plan for the full term of the plan.

Section C. This section authorizes the trustee to secure any amount of your future property or income necessary to pay certain claims that arise after you file—principally tax claims, but also debts you incur in order to successfully complete your Chapter 13 plan, such as payments to an attorney. Because you can't know whether you will have these types of claims or how much you will have to pay, this section doesn't ask you to give a dollar amount.

C. Amounts necessary for the payment of postpetition claims allowed under 11 U.S.C. Section 1305.

Section D. The trustee will get your tax refunds, to add to the other payments you make under the plan, unless your plan provides for payment of 100% of your nonpriority, unsecured claims. Again, you don't have to provide an amount here; you won't know how much your tax refunds will be, or perhaps even that you will be entitled to receive any, at this point.

D. If the plan provides for less than 100% payment of nonpriority unsecured claims, all postpetition tax refunds received by the debtor during the plan term.

Section E. Because a long time can elapse between your bankruptcy filing and your plan confirmation, secured creditors may demand a premium (called adequate protection payments) to protect their property interests before the plan is confirmed. The trustee

typically pays these amounts out of your first plan payment. (See Ch. 10 for more information.)

E. Preconfirmation Adequate Protection Payments for any creditor who holds an allowed claim secured by personal property: $_____ .

Section F. The "other property" blank refers to additional property that the trustee may require control over. This might include unexpected receipts of an ongoing business or royalties that have not been included as part of your current monthly income.

F. Other property: _____ .

Classification and Treatment of Claims

In this section, you list all of your debts according to category, and calculate how much you will pay on each during your plan. We have divided our discussion into classes of claims.

Class 1. List each of your priority claims (from Schedule E) here, in the appropriate category. Fill in the columns as follows:

- In column one, list the total amount due.
- List the interest rate on the loan in column two.
- Typically, you won't have to pay interest on a priority debt. However, you may have to add interest to your payment—if, for example, you signed a contract that requires interest.
- To calculate your monthly payment of loan plus interest, either use your own calculator or go to www.bankrate.com (or another online calculator site). Select a calculator that allows you to calculate interest on an annual basis. Enter the amount of the claim, the interest rate, and the length of the claim, then click the "calculate" button. The result will be your monthly payment.
- In column 4, indicate how long your plan will last.
- Multiply the monthly payment in column 3 by the number of months in column 4, and place the total in column 5.

Classification and Treatment of Claims

Class 1: Allowed unsecured claims entitled to priority under 11 U.S.C. 507

The debtor will pay Class 1 allowed claims in full; except the debtor may provide for less than full payment of domestic support obligations assigned to a government agency.

Category	1. Amount of Priority Claim	2. Interest Rate If Any	3. Monthly Payment	4. Number of Months	5. Total Payment
Administrative					
1. Trustee's fee					
2. Attorney fees					
3. Ch. 7 trustee fees					
4. Other Admin.					
5. IRS					
6. State Tax					
7. Support					
8. Other					
9. Support not to be paid in full					
Totals					

Class 2. In the first section, choose whether you will make the mortgage payment directly to the creditor or whether the trustee will make the mortgage payment out of the plan. As explained above, most debtors choose to pay the lender directly, if they have a choice. If you owe an arrearage on your mortgage, you will have to pay it to the trustee, however.

In the second section, list any arrearages you owe on debts secured by your home. Complete this section as follows:

- In column 1, list the lender's name.
- In column 2, list the last four digits of the loan number.
- In column 3, list the total amount of the arrearage.
- In column 4, if your mortgage was written before 1994, you don't have to pay interest on the arrearage; the interest on the mortgage is included in the mortgage. Otherwise, enter the contract interest rate.

- In column 5, list your monthly payment. Assuming your mortgage was written before 1994, you can divide the total amount in column 3 by how many months your plan will last. Otherwise, calculate your monthly payment using the instructions for Class 1 claims.
- In column 6, enter the number of months your plan will last.
- Multiply the amount in column 5 by the amount in column 6, and list the total in column 7.

Class 3. In the first set of boxes, enter all secured claims that must be paid in full under the plan. These are tax liens, mechanic's liens, judicial liens that can't be avoided, and secured claims that are to be paid in full under a contract that expires during the plan period. For example, if you owe $20,000 on a claim for a secured debt under a contract that will expire in three years, and you are drafting a five-year plan, the claim must be paid in full unless it qualifies for a cramdown. (See Class 4, below.)

You don't have to list secured claims that will outlive your plan—you can pay these on your own, to keep the trustee's fee down.

Complete this section as follows:

- In column 1, enter the name of the creditor.
- In column 2, enter the last four digits of the account number for the debt.
- In column 3, enter the total claim.
- In column 4, enter the interest rate you must pay on the claim. (See "Determining Interest Rates for Secured Debts in Chapter 13 Plans," below.)
- In column 5, calculate your monthly payment, using the instructions for Class 1 claims.

- In column 6 enter the number of months in your plan.
- In column 7, multiply the monthly payment by the number of months in your plan.

The second section is for arrearages on secured debts. If your secured debt is contractual and secures collateral you are keeping, you can pay any arrearage on the debt under your plan. For example, if you have fallen behind on your car payments, you can use your plan to pay the arrearage off in equal monthly payments over the life of your plan.

Complete these boxes following the instructions for Class 2 claims, above.

Class 2: Claims secured solely by real property that is the debtor's principal residence

☐ 1. The postconfirmation monthly mortgage payment will be made by the trustee from the plan payment to: _____

_____ .

☐ 1.2. The postconfirmation monthly mortgage payment will be made by the debtor directly to: _____ .

The debtor will cure all prepetition arrearages for the primary residence through the plan payment as set forth below. If the debtor pays the cure amount while timely making all required postpetition payments, the mortgage will be reinstated according to its original terms, extinguishing any right of the mortgagee to recover any amount alleged to have arisen prior to the filing of the petition.

1. Name of Creditor	2. Last Four Digits of Loan #	3. Amount of Arrearage	4. Interest Rate	5. Monthly Payment	6. Number of Months	7. Total Payment

---

Class 3: Secured claims to be paid in full through the plan

1. Name of Creditor	2. Last Four Digits of Loan #	3. Amount of Claim	4. Interest Rate	5. Monthly Payment	6. Number of Months	7. Total Payment

The debtor will cure all prepetition arrearages on these claims through the plan payment as set forth below:

1. Name of Creditor	2. Last Four Digits of Loan #	3. Amount of Arrearage	4. Interest Rate	5. Monthly Payment	6. Number of Months	7. Total Payment

Determining Interest Rates for Secured Debts in Chapter 13 Plans

Until recently, the question of how to set an interest rate for secured claims other than mortgages was hotly debated, with various bankruptcy courts issuing inconsistent rulings. In 2004, however, the U.S. Supreme Court settled the matter and announced a formula to be used in Chapter 13 cases. (*Till v. SCS Credit Corporation*, 541 U.S 465 (2004).) The Court said the rate should be the national prime rate, adjusted upward slightly for the additional risk of lending to a bankruptcy debtor. In that case, the risk was deemed to be 1.5% over prime. Lower courts have generally approved adjustments in the range of 1%–3% over prime. The new bankruptcy law did not address the *Till* case, so its holding still stands.

The bankruptcy court in your district may already have a rate stated on its standard Chapter 13 plan form. If your court has not set an interest rate, you and your creditor will have to negotiate a rate or ask the court to decide, using the formula announced by the Supreme Court.

Class 4. This class of claims is for secured debts on which you owe more than the value of the collateral. For example, you might owe $10,000 on a car that is worth only $6,000. In some cases, you can modify the claim so that the secured portion is reduced to the value of the property ($6,000 in this case). The rest of the claim ($4,000 in this example) is treated as an unsecured, nonpriority claim. This is called a cramdown.

As a general rule, you can't cram down your mortgage, but there are exceptions. (See "Modifying Mortgages," below.) If you don't qualify for a cramdown of a debt that secures collateral, include the debt in Class 3 above or Class 5 below (if the contract extends beyond the length of the plan).

Fill out the first set of boxes as follows:

- In column 1, enter the name of the creditor.
- In column 2, enter the last four digits of the account number for the debt.
- In column 3, enter the total amount due.
- In column 4, enter the amount of the debt that is secured—in other words, the value of the property. You are supposed to use the property's replacement value—what a retail merchant would get for the property given its age and condition. If you use the *Kelley Blue Book* middle value for a car and secondhand stores or eBay for other types of property, you should be okay. But again, if the creditor argues with your amount, you are free to negotiate or even have the judge decide the issue.

Class 4: Secured claims to be bifurcated under the plan

1. Name of Creditor	2. Last Four Digits of Loan #	3. Claim Total	4. Secured Claim	5. Unsecured Claim	6. Interest Rate	7. Equal Monthly Payments	8. Number of Months	9. Total Payment	10. Purchase for Debtor's Personal Use?	11. Date of Purchase	12. Purchase Money Loan?
									Y ☐ N ☐		Y ☐ N ☐

The debtor will cure all prepetition arrearages on these claims through the plan payment as set forth below:

1. Name of Creditor	2. Last Four Digits of Loan #	3. Amount of Arrearage	4. Interest Rate	5. Monthly Payment	6. Number of Months	7. Total Payment

- In column 5, enter the amount you will treat as an unsecured claim. This is the total amount due minus the value of the property.

- In column 6, enter an interest rate based on the national prime rate, in accordance with the formula described in "Determining Interest Rates for Secured Debts in Chapter 13 Plans," above.

- Calculate your monthly payment based on the amount of the secured claim and the interest rate, using the instructions for Class 1 claims.

- In column 8, enter the number of months your plan will last.

- Multiply the monthly amount in column 7 by the number of months in column 8, and list the total in column 9.

- In column 10, check the appropriate box to indicate whether the property was intended for your personal use when you bought it. If it wasn't acquired for your personal use (for example, it was intended to be used in your business or by another member of your household as evidenced on the title agreement), you can cram down the debt no matter when you bought it.

- In column 11, enter the date of purchase. Subject to column 10, you may cram down debts for all property (other than cars) only if you incurred them at least a year before you filed for bankruptcy. For cars, you must have incurred the debt at least 910 days before you filed for bankruptcy in order to cram down the debt. Some courts have held that you still owe the unsecured part of a loan when you bifurcate it into secured and unsecured portions—that is, when you cram it down. (See, for example, *In re Rodriguez*, 375 B.R. 535 (9th Cir. B.A.P. 2007).) If, on the other hand, you don't qualify for a cramdown and you simply give your car back to the lender, your entire debt may be cancelled. (See, for example, *In re Ezell*, 338 B.R. 330 (E.D. Tenn. 2006).)

- In column 12, check the appropriate box. If you used the loan to purchase the property that secures the debt, it's a purchase-money loan. You can cram down a debt only if it is not a purchase-money loan—that is, if you secured the debt with property you already owned, not property you bought with the loan.

Modifying Mortgages

You can modify your mortgage to the actual value of your home if any of the following is true:

- Your loan was for the purchase of a multiunit building.
- Your loan was for other buildings or an adjacent lot that is not likely to be considered part of your residence, such as farmland.
- Your loan was for a mobile home you live in that is considered personal property.
- The mortgage loan is not secured solely by your residence.

If you do modify your mortgage, you will have to pay it off completely in your plan. For instance, if the contract value of your mortgage is $150,000 and you modify it to $110,000 (the value of your home), you'll have to pay the entire $110,000 off as part of your plan. This fact alone prevents most mortgages from being crammed down, even if they meet one of the criteria above.

You can also reclassify secured debts as unsecured debts if you owe more than your property is worth when you file your bankruptcy petition. For example, assume you have a first mortgage on your home for $200,000. Several years ago, when your home was worth $300,000, you incurred a second mortgage for $45,000. When you file for bankruptcy, however, your home's value has declined to $200,000. Because the second mortgage is no longer secured by your property, you can classify the debt as unsecured and pay if off along with your other unsecured debts in Class 6. This reclassification means that you most likely won't have to pay off the second mortgage in full, but can instead pay whatever percentage your plan devotes to unsecured creditors.

The second set of boxes allows you to pay off arrearages on loans you intend to cram down. Complete the boxes as follows:

- In column 1, enter the name of the creditor.
- In column 2, enter the last four digits of the account number for the debt.
- In column 3, enter the total arrearage.
- In column 4, enter the interest rate you must pay on the claim. As mentioned earlier, this is an area ripe for negotiation.

- In column 5, list your monthly payment, following the instructions for Class 1 claims.
- In column 6 enter the number of months in your plan.
- In column 7, multiply the monthly payment by the number of months in your plan.

Class 5. These debts are typically arrearages on leases or licenses, six- or seven-year car notes, and long-term secured and unsecured promissory notes that last beyond five years. If your mortgage is being paid through the plan, enter the mortgage terms here. The trustee will pay this amount unless you check the second button.

The boxes allow you to pay off arrearages on these amounts. Complete the boxes as follows:

- In column 1, enter the name of the creditor.

- In column 2, enter the last four digits of the account number for the debt.
- In column 3, enter the total claim.
- In column 4, enter the interest rate you must pay on the claim. As mentioned earlier, this is an area ripe for negotiation.
- In column 5, list your monthly payment including interest, calculated according to the instructions for Class 1 claims.
- In column 6 enter the number of months in your plan.
- In column 7, multiply the monthly payment by the number of months in your plan.

Class 6. In the first space, enter the total of the debts you listed on Schedule F, plus the unsecured portion of any bifurcated secured claim (listed in Class 4, above).

Class 5: Secured or unsecured claims other than residential mortgages on which the last payment is due after date on which final payment under the plan is due

☐ 3. The postconfirmation monthly payment pursuant to the promissory note will be made by the trustee from the plan payment to: _____ .

☐ 3.4. The postconfirmation monthly payment pursuant to the promissory note will be made by the debtor directly to: _____ .

The debtor will cure all prepetition arrearages on these claims through the plan payment as set forth below:

1. Name of Creditor	2. Last Four Digits of Loan #	3. Amount of Arrearage	4. Interest Rate	5. Monthly Payment	6. Number of Months	7. Total Payment

Class 6: Nonpriority unsecured claims

The debtor estimates that allowed nonpriority unsecured claims will be the sum of $_____ .

Class 6 claims will be paid as follows:

Check one box only

☐ Class 6 claims (including the unsecured claims in Class 4) are of one class and will be paid pro rata.

☐ Class 6 claims will be divided into subclasses as shown below and the creditors in each class will be paid pro rata.

Claim	Reason for Subclass	Amount

If you don't have a cosigner for any of your debts, and all of your debts in this category are dischargeable, you are probably safe in checking the first box and not breaking this class into subclasses. If you have nonpriority, unsecured debts that you want to treat differently than others, check the second box and prepare an exhibit to accompany the plan. You might want to create subclasses to:

- separately classify debts that have cosigners, so you can pay those debts in full and take your cosigners off the hook
- separately classify certain debts you've incurred after you filed your petition, because those debts must be paid off in full with interest
- separately classify certain business debts so that you can continue your business
- separately classify debts based on how much you owe (for example, you might want to pay 100% of debts for less than $1,000 and a lesser percentage of larger debts), or
- separately classify certain nondischargeable debts so you can pay them in full (for example, a student loan or child support owed to a government entity).

Comparison With Chapter 7

Here, you must enter two values: The total value of property that would be nonexempt in a Chapter 7 case (see Ch. 4) and what percentage of your total allowed unsecured, nonpriority debt (the debts listed in Schedule F) that amount would pay off over the course of your plan.

Comparison With Chapter 7

The value as of the effective date of the plan of property to be distributed under the plan on account of each allowed claim is not less than the amount that would be paid on such claim if the estate of the debtor were liquidated under Chapter 7 of the Bankruptcy Code on such date. The amount distributed to nonpriority unsecured creditors in Chapter 7 would be $_____ , which is estimated to pay _____% of the scheduled nonpriority debt. The plan proposes to pay _____% of the debtor's nonpriority unsecured debt.

Plan Analysis

This section summarizes your payments for each class of debts. Enter the amounts in each class that will be paid under the plan. Payments you will make directly to the creditor, such as your car note or mortgage, should not be included here. The total payment, divided by the number of months your plan will last, is the amount you should enter in the very first blank in the "Plan Payments" section, below. This is the total monthly payment you will have to make to the trustee.

Plan Analysis

Total Payments Provided for Under the Plan	
Class 1 (Priority Claims)	
Class 2 Residence (current and arrearage)	
Class 3 (Secured claims paid in full)	
Class 4 (Secured claims bifurcated)	
Class 5 (Claims due beyond final payment)	
Class 6 (Nonpriority unsecured)	
Subtotal	
Trustee's Fee (10% unless otherwise)	
Total Payment	

Order of Payment

This section tells the trustee how to prioritize the creditors to be paid under your plan. Much of it is self-explanatory. In the third item, if you have any administrative expenses other than the trustee's fees, you must enter the percentage of each plan payment that will be paid to that creditor. Other administrative expenses typically include attorney fees. The percentage is typically somewhere around 10% or 11%, but may be less in your district.

The fourth item should be included only if the trustee will make your payments on secured debts, such as a car note or mortgage. If you will make these payments yourself, delete this paragraph and renumber the remaining items.

Order of Payment

Except as otherwise provided in the plan or by court order, the Chapter 13 trustee shall disburse all available funds for the payment of claims in the following order:

First: The Chapter 13 trustee's fee up to but not more than the amount accrued on payments made to date.

Second: Any domestic support orders.

Third: Administrative expenses (including, but not limited to, attorneys' fees) in an amount up to but not more than 10% of each plan payment until paid in full.

Fourth: Ongoing payments on secured debts that are to be made by the trustee from the plan payment.

Fifth: Pro rata to all other claims except as otherwise provided in the plan.

Sixth: No payment shall be made on general unsecured claims until all secured and priority claims have been paid in full.

Other Plan Provisions

There are a number of provisions that are standard in repayment plans. You may not need to use all of the following language. Read the instructions carefully to figure out whether the provision applies to you.

Section A. This clause provides you the opportunity to get out of any contracts and leases still in effect (like a car lease) that you described in Schedule G. If you have collateral that you are leasing (such as a car), you will have to return it to the creditor as provided in Section D, below.

Other Plan Provisions

A. The debtor rejects the following executory contracts and unexpired leases: _____ .

Section B. This clause provides you the opportunity to assume live contracts or leases, which means they will continue in effect. If you have arrearages under the contract or lease, you can make them up as part of your plan. All ongoing payments should be made directly to the lessor; arrearages must be paid through your plan.

B. The debtor assumes the executory contracts or unexpired leases set forth in this section. The debtor has a leasehold interest in personal property and will make all postpetition payments directly to the lessor(s): _____
_____ .

Section C. This clause allows you to specify that you will make direct payments to any creditor not listed in Class 2 and Class 5 above.

C. In addition to the payments specified in Class _____ and Class _____, the debtor will make regular payments directly to the following: _____
_____ .

Section D. This clause allows you to surrender any personal property and real property that you don't want to continue making payments on in your Chapter 13 plan. According to one court (*In re Ezell,* E.D. Tenn. 2006), if the property surrendered is a car purchased within 910 days or other property purchased within one year of your bankruptcy filing, giving it back to the lender extinguishes the debt. If the property can be crammed down, giving the property back extinguishes the portion of the debt that is secured by the property. The amount of debt that exceeds the property's actual value will be treated as an unsecured debt, payable in the same way as your other unsecured debts.

D. The debtor hereby surrenders the following personal or real property (identify property and creditor to which it is surrendered):

Property	Creditor

Section E. In the table, insert the creditor's name and the amount required by the creditor for adequate assurance. The last paragraph explains how preconfirmation adequate protection plan payments shall be disbursed to the creditor and how the trustee shall be paid.

E. Preconfirmation Adequate Protection Payments will be paid to the trustee for the following creditor(s) in the following amounts:

Creditor Name	Amount

Each adequate protection payment will commence on the 30th day from the date of filing of the case. The trustee shall deduct the foregoing adequate protection payment(s) from the debtor's plan payment and disburse the adequate protection payment to the secured creditor(s) at the next available disbursement or as soon as practicable after the payment is received and posted to the trustee's account. The trustee will take his or her statutory fee on all disbursements made for preconfirmation adequate protection payments.

Section F. This clause limits the amount of credit you can incur during the life of your plan. The Central District of California plan limits credit to $250, for example. However, that seems low. Different courts will have different limits. If your court has no limit, don't include this provision in your plan.

F. The debtor shall incur no debt greater than $_____ unless the debt is incurred in the ordinary course of business pursuant to 11 U.S.C. Section 1304(b) or for medical emergencies.

Section G. This clause implements a provision of the new bankruptcy law, which requires Chapter 13 debtors to remain current on their taxes.

G. The debtor will pay timely all postconfirmation tax liabilities directly to the appropriate taxing authorities as they come due.

Section H. This clause authorizes the trustee to disburse funds as provided in your plan.

H. The trustee is authorized to disburse funds after the date of confirmation in open court.

Section I. This clause implements the new law requiring Chapter 13 debtors to remain current on their support orders.

I. The debtor will pay all amounts required to be paid under a domestic support obligation that first became payable after the date of the filing of the petition.

Revestment of Property. This clause sorts out legal relationships between you, the trustee, and your creditors after plan confirmation and discharge.

Revestment of Property

Property of the estate shall not revest in the debtor until such time as a discharge is granted or the case is dismissed or closed without discharge. Revestment shall be subject to all liens and encumbrances in existence when the case was filed, except those liens avoided by court order extinguished by operation of law. In the event the case is converted to a case under Chapter 7, 11, or 12 of the Bankruptcy Code, the property of the estate shall vest in accordance with applicable law. After confirmation of the plan, the Chapter 13 trustee shall have no further authority or fiduciary duty regarding use, sale, or refinance of property of the estate except to respond to any motion for proposed use, sale, or refinance as required by the Local Bankruptcy Rules. Prior to any discharge or dismissal, the debtor must seek approval of the court to purchase, sell, or refinance real property.

Sample Plan

Here is a sample Chapter 13 repayment plan. The debtor is Carrie Ann Edwards, divorced mother of two children who lives in Lakeport, California. The numbers in her plan are based on the information in the sample bankruptcy forms, especially Form 22C, which you'll find in Ch. 5. Carrie was forced into Chapter 13 by the new bankruptcy rules. Also, she was faced with possible foreclosure on her mortgage because of an arrearage—which can be paid off over time in a Chapter 13 bankruptcy.

UNITED STATES BANKRUPTCY COURT

_____ [*Name of district*] _____ DISTRICT OF _____ [*Your state*] _____

In re _____ Edwards, Carrie Anne _____)
      [*Set forth here all names including married,*)
      maiden, and trade names used by debtor)
      within last 8 years.])
                                Debtor)   Case No. _____
)
Address _____ 3045 Berwick St. _____)
)
Lakeport, CA 95453 _____)   Chapter 13
)
Last four digits of Social Security or Individual)
Tax Payer Identification (ITIN) No(s). (if any): _____ 6287 _____)
)
Employer's Tax Identification (EIN) No(s). (if any):)
_____)

Chapter 13 Repayment Plan

Notice

This plan is proposed by the above debtor under penalty of perjury. Any creditor can object to this plan being confirmed by written notice filed with the court and served upon the debtor, the trustee, and other parties in interest not less than 8 days before the date set for the meeting of creditors. Absent a timely objection, the court may confirm this plan as drafted. The plan, and payments under the plan, will be subject to all relevant Bankruptcy Code provisions.

    With certain exceptions, a confirmed plan holds the debtor and creditors to the treatment provided in the plan—even if the plan modifies rights and duties held by the debtor and creditor. The exceptions are:

    a. Each creditor will retain its lien until the earlier of payment of the underlying debt determined under nonbankruptcy law or discharge under Section 1328. If the case under this chapter is dismissed or converted without completion of the plan, the holder of such lien shall retain it to the extent recognized by applicable nonbankruptcy law.

    b. Defaults will be cured using the interest rate set forth below in the plan. Any ongoing obligation will be paid according to the terms of the plan.

    c. Holders of secured claims and Class 1 claimants will be paid according to the plan after confirmation unless the secured creditor or Class 1 claimant files a proof of claim in a different amount than that provided in the plan.

    d. If a secured creditor files a proof of claim, that creditor will be paid according to that creditor's proof of claim, unless the court orders otherwise. Holders of all other claims must timely file proofs of claims, if the code so requires, or they will not be paid any amount. A debtor who confirms a Chapter 13 plan may be eligible thereafter to receive a discharge of debts to the extent specified in 11 U.S.C. Section 1328.

Plan Payments

The debtor proposes the following Chapter 13 plan and makes the following declarations:

Monthly Amounts Paid to Trustee Under the Plan

The debtor submits the following to the supervision and control of the trustee:

A. Payments by debtor of $ ___3,613.75___ per month for sixty (60) months. The monthly payment will begin within 30 days of the date the petition was filed.

B. The base plan amount is $ ___86,760 (disposable income x 60)___, which will pay ___41___% of the allowed claims of nonpriority unsecured creditors. If that percentage is less than 100%, the debtor will pay the plan payment stated in this plan for the full term of the plan.

C. Amounts necessary for the payment of postpetition claims allowed under 11 U.S.C. Section 1305.

D. If the plan provides for less than 100% payment of nonpriority unsecured claims, all postpetition tax refunds received by the debtor during the plan term.

E. Preconfirmation Adequate Protection Payments for any creditor who holds an allowed claim secured by personal property:

_____ .

F. Other property: _____ .

Classification and Treatment of Claims

Class 1: Allowed unsecured claims entitled to priority under 11 U.S.C. 507

The debtor will pay Class 1 allowed claims in full; except the debtor may provide for less than full payment of domestic support obligations assigned to a government agency.

Category	1. Amount of Priority Claim	2. Interest Rate If Any	3. Monthly Payment	4. Number of Months	5. Total Payment
Administrative					
1. Trustee's fee	$155		$155.00	60	$9,526
2. Attorney fees					
3. Ch. 7 trustee fees					
4. Other Admin.					
5. IRS	$3,000	7%	$59.50	60	$3,570
6. State Tax					
7. Support	$2,500	7%	$49.50	60	$2,970
8. Other					
9. Support not to be paid in full					
Totals					$16,066

Class 2: Claims secured solely by real property that is the debtor's principal residence

☑ 1. The postconfirmation monthly mortgage payment will be made by the trustee from the plan payment to: _____

_____ .

☐ 1.2. The postconfirmation monthly mortgage payment will be made by the debtor directly to: _____ .

The debtor will cure all prepetition arrearages for the primary residence through the plan payment as set forth below. If the debtor pays the cure amount while timely making all required postpetition payments, the mortgage will be reinstated according to its original terms, extinguishing any right of the mortgagee to recover any amount alleged to have arisen prior to the filing of the petition.

1. Name of Creditor	2. Last Four Digits of Loan #	3. Amount of Arrearage	4. Interest Rate	5. Monthly Payment	6. Number of Months	7. Total Payment
GJM	2345	$3,234.40	7%	$57.66	60	$3,460.81

Class 3: Secured claims to be paid in full through the plan

1. Name of Creditor	2. Last Four Digits of Loan #	3. Amount of Claim	4. Interest Rate	5. Monthly Payment	6. Number of Months	7. Total Payment
LT	9876	$6,000	7%	$118.81	60	$7,128.60

The debtor will cure all prepetition arrearages on these claims through the plan payment as set forth below:

1. Name of Creditor	2. Last Four Digits of Loan #	3. Amount of Arrearage	4. Interest Rate	5. Monthly Payment	6. Number of Months	7. Total Payment

Class 4: Secured claims to be bifurcated under the plan

1. Name of Creditor	2. Last Four Digits of Loan #	3. Claim Total	4. Secured Claim	5. Unsecured Claim	6. Interest Rate	7. Equal Monthly Payments	8. Number of Months	9. Total Payment	10. Purchase for Debtor's Personal Use?	11. Date of Purchase	12. Purchase Money Loan?
GMAC	2753	$15,000	$8,000	$7,000	7%	$158.41	60	$9,504.60	Y ☐ N ☐	03/05/xx	Y ☑ N ☐

The debtor will cure all prepetition arrearages on these claims through the plan payment as set forth below:

1. Name of Creditor	2. Last Four Digits of Loan #	3. Amount of Arrearage	4. Interest Rate	5. Monthly Payment	6. Number of Months	7. Total Payment

Class 5: Secured or unsecured claims other than residential mortgages on which the last payment is due after date on which final payment under the plan is due

☑ 3. The postconfirmation monthly payment pursuant to the promissory note will be made by the trustee from the plan payment to: _____ .

☐ 3.4. The postconfirmation monthly payment pursuant to the promissory note will be made by the debtor directly to:

_____ .

The debtor will cure all prepetition arrearages on these claims through the plan payment as set forth below:

1. Name of Creditor	2. Last Four Digits of Loan #	3. Amount of Arrearage	4. Interest Rate	5. Monthly Payment	6. Number of Months	7. Total Payment

Class 6: Nonpriority unsecured claims

The debtor estimates that allowed nonpriority unsecured claims will be the sum of $ __210,105__ .

Class 6 claims will be paid as follows:

Check one box only

☑ Class 6 claims (including the unsecured claims in Class 4) are of one class and will be paid pro rata.

☐ Class 6 claims will be divided into subclasses as shown below and the creditors in each class will be paid pro rata.

Claim	Reason for Subclass	Amount

Comparison With Chapter 7

The value as of the effective date of the plan of property to be distributed under the plan on account of each allowed claim is not less than the amount that would be paid on such claim if the estate of the debtor were liquidated under Chapter 7 of the Bankruptcy Code on such date. The amount distributed to nonpriority unsecured creditors in Chapter 7 would be $ _2,425_ , which is estimated to pay __1.2__ % of the scheduled nonpriority debt. The plan proposes to pay __41__ % of the debtor's nonpriority unsecured debt.

Plan Analysis

Total Payments Provided for Under the Plan	
Class 1 (Priority Claims)	$6,540
Class 2 Residence (current and arrearage)	$3,460.81 (arrearage) and $93,900 (current over five years)
Class 3 (Secured claims paid in full)	$7,128
Class 4 (Secured claims bifurcated)	$9,504.60
Class 5 (Claims due beyond final payment)	
Class 6 (Nonpriority unsecured)	$86,760
Subtotal	$207,298.81
Trustee's Fee (10% unless otherwise)	$9,526
Total Payment	$216,824

Order of Payment

Except as otherwise provided in the plan or by court order, the Chapter 13 trustee shall disburse all available funds for the payment of claims in the following order:

First: The Chapter 13 trustee's fee up to but not more than the amount accrued on payments made to date.

Second: Any domestic support orders.

Third: Administrative expenses (including, but not limited to, attorneys' fees) in an amount up to but not more than 10% of each plan payment until paid in full.

Fourth: Ongoing payments on secured debts that are to be made by the trustee from the plan payment.

Fifth: Pro rata to all other claims except as otherwise provided in the plan.

Sixth: No payment shall be made on general unsecured claims until all secured and priority claims have been paid in full.

Other Plan Provisions

A. The debtor rejects the following executory contracts and unexpired leases: _____
_____ .

B. The debtor assumes the executory contracts or unexpired leases set forth in this section. The debtor has a leasehold interest in personal property and will make all postpetition payments directly to the lessor(s): _____

C. In addition to the payments specified in Class _____ and Class _____, the debtor will make regular payments directly to the following: _____

D. The debtor hereby surrenders the following personal or real property (identify property and creditor to which it is surrendered):

Property	Creditor

E. Preconfirmation Adequate Protection Payments will be paid to the trustee for the following creditor(s) in the following amounts:

Creditor Name	Amount

Each adequate protection payment will commence on the 30th day from the date of filing of the case. The trustee shall deduct the foregoing adequate protection payment(s) from the debtor's plan payment and disburse the adequate protection payment to the secured creditor(s) at the next available disbursement or as soon as practicable after the payment is received and posted to the trustee's account. The trustee will take his or her statutory fee on all disbursements made for preconfirmation adequate protection payments.

F. The debtor shall incur no debt greater than $_____ unless the debt is incurred in the ordinary course of business pursuant to 11 U.S.C. Section 1304(b) or for medical emergencies.

G. The debtor will pay timely all postconfirmation tax liabilities directly to the appropriate taxing authorities as they come due.

H. The trustee is authorized to disburse funds after the date of confirmation in open court.

I. The debtor will pay all amounts required to be paid under a domestic support obligation that first became payable after the date of the filing of the petition.

Revestment of Property

Property of the estate shall not revest in the debtor until such time as a discharge is granted or the case is dismissed or closed without discharge. Revestment shall be subject to all liens and encumbrances in existence when the case was filed, except those liens avoided by court order extinguished by operation of law. In the event the case is converted to a case under Chapter 7, 11, or 12 of the Bankruptcy Code, the property of the estate shall vest in accordance with applicable law. After confirmation of the plan, the Chapter 13 trustee shall have no further authority or fiduciary duty regarding use, sale, or refinance of property of the estate except to respond to any motion for proposed use, sale, or refinance as required by the Local Bankruptcy Rules. Prior to any discharge or dismissal, the debtor must seek approval of the court to purchase, sell, or refinance real property .

Filing Your Bankruptcy Papers

Now that you've prepared all the necessary forms and drafted your repayment plan, it's time to file your case. Filing your papers with the court should be simple. This chapter explains how to gather the documents and information you'll need and file your case.

Gather the Necessary Documents

In addition to completing a sizable stack of official bankruptcy forms and your repayment plan, you must also submit a number of other papers. Along with your bankruptcy forms you will have to file:

- Exhibit D to your Petition, explaining your credit counseling status (see Ch. 7)
- your most recent tax return or a transcript of the return, and
- your wage stubs for the last 60 days, if you were working.

Credit Counseling

As explained in Ch. 1, almost everyone who files a consumer bankruptcy must first attend credit counseling. This credit counseling must be provided by an agency approved by the United States Trustee's Office within the 180-day period before you file for bankruptcy. The counseling can be done by phone, on the Internet, or in person. You can obtain a list of approved counselors by visiting the U.S Trustee's Office website at www.usdoj.gov/ust (click "Credit Counseling & Debtor Education"). The agencies are listed by state, but you can use any agency in any state or region that is on the list.

Repayment Plans

The purpose of this counseling is to get you to sign up for a debt repayment plan instead of filing for bankruptcy. Indeed, if the plan makes sense and you believe you can faithfully make the payments required to complete it, you might reasonably consider signing up for it. However, keep in mind that even if you make the required payments on the plan month after month, the creditors can pull out of the plan if you later fall behind—and they can go after you for the remaining debt. If you then decide to file for bankruptcy protection, you will have paid back all that money for no good reason. This is why most bankruptcy professionals—including the authors of this book—discourage their clients from signing up for a debt repayment plan.

Counseling Fees

Most of these credit-counseling agencies charge a modest sum ($50–$100 is common) for the counseling, creating a repayment plan (if it gets that far), and the certificate of completion that you'll need to file with your other bankruptcy papers.

Agencies are legally required to offer their services without regard to your ability to pay. (11 U.S.C. § 111(c)(2)(B).) If an agency wants to charge more than you can afford, inform the agency of this legal requirement. If the agency doesn't back down, make notes of your conversations (including whom you talked to, what they said, and the date when you talked), and then inform the agency that you are going to report it to the U.S. Trustee's office for failing to take your poverty into account. If that doesn't bring down the price, go ahead and report the agency. You'll be doing others in your same situation a great favor. You can report problems sending an email to ust.CCDE.complaint.help@usdoj.gov.

Exceptions to the Counseling Requirement

You don't have to get counseling if the U.S. Trustee certifies that there is no appropriate agency available to you in the district where you will be filing. However, counseling can be provided by telephone or online if the U.S. Trustee approves, so it is unlikely that approved debt counseling will ever be "unavailable."

You can also avoid the requirement if you move the court to grant an exception and prove to the court's satisfaction that "exigent circumstances" prevented you from meeting the counseling requirement. This means that:

- you had to file for bankruptcy immediately, and
- you were unable to obtain counseling within five days after requesting it.

Many of the agencies on the U.S. Trustee's list will counsel you the same day you ask for it, so it will be tough to show that you couldn't get counseling when you requested it. In other words, once you decide to file for Chapter 13 bankruptcy, you should immediately seek credit counseling and don't rely on the exigent circumstances exception.

> **CAUTION**
> **A foreclosure may not be "exigent" enough.** Some courts have found that a debtor who waits until the last minute to seek credit counseling might not qualify for an exception to the counseling requirement. For example, one court found that no exigent circumstances existed when a debtor filed for bankruptcy on the day of a scheduled foreclosure sale. In that case, the debtor claimed to have learned that he could file for bankruptcy—and that he would have to complete credit counseling—on the night before he filed.

If you can prove that you didn't receive credit counseling for this reason, you must file a certification with the court explaining your situation, then complete the counseling within 30 days after you file (you can ask the court to extend this deadline by 15 days).

You may also escape the credit counseling requirement if, after notice and hearing, the bankruptcy court determines that you couldn't participate because of:

- a physical disability that prevents you from attending counseling (this exception probably won't apply if the counseling is available on the Internet or over the phone)
- mental incapacity (you are unable to understand and benefit from the counseling), or
- your active duty in a military combat zone.

> **CAUTION**
> **"Same-day" counseling might not count.** Some courts have ruled that getting credit counseling on the same day you file for bankruptcy does not satisfy the requirement that the counseling take place "within 180 days prior to your filing date." Other courts have allowed same-day counseling.

Your Tax Return or Transcript

Under the new bankruptcy law, you are supposed to give the trustee your most recent IRS tax return no later than seven days before your creditors meeting.

(11 U.S.C. § 521(e)(2).) You also have to provide the return to any creditor who asks for it. To protect your privacy, you can redact (black out) your date of birth and Social Security number. If you don't provide your tax return on time, your case will likely be dismissed.

If you can't find a copy of your most recent tax return, you can ask the IRS to give you a transcript of the basic information in your return—and you can use the transcript as a substitute for your return. Because it can take some time to receive the transcript (the IRS says two weeks), you should make your request as soon as you can. Of course, if you already have a copy of your most recent return, you needn't worry.

> **CAUTION**
> **Your taxes must be current for the last four years.** Before you file for Chapter 13 bankruptcy, you must be able to show that you have filed tax returns for the previous four years. If you are behind on your tax filings, contact an accountant, enrolled tax agent, or tax preparation service right away.

Wage Stubs

If you are employed, you receive stubs or "advisements" with your paycheck. You are required to produce these stubs for the 60-day period before you file. If you have already tossed your stubs, you have three options: Ask your employer for copies; wait 60 days (and keep your stubs) before filing; or go ahead and file, hand over the stubs you have, and explain why you don't have 60 days' worth.

If you do not have an employer—for instance you are self-employed or operate a business as a sole proprietor—you won't have to produce wage stubs. However, most courts have a local form requiring you to declare the reason you aren't submitting wage stubs. Make sure to check for this local form before filing.

Get Filing Information From the Court

Every bankruptcy court has its own requirements for filing bankruptcy papers. If your papers don't meet these local requirements, the court clerk may reject them.

Follow These Rules to Stay Out of Trouble

- If you keep these golden rules in mind, you'll save yourself a lot of time and trouble:
- Don't file for Chapter 13 bankruptcy unless you are sure it is the right choice (Ch. 1 explains how to decide whether bankruptcy makes sense and, if so, which type of bankruptcy will best suit your situation; also see Ch. 6).
- Don't file until you have completed all of your forms, prepared your repayment plan, and gathered your documents.
- Don't file until you have a certificate showing that you have completed your credit-counseling workshop.
- If you can, pay your filing fee in full rather than in installments, so you don't have to worry about your case being dismissed if you miss a payment.
- Be absolutely complete and honest in filling out your paperwork.
- File all of your documents at the same time (unless you have to file an emergency petition to stop an impending foreclosure, wage garnishment, or repossession, and you can't get all the paperwork done in time).
- If possible, don't file your case until you have your most recent federal tax return (or a transcript) in your hands, as well as proof that you have filed returns for the previous four years. If you haven't filed in the previous four years, contact an accountant, enrolled tax agent, or tax preparation service. You can still file if you are delinquent for these years, but you will have to prove currency by the date scheduled for your creditors' meeting, or, if the meeting is continued, no later than 120 days after you file. (11 U.S.C. § 1308.)
- Serve your most recent tax return (or transcript) on the trustee and any creditors who request it as soon after you file as possible. If you don't serve it on the trustee at least seven days before the creditors' meeting, your case could be dismissed.
- Immediately amend your paperwork if the trustee asks you to.
- Don't forget your personal financial management counseling. You won't receive a discharge until you get a certificate showing that you have completed this counseling, which you must file before the last payment is due under your Chapter 13 plan.

Number of Copies

Before filing your papers, find out how many copies your court requires. Most ask for an original and one copy. The original will be scanned into the court's database, and your copy will be "conformed" for your records. (A conformed copy is either stamped or receives a computer-generated label, with information showing that you filed, the date of your filing, your case number, and the tentative date of your creditors' meeting.) A few courts still require you to provide an original and four copies.

Order of Papers and Other Details

Every court has a preferred order in which it wants to receive the forms in the package you submit for filing. Most courts also have rules indicating whether the forms should be hole-punched or stapled, and other details. If you mess up, most clerks will put your forms in the correct order or punch and staple your papers in the right way. Some, however, will make you do it yourself. This can be a major pain if you are filing by mail. Every court has an exhibit of the standard Chapter 13 filing with the forms arranged correctly. If you want to get it right the first time, visit the court and carefully examine the court's sample filing, taking notes of which forms fall in which order.

How to File Your Papers

Gather up all of your forms and documents (make sure you have everything by checking your stack against the Bankruptcy Forms Checklist and Bankruptcy Documents Checklist, below). Then follow the instructions in this section to get everything properly filed.

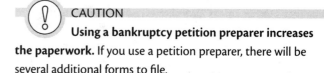

CAUTION
Using a bankruptcy petition preparer increases the paperwork. If you use a petition preparer, there will be several additional forms to file.

Bankruptcy Forms Checklist

☐ Form 1—Voluntary Petition

☐ Form 3A—(only if you are paying your filing fee in installments)

☐ Form 6, which consists of:

    ☐ Schedule A—Real Property

    ☐ Schedule B—Personal Property

    ☐ Schedule C—Property Claimed as Exempt

    ☐ Schedule D—Creditors Holding Secured Claims

    ☐ Schedule E—Creditors Holding Unsecured Priority Claims

    ☐ Schedule F—Creditors Holding Unsecured Nonpriority Claims

    ☐ Schedule G—Executory Contracts and Unexpired Leases

    ☐ Schedule H—Codebtors

    ☐ Schedule I—Current Income

    ☐ Schedule J—Current Expenditures

    ☐ Summary of Schedules A through J

    ☐ Declaration Concerning Debtor's Schedules

☐ Form 7—Statement of Financial Affairs

☐ Form 21—Full Social Security Number Disclosure

☐ Form 22C—Statement of Current Monthly Income and Disposable Income Calculation

☐ Form 201—Notice to Individual Consumer Debtor Under § 342 of the Bankruptcy Code

☐ Mailing Matrix

Bankruptcy Documents Checklist

☐ Your Chapter 13 repayment plan

☐ Required local forms, if any

☐ Your most recent federal tax return (or a transcript of the return obtained from the IRS)

☐ Proof that you've filed your tax returns for the last four years with the IRS

☐ Your credit counseling certificate

☐ Any repayment plan that was developed during your credit counseling session

☐ Your pay stubs for the previous 60 days (along with any accompanying local form your local court requires)

Basic Filing Procedures

Step 1: Put all your bankruptcy forms in the proper order.

Step 2: Check that you, and your spouse if you're filing a joint petition, have signed and dated each form where required.

Step 3: Make the required number of copies, plus one additional copy for you to keep.

Step 4: Unless the court clerk will hole-punch your papers when you file them, use a standard two-hole punch (copy centers have them) to punch the top center of your original set of bankruptcy papers. Don't staple any forms together.

Step 5: If you plan to mail your documents to the court, address a 9" x 12" envelope to yourself and affix adequate postage to handle one copy of all the paperwork. Although many people prefer to file by mail, we recommend that you personally take your papers to the bankruptcy court clerk if at all possible. Going to the court will give you a chance to correct minor mistakes on the spot.

Step 6: If you can pay the entire fee when you file, clip or staple a money order (courts don't accept checks), payable to "U.S. Bankruptcy Court," to your original set of papers. If you want to pay in installments, attach a completed Application and Order to Pay Filing Fee in Installments, plus any additional papers required by local rules. (See "Paying in Install-ments," below.) Be aware that many courts will require you to appear in court and justify your request to file in installments. If at all possible, it's a lot easier to pay the filing fee in full at the time of filing.

Step 7: Take or mail the original and copies of all forms to the correct bankruptcy court. (See Ch. 7 for more on finding the right court.)

Paying in Installments

You can pay in up to four installments over 120 days. You can ask the judge to give you extra time for a particular installment, but your entire fee must be paid within 180 days after you file. Some courts will require you to appear at a separate hearing a couple of weeks after you file to make your case for installment payments before the bankruptcy judge. If the judge refuses your request, you will be given some time to come up with the fees (probably ten days, perhaps longer). Because of this "appearance before the judge" requirement, many debtors prefer to raise the whole fee before filing and avoid the judge altogether.

If you are applying to pay in installments, you must file a completed Official Form 3A (*Application and Order to Pay Filing Fee in Installments*) when you file your petition. You can find a blank copy of this form in Appendix B.

! **CAUTION**

If you are paying in installments, you can't pay for the services of an attorney or bankruptcy petition preparer until you've completed your payments. This means you won't be able to pay an attorney to help you with your plan when you need it most. This is another reason why it is better to pay your filing fee all at once if possible.

The Application is easy to fill out. At the top, fill in the name of the court (this is on Form 1—*Voluntary Petition*), your name (and your spouse's name if you're filing jointly), and "13" following the blank "Chapter." Leave the Case No. space blank. Then enter:

- the total filing fee you must pay: $274 (item 1)
- the amount you propose to pay when you file the petition (item 4, first blank), and

- the amount and date you propose for each installment payment (item 4, second, third, and fourth blanks).

You (and your spouse, if you're filing jointly) must sign and date the Application. Leave the rest blank. As mentioned, the judge may require you to appear for a hearing at which the judge will decide whether to approve or modify your application.

Emergency Filing

If you want to file for bankruptcy in a hurry—typically, to get the protection of the automatic stay—you can accomplish that (in most places) by filing your bank-ruptcy petition, mailing matrix and cover sheet (if required by local rules), Form 21 (*Statement of Social Security Number*), and your credit counseling certifi-cate. Some courts also require you to file a cover sheet and an order dismissing your Chapter 13 case, which will be processed if you don't file the rest of your papers within 15 days. If the bankruptcy court for your district requires this form, you can get it from the court (possibly on its website), a local bankruptcy attorney, or a bankruptcy petition preparer.

If you don't follow up by filing the additional docu-ments within 15 days, your bankruptcy case will be dismissed. You can file again, if necessary. However, if your case was dismissed when you opposed a credi-tor's request to lift the stay, you'll have to wait 180 days to refile. And even if you don't have to wait to file, you'll have to ask the court to keep the automatic stay in effect once 30 days have passed after you file. (See Ch. 2.)

For an emergency filing, follow these steps:

Step 1: Check with the court to find out which local forms you must submit for an emergency filing.

Step 2: Fill in Form 1—*Voluntary Petition* (as directed in Ch. 7).

Step 3: On a Mailing Matrix (or whatever other form is required by your court), list all your creditors, as well as collection agencies, sheriffs, attorneys, and others who are seeking to collect debts from you. (See Ch. 7 for more information.)

Step 4: Fill in the *Statement of Social Security Number* (Official Form 21).

Step 5: Make copies of your certificate of credit counseling.

Step 6: File the originals and the required number of copies, accompanied by your fee (or an application for payment of fee in installments) and a self-addressed envelope with the bankruptcy court. Keep copies of everything for your records.

Step 7: File all other required forms within 15 days. If you don't, your case will be dismissed.

 CAUTION

Don't miss your deadline for the rest of your paperwork. Debtors who file under the emergency provisions often have their cases dismissed because they fail to get all of their paperwork filed within the 15-day deadline. If you file an emergency petition, calendar your filing deadline and make sure you get your papers in on time.

After You File

Filing a bankruptcy petition has a dramatic effect on your creditors and your property.

The Automatic Stay

The instant you file for Chapter 13 bankruptcy, your creditors are subject to the automatic stay, as described in detail in Ch. 2. If you haven't read that chapter, now is the time to do it.

Property Ownership

When you file your bankruptcy papers, the trustee becomes the owner of all the property in your bankruptcy estate as of that date. However, the trustee won't actually take physical control of the property; it will return to your legal possession after your plan is confirmed. Until your plan is confirmed, do not throw out, give away, sell, or otherwise dispose of property you owned as of your filing date, unless and until the bankruptcy trustee says otherwise. If you have any questions about dealing with property after you file, ask the trustee or the trustee's staff.

If you are a sole proprietor with business inventory, the trustee takes legal control of your inventory, although you still keep physical control of it. Ask the trustee if you can continue running your business. Usually you can, but you must be prepared to account for any inventory you sell before your Chapter 13 plan is confirmed. If your business is a corporation or other entity, you will need to consult an attorney.

In a Chapter 13 case, with a few exceptions, the trustee has no claim to property you acquire or income you earn after you file. You are free to spend it as you please. The exceptions are: property from an insurance settlement, marital settlement agreement, or inheritance that you become entitled to receive within 180 days after your filing date. (See "Understanding Property Exemptions," in Ch. 5, for more information.) To the extent that this property is not exempt, it can determine the amount you have to pay your non-priority, unsecured creditors in your plan.

You Can Pay Creditors After You File

- You may be tempted to leave some creditors (like your doctor, dentist, or favorite electrician) off of your bankruptcy schedules, in order to stay in their good graces. That's not a good idea. You must list all of your creditors. But there is nothing to prevent you from paying a dischargeable debt after you file—as long as you don't do so with money from your bankruptcy estate.

- If you plan to pay certain creditors despite your bankruptcy, let them know. This will lessen the sting from the notice of filing that they'll receive from the bankruptcy court. Although your promise is unenforceable, creditors will gladly accept your money.

Handling Routine Matters
After You File

Once you have filed all of your Chapter 13 bankruptcy papers, including your repayment plan, the bankruptcy trustee and the court take over. They will examine your papers and schedule court hearings. Your creditors also get into the act; it's time for them to file their claims, so they can get paid by the trustee once you start making plan payments. They may also object to your plan if they think they are getting shortchanged.

This chapter tells you how to move your bankruptcy case along once you file. You will probably have to make two or three brief court appearances and do some negotiating with creditors.

> ! CAUTION
>
> **Emergency filing reminder.** If you have not filed all your bankruptcy papers, you must do so within 15 days of when you filed your petition. (Bankruptcy Rules 1007(c), 3015(b).) If you do not, the bankruptcy court will dismiss your case and might even fine you.

The Automatic Stay

When you file your bankruptcy papers, the automatic stay will go into effect. (See Ch. 2 for detailed information on how the automatic stay works.) Creditors won't know about your case until they receive notice of your bankruptcy filing from the court, however. It might take several days—or weeks—for this notice to reach your creditors. If you want quicker results (particularly if you are facing aggressive collection efforts), you can send out your own notice. A sample letter is shown below.

The court almost always lifts (removes) the stay at the end of the confirmation hearing, because your creditors are now bound by your plan. This means they cannot sue you or take other action to get paid. Their only means of being paid is through the terms of the confirmed plan.

Notice to Creditor of Filing for Bankruptcy

Lynn Adams
18 Orchard Park Blvd.
East Lansing, MI 48823

June 15, 20xx

Cottons Clothing Store
745 Main Street
Lansing, MI 48915

Dear Cottons Clothing:

On June 14, 20xx, I filed a voluntary petition under Chapter 13 of the U.S. Bankruptcy Code in the Bankruptcy Court for the Eastern District of Michigan. The case number is 123-456-7890. No attorney is representing me. Under 11 U.S.C. § 362(a), you may not:

- take any action against me or my property to collect any debt

- file or pursue any lawsuit against me

- place a lien on my real or personal property

- take any property to satisfy an already recorded lien

- repossess any property in my possession

- discontinue any service or benefit currently being provided to me, or

- take any action to evict me from where I live.

A violation of these prohibitions may be considered contempt of court and punished accordingly.

Very truly yours,

Lynn Adams

Lynn Adams

Dealing With the Trustee

Within a few days after you file your bankruptcy petition, the bankruptcy court assigns a Chapter 13 trustee to oversee your case. You will receive a Notice of Appointment of Trustee from the court, giving the name, address, and phone number of the trustee. It may also include a list of any financial documents the trustee wants copies of, such as bank statements, canceled checks, and tax returns, and the date by which the trustee wants them.

Within a few days after the trustee is appointed, the court will send you and your creditors a Notice of Chapter 13 Bankruptcy Case. This notice usually contains:

- a summary of your Chapter 13 plan (if you filed it with your petition)
- an explanation of the automatic stay
- the date, time, and place of the meeting of creditors (see below)
- the date, time, and place of the confirmation hearing (see below), and
- the date by which creditors must file their claims (see below).

You may also receive a letter of introduction from the trustee explaining how this trustee runs a Chapter 13 case. For example, many trustees require you to make your payments by cashier's check or money order, and don't accept personal checks or cash. The letter will probably remind you to make your first payment within 30 days of when you filed your petition.

Many Chapter 13 trustees play a fairly active role in the cases they administer. This is especially true in small suburban or rural judicial districts or districts with a lot of Chapter 13 bankruptcy cases. For example, a trustee may:

- give you financial advice and assistance, such as helping you create a realistic budget (the trustee cannot, however, give you legal advice)
- actively participate in modifying your plan at the meeting of the creditors, and
- participate at any hearing on the value of an item of secured property, possibly even hiring an appraiser.

For more information on the role of the Chapter 13 trustee, see Ch. 1.

Hold on to Property You Owned Before Filing

Once you file your bankruptcy papers, the property you owned before filing is under the supervision of the bankruptcy court. Don't throw out, give away, sell, or otherwise dispose of any property unless and until the bankruptcy trustee says otherwise.

Report Certain Property You Receive After Filing

Despite the trustee's great interest in your finances, your financial relationship with the trustee is not as stifling as it may sound. In general, you still have complete control over money and property you acquire after filing—as long as you make the payments called for under your repayment plan and you make all regular payments on your secured debts. If you don't make those payments, your creditors may object at the confirmation hearing or even file a motion to dismiss your case.

You can use income you earn after filing that's not going toward your plan payments to purchase everyday items such as groceries, personal effects, and clothing. If you have any questions about using your postfiling income, ask the Chapter 13 bankruptcy trustee.

If you receive certain kinds of property (or become entitled to receive it), within 180 days after filing for bankruptcy, you must report it to the bankruptcy trustee. Here's the list:

- property you inherit or become entitled to inherit
- property from a marital settlement agreement or divorce decree, or
- death benefits or life insurance policy proceeds.

If any of this property is nonexempt, you might have to modify your plan to increase the amount your unsecured creditors receive, if they would no longer be receiving at least the value of your nonexempt property.

Provide the Trustee With Proof of Insurance

If you are behind on payments on a secured debt, such as a car loan, and you plan to make up the payments and get back on track during your Chapter 13 case, you may have to give the trustee proof that you have adequate insurance on the collateral. This requirement is meant to protect the creditor if the collateral is destroyed or damaged.

Make Adequate Protection Payments

Within 30 days after you file for bankruptcy, you will have to start making payments (called "adequate assurance payments" or "adequate protection payments") to secured creditors to cover the period between the date you file and the date your plan is confirmed. Usually, you will have to pay the same amount you were obligated to pay before you filed for bankruptcy. These payments are intended to protect the creditor's rights: The creditor cannot repossess the property or go after you for payment because of the automatic stay, so these payments protect the creditor's interest in the property before your repayment plan kicks in.

Make Your First Payment

Within 30 days after you file your petition, you must make the first payment proposed in your Chapter 13 repayment plan. (11 U.S.C. § 1326.) This deadline usually comes up before the meeting of creditors, and always before your confirmation hearing. The reason you must make the payment so early is to show that you can, in fact, make the payments.

It's crucial to meet this first deadline. So that you don't forget, count out 30 days from the date you filed your petition and mark the deadline on a calendar. It might be better, though, to make the payment a little earlier—for example, the day after you get paid, so you'll be sure to have the funds. If your wages are currently subject to wage attachments, garnishments, or voluntary payroll deductions, call the trustee and ask for help in getting those removed so that you have the money to make your Chapter 13 payments.

If you do not make your first payment on time, the bankruptcy court can convert your case to Chapter 7 bankruptcy, dismiss your case, or deny confirmation of your plan. A few courts consider the failure to make the first payment evidence that the plan was not submitted in good faith and is an abuse of the Chapter 13 bankruptcy system. In that case, the court would lift the automatic stay and allow your creditors to continue their collection efforts. If the court felt you were egregiously abusing the system—for example, this is the fourth Chapter 13 bankruptcy case you've filed without making payments in any of them—the court would likely dismiss your case, and possibly fine you and bar you from ever filing for Chapter 13 bankruptcy again.

How a Typical Chapter 13 Bankruptcy Proceeds	
Step	When It Happens
1. You file for Chapter 13 bankruptcy.	
2. The automatic stay takes effect. It bars your creditors, once they learn of your filing, from taking any actions to collect what you owe.	When you file the bankruptcy petition.
3. The court appoints a trustee to oversee your case. You will receive a Notice of Appointment of Trustee from the court.	Within a few days after you file the bankruptcy petition.
4. The court sends you and your creditors a Notice of Chapter 13 Case, which usually contains: • general information about Chapter 13 bankruptcy • a summary of your Chapter 13 plan • the date of the meeting of creditors • the date of the confirmation hearing, and • the deadline by which creditors must file their claims.	Within a few days after you file your Chapter 13 plan.
5. You provide your most recent tax return to the trustee. You may black out certain personal information, such as your Social Security number.	At least seven days before the scheduled date of the first meeting of creditors.

How a Typical Chapter 13 Bankruptcy Proceeds (continued)	
Step	**When It Happens**
6. You begin making payments under your repayment plan. (If your plan is never approved, the trustee will return your money, less administrative costs.)	Within 30 days after you file the bankruptcy petition.
7. You attend the meeting of the creditors, where the trustee and any creditors who show up can ask you about information in your papers. A creditor may raise objections to your plan with the hope of getting you to modify it before the confirmation hearing. You must bring any documents the trustee requests and proof that you've filed tax returns for the last four years.	Within 40 days after you file the bankruptcy petition.
8. You file a modified plan, if you wish.	Anytime before the confirmation hearing. You must send a copy of the modified plan to all creditors, who are entitled to 20 days' notice before the confirmation hearing. If you don't give 20 days' notice, you will have to schedule a new hearing date.
9. Creditors file written objections to your plan, if they wish.	At least 25 days before the confirmation hearing.
10. You attend the confirmation hearing, where the court addresses any objections raised by creditors or the trustee and approves your repayment plan.	The hearing must be held between 20 and 45 days after the creditors' meeting, unless the court wants to hold it earlier and there is no objection to the earlier date.
11. Creditors file their "proofs of claims," specifying how much they are owed. You may also have to file proofs of claims for creditors.	Within 90 days after the creditor's meeting (180 days for creditors that are government agencies). If you have to file proofs of claim on behalf of creditors, you must do so within 30 days after the 90-day or 180-day limit.
12. You or the trustee file written objections to creditors' claims, if you have a reason to object.	As soon as possible after the creditors file their claims. You must notify your creditors at least 30 days in advance of the hearing on your objections.
13. The trustee sends you periodic statements, showing: • who has filed claims and for how much • how much money has been paid to each creditor, and • the balance due each creditor.	Commonly, twice a year.
14. You give the trustee annual income and expense statements.	Every year while your Chapter 13 plan is in effect, if requested by the court, trustee, U.S. Trustee, or a creditor.
15. You file a certificate (Form 23) showing that you completed a course in personal financial management.	Before you make your last plan payment.
16. The court grants your discharge. The court may schedule a brief final court appearance called a "discharge hearing." If there's no discharge hearing, you'll be mailed formal notice of your discharge.	36 to 60 months after you file if you complete your plan payments; sooner if you seek and obtain a hardship discharge.

If You Operate a Business

If you operate a business, by all means keep running it after you file your Chapter 13 papers. If your business has employees, don't forget to make all required payroll tax and withholding deposits with the IRS and your state taxing authority.

The trustee can require the following from you:

- an inventory of your business property, and
- a report on the recent operation of the business, including a statement of receipts and disbursements, if you didn't include one in your bankruptcy papers (you may have attached one to Schedule I—*Current Income of Individual Debtor(s)*, or Form 7—*Statement of Financial Affairs*). (11 U.S.C. § 1304; Bankruptcy Rule 2015(c).)

The trustee may also direct you to send notification of your bankruptcy case to all entities who hold money or property that belongs to you. This includes financial institutions where you have accounts, landlords and utility companies who hold security deposits, and insurance companies where you have business insurance with a cash surrender value. If the balance of the money or value of the property is high and your plan provides little or no payment to your unsecured creditors, the trustee might try to take this money or property for them.

The Meeting of Creditors

Your first court appearance is a fairly informal one; the bankruptcy judge isn't even present. The purpose of the creditors' meeting is to allow the trustee and your creditors to ask you about the information in your bankruptcy papers, including your repayment plan. The trustee will want to be sure that you can make the payments you've proposed in your plan.

You (and your spouse, if you are filing jointly) must attend. If you don't, you may be fined $100 or so by the judge. Even worse, your case may be dismissed. If you know in advance that you can't attend the creditors' meeting, call the trustee and try to reschedule it.

Prepare for the Meeting

Before the meeting, call the trustee. Explain that you're proceeding without a lawyer and ask what records you're required to bring. Some courts require you to bring at least the following documents:

- file-stamped copies of all the papers you've filed with the bankruptcy court
- copies of all documents that describe your debts and property, such as bills, deeds, contracts, and licenses, and
- financial records, such as recent tax returns, checkbooks, and bank statements.

Bring proof of your state and federal tax filings for the previous four years to the creditors' meeting. Also be prepared for the trustee to ask you to hand over all of your major credit cards. (Not all trustees require this.) You should be able to hold on to your bank check cards that have the Visa or MasterCard logo on them. This will give you a card to use for your online accounts and rental cars.

If you lack the necessary documents at the creditors' meeting, the trustee will postpone the meeting to a later date when you can produce them. Often, if you get the documents to the trustee before the rescheduled meeting, you won't have to appear again; the trustee will simply review your documents, then close the meeting.

If you are feeling anxious about the meeting of creditors, ask the trustee when and where the next scheduled meeting will occur. Then, attend the meeting. That way, you can observe the proceedings and get comfortable with the process before you have to attend your own meeting.

The night before the creditors' meeting, thoroughly review the papers you filed with the bankruptcy court. If you discover mistakes, make careful note of them. You'll probably have to correct your papers after the meeting, an easy process. (Instructions are below.)

If your papers are internally consistent and there are no problem areas, the trustee is likely to ask you very few questions, perhaps nothing more than whether you have provided complete and accurate information. But sometimes the trustee may delve into a particular subject in more detail. For instance, the trustee may be interested in how you put a value on property such as real estate or a business. Or, if you recently sold some property, the trustee may want to know the details of the transaction and what you did with the proceeds. Or, if one part of your bankruptcy papers shows that you owe a debt but that debt hasn't been identified on the appropriate schedule, the trustee will want to know why. And finally, the trustee may want a better understanding of how your plan will pay your creditors.

Clearly there are an infinite number of situations where the trustee may want to go deeper into the facts. So how can you prepare for this? The single best way is to do a complete and accurate job of preparing your bankruptcy papers in the first place. Then, as mentioned, carefully review your papers before the meeting to make sure you understand all the information they contain and how you arrived at particular estimates and appraisals. Even if you had your papers prepared by someone else, you and you alone are responsible for what goes in them.

Getting to the Meeting

Most creditors' meetings take place in a room in or near the bankruptcy courthouse or federal courthouse. The date and time of the meeting are commonly stated on the notice sent out by the court; if they are not, call the trustee to find out. Give yourself at least an extra 30 minutes to find the right place, park, find the right building, go through security, and find the right room.

> **CAUTION**
>
> **You'll have to prove your identity.** To show that you are really who you say you are, you'll need to produce a solid picture ID and official proof of your Social Security number, such as a Social Security card, wage stubs, or a passport. Failure to produce such a document will result in your meeting being reset for a later date. Also, you'll need your picture ID to gain entrance to the federal building where the meeting is being held.

When you get to the right room, look for the trustee. The trustee will probably be sitting at a table; lawyers may be milling around, waiting to ask questions. Ask the trustee if you have to "check in"—that is, give your name so the trustee knows you are present. Then just sit down and wait your turn.

Tight Court Security

On your way to any court hearing, you will probably spend some time getting through security. Like airports, federal buildings have metal detectors, but set to an even higher sensitivity. If you set the detector off, you'll have to empty your pockets, take off any offending articles, such as a jacket or belt, and go through again. If you set it off again, the security guard may scan your body with a hand-held metal detector. In addition, items you're carrying—such as a purse, briefcase, or knapsack—must go through an X-ray scanner. The security guard may confiscate objects such as pocket knives; you can reclaim them after your hearing. You should also be prepared to show a picture ID to gain entrance.

What Happens at the Meeting

Most bankruptcy trustees set aside one or two days a month to hold Chapter 13 bankruptcy creditors' meetings. This means that when you show up for your meeting, many other people who have filed for bankruptcy will be there, too. And commonly, everyone is told to come at the same time. That means that 25–30 cases may all be scheduled for 9:00 a.m.

To get a rough idea of when your name will be called, check the schedule that should be posted outside the door. If your name is near the top of the list, you may not have too long to wait. If you're toward the bottom, you may be sitting there for quite some time. This time doesn't have to be wasted. The opportunity to observe other people at their meetings can be to your advantage; you'll quickly find out what to expect, where to stand, and maybe even what to say. And if you're nervous, watching other cases will probably help you calm down.

Your creditors' meeting, if it's typical, will last less than 15 minutes. When your name is called, you'll be asked to sit at a table near the front of the room. The trustee will swear you in and ask your name, address, and other identifying information. The trustee will also ask to see your photo ID and proof of Social Security number.

The trustee will briefly go over your forms with you, probably asking at least a few questions. Your answers should be both truthful and consistent with your bankruptcy papers. The trustee is likely to be most interested in the fairness of your plan (that is, that it treats all similarly situated creditors the same) and your ability to make the payments you have proposed.

When the trustee is finished, any creditors who showed up will have a chance to question you. Often, secured creditors come, especially if they have any objections to the plan—for example, that the interest rate you propose is too low, the schedule takes too long to pay your arrearage, or the value you assigned the collateral is wrong (if you are proposing a cramdown). An unsecured creditor who is receiving very little under your plan might show up too, if that creditor thinks you can cut your expenses and increase your disposable income. (See below for a discussion on the types of objections creditors raise to repayment plans.)

At the end of the meeting, be ready to negotiate. If you agree to make changes to accommodate a creditor's objections, you must submit a modified plan.

Modifying Your Plan Before the Confirmation Hearing

You have an absolute right to file modified plans with the bankruptcy court any time before the confirmation hearing, and most Chapter 13 debtors modify their plan at least once. (11 U.S.C. § 1323(a).) You must file the new plan with the bankruptcy court clerk, give a copy to the trustee, and send notice of the new plan to all of your creditors. The new plan replaces the old one.

Here are some common reasons to modify a plan:

- To correct errors—such as to add overlooked creditors or debts.
- To reflect financial changes—such as a new job, raise, inheritance or insurance settlement, reduction in income, or destruction of property secured by a debt.
- To reduce your proposed payments—for example, if you just lost your job or had your income reduced.
- To respond to creditors' objections or include terms you negotiated with a creditor at the end of the meeting of the creditors.

- To add debts you incurred after filing. In general, you should not incur debts after you file, other than day-to-day expenses. You can modify your plan, however, to add any debts that are necessary for you to keep following your plan (such as a medical bill) or unanticipated debts (such as a tax bill). (This is covered in Ch. 12.)

Your creditors have a right to be notified about your proposed modifications—and your notice must be fairly specific. At a minimum the notice must:

- identify the debtor (you)
- identify each creditor whose claim is affected by your modification
- describe your proposed modification with particularity (for instance, if you're proposing to reduce your payment to a creditor, your notice has to make that clear), and
- if secured property is involved, state whether you plan to keep making payments or surrender the collateral.

(See *In re Friday*, 304 B.R. 537 (N.D. Ga. 2003).)

Rules for Providing Notice

Your notice to creditors must contain the last four digits of your Social Security number and the creditor's account number (if any). You must send the notice to the contact address the creditor listed in its communications with the bankruptcy court. Alternatively, you may send it to the address listed on at least two written communications received from the creditor within the 90 days before you filed for bankruptcy. If you have not received any communications from the creditor during the 90-day period before you filed (because, for example, you have asserted your right to prohibit the creditor from contacting you), you may send the notice to the address listed on the two most recent written communications from the creditor.

You'll find a blank "Notice of Plan Amendment" form in Appendix B, which you can use to notify creditors of your intent to amend the plan, and the date and time of the new confirmation hearing.

The Confirmation Hearing

A judge must approve your Chapter 13 plan for it to be valid. This is done at a confirmation hearing, where the judge addresses any objections raised by creditors or the trustee. If you are representing yourself, you (and your spouse, if you are filing jointly) must attend. In a few courts, a confirmation hearing is held only if a creditor has filed a formal motion objecting to the plan. If no hearing is scheduled, it means your plan is approved as filed.

The confirmation hearing must be held no sooner than 20 or later than 45 days after the creditors' meeting, unless the court wants to hold it earlier and no one objects. However, the deadline for filing proofs of claims—which creditors must file to get paid through your plan—is 90 days after the date set for the first creditors' meeting. Assuming that the creditors' meeting is actually held on the scheduled date (it usually is), creditors might not have to file their proofs of claim until 45 to 70 days after the confirmation hearing. This means that plans up for confirmation often have to estimate which debts will be paid, and in what amounts. If creditors file claims after the court approves your plan, you may need to pay more into the plan than you expected.

Dealing With Disputed Debts

If you want to dispute whether you actually owe a particular debt, you'll need to file your objection with the court. The court will issue a ruling on whether you owe the debt. Similarly, you may need to ask the court to rule on whether a nondischargeable debt is dischargeable in your particular circumstances.

Ideally, you want the court to rule on your objection before your plan is confirmed. Otherwise you'll have to modify your plan if the court ultimately agrees with your objection. And until you get the court's ruling, you'll also have to start paying off the debt if these payments come due under your Chapter 13 plan. Unfortunately, many courts hold confirmation hearings early in the case—even as early as the creditors' meeting—so it may be difficult if not impossible to get a ruling prior to confirmation.

Prepare for the Confirmation Hearing

A few days before the confirmation hearing, review your plan and the objections raised by your creditors or trustee. If you're confident that you can make the payments under your plan and your plan is fair to your creditors, gather the documents that support your plan—such as pay stubs you filed with the court. You're ready to go.

If you think the objections might have some merit, you'll probably need to hit the law library. There, you can do a little legal research to see how bankruptcy appeals and federal appeals courts for your district have ruled in similar disputes. Ch. 15 suggests some excellent resources to help you do your bankruptcy research.

If you find cases that support your position, photocopy them and bring them to court. If you find material that supports the objection, be ready to modify your plan.

What Happens at the Confirmation Hearing

Most bankruptcy districts set aside one or two days a month to hold Chapter 13 bankruptcy confirmation hearings—and in many courts, confirmation hearings are scheduled at the same time as other hearings, such as hearings on motions to dismiss, motions to convert to Chapter 7, and motions to establish the value of property. The courtroom will probably be filled with people who have all been told to come at the same time.

Watch the cases before yours so you know where to go when your name is called. If your case is called first, just ask the judge, clerk, or trustee—whoever is calling the cases—where you should stand. The judge or court clerk will ask you to state your name.

Unlike a creditors' meeting, the confirmation hearing usually is run by a bankruptcy judge. Judges like to get easy cases in and out of their courtrooms as quickly as possible. This means that all uncontested matters will be heard first. Next will be cases where the outcome is fairly obvious—often motions to dismiss in cases where the plans were approved but the debtors have missed several payments. If the trustee or a creditor has filed an objection in your case, your confirmation hearing will probably be toward the end. Bring a big book with you.

The judge is most interested in your ability to make the payments under your plan, and will question you about that or about plan provisions that are unclear.

After these questions, the judge will ask you whether any objections raised by the trustee or creditors have been resolved. If they haven't, the judge may ask the trustee or creditors to elaborate on their objections, ask you for any response, and then make a ruling. If the trustee doesn't think your plan is feasible, the trustee will raise that issue now. If the judge still has a lot of cases to get through, the judge may reschedule the rest of your hearing to a less busy day.

If the judge agrees with an objection, you will probably be allowed to submit a modified plan. (See "Modifying Your Plan After the Confirmation Hearing," below.) But if it's obvious that Chapter 13 bankruptcy just isn't realistic for you—for example, you earn very little money to pay into a plan—the judge will order that your case be dismissed or converted to Chapter 7 bankruptcy.

> **TIP**
>
> **If you were already forced out of Chapter 7.** If you had to file for Chapter 13 because you couldn't pass the means test (see Ch. 4), you may also be unable to propose a confirmable Chapter 13 repayment plan. If your income has declined since the six-month period before you filed, however, you may now find yourself eligible to use Chapter 7. (Remember, the means test is based on your average monthly income in the six months before you file.) Some lawyers believe that you can voluntarily convert to Chapter 7 regardless of your income, because the new law that creates the means test seems to apply only to those who file for Chapter 7 in the first place—not to people who convert from Chapter 13 to Chapter 7. (See, for example, *In re Fox*, 370 B.R. 639 (D. N.J. 2007).)

Income Deduction Orders

If you have a regular job with regular income, the bankruptcy judge may order, at the confirmation hearing, that your monthly plan payments be automatically deducted from your wages and sent to the bankruptcy court. (11 U.S.C. § 1325(c).) This is called an income deduction order. Income deduction orders work if you are regularly paid a salary or wages. They are almost impossible to issue, however, if you are:

- self-employed
- funding your plan with public benefits, such as Social Security—the Social Security Act prohibits the Social Security Administration from complying with an income deduction order, or
- funding your plan with pension benefits— many pension plans prohibit the administrator from paying proceeds to anyone other than the beneficiary (you), which means that the administrator will ignore the income deduction order.

In many districts, the bankruptcy court automatically issues an income deduction order at the confirmation hearing—and possibly even earlier. In some districts, the bankruptcy court leaves it up to the debtor whether or not to issue an order. And in a few districts, the court doesn't issue the order unless you miss a payment in your plan.

You may not like the idea of the order, but the court is likely to deny your plan for lack of feasibility if you refuse to comply with it. And you should realize that the order will probably make it easier for you to complete your plan. The success rate of Chapter 13 cases is higher for debtors with income deduction orders than for debtors who pay the trustee themselves.

One benefit of an income deduction order is that it usually forbids your employer from making other deductions from your paycheck. This means that all wage attachments, garnishments, and voluntary payroll deductions will end (if they haven't already) when the order takes effect.

If the court does issue an income deduction order, you will have to find out from the court clerk or trustee who is responsible for preparing and giving your employer the order—the clerk, the trustee, or you. You might inform the payroll department at your job that you've filed for Chapter 13 bankruptcy and to expect an income deduction order from the bankruptcy court.

Once the income deduction order takes effect, you will need to tell the trustee if you change jobs. You can just call, or write a letter if you'd prefer.

Your Employer Can't Fire You for Filing for Bankruptcy

Don't be worried that your employer, who will learn of your bankruptcy when the income deduction order arrives, will fire you because you filed for bankruptcy. Employers rarely care. If your employer does punish you for having filed for bankruptcy, let someone in charge know that the Bankruptcy Act prohibits all private and public employers from terminating you or otherwise discriminating against you solely because you filed for bankruptcy. (See Ch. 14 for more on the laws against this kind of discrimination.)

The Judge's Order Confirming Your Plan

A court order granting confirmation of your repayment plan is binding on your creditors; they must accept the payments the trustee will make to them under the terms of your plan. This includes creditors who do not file claims by the deadline and creditors who objected to your plan. (11 U.S.C. § 1327(a).)

Exception for Student Loans

In the past, some debtors tried to get student loans discharged by including them in their plan as just another unsecured debt. Because student loans are nondischargeable unless the debtor comes forward to establish hardship, the student loan creditor wouldn't object to the confirmation. The debtor would then argue that the confirmation was final and the debt was discharged as a result. This agrument has been rejected by a number of courts. (See *In re Ruehle*, 307 B.R. 28 (6th Cir. B.A.P. Ohio 2004); *In re Banks*, 299 F.3d 296 (4th Cir. 2002).)

When the court approves your plan, you usually have to file an Order Confirming Chapter 13 Plan with the bankruptcy court clerk and send notice that your plan was confirmed to all your creditors. If the judge doesn't say anything, ask the judge if you must prepare the order and send notice.

Below are a sample order and sample notice form. To complete your own, type up the samples—filling in the information requested in italics. Attach a copy of your confirmed plan to the order, and then file the order and notice with the bankruptcy court clerk. After you've filed the papers, you must send a copy of the notice to each of your creditors.

Modifying Your Plan After the Confirmation Hearing

If your plan isn't confirmed at the hearing, the court will usually give you a certain amount of time in which to try again. If you don't submit a modified plan by the deadline (or if the court found that you acted in bad faith or that Chapter 13 is not a feasible option for you), the court will dismiss your case or convert it to a Chapter 7 bankruptcy case. In that situation, the trustee must return your payments to you, less administrative expenses.

If you want to submit a modified plan, call the trustee and ask for an appointment. Then, if you don't already know, find out from the trustee what it will take to get your plan confirmed. If you do know, ask the trustee if the ideas you have to modify your plan are likely to be approved by the judge.

In most cases, you'll need to do one or more of the following to get your modified plan confirmed:

- extend your plan (if it's for less than five years)
- arrange to pay off your secured debt arrears faster
- change an interest rate on secured debt arrears
- increase the secured portion of a debt that is partially secured and partially unsecured
- create or eliminate a class of unsecured creditors, or
- increase the amount a particular class of creditors receives.

After you type up your modified plan, call the court and ask how many copies you need to submit when filing a modified Chapter 13 plan. (You may need to submit more than you did when you filed the original.) Next, call the trustee and ask who sends the modified plan to your creditors—you or the court. (If it's you, ask the trustee what procedure you should follow.) As with modifications before confirmation, it's very important that you give your creditors exact notice of

B230B (Form 230B) (08/07)

United States Bankruptcy Court

_____ District Of _____

In re _____
                    Debtor*

Address: _____

_____

Last four digits of Social-Security or Individual Taxpayer-
Identification (ITIN) No(s).,(if any): _____
Employer Tax-Identification (EIN) No(s).(if any): ____

_____

Case No. _____

Chapter 13

ORDER CONFIRMING CHAPTER 13 PLAN

The debtor's plan was filed on _____ (date), and was modified on _____ (date). The plan or a summary of the plan was transmitted to creditors pursuant to Bankruptcy Rule 3015. The court finds that the plan meets the requirements of 11 U.S.C. § 1325.

IT IS ORDERED THAT:

The debtor's chapter 13 plan is confirmed, with the following provisions:

1. Payments:
Amount of each payment: $_____

Due date of each payment: the   ☐ _____day of each month, or
                                 ☐ _____

Period of payments: ☐ _____ months,
                                 ☐ until a _____% dividend is paid to creditors holding
                                 allowed unsecured claims, or
                                 ☐ _____

Payable to:
_____Standing Trustee
_____
_____

2. Attorney's Fees:
The debtor's attorney is awarded a fee in the amount of $_____, of which
$_____ is due and payable from the estate.

3. [Other provisions as needed] _____

_____   _____
         Date   *Bankruptcy Judge*

* *Set forth all names, including trade names, used by the debtor(s) within the last 8 years. For joint debtors, set forth the last four digits of both social-security numbers or individual taxpayer-identification numbers.*

UNITED STATES BANKRUPTCY COURT

_____ [_Name of district_] _____ DISTRICT OF _____ [_Your state_] _____

In re _____)
      [_Set forth here all names including married,_)
      maiden, and trade names used by debtor)
      within last 8 years.])
                        Debtor)   Case No. _____
)
Address _____)
)
_____)   Chapter 13
)
Last four digits of Social Security or Individual)
Tax Payer Identification (ITIN) No(s). (if any):_____)
)
Employer's Tax Identification (EIN) No(s). (if any):)
_____)

NOTICE OF ENTRY OF ORDER CONFIRMING CHAPTER 13 PLAN
TO ALL INTERESTED PARTIES AND THEIR ATTORNEYS OF RECORD

NOTICE IS HEREBY GIVEN pursuant to Bankruptcy Rule 3020(c) of the Order Confirming Chapter 13 Plan

entered on ___ [_date judge signed order_] ___ .

Dated: _____   _____
                                        Debtor in Propria Persona

your intended modifications. (See *In re Friday*, 304 B.R. 537 (N.D. Ga. 2003).) Otherwise, your modification may not be binding on any creditor who didn't get adequate notice.

When you file the modified plan, you will also need to schedule a new confirmation hearing. The hearing must be at least 25 days after you file the plan, so your creditors will have an opportunity to object. Call the court clerk to find out which dates are available for a hearing. Include the date and time of the hearing in your notice. (You'll find a blank "Notice of Plan Amendment" form in Appendix B, which you can use to notify creditors of the new hearing date and time.)

Amending Your Bankruptcy Forms

You have a right to amend the bankruptcy forms you have filed at any time before your final discharge. (You can also modify your plan after it's confirmed if the judge consents.) This means that if you made a mistake on your schedules, you can correct it easily. Also, you must amend your papers if you receive certain property within 180 days after filing. (These are described in "Dealing With the Trustee," above.) Some courts have local forms you must use for this purpose. Otherwise, all you do is file a corrected document, labeling it, for example, "Amended Schedule B."

SEE AN EXPERT

If the judge says "no." Bankruptcy rules state clearly that you have a right to amend any time before your case is closed. (Bankruptcy Rule 1009.) But judges sometimes balk. For instance, some courts may not let you amend your exemption schedule if it's too late for creditors to object to the exemptions you claimed. If you run into this problem, consult a bankruptcy attorney.

If your mistake means that notice of your bankruptcy filing must be sent to additional creditors (for instance, if you inadvertently left off a creditor who must be notified), you'll have to pay a fee to file the amendment. If your mistake doesn't require new notice (for example, you just add information about property you owned when you filed), you may not have to pay an additional filing fee. If you amend your schedules

to add creditors before the meeting of creditors, you'll usually be required to provide the newly listed creditors with notice of the meeting as well as notice of your amendment.

If you become aware of debts or property that you should have included in your papers, amending your papers will help you avoid any suspicion that you're trying to conceal things from the trustee. If you fail to amend your papers in this situation and someone else discovers your error, the judge may dismiss your bankruptcy petition or rule that one or more of your debts is nondischargeable.

Common Amendments

Here are some of the more common reasons for amendments and the forms that you may need to amend.

CAUTION

Amend all relevant forms. Even a simple change in one form may require changes in several other forms. Exactly what forms you'll have to change depends on your court's rules.

Add or Delete Exempt Property on Schedule C

If you want to add or delete property from your list of exemptions, you must file an amended Schedule C. You may also need to change:

- Schedule A, if the property is real estate and not listed there
- Schedule B, if the property is personal property and not listed there
- Schedule D, if the property is collateral for a secured debt and isn't already listed
- Form 7—*The Statement of Financial Affairs*, if any transactions regarding the property weren't described on that form, or
- the mailing matrix (if your court requires one), if the exempt item is tied to a particular creditor who isn't listed.

Add or Delete Property on Schedules A or B

If you forgot to list some of your property on your schedules or you receive certain property within six months after filing (see "Dealing With the Trustee," above), you may need to file amendments to:

- Schedule A, if the property is real estate
- Schedule B, if the property is personal property
- Schedule C, if the property was claimed as exempt or you want to claim it as exempt
- Schedule D, if the property is collateral for a secured debt
- Form 7—*The Statement of Financial Affairs*, if any transactions regarding the property haven't been described as required by that form, or
- the mailing matrix (if your court requires one), if the item is tied to a particular creditor who isn't listed.

Correct Your List of Creditors

To correct your list of creditors, you may need to amend:

- Schedule C, if the debt is secured and you plan to claim the collateral as exempt
- Schedule D, if the debt is a secured debt
- Schedule E, if the debt is a priority debt
- Schedule F, if the debt is unsecured
- Form 7—*The Statement of Financial Affairs*, if any transactions regarding the creditor haven't been described on that form, or
- the mailing matrix (if your court uses it), which contains the names and addresses of all your creditors.

How to File an Amendment

To make an amendment, take these steps:

Step 1: Fill out the Amendment Cover Sheet in Appendix B, if no local form is required. Otherwise, use the local form.

Step 2: Make copies of the blank forms you need to amend.

Step 3: Check your local court rules or ask the court clerk whether you must retype the whole form to make the correction, or if you can just type the new information on another blank form. If you can't find the answer, ask a local bankruptcy lawyer or bankruptcy petition preparer. If it's acceptable to just type the new information, precede the information you're typing with "ADD:," "CHANGE:," or "DELETE:"

as appropriate. At the bottom of the form, type "AMENDED" in capital letters.

Step 4: Call or visit the court and ask what order you should put the papers in and how many copies it requires for amendments.

Step 5: Make the required number of copies, plus one copy for yourself, one for the trustee, and one for each creditor affected by your amendment.

Step 6: Have a friend or relative mail, first class, a copy of your amended papers to the bankruptcy trustee and to each creditor affected by your amendment.

Step 7: Enter the name and complete address of every new creditor affected by your amendment on the Proof of Service by Mail (a copy is in Appendix B). Also enter the name and address of the bankruptcy trustee. Then have the person who mailed the Amendments sign and date the Proof of Service.

Step 8: Mail or take the original Amendment and Proof of Service and copies to the bankruptcy court. Enclose or take a money order for the filing fee, if required. If you use the mail, enclose a self-addressed envelope so the clerk can return a file-stamped set of papers to you.

Filing a Change of Address

If you move while your bankruptcy case is still open, you must give the court, the trustee, and your creditors your new address. Here's how to do it:

Step 1: Make one or two photocopies of the blank Notice of Change of Address and Proof of Service forms in Appendix B.

Step 2: Fill in the Change of Address form.

Step 3: Make one photocopy for the trustee, one for your records, and one for each creditor listed in Schedules D, E, and F or the mailing matrix.

Step 4: Have a friend or relative mail a copy of the Notice of Change of Address to the trustee and to each creditor.

Step 5: Complete the Proof of Service by Mail form, listing the bankruptcy trustee and the names and addresses of all creditors the Notice was mailed to. Have the person who did the mailing sign it.

Step 6: File the original Notice of Change of Address and original Proof of Service with the bankruptcy court.

Filing Tax Returns

The court, a creditor, the trustee, or the U.S. Trustee may request that you file copies of your federal tax returns (or transcripts) with the bankruptcy court when you file those returns with the IRS, while your case is pending. This rule applies to returns for current years and for the three years before you file your bankruptcy petition. Because this rule is new, it's too soon to know whether these requests will be common or rare. But this much is clear: If you don't comply with a request to file your returns, your case will be dismissed.

Before you provide your returns to the court or a creditor, you can redact (black out) information that identifies you personally. The following information may be redacted:

- **Social Security number.** You may redact all but the last four digits of any Social Security number that appears in the documents.
- **Names of minor children.** You may redact the names and use only initials.
- **Dates of birth.** You may redact the day and month of birth, and use only the year.
- **Financial account numbers.** If any account numbers are included, you may redact all but the last four digits.

Filing Annual Income and Expense Statements

The court, a creditor, the trustee, or the U.S. Trustee may request that you file an annual income and expense statement. This statement must include your income and expenditures during the most recent concluded tax year, and it must show how you calculated your income (both monthly and annually) and your expenses.

You must file the first statement 90 days after the end of the last tax year or one year after the date you filed your case (whichever is later), if your plan has not yet been confirmed by the later date. Once your plan is confirmed, you must file an annual statement at least 45 days before the anniversary of the date your plan is confirmed. It's hard to imagine that anyone will be paying close attention to these dates, as long as you are proceeding in good faith. Still, you should mark these dates on your calendar, just in case someone makes the request.

The income and expense statement must identify the amount and sources of your income, any person who contributed money to your household, and the amount that person contributed. Unless the trustee tells you otherwise, the best way to prepare this statement is to use blank copies of Schedules I and J to compute your annual and monthly income and your expenses.

Personal Financial Management Counseling

Before your last plan payment is due, you must complete a two-hour course in financial management and file a certificate of completion with the court. If you don't complete the course and file the certificate, the court can close your case without granting you a discharge. Although it isn't terribly difficult to reopen your case and file the certificate, it's better to avoid that extra step. When you file the certificate, you must also file Form 23; you'll find a sample copy below (Appendix B contains a blank copy).

You must use an agency that's been approved by the U.S. Trustee's office. You can find a list of approved providers at the U.S. Trustee's website, www.usdoj.gov/ust. If you were satisfied with the agency that provided you with credit counseling before you filed your case, you can probably use it again—typically, the same agencies are approved to provide both types of counseling.

You might think that requiring you to complete this course is overkill. After all, to complete your repayment plan, you have had to live on a pretty strict budget for three to five years. Nevertheless, the court will require proof that you've completed this counseling before it will grant your discharge.

B23 (Official Form 23) (12/07)

United States Bankruptcy Court
Northern District of California

In re   **Carrie Anne Edwards**

Debtor(s)

Case No. _____

Chapter   **13**

DEBTOR'S CERTIFICATION OF COMPLETION OF POSTPETITION INSTRUCTIONAL COURSE CONCERNING PERSONAL FINANCIAL MANAGEMENT

Every individual debtor in a chapter 7, chapter 11 in which § 1141(d)(3) applies, or chapter 13 case must file this certification. If a joint petition is filed, each spouse must complete and file a separate certification. Complete one of the following statements and file by the deadline stated below:

■ I, **Carrie Anne Edwards**, the debtor in the above-styled case, hereby certify that on **01/01/2009**, I completed an instructional course in personal financial management provided by **Consumer Credit Counseling Service**, an approved personal financial management provider.

Certificate No. (if any): **4565433**.

☐ I, _____, the debtor in the above-styled case, hereby certify that no personal financial management course is required because of *[Check the appropriate box.]*:

☐ Incapacity or disability, as defined in 11 U.S.C.§ 109(h);

☐ Active military duty in a military combat zone; or

☐ Residence in a district in which the United States trustee (or bankruptcy administrator) has determined that the approved instructional courses are not adequate at this time to serve the additional individuals who would otherwise be required to complete such courses.

Signature of Debtor: *Carrie Anne Edwards*
                              Carrie Anne Edwards

Date: *October 3, 2008*

Instructions: Use this form only to certify whether you completed a course in personal financial management. (Fed. R. Bankr. P. 1007(b)(7).) Do NOT use this form to file the certificate given to you by your prepetition credit counseling provider and do NOT include with the petition when filing your case.

Filing Deadlines: In a chapter 7 case, file within 45 days of the first date set for the meeting of creditors under § 341 of the Bankruptcy Code. In a chapter 11 or 13 case, file no later than the last payment made by the debtor as required by the plan or the filing of a motion for entry of a discharge under § 1328(b) of the Code. (See Fed. R. Bankr. P. 1007(c).)

Making Your Plan Work

Handling Legal Issues

Hopefully, your bankruptcy case will go smoothly, without any challenges or unexpected complications. In some situations, however, you might have to make an extra court appearance or two. This might happen if you need to ask the court to rule in your favor on an issue—for example, to eliminate a lien from your property. You might also have to defend against a creditor's objections to your plan or object to a creditor's claim for repayment. This chapter explains how to handle these types of contingencies.

Filing Motions

While your bankruptcy case is pending, you may learn that you need the judge to rule on a particular point. For example, you may have to modify your repayment plan (see Ch. 10) or have your debts discharged on the basis of hardship because you can't complete your plan (see Ch. 13). Requests for the court to intervene in your case—to make a decision or take some action, for example—are called motions.

This chapter includes detailed instructions on filing motions to eliminate liens (see "Asking the Court to Eliminate Liens," below), and much of that information applies no matter what type of motion you have to file. In this section, we briefly review the general requirements that apply to all motions brought in bankruptcy court.

There are two basic types of motions:
- ex parte motions, which are typically decided by the judge on the application of one party, without a hearing, and
- noticed motions, which give the other side enough time to come into court and oppose your request.

Ex Parte Motions

Ex parte motions are typically used when you are clearly entitled to the action you are asking the court to take. For example, let's say you want to file a noticed motion to modify your repayment plan, but you can only give the creditor 20 days' notice, rather than the 25 days generally required for a noticed motion. In this situation, you could file an ex parte motion seeking an "order shortening time." With your motion, you also include an order for the judge to sign and a declaration—a statement you sign under penalty of perjury—explaining that you have contacted or tried to contact the other side and let them know what you are doing.

Ex parte motions can also be used to dismiss your Chapter 13 bankruptcy case, because you have an absolute right to do so.

Noticed Motions

Noticed motions are much more common. There are two basic types of notice:
- notice of the date and time of the hearing, and
- notice that the other side must schedule a hearing if it wants to contest your motion.

If you will schedule the hearing yourself, you will need to complete these papers:
- The notice of motion (you can use Form 20A—an official bankruptcy court form that we've included in Appendix B—as a template for your notice). Typically, you have to give the other side at least 25 days' notice; if you don't provide enough time, you'll have to reschedule the hearing.
- The motion itself, which explains what you want the court to do and why.
- A declaration, which is a statement of facts written by a person with firsthand knowledge. The declaration must be signed under penalty of perjury.
- A memorandum of points and authorities that briefly sets out the applicable law and explains why the motion should be granted.
- A proof of service, which shows that someone (other than you) mailed the notice and motion to the other side.

To present a motion for which the other side has to schedule a hearing, you must file similar papers, but your notice won't include the time and date of the hearing. Instead, it will tell the other side what to do if it wants to oppose your request. If the other side doesn't respond within the 25-day notice period, you can file a request for default, asking the court to grant your motion. If you don't file this request for default, nothing will happen to your motion. It will just sit there. (You'll find a sample notice and motion, as well as a sample request for default in "Asking the Court to Eliminate Liens," below.)

The party you bring the motion against can file a written opposition to the motion if it wishes, but it must do so at least five days before any hearing that has been scheduled. At the hearing, the judge will listen to you and the other side argue your points. Then, the judge will either announce a decision or take the matter under submission (think about it for a while). The judge typically files a written memorandum explaining the decision. The judge will also ask the party that won the motion to prepare a formal order.

Dealing With Creditors' Motions

In most Chapter 13 cases, you'll be able to work out any minor glitches as they arise. On rare occasions, however, a creditor throws a monkey wrench into the works by filing a motion that, if successful, could mean a major disruption or even a dismissal of your case.

If you are faced with a creditor motion, take heart: Even when creditors file motions to challenge your right to file a Chapter 13 bankruptcy or discharge a particular debt, few Chapter 13 trustees want to deal with them. Most trustees handle thousands of cases a year. They do not want to get involved in drawn-out court battles unless the result is likely to have an impact on many other debtors in your district. In most cases, the trustee will encourage you and the creditor to work things out without a hearing. Some trustees even discourage creditors from filing a lot of motions (and creditors need to stay on the trustee's good side).

If you receive a motion from a creditor, you will have a certain period of time to file a written response. If you don't respond, you will automatically lose the motion. You will probably need to consult with a bankruptcy lawyer to help you prepare the response. You should also appear at the hearing. This is your opportunity to explain your position to the judge.

Here are a few common types of motions a creditor might file.

Objections to Your Eligibility to Use Chapter 13

A creditor might file a motion claiming that your debts exceed the Chapter 13 bankruptcy limits; as explained in Ch. 3, these limits are $336,900 for unsecured debts and $1,010,650 for secured debts. A creditor may raise this kind of objection if your liability for a debt is relatively certain (even though it hasn't yet been determined), and the creditor is afraid you'll wipe it out in bankruptcy.

> **EXAMPLE:** A few years ago, you and a partner started a business. It failed, you both lost a lost of money, and your former partner blames you for the whole mess, with some justification. He has been threatening to sue you for the money he claims you are responsible for causing him to lose. During your business's lean times, you missed several house payments, didn't pay your personal income taxes, and charged up your credit cards. You have filed for Chapter 13 bankruptcy, and your plan proposes to pay only 10% of your unsecured debts. Your ex-partner objects, claiming that you owe him at least $400,000, which puts you over the limit for unsecured debts.

Motion for Adequate Protection

Your secured creditors will probably insist that you agree to protect the property securing their debts against loss, damage, or general depreciation. This is called providing "adequate protection." (See Ch. 10 for more information.) The protection you provide could take the form of money, additional liens, or proof of insurance. If you refuse to provide adequate protection, the creditor may file a motion asking the court to order you to do so. If this happens, you might as well comply—because the creditor has a right to protect its interest in the property, you have no chance of winning this type of motion.

Motion for Relief From the Automatic Stay

When you file for bankruptcy, the automatic stay prohibits most creditors from taking any action to collect the debts you owe them, unless and until the court says otherwise. If you have had two or more dismissals entered in bankruptcy cases within the past year, you are not protected by the automatic stay and will need a court order to protect you against creditor actions. If you have one dismissal entered in the past year, the automatic stay only lasts for 30 days, absent a court order. (For more on the automatic stay, see Ch. 2.)

In a Chapter 13 bankruptcy, the automatic stay bars creditors from going after the property and wages you acquire after you file your petition and before your confirmation hearing. The court almost always removes (lifts) the stay after the confirmation hearing, because your creditors are bound by your plan at that point. If the confirmation hearing is delayed, however, your creditors may file a motion asking the judge to lift the stay early. The court is likely to grant such a motion if any of the following are true:

- You refuse to provide adequate protection to a secured creditor. (See "Motion for Adequate Protection," above.)
- Your filing is obviously in bad faith, or your plan is completely unfeasible.
- You have no equity in an item of secured property, and the creditor (who wants to repossess it) claims that you don't need the item to carry out your Chapter 13 plan. You may be able to get around a motion that makes this argument if:
  - Your plan includes payments on the secured item.
  - You can show that you need the property to generate income. For example, you could argue that you need to keep a car because you have to drive to work and have no adequate alternative means of transportation.
  - The property is your family home. Many courts rule that the family home is always necessary. Some courts rule otherwise, however, if the creditor can show that comparable housing is available to you for less money. You would have to emphasize your children's ties to their school and neighborhood, your proximity to work, and/or the cost of finding new housing and moving.

Motion to Lift Stay to Proceed With Foreclosure

If your mortgage lender initiated foreclosure proceedings before you filed for bankruptcy, and the notice period required by your state law has passed (for example, three months in California), the lender will likely ask the court to lift the automatic stay so the lender can sell your property. Probably your only defense is to challenge the lender's paper trail. For instance, because ownership of the mortgage may have been established by various electronic transactions, the lender may not now be able to prove ownership by presenting your original promissory note and security agreement or the necessary assignments to link itself to those original documents. If there isn't a proper paper trail, the court may reject the motion to lift the stay because the house could not be sold. Because it will probably take the creditor some time to get the proper paperwork in order, this will give you extra time in your home.

Motions to Dismiss by the Trustee and Others

Under the new bankruptcy law, creditors and trustees can file a variety of motions to dismiss your case. Typically, these motions argue that the filer failed to comply with procedural bankruptcy rules. For example, you might face:

- A motion by the trustee to dismiss your case because you failed to provide your most recent tax return at least seven days before the creditors' meeting.
- A motion by the trustee to dismiss or convert your case (to Chapter 7) if you fail to prove that you filed your tax returns for the previous four years.
- A motion by the trustee, the U.S. Trustee, or a creditor to dismiss you case because you failed to provide them, on their request, with the income tax returns you filed while your case was pending.
- A motion by the trustee to dismiss your case because you didn't stay current on your income tax filings.

- A motion by an ex-spouse or the trustee to dismiss your case because you didn't stay current on your child support or alimony payments while your case was pending.

If the person bringing this type of motion is right—that is, you really didn't file your tax returns or stay current on your child support payments—your only defense is that the failure was beyond your control. If you can show, for example, that a natural disaster (such as Hurricane Katrina) prevented you from filing your tax return on time, you might have a shot at success.

If an Unsecured Creditor Objects to Your Plan

It might seem odd to you that an unsecured creditor would object to your Chapter 13 plan. After all, in a Chapter 13 case, the creditor might get some money. By contrast, if you ignored the creditor or filed for Chapter 7 bankruptcy, the creditor probably wouldn't get anything.

A creditor who objects to your plan isn't trying to derail your bankruptcy, however: Instead, the creditor wants you to modify your plan to ensure that you will be able to make the payments it requires. Because so many Chapter 13 filers eventually dismiss their cases or convert to Chapter 7, your creditors have good reason to doubt that you'll be able to follow through. A creditor objects to a plan precisely because the creditor wants it to succeed.

A creditor who objects to your plan will probably attend the creditors' meeting and try to convince you to modify your plan before the confirmation hearing, which typically takes place from 20 to 40 days after the creditors' meeting. For example, the mortgage holder on your home might want you to add attorney fees to the arrearage you'll pay—perhaps $50 more per month.

The creditor will probably also file formal papers, either a motion or an objection, with the bankruptcy court, asking the judge not to modify or confirm your plan as written. That way, in case you and the creditor can't reach an informal agreement, the judge will decide the issue. If the creditor doesn't file a motion or objection, the creditor can't raise the objection at your confirmation hearing.

CAUTION

If a creditor requests a deposition. It's rare, but a creditor who thinks you are hiding assets and could pay more into your plan might try to gather evidence about your finances through a formal legal process called "discovery." The discovery technique the creditor is most likely to use is a deposition: a proceeding in which you answer questions posed by the creditor's attorney orally, under oath, before a court reporter. If a creditor sends you a discovery request, the court will postpone the confirmation hearing to give the creditor time to gather evidence. If the creditor decides to take your deposition, pick up a copy of *Nolo's Deposition Handbook*, by Paul Bergman and Albert Moore.

This section describes the four most common objections creditors raise to Chapter 13 plans.

The Plan Is Not Submitted in Good Faith

Probably the most common objection creditors raise is that a Chapter 13 plan was not proposed in good faith. The bankruptcy rules don't define good faith, but bankruptcy courts will take this type of objection seriously if you have proposed a plan that appears to be impossible for you to carry through. If you filed your papers with the honest intention of getting back on your feet and making all payments required in a Chapter 13 case by the bankruptcy code (11 U.S.C. §§ 1322 and 1325), you should be able to overcome this objection.

Occasionally, creditors make a good faith objection as a negotiating ploy. They want you to change your plan to satisfy them rather than argue the issue to the judge. If you think this is going on, you may need the help of a bankruptcy lawyer to figure out whether you have anything to worry about—that is, whether there are any valid, good faith objections to your plan.

When creditors make a good faith objection, most bankruptcy courts look at these factors:

- **How often you have filed for bankruptcy.** Filing multiple bankruptcies in and of itself does not show bad faith. If, however, you've filed and dismissed two or more other bankruptcy cases within a year, the court may find that you lack good faith if your papers are inconsistent or you can't show that your circumstances have changed since the previous dismissal. Changed circumstances sufficient to support a refiling might include:

- an increase in your income
- a reduction of your debt
- a new job that will permit use of an income deduction order
- your spouse's decision to file jointly with you, or
- the end of a condition that required your previous dismissal, such as illness or unemployment.

The court might also find a lack of good faith if you file for Chapter 13 bankruptcy within four years after filing a case in which you received a Chapter 7 discharge, and you propose to pay your unsecured creditors substantially less than what you owe them. In this situation, the court may well find that you are using Chapter 13 to circumvent Chapter 7's prohibition on filing a second Chapter 7 case within eight years of receiving a prior discharge.

- **The accuracy of your bankruptcy papers and statements.** The court is likely to find a lack of good faith if you misrepresent your income, debts, expenses, or assets, or you lie at the creditors' meeting or a deposition. Creditors will look for discrepancies by comparing your written and oral statements with credit applications and financial data you submitted to them—such as tax returns and bank statements. Even if your mistakes were purely accidental, the appearance of sloppiness (such as failing to mention property or minor debts, providing the wrong Social Security number, listing insufficient or incorrect information about creditors, or incorrectly valuing your property) will lead some courts to dismiss your case on the ground that you failed to meet your obligations as a debtor. If you discover any inaccuracy in your papers after you file them, be sure to point it out to the trustee at the creditors' meeting and promptly make the appropriate amendments.

- **Your motive for filing for Chapter 13 bankruptcy.** If you want to cure your mortgage default and get back on track with your house payments, pay off a tax debt, or get some breathing room to pay off your creditors, you have nothing to worry about. If the courts finds that you have either of the following motives, however, it might also find a lack of good faith:

  - You filed for bankruptcy solely to reject a lease or contract, such as a time-share or car lease.
  - You filed for bankruptcy to handle only one debt, other than mortgage arrears or back taxes. The court is particularly likely to find lack of good faith if you file only to pay a nondischargeable debt, such as a student loan or criminal fine.

- **Your efforts to repay your debts.** If you will pay your nonpriority, unsecured creditors less than the full amount you owe, you will have to show the court that you are stretching your budget as much as you can. The court will want to see that the expenses you deduct from your income when calculating your disposable income are reasonably necessary to support yourself and your dependents. You'll have few problems if you can show that you've eliminated payments on luxury items, depleted your investments, canceled your country club membership, brought down your living expenses, and increased your hours at work.

- **The cause of your financial trouble.** Bankruptcy courts are reluctant to find bad faith if your financial problems are due to events beyond your control, such as exceptional medical expenses, or an accident, job loss, or death in the family.

The Plan Is Not Feasible

The second most likely objection is that your plan is not feasible—that is, that you won't be able to make required payments or comply with the other terms of the plan.

There are two arguments a creditor might make:

- Your Form 22C does not show that you have enough income to pay all required debts. For instance, if you owe $35,000 in priority taxes but your current monthly income won't allow you to pay $583 a month ($34,980) for the next five years, you can't propose a feasible plan.
- Your income as shown in Schedule I (your actual current income) does not exceed your expenses as listed in Schedule J by enough to pay all required debts. If, on the other hand,

your Schedule I income, when compared to your Schedule J expenses, is sufficient to pay all your mandatory debts, you may be able to propose a feasible plan even if you have nothing left over to pay your unsecured creditors. This will depend on whether or not your bankruptcy court lets you use your Schedules I and J to propose a feasible plan or whether you are forced to use the figures listed on Form 22C. (See Ch. 5 for more information.)

To contest a feasibility objection, you should assemble the documents that support your calculations. Bring your worksheets and any other documents (such as pay stubs, monthly bills, and so on) that show your income and expenses.

Your creditors might also question your job stability, the likelihood that you'll incur extraordinary expenses, and whether you have any outside sources of money. The court will likely find that your plan is not feasible—and refuse to confirm it—if any of the following is true:

- Your business has been failing, but you have predicted a rebound (on a wing and a prayer) and intend to use the proceeds to make your plan payments.
- You propose making plan payments from the proceeds of the sale of certain property, but a sale isn't imminent. For example, if your house has been on the market for a long time and you haven't received any offers, the court probably won't confirm a plan that depends on your house selling.
- Your plan includes a balloon payment, but you haven't identified a source of money you'll use to make the payment.
- You owe back child support or alimony and have been held in contempt of court for failing to pay.
- You've been convicted of a crime and face a likely jail sentence.

The Plan Is Not in the Best Interests of the Creditors

When you file for Chapter 13 bankruptcy, you must pay your unsecured creditors at least as much as they would have received if you had filed for Chapter 7 bankruptcy—in other words, you must pay them at least as much as the value of your nonexempt property.

(See Ch. 5 for more information on this requirement). This is called the "best interests of the creditors" test.

If a creditor raises this objection, gather your worksheets from Ch. 5 and any other documents you have regarding the value of your nonexempt property, such as recent appraisals or the published value of your car. Bring these documents to the confirmation hearing. If you lose on this point, you'll need to raise the amount of your monthly payments to your nonpriority, unsecured creditors, or extend the life of your plan (if it doesn't already last for five years).

The Plan Unfairly Discriminates

In your plan, you must specify which unsecured creditors will be paid in full and which, if any, will get less. To do that, you can create classes of unsecured creditors, specifying how much (or what percentage of your payments) each class will receive, as long as you do not unfairly discriminate against any particular creditor. (Classes of creditors are explained in Ch. 8.)

If a creditor objects to classes you've created, you can either fight it out in court at the confirmation hearing or amend your plan to eliminate the class. If you decide to fight, you'll need to research how courts in your bankruptcy district have ruled in similar cases. (See Ch. 15 for more on legal research.)

Handling Creditors' Claims

After you file for bankruptcy, the trustee sends a notice of your bankruptcy filing to all the creditors you listed in your papers. In general, creditors who want to be paid must file a claim within 90 days after the meeting of creditors is first scheduled to be held. If the meeting is rescheduled, the deadline is still 90 days from the originally scheduled date.

Sometimes, a creditor you want to pay through your Chapter 13 plan forgets to file a claim. If this happens, you may have to file a Proof of Claim on behalf of the creditor. For example, if you want the trustee to pay the creditor under your plan and the trustee won't make the payment without a Proof of Claim, you will have to file one for the creditor. The time limit for filing a Proof of Claim on a creditor's behalf is short—you have only 30 days after the deadline the creditor missed to file your papers. (Bankruptcy Rule 3004.)

Filing a Proof of Claim on Behalf of a Creditor

Most claims are filed on an official court form. Most bankruptcy courts will also accept an informal document or letter, as long as it shows that the creditor intends to assert a claim.

A blank Proof of Claim form is in Appendix B. You must attach to the form evidence of your debt, such as your mortgage agreement, and any notice of default. Ask the trustee whether you should file it with the court clerk or directly with the trustee.

How the claim procedure works depends on whether the creditor is classified as secured, priority, or unsecured.

Secured creditors. The bankruptcy code does not expressly require secured creditors to file claims in order to be paid, but few trustees will pay secured creditors unless there's a claim on file. (Even if a secured creditor doesn't file a claim, however, the creditor's lien stays on the property.)

 CAUTION

To pay arrearages on a secured debt, you must file a proof of claim. If you want to make up missed payments on a secured debt in your Chapter 13 case and the secured creditor doesn't file a claim, you will have to file it on the creditor's behalf. For example, if you have missed three house payments, but the lender doesn't file a claim, the trustee won't pay your arrears through your plan unless you file the claim yourself. If you don't, the lender would probably ask the court for permission to proceed with a foreclosure.

Priority creditors. Priority creditors must file a claim to be paid. Most priority creditors must file the claim within 90 days after the date set for the first meeting of creditors. Government agencies must file a Proof of Claim within 180 days after the date you filed your case. The government can get an extension if it formally requests one before the 180 days expire. (Bankruptcy Rule 3002(c)(1).) The IRS is notoriously late at filing claims, but it is usually granted extensions.

Nonpriority, unsecured creditors. Nonpriority, unsecured creditors must file a claim to be paid. If a nonpriority, unsecured creditor does not, that creditor's debt will be discharged when you complete your plan, unless the debt is nondischargeable.

If you want to pay a nondischargeable unsecured debt through your Chapter 13 plan (to avoid having the debt remain after your case ends) and the creditor doesn't file a claim, you will have to file it on the creditor's behalf.

Objecting to a Creditor's Claim

Unless you file a written objection to a creditor's claim, the trustee will pay the claim. (In bankruptcy legalese, claims the trustee pays are called "allowed" claims.) You can file an objection at any time, but the sooner the better. You'll have to give notice and schedule a court hearing, at which the creditor must prove you owe the claim. This is where you get to contest the validity of a disputed debt, such as a tax debt.

Use Form 20A to give notice of your objection; you'll find a blank copy in Appendix B.

Possible reasons for objecting to a creditor's claim include:

- You owe less than the creditor claims you do.
- A secured creditor has overstated the value of the collateral.
- The creditor has characterized the debt as secured (meaning you'll have to pay it in full), and you think it's unsecured.
- The claim was filed late. Most courts disallow late claims. Some, however, allow late claims if the creditor shows "excusable neglect" or another good reason for the failure to file on time.
- The creditor hasn't provided a paper trail proving that it owns the lien—for example, the creditor can't come up with a copy of your original promissory note and security agreement or can't produce assignments linking itself to those original documents.

Objecting to a Proof of Claim for a Credit Card Debt

The court will presume that a proof of claim submitted on a credit card debt (most likely by your credit card company) is valid if it is accompanied by a summary statement that:

- identifies the debtor's (your) name and account number
- states the amount of the debt before the bankruptcy filing date
- is presented in the form of a business record or other reliable format, and
- breaks down any added charges, such as interest, late fees, and attorney's fees.

If the proof of claim includes this information, then you have the burden of refuting the claim as part of your objection. If the proof of claim doesn't include this information, the creditor must prove the claim. Finally, if the holder of the claim is not the original creditor, the creditor must provide documentation that ownership of the claim has been transferred, in addition to providing the other information. (See *In re Armstrong*, 320 B.R. 97 (N.D. Tex. 2005).)

If you are proposing to pay a very small percentage of your nonpriority, unsecured debt, it may not be worth your time to object to a credit card claim. Even if you win, that just means you will have to pay your other nonpriority, unsecured creditors a little more. Remember, the amount you have to pay to these creditors is based on your disposable income. You shouldn't spend time worrying about which creditors get what. Or, as the old saying goes, "Don't sweat the small stuff."

Asking the Court to Eliminate Liens

During your Chapter 13 case, you may be able to get the court to reduce or eliminate liens on your property. If you succeed, you'll still owe the debt, but it will be unsecured. The creditor then shares in what you are paying your other unsecured creditors and you keep the property. Even if you're paying your other unsecured creditors 100%, avoiding the lien is still worthwhile, because you get to keep your property with clear title. (See *In re Lane*, 280 F.3d 663 (6th Cir. 2002).)

Which Liens Can Be Avoided

Lien avoidance is a procedure by which you ask the bankruptcy court to allow you to "avoid" (eliminate or reduce) certain liens. If your Chapter 13 repayment plan proposes to pay nothing or very little on your unsecured debts, lien avoidance makes a lot of sense. As long as there's a lien, you have to pay it in full to keep your secured property.

Lien avoidance is available only in very limited circumstances, and only for certain types of liens.

Security Interest Liens

A security interest is a secured debt you take on voluntarily, by pledging property as collateral for the debt. The creditor's interest in the collateral is secured by a lien. Common security interests include mortgages, home equity loans, car loans, store charges that contain a security agreement, and bank loans for which you pledge collateral.

You can avoid a security interest lien only if it meets these criteria:

1. **You obtained the loan by pledging property you already own (not property you purchased with the loan).** This is called a nonpossessory, nonpurchase-money security interest. It sounds complicated, but it's easier to understand when you break it down:
   - Nonpossessory means the creditor does not physically keep the property you pledge as collateral—you do. (In contrast, if you leave you property at a pawn shop to get a loan, that would be a possessory security interest, for which lien avoidance is not available.)
   - Nonpurchase money means you didn't use the money from the loan to buy the collateral.
   - Security interest means the lien was created by agreement between you and the creditor.
2. **The property you pledged is exempt.** Exemptions are explained in Ch. 5.
3. **The collateral you pledged fits into certain categories of property.** These categories are:
   - household furnishings, household goods, clothing, appliances, books, musical instruments, or jewelry that are primarily for your personal, family, or household use

- health aids professionally prescribed for you or a dependent
- animals or crops held primarily for your personal, family, or household use (but only the first $5,000 of the lien can be avoided), or
- implements, professional books, or tools used in a trade (yours or a dependent's), but only the first $5,000 of the lien can be avoided.

These rules prevent you from eliminating liens on real estate or on motor vehicles, unless the vehicle is a tool of your trade. Generally, a vehicle is not considered a tool of the trade unless it is an integral part of your business—for example, you are a door-to-door salesperson or make deliveries. If you just use your vehicle to get to and from work, it isn't considered a tool of the trade, even if you have no other way to commute.

If you owe a lot more than your home is worth, you may be able to strip off a real estate lien and reclassify what you owe that creditor as unsecured debt. You may do this only if the lien is for a secured debt that was no longer secured by your home—that is, you didn't have any equity to cover the lien—when you filed for bankruptcy. For example, let's say you have a mortgage of $200,000 on your home, and a home equity loan of $25,000. Your home is worth only $200,000 when you filed your bankruptcy petition. In this situation, the home equity loan is not secured by your home, because the entire value of your home is covered by your mortgage.

Nonconsensual Liens

A nonconsensual lien—a secured debt that you didn't agree to—can be avoided only if:

- it's a judicial lien
- you can claim the property as exempt, and
- the lien, if honored, would deprive you of your full exemption.

You can remove judicial liens from any exempt property, including real estate and cars.

Tax Liens

If your federal tax debt is secured, you may have a basis for challenging the lien. Quite often, the IRS makes mistakes when it records a notice of federal tax lien.

 **SEE AN EXPERT**

Talk to a lawyer. You will need the help of a tax or bankruptcy attorney—preferably one who has experience in both areas—to challenge a tax lien.

Here are some possible grounds for asking the court to remove a tax lien:

- The notice of federal tax lien was never recorded, though the IRS claims it was.
- The notice of federal tax lien was recorded after the automatic stay took effect.
- The notice of federal tax lien was recorded in the wrong county—it must be recorded where you own real estate for it to attach to the real estate in that county.
- The notice of federal tax lien was recorded against the wrong assets, such as your child's house, not yours.

Even if the notice of federal tax lien was recorded correctly, you still may have a basis to fight it if:

- the lien expired (liens last only ten years), or
- the lien is based on an invalid tax assessment by the IRS.

Making a Motion to Avoid a Lien

You request lien avoidance by typing and filing a motion. It is quite simple and can be done without a lawyer. In most courts, you must file your motion with the court within 30 days after you file for bankruptcy. But some courts require you to file these motions before the creditors' meeting. Check your local rules.

You will need to fill out one complete set of forms for each affected creditor—generally, each creditor holding a lien on that property. Sample forms are shown below. Some courts have their own forms; if yours does, use them and adapt these instructions to fit.

Most courts consider a motion to avoid a lien as a matter that can be settled by default—in other words, if the creditor doesn't bother to respond, the judge can rule in your favor. The law is very clear about when a lien can be avoided. If your papers indicate that you meet these requirements, the creditor will most likely see no point in opposing ("contesting") the matter. This means that your first set of papers should notify the creditor that if he or she hasn't filed a response to your motion within a particular period of time—usually 25 days—the court will rule in your favor. Your notice should also explain that if the creditor wants to contest your motion, it's the creditor's job to arrange a hearing on the matter.

Although we provide sample motions to avoid liens below, you'll also need to check the local rules issued by your district's bankruptcy court. Local rules can get into some picayune details, from the exact wording of the notice you must send the creditor to the procedures for setting up a hearing if the creditor contests your motion. In some areas the rules require you to set a hearing, on the assumption that the creditor will want to contest your motion. Local rules also govern such mundane matters as whether numbered papers must be used and how to attach any exhibits that accompany the papers.

If the creditor requests a hearing, the local rules will explain what actions you should take, if any. In addition to procedural actions, such as filing a response to the creditor's request, you'll be required to prove, at a minimum, that the lien would impair your exemption on the property if you were required to pay it.

If the creditor doesn't request a hearing, you'll be required to file a proposed order and a request to enter a default. Your local rules will also govern this procedure.

The sample papers provided below assume that you are in a district where numbered paper is required and where motions to avoid liens may proceed without the creditor's reply ("by default"). The language in the sample notice is based on Local Rule 9014-1 for the Northern District of California bankruptcy court.

In Chapter 13 cases, the most common type of motion to avoid a lien involves a lien that a creditor has placed on a house as a result of a court judgment. This motion is titled Motion to Avoid Judicial Lien on Real Estate, so our samples are based on this scenario. Other types of motions to avoid liens will normally follow the same procedures, although the exact wording of the motions will differ.

Step 1: If your court publishes local rules, refer to them for time limits, format of papers, and other details of a motion proceeding.

Step 2: Type the top half of the pleading form (where you list your name, the court, case number, etc.), following the examples shown below. This part of the form is known as the "caption." It is the same for all pleadings.

Step 3: If you're using a computer to prepare the forms, save the caption portion and reuse it for other pleadings. If you're using a typewriter to prepare the forms, stop when you've typed the caption, and photocopy the page you've made so far, so you can reuse it for other pleadings.

Step 4: Using one of the copies that you just made, start typing again just below the caption and prepare a Notice of Motion and Motion to Avoid Judicial Lien on Real Estate as shown in the sample.

Step 5: Prepare a separate proof of service as shown in the example. Note that the proof of service must include the trustee and the U.S. Trustee as well as the creditor. If the creditor is a corporation, the proof of service must identify a specific person as the object of the service. This involves calling the corporation and asking the name and title of the person who accepts service for it. If the corporation holding the lien is no longer active—for instance it has merged with another corporation—ask the current corporation who should be served for the defunct corporation. You can also often get the name of the person who should be served by contacting the agency responsible for corporate filings in your state (usually the secretary of state). They will usually be able to give you the appropriate person to be served.

Step 6: Make at least three extra copies of all forms.

Step 7: Keep the proofs of service. Have your friend mail one copy of the motion, notice of motion, and proposed order to each affected creditor and the trustee.

Step 8: File (in person or by mail) the original (signed) notice of motion, motion, and proof of service with the bankruptcy court. There should be no fee.

Step 9: Wait the required period of time for a response from the creditor (usually 20–25 calendar days). If no response arrives, prepare a Request for Entry of Default, a proposed order, and a proof of service, as shown in the samples. If you receive a response, the response will, in most districts, provide you with notice of a hearing that has been scheduled by the creditor. Under most local rules, the creditor's response will also contain a memorandum of points and authorities as to why your motion should be denied. However, your local rules may instead require you to set the hearing and to provide points and authorities as to why your motion should be granted.

Scheduling a Hearing

To schedule a hearing, call the court clerk and give your name and case number. Say that you'd like to file a motion to avoid a lien and need to find out when and where the judge will hear arguments on your motion. In some districts, the court hears certain matters on certain days, and you will be able to choose the available day and time when you want your motion heard. In other districts, the local rules require the clerk to set a hearing date for you. In either case, ask for a date at least 31 days in the future, because you'll have to mail notice of your motion to the creditor at least 30 days' in advance of the hearing—in order to ensure the 25-day notice—unless your local rules require something different. Write down the information the clerk gives you.

If the clerk won't permit you to take care of these matters by phone, go to the court with a copy of your motion filled out. File the form and schedule the hearing. Write down the information about when and where your motion will be heard by the judge and then serve the papers by mail.

Step 10: Assuming no response to your motion, serve the Request for Entry of Default and proposed order on the creditor, trustee, and U.S. Trustee.

Step 11: File the Request for Entry of Default and proposed order with the court, including the proof of service as shown in the sample.

Step 12: The court should sign your proposed order and mail it back to you.

Step 13: Obtain a certified copy of the order from the court clerk. Ask the clerk what the fees are for this service.

Step 14: Even though the court's order requires the creditor to remove the lien from your records, you should independently record the certified copy of the order with the land records office where your real estate is recorded. This will operate to remove the lien from the official records.

Sample Notice of Motion and Motion to Avoid Judicial Lien on Real Estate

UNITED STATES BANKRUPTCY COURT

_____ DISTRICT OF _____

In re _____)
    [*Set forth here all names including married,*)
    maiden, and trade names used by debtor)
    within last 8 years.])
                      Debtor)
) Case No. _[*Bankruptcy Case #*]_
) [*Special number for Avoidance of Lien motions, if any*]
Address _____)
)
_____) Chapter 13
)
Last four digits of Social Security or Individual)
Tax Payer Identification (ITIN) No(s). (if any):_____)
)
Employer's Tax Identification (EIN) No(s). (if any):)
_____)

NOTICE OF MOTION AND
MOTION TO AVOID JUDICIAL LIEN ON REAL ESTATE

    PLEASE TAKE NOTICE that Debtor _____[*debtor's name*]_____ is moving the court to avoid a judicial

lien held by _____[*name of lien owner*]_____ on certain real property owned by the Debtor.

    This motion is being brought under procedures prescribed by Bankruptcy Local Rule 9414-1 of the United States

Bankruptcy Court for the Northern District of California.

    If you wish to object to the motion, or request a hearing on the motion, your objection and/or request must be

filed and served upon Debtor within 20 days of the date this notice was mailed;

    You must accompany any request you make for a hearing, or any objection to the relief sought by Debtor(s), with

any declarations or memoranda of law you wish to present in support of your position.

    If you do not make a timely objection to the requested relief, or a timely request for hearing, the court may enter

an order granting the relief by default and either 1) set a tentative hearing date or 2) require that Debtors provide you at

least 10 days written notice of hearing (in the event an objection or request for hearing is timely made).

    1. Debtor _____[*debtor's name*]_____ commenced this case on [*date of bankruptcy*

filing] by filing a voluntary petition for relief under Chapter 13 of Title 11 of the United States Bankruptcy Code.

    2. This court has jurisdiction over this motion, filed pursuant to 11 U.S.C. Sec. 522(f), to avoid and cancel a judicial

lien held by [*name of lien owner*] on real property used as the debtors' residence, under 28 U.S.C. Sec. 1334.

Sample Notice of Motion and Motion to Avoid Judicial Lien on Real Estate (continued)

3. On ___[date of lien being recorded]___ , creditors recorded a judicial lien against the debtors' residence at

_____[address]_____ . The said judicial lien is entered of

record as follows: _____[describe how lien appears in public records]_____ .

4. The Debtors' interest in the property referred to in the preceding paragraph and encumbered by the lien has

been claimed as fully exempt in their bankruptcy case.

5. The existence of _____[lien owner's name]_____ lien on Debtors' real property impairs

exemptions to which the Debtors would be entitled under 11 U.S.C. Sec. 522(b).

WHEREFORE, Debtors pray for an order against _____[lien owner's name]_____ avoiding

and canceling the judicial lien in the above-mentioned property, and for such additional or alternative relief as may be

just and proper.

Date: _____   Signed by: _____

Sample Request for Entry of Order by Default and Proposed Order

UNITED STATES BANKRUPTCY COURT

_____DISTRICT OF _____

In re _____)
      [Set forth here all names including married,)
      maiden, and trade names used by debtor)
      within last 8 years.])
                        Debtor) Case No. _[*Bankruptcy Case #*]_
) [*Special number for Avoidance of Lien motions, if any*]

Address _____)
)
_____) Chapter 13
)

Last four digits of Social Security or Individual)
Tax Payer Identification (ITIN) No(s). (if any):_____)
)
Employer's Tax Identification (EIN) No(s). (if any):)
_____)

REQUEST FOR ENTRY OF ORDER BY DEFAULT AND PROPOSED ORDER

Now comes _____[*debtor's name*]_____ who declares and says under penalty of

perjury this [*date of request*] that the following statements are true and correct:

    1. On [*date notice and motion served*], Debtor _____[*debtor's name*]_____

caused a Notice of Motion and Motion to Avoid Judicial Lien on Real Estate to be served on _____[*name of

person served on behalf of lien owner]*_____ .

    2. A copy of the Notice of Motion and Motion and a proposed order are attached to this request. Also attached

is a Proof of Service of this request on _____[*name of lien owner*]_____ , the Trustee, and the

U.S. Trustee.

    3. The Trustee and the U.S. Trustee were also served with the Notice of Motion and Motion on [*date notice and

motion served*].

    4. A proof of service duly executed by _____[*name of person who mailed the notice*]_____

as to service of the Notice of Motion and Motion is on file with the court.

    5. The Notice of Motion and Motion complies in all respects with Bankruptcy Local Rule 9414-1 of the United

States Bankruptcy Court for the Northern District of California.

Sample Request for Entry of Order by Default and Proposed Order (continued)

6. The Debtor has received no response from any of the served parties as of the date of this request, more than 20 days after the service of the Notice of Motion and Motion.

WHEREFORE, Debtor respectfully requests that the court enter by default the attached Order to Avoid Judicial Lien on Real Estate.

Date: _____   Signed by: _____

Sample Order to Avoid Judicial Lien on Real Estate

UNITED STATES BANKRUPTCY COURT

_____DISTRICT OF _____

In re _____)
    [Set forth here all names including married,)
    maiden, and trade names used by debtor)
    within last 8 years.])
                              Debtor) Case No. *[Bankruptcy Case #]*
) *[Special number for Avoidance of Lien motions, if any]*

Address _____)
)
_____) Chapter 13
)

Last four digits of Social Security or Individual)
Tax Payer Identification (ITIN) No(s). (if any):_____)
)
Employer's Tax Identification (EIN) No(s). (if any):)
_____)

ORDER TO AVOID JUDICIAL LIEN ON REAL ESTATE

Upon request of Debtor for relief by default under Bankruptcy Local Rule 9014(b)(4), and good cause appearing

therefore, the motion of the above-named debtor *[debtor's name]* to avoid the lien of respondent *[creditor's name]* is

sustained.

It is hereby ORDERED AND DECREED that the judicial lien held by *[creditor's name]* in and on Debtor's residential

real estate at_____*[address of real estate]*_____ recorded *[date lien recorded and description of lien as it appears*

in the records] and any other amounts due under the lien be hereby canceled.

It is further ORDERED that unless Debtor's bankruptcy case is dismissed, _____*[creditor's name]*_____

and its successors shall take all steps necessary and appropriate to release the judicial lien and remove it from the local

judgment index.

Date: _____   Signed by: _____
                                                   U.S. Bankruptcy Judge

Sample Proof of Service by Mail

UNITED STATES BANKRUPTCY COURT

_____ DISTRICT OF _____

In re _____)
    [Set forth here all names including married,)
    maiden, and trade names used by debtor)
    within last 8 years.])
                     Debtor)   Case No. _____
)
Address _____)
)
_____)   Chapter 13
)
Last four digits of Social Security or Individual)
Tax Payer Identification (ITIN) No(s). (if any):_____)
)
Employer's Tax Identification (EIN) No(s). (if any):)
_____)

PROOF OF SERVICE BY MAIL

I, _____ *[name of server]* _____, declare that: I am a

resident or employed in the County of _____ *[server's county]* _____ , State of _____ *[server's state]* _____ .

My residence/business address is_____ *[server's addresss]* _____

_____ . I am over the age of eighteen years and not a party to this case.

    On _____ *[date request served]* _____ , 20____ , I served the enclosed `Request for Entry of Order by`

`_____ Default`

on the following parties by placing true and correct copies thereof enclosed in a sealed envelope with postage thereon fully

prepaid in the United States Mail at _____ *[city and state]* _____ , addressed as follows:

    [Name and address of lien owner]

    [Name and address of trustee]

    [Address of U.S. Trustee}

I declare under penalty of perjury that the foregoing is true and correct, and that this declaration was executed on

Date: _____ *[date Proof of Service signed]* _____ , 20____ at _____
                                            City and State

                                      [Server's signature] _____
                                            Signature

Carrying Out Your Plan

Once the court has approved your repayment plan, you should be in for smooth sailing as long as you make your monthly payments. If an unforeseen problem arises, and you think you're going to have trouble making a payment, notify the trustee as quickly as you can. The trustee wants you to succeed and will help you over the rough spots.

You may be wondering why the trustee cares whether you are successful with your Chapter 13 plan. The answer, of course, is money. Remember, the trustee gets a cut of everything paid to creditors under your plan. If you have to convert to Chapter 7 or your case is dismissed, the trustee's income from your case will be cut off.

Making Plan Payments

By the time your plan is confirmed, you will have made at least one plan payment, and probably more. The hardest part of Chapter 13 bankruptcy is making those payments.

Prepare for Postconfirmation Creditor Claims

You probably feel like you are stretching as far as you can to make your plan payments every month and still have enough to take care of your day-to-day needs. But sometimes it's a good idea to reach even a little deeper into your pocket and come up with a few extra dollars to add to each payment. Here's why.

Creditors often file claims with the bankruptcy court after the judge approves your repayment plan at the confirmation hearing. Unless you regularly ask the trustee for a list of claims filed by creditors, you won't know who has filed claims.

Claims filed after your plan is confirmed can cause problems, for a number of reasons:

- If you forgot about a creditor (didn't list the creditor in your papers), but the creditor somehow hears about your bankruptcy and files a claim, the trustee will probably pay that creditor.
- If a creditor files a claim for more than the amount you think you owe, the trustee could end up paying out more than you had anticipated, especially if your plan pays each creditor a percentage of their claim, not a set dollar amount.

- If a creditor files a claim for payment of a secured debt (meaning you'll have to pay it in full) and you mistakenly thought it was unsecured, the trustee will probably pay that creditor more than you planned. This is often the situation with Sears—someone charges items on a Sears card and assumes the debt is unsecured. Sears's paperwork states, however, that Sears takes a security interest in all items paid for using its card, so those debts are secured.

To avoid underpaying your creditors in your Chapter 13 plan, it's a good idea to include an extra few dollars ($5, $10, $25—whatever you can afford) in each payment. Keep this up until the time for making claims has passed. If you're paying the trustee directly, tell the trustee why you're adding a few dollars. If the court has issued an income deduction order, send the trustee a few extra dollars yourself each month.

If no creditor files a claim you hadn't anticipated, you will simply complete your plan early. On the other hand, if you don't add the money and creditors you hadn't thought of do file claims, you will probably still owe some money at the end of your Chapter 13 case. You will have to either pay a lump sum to make up what you still owe or ask the court to extend your plan (but only if it lasted less than five years; plans may not last longer than that).

To keep track of the new claims, you can monitor your case file at the bankruptcy court during the 90 days following the meeting of the creditors (the deadline for creditors other than governmental agencies to file proofs of claims). If you disagree with any of the claims filed, you will have to file a motion objecting to the claim. (See Ch. 11 for more information on objecting to a claim.)

If Your Income Increases

There are a couple of ways for the trustee to keep track of your income as your case proceeds. You may be asked to submit an annual income and expense statement to the trustee (and to any creditor who requests one). In addition, you must remain current on your tax returns throughout your case, and provide a copy of your tax return to the trustee (and to any creditor who makes a request). (For more information on these requirements, see Ch. 10.) From these documents, the trustee can determine whether your income has increased.

If your financial condition improves sufficiently to allow you to pay more to your unsecured creditors (assuming your plan doesn't provide for them to be paid in full), the trustee or an unsecured creditor may file a motion with the bankruptcy court to amend your plan. The motion will request that the court order you to increase each payment, pay a lump sum amount (especially if you've inherited valuable property or won the lottery), or extend your plan (unless it already lasts for five years). The bankruptcy court will most likely grant the motion.

If You Get a Windfall

If you win the lottery, get a substantial raise, or receive an inheritance, or if your house goes way up in value, you may be able to dismiss your case and pay off your debts outside of bankruptcy. But keep in mind that the interest (and sometimes the penalties) on your debts that stopped accruing while you were in bankruptcy can be added back when you dismiss your case. In addition, before assuming you can use the equity in your home to apply for and obtain the loan. Don't dismiss your case and then apply for the loan. If you are rejected, you'll just have to refile for bankruptcy.

Selling Property

Certain property remains under the control of the bankruptcy court even after your plan is approved. (See Ch. 10 for more information.) If you want to sell any of this property, the court (or in some cases, the trustee) will have to approve the sale. And your unsecured creditors might object if you'd pocket any cash left over after paying off any liens on the property, rather than use it to pay their claims.

Modifying Your Plan When Problems Come Up

Chapter 13 bankruptcy isn't easy. You must live under a strict budget for three to five years. Problems are bound to arise. Fortunately, the Chapter 13 bankruptcy system has built-in procedures designed to handle the disruptions. Any time after your plan is confirmed, you, the trustee, or an unsecured creditor who filed a claim can file a motion with the court, asking permission to modify the plan.

This section discusses five common situations in which you might need to modify your plan. If you think you want to modify your plan, call the trustee and ask for help in filing your motion and scheduling your hearing before the judge. Your creditors will have to be sent notice of your motion at least 20 days before the hearing date. (Bankruptcy Rule 2002(a)(6).) Ask the trustee whether you or the trustee will send the notice.

The court hearing on modification of the plan is just like the original confirmation hearing. The rules and procedures are discussed in Ch. 10.

Your modified plan cannot last more than five years after the date your plan originally began.

You Miss a Payment

If the trustee doesn't receive a plan payment, expect a phone call. Sometimes, the problem will be easy to solve—the payment got lost in the mail, your employer forgot to send it (if there is an income deduction order), or you changed jobs and forgot to change the income deduction order.

If you missed the payment because you are struggling to make ends meet, resolving the problem may be more complicated. But don't lose heart. If the problem looks temporary, and you are several months or years into your plan, the trustee may suggest that you modify your plan to do any of the following:

- skip a few payments altogether, meaning your unsecured creditors would receive less than you originally proposed
- skip a few payments now and extend your plan to make them up, assuming your plan is not already scheduled to last five years
- make a lump sum payment to make up the payments you've missed, or
- increase several payments to cover the payments you missed.

If the problem looks likely to continue, or it happens very early in your Chapter 13 case, the trustee is less likely to support a modification of your plan. Instead, the trustee (or a creditor) is likely to file a motion to have your case dismissed or require you to convert to Chapter 7.

If you file a motion to modify your plan because you've missed some payments, a creditor may ask that the modified plan contain what is called a "drop dead" clause. Such a clause provides that if you miss another payment, your case will automatically convert to Chapter 7 bankruptcy or be dismissed by the court. Many courts include drop dead clauses in modified plans.

Your plan payment isn't the only payment you might miss. If the court approved your request to make direct payments to certain creditors (such as a mortgage lender) and you miss a payment, the creditor will run to the court. Most likely, the creditor will file a motion to have the automatic stay lifted, which would let the creditor go after any property you've acquired since filing for bankruptcy. Alternatively, the creditor may ask the court to dismiss your case or convert it to Chapter 7. If it's early in your plan and you haven't missed any other payments, ask the court for permission to modify your plan to pay the new arrears immediately.

Your Disposable Income Decreases

You wouldn't have filed for Chapter 13 bankruptcy if you hadn't had debt problems in your past—perhaps because of job losses or reduced work hours. Filing for bankruptcy doesn't make those kinds of problems go away.

If your income goes down, you or your spouse suffer a serious illness, go on maternity leave, or incur an extraordinary expense, call the trustee. The trustee is likely to suggest that you suspend payments for a month or two. You can make up the difference by modifying your plan to:

- make a lump sum payment when your income goes back up
- extend your plan, if it is scheduled to last less than five years, or
- decrease the amount or percentage that a certain class of creditor receives—for example, you might have originally proposed to pay your general unsecured creditors 75% of what you owe but will now file a modified plan that calls for them to get only 45%.

Creditors rarely object to a short suspension in payments, and bankruptcy courts routinely grant those modifications. If you propose a longer-term suspension, however, your secured creditors may object, especially if the collateral is decreasing in value. You may have to continue your payments on secured debts and suspend only the unsecured portion for a while.

You Need to Replace Your Car

A lot can go wrong with a car during the three to five years you're paying into your Chapter 13 plan—especially if you bought a used car before you filed to minimize your expenses. Chapter 13 trustees often hear from debtors whose cars have died or are on their last legs. This situation raises several issues in a Chapter 13 bankruptcy case.

Taking out a new loan. Let's say your car dies, you need another one, and you want to take out a loan to pay for it. You file a motion to modify your plan to include payments for the new loan. Will the court confirm the new plan? The court is likely to say "yes" if you *must* have the car to complete your plan—for example, you're a salesperson. If, however, the car is just a convenience, the payments will significantly increase your monthly expenses, and you've had trouble making your plan payments, the court will probably turn you down.

For most people, the need for a car isn't all or nothing. In that case, the court will probably allow you to take out the loan if the effect is to lower your bills (for example, you were still making payments on your previous car and the loan will reduce your payments) or to increase your income (for instance, it would take two hours each way to get to work by public transit and only 30 minutes by car, so with a car you can get paid for three more hours' work a day).

Giving back a wrecked car. Now let's assume that after your plan is confirmed, your car is wrecked or won't run. You want to give the car back to the lender and modify your plan to treat the balance due (called a deficiency) as an unsecured claim. Several courts have allowed this. (*In re Hernandez*, 282 B.R. 200 (Bankr. S.D. Tex. 2002); *In re Knappen*, 281 B.R. 714 (Bankr. D. N.M. 2002); *In re Townley*, 256 B.R. 697 (Bankr. D. N.J. 2000); *In re Rincon*, 133 B.R. 594 (N.D. Tex. 1991).)

Other courts have ruled that a secured creditor cannot be reclassified into an unsecured creditor after a plan has been confirmed, and that the debtor still must pay the full balance owed the lender. (*In re Nolan*, 232 F.3d 528 (6th Cir. 2000); *In re Wilcox*, 295 B.R. 155 (Bankr. W.D. Okla. 2003); *In re Meeks*, 237 B.R. 856 (Bankr. M.D. Fla. 1999); *In re Coleman*, 231 B.R. 397 (Bankr. S.D. Ga. 1999); *In re Dunlap*, 215 B.R. 867 (Bankr. E.D. Ark. 1997); *In re Holt*, 136 B.R. 260 (Bankr. D. Idaho 1992); and *In re Abercrombie*, 39 B.R. 178 (N.D. Ga. 1984).)

A court might look at how you got into the situation. If your negligence or recklessness caused the problem, the court may be more inclined to deny modification of your plan.

What happens to insurance proceeds. If your car was all paid off and is damaged in an accident, you may get some insurance money. The court will probably want you to use that money to get the new car you need. If your car wasn't paid off, the insurance money will go to pay off your lender. If the insurance proceeds exceed what you owe the lender under your plan, you get to keep the difference. Remember, once the court determines the amount a secured creditor is entitled to get under the plan, that's all the creditor gets.

You Incur New Debt

If you fail to pay debts you incur after your plan is confirmed, you can amend your plan so these creditors are paid through your plan. You may have anticipated this by creating a class of postpetition creditors in your plan. If so, your plan should specify that these creditors receive 100% of what they are owed, plus interest. If you didn't create such a class, you'll have to handle postpetition debts as they arise.

No matter what your plan provides, your postpetition creditors will need to file a claim with the trustee in order to get paid through your plan.

If Your Plan Includes a Class of Postpetition Creditors

If your plan includes 100% payment of your post-petition debts, your postpetition creditors are unlikely to object to being paid through the trustee.

If, however, the creditor disagrees with the terms of your plan or you miss a plan payment, the creditor might object. If this happens, you will have to modify your plan to handle the creditor's objection. If the creditor is still not satisfied, the creditor might file a motion with the bankruptcy court asking the court to lift the automatic stay. If the court grants the motion, the creditor would be allowed to go after your post-petition property and income for payment.

> **EXAMPLE:** For the first year and a half of your plan, you will be paying your priority tax debt and your mortgage arrears. Not until month 19 will the trustee pay your unsecured creditors, including a class of postpetition creditors. Three months into your plan, the court lets you incur a medical debt. The doctor objects to being paid through the plan because the first payment won't come for at least 16 months. You will probably have to amend your plan to add the medical debt to the other debts that will be paid off early in the plan.

Your Plan Does Not Include a Class of Postpetition Creditors

If your plan does not include a class of postpetition creditors, and you want to pay a new creditor through your plan, you will have to modify your plan. Sometimes, postpetition creditors file a motion to be included in a modified Chapter 13 plan. The motion is likely to be granted.

If you don't modify your plan to include postpetition creditors to whom you default, the creditor may be able to take collection efforts against property you acquired after filing for bankruptcy.

You Buy Health Insurance

In the new bankruptcy law, Congress provided that Chapter 13 debtors can reduce what they pay into their repayment plans by the actual amount they spend to buy health insurance for themselves and their families. This measure is intended to help reduce the number of people who go without health insurance.

To take advantage of this new rule, you have to demonstrate a number of facts, including:

- the insurance is necessary
- the cost of the insurance is reasonable
- the cost is not significantly more than the cost of your previous policy or the cost necessary to

maintain the lapsed policy (if you were previously insured)

- you have not already claimed the cost as an expense for purposes of determining your disposable income (on Form 22C or Schedule J), and

- you actually purchased the policy.

Attempts to Revoke Your Confirmation

If a creditor or the trustee thinks you obtained your confirmation fraudulently—for example, because you used a false name, address, or Social Security number—one of them may file something called an "adversary proceeding" asking the court to revoke your confirmation. This is extremely rare. An adversary proceeding to revoke a confirmation must be filed within 180 days of the confirmation.

An adversary proceeding is much more formal than a motion. It creates an entirely new lawsuit, separate from your bankruptcy case, and proceeds like any other lawsuit. You will need a lawyer to help you.

The bankruptcy court won't revoke your confirmation because of fraud unless it finds that:

- you made a material (significant) false statement in your papers, in a deposition, or in court

- you either knew the statement was false or made the statement with reckless disregard to its truth

- you intended to induce the court into relying on the statement, and

- the court did rely on the statement.

When You Complete Your Plan

It's quite an accomplishment—and something to be proud of—to stick with a Chapter 13 plan to the end. After you have made all of your payments under your plan, filed a certificate showing that you have completed your financial management counseling, and certified that you are current on your domestic support obligations (if any), the court grants a "full payment" discharge. In most courts, the trustee simply files the discharge order on behalf of the court after determining that all payments have been made. In other courts, you must ask the trustee (by phone is fine) to file the discharge order.

TIP

File Form 23 right away. You must complete a financial management counseling course—and file a certification, Form 23, stating that you have done so—before you make your last plan payment. If you don't file Form 23 on time, the court will close your case without granting you a discharge. To get your discharge, you will have to reopen the case and pay fees. To avoid this fate, file Form 23 as soon as you complete your counseling, even if you haven't yet reached your final plan payment.

Debts Covered by the Discharge

Your Chapter 13 discharge wipes out the balance owed on all of your debts, as long as the debt is included in your plan and does not fall into one of these categories:

- Long-term obligations for which the last payment is still due—that is, it will be paid after you've made the final payment on your plan.

- Nondischargeable debts, as described in Ch. 1.

- Debts you incurred after filing your Chapter 13 case, if the creditor was not paid or was only partially paid through the plan.

The Discharge Hearing

After struggling for years to repay your debts, the long-awaited end of your bankruptcy case may be a little anticlimactic. The court may hold a brief hearing, called a discharge hearing, and require you to attend. At the hearing, the judge explains the effects of discharging your debts in bankruptcy and may lecture you about staying clear of debt.

Few courts, however, schedule a discharge hearing in Chapter 13 cases. Whether or not you must attend a discharge hearing, you'll receive a copy of your discharge order from the court within about four weeks after you complete your payments. If you don't, call the trustee. Make several photocopies of the order and keep them in a safe place. If it's necessary, send copies to creditors who attempt to collect their debt after your case is over or to credit bureaus that continue to report that you owe a discharged debt.

Ending the Income Deduction Order

The trustee will probably remember to stop your income deduction order after you've made your last payment. If the trustee forgets, however, you may need to call and raise the issue.

Debtor Rehabilitation Program

A few Chapter 13 bankruptcy courts have created debtor rehabilitation/credit reestablishment programs. The purpose is to reward people who choose Chapter 13 bankruptcy instead of Chapter 7 bankruptcy and who succeed in completing their Chapter 13 cases.

If you have paid off a high percentage of your unsecured debts (often 75% or more), you may apply for credit from certain creditors.

In the typical program, the court staff includes a "credit liaison." This person will help you:

- acquire, review, and correct your credit file—in particular, to get your credit file to show that you completed a Chapter 13 bankruptcy in which you paid back a high percentage of your debts
- set up a budget
- analyze your ability to repay new debts
- understand the different types of credit
- identify possible sources of credit and credit limits
- fill out credit applications
- obtain information to support your application, such as your Chapter 13 payment history and completed plan
- prepare for any in-person interview with a creditor (for a car loan, for example), and
- understand how creditors make their decisions about extending credit.

Ask the trustee whether your court has a rehabilitation program. If it doesn't, find out from the trustee if a nearby bankruptcy court has one in which you might participate. If there's nothing nearby, you'll have to take your own steps to rebuild your credit. (See Ch. 14.)

If You Cannot Complete Your Plan

Despite your best efforts to keep a handle on your finances and make your regular plan payments, you may be unable to complete your plan. If this happens to you, take solace in the fact that you aren't alone—a significant percentage of Chapter 13 debtors eventually find themselves in this position.

If you can't complete your plan, you have three options: dismiss your case, convert it to a Chapter 7 bankruptcy, or ask the court to grant you a hardship discharge.

Dismiss Your Case

You have the absolute right to dismiss your Chapter 13 bankruptcy case at any time, as long as:

- the court doesn't believe that you filed your bankruptcy case in bad faith (see Ch. 11), and
- you didn't start in another type of bankruptcy (typically, Chapter 7) and then convert to Chapter 13 bankruptcy.

To dismiss your case, you have to file a simple ex parte motion with the court (see Ch. 11 for a brief discussion of ex parte motions). The court may have a preprinted dismissal form you can use; if it does not, ask the trustee for help. There won't be any court hearing. Because you have the right to dismiss your case (unless one of the exceptions discussed above applies), the motion will automatically be granted. A creditor or the trustee can also file a noticed motion to have your case dismissed.

If you converted to Chapter 13 from a different type of bankruptcy, you have to file a noticed motion asking the court for permission to dismiss your case. (See Ch. 11 for information on noticed motions.) The court may deny your request—and order you to convert to Chapter 7 bankruptcy—if it feels that you are abusing the bankruptcy system. Or, it may grant your request, but sanction (fine) you or issue an order barring you from filing for bankruptcy again for a certain period of time.

If your case is dismissed, there are several important consequences:

- All liens that you had removed from your property in your Chapter 13 case are reinstated.
- All money you have paid the trustee that has not yet been disbursed to your creditors will be returned to you, less the trustee's expenses.
- The automatic stay ends, which means that your creditors are free to go after you and your assets for payment.
- Interest (and in some cases penalties) that stopped accruing during your bankruptcy will be added on to your debts.
- You cannot refile for bankruptcy—Chapter 13, Chapter 7, or any other kind—within 180 days if you dismissed your case because a creditor filed a motion asking the bankruptcy court to lift the automatic stay.

If you change your mind and decide that you want your case to proceed, you can file a motion with the bankruptcy court within ten days of the dismissal asking that your case be reinstated. Unless you have a history of filing and dismissing, or you've had serious problems making the payments under this plan, the court will probably grant your motion.

Convert Your Case to Chapter 7 Bankruptcy

You have an absolute right to convert your Chapter 13 bankruptcy case to a Chapter 7 bankruptcy case at any time, as long as you haven't received a Chapter 7 discharge within the previous eight years.

You convert your case by filing an ex parte motion with the court. The court may have a preprinted form you can use; if it does not, ask the trustee for help. There won't be a court hearing, and your motion will automatically be granted. A creditor, the trustee, or the U.S. Trustee can also file a motion to have your case converted.

If you want to convert your case to a Chapter 7 bankruptcy, ask the trustee whether you have to notify your creditors. When you convert your case, all money that you have paid the trustee but has not yet been disbursed to your creditors will be returned to you, less the trustee's expenses.

In addition, the bankruptcy forms you filed for your Chapter 13 case will usually become a part of your new case. (These are the forms in Ch. 7 of this book.) A few bankruptcy courts, however, require you to file an entire new set of schedules, even if nothing has changed. Within 30 days after you convert, you must file one additional bankruptcy form called the Statement of Intention. It tells the court what you plan to do with your secured debts. You will also have to attend a new meeting of creditors.

Because any debts you incurred after filing your Chapter 13 case can be discharged in your Chapter 7 case (if they are otherwise dischargeable), you must amend the appropriate forms to list these new debts. You might have to amend:

- Schedule D (if you've incurred new secured debts)
- Schedule E (if you've incurred new unsecured priority debts)
- Schedule F (if you've incurred new unsecured nonpriority debts)
- Schedule G (if you entered into any new contracts or leases), and
- Schedule H (if you have new codebtors).

If, in your Chapter 13 case, the court established a value for certain items of property or determined the amount of a secured claim, those values and amounts will not apply in the converted case. (11 U.S.C. § 348(f)(1)(B).)

Some courts determine your exemptions as of the date you filed for Chapter 13 bankruptcy, while other courts determine them as of the date you convert to Chapter 7. In the latter situation, if you've acquired nonexempt property after filing your Chapter 13 case, you will be at risk of losing it in your Chapter 7 case. In addition, if the court determines that your conversion to Chapter 7 bankruptcy is in bad faith, the court can order that the new property be included in your Chapter 7 bankruptcy estate. (11 U.S.C. § 348(f)(2).)

If your creditors have filed proofs of claim, those claims carry over to your Chapter 7 case. However, if you dismiss your Chapter 13 case and refile a Chapter 7 case, your creditors will have to file new claims, assuming you have assets to be distributed. People with nonexempt assets sometimes use this strategy (dismissing the Chapter 13 case and refiling under Chapter 7) with the hope that creditors won't file new claims and therefore won't be paid in the Chapter 7 case. Even if you have nonexempt assets to be distributed, however, you would seldom care about who gets paid what, unless your nonexempt assets are so valuable that you might get to keep some of them if a creditor doesn't file a claim. For example, if you have nonexempt assets worth $100,000 and you owe only $80,000 to the creditors who file proofs of claim, you could keep the remaining $20,000.

RESOURCE

Resource for Chapter 7 bankruptcy. *How to File for Chapter 7 Bankruptcy*, by Stephen Elias, Albin Renauer, and Robin Leonard (Nolo), contains detailed information on Chapter 7 bankruptcy. It includes the forms and instructions you will need to file the additional form (the "Statement of Intention") and to amend the forms you've already filed.

Seek a Hardship Discharge

If you cannot complete your Chapter 13 repayment plan, you can file a motion with the bankruptcy court asking for a hardship discharge. (11 U.S.C. § 1328(b).) The court will grant your request only if three conditions are met:

1. You failed to complete your plan payments due to circumstances "for which you should not justly be held accountable." Your burden is to show the maximum possible misery and the worst of awfuls—that is, more than just a temporary job loss or temporary physical disability. Proving that your condition is permanent is usually key; you may need to bring medical evidence to court.

2. Based on what you have already paid into the plan, your unsecured creditors have received at least what they would have received if you had filed for Chapter 7—that is, the value of your nonexempt property. (This is typically a hard condition to meet unless you have little or no nonexempt property.)

3. Modification of your plan is not practical. To meet this requirement, you do not have to file a motion for modification and lose it; you just have to show the bankruptcy court that you wouldn't be able to make payments even under a modified plan. For example, in the aftermath of the Katrina disaster, a New Orleans debtor in a Chapter 13 plan could easily establish that modification wasn't practical.

Debts That Are Not Discharged

If the court grants your motion for a hardship discharge, only unsecured, nonpriority dischargeable debts are discharged. The following debts typically are not wiped out in a hardship discharge:

- priority debts
- secured debts
- arrears on secured debts
- debts you didn't list in your bankruptcy papers
- student loans
- most federal, state, and local taxes, as well as any amounts you borrowed or charged on a credit card to pay those taxes
- child support, alimony, and debts resulting from a divorce or separation decree
- fines or restitution imposed in a criminal-type proceeding
- debts for death or personal injury resulting from your intoxicated driving
- debts for dues or special assessments you owe to a condominium or cooperative association
- debts you couldn't discharge in a previous bankruptcy that was dismissed due to fraud or misfeasance, and
- debts you owe to a pension, profit-sharing, stock bonus, or other plan established under various sections of the Internal Revenue Code.

Debts That Are Not Discharged If the Creditor Successfully Objects

Some debts will be discharged in a hardship discharge unless the creditor files a successful objection to the discharge in court. These debts include:

- debts incurred through your fraudulent acts, including using a credit card when you knew you would be unable to pay the bill
- debts from willful and malicious injury you caused to another person or property, and
- debts from embezzlement, larceny, or breach of trust (fiduciary duty).

If you have a debt that falls into one of these categories, your best strategy is to do nothing and hope the creditor does the same. If the creditor objects, the court will examine the circumstances in which you incurred the debt to determine whether or not it can be legally eliminated. If you want the debt to be discharged, you should respond to the creditor's objection. If the debt is large enough to justify the fees, consider hiring a bankruptcy attorney to help you. See Ch. 15 for information on hiring a lawyer or doing your own legal research.

Life After Bankruptcy

Congratulations! After you receive your final discharge and your case is closed, you can get on with your life and enjoy the fresh start that bankruptcy offers. This chapter explains how you can start to rebuild your credit and how to deal with any problems that come up.

Rebuilding Your Credit

A bankruptcy filing can legally remain on your credit record for ten years after you filed your papers, although most credit bureaus remove a Chapter 13 bankruptcy filing after seven years. (Major creditors, such as banks and department stores, have pressured bureaus to remove the notations after seven years as an incentive to debtors to choose Chapter 13 bankruptcy over Chapter 7 bankruptcy.) Many creditors disregard Chapter 13 bankruptcy after three or four years.

In about two years, you can probably rebuild your credit to the point that you won't be turned down for a major credit card or loan. Most creditors look for steady employment and a history, since bankruptcy, of making and paying for purchases on credit.

RESOURCE

Resource for rebuilding credit. For more information on rebuilding your credit—including obtaining a copy of your credit file, requesting that the credit bureau correct mistakes, contacting creditors directly for help in cleaning up your credit, and getting positive information into your credit file—see *Credit Repair*, by John Lamb and Robin Leonard (Nolo).

If your debt problems led to a foreclosure, your credit will suffer for a number of years. If the foreclosure occurs in the midst of the housing crisis (2007-2008), however, you might be able to reestablish credit sooner than would otherwise be the case. Because so many foreclosures are occurring in this period—often without the borrower's fault—lenders may be more willing to extend credit with a foreclosure on your record than they would have been in the past.

TIP

Using a check card instead of a credit card. Many people mistakenly believe that they have to have a regular credit card to do simple things like charge a meal in a restaurant, get gas at the pump, or buy a book on the Internet. In fact, simply by maintaining a checking account with your bank, you will usually be issued a "check card" that doubles as a Visa or MasterCard—except that your ability to charge things on the card is limited by how much you have in your bank account when you use the card. Alas, the check card doesn't work for everything. Some car rental companies require a major credit card and won't accept your check card unless you post a sizable deposit. Also, if you don't keep track of your spending, using a check card can make it easier to overdraw your account, often resulting in steep penalties.

Don't Take on Too Much Debt Too Soon

Habitual overspending can be just as hard to overcome as excessive gambling or drinking. If you think you may be a compulsive spender, one of the worst things you might do is rebuild your credit. Instead, you need to get a handle on your spending habits.

Debtors Anonymous, a 12-step support program similar to Alcoholics Anonymous, has programs nationwide. If a Debtors Anonymous group or a therapist recommends that you stay out of the credit system for a while, follow that advice. Even if you don't feel you're a compulsive spender, paying as you spend may still be the way to go.

To find a Debtors Anonymous meeting close by, go to www.debtorsanonymous.org or call 781-453-2743.

Create a Budget

The first step in rebuilding your credit is to create a budget. Making a budget will help you control impulses to overspend and help you start saving money—an essential part of rebuilding your credit.

Fortunately, the bankruptcy law requires you to participate in budget counseling prior to getting a discharge. You will be able to apply what you learn in your budget counseling class to our suggestions in this chapter.

Before you try to limit how much you spend, take some time to find out exactly how much money you spend now, using a form like the one shown below. Make copies of the form, which is in Appendix B, and fill one out for 30 days. Write down every cent you spend—50¢ for the paper, $3 for your morning coffee and muffin, $5 for lunch, $2 for the bridge or tunnel toll, and so on. If you omit any money spent, your picture of how much you spend, and your budget, will be inaccurate. If you're married or combine your finances with someone, make sure each person fills out a form.

At the end of the 30 days, review your sheets. Are you surprised? Are you impulsively buying things, or do you tend to buy the same types of things consistently? If the latter, you'll have an easier time planning a budget than if your spending varies tremendously from day to day.

Think about the changes you need to make to put away a few dollars at the end of every week. Even if you think there's nothing to spare, try to set a small goal—even $5 a week. It will help. If you spend $3 each day on coffee and a muffin, that adds up to $15 per week and at least $60 per month. Eating breakfast at home might save you most of that amount. If you buy the newspaper at the corner store every day, consider subscribing. A subscription doesn't require the company to extend you credit; if you don't pay, they simply stop delivering.

Once you understand your spending habits and identify the changes you need to make, you're ready to make a budget. At the top of a sheet of paper, write down your monthly net income—that is, the amount you bring home after taxes and other mandatory deductions. At the left, list everything you spend money on in a month, any investments you plan to make (including into a savings or money market account), and any nondischargeable or other debts you make payments on. To the right of each item, write down the amount of money you spend, deposit, or pay each month. Finally, total up the amount. If it exceeds your monthly income, make some changes—eliminate or reduce expenditures for nonnecessities—and start over. Once your budget is final, stick to it.

When you examine your budget, you'll see that some of the things you spend money on are essential—and some are not. Essential items might include your rent or mortgage payments, taxes, utilities, child support, car payments, payments on other collateral (such as furniture or a boat), and medical and auto insurance. If you can, it's a good idea to prepay these essential items—in order of importance—for as long a period as possible. The more essential items you can prepay, the less you have to worry about going over your budget. For example, if you have paid several months of rent in advance, you won't have to worry about coming up with that money for several months.

Of course, the wisdom of prepaying debts depends on the prevailing interest rate, which determines how much you can make by keeping your money rather than spending it to pay off bills early. If the prevailing interest rate is 12%, then you may be losing some significant cash by prepaying your debts instead of keeping that money in the bank. If, on the other hand, the interest rate is closer to 5% or 6%, you won't lose much by prepaying your debts—and you'll gain plenty of peace of mind.

Keep Your Credit Report Accurate

When you apply for credit, the creditor will contact a credit reporting agency (also called a credit bureau) and request a copy of your credit report. The information in the report—and the numerical score the agency computes from that information—is used by creditors to decide whether to grant or deny your credit requests. In addition, some insurance companies, landlords, and employers obtain credit reports when evaluating potential insurance policyholders, tenants, or employees.

To make sure that creditors and others who use your credit report see you in the best light, you should keep incorrect and outdated information out of your credit report, and get current positive information into your report.

Start by obtaining a copy of your report from each of the "big three" reporting agencies (Equifax, Experian, and TransUnion). You are entitled to a free copy of your report from each agency every 12 months. To get your copies, go to www.annualcreditreport.com. You can get your reports online, by phone (877-322-8228), or by mail. To get reports by mail, you must submit

Daily Expenses

Date: _____8/1_____

Item	Cost
coffee	1.20
paper	.35
lunch	6.16
toll	3.00
rent	650.00
Daily Total	660.71

Date: _____8/2_____

Item	Cost
coffee	2.75
paper	.35
toll	3.00
CD	17.58
Daily Total	23.68

Date: _____8/3_____

Item	Cost
coffee	1.20
paper	.35
lunch	8.00
hardware—light switches	3.00
fabric—sewing gadgets	19.06
toll	3.00
Daily Total	34.61

Date: _____8/4_____

Item	Cost
brunch	11.50
haircut	25.00
movie rental	2.99
Daily Total	39.49

Avoiding Financial Problems

These nine rules, suggested by people who have been through bankruptcy, will help you stay out of financial hot water.

1. Create a realistic budget and stick to it.

2. Don't buy on impulse. When you see something you hadn't planned to purchase, go home and think it over. It's unlikely you'll return to the store and buy it.

3. Avoid sales unless you are looking for something you absolutely need. Buying a $500 item on sale for $400 isn't a $100 savings if you didn't need the item in the first place—it's spending $400 unnecessarily.

4. Get medical insurance. You can't avoid medical emergencies, but living without medical insurance is an invitation to financial ruin.

5. Charge items only if you could pay for them now. Don't charge based on future income—sometimes that income doesn't materialize.

6. Avoid large house payments. Obligate yourself only for what you can now afford and increase your mortgage payments only as your income increases. Again, don't obligate yourself based on future income that you might not have.

7. Think long and hard before agreeing to cosign or guarantee a loan for someone. Your signature obligates you as if you were the primary borrower. You can't be sure that the other person will pay.

8. If possible, avoid joint obligations with people who have questionable spending habits. If you incur a joint debt, you're probably liable for it all if the other person defaults.

9. Avoid high-risk investments, such as speculative real estate, penny stocks, and junk bonds. Invest conservatively in things such as certificates of deposit, money market funds, and government bonds. And never invest more than you can afford to lose.

a written request form, which you can download from the website, and send it to Annual Credit Report Request Service, P.O. Box 105281, Atlanta, GA 30348-5281.

In addition to your credit history, your credit report will contain the sources of the information and the names of people who have received your report within the last year, or within the last two years if those people sought your report for employment reasons.

Credit reports can contain negative information for up to seven years, except for bankruptcy filings, which can stay for ten. As mentioned earlier, most credit bureaus report Chapter 13 bankruptcies for only seven years. You will want to challenge outdated, as well as incorrect or incomplete, information. The bureau must investigate the accuracy of anything you challenge within 30 days. Then the bureau must either correct it or, if it can't verify the item, remove it.

If, after the investigation, the bureau keeps information in your file you still believe is wrong, you are entitled to write a brief statement giving your side of the story, to be included in your report. Be sure the statement is tied to a particular item in your report. When the item eventually is removed from your report or corrected, the statement will be taken out. If you write a general "my life was a mess and I got into debt" statement, however, it will stay for a full seven years from the date you place it, even if the negative items come out sooner. An example of a statement is shown below.

Sample Statement to Credit Bureau

September 12, 20xx

Your records show that I am unemployed. That's incorrect. I am a self-employed cabinetmaker and carpenter. I work out of my home and take orders from people who are referred to me through various sources. My work is known in the community and that's how I earn my living.

Denny Porter
Denny Porter

The agency must give the statement, or a summary of it, to anyone who's given your credit report. In addition, if you request it, the agency must pass on a copy or summary of your statement to any person who received your report within the past year, or two years if it involved employment.

You also want to keep new negative information out of your report. To do this, remain current on your bills. What you owe, as well as how long it takes you to pay, will go in your report.

In addition to information about credit accounts, credit reports also contain information from public records, including criminal records. After receiving your bankruptcy discharge, be sure to modify public records to reflect what occurred in the bankruptcy, so wrong information won't appear in your credit report. For example, if a court case was pending against you at the time you filed for bankruptcy, and, as part of the bankruptcy, the potential judgment against you was discharged, be sure the court case is formally dismissed. You may need the help of an attorney. (See Ch. 15 for information on finding one.)

Avoid Credit Repair Agencies

You've probably seen ads for companies that claim they can fix your credit, qualify you for a loan, and get you a credit card. Stay clear of these companies. Their practices are almost always deceptive and sometimes illegal. Some steal the credit reports or Social Security numbers of people who have died or live in places like Guam or the U.S. Virgin Islands and replace your report with these other reports. Others create new identities for debtors by applying to the IRS for a taxpayer I.D. number and telling debtors to use it in place of their Social Security number (which is illegal).

Even the legitimate companies can't do anything for you that you can't do yourself. If items in your credit report are correct, these companies cannot get them removed. About the only difference between using a legitimate credit repair agency and doing it yourself is the money you save by doing it yourself.

Negotiate With Current Creditors

If you owe any debts that show up as past due on your credit report (perhaps the debt wasn't discharged in your bankruptcy or was incurred after you filed), you can take steps to make them current. Contact the creditor and ask that the item be removed in exchange for full or partial payment. On a revolving account (with a department store, for example), ask the creditor to "re-age" the account so that it is shown as current. For help in negotiating with your creditors, consider contacting a local consumer credit counseling service office.

Stabilize Your Income and Employment

Your credit history and score are not the only thing lenders will consider in deciding whether to give you credit. They also look carefully at the stability of your income and employment. Plus, if you start getting new credit before you're back on your feet financially, you'll end up in the same mess that led you to file for bankruptcy in the first place.

Get a Credit Card

Once you have your budget and some money saved, you can begin to get some positive information in your credit report. One way is to get a secured credit card. In a few years, banks and other large creditors will be more apt to grant you credit if, since your bankruptcy, you've made and paid for purchases on credit.

Some banks will give you a credit card and a line of credit if you deposit money into a savings account. In exchange, you cannot remove the money from your account. If you don't pay your bill, the bank uses the money in your account to cover what you owe. Get such a card if you truly believe you'll control any impulses to overuse it.

A major drawback with these cards is that the interest rate often nears 25%–30%. So use the card only to cash checks, buy inexpensive items you can pay for when the bill arrives, or guarantee a hotel reservation or car rental. Otherwise, you're going to pay a bundle in interest and may end up in financial trouble again.

Be sure to shop around before signing up for a secured credit card. Even though you just filed for bankruptcy, you'll probably still get lots of offers for unsecured cards in the mail. Often, these cards have better terms than do secured cards. If you do choose a secured credit card, be sure it isn't secured by your home.

CAUTION
Avoid look-alike credit cards. Some lesser-known mail-order companies issue cards that look like credit cards, but allow you to make purchases only from their own catalogues. The items in the catalogue tend to be overpriced and of mediocre (if not poor) quality. And your use of the card isn't reported to credit bureaus, so you won't be rebuilding your credit.

Borrow From a Bank

Bank loans provide an excellent way to rebuild credit. A few banks offer something called a passbook savings loan, which is a lot like a secured credit card. You deposit a sum of money into a savings account, and in exchange the bank makes you a loan. You have no access to your savings account while your loan is outstanding. If you don't repay it, the bank will use the money in your savings account. The amount you can borrow depends on how much the bank requires you to deposit.

In most cases, though, you'll have to apply for a standard bank loan. You probably won't qualify unless you bring in a cosigner, offer some property as collateral, or agree to a very high rate of interest.

Banks that offer passbook loans typically give you one to three years to repay the loan. But don't pay the loan back too soon—give it about six to nine months to appear on your credit report. Standard bank loans are paid back on a monthly schedule, usually for a year or two.

Before you take out any loan, be sure you understand the terms:

- **Interest rate.** The interest rate on the loan is usually between two and six percentage points more than what the bank charges its customers with the best credit.

- **Prepayment penalties.** Usually, you can pay the loan back as soon as you want without incurring any prepayment penalties. Prepayment penalties are fees banks sometimes charge if you pay back a loan early and the bank doesn't collect as much interest from you as it had expected. The penalty is usually a small percentage of the loan amount.

- **Whether the bank reports the loan to a credit bureau.** This is key; the whole reason you take out the loan is to rebuild your credit. You may have to make several calls to find a bank that reports the loan.

Work With a Local Merchant

Another step to consider in rebuilding your credit is to approach a local merchant, such as a jewelry or furniture store, about purchasing an item on credit. Many local stores will work with you in setting up a payment schedule, but be prepared to put down a deposit of up to 30%, pay a high rate of interest, or find someone to cosign the loan. This isn't an ideal way to rebuild your credit, but if all other lenders turn you down, it may be your only option.

Attempts to Collect Clearly Discharged Debts

If a debt was discharged in bankruptcy, the law prohibits creditors from filing a lawsuit, sending you collection letters, calling you, withholding credit, or threatening to file or actually filing a criminal complaint against you. (11 U.S.C. § 524.) If a creditor tries to collect a debt that clearly was discharged in your bankruptcy, you should respond at once with a letter like the one shown below.

The court doesn't give you a list of debts that were discharged. But you can assume a debt was discharged if you listed it in your bankruptcy papers, the creditor didn't successfully object to its discharge, and it isn't in one of the nondischargeable categories listed in Ch. 1. Also, if you live in a community property state and your spouse filed alone, you can assume that your share of the community debts was also discharged.

Letter to Creditor

1905 Fifth Road
N. Miami Beach, FL 35466

March 18, 20xx

Bank of Miami
2700 Finances Highway
Miami, FL 36678

To Whom It May Concern:

I've been contacted once by letter and once by phone by Rodney Moore of your bank. Mr. Moore claims that I owe $4,812 on Visa account number 1234 567 890 123.

As you're well aware, this debt was discharged in bankruptcy (case number 111-999 in the Western District of Tennessee) on February 1, 20xx. Thus, your collection efforts violate federal law, 11 U.S.C. § 524. If they continue, I won't hesitate to pursue my legal rights, including bringing a lawsuit against you for harassment.

Sincerely,

Dawn Schaffer

Dawn Schaffer

If the collection efforts don't immediately stop, you may want to hire a lawyer to write the creditor again—sometimes, a lawyer's letterhead gets results. If that doesn't work, you can sue the creditor for harassment. You can bring a lawsuit in state court or in the bankruptcy court. The bankruptcy court should be more familiar with the prohibitions against collection and more sympathetic to you.

If the creditor sues you over the debt, you'll want to raise the discharge as a defense and sue the creditor yourself to stop the illegal collection efforts. The court has the power to hold the creditor in contempt of court. The court may also fine the creditor for the humiliation, inconvenience, and anguish caused you and order the creditor to pay your attorney's fees. For example, a bankruptcy court in North Carolina fined a creditor $900 for attempting to collect a discharged debt. (*In re Barbour*, 77 B.R. 530 (E.D. N.C. 1987).)

If the creditor sues you (almost certainly in state court), you or your attorney can file papers requesting that the case be transferred ("removed") to the bankruptcy court.

Anticipating Postbankruptcy Debt Collections

Sometimes you can anticipate that a particular creditor will consider a debt to be nondischargeable and go after you for it after your bankruptcy case is closed. In that event, you can file an action in the bankruptcy court while your case is still open to obtain a determination of whether the debt is dischargeable. If the court rules in your favor, the creditor will be prevented from pursuing the debt in state court. How to do this is beyond the scope of this book. However, *Represent Yourself in Court*, by Bergman and Barrett (Nolo), has a chapter on the subject.

Postbankruptcy Discrimination

Although filing for bankruptcy has serious consequences, it might not be as bad as you think. There are laws that will protect you from most types of postbankruptcy discrimination by the government and by private employers.

Government Discrimination

All federal, state, and local governmental units are prohibited from discriminating against you solely because you filed for bankruptcy. (11 U.S.C. § 525(a).) This includes denying, revoking, suspending, or refusing to renew a license, permit, charter, franchise, or other similar grant. This part of the Bankruptcy Code provides important protections, but it does not insulate debtors from all adverse consequences of filing for bankruptcy. Lenders, for example, can consider a debtor's bankruptcy filing when reviewing an application for a government loan or extension of credit. (See, for example, *Watts v. Pennsylvania Housing Finance Co.*, 876 F.2d 1090 (3d Cir. 1989) and *Toth v. Michigan State Housing Development Authority*, 136 F.3d 477 (6th Cir. 1998).) Still, under this provision of the Bankruptcy Code, the government cannot:

- deny you a job or fire you
- deny you or terminate your public benefits
- evict you from public housing (although if you have a Section 8 voucher, you may not be protected)
- deny you or refuse to renew your state liquor license
- withhold your college transcript
- deny you a driver's license, or
- deny you a contract, such as a contract for a construction project.

In addition, lenders can't exclude you from participating in a government-guaranteed student loan program. (11 U.S.C. § 525(c).)

In general, once any government-related debt has been discharged, all acts against you that arise out of that debt also must end. If, for example, you lost your driver's license because you didn't pay a court judgment that resulted from a car accident, once the debt is discharged, you must be granted a license. If, however, the judgment wasn't discharged, you can still be denied your license until you pay up.

Keep in mind that only denials based solely on your bankruptcy are prohibited. You may be denied a loan, job, or apartment for reasons unrelated to the bankruptcy or for reasons related to your future creditworthiness—for example, because the government concludes you won't be able to repay a Small Business Administration loan.

Nongovernment Discrimination

Private employers may not fire you or otherwise discriminate against you solely because you filed for bankruptcy. (11 U.S.C. § 525(b).) While the Bankruptcy Code expressly prohibits employers from firing you, it is unclear whether or not the act prohibits employers from refusing to hire you because you went through bankruptcy.

Other forms of discrimination in the private sector aren't illegal. If you seek to rent an apartment and the landlord does a credit check, sees your bankruptcy, and refuses to rent to you, there's not much you can do other than try to show that you'll pay your rent and be a responsible tenant. Paying several months rent in advance can work wonders in these situations.

If you suffer illegal discrimination because of your bankruptcy, you can sue in state court or in the bankruptcy court. You'll probably need the assistance of an attorney.

Attempts to Revoke Your Discharge

In extremely rare instances, the trustee or a creditor can ask the bankruptcy court to revoke your discharge. The trustee or creditor must file a complaint within one year of your discharge.

Your discharge can be revoked only if the creditor or trustee proves that you obtained the discharge through fraud, which was discovered after your discharge. If your discharge is revoked, you'll owe your creditors as if you had not filed for bankruptcy. Any payment your creditors received from the trustee, however, will be credited against what you owe.

 SEE AN EXPERT

Help from a lawyer. If someone asks the bankruptcy court to revoke your discharge, consult a bankruptcy attorney right away.

Help Beyond the Book

lthough this book covers routine Chapter 13 bankruptcy procedures in some detail, it doesn't come close to covering everything. That would require a much longer tome, most of which would be irrelevant for nearly all readers. That said, here are some suggestions if you need more information or advice than this book provides.

The major places to go for follow-up help are:

- **Bankruptcy petition preparers,** if you're ready to file for bankruptcy, but need assistance in typing the forms and organizing them for filing in your district.
- **Lawyers,** if you want information, advice, or legal representation for some or all of your case.
- **Law libraries and the Internet,** if you want to do your own research on issues raised in the course of your bankruptcy.

Before we discuss each of these resources in more detail, here's a general piece of advice: Maintain control of your case whenever possible. By getting this book and filing for Chapter 13 bankruptcy, you've taken responsibility for your own legal affairs. If you decide to get help from others, shop around until you find someone who respects your efforts as a self-helper and recognizes your right to participate in the case as a valuable partner.

Debt Relief Agencies

Under the new bankruptcy law, any person, business, or organization that you pay or otherwise compensate for help with your bankruptcy is considered a debt relief agency—and must identify itself as such. The two main types of debt relief agencies are lawyers and bankruptcy petition preparers (BPPs). Credit-counseling agencies and budget counseling agencies are not debt relief agencies. Nor are any of the following:

- employers or employees of debt relief agencies (for instance, legal secretaries)
- nonprofit organizations that have federal 501(c)(3) tax-exempt status
- any creditor who works with you to restructure your debt
- banks, credit unions, and other deposit institut-ions, or

- an author, publisher, distributor, or seller of works subject to copyright protection when acting in that capacity (in other words, Nolo and the stores that sell its books aren't debt relief agencies).

BPPs and lawyers are covered separately below. This section explains what the new bankruptcy law requires of debt relief agencies generally, so you'll know what you can expect for your money.

Mandatory Contract

Within five days after a debt relief agency assists you, it (or he or she) must enter into a contract with you that explains, clearly and conspicuously:

- what services the agency will provide
- what the agency will charge for the services, and
- the terms of payment.

The agency must give you a copy of the completed, signed contract.

Mandatory Disclosures and Notices

Debt relief agencies must inform you, in writing, that:

- All information you are required to provide in your bankruptcy papers must be complete, accurate, and truthful.
- You must completely and accurately disclose your assets and liabilities in the documents you file to begin your case.
- You must undertake a reasonable inquiry to establish the replacement value of any item you plan to keep, before you provide that value on your forms.
- Your current monthly income and your computa-tion of projected disposable income as stated in your bankruptcy papers (if your income is more than the state median), must be based on a reasonable inquiry into their accuracy.
- Your case may be audited, and your failure to cooperate in the audit may result in dismissal of your case or some other sanction, including a possible criminal penalty.

In addition to these stark warnings—which most debt relief agencies would rather not have to give—a debt relief agency must also give you a general notice regarding some basic bankruptcy requirements and your options for help in filing and pursuing your case.

Sample Notice From Debt Relief Agency

IMPORTANT INFORMATION ABOUT BANKRUPTCY ASSISTANCE SERVICES FROM AN ATTORNEY OR BANKRUPTCY PETITION PREPARER.

If you decide to seek bankruptcy relief, you can represent yourself, you can hire an attorney to represent you, or you can get help in some localities from a bankruptcy petition preparer who is not an attorney. THE LAW REQUIRES AN ATTORNEY OR BANKRUPTCY PETITION PREPARER TO GIVE YOU A WRITTEN CONTRACT SPECIFYING WHAT THE ATTORNEY OR BANKRUPTCY PETITION PREPARER WILL DO FOR YOU AND HOW MUCH IT WILL COST. Ask to see the contract before you hire anyone.

The following information helps you understand what must be done in a routine bankruptcy case to help you evaluate how much service you need. Although bankruptcy can be complex, many cases are routine.

Before filing a bankruptcy case, either you or your attorney should analyze your eligibility for different forms of debt relief available under the Bankruptcy Code and which form of relief is most likely to be beneficial for you. Be sure you understand the relief you can obtain and its limitations. To file a bankruptcy case, documents called a Petition, Schedules and Statement of Financial Affairs, as well as in some cases a Statement of Intention need to be prepared correctly and filed with the bankruptcy court. You will have to pay a filing fee to the bankruptcy court. Once your case starts, you will have to attend the required first meeting of creditors where you may be questioned by your creditors.

If you choose to file a chapter 7 case, you may be asked by a creditor to reaffirm a debt. You may want help deciding whether to do so. A creditor is not permitted to coerce you into reaffirming your debts.

If you choose to file a chapter 13 case in which you repay your creditors what you can afford over 3 to 5 years, you may also want help with preparing your chapter 13 plan and with the confirmation hearing on your plan which will be before a bankruptcy judge.

If you select another type of relief under the Bankruptcy Code other than chapter 7 or chapter 13, you will want to find out what should be done from someone familiar with that type of relief.

Your bankruptcy case may also involve litigation. You are generally permitted to represent yourself in litigation in bankruptcy court, but only attorneys, not bankruptcy petition preparers, can give you legal advice.

Here is the notice that you can expect to receive from any debt relief agency within three business days after the agency first offers to provide you with services. Failure to give you this notice—in a timely manner—can land the agency in big trouble.

Finally, every debt relief agency has to give you some plain-English written information about the basic tasks associated with most bankruptcies, such as how to deal with secured debts and choose exemptions. Ideally, debt relief agencies would freely distribute this book, which has all of the information required (and much more, of course).

Restrictions on Debt Relief Agencies

Under the new law, a debt relief agency may not:

- fail to perform any service that the agency informed you it would perform in connection with your bankruptcy case
- counsel you to make any statement in a document that is untrue and misleading or that the agency should have known was untrue or misleading, or
- advise you to incur more debt in order to pay for the agency's services (for instance, accepting a credit card or steering you to a cash advance business).

Any contract that doesn't comply with the new requirements on debt relief agencies may not be enforced against you. A debt relief agency is liable to you for costs and fees, including legal fees, if the agency negligently or intentionally:

- fails to comply with the new law's restrictions on debt relief agencies, or
- fails to file a document that results in dismissal of your case or conversion to another bankruptcy chapter.

In sum, debt relief agencies are on the hook if they are negligent in performing the services required by the bankruptcy law or other services they have agreed to provide.

Bankruptcy Petition Preparers

Even though you should be able to handle routine bankruptcy procedures yourself, you may want someone familiar with the bankruptcy forms and courts in your area to use a computer to enter your data in the official forms and print them out for filing with the court. For this level of assistance—routine form preparation and organization—consider using a bankruptcy petition preparer (BPP).

Limits on Bankruptcy Petition Preparers

BPPs are very different from lawyers. BPPs are legally prohibited from giving you legal advice, which includes a lot of the information in this book, such as:

- whether to file a bankruptcy petition or which Chapter (7, 11, 12, or 13) is appropriate
- whether your debts will be discharged under a particular Chapter
- whether you will be able to hang on to your home or other property if you file under a particular Chapter (that is, which exemptions you should choose)
- information about the tax consequences of a case brought under a particular Chapter or whether tax claims in your case can be discharged
- whether you should offer to repay or agree to reaffirm a debt
- how to characterize the nature of your interest in property or debts, and
- information about bankruptcy procedures and rights.

Most important, BPPs cannot tell you how to draft your Chapter 13 repayment plan. Even if you hire a BPP to help you with the rest of your paperwork, you may need at least some help from a lawyer to draft your plan.

Fees

All fees charged by debt relief agencies are reviewed by the U.S. Trustee for reasonableness. However, unlike lawyers' fees, which can vary widely according to the circumstances, a BPP's fees are subject to a strict cap, somewhere between $100 and $200, depending on the district. The rationale offered by the U.S. Trustee for this cap—and by the courts that have upheld it—is that BPP fees can be set according to what general typists charge per page in the community. Because BPPs aren't supposed to be doing anything other than "typing" the forms, the argument goes, they shouldn't be able to charge rates for professional services.

Rates allowed for BPPs are far less than lawyers charge. For that reason, BPPs are a good choice for people who want some help getting their basic Chapter 13 forms typed and organized in a way that will please the court clerk.

How Bankruptcy Petition Preparers Are Regulated

Anyone can be a BPP. Yes, anyone. There is nothing in the bankruptcy code that requires BPPs to have any particular level of education, training, or experience. Unlike most other jobs, a prison record is no handicap to becoming a BPP. How, then, are BPPs regulated? Regulation is provided by the U.S. Trustee's office, which reviews all bankruptcy petitions prepared by a BPP. BPPs must provide their name, address, telephone number, and Social Security number on the bankruptcy petition, as well as on every other bankruptcy document they prepare. The U.S. Trustee uses this information to keep tabs on BPPs.

BPPs are also regulated at the creditors' meeting, where the bankruptcy trustee can ask you about the manner in which the BPP conducts his or her business. For instance, if you are representing yourself, the trustee might ask how you got the information necessary to choose your exemptions (see Ch. 3) or decide which bankruptcy Chapter to use.

If the BPP provided you with this information, the trustee may refer the case to the U.S. Trustee's office and the BPP will be hauled into court to explain why he or she violated the rules against giving legal advice. The BPP may be forced to return the fee you paid and may even be banned from practicing as a BPP, if it's not the first offense. None of this will have any effect on your case, however, other than the inconvenience of being dragged into court.

BPPs can be fined for certain actions and inactions spelled out in the Bankruptcy Code (11 U.S.C. § 110). These are:

- failing to put their name, address, and Social Security number on your bankruptcy petition
- failing to give you a copy of your bankruptcy documents when you sign them

- using the word "legal" or any similar term in advertisements, or advertising under a category that includes such terms, and
- accepting court filing fees from you—you must pay the filing fee to the court yourself or, in some districts, give the BPP a cashier's check made out to the court.

Finally, under the new law, BPPs must submit a statement under oath with each petition they prepare stating how much you paid them in the previous 12 months and any fees that you owe them but haven't yet paid them. If they charge more than they are permitted, they will be ordered to return the excess fees to you.

If a BPP engages in any fraudulent act in regard to your case or fails to comply with the rules governing their behavior listed above, he or she may be required to return your entire fee as well as pay a $500 fine for each transgression. If they engage in serious fraud, they may be fined up to $2,000 and triple your fee, and even be ordered to cease providing BPP services. Simply put, fraudulent BPPs (those who would take your money without providing promised services or counsel you to play fast and loose with the bankruptcy system) are likely to be weeded out in a hurry.

Can BPPs Give You Written Information?

Under the Bankruptcy Code, BPPs are supposed to prepare your bankruptcy forms under your direction. This means you are supposed to tell the BPP what exemptions to choose, whether to file under Chapter 7 or Chapter 13, what approach to take in respect to your secured debts (car note, mortgage) and what values to place on your property. That's fine in theory, but unless you have the benefit of this book or another source of legal information, there is no way you would have adequate bankruptcy expertise to tell the BPP how to proceed. In an attempt to bridge this gap, many BPPs hand their customers written materials that contain all the information their customers need to direct the case. Unfortunately, providing a customer with written legal information about bankruptcy has itself been held to be the unauthorized practice of law in many states (California is an important exception). Whether these holdings will continue under the new bankruptcy law remains to be seen.

How to Find Bankruptcy Petition Preparers

BPP services are springing up all over the country to help people who don't want or can't afford to hire a lawyer, but you're still more likely to find a BPP if you live on the West Coast. The best way to find a reputable BPP in your area is to get a recommendation from someone who has used a particular BPP and been satisfied with his or her work.

BPPs sometimes advertise in classified sections of local newspapers and in the yellow pages. You may have to look hard to spot their ads, however, because they go by different names in different states. In California, your best bet is to find a legal document assistant (the official name given to independent paralegals in California) who also provide BPP services. Check the website maintained by the California Association of Legal Document Assistants (www.calda.org). In Arizona, hunt for a legal document preparer. In other states, especially Florida, search for paralegals who directly serve the public (often termed independent paralegals or legal technicians). In many states, an independent paralegal franchise called We the People offers BPP services.

Some BPPs Don't Prepare Chapter 13 Paperwork

As a general rule, BPPs don't often work on Chapter 13 cases. Because there are strict limits on the fees a BPP can charge, BPPs are unable to earn a profit from working on Chapter 13 bankruptcies. Also, BPPs are not legally allowed to draft Chapter 13 plans—such work is considered to be practicing law, and therefore reserved only for attorneys—and few of their clients are able to draft a plan on their own. If you are using this book and assure the BPP that you can draft your own plan, the BPP might be willing to prepare the rest of your paperwork, however.

Combining Lawyers and Bankruptcy Petition Preparers

In California and some other parts of the country, it is possible to use a BPP to grind out your paperwork and a lawyer to provide you with all the legal savvy you need to direct your own case. Under this arrangement, you are still representing yourself, but you are combining legal and secretarial resources to get the job done. This is what is known as unbundled legal service, where you hire an attorney for a discrete task (legal advice in this case) rather than for the whole enchilada we know as "legal representation." For example, the National Bankruptcy Law Project offers folks using a BPP the services of a knowledgeable lawyer for a flat fee for all questions related to the bankruptcy. This works a little like prepaid insurance. However, you don't pay for the service until it is clear that you need an attorney, and the service is very specialized. For more information on how this type of service works, see "Unbundled Services," below. For information on the services offered by the National Bankruptcy Law Project, go to www.bankruptcylawproject.com.

A Bankruptcy Petition Preparer Cannot Represent You

If you decide to use a BPP, remember that you are representing yourself and are responsible for the outcome of your case. This means not only learning about your rights under the bankruptcy law and understanding the proper procedures to be followed, but also accepting responsibility for correctly and accurately filling in the bankruptcy petition and schedules and preparing a confirmable Chapter 13 repayment plan. The point is, unless you hire a lawyer to represent you, you are solely responsible for acquiring the information necessary to competently pursue your case.

Bankruptcy Lawyers

Bankruptcy lawyers (a type of debt relief agency under the law) are regular lawyers who specialize in handling bankruptcy cases. Under the old law, it was usually possible to find an affordable bankruptcy lawyer who would provide at least a minimal level of representation throughout your case. However, for the reasons discussed below, lawyers are charging more to represent clients in bankruptcies filed under the new law.

If you aren't represented by a lawyer but want to file for bankruptcy, you will need to represent yourself. While this will involve a fair amount of work—much more than under the old law—it is certainly possible. And there is help available for you. In addition to books published by Nolo, you can use a combination of bankruptcy petition preparers and telephone legal advice from a lawyer to help you over the clerical and legal humps and get you through the process in reasonably good shape—for far less than a lawyer would charge to represent you.

Full-Service Lawyer Representation

In a general sense, you are represented by a lawyer if you contract with the lawyer to handle some or all of your bankruptcy case for you. More specifically, there are two types of representation—the type where you hire a lawyer to assume complete responsibility for your bankruptcy, and the type where you represent yourself but hire a lawyer to handle one particular aspect of your bankruptcy case. We refer to the first type of representation as "full-service representation" and the second type of representation as unbundled services (discussed below).

When providing full-service representation, a bankruptcy lawyer is responsible for making sure that all of your paperwork is filed on time, that the information in your paperwork is accurate, and that you propose a repayment plan the judge will confirm. These duties require the lawyer to review various documents—for instance, your credit report, tax returns, and home value appraisal—both to assure the accuracy of your paperwork and to make sure that you are filing for bankruptcy under the appropriate chapter.

In exchange for their basic fee, full-service bankruptcy lawyers also are typically responsible for appearing on your behalf at the creditors' meeting and confirmation hearing, representing you if a creditor objects to your plan or opposes the discharge of a debt, and eliminating any liens that the bankruptcy laws allow to be stripped from your property.

Often, it will be very clear from the start that you will be able to draft your own repayment plan (with the help of Ch. 8) and that there are no complications—such as a lien that must be stripped from your property—that require the skills of a lawyer. In this situation, you can get by with the help of this book and, if you wish, other support resources described in this chapter.

In many Chapter 13 cases, however, the opposite is true: Either you cannot put together a confirmable repayment plan in the court's required format, or you can tell from the very beginning that you—or an attorney representing you—will have to appear before a bankruptcy judge several times to keep your bankruptcy on track and fully assert your rights under the bankruptcy laws. And that can be intimidating. For instance, if you want to discharge a student loan, you might want to hire a full-service attorney at the very beginning of your case. As a general rule, you might also consider hiring a full-service lawyer at the beginning of your case if you know that you will need to prepare custom-made court papers (for which there aren't any official forms) or to negotiate with creditors in situations where a lot is at stake and you don't have confidence in your own negotiating skills.

Lawyers Can Amend Your Paperwork

Despite your best efforts to represent yourself, there may come a time when you realize that you are in over your head. If this happens, it is most likely to take place at the Chapter 13 confirmation hearing—the first time you appear before a judge. The judge might make it painfully clear that you are going to need a lawyer's help if you want to continue with your case.

Fortunately, the bankruptcy rules make it very easy to amend your paperwork—and your repayment plan—if necessary. Don't be afraid to consult with a lawyer about your case, if you feel like you need help. If you decide to hire the lawyer to take over, he or she can make any necessary amendments. Also, you can pay the lawyer's fees as part of your repayment plan, rather than having to come up with the whole fee up front.

Sometimes, a case appears to be simple at the beginning but turns out to be complicated later on. In that event, you might start out representing yourself but later decide to hire an attorney to handle a tricky issue that arises. (See "Unbundled Services," below, for more on hiring a lawyer on a limited basis.)

Because full-service lawyer duties for even a simple bankruptcy case have drastically increased under the new bankruptcy law, typical lawyer fees have gone way up. For this reason, many people who would have used lawyers in the past will now be forced to represent themselves—with or without the help of outside resources. And many readers of this book are likely to find themselves in this boat.

Unbundled Services

As mentioned earlier, the recent changes in bankruptcy law means that many people who would have hired a full-service lawyer in the past will now have to represent themselves. However, this doesn't mean that they can't get a lawyer to help out with some aspect of the case. Since the 1990s, lawyers have been increasingly willing to offer their services on a piecemeal basis and provide legal advice over the telephone and Internet to help people who are representing themselves. In bankruptcy cases, lawyers are increasingly willing to step in and handle a particular matter, such as stripping liens from your property or handling a dischargeability action brought by you or a creditor.

When lawyers do specific jobs at a client's request but don't contract for full-service representation in the underlying case, they are said to be providing an unbundled service. For example, you may be able to hire an attorney to handle a specific procedure—such as drafting a confirmable repayment plan or defending against a motion for relief from stay—while you handle the main part of the bankruptcy yourself.

Few cases discuss the boundaries of unbundled services. Some courts have held that attorneys can't "ghostwrite" legal documents for nonlawyers—because that would be a type of fraud on the court—but the issue has not been decided by most courts. Also, nothing prevents a lawyer from appearing for you in a limited capacity and putting his or her own name on associated documents.

Lawyers providing unbundled services usually charge an hourly fee. As a general rule, you should bring an attorney into the case for an unbundled service only if the service is necessary for your bankruptcy to succeed (for example, drafting a confirmable repayment plan) or involves something valuable enough to justify the attorney's fees. If a creditor objects to the discharge of a $500 debt, and it will cost you $400 to hire an attorney, you may be better off trying to handle the matter yourself, even though this increases the risk that the creditor will win. If, however, the dispute is worth $2,000 and the attorney will cost you $400, hiring the attorney makes better sense.

Unfortunately, some bankruptcy attorneys do not like to appear or do paperwork on a piecemeal basis. Justified or not, these attorneys believe that by doing a little work for you, they might be on the hook if something goes wrong in another part of your case—that is, if they are in for a penny, they are in for a pound. Also, the bar associations of some states frown on unbundled services on ethical grounds. On the other hand, a number of other state bar associations are starting to encourage their attorneys to offer unbundled services simply because so many people—even middle-income people—are unable to afford full representation.

Bankruptcy Consultants

Under the old bankruptcy law, many people were able to represent themselves with a Nolo book as their main source of information. Bankruptcy under the new law is more complex, but in many cases, it's still just a matter of knowing what to put in the forms and what forms to file. For many people, however, a book just won't do the trick, no matter how well written and complete: You want to talk to a human being. Because of unauthorized practice laws and restrictions in the bankruptcy law, however, there is only one kind of human being who is authorized to answer your questions about bankruptcy law and procedure—a lawyer.

Fortunately, there are lawyers who provide bankruptcy consultations (a category of unbundled service) for a transaction fee (for example, a $39.95 flat rate) or a fee based on the amount of time your call takes (for example, $3 a minute). There are also free consultations offered by private attorneys and bar associations. Similar services—free and paid—are available on the Internet. To find a telephonic or online consultation service, in addition to those mentioned here, go to Google or another search engine and look for "bankruptcy legal advice telephone or Internet."

Even if you use a BPP to prepare your paperwork, and are using this book, you may wish to talk to a lawyer to get the information you need to make your own choices and tell the BPP what you want in your papers. For instance, a BPP can't choose your exemptions for you, because that would be considered the practice of law—something only lawyers can do. However, a lawyer can help you decide which exemptions to pick so you can tell the BPP what to put in the form that lists your exemptions.

As with other debt relief agencies, lawyers offering telephonic services are considered debt relief agencies and will have to offer you a contract detailing their services and provide the other notices described in "Debt Relief Agencies," above.

How to Find a Bankruptcy Lawyer

Where there's a bankruptcy court, there are bankruptcy lawyers. They're listed in the yellow pages under "Attorneys," and often advertise in newspapers. You should use an experienced bankruptcy lawyer, not a general practitioner, to advise you or handle matters associated with bankruptcy.

There are several ways to find the best bankruptcy lawyer for your job:

- **Personal referrals.** This is your best approach. If you know someone who was pleased with the services of a bankruptcy lawyer, call that lawyer first.
- **Bankruptcy petition preparers.** If there's a BPP in your area, he or she may know some bankruptcy attorneys who are both competent and sympathetic to self-helpers. It is here that you are most likely to find a good referral to attorneys who are willing to deliver unbundled services, including advice over the telephone.
- **Legal Aid.** Legal Aid offices are partially funded by the federal Legal Services Corporation and offer legal assistance in many areas. A few offices may do bankruptcies, although most do not. To qualify for Legal Aid, you must have a very low income.
- **Legal clinics.** Many law schools sponsor legal clinics and provide free legal advice to consumers. Some legal clinics have the same income requirements as Legal Aid; others offer free services to low- and moderate-income people.
- **Group legal plans.** If you're a member of a plan that provides free or low-cost legal assistance and the plan covers bankruptcies, make that your first stop in looking for a lawyer.
- **Lawyer-referral panels**. Most county bar associations will give you the names of bankruptcy attorneys who practice in your area. But bar associations may not provide much screening. Take the time to check out the credentials and experience of the person to whom you're referred.
- **Internet directories.** Both bar associations and private companies provide lists of bankruptcy lawyers on the Internet, with a lot more information about the lawyer than you're likely to get in a yellow pages ad. One good place to start is Nolo's lawyer directory, at http://lawyers.nolo.com. We provide a variety of information on listed lawyers. Simply select "bankruptcy" and enter your zip code to get started. Also, check out www.legalconsumer.com, a site that provides a variety of free services and information, including bankruptcy lawyer listings by zip code.

TIP

Look for a member of the National Association of Consumer Bankruptcy Attorneys. Because of the massive changes enacted by the new bankruptcy law, you will want to find an attorney who has a means of keeping up to date and communicating with other bankruptcy lawyers. Membership in the National Association of Consumer Bankruptcy Attorneys (NACBA) is a good sign that your lawyer will be tuned in to the nuances of the new law and the court interpretations of the law that are sure to come.

Fees

For a routine Chapter 13 bankruptcy, a full-service lawyer will likely charge you somewhere between $2,500 and $4,000 (plus the $274 filing fee and the fees you'll have to pay for credit counseling and personal debt management counseling, about $50 each).

Some lawyers allow you to pay the full fee through your repayment plan, without paying anything up front. Other lawyers require an initial payment—for example, $1,000—and let you pay the rest through your plan. A lawyer might decide how you should pay by considering the likelihood that your plan will be confirmed and you will be able to complete it. For example, if you clearly have enough income to cover your mandatory debts and you are filing for Chapter 13 to save your home, the lawyer might charge only a minimal initial fee, because you are likely to complete your plan and finish paying the fee that way. On the other hand, if you barely have enough income to propose a confirmable plan and you don't own a home, the lawyer might be skeptical of your ability to complete the plan—and might demand the entire fee up front.

On your bankruptcy papers, you must state the amount you are paying your bankruptcy lawyer. Because every penny you pay to a bankruptcy lawyer is a penny not available to your creditors (at least in theory), the court has the legal authority to make the attorney justify his or her fee. This rarely happens, however, because attorneys know the range of fees generally allowed by local bankruptcy judges, and set their fees accordingly. This means that you probably won't find much variation in the amounts charged by lawyers in your area (although it never hurts to shop around).

Bankruptcy Lawyer Fees Are Not Fixed

Despite what many believe, bankruptcy lawyer fees are not fixed—individual lawyers are free to decide what to charge, based on what services you want and how complicated your case is likely to be. This is why it pays to shop around: You are likely to hear a range of fee quotes and options for payment.

The scope and range of services that the attorney promises you in return for your initial fee will be listed in what's called a "Rule 2016 Attorney Fee Disclosure Form." This form is filed as part of your bankruptcy papers. In the typical Chapter 13 case, the attorney's fee will include the routine tasks associated with a bankruptcy filing: counseling, preparing bankruptcy and forms, drafting your repayment plan, and attending the creditors' meeting and confirmation hearing. Any task not included in the Rule 2016 disclosure form is subject to a separate fee.

If your case will likely require more attorney time, you may—and probably will—be charged extra, according to the attorney's hourly fee or other criteria he or she uses. A typical bankruptcy attorney charges between $200 and $300 an hour (rural and urban) and would charge a minimum of roughly $400 to $600 for a court appearance. Some attorneys will add these fees to their standard fee and require you to pay it all in advance. For instance, if the attorney's standard fee is $1,400, but the attorney sees extra work down the line, you may be charged $2,000 or even $2,500 in anticipation of the additional hours.

Other attorneys will happily just charge you their standard fee up front and wait until after you file to charge you for the extra work. Because these fees are earned after your bankruptcy filing, they won't be discharged in your bankruptcy and the attorney need not collect them up front; they will be added to your plan payments. However the attorney charges you, you are protected against fee gouging. An attorney must file a supplemental Rule 2016 form to obtain the court's permission for any postfiling fees.

What to Look for in a Lawyer

No matter how you find a lawyer, these three suggestions will help you make sure you have the best possible working relationship.

First, fight any urge you may have to surrender to, or be intimidated by, the lawyer. You should be the one who decides what you feel comfortable doing about your legal and financial affairs. Keep in mind that you're hiring the lawyer to perform a service for you, so shop around if the price or personality isn't right.

Second, make sure you have good "chemistry" with any lawyer you hire. When making an appointment, ask to talk directly to the lawyer. If you can't, this may give you a hint as to how accessible he or she is. Of course, if you're told that a paralegal will be handling the routine aspects of your case under the supervision of a lawyer, you may be satisfied with that arrangement. If you do talk directly, ask some specific questions. Do you get clear, concise answers? If not, try someone else. Also pay attention to how the lawyer responds to your knowledge. If you've read this book, you're already better informed than most clients (and some lawyers are threatened by clients who have done their homework).

Finally, once you find a lawyer you like, make an hour-long appointment to discuss your situation fully. The lawyer or a paralegal in the lawyer's office will tell you what to bring to the meeting, if anything (if not, be sure to ask ahead of time). Some lawyers will want to see a recent credit report and tax return, while others will send you a questionnaire to complete prior to your visit. Depending on the circumstances, you may also be asked to bring your bills and documents pertaining to your home and other real estate you own. Some lawyers prefer not to deal with details during the first visit, and will simply ask you to come as you are.

Your main goal at the initial conference is to find out what the lawyer recommends in your particular case and how much it will cost. Go home and think about the lawyer's suggestions. If they don't make sense or you have other reservations, call someone else.

Legal Research

Legal research can vary from the very simple to the hopelessly complex. In this section, we are staying on the simple side. If you would like to learn more about legal research or if you find that our suggestions come up a bit short in your particular case, we recommend that you obtain a copy of *Legal Research: How to Find & Understand the Law*, by Stephen Elias and Susan Levinkind (Nolo), which provides a plain-English tutorial on legal research in the law library and on the Internet.

Sources of Bankruptcy Law

Bankruptcy law comes from a variety of sources:
- federal bankruptcy statutes passed by Congress
- federal rules about bankruptcy procedure issued by a federal judicial agency
- local rules issued by individual bankruptcy courts
- federal and bankruptcy court cases applying bankruptcy laws to specific disputes
- laws (statutes) passed by state legislatures that define the property you can keep in bankruptcy, and

- state court cases interpreting state exemption statutes.

Not so long ago, you would have had to visit a law library to find these resources. Now you can find most of them on the Internet. However, if you are able to visit a decent-sized law library, your research will be the better for it. Using actual books allows you to more easily find and read relevant court interpretations of the underlying statutes and rules—which are crucial to getting a clear picture of what the laws and rules really mean.

How to Use Law Libraries

Law libraries that are open to the public are most often found in and around courthouses. Law schools also frequently admit the public at least some of the time (typically not during exam time, over the summer, or during other breaks in the academic year).

If you're using a library as a member of the public, find a way to feel at home, even if it seems that the library is run mostly to serve members of the legal community: law students, judges, lawyers, and paralegals. Almost without exception, law libraries come with law librarians. The law librarians will be helpful as long as you ask them the right questions. For example, the law librarians will help you find specific library resources (for instance, where you can find the federal bankruptcy statutes or rules), but they normally won't teach you the ins and outs of legal research. Nor will they give an opinion about what a law means, how you should deal with the court, or how your particular question should be answered. For instance, if you want to find a state case interpreting a particular exemption, the law librarian will show you where your state code is located on the shelves and may even point out the volumes that contain the exemptions. The librarian won't, however, help you interpret the exemption, apply the exemption to your specific facts, or tell you how to raise the exemption in your bankruptcy case. Nor is the librarian likely to tell you what additional research steps you can or should take. When it comes to legal research in the law library, self help is the order of the day.

There is another important reason to visit the law library. Many have computer terminals that offer access to one or both of the major online legal research libraries: Westlaw and LexisNexis. With proper training, you can find just about anything in these online libraries that you could find in the law library itself. In fact, some libraries have started replacing hardcopy books with online materials, to save money and space. When visiting your local library, ask the librarian whether it has access to Westlaw or Lexis and, if so, for some tips on using the bankruptcy materials the online library carries. For example, Westlaw offers a set of materials under a tab called "Bankruptcy Practitioner," with forms, cases, articles, and treatises, all searchable by key words. Learning how to use these materials will be an enormous timesaver in your research.

Below, we show you how to get to the resources you'll most likely be using, whether you are doing your research on the Internet or in the law library.

Bankruptcy Background Materials: Overviews, Encyclopedias, and Treatises

Before digging into the primary law sources (statutes, rules, cases, and so on) that we discuss below, you may want to do some background reading to get a firm grasp of your issue or question.

The Internet

A number of Internet sites contain large collections of articles written by experts about various aspects of bankruptcy. A good starting place is Nolo's website, at www.nolo.com (click the "Property and Money" tab to get started). Our next favorite jumping-off site for this type of research is The Bankruptcy Law Trove page at www.lawtrove.com/bankruptcy. You might also want to visit www.bankruptcyfinder.com, a comprehensive site that provides links to hundreds of bankruptcy articles, reference materials, statutes, and more.

If you are using Westlaw at your local library, head for the information under the tab "Bankruptcy Practitioner."

The Law Library

Providing you with a good treatise or encyclopedia discussion of bankruptcy is where the law library shines. You can find these materials in hardcopy, or on the Westlaw or Lexis online research libraries.

Collier on Bankruptcy

It's a good idea to get an overview of your subject before trying to find a precise answer to a precise question. The best way to do this is to find a general commentary on your subject by a bankruptcy expert. For example, if you want to find out whether a particular debt is nondischargeable, you should start by reading a general discussion about the type of debt you're dealing with. Or, if you don't know whether you're entitled to claim certain property as exempt, a good overview of your state's exemptions would get you started on the right track.

The most complete source of this type of background information is a set of books known as *Collier on Bankruptcy*, by Lawrence P. King, et al. (Matthew Bender). It's available in virtually all law libraries. *Collier* is both incredibly thorough and meticulously up to date; semiannual supplements, with all the latest developments, are in the front of each volume. In addition to comments on every aspect of bankruptcy law, *Collier* contains the bankruptcy statutes, rules, and exemption lists for every state.

Collier is organized according to the bankruptcy statutes. This means that the quickest way to find information in it is to know what statute you're looking for. (See the Bankruptcy Code sections set out below.) If you still can't figure out the governing statute, start with the *Collier* subject-matter index. Be warned, however, that the index can be difficult to use because it contains a lot of bankruptcy jargon you may be unfamiliar with. A legal dictionary will be available in the library.

Bankruptcy (The Rutter Group)

This is a four-volume set of looseleaf binders that covers every aspect of bankruptcy. Although these books are written for lawyers, they aren't too difficult to understand and use. You'll find information on exemptions, Chapter 13 plans, lien stripping, filing and opposing motions, and much more. The books are geared especially for those in California, and include numerous forms.

Other Background Resources

For general discussions of bankruptcy issues, there are several other good places to start. An excellent all-around resource is called *Consumer Bankruptcy Law and Practice*. This volume, published by the National Consumer Law Center, is updated every year. It contains a complete discussion of Chapter 13 bankruptcy procedures, the official bankruptcy forms, and a marvelous bibliography.

Another good treatise is a legal encyclopedia called *American Jurisprudence*, 2nd Series. Almost all law libraries carry it. The article on bankruptcy has an extensive table of contents, and the entire encyclopedia has an index. Between these two tools, you should be able to zero in on helpful material. Finally, some large and well-stocked law libraries carry a looseleaf publication known as the Commerce Clearing House (CCH) *Bankruptcy Law Reporter* (BLR). In this publication, you can find all three primary source materials relating to bankruptcy: statutes, rules, and cases.

If you are looking for information on adversary proceedings (such as how to defend against a creditor's challenge to the dischargeability of a debt), turn to *Represent Yourself in Court*, by Paul Bergman and Sara J. Berman-Barrett (Nolo). It has an entire chapter on representing yourself in adversary proceedings in bankruptcy court. If you need information on court procedures or the local rules of a specific court, consult the *Collier Bankruptcy Practice Manual*.

Finding Federal Bankruptcy Statutes

Title 11 of the United States Code contains all the statutes that govern your bankruptcy.

The Internet

You can find the complete Bankruptcy Code online, free. One of our favorite legal research resources, the Legal Information Institute of Cornell University Law School, lets you browse laws by subject matter and also offers a keyword search. To find the Bankruptcy Code, go to www.law.cornell.edu, select "U.S. Code" from the menu available under the "Constitutions and Codes" tab, then select Title 11. Use the table below to find the code sections you need.

Bankruptcy Code Sections (11 U.S.C.)	
§ 101	Definitions
§ 109	Who May File for Which Type of Bankruptcy; Credit Counseling Requirements
§ 110	Rules for Bankruptcy Petition Preparers
§ 111	Budget and Credit Counseling Agencies
§ 302	Who Can File Joint Cases
§ 326	How Trustees Are Compensated
§ 332	Consumer Privacy Ombudsmen
§ 341	Meeting of Creditors
§ 342	Notice of Creditors' Meeting; Informational Notice to Debtors; Requirements for Notice by Debtors
§ 343	Examination of Debtor at Creditors' Meeting
§ 348	Converting From One Type of Bankruptcy to Another
§ 349	Dismissing a Case
§ 350	Closing and Reopening a Case
§ 362	The Automatic Stay
§ 365	How Leases and Executory Contracts Are Treated in Bankruptcy
§ 366	Continuing or Reconnecting Utility Service
§ 501	Filing of Creditors' Claims
§ 506	Allowed Secured Claims and Lien Avoidance
§ 507	Priority Claims
§ 521	Paperwork Requirements and Deadlines
§ 522	Exemptions; Residency Requirements for Homestead Exemption; Stripping Liens From Property
§ 523	Nondischargeable Debts
§ 524	Effect of Discharge and Reaffirmation of Debts
§ 525	Prohibited Post-Bankruptcy Discrimination
§ 526	Restrictions on Debt Relief Agencies
§ 527	Required Disclosures by Debt Relief Agencies
§ 528	Requirements for Debt Relief Agencies
§ 541	What Property Is Part of the Bankruptcy Estate
§ 547	Preferences
§ 548	Fraudulent Transfers
§ 554	Trustee's Abandonment of Property in the Bankruptcy Estate
§ 707	The Means Test
§ 1301	Stay of Action Against Codebtor
§ 1305	Proof of Claims

The Bankruptcy Code is also available at the website of the American Bankruptcy Institute, www.abiworld. org. Find the link to view the code online from ABI's home page or go straight to the wiki: www.abiworld. org/wiki/index.html.

The Law Library

Virtually every law library has at least one complete set of the annotated United States Code ("annotated" means that each statute is followed by citations and summaries of cases interpreting that provision). If you already have a citation to the statute you are seeking, you can use the citation to find the statute. However, if you have no citation—which is frequently the case—you can use either the index to Title 11 (the part of the Code that applies to bankruptcy) or the table we set out above, which matches various issues that are likely to interest you with specific sections of Title 11.

Once you have found and read the statute, you can browse the one-paragraph summaries of written opinions issued by courts that have interpreted that particular statute. You will be looking to see whether a court has addressed your particular issue. If so, you can find and read the entire case in the law library. Reading what a judge has had to say about the statute regarding facts similar to yours is an invaluable guide to understanding how a judge is likely to handle the issue in your case, although when and where the case was decided may be important.

Finding the Federal Rules of Bankruptcy Procedure (FRBP)

The Federal Rules of Bankruptcy Procedure govern what happens if an issue is contested in the bankruptcy court. They also apply to certain routine bankruptcy procedures, such as deadlines for filing paperwork. Because most cases sail through the court without any need for the bankruptcy judge's intervention, you may not need to be familiar with these rules. However, certain types of creditor actions in the bankruptcy court must proceed by way of a regular lawsuit conducted under both these rules and the Federal Rules of Civil Procedure—for example, complaints to determine dischargeability of a debt. If you are representing yourself in such a lawsuit, you'll want to know these rules and look at the cases interpreting them. Any law

library will have these rules. Your bankruptcy court's website will have a link to the rules, as does www.law. cornell.edu.

Finding Local Court Rules

Every bankruptcy court operates under a set of local rules that govern how it does business and what is expected of the parties who use it. Each court also has its own forms that debtors must use, and these forms vary from court to court. Throughout this book, we have cautioned you to read the rules and review the local forms for your particular court so that your dealings with the court will go smoothly—and so you won't end up getting tossed out of court if you become involved in litigation, such as an action to determine the dischargeability of a debt or a creditor's motion to lift the automatic stay.

Your bankruptcy court clerk's office will have the local rules available for you. Most courts also post their local rules and forms on their own websites. To find the website for your court, take these steps:

Step 1: Go to www.uscourts.gov/links.html.

Step 2: Click the number on the map that is closest to where you live.

Step 3: Browse the list until you find your court and click on it.

Step 4: Click on the local rules and forms link.

These court websites usually contain other helpful information as well, including case information, official bankruptcy forms, court guidelines (in addition to the local rules), information for lawyers and BPPs, information about the court and its judges, and the court calendar.

At the law library, the *Collier Bankruptcy Practice Manual* has the local rules for most (if not all) of the nation's bankruptcy courts.

Finding Federal Court Bankruptcy Cases

Court opinions are vital to understanding how a particular law might apply to your individual case. The following levels of federal courts issue bankruptcy-related opinions:

- the U.S. Supreme Court
- the U.S. Courts of Appeals
- the Bankruptcy Appellate Panels

- the U.S. District Courts, and
- the bankruptcy courts.

Most bankruptcy-related opinions are, not surprisingly, issued by the bankruptcy courts. By comparison, very few bankruptcy opinions come out of the U.S. Supreme Court. The other courts are somewhere in the middle.

The Internet

Depending on the date the case was decided, U.S. Supreme Court decisions and U.S. Court of Appeals decisions are available for free on the Internet. For $13.95 a month you can also subscribe to VersusLaw (at www.versuslaw.com), which provides U.S. Court of Appeals cases for an earlier period than you can get for free—often back to 1950. VersusLaw doesn't require you to sign a long-term contract. So, one payment of $13.95 gets you a month's worth of research. Not too shabby. VersusLaw also publishes many U.S. District Court cases on its website. Westlaw and Lexis are generally too costly to use from home, unless you do a lot of research. However, you will be able to find either or both of these online megaresources at your local law library.

U.S. Supreme Court. To find a Supreme Court case, go to www.findlaw.com/casecode/supreme.html. Use one of the search options to locate a particular case. If you don't know the case name and you don't have a citation, enter some relevant words relating to your issue and see what you pull up. You can search cases all the way back to 1893.

U.S. Court of Appeals. You can find a U.S Circuit Court of Appeals case back to roughly 1996. Follow these steps:

Step 1: Go to www.findlaw.com/casecode/index.html.

Step 2: Scroll down to U.S Courts of Appeals— Opinions and Websites.

Step 3: Click on the link that contains your state's abbreviation.

Step 4: Use one of the search options to find the case.

Again, if you are looking for a case decided prior to 1996, your best bet is to sign up for VersusLaw, described just above.

U.S. District Court and Bankruptcy Court. Cases reported by the bankruptcy courts are generally not available online unless you use Westlaw or Lexis. However, if you know the name of a particular case, a Google search might lead you to a court's website, where some judges post their decisions. You will probably have to take a trip to a law library if you want to know what the judges are doing in these courts— where the legal rubber meets the judicial road.

The Law Library

U.S. Supreme Court cases are published in three different book series:

- Supreme Court Reports
- Supreme Court Reporter, and
- Supreme Court Lawyer's Edition.

Some law libraries carry all three of these publications; others have only one. The cases are the same, but each series has different editorial enhancements.

U.S. Court of Appeals cases are published in the Federal Reporter (abbreviated simply as "F."). Most law libraries, large and small, carry this series.

Many U.S. District Court cases are published in the Federal Supplement (F.Supp.), a series available in most law libraries.

Written opinions of bankruptcy judges, and related appeals, are published in the Bankruptcy Reporter (B.R.), available in most mid- to large-sized libraries. To accurately understand how your bankruptcy court is likely to interpret the laws in your particular case, sooner or later you will need access to the Bankruptcy Reporter.

State Statutes

The secret to understanding what property you can keep frequently lies in the exemptions that your state allows you to claim. These exemptions are found in your state's statutes.

The Internet

Every state has its statutes online, including its exemption statutes. This means that you can read your state's exemption statutes for yourself. Follow these steps:

Step 1: Go to Appendix A. At the top of your state's exemption table, you'll see a general reference to the collection of state laws for your state that contain the exemption statutes.

Step 2: Go to www.nolo.com.

Step 3: Click "Site Map" at the bottom of the page.

Step 4: Select "State Statutes" under the "Legal Research" heading.

Step 5: Click on your state.

Step 6: Locate the collection of statutes mentioned in Appendix A.

Step 7: Use the exemption citation to the far right of your state's exemption table to search for the statute.

The Law Library

Your law library will have your state's statutes in book form, usually referred to as your state's code, annotated statutes, or compiled laws. Use Appendix A in this book to find a reference to the exemption statute you want to read, then use that reference to locate the exemption statute in the code. Once you find and read the statute, you can browse the summaries of court opinions interpreting the statute and, if you wish, read the cases in their entirety.

Alternatively, if your library has a copy of *Collier on Bankruptcy* (see above), you can find the exemptions for your state, accompanied by annotations summarizing state court interpretations.

State Court Cases

State courts are sometimes called on to interpret exemption statutes. If a court has interpreted the statute in which you are interested, you'll definitely want to chase down the relevant case and read it for yourself.

The Internet

All states make their more recent cases available free on the Internet—usually back to about 1996. To find these cases for your state:

Step 1: Go to www.law.cornell.edu/opinions.html#state.

Step 2: Click on your state.

Step 3: Locate the link to the court opinions for your state. This may be one link, or there may be separate links for your state's supreme court and your state's courts of appeal (the lower trial courts seldom publish their opinions, so you probably won't be able to find them).

If you want to go back to an earlier case, consider subscribing to VersusLaw at www.versuslaw.com. As mentioned earlier, you don't have to sign a long-term contract.

The Law Library

Your law library will have a collection of books that contain opinions issued by your state's courts. If you have a citation, you can go right to the case. If you don't have a citation, you'll need to use a digest to find relevant bankruptcy cases. Finding cases by subject matter is a little too advanced for this brief summary. See *Legal Research: How to Find & Understand the Law*, by Stephen Elias and Susan Levinkind (Nolo), for more help.

Other Helpful Resources

Probably the most helpful bankruptcy website is maintained by the Office of the United States Trustee, at www.usdoj.gov/ust. This site provides lists of approved credit and financial management counseling agencies, median income figures for every state, the IRS national, regional, and local expenses you will need to complete the means test, and all of the forms you will need to file, in fill-in-the-blanks, PDF format. You can also download official bankruptcy forms from www.uscourts.gov/bkforms/index.html. However, this site doesn't include required local forms; for those, you'll have to visit your court or its website.

As part of the bankruptcy process, you are required to give the replacement (retail) value for all of the property you list in Schedule A (real property) and Schedule B (personal property). These figures are also the key to figuring out which of your property is exempt. Here are some tips on finding these values:

- **Cars:** Use the *Kelley Blue Book*, at www.kbb.com, or the website of the National Auto Dealers Association, www.nada.com.
- **Other personal property:** Check prices on eBay, www.ebay.com.
- **Homes:** To value your property, compare it to similar real estate parcels in your neighborhood that have recently sold (comparables). For a modest fee, you can get details on comparables—including neighborhood information, sales history,

address, number of bedrooms and baths, square footage, and property tax information—from SmartHomeBuy at www.smarthomebuy.com. Less detailed information (purchase price, sales date, and address) is available free from sites such as www.homevalues.com, www.zillow.com, www. domania.com, www.homeradar.com, and http:// list.realestate.yahoo.com/re/homevalues. Simply enter the home's address or zip code. In an era of falling home prices, it is harder to pin a value on real estate than it used to be. For example, if a comparable sold three months ago for $250,000, your home may not be worth that much today (although it can be tough to figure out how to translate this change into dollars and cents).

Our Websites

Nolo's website, www.nolo.com, offers lots of free information on bankruptcy, credit repair, student loans, and much more. (Click the "Property and Money" tab to get started.) You can also view information on the Nolo products mentioned in this book, including links to legal updates highlighting important developments that occurred after this book went to press.

In addition, two Nolo authors maintain their own websites, both of which provide plenty of free information on a variety of bankruptcy topics.

- www.bankruptcylawproject.com, created by Stephen Elias, provides information on bankruptcy petition preparers and unlimited legal advice by telephone at a flat rate (currently $100).
- www.legalconsumer.com, created by Albin Renauer, provides free bankruptcy information and resources organized by the user's zip code. The site offers a means test calculator; state and federal exemption laws; contact information for your local bankruptcy court; links to official court forms and instructions; links to resources; and more.

Glossary

341 meeting. See "meeting of creditors."

341 notice. A notice sent to the debtor and the debtor's creditors announcing the date, time, and place for the first meeting of creditors. The 341 notice is sent along with the notice of bankruptcy filing and information about important deadlines by which creditors have to take certain actions, such as filing objections.

342 notice. A notice that the court clerk is required to give to debtors pursuant to Section 342 of the Bankruptcy Code, to inform them of their obligations as bankruptcy debtors and the consequences of not being completely honest in their bankruptcy case.

707(b) action. An action taken by the U.S. Trustee, the regular trustee, or any creditor, under authority of Section 707(b) of the Bankruptcy Code, to dismiss a debtor's Chapter 7 filing on the ground of abuse.

Abuse. Misuse of the Chapter 7 bankruptcy remedy. This term is typically applied to Chapter 7 bankruptcy filings that should have been filed under Chapter 13 because the debtor appears to have enough disposable income to fund a Chapter 13 repayment plan.

Accounts receivable. Money or other property that one person or business owes to another for goods or services. Accounts receivable most often refer to the debts owed to a business by its customers.

Administrative expenses. The trustee's fee, the debtor's attorney fee, and other costs of bringing a bankruptcy case that a debtor must pay in full in a Chapter 13 repayment plan. Administrative costs are typically 10% of the debtor's total payments under the plan.

Administrative Office of the United States Courts. The federal government agency that issues court rules and forms to be used by the federal courts, including bankruptcy courts.

Adversary action. Any lawsuit that begins with the filing of a formal complaint and formal service of process on the parties being sued. In a bankruptcy case, adversary actions are often brought to determine the dischargeability of a debt or to recover property transferred by the debtor shortly before filing for bankruptcy.

Affidavit. A written statement of facts, signed under oath in front of a notary public.

Allowed secured claim. A debt that is secured by collateral or a lien against the debtor's property, for which the creditor has filed a proof of claim with the bankruptcy court. The claim is secured only to the extent of the value of the property—for example, if a debtor owes $5,000 on a note for a car that is worth only $3,000, the remaining $2,000 is an unsecured claim.

Amendment. A document filed by the debtor that changes one or more documents previously filed with the court. A debtor often files an amendment because the trustee requires changes to the debtor's paperwork based on the testimony at the meeting of creditors.

Animals. An exemption category in many states. Some states specifically exempt pets or livestock and poultry. If your state simply allows you to exempt "animals," you may include livestock, poultry, or pets. Some states exempt only domestic animals, which are usually considered to be all animals except pets.

Annuity. A type of insurance policy that pays out during the life of the insured, unlike life insurance, which pays out at the insured's death. Once the insured reaches the age specified in the policy, he or she receives monthly payments until death.

Appliance. A household apparatus or machine, usually operated by electricity, gas, or propane. Examples include refrigerators, stoves, washing machines, dishwashers, vacuum cleaners, air conditioners, and toasters.

Arms and accoutrements. Arms are weapons (such as pistols, rifles, and swords); accoutrements are the furnishings of a soldier's outfit, such as a belt or pack, but not clothes or weapons.

Arms-length creditor. A creditor with whom the debtor deals in the normal course of business, as opposed to an insider (a friend, relative, or business partner).

Articles of adornment. See "jewelry."

Assessment benefits. See "stipulated insurance."

Assisted person. Any person contemplating or filing for bankruptcy who receives bankruptcy assistance, whose debts are primarily consumer debts, and whose nonexempt property is valued at less than $150,000. A person or entity that offers help to an assisted person is called a "debt relief agency."

Automatic stay. An injunction automatically issued by the bankruptcy court when a debtor files for bankruptcy. The automatic stay prohibits most creditor collection activities, such as filing or continuing lawsuits, making written requests for payment, or notifying credit reporting bureaus of an unpaid debt.

Avails. Any amount available to the owner of an insurance policy other than the actual proceeds of the policy. Avails include dividend payments, interest, cash or surrender value (the money you'd get if you sold your policy back to the insurance company), and loan value (the amount of cash you can borrow against the policy).

Bankruptcy Abuse Prevention and Reform Act of 2005. The formal name of the new bankruptcy law that took effect on October 17, 2005.

Bankruptcy administrator. The official responsible for supervising the administration of bankruptcy cases, estates, and trustees in Alabama and North Carolina, where there is no U.S. Trustee.

Bankruptcy Appellate Panel. A specialized court that hears appeals of bankruptcy court decisions (available only in some regions).

Bankruptcy assistance. Goods or services provided to an "assisted person" for the purpose of providing information, advice, counsel, document preparation or filing, or attendance at a creditors' meeting; appearing in a case or proceeding on behalf of another person; or providing legal representation.

Bankruptcy Code. The federal law that governs the creation and operation of the bankruptcy courts and establishes bankruptcy procedures. (You can find the Bankruptcy Code in Title 11 of the United States Code.)

Bankruptcy estate. All of the property you own when you file for bankruptcy, except for most pensions and educational trusts. The trustee technically takes control of your bankruptcy estate for the duration of your case.

Bankruptcy lawyer. A lawyer who specializes in bankruptcy and is licensed to practice law in the federal courts.

Bankruptcy petition preparer. Any nonlawyer who helps someone with his or her bankruptcy. Bankruptcy petition preparers (BPPs) are a special type of debt relief agency, regulated by the U.S. Trustee. Because they are not lawyers, BPPs can't represent anyone in bankruptcy court or provide legal advice.

Bankruptcy Petition Preparer Fee Declaration. An official form bankruptcy petition preparers must file with the bankruptcy court to disclose their fees.

Bankruptcy Petition Preparer Notice to Debtor. A written notice that bankruptcy petition preparers must provide to debtors who use their services. The notice explains that bankruptcy petition preparers aren't attorneys and that they are permitted to perform only certain acts, such as entering information in the bankruptcy petition and schedules under the direction of their clients.

Benefit or benevolent society benefits. See "fraternal benefit society benefits."

Building materials. Items, such as lumber, brick, stone, iron, paint, and varnish, that are used to build or improve a structure.

Burial plot. A cemetery plot.

Business bankruptcy. A bankruptcy in which the debts arise primarily from the operation of a business, including bankruptcies filed by corporations, limited liability companies, and partnerships.

Certification. The act of signing a document under penalty of perjury. (The document that is signed is also called a certification.)

Chapter 7 bankruptcy. A liquidation bankruptcy, in which the trustee sells the debtor's nonexempt property and distributes the proceeds to the debtor's creditors. At the end of the case, the debtor receives a discharge of all remaining debts, except those that cannot legally be discharged.

Chapter 9 bankruptcy. A type of bankruptcy restricted to governmental units.

Chapter 11 bankruptcy. A type of bankruptcy intended to help businesses reorganize their debt load in order to remain in business. A Chapter 11 bankruptcy is typically much more expensive than a Chapter 7 or 13 bankruptcy because all of the lawyers must be paid out of the bankruptcy estate.

Chapter 12 bankruptcy. A type of bankruptcy designed to help small farmers reorganize their debts.

Chapter 13 bankruptcy. A type of consumer bankruptcy designed to help individuals reorganize their debts and pay all or a portion of them over three to five years.

Chapter 13 plan. A document filed in a Chapter 13 bankruptcy in which the debtor shows how all of his or her projected disposable income will be used over a three- to five-year period to pay all mandatory debts—for example, back child support, taxes, and mortgage arrearages—as well as some or all unsecured, nonpriority debts, such as medical and credit card bills.

Claim. A creditor's assertion that the bankruptcy filer owes it a debt or obligation.

Clothing. As an exemption category, the everyday clothes you and your family need for work, school, household use, and protection from the elements. In many states, luxury items and furs are not included in the clothing exemption category.

Codebtor. A person who assumes an equal responsibility, along with the debtor, to repay a debt or loan.

Collateral. Property pledged by a borrower as security for a loan.

Common law property states. States that don't use a community property system to classify marital property.

Community property. Certain property owned by married couples in Arizona, California, Idaho, Louisiana, New Mexico, Nevada, Texas, Washington, Wisconsin, and, if both spouses agree, Alaska. Very generally, all property acquired during the marriage is considered community property, belonging equally to both spouses, except for gifts and inheritances by one spouse. Similarly, all debts incurred during the marriage are considered community debts, owed equally by both spouses, with limited exceptions.

Complaint. A formal document that initiates a lawsuit.

Complaint to determine dischargeablity. A complaint initiating an adversary action in bankruptcy court that asks the court to decide whether a particular debt should be discharged at the end of the debtor's bankruptcy case.

Condominium. A building or complex in which separate units, such as townhouses or apartments, are owned by individuals, and the common areas (lobby, hallways, stairways, and so on) are jointly owned by the unit owners.

Confirmation. The bankruptcy judge's ruling approving a Chapter 13 plan.

Confirmation hearing. A court hearing conducted by a bankruptcy judge in which the judge decides whether a debtor's proposed Chapter 13 plan appears to be feasible and meets all applicable legal requirements.

Consumer bankruptcy. A bankruptcy in which most of the debt was incurred for personal, family, or household purposes.

Consumer debt. A debt incurred by an individual for personal, family, or household purposes.

Contingent debts. Debts that may be owed if certain events happen or conditions are satisfied.

Contingent interests in the estate of a decedent. The right to inherit property if one or more conditions to the inheritance are satisfied. For example, a debtor who will inherit property only if he survives his brother has a contingent interest.

Conversion. When a debtor who has filed one type of bankruptcy switches to another type—as when a Chapter 7 debtor converts to a Chapter 13 bankruptcy, or vice versa.

Cooperative housing. A building or other residential structure that is owned by a corporation formed by the residents. In exchange for purchasing stock in the corporation, the residents have the right to live in particular units.

Cooperative insurance. Compulsory employment benefits provided by a state or federal government, such as old age, survivors, disability, and health insurance, to assure a minimum standard of living for lower- and middle-income people. Also called social insurance.

Court clerk. The court employee who is responsible for accepting filings and other documents, and generally maintaining an accurate and efficient flow of paper and information in the court.

Cramdown. In a Chapter 13 bankruptcy, the act of reducing a secured debt to the replacement value of the collateral securing the debt.

Credit and debt counseling. Counseling that explores the possibility of repaying debts outside of bankruptcy and educates the debtor about credit, budgeting, and financial management. Under the new bankruptcy law, a debtor must undergo credit counseling with an approved provider before filing for bankruptcy.

Credit insurance. An insurance policy that covers a borrower for an outstanding loan. If the borrower dies or becomes disabled before paying off the loan, the policy will pay off the balance due.

Creditor. A person or institution to whom money is owed.

Creditor committee. In a Chapter 11 bankruptcy, a committee that represents the unsecured debtors in reorganization proceedings.

Creditor matrix. A specially formatted list of creditors that a debtor must file with the bankruptcy petition. The matrix helps the court notify creditors of the bankruptcy filing and the date and time set for the first meeting of creditors.

Creditors' meeting. See "meeting of creditors."

Crops. Products of the soil or earth that are grown and raised annually and gathered in a single season. Thus, oranges (on the tree or harvested) are crops; an orange tree isn't.

Current market value. What property could be sold for. This is how a debtor's property was previously valued for purposes of determining whether the property is protected by an applicable exemption. Under the new bankruptcy law, property must be valued at its "replacement cost."

Current monthly income. As defined by the new bankruptcy law, a bankruptcy filer's total gross income (whether taxable or not), averaged over the six-month period immediately preceding the month in which the bankruptcy is filed. The current monthly income is used to determine whether the debtor can file for Chapter 7 bankruptcy, among other things.

Debt. An obligation of any type, including a loan, credit, or promise to perform a contract or lease.

Debt relief agency. An umbrella term for any person or agency—including lawyers and bankruptcy petition preparers, but excluding banks, nonprofit and government agencies, and employees of debt relief agencies—that provides "bankruptcy assistance" to an "assisted person."

Debtor. Someone who owes money to another person or business. Also, the generic term used to refer to anyone who files for bankruptcy.

Declaration. A written statement that is made under oath but not witnessed by a notary public.

Declaration of homestead. A form filed with the county recorder's office to put on record your right to a homestead exemption. In most states, the homestead exemption is automatic—that is, you are not required to record a homestead declaration in order to claim the homestead exemption. A few states do require such a recording, however.

Deed in lieu of foreclosure. The document created when a homeowner dissolves his or her responsibility for a mortgage by deeding the property over to the mortgage owner. The homeowner's credit report will be negatively affected just as if the home were lost through foreclosure.

Disability benefits. Payments made under a disability insurance or retirement plan when the insured is unable to work (or retires early) because of disability, accident, or sickness.

Discharge. A court order, issued at the conclusion of a Chapter 7 or Chapter 13 bankruptcy case, which legally relieves the debtor of personal liability for debts that can be discharged in that type of bankruptcy.

Discharge exceptions. Debts that are not discharged in a bankruptcy case. The debtor continues to owe these debts even after the bankruptcy is concluded.

Discharge hearing. A hearing conducted by a bankruptcy court to explain the discharge, urge the debtor to stay out of debt, and review reaffirmation agreements to make sure they are feasible and fair.

Dischargeability action. An adversary action brought by a party who asks the court to determine whether a particular debt qualifies for discharge.

Dischargeable debt. A debt that is wiped out at the conclusion of a bankruptcy case, unless the judge decides that it should not be.

Dismissal. When the court orders a case to be closed without providing the relief available under the bankruptcy laws. For example, a Chapter 13 case might be dismissed because the debtor fails to propose a feasible plan; a Chapter 7 case might be dismissed for abuse.

Disposable income. The difference between a debtor's "current monthly income" and allowable expenses. This is the amount that the bankruptcy law deems available to pay into a Chapter 13 plan.

Domestic animals. See "animals."

Domestic support obligation. An obligation to pay alimony or child support to a spouse, child, or government entity pursuant to an order by a court or other governmental unit.

Doubling. The ability of married couples to double the amount of certain property exemptions when filing for bankruptcy together. The federal bankruptcy exemptions allow doubling. State laws vary—some permit doubling and some do not.

Education Individual Retirement Account. A type of account to which a person can contribute a certain amount of tax-deferred funds every year for the educational benefit of the debtor or certain relatives. Such an account is not part of the debtor's bankruptcy estate.

Emergency bankruptcy filing. An initial bankruptcy filing that includes only the petition and the creditor matrix, filed right away because the debtor needs the protection of the automatic stay to prevent a creditor from taking certain action, such as a foreclosure. An emergency filing case will be dismissed if the other required documents and forms are not filed in a timely manner.

Endowment insurance. An insurance policy that gives an insured who lives for a specified time (the endowment period) the right to receive the face value of the policy (the amount paid at death). If the insured dies sooner, the beneficiary named in the policy receives the proceeds.

Equity. The amount you get to keep if you sell property —typically the property's market value, less the costs of sale and the value of any liens on the property.

ERISA-qualified benefits. Pensions that meet the requirements of the Employee Retirement Income Security Act (ERISA), a federal law that sets minimum standards for such plans and requires beneficiaries to receive certain notices.

Executory contract. A contract in which one or both parties still have a duty to carry out one or more of the contract's terms.

Exempt property. Property described by state and federal laws (exemptions) that a debtor is entitled to keep in a Chapter 7 bankruptcy. Exempt property cannot be taken and sold by the trustee for the benefit of the debtor's unsecured creditors.

Exemptions. State and federal laws specifying the types of property creditors are not entitled to take to satisfy a debt, and the bankruptcy trustee is not entitled to take and sell for the benefit of the debtor's unsecured creditors.

Farm tools. Tools used by a person whose primary occupation is farming. Some states limit farm tools of the trade to items that can be held in the hand, such as hoes, axes, pitchforks, shovels, scythes, and the like. In other states, farm tools also include plows, harnesses, mowers, reapers, and so on.

Federal exemptions. A list of exemptions contained in the federal Bankruptcy Code. Some states give debtors the option of using the federal exemptions rather than the state exemptions.

Federal Rules of Bankruptcy Procedure. A set of rules issued by the Administrative Office of the United States Courts, which govern bankruptcy court procedures.

Filing date. The date a bankruptcy petition in a particular case is filed. With few exceptions, debts incurred after the filing date are not discharged. Similarly, property owned before the filing date is part of the bankruptcy estate, while property acquired after the filing date is not.

Fines, penalties, and restitution. Debts owed to a court or a victim as a result of a sentence in a criminal matter. These debts are generally not dischargeable in bankruptcy.

Foreclosure. The process by which a creditor with a lien on real estate forces a sale of the property in order to collect on the lien. Foreclosure typically occurs when a homeowner defaults on a mortgage.

Fraternal benefit society benefits. Benefits, often group life insurance, paid for by fraternal societies, such as the Elks, Masons, Knights of Columbus, or the Knights of Maccabees, for their members. Also called benefit society, benevolent society, or mutual aid association benefits.

Fraud. Generally, an act that is intended to mislead another for the purpose of financial gain. In a bankruptcy case, fraud is any writing or representation intended to mislead creditors for the purpose of obtaining a loan or credit, or any act intended to mislead the bankruptcy court or the trustee.

Fraudulent transfer. In a bankruptcy case, a transfer of property to another for less than the property's value for the purpose of hiding the property from the bankruptcy trustee—for instance, when a debtor signs a car over to a relative to keep it out of the bankruptcy estate. Fraudulently transferred property can be recovered and sold by the trustee for the benefit of the creditors.

Fraudulently concealed assets. Property that a bankruptcy debtor deliberately fails to disclose as required by the bankruptcy rules.

Furnishings. An exemption category recognized in many states, which includes furniture, fixtures in your home (such as a heating unit, furnace, or built-in lighting), and other items with which a home is furnished, such as carpets and drapes.

Good faith. In a Chapter 13 case, when a debtor files for bankruptcy with the sincere purpose of paying off debts over the period of time required by law rather than for manipulative purposes—such as to prevent a foreclosure that by all rights should be allowed to proceed.

Goods and chattels. See "personal property."

Group life or group health insurance. A single insurance policy covering individuals in a group (for example, employees) and their dependents.

Head of household. A person who supports and maintains, in one household, one or more people who are closely related to the person by blood, marriage, or adoption. Also referred to as "head of family."

Health aids. Items needed to maintain their owner's health, such as a wheelchair, crutches, prosthesis, or a hearing aid. Many states require that health aids be prescribed by a physician.

Health benefits. Benefits paid under health insurance plans, such as Blue Cross/Blue Shield, to cover the costs of health care.

Heirloom. An item with special monetary or sentimental value, which is passed down from generation to generation.

Home equity loan. A loan made to a homeowner on the basis of the equity in the home—and secured by the home in the same manner as a mortgage.

Homestead. A state or federal exemption applicable to property where the debtor lives when he or she files bankruptcy—usually including boats and mobile homes.

Homestead declaration. See "declaration of homestead."

Household good. As an exemption category, an item of permanent nature (as opposed to items consumed, like food or cosmetics) used in or about the house. This includes linens, dinnerware, utensils, pots and pans, and small electronic equipment like radios. Many state laws specifically list the types of household goods that fall within this exemption, as do the federal bankruptcy laws.

Householder. A person who supports and maintains a household, with or without other people. Also called a "housekeeper."

Impairs an exemption. When a lien, in combination with any other liens on the property and the amount the debtor is entitled to claim as exempt, exceeds the value of the property the debtor could claim in the absence of any liens. For example, if property is worth $15,000, there are $5,000 worth of liens on the property, and the debtor is entitled to a $5,000 exemption in the property, another lien that exceeded $5,000 would impair the debtor's exemption. Certain types of liens that impair an exemption may be removed (avoided) by the debtor if the court so orders.

Implement. As an exemption category, an instrument, tool, or utensil used by a person to accomplish his or her job.

In lieu of homestead (or burial) exemption. Designates an exemption that is available only if you don't claim the homestead (or burial) exemption.

Individual Debtor's Statement of Intention. An official bankruptcy form that debtors with secured debts must file to indicate what they want to do with the property that secures the debt. For instance, a debtor with a car note must indicate whether he or she wants to keep the car and continue the debt (reaffirmation), pay off the car note at a reduced price (redemption), or give the car back to the creditor and cancel the debt.

Injunction. A court order prohibiting a person or entity from taking specified actions—for example, the automatic stay (in reality an automatic injunction), which prevents most creditors from trying to collect their debts.

Insider creditor. A creditor with whom the debtor has a personal relationship, such as a relative, friend, or business partner.

Intangible property. Property that cannot be physically touched, such as an ownership share in a corporation or a copyright. Documents—such as a stock certificate—may provide evidence of intangible property.

Involuntary dismissal. When a bankruptcy judge dismisses a case because the debtor fails to carry out his or her duties—such as filing papers in a timely manner and cooperating with the trustee—or because the debtor files the bankruptcy in bad faith or engages in abuse by wrongfully filing for Chapter 7 when he or she should have filed for Chapter 13.

Involuntary lien. A lien that is placed on the debtor's property without the debtor's consent—for instance, when the IRS places a lien on property for back taxes.

IRS expenses. A table of national and regional expense estimates published by the IRS. Debtors whose "current monthly income" is more than their state's "median family income" must use the IRS expenses to calculate their average net income in a Chapter 7 case, or their disposable income in a Chapter 13 case.

Jewelry. Items created for personal adornment; usually includes watches. Also called "articles of adornment."

Joint debtors. Married people who file for bankruptcy together and pay a single filing fee.

Judgment proof. A description of a person whose income and property are such that a creditor can't (or won't) seize them to enforce a money judgment—for example, a dwelling protected by a homestead exemption or a bank account containing only a few dollars.

Judicial foreclosure. A foreclosure that occurs through a court proceeding, usually when the party seeking the foreclosure files a complaint in court seeking a court order authorizing it.

Judicial lien. A lien created by the recording of a court money judgment against the debtor's property, usually real estate.

Lease. A contract that governs the relationship between an owner of property (such as a car or real estate) and a person who wishes to use the property for a specific period of time.

Lien. A legal claim against property that must be paid before title to the property can be transferred. Liens can also often be collected through repossession (personal property) or foreclosure (real estate), depending on the type of lien.

Lien avoidance. A bankruptcy procedure in which certain types of liens can be removed from certain types of property. Liens that are not avoided survive the bankruptcy even though the underlying debt may be cancelled—for instance, a lien remains on a car even if the debt evidenced by the car note is discharged in the bankruptcy.

Life estate. The right to live in, but not own, a specific home until your death.

Life insurance. A policy that provides for the payment of money to an individual (called the beneficiary) in the event of the death of another (called the insured). The policy matures (becomes payable) only when the insured dies.

Lifting the stay. When a bankruptcy court allows a creditor to continue with debt collection or other activities that are otherwise banned by the automatic stay. For instance, the court might allow a landlord to proceed with an eviction or a lender to repossess a car because the debtor has defaulted on the note.

Liquid assets. Cash or items that are easily convertible into cash, such as a money market account, stock, U.S. Treasury bill, or bank deposit.

Liquidated debt. An existing debt for a specified amount arising out of a contract or court judgment. In contrast, an unliquidated debt is a claim for an as-yet uncertain amount, such as for injuries suffered in a car accident before the case goes to court.

Lost future earnings. The portion of a lawsuit judgment intended to compensate an injured person for the money he or she won't be able to earn in the future because of the injury. Also called lost earnings payments or recoveries.

Luxuries. In bankruptcy, goods or services purchased by the debtor that a court decides were not appropriate in light of the debtor's insolvency. This might include vacations, jewelry, costly cars, or frequent meals at expensive restaurants.

Mailing matrix. See "creditor matrix."

Marital debts. Debts owed jointly by a married couple.

Marital property. Property owned jointly by a married couple.

Marital settlement agreement. An agreement between a divorcing couple that sets out who gets what percentage (or what specific items) of the marital property, who pays what marital debts, and who gets custody and pays child support if there are children of the marriage.

Materialmen's and mechanics' liens. Liens imposed by statute on real estate when suppliers of materials, labor, and contracting services used to improve the real estate are not properly compensated.

Matured life insurance benefits. Insurance benefits that are currently payable because the insured person has died.

Means test. A formula that uses predefined income and expense categories to determine whether a debtor whose income is more than the median family income for his or her state should be allowed to file a Chapter 7 bankruptcy.

Median family income. An annual income figure for which there are as many families with incomes below that level as there are above that level. The U.S. Census Bureau publishes median family income figures for each state and for different family sizes. In bankruptcy, the median family income is used as a basis for determining whether a debtor must pass the means test to file Chapter 7 bankruptcy, and whether a debtor filing a Chapter 13 bankruptcy must commit all his or her projected disposable income to a five-year repayment plan.

Meeting of creditors. A meeting that the debtor is required to attend in a bankruptcy case, at which the trustee and creditors may ask the debtor questions about his or her property, information in the documents and forms he or she filed, and his or her debts.

Mortgage. A contract in which a loan to purchase real estate is secured by the real estate as collateral. If the borrower defaults on loan payments, the lender can foreclose on the property.

Motion. A formal legal procedure in which the bankruptcy judge is asked to rule on a dispute in the bankruptcy case. To bring a motion, a party must file a document explaining what relief is requested, the facts of the dispute, and the legal reasons why the court should grant the relief. The party bringing the motion must mail these documents to all affected parties and let them know when the court will hear argument on the motion.

Motion to avoid judicial lien on real estate. A motion brought by a bankruptcy debtor that asks the bankruptcy court to remove a judicial lien on

real estate because the lien impairs the debtor's homestead exemption.

Motion to lift stay. A motion in which a creditor asks the court for permission to continue a court action or collection activities in spite of the automatic stay.

Motor vehicle. A self-propelled vehicle suitable for use on a street or road. This includes a car, truck, motorcycle, van, and moped. See also "tools of the trade."

Musical instrument. An instrument having the capacity, when properly operated, to produce a musical sound. Pianos, guitars, drums, drum machines, synthesizers, and harmonicas are all musical instruments.

Mutual aid association benefits. See "fraternal benefit society benefits."

Mutual assessment or mutual life. See "stipulated insurance."

Necessities. Articles needed to sustain life, such as food, clothing, medical care, and shelter.

Newly discovered creditors. Creditors who the debtor discovers after the bankruptcy is filed. If the case is still open, the debtor can amend the list to include the creditor; if the case is closed, it usually can be reopened to accommodate the amendment.

Nonbankruptcy federal exemptions. Federal laws that allow a debtor who has not filed for bankruptcy to keep creditors away from certain property. The debtor can also use these exemptions in bankruptcy if the debtor is using a state exemption system.

Nondischargeable debt. Debt that survives bankruptcy, such as back child support and most student loans.

Nonexempt property. Property in the bankruptcy estate that is unprotected by the exemption system available to the debtor (this is typically—but not always—the exemption system in the state where the debtor files bankruptcy). In a Chapter 7 bankruptcy, the trustee may sell it for the benefit of the debtor's unsecured creditors. In a Chapter 13 bankruptcy, debtors must propose a plan that pays their unsecured creditors at least the value of their unsecured property.

Nonjudicial foreclosure. A foreclosure that occurs outside of court, usually when a trustee of a deed of trust first records a notice of default and then a notice of sale in an auction, typically held on the courthouse steps.

Nonpossessory, nonpurchase-money lien. A lien placed on property that is already owned by the debtor and is used as collateral for the loan without being possessed by the lender. In contrast, a nonpurchase-money, possessory lien exists on collateral that is held by a pawnshop.

Nonpriority debt. A type of debt that is not entitled to be paid first in bankruptcy, as priority debts are. Nonpriority debts do not have to be paid in full in a Chapter 13 case.

Nonpriority, unsecured claim. A claim that is not for a priority debt (such as child support) and is not secured by collateral or other property. Typical examples include credit card debt, medical bills, and student loans. In a Chapter 13 repayment plan, nonpriority, unsecured claims are paid only after all other debts are paid.

Notice of appeal. A form that must be filed with a court when a party wishes to appeal a judgment or order issued by the court. Often, the notice of appeal must be filed within ten days of the date the order or judgment is entered in the court's records.

Objection. A document one party files to oppose a proposed action by another party—for instance, when a creditor or trustee files an objection to a bankruptcy debtor's claim of exemption.

Order for relief. The court's automatic injunction against certain collection and other activities that might negatively affect the bankruptcy estate. Another name for the "automatic stay."

Oversecured debt. A debt that is secured by collateral that is worth more than the amount of the debt.

PACER. An online, fee-based database containing bankruptcy court dockets (records of proceedings in bankruptcy cases) and federal court documents, such as court rules and recent appellate court decisions.

Pain and suffering damages. The portion of a court judgment intended to compensate for past, present, and future mental and physical pain, suffering, impairment of ability to work, and mental distress caused by an injury.

Partially secured debt. A debt secured by collateral that is worth less than the debt itself—for instance, when a person owes $15,000 on a car that is worth only $10,000.

Party in interest. Any person or entity that has a financial interest in the outcome of a bankruptcy case, including the trustee, the debtor, and all creditors.

Pension. A fund into which payments are made to provide an employee income after retirement. Typically, the beneficiary can't access the account without incurring a significant penalty, usually a tax. There are many types of pensions, including defined benefit pensions provided by many large corporations and individual pensions (such as 401(k) and IRA accounts). In bankruptcy, most pensions are not considered part of the bankruptcy estate and are therefore not affected by a bankruptcy filing.

Personal financial management counseling. Under the new bankruptcy law, a two-hour class intended to teach budget skills. Every consumer bankruptcy filer must attend such a class in order to obtain a discharge in Chapter 7, Chapter 12, or Chapter 13 bankruptcy.

Personal injury cause of action. The right to seek compensation for physical and mental suffering, including injury to body, reputation, or both. For example, someone who is hit and injured by a car might have a personal injury cause of action against the driver.

Personal injury recovery. The portion of a lawsuit judgment or insurance settlement that is intended to compensate someone for physical and mental suffering, including physical injury, injury to reputation, or both. Bankruptcy exemptions usually do not apply to compensation for pain or suffering or punitive damages—in other words, that part of the recovery can be taken by the trustee in a Chapter 7 case.

Personal property. All property not classified as real property, including tangible items such as cars and jewelry, and intangible property such as stocks and pensions.

Petition. The document a debtor files to officially begin a bankruptcy case and ask for relief. Other documents and schedules must be filed to support the petition at the time it is filed, or shortly afterwards.

Pets. See "animals."

Preference. A payment made by a debtor to a creditor within a defined period prior to filing for bankruptcy—within three months for arms-length creditors (regular commercial creditors) and one year for insider creditors (friends, family, business associates). Because a preference gives that debtor an edge over other debtors in the bankruptcy case, the trustee can recover the preference and distribute it among all of the creditors.

Prepetition. Any time prior to the moment the bankruptcy petition is filed.

Prepetition counseling. Debt or credit counseling that occurs before the bankruptcy petition is filed—as opposed to personal financial management counseling, which occurs after the petition is filed.

Presumed abuse. In a Chapter 7 bankruptcy, when the debtor has a current monthly income in excess of the family median income for the state where the debtor lives, and has sufficient income to propose a Chapter 13 plan under the "means test." If abuse is presumed, the debtor has to prove that his or her Chapter 7 filing is not abusive in order to proceed further.

Primarily business debts. When the majority of debt owed by a bankruptcy debtor—in dollar terms—arises from debts incurred to operate a business.

Primarily consumer debts. When the majority of debt owed by a bankruptcy debtor—in dollar terms—arises from debts incurred for personal or family purposes.

Priority claim. See "priority debt."

Priority creditor. A creditor who has filed a "Proof of Claim" showing that the debtor owes it a priority debt.

Priority debt. A type of debt that is paid first if there are distributions to be made from the bankruptcy estate. Priority debts include alimony and child support, fees owed to the trustee and attorneys in the case, and wages owed to employees. With one exception (back child support obligations assigned to government entities), priority claims must be paid in full in a Chapter 13 bankruptcy.

Proceeds for damaged exempt property. Money received through insurance coverage, arbitration, mediation, settlement, or a lawsuit to pay for exempt property that has been damaged or destroyed. For example, if a debtor had the right to use a $30,000 homestead exemption, but his or her home was destroyed by fire, the debtor can instead exempt $30,000 of the insurance proceeds.

Projected disposable income. The amount of income a debtor will have left over each month, after deducting allowable expenses, payments on mandatory debts, and administrative expenses from his or her current monthly income. This is the amount the debtor must pay toward his or her unsecured nonpriority debts in a Chapter 13 plan.

Proof of Claim. A formal document filed by bankruptcy creditors in a bankruptcy case to assert their right to payments from the bankruptcy estate, if any payments are made.

Proof of service. A document signed under penalty of perjury by the person serving a document showing how the service was made, who made it, and when.

Property of the estate. See "bankruptcy estate."

Purchase-money loans. Loans that are made to purchase specific property items, and that use the property as collateral to assure repayment, such as car loans and mortgages.

Purchase-money security interest. A claim on property owned by the holder of a loan that was used to purchase the property and that is secured by the property (as collateral).

Reaffirmation. An agreement entered into after a bankruptcy filing (postpetition) between the debtor and a creditor in which the debtor agrees to repay all or part of a prepetition debt after the bankruptcy is over. For instance, a debtor makes an agreement with the holder of a car note that the debtor can keep the car and must continue to pay the debt after bankruptcy.

Real property. Real estate (land and buildings on the land, usually including mobile homes attached to a foundation).

Reasonable investigation. A bankruptcy attorney's obligation, under the new bankruptcy law, to look into the information provided to them by their clients.

Redemption. In a Chapter 7 bankruptcy, when the debtor obtains legal title to collateral for a secured debt by paying the secured creditor the replacement value of the collateral in a lump sum. For example, a debtor may redeem a car note by paying the lender the replacement value of the car (what a retail vendor would charge for the car, considering its age and condition).

Reopen a case. To open a closed bankruptcy case, usually for the purpose of adding an overlooked creditor or filing a motion to avoid an overlooked lien. A debtor must request that the court reopen the case.

Repayment plan. An informal plan to repay creditors most or all of what they are owed outside of bankruptcy. Also refers to the plan proposed by a debtor in a Chapter 13 case.

Replacement cost. What it would cost to replace a particular item by buying it from a retail vendor, considering its age and condition—for instance, when buying a car from a used car dealer, furniture from a used furniture shop, or electronic equipment on eBay.

Repossession. When a secured creditor takes property used as collateral because the debtor has defaulted on the loan secured by the collateral.

Request to lift the stay. A written request filed in bankruptcy court by a creditor, which seeks permission to engage in debt collection activity otherwise prohibited by the automatic stay.

Schedule A. The official bankruptcy form a debtor must file to describe all of his or her real property.

Schedule B. The official bankruptcy form a debtor must file to describe all personal property owned by the debtor, including tangible property, such as jewelry and vehicles, and intangible property, such as investments and accounts receivable.

Schedule C. The official bankruptcy form a debtor must file to describe the property the debtor is claiming as exempt, and the legal basis for the claims of exemption.

Schedule D. The official bankruptcy form a debtor must file to describe all secured debts owed by the debtor, such as car notes and mortgages.

Schedule E. The official bankruptcy form a debtor must file to describe all priority debts owed by the debtor, such as back child support and taxes.

Schedule F. The official bankruptcy form a debtor must file to describe all nonpriority, unsecured debts owed by the debtor, such as most credit card and medical bills.

Schedule G. The official bankruptcy form a debtor must file to describe any leases and executory contracts (contracts under which one or both parties still have obligations) to which the debtor is a party.

Schedule H. The official bankruptcy form a debtor must file to describe all codebtors that might be affected by the bankruptcy.

Schedule I. The official bankruptcy form a debtor must file to describe the debtor's income.

Schedule J. The official bankruptcy form a debtor must file to describe the debtor's actual monthly expenses.

Schedules. Official bankruptcy forms a debtor must file, detailing the debtor's property, debts, income, and expenses.

Second deed of trust. A loan against real estate made after the original mortgage (or first deed of trust). Most home equity loans are second deeds of trust.

Secured claim. A debt secured by collateral under a written agreement (for instance, a mortgage or car note) or by operation of law—such as a tax lien.

Secured creditor. The owner of a secured claim.

Secured debt. A debt secured by collateral.

Secured interest. A claim to property used as collateral. For instance, a lender on a car note retains legal title to the car until the loan is paid off.

Secured property. Property that is collateral for a secured debt.

Serial bankruptcy filing. A practice used by some debtors to file and dismiss one bankruptcy after another to obtain the protection of the automatic stay, even though the bankruptcies themselves offer no debt relief—for instance, when a debtor files successive Chapter 13 cases to prevent foreclosure of his or her home even though there are no debts to repay.

Short sale. When a homeowner sells his or her home for less than is owed on the mortgage and turns the proceeds over to the mortgage owner. The homeowner's credit report will be negatively affected just as if the home were lost through foreclosure.

Sickness benefits. See "disability benefits."

State exemptions. State laws that specify the types of property creditors are not entitled to take to satisfy a debt, and the bankruptcy trustee is not entitled to take and sell for the benefit of the debtor's unsecured creditors.

Statement of Affairs. The official bankruptcy form a debtor must file to describe the debtor's legal, economic, and business transactions for the several years prior to filing, including gifts, preferences, income, closing of deposit accounts, lawsuits, and other information that the trustee needs to assess the legitimacy of the bankruptcy and the true extent of the bankruptcy estate.

Statement of Current Monthly Income and Disposable Income Calculation. The official bankruptcy form a debtor must file in a Chapter 13 case, setting out the debtor's current monthly income and calculating the debtor's projected disposable income that will determine how much will be paid to the debtor's unsecured creditors.

Statement of Current Monthly Income and Means Test Calculation. The official bankruptcy form a debtor must file in a Chapter 7 filing that shows the debtor's current monthly income, calculates whether the debtor's income is higher than the state's median family income, and, if so, uses the means test to determine whether a Chapter 7 bankruptcy would constitute abuse.

Statement of Intention. The official bankruptcy form a debtor must file in a Chapter 7 case to tell the court and secured creditors how the debtor plans to treat his or her secured debts—that is, reaffirm the debt, redeem the debt, or surrender the property and discharge the debt.

Statement of Social Security Number. The official bankruptcy form a debtor must file to disclose the debtor's complete Social Security number.

Statutory lien. A lien imposed on property by law, such as tax liens and mechanics' liens, as opposed to voluntary liens (such as mortgages) and liens arising from court judgments (judicial liens).

Stay. See "automatic stay."

Stipulated insurance. An insurance policy that allows the insurance company to assess an amount on the insured, above the standard premium payments, if the company experiences losses worse than had been calculated into the standard premium. Also called assessment, mutual assessment, or mutual life insurance.

Stock options. A contract between a corporation and an employee that gives the employee the right to purchase corporate stock at a specific price mentioned in the contract (the strike price).

Strip down of lien. In a Chapter 13 bankruptcy, when the amount of a lien on collateral is reduced to the collateral's replacement value. See "cramdown."

Student loan. A type of loan made for educational purposes by nonprofit or commercial lenders with repayment and interest terms dictated by federal law. Student loans are not dischargeable in bankruptcy unless the debtor can show that repaying the loan would impose an "undue hardship."

Substantial abuse. Under the old bankruptcy law, filing a Chapter 7 bankruptcy when a Chapter 13 bankruptcy was feasible.

Suits, executions, garnishments, and attachments. Activities engaged in by creditors to enforce money judgments, typically involving the seizure of wages and bank accounts.

Summary of Schedules. The official bankruptcy form a debtor must file to summarize the property and debt information contained in a debtor's schedules

Surrender value. See "avails."

Surrendering collateral. In Chapter 7 bankruptcy, the act of returning collateral to a secured lender in order to discharge the underlying debt—for example, returning a car to discharge the car note.

Tangible personal property. See "tangible property" and "personal property."

Tangible property. Property that may be physically touched. Examples include money, furniture, cars, jewelry, artwork, and houses. Compare "intangible property."

Tax lien. A statutory lien imposed on property to secure payment of back taxes—typically income and property taxes.

Tenancy by the entirety. A way that married couples can hold title to property in about half of the states. When one spouse dies, the surviving spouse automatically owns 100% of the property. In most cases, this type of property is not part of the bankruptcy estate if only one spouse files.

To ____ acres. A limitation on the size of a homestead that may be exempted.

Tools of the trade. Items needed to perform a line of work that you are currently doing and relying on for support. For a mechanic, plumber, or carpenter, for example, tools of trade are the implements used to repair, build, and install. Traditionally, tools of the trade were limited to items that could be held in the hand. Most states, however, now embrace a broader definition, and a debtor may be able to fit many items under a tool of trade exemption.

Transcript of tax return. A summary of a debtor's tax return provided by the IRS upon the debtor's request, usually acceptable as a substitute for the return in the instances when a return must be filed under the new bankruptcy law.

Trustee. An official appointed by the bankruptcy court to carry out the administrative tasks associated with a bankruptcy and to seize and sell nonexempt property in the bankruptcy estate for the benefit of the debtor's unsecured creditors.

U.S. Trustee. An official employed by Office of the U.S. Trustee (a division of the U.S. Department of Justice) who is responsible for overseeing the bankruptcy trustees, regulating credit and personal financial management counselors, regulating bankruptcy petition preparers, auditing bankruptcy cases, ferreting out fraud, and generally making sure that the bankruptcy laws are obeyed.

Undersecured debt. A debt secured by collateral that is worth less than the debt.

Undue hardship. The conditions under which a debtor may discharge a student loan—for example, when the debtor has no income and little chance of earning enough to repay the loan in the future.

Unexpired lease. A lease that is still in effect.

Unmatured life insurance. A policy that is not yet payable because the insured is still alive.

Unscheduled debt. A debt that is not included in the schedules accompanying a bankruptcy filing, perhaps because it was overlooked or intentionally left out.

Unsecured creditor. A creditor whose debt is not secured by collateral, and who therefore has no right to seize a particular item of the debtor's property if the debtor defaults on the debt.

Unsecured priority claims. Priority claims that aren't secured by collateral, such as back child support or taxes for which no lien has been placed on the debtor's property.

Valuation of property. The act of determining the replacement value of property for the purpose of describing it in the bankruptcy schedules, determining whether it is protected by an applicable exemption, redeeming secured property, or cramming down a lien in Chapter 13 bankruptcy.

Voluntary dismissal. When a bankruptcy debtor dismisses his or her Chapter 7 or Chapter 13 case on his or her own, without coercion by the court.

Voluntary lien. A lien agreed to by the debtor, as when the debtor signs a mortgage, car note, or second deed of trust.

Weekly net earnings. The earnings a debtor has left after mandatory deductions, such as income tax, mandatory union dues, and Social Security contributions, have been subtracted from his or her gross income.

Wildcard exemption. A dollar value that the debtor can apply to any type of property to make it—or more of it—exempt. In some states, filers may use the unused portion of a homestead exemption as a wildcard exemption.

Willful and malicious act. An act done with the intent to cause harm. In a Chapter 7 bankruptcy, a debt arising from the debtor's willful and malicious act is not discharged if the victim proves to the bankruptcy court's satisfaction that the act occurred.

Willful or malicious act resulting in a civil judgment. A bad act that was careless or reckless, but was not necessarily intended to cause harm. In a Chapter 13 case, a debt arising from the debtor's act that was either willful or malicious is not discharged if it is part of a civil judgment.

Wrongful death cause of action. The right to seek compensation for having to live without a deceased person. Usually only the spouse and children of the deceased have a wrongful death cause of action.

Wrongful death recoveries. The portion of a lawsuit judgment intended to compensate a plaintiff for having to live without a deceased person. The compensation is intended to cover the earnings and the emotional comfort and support the deceased would have provided.

State and Federal Exemption Charts

The charts in this appendix summarize the laws that determine how much property people can keep when they file for Chapter 7 bankruptcy. When you file for Chapter 13 bankruptcy, your repayment plan must pay at least the value of your nonexempt property—the property that you would not get to keep if you had filed under Chapter 7—to your unsecured, nonpriority creditors. (See Chs. 3, 4, and 5 for more on this requirement.)

As you will see, the charts are divided into categories of property, such as insurance, personal property, and wages. Following each exemption, we provide the numerical citation to the state statute that includes the exemption.

The states are listed alphabetically, followed by the federal exemptions. We also note which states allow you to choose between the federal and state bankruptcy exemptions.

> **CROSS-REFERENCE**
>
> **Need help understanding a term?** Many of the categories, types of property, and other terms used in these charts are defined in the Glossary, which you'll find right before this appendix.

Doubling

When married couples file for bankruptcy jointly, federal law and the laws of some states allow them each to claim the full amount of an exemption. (11 U.S.C. § 522.) Because these couples get to claim twice the amount available to those who file alone, this practice is informally known as "doubling."

Not all states allow doubling, however. And some states allow married filers to double only certain exemptions (for example, they can double personal property exemptions but not the homestead exemption). In the charts that follow, we indicate exemptions that cannot be doubled (and states that don't allow doubling at all). Unless you see a note stating that you cannot double, assume that you can.

> **CAUTION**
>
> **These charts provide general information only.** There are exceptions to state exemption laws that are much too detailed to include here. Consider doing further legal research or consulting an attorney about the exemptions you plan to claim, particularly if you anticipate—or are facing—a challenge to your exemption claims.

Residency Requirements for Claiming State Exemptions

Prior to the new bankruptcy law, filers could use the exemptions of the state where they lived when they filed for bankruptcy. Under the new rules, however, some filers will have to use the exemptions of the state where they used to live. These residency requirements are explained in "Understanding Property Exemptions," in Ch. 5.

Exemptions for Retirement Accounts

Under the new bankruptcy law, virtually all types of tax-exempt retirement accounts are exempt in bankruptcy, whether you use the state or federal exemptions. You can exempt 401(k)s, 403(b)s, profit-sharing and money purchase plans, IRAs (including Roth, SEP, and SIMPLE IRAs), and defined-benefit plans.

These exemptions are unlimited—that is, the entire account is exempt, regardless of how much money is in it—except in the case of traditional and Roth IRAs. For these types of IRAs only, the exemption is limited to a total value of $1,095,000 per person (this figure will be adjusted every three years for inflation). If you have more than one traditional or Roth IRA, you don't get to exempt $1,095,000 per account: Your total exemption, no matter how many accounts you have, is $1,095,000.

If you are using the federal bankruptcy exemptions, you can find this new retirement account provision at 11 U.S.C. § 522(d)(12). If you are using state exemptions, cite 11 U.S.C. § 522(b)(3)(C) as the applicable exemption when you complete your bankruptcy papers.

Alabama

Federal bankruptcy exemptions not available. All law references are to Alabama Code unless otherwise noted.

ASSET	EXEMPTION	LAW
homestead	Real property or mobile home to $5,000; property cannot exceed 160 acres	6-10-2
	Must record homestead declaration before attempted sale of home	6-10-20
insurance	Annuity proceeds or avails to $250 per month	27-14-32
	Disability proceeds or avails to an average of $250 per month	27-14-31
	Fraternal benefit society benefits	27-34-27
	Life insurance proceeds or avails	6-10-8; 27-14-29
	Life insurance proceeds or avails if clause prohibits proceeds from being used to pay beneficiary's creditors	27-15-26
	Mutual aid association benefits	27-30-25
pensions	Tax-exempt retirement accounts, including 401(k)s, 403(b)s, profit-sharing and money purchase plans, SEP and SIMPLE IRAs, and defined-benefit plans	11 U.S.C. § 522(b)(3)(C)
	Traditional and Roth IRAs to $1,095,000 per person	11 U.S.C. § 522(b)(3)(C); (n)
	IRAs & other retirement accounts	19-3B-508
	Judges (only payments being received)	12-18-10(a),(b)
	Law enforcement officers	36-21-77
	Spendthrift trusts (with exceptions)	19-3B-501 to 503
	State employees	36-27-28
	Teachers	16-25-23
personal property	Books of debtor & family	6-10-6
	Burial place for self & family	6-10-5
	Church pew for self & family	6-10-5
	Clothing of debtor & family	6-10-6
	Family portraits or pictures	6-10-6
public benefits	Aid to blind, aged, disabled; & other public assistance	38-4-8
	Crime victims' compensation	15-23-15(e)
	Southeast Asian War POWs' benefits	31-7-2
	Unemployment compensation	25-4-140
	Workers' compensation	25-5-86(b)
tools of trade	Arms, uniforms, equipment that state military personnel are required to keep	31-2-78
wages	With respect to consumer loans, consumer credit sales, & consumer leases, 75% of weekly net earnings or 30 times the federal minimum hourly wage; all other cases, 75% of earned but unpaid wages; bankruptcy judge may authorize more for low-income debtors	5-19-15; 6-10-7
wildcard	$3,000 of any personal property, except wages	6-10-6

Alaska

Alaska law states that only the items found in Alaska Statutes §§ 9.38.010, 9.38.015(a), 9.38.017, 9.38.020, 9.38.025, and 9.38.030 may be exempted in bankruptcy. In *In re McNutt*, 87 B.R. 84 (9th Cir. 1988), however, an Alaskan debtor used the federal bankruptcy exemptions. All law references are to Alaska Statutes unless otherwise noted.

Alaska exemption amounts are adjusted regularly by administrative order. Current amounts are found at 8 Alaska Admin. Code tit. 8, § 95.030.

ASSET	EXEMPTION	LAW
homestead	$67,500 (joint owners may each claim a portion, but total can't exceed $67,500)	09.38.010(a)
insurance	Disability benefits	09.38.015(b); 09.38.030(e)(1),(5)
	Fraternal benefit society benefits	21.84.240
	Life insurance or annuity contracts, total avails to $12,500	09.38.025
	Medical, surgical, or hospital benefits	09.38.015(a)(3)
miscellaneous	Alimony, to extent wages exempt	09.38.030(e)(2)
	Child support payments made by collection agency	09.38.015(b)
	Liquor licenses	09.38.015(a)(7)
	Property of business partnership	09.38.100(b)
pensions	Tax-exempt retirement accounts, including 401(k)s, 403(b)s, profit-sharing and money purchase plans, SEP and SIMPLE IRAs, and defined-benefit plans	11 U.S.C. § 522(b)(3)(C)
	Traditional and Roth IRAs to $1,095,000 per person	11 U.S.C. § 522(b)(3)(C); (n)
	Elected public officers (only benefits building up)	09.38.015(b)
	ERISA-qualified benefits deposited more than 120 days before filing bankruptcy	09.38.017
	Judicial employees (only benefits building up)	09.38.015(b)
	Public employees (only benefits building up)	09.38.015(b); 39.35.505
	Roth & traditional IRAs, medical savings accounts	09.38.017(e)(3)
	Teachers (only benefits building up)	09.38.015(b)
	Other pensions, to extent wages exempt (only payments being received)	09.38.030(e)(5)
personal property	Books, musical instruments, clothing, family portraits, household goods, & heirlooms to $3,750 total	09.38.020(a)
	Building materials	34.35.105
	Burial plot	09.38.015(a)(1)
	Cash or other liquid assets to $1,750; for sole wage earner in household, $2,750 (restrictions apply—see *wages*)	09.38.030(b)
	Deposit in apartment or condo owners' association	09.38.010(e)
	Health aids needed	09.38.015(a)(2)
	Jewelry to $1,250	09.38.020(b)
	Money held in mortgage escrow accounts after July 1, 2008	09.38.015(e)
	Motor vehicle to $3,750; vehicle's market value can't exceed $25,000	09.38.020(e)
	Personal injury recoveries, to extent wages exempt	09.38.030(e)(3)
	Pets to $1,250	09.38.020(d)
	Proceeds for lost, damaged, or destroyed exempt property	09.38.060
	Tuition credits under an advance college tuition payment contract	09.38.015(a)(8)
	Wrongful death recoveries, to extent wages exempt	09.38.030(e)(3)

public benefits	Adult assistance to elderly, blind, disabled	47.25.550
	Alaska benefits for low-income seniors	09.38.015(a)(11)
	Alaska longevity bonus	09.38.015(a)(5)
	Crime victims' compensation	09.38.015(a)(4)
	Federally exempt public benefits paid or due	09.38.015(a)(6)
	General relief assistance	47.25.210
	Senior care (prescription drug) benefits	09.38.015(a)(10)
	20% of permanent fund dividends	43.23.065
	Unemployment compensation	09.38.015(b); 23.20.405
	Workers' compensation	23.30.160
tools of trade	Implements, books, & tools of trade to $3,500	09.38.020(c)
wages	Weekly net earnings to $438; for sole wage earner in a household, $688; if you don't receive weekly or semimonthly pay, can claim $1,750 in cash or liquid assets paid any month; for sole wage earner in household, $2,750	9.38.030(a),(b); 9.38.050(b)
wildcard	None	

Arizona

Federal bankruptcy exemptions not available. All law references are to Arizona Revised Statutes unless otherwise noted.

ASSET	EXEMPTION	LAW
homestead	Real property, an apartment, or mobile home you occupy to $150,000; sale proceeds exempt 18 months after sale or until new home purchased, whichever occurs first (husband & wife may not double)	33-1101(A)
	May record homestead declaration to clarify which one of multiple eligible parcels is being claimed as homestead	33-1102
insurance	Fraternal benefit society benefits	20-877
	Group life insurance policy or proceeds	20-1132
	Health, accident, or disability benefits	33-1126(A)(4)
	Life insurance cash value or proceeds, or annuity contract if owned at least two years and beneficiary is dependent family member	33-1126(A)(6); 20-1131(D)
	Life insurance proceeds to $20,000 if beneficiary is spouse or child	33-1126(A)(1)
miscellaneous	Alimony, child support needed for support	33-1126(A)(3)
	Minor child's earnings, unless debt is for child	33-1126(A)(2)
pensions *see also wages*	Tax-exempt retirement accounts, including 401(k)s, 403(b)s, profit-sharing and money purchase plans, SEP and SIMPLE IRAs, and defined-benefit plans	11 U.S.C. § 522(b)(3)(C)
	Traditional and Roth IRAs to $1,095,000 per person	11 U.S.C. § 522(b)(3)(C); (n)
	Board of regents members, faculty & administrative officers under board's jurisdiction	15-1628(I)
	District employees	48-227
	ERISA-qualified benefits deposited over 120 days before filing	33-1126(B)
	IRAs & Roth IRAs	33-1126(B) *In re Herrscher*, 121 B.R. 29 (D. Ariz. 1989)
	Firefighters	9-968
	Police officers	9-931
	Rangers	41-955
	State employees retirement & disability	38-792; 38-797.11

personal property *husband & wife may double all personal property*	2 beds & bedding; 1 living room chair per person; 1 dresser, table, lamp; kitchen table; dining room table & 4 chairs (1 more per person); living room carpet or rug; couch; 3 lamps; 3 coffee or end tables; pictures, paintings, personal drawings, family portraits; refrigerator, stove, washer, dryer, vacuum cleaner; TV, radio, stereo, alarm clock to $4,000 total	33-1123
	Bank deposit to $150 in one account	33-1126(A)(9)
	Bible; bicycle; sewing machine; typewriter; burial plot; rifle, pistol, or shotgun to $500 total	33-1125
	Books to $250; clothing to $500; wedding & engagement rings to $1,000; watch to $100; pets, horses, milk cows, & poultry to $500; musical instruments to $250	33-1125
	Food & fuel to last 6 months	33-1124
	Funeral deposits to $5,000	32-1391.05(4)
	Health aids	33-1125(9)
	Motor vehicle to $5,000 ($10,000, if debtor is physically disabled)	33-1125(8)
	Prepaid rent or security deposit to $1,000 or 1½ times your rent, whichever is less, in lieu of homestead	33-1126(C)
	Proceeds for sold or damaged exempt property	33-1126(A)(5),(8)
	Wrongful death awards	12-592
public benefits	Unemployment compensation	23-783(A)
	Welfare benefits	46-208
	Workers' compensation	23-1068(B)
tools of trade *husband & wife may double*	Arms, uniforms, & accoutrements of profession or office required by law	33-1130(3)
	Farm machinery, utensils, seed, instruments of husbandry, feed, grain, & animals to $2,500 total	33-1130(2)
	Library & teaching aids of teacher	33-1127
	Tools, equipment, instruments, & books to $2,500	33-1130(1)
wages	75% of earned but unpaid weekly net earnings or 30 times the federal minimum hourly wage; 50% of wages for support orders; bankruptcy judge may authorize more for low-income debtors	33-1131
wildcard	None	

Arkansas

Federal bankruptcy exemptions available. All law references are to Arkansas Code Annotated unless otherwise noted.

Note: *In re Holt*, 894 F.2d 1005 (8th Cir. 1990) held that Arkansas residents are limited to exemptions in the Arkansas Constitution. Statutory exemptions can still be used within Arkansas for nonbankruptcy purposes, but they cannot be claimed in bankruptcy

ASSET	EXEMPTION	LAW
homestead *choose Option 1 or 2*	1. For married person or head of family: unlimited exemption on real or personal property used as residence to ¼ acre in city, town, or village, or 80 acres elsewhere; if property is between ¼–1 acre in city, town, or village, or 80-160 acres elsewhere, additional limit is $2,500; homestead may not exceed 1 acre in city, town, or village, or 160 acres elsewhere (husband & wife may not double)	Constitution 9-3; 9-4, 9-5; 16-66-210; 16-66-218(b)(3), (4) *In re Stevens*, 829 F.2d 693 (8th Cir. 1987)
	2. Real or personal property used as residence to $800 if single; $1,250 if married	16-66-218(a)(1)

insurance	Annuity contract	23-79-134
	Disability benefits	23-79-133
	Fraternal benefit society benefits	23-74-403
	Group life insurance	23-79-132
	Life, health, accident, or disability cash value or proceeds paid or due to $500	16-66-209; Constitution 9-1, 9-2; *In re Holt*, 894 F.2d 1005 (8th Cir. 1990)
	Life insurance proceeds if clause prohibits proceeds from being used to pay beneficiary's creditors	23-79-131
	Life insurance proceeds or avails if beneficiary isn't the insured	23-79-131
	Mutual assessment life or disability benefits to $1,000	23-72-114
	Stipulated insurance premiums	23-71-112
pensions	Tax-exempt retirement accounts, including 401(k)s, 403(b)s, profit-sharing and money purchase plans, SEP and SIMPLE IRAs, and defined-benefit plans	11 U.S.C. § 522(b)(3)(C)
	Traditional and Roth IRAs to $1,095,000 per person	11 U.S.C. § 522(b)(3)(C); (n)
	Disabled firefighters	24-11-814
	Disabled police officers	24-11-417
	Firefighters	24-10-616
	IRA deposits to $20,000 if deposited over 1 year before filing for bankruptcy	16-66-218(b)(16)
	Police officers	24-10-616
	School employees	24-7-715
	State police officers	24-6-205; 24-6-223
personal property	Burial plot to 5 acres, if choosing federal homestead exemption (Option 2)	16-66-207; 16-66-218(a)(1)
	Clothing	Constitution 9-1, 9-2
	Motor vehicle to $1,200	16-66-218(a)(2)
	Prepaid funeral trusts	23-40-117
	Wedding rings	16-66-219
public benefits	Crime victims' compensation	16-90-716(e)
	Unemployment compensation	11-10-109
	Workers' compensation	11-9-110
tools of trade	Implements, books, & tools of trade to $750	16-66-218(a)(4)
wages	Earned but unpaid wages due for 60 days; in no event less than $25 per week	16-66-208; 16-66-218(b)(6)
wildcard	$500 of any personal property if married or head of family; $200 if not married	Constitution 9-1, 9-2; 16-66-218(b)(1),(2)

California—System 1

Federal bankruptcy exemptions not available. California has two systems; you must select one or the other. All law references are to California Code of Civil Procedure unless otherwise noted. Many exemptions do not apply to claims for child support.

Note: California's exemption amounts are no longer updated in the statutes themselves. California Code of Civil Procedure Section 740.150 deputized the California Judicial Council to update the exemption amounts every three years.

(The next revision will be in 2010.) As a result, the amounts listed in this chart will not match the amounts that appear in the cited statutes. The current exemption amounts can be found on the California Judicial Council website, www.courtinfo. ca.gov/forms/exemptions.htm.

ASSET	EXEMPTION	LAW
homestead	Real or personal property you occupy including mobile home, boat, stock cooperative, community apartment, planned development, or condo to $50,000 if single & not disabled; $75,000 for families if no other member has a homestead (if only one spouse files, may exempt one-half of amount if home held as community property & all of amount if home held as tenants in common); $150,000 if 65 or older, or physically or mentally disabled; $150,000 if 55 or older, single, & earn under $15,000 or married & earn under $20,000 & creditors seek to force the sale of your home; forced sale proceeds received exempt for 6 months after (husband & wife may not double); separated married debtor may claim homestead in community property homestead occupied by other spouse.	704.710; 704.720; 704.730; *In re McFall*, 112 B.R. 336 (9th Cir. B.A.P. 1990)
	May file homestead declaration to protect exemption amount from attachment of judicial liens and to protect proceeds of voluntary sale for 6 months	704.920
insurance	Disability or health benefits	704.130
	Fidelity bonds	Labor 404
	Fraternal benefit society benefits	704.170
	Fraternal unemployment benefits	704.120
	Homeowners' insurance proceeds for 6 months after received, to homestead exemption amount	704.720(b)
	Life insurance proceeds if clause prohibits proceeds from being used to pay beneficiary's creditors	Ins. 10132; Ins. 10170; Ins. 10171
	Matured life insurance benefits needed for support	704.100(c)
	Unmatured life insurance policy cash surrender value completely exempt. Loan value exempt to $10,775	704.100(b)
miscellaneous	Business or professional licenses	695.060
	Inmates' trust funds to $1,350 (husband & wife may not double)	704.090
	Property of business partnership	Corp. 16501-04
pensions	Tax-exempt retirement accounts, including 401(k)s, 403(b)s, profit-sharing and money purchase plans, SEP and SIMPLE IRAs, and defined-benefit plans	11 U.S.C. § 522(b)(3)(C)
	Traditional and Roth IRAs to $1,095,000 per person	11 U.S.C. § 522(b)(3)(C); (n)
	County employees	Gov't 31452
	County firefighters	Gov't 32210
	County peace officers	Gov't 31913
	Private retirement benefits, including IRAs & Keoghs	704.115
	Public employees	Gov't 21255
	Public retirement benefits	704.110

personal property	Appliances, furnishings, clothing, & food	704.020
	Bank deposits from Social Security Administration to $2,700 ($4,050) for husband & wife); unlimited if SS funds are not commingled with other funds	704.080
	Bank deposits of other public benefits to $1,350 ($2,025 for husband & wife)	
	Building materials to repair or improve home to $2,700 (husband & wife may not double)	704.030
	Burial plot	704.200
	Funds held in escrow	Fin. 17410
	Health aids	704.050
	Jewelry, heirlooms, & art to $6,750 total (husband & wife may not double)	704.040
	Motor vehicles to $2,550, or $2,550 in auto insurance for loss or damages (husband & wife may not double)	704.010
	Personal injury & wrongful death causes of action	704.140(a); 704.150(a)
	Personal injury & wrongful death recoveries needed for support; if receiving installments, at least 75%	704.140(b),(c),(d); 704.150(b),(c)
public benefits	Aid to blind, aged, disabled; public assistance	704.170
	Financial aid to students	704.190
	Relocation benefits	704.180
	Unemployment benefits	704.120
	Union benefits due to labor dispute	704.120(b)(5)
	Workers' compensation	704.160
tools of trade	Tools, implements, materials, instruments, uniforms, books, furnishings, & equipment to $6,750 total ($13,475 total if used by both spouses in same occupation)	704.060
	Commercial vehicle (Vehicle Code § 260) to $4,850 ($9,700 total if used by both spouses in same occupation)	704.060
wages	Minimum 75% of wages paid within 30 days prior to filing	704.070
	Public employees' vacation credits; if receiving installments, at least 75%	704.113
wildcard	None	

California—System 2

Refer to the notes for California—System 1, above.

Note: Married couples may not double any exemptions. (*In re Talmadge*, 832 F.2d 1120 (9th Cir. 1987); *In re Baldwin*, 70 B.R. 612 (9th Cir. B.A.P. 1987).)

ASSET	EXEMPTION	LAW
homestead	Real or personal property, including co-op, used as residence to $20,725; unused portion of homestead may be applied to any property	703.140(b)(1)
insurance	Disability benefits	703.140(b)(10)(C)
	Life insurance proceeds needed for support of family	703.140(b)(11)(C)
	Unmatured life insurance contract accrued avails to $11,075	703.140(b)(8)
	Unmatured life insurance policy other than credit	703.140(b)(7)
miscellaneous	Alimony, child support needed for support	703.140(b)(10)(D)

pensions	Tax-exempt retirement accounts, including 401(k)s, 403(b)s, profit-sharing and money purchase plans, SEP and SIMPLE IRAs, and defined-benefit plans	11 U.S.C. § 522(b)(3)(C)
	Traditional and Roth IRAs to $1,095,000 per person	11 U.S.C. § 522(b)(3)(C); (n)
	ERISA-qualified benefits needed for support	703.140(b)(10)(E)
personal property	Animals, crops, appliances, furnishings, household goods, books, musical instruments, & clothing to $525 per item	703.140(b)(3)
	Burial plot to $20,725, in lieu of homestead	703.140(b)(1)
	Health aids	703.140(b)(9)
	Jewelry to $1,350	703.140(b)(4)
	Motor vehicle to $3,300	703.140(b)(2)
	Personal injury recoveries to $20,725 (not to include pain & suffering; pecuniary loss)	703.140(b)(11)(D),(E)
	Wrongful death recoveries needed for support	703.140(b)(11)(B)
public benefits	Crime victims' compensation	703.140(b)(11)(A)
	Public assistance	703.140(b)(10)(A)
	Social Security	703.140(b)(10)(A)
	Unemployment compensation	703.140(b)(10)(A)
	Veterans' benefits	703.140(b)(10)(B)
tools of trade	Implements, books, & tools of trade to $2,075	703.140(b)(6)
wages	None (use federal nonbankruptcy wage exemption)	
wildcard	$1,100 of any property	703.140(b)(5)
	Unused portion of homestead or burial exemption of any property	703.140(b)(5)

Colorado

Federal bankruptcy exemptions not available. All law references are to Colorado Revised Statutes unless otherwise noted.

ASSET	EXEMPTION	LAW
homestead	Real property, mobile home, manufactured home, or house trailer you occupy to $60,000; $90,000 if owner, spouse, or dependent is disabled or at least 60 years old; sale proceeds exempt 2 years after received	38-41-201; 38-41-201.6; 38-41-203; 38-41-207; *In re Pastrana*, 216 B.R. 948 (Colo., 1998)
	Spouse or child of deceased owner may claim homestead exemption	38-41-204
insurance	Disability benefits to $200 per month; if receive lump sum, entire amount exempt	10-16-212
	Fraternal benefit society benefits	10-14-403
	Group life insurance policy or proceeds	10-7-205
	Homeowners' insurance proceeds for 1 year after received, to homestead exemption amount	38-41-209
	Life insurance cash surrender value to $50,000, except contributions to policy within past 48 months	13-54-102(1)(l)
	Life insurance proceeds if clause prohibits proceeds from being used to pay beneficiary's creditors	10-7-106

miscellaneous	Child support or domestic support obligation	13-54-102(u) 13-54-102.5
	Property of business partnership	7-60-125
pensions *see also wages*	Tax-exempt retirement accounts, including 401(k)s, 403(b)s, profit-sharing and money purchase plans, SEP and SIMPLE IRAs, and defined-benefit plans	11 U.S.C. § 522(b)(3)(C)
	Traditional and Roth IRAs to $1,095,000 per person	11 U.S.C. § 522(b)(3)(C); (n)
	ERISA-qualified benefits, including IRAs & Roth IRAs	13-54-102(1)(s)
	Firefighters & police officers	31-30.5-208; 31-31-203
	Public employees' pensions & defined contribution plans as of 2006	24-51-212
	Public employees' deferred compensation	24-52-105
	Teachers	22-64-120
	Veteran's pension for veteran, spouse, or dependents if veteran served in war or armed conflict	13-54-102(1)(h); 13-54-104
personal property	1 burial plot per family member	13-54-102(1)(d)
	Clothing to $1,500	13-54-102(1)(a)
	Food & fuel to $600	13-54-102(1)(f)
	Health aids	13-54-102(1)(p)
	Household goods to $3,000	13-54-102(1)(e)
	Jewelry & articles of adornment to $2,000	13-54-102(1)(b)
	Motor vehicles or bicycles used for work to $5,000; to $10,000 if used by a debtor or by a dependent who is disabled or 60 or over	13-54-102(j) (I), (II)
	Personal injury recoveries	13-54-102(1)(n)
	Family pictures & books to $1,500	13-54-102(1)(c)
	Proceeds for damaged exempt property	13-54-102(1)(m)
	Security deposits	13-54-102(1)(r)
public benefits	Aid to blind, aged, disabled; public assistance	26-2-131
	Crime victims' compensation	13-54-102(1)(q); 24-4.1-114
	Disability benefits to $3,000	13-54-102(v)
	Earned income tax credit or refund	13-54-102(1)(o)
	Unemployment compensation	8-80-103
	Veteran's benefits for veteran, spouse, or child if veteran served in war or armed conflict	13-54-102(1)(h)
	Workers' compensation	8-42-124
tools of trade	Livestock or other animals, machinery, tools, equipment, & seed of person engaged in agriculture, to $50,000 total	13-54-102(1)(g)
	Professional's library to $3,000 (if not claimed under other tools of trade exemption)	13-54-102(1)(k)
	Stock in trade, supplies, fixtures, tools, machines, electronics, equipment, books, & other business materials, to $20,000 total	13-54-102(1)(i)
	Military equipment personally owned by members of the National Guard	13-54-102(1)(h.5)
wages	Minimum 75% of weekly net earnings or 30 times the federal or state minimum wage, whichever is greater, including pension & insurance payments	13-54-104
wildcard	None	

Connecticut

Federal bankruptcy exemptions available. All law references are to Connecticut General Statutes Annotated unless otherwise noted.

ASSET	EXEMPTION	LAW
homestead	Real property, including mobile or manufactured home, to $75,000; applies only to claims arising after 1993, but to $125,000 in the case of a money judgment arising out of services provided at a hospital	52-352a(e); 52-352b(t)
insurance	Disability benefits paid by association for its members	52-352b(p)
	Fraternal benefit society benefits	38a-637
	Health or disability benefits	52-352b(e)
	Life insurance proceeds if clause prohibits proceeds from being used to pay beneficiary's creditors	38a-454
	Life insurance proceeds or avails	38a-453
	Unmatured life insurance policy avails to $4,000 if beneficiary is dependent	52-352b(s)
miscellaneous	Alimony, to extent wages exempt	52-352b(n)
	Child support	52-352b(h)
	Farm partnership animals & livestock feed reasonably required to run farm where at least 50% of partners are members of same family	52-352d
pensions	Tax-exempt retirement accounts, including 401(k)s, 403(b)s, profit-sharing and money purchase plans, SEP and SIMPLE IRAs, and defined-benefit plans	11 U.S.C. § 522(b)(3)(C)
	Traditional and Roth IRAs to $1,095,000 per person	11 U.S.C. § 522(b)(3)(C); (n)
	ERISA-qualified benefits, including IRAs, Roth IRAs, & Keoghs, to extent wages exempt	52-321a; 52-352b(m)
	Medical savings account	52-321a
	Municipal employees	7-446
	State employees	5-171; 5-192w
	Teachers	10-183q
personal property	Appliances, food, clothing, furniture, bedding	52-352b(a)
	Burial plot	52-352b(c)
	Health aids needed	52-352b(f)
	Motor vehicle to $3,500	52-352b(j)
	Proceeds for damaged exempt property	52-352b(q)
	Residential utility & security deposits for 1 residence	52-3252b(l)
	Spendthrift trust funds required for support of debtor & family	52-321(d)
	Transfers to a nonprofit debt adjuster	52-352b(u)
	Tuition savings accounts	52-321a(E)
	Wedding & engagement rings	52-352b(k)
public benefits	Crime victims' compensation	52-352b(o); 54-213
	Public assistance	52-352b(d)
	Social Security	52-352b(g)
	Unemployment compensation	31-272(c); 52-352b(g)
	Veterans' benefits	52-352b(g)
	Workers' compensation	52-352b(g)

tools of trade	Arms, military equipment, uniforms, musical instruments of military personnel	52-352b(i)
	Tools, books, instruments, & farm animals needed	52-352b(b)
wages	Minimum 75% of earned but unpaid weekly disposable earnings, or 40 times the state or federal hourly minimum wage, whichever is greater	52-361a(f)
wildcard	$1,000 of any property	52-352b(r)

Delaware

Federal bankruptcy exemptions not available. All law references are to Delaware Code Annotated (in the form title number-section number) unless otherwise noted.

Note: A single person may exempt no more than $25,000 total in all exemptions (not including retirement plans); a husband & wife may exempt no more than $50,000 total (10-4914).

ASSET	EXEMPTION	LAW
homestead	Real property or manufactured home used as principal residence to $50,000 (spouses may not double)	10-4914(c)
	Property held as tenancy by the entirety may be exempt against debts owed by only one spouse	*In re Kelley*, 289 B.R. 38 (Bankr. D. Del. 2003)
insurance	Annuity contract proceeds to $350 per month	18-2728
	Fraternal benefit society benefits	18-6218
	Group life insurance policy or proceeds	18-2727
	Health or disability benefits	18-2726
	Life insurance proceeds if clause prohibits proceeds from being used to pay beneficiary's creditors	18-2729
	Life insurance proceeds or avails	18-2725
pensions	Tax-exempt retirement accounts, including 401(k)s, 403(b)s, profit-sharing and money purchase plans, SEP and SIMPLE IRAs, and defined-benefit plans	11 U.S.C. § 522(b)(3)(C)
	Traditional and Roth IRAs to $1,095,000 per person	11 U.S.C. § 522(b)(3)(C); (n)
	IRAs, Roth IRAs, & any other retirement plans	*In re Yuhas*, 104 F.3d 612 (3rd Cir. 1997)
	Kent County employees	9-4316
	Police officers	11-8803
	State employees	29-5503
	Volunteer firefighters	16-6653
personal property	Bible, books, & family pictures	10-4902(a)
	Burial plot	10-4902(a)
	Church pew or any seat in public place of worship	10-4902(a)
	Clothing, includes jewelry	10-4902(a)
	College investment plan account (limit for year before filing is $5,000 or average of past two years' contribution, whichever is more)	10-4916
	Principal and income from spendthrift trusts	12-3536
	Pianos & leased organs	10-4902(d)
	Sewing machines	10-4902(c)

public benefits	Aid to blind	31-2309
	Aid to aged, disabled, general assistance	31-513
	Crime victims' compensation	11-9011
	Unemployment compensation	19-3374
	Workers' compensation	19-2355
tools of trade	Tools of trade and/or vehicle necessary for employment to $15,000 each	10-4914(c)
	Tools, implements, & fixtures to $75 in New Castle & Sussex Counties; to $50 in Kent County	10-4902(b)
wages	85% of earned but unpaid wages	10-4913
wildcard	$500 of any personal property, except tools of trade, if head of family	10-4903

District of Columbia

Federal bankruptcy exemptions available. All law references are to District of Columbia Code unless otherwise noted.

ASSET	EXEMPTION	LAW
homestead	Any property used as a residence or co-op that debtor or debtor's dependent uses as a residence	15-501(a)(14)
	Property held as tenancy by the entirety may be exempt against debts owed by only one spouse	*Estate of Wall*, 440 F.2d 215 (D.C. Cir. 1971)
insurance	Disability benefits	15-501(a)(7); 31-4716.01
	Fraternal benefit society benefits	31-5315
	Group life insurance policy or proceeds	31-4717
	Life insurance payments	15-501(a)(11)
	Life insurance proceeds if clause prohibits proceeds from being used to pay beneficiary's creditors	31-4719
	Life insurance proceeds or avails	31-4716
	Other insurance proceeds to $200 per month, maximum 2 months, for head of family; else $60 per month	15-503
	Unmatured life insurance contract other than credit life insurance	15-501(a)(5)
miscellaneous	Alimony or child support	15-501(a)(7)
pensions *see also wages*	Tax-exempt retirement accounts, including 401(k)s, 403(b)s, profit-sharing and money purchase plans, SEP and SIMPLE IRAs, and defined-benefit plans	11 U.S.C. § 522(b)(3)(C)
	Traditional and Roth IRAs to $1,095,000 per person	11 U.S.C. § 522(b)(3)(C); (n)
	ERISA-qualified benefits, IRAs, Keoghs, etc. to maximum deductible contribution	15-501(b)(9)
	Any stock bonus, annuity, pension, or profit-sharing plan	15-501(a)(7)
	Judges	11-1570(f)
	Public school teachers	38-2001.17; 38-2021.17
personal property	Appliances, books, clothing, household furnishings, goods, musical instruments, pets to $425 per item or $8,625 total	15-501(a)(2)
	Cemetery & burial funds	43-111
	Cooperative association holdings to $50	29-928
	Food for 3 months	15-501(a)(12)
	Health aids	15-501(a)(6)

personal property (continued)	Higher education tuition savings account	47-4510
	Residential condominium deposit	42-1904.09
	All family pictures; & all the family library, to $400	15-501(a)(8)
	Motor vehicle to $2,575	15-501(a)(1)
	Payment including pain & suffering for loss of debtor or person depended on	15-501(a)(11)
	Uninsured motorist benefits	31-2408.01(h)
	Wrongful death damages	15-501(a)(11); 16-2703
public benefits	Aid to blind, aged, disabled; general assistance	4-215.01
	Crime victims' compensation	4-507(e); 15-501(a)(11)
	Social Security	15-501(a)(7)
	Unemployment compensation	51-118
	Veterans' benefits	15-501(a)(7)
	Workers' compensation	32-1517
tools of trade	Library, furniture, tools of professional or artist to $300	15-501(a)(13)
	Tools of trade or business to $1,625	15-501(a)(5)
	Mechanic's tools to $200	15-503(b)
	Seal & documents of notary public	1-1206
wages	Minimum 75% of earned but unpaid wages, pension payments; bankruptcy judge may authorize more for low-income debtors	16-572
	Nonwage (including pension & retirement) earnings to $200/mo for head of family; else $60/month for a maximum of two months	15-503
	Payment for loss of future earnings	15-501(e)(11)
wildcard	Up to $850 in any property, plus up to $8,075 of unused homestead exemption	15-501(a)(3)

Florida

Federal bankruptcy exemptions not available. All law references are to Florida Statutes Annotated unless otherwise noted.

ASSET	EXEMPTION	LAW
homestead	Real or personal property including mobile or modular home to unlimited value; cannot exceed half acre in municipality or 160 acres elsewhere; spouse or child of deceased owner may claim homestead exemption	222.01; 222.02; 222.03; 222.05; Constitution 10-4 *In re Colwell*, 196 F.3d 1225 (11th Cir. 1999)
	May file homestead declaration	222.01
	Property held as tenancy by the entirety may be exempt against debts owed by only one spouse	*Havoco of America, Ltd. v. Hill*, 197 F.3d 1135 (11th Cir. Fla.,1999)
insurance	Annuity contract proceeds; does not include lottery winnings	222.14; *In re Pizzi*, 153 B.R. 357 (S.D. Fla. 1993)
	Death benefits payable to a specific beneficiary, not the deceased's estate	222.13
	Disability or illness benefits	222.18
	Fraternal benefit society benefits	632.619
	Life insurance cash surrender value	222.14
miscellaneous	Alimony, child support needed for support	222.201
	Damages to employees for injuries in hazardous occupations	769.05

pensions *see also wages*	Tax-exempt retirement accounts, including 401(k)s, 403(b)s, profit-sharing and money purchase plans, SEP and SIMPLE IRAs, and defined-benefit plans	11 U.S.C. § 522(b)(3)(C)
	Traditional and Roth IRAs to $1,095,000 per person	11 U.S.C. § 522(b)(3)(C); (n)
	County officers, employees	122.15
	ERISA-qualified benefits, including IRAs & Roth IRAs	222.21(2)
	Firefighters	175.241
	Police officers	185.25
	State officers, employees	121.131
	Teachers	238.15
personal property	Any personal property to $1,000 (husband & wife may double); to $4,000 if no homestead claimed	Constitution 10-4 *In re Hawkins*, 51 B.R. 348 (S.D. Fla. 1985)
	Federal income tax refund or credit	222.25
	Health aids	222.25
	Motor vehicle to $1,000	222.25
	Pre-need funeral contract deposits	497.56(8)
	Prepaid college education trust deposits	222.22(1)
	Prepaid hurricane savings accounts	222.22(4)
	Prepaid medical savings account deposits	222.22(2)
public benefits	Crime victims' compensation, unless seeking to discharge debt for treatment of injury incurred during the crime	960.14
	Public assistance	222.201
	Social Security	222.201
	Unemployment compensation	222.201; 443.051(2),(3)
	Veterans' benefits	222.201; 744.626
	Workers' compensation	440.22
tools of trade	None	
wages	100% of wages for heads of family up to $500 per week either unpaid or paid & deposited into bank account for up to 6 months	222.11
	Federal government employees' pension payments needed for support & received 3 months prior	222.21
wildcard	See personal property	

Georgia

Federal bankruptcy exemptions not available. All law references are to the Official Code of Georgia Annotated unless otherwise noted.

ASSET	EXEMPTION	LAW
homestead	Real or personal property, including co-op, used as residence to $10,000 (to $20,000 if married, whether or not spouse is filing); up to $5,000 of unused portion of homestead may be applied to any property	44-13-100(a)(1); 44-13-100(a)(6); *In re Burnett*, 303 B.R. 684 (M.D. Ga. 2003)
insurance	Annuity & endowment contract benefits	33-28-7
	Disability or health benefits to $250 per month	33-29-15
	Fraternal benefit society benefits	33-15-62

insurance (continued)	Group insurance	33-30-10
	Proceeds & avails of life insurance	33-26-5; 33-25-11
	Life insurance proceeds if policy owned by someone you depended on, needed for support	44-13-100(a)(11)(C)
	Unmatured life insurance contract	44-13-100(a)(8)
	Unmatured life insurance dividends, interest, loan value, or cash value to $2,000 if beneficiary is you or someone you depend on	44-13-100(a)(9)
miscellaneous	Alimony, child support needed for support	44-13-100(a)(2)(D)
pensions	Tax-exempt retirement accounts, including 401(k)s, 403(b)s, profit-sharing and money purchase plans, SEP and SIMPLE IRAs, and defined-benefit plans	11 U.S.C. § 522(b)(3)(C)
	Traditional and Roth IRAs to $1,095,000 per person	11 U.S.C. § 522(b)(3)(C); (n)
	Employees of nonprofit corporations	44-13-100(a)(2.1)(B)
	ERISA-qualified benefits & IRAs	18-4-22
	Public employees	44-13-100(a)(2.1)(A); 47-2-332
	Payments from IRA necessary for support	44-13-100(a)(2)(F)
	Other pensions needed for support	18-4-22; 44-13-100(a)(2)(E); 44-13-100(a)(2.1)(C)
personal property	Animals, crops, clothing, appliances, books, furnishings, household goods, musical instruments to $300 per item, $5,000 total	44-13-100(a)(4)
	Burial plot, in lieu of homestead	44-13-100(a)(1)
	Compensation for lost future earnings needed for support to $7,500	44-13-100(a)(11)(E)
	Health aids	44-13-100(a)(10)
	Jewelry to $500	44-13-100(a)(5)
	Motor vehicles to $3,500	44-13-100(a)(3)
	Personal injury recoveries to $10,000	44-13-100(a)(11)(D)
	Wrongful death recoveries needed for support	44-13-100(a)(11)(B)
public benefits	Aid to blind	49-4-58
	Aid to disabled	49-4-84
	Crime victims' compensation	44-13-100(a)(11)(A)
	Local public assistance	44-13-100(a)(2)(A)
	Old age assistance	49-4-35
	Social Security	44-13-100(a)(2)(A)
	Unemployment compensation	44-13-100(a)(2)(A)
	Veterans' benefits	44-13-100(a)(2)(B)
	Workers' compensation	34-9-84
tools of trade	Implements, books, & tools of trade to $1,500	44-13-100(a)(7)
wages	Minimum 75% of earned but unpaid weekly disposable earnings, or 40 times the state or federal hourly minimum wage, whichever is greater, for private & federal workers; bankruptcy judge may authorize more for low-income debtors	18-4-20; 18-4-21
wildcard	$600 of any property	44-13-100(a)(6)
	Unused portion of homestead exemption to $5,000	44-13-100(a)(6)

Hawaii

Federal bankruptcy exemptions available. All law references are to Hawaii Revised Statutes unless otherwise noted.

ASSET	EXEMPTION	LAW
homestead	Head of family or over 65 to $30,000; all others to $20,000; property cannot exceed 1 acre; sale proceeds exempt for 6 months after sale (husband & wife may not double)	651-91; 651-92; 651-96
	Property held as tenancy by the entirety may be exempt against debts owed by only one spouse	*Security Pacific Bank v. Chang*, 818 F.Supp. 1343 (D. Haw. 1993)
insurance	Annuity contract or endowment policy proceeds if beneficiary is insured's spouse, child, or parent	431:10-232(b)
	Accident, health, or sickness benefits	431:10-231
	Fraternal benefit society benefits	432:2-403
	Group life insurance policy or proceeds	431:10-233
	Life insurance proceeds if clause prohibits proceeds from being used to pay beneficiary's creditors	431:10D-112
	Life or health insurance policy for spouse or child	431:10-234
miscellaneous	Property of business partnership	425-125
pensions	Tax-exempt retirement accounts, including 401(k)s, 403(b)s, profit-sharing and money purchase plans, SEP and SIMPLE IRAs, and defined-benefit plans	11 U.S.C. § 522(b)(3)(C)
	Traditional and Roth IRAs to $1,095,000 per person	11 U.S.C. § 522(b)(3)(C); (n)
	IRAs, Roth IRAs, and ERISA-qualified benefits deposited over 3 years before filing bankruptcy	651-124
	Firefighters	88-169
	Police officers	88-169
	Public officers & employees	88-91; 653-3
personal property	Appliances & furnishings	651-121(1)
	Books	651-121(1)
	Burial plot to 250 sq. ft. plus tombstones, monuments, & fencing	651-121(4)
	Clothing	651-121(1)
	Jewelry, watches, & articles of adornment to $1,000	651-121(1)
	Motor vehicle to wholesale value of $2,575	651-121(2)
	Proceeds for sold or damaged exempt property; sale proceeds exempt for 6 months after sale	651-121(5)
public benefits	Crime victims' compensation & special accounts created to limit commercial exploitation of crimes	351-66; 351-86
	Public assistance paid by Dept. of Health Services for work done in home or workshop	346-33
	Temporary disability benefits	392-29
	Unemployment compensation	383-163
	Unemployment work relief funds to $60 per month	653-4
	Workers' compensation	386-57

tools of trade	Tools, implements, books, instruments, uniforms, furnishings, fishing boat, nets, motor vehicle, & other property needed for livelihood	651-121(3)
wages	Prisoner's wages held by Dept. of Public Safety (except for restitution, child support, & other claims)	353-22.5
	Unpaid wages due for services of past 31 days	651-121(6)
wildcard	None	

Idaho

Federal bankruptcy exemptions not available. All law references are to Idaho Code unless otherwise noted.

ASSET	EXEMPTION	LAW
homestead	Real property or mobile home to $100,000; sale proceeds exempt for 6 months (husband & wife may not double)	55-1003; 55-1113
	Must record homestead exemption for property that is not yet occupied	55-1004
insurance	Annuity contract proceeds to $1,250 per month	41-1836
	Death or disability benefits	11-604(1)(a); 41-1834
	Fraternal benefit society benefits	41-3218
	Group life insurance benefits	41-1835
	Homeowners' insurance proceeds to amount of homestead exemption	55-1008
	Life insurance proceeds if clause prohibits proceeds from being used to pay beneficiary's creditors	41-1930
	Life insurance proceeds or avails for beneficiary other than the insured	11-604(d); 41-1833
	Medical, surgical, or hospital care benefits	11-603(5)
	Unmatured life insurance contract, other than credit life insurance, owned by debtor	11-605(8)
	Unmatured life insurance contract interest or dividends to $5,000 owned by debtor or person debtor depends on	11-605(9)
miscellaneous	Alimony, child support	11-604(1)(b)
	Liquor licenses	23-514
pension *see also wages*	Tax-exempt retirement accounts, including 401(k)s, 403(b)s, profit-sharing and money purchase plans, SEP and SIMPLE IRAs, and defined-benefit plans	11 U.S.C. § 522(b)(3)(C)
	Traditional and Roth IRAs to $1,095,000 per person	11 U.S.C. § 522(b)(3)(C); (n)
	ERISA-qualified benefits	55-1011
	Firefighters	72-1422
	Government & private pensions, retirement plans, IRAs, Roth IRAs, Keoghs, etc.	11-604A
	Police officers	50-1517
	Public employees	59-1317
personal property	Appliances, furnishings, books, clothing, pets, musical instruments, 1 firearm, family portraits, & sentimental heirlooms to $500 per item, $5,000 total	11-605(1)
	Building materials	45-514

personal property (continued)	Burial plot	11-603(1)
	College savings program account	11-604A(4)(b)
	Crops cultivated on maximum of 50 acres, to $1,000; water rights to 160 inches	11-605(6)
	Health aids	11-603(2)
	Jewelry to $1,000	11-605(2)
	Motor vehicle to $3,000	11-605(3)
	Personal injury recoveries	11-604(1)(c)
	Proceeds for damaged exempt property for 3 months after proceeds received	11-606
	Wrongful death recoveries	11-604(1)(c)
public benefits	Aid to blind, aged, disabled	56-223
	Federal, state, & local public assistance	11-603(4)
	General assistance	56-223
	Social Security	11-603(3)
	Unemployment compensation	11-603(6)
	Veterans' benefits	11-603(3)
	Workers' compensation	72-802
tools of trade	Arms, uniforms, & accoutrements that peace officer, National Guard, or military personnel is required to keep	11-605(5)
	Implements, books, & tools of trade to $1,500	11-605(3)
wages	Minimum 75% of earned but unpaid weekly disposable earnings, or 30 times the federal hourly minimum wage, whichever is greater; pension payments; bankruptcy judge may authorize more for low-income debtors	11-207
wildcard	$800 in any tangible personal property	11-605(10)

Illinois

Federal bankruptcy exemptions not available. All law references are to Illinois Compiled Statutes Annotated unless otherwise noted.

ASSET	EXEMPTION	LAW
homestead	Real or personal property including a farm, lot, & buildings, condo, co-op, or mobile home to $15,000; sale proceeds exempt for 1 year	735-5/12-901; 735-5/12-906
	Spouse or child of deceased owner may claim homestead exemption	735-5/12-902
	Illinois recognizes tenancy by the entirety, with limitations	750-65/22; 765-1005/1c; *In re Gillissie*, 215 B.R. 370 (Bankr. N.D. Ill. 1998); *Great Southern Co. v. Allard*, 202 B.R. 938 (N.D. Ill. 1996).
insurance	Fraternal benefit society benefits	215-5/299.1a
	Health or disability benefits	735-5/12-1001(g)(3)
	Homeowners' proceeds if home destroyed, to $15,000	735-5/12-907
	Life insurance, annuity proceeds, or cash value if beneficiary is insured's child, parent, spouse, or other dependent	215-5/238; 735-5/12-1001(f)
	Life insurance proceeds to a spouse or dependent of debtor to extent needed for support	735-5/12-1001(f),(g)(3)
miscellaneous	Alimony, child support	735-5/12-1001(g)(4)
	Property of business partnership	805-205/25

pensions	Tax-exempt retirement accounts, including 401(k)s, 403(b)s, profit-sharing and money purchase plans, SEP and SIMPLE IRAs, and defined-benefit plans	11 U.S.C. § 522(b)(3)(C)
	Traditional and Roth IRAs to $1,095,000 per person	11 U.S.C. § 522(b)(3) (C); (n)
	Civil service employees	40-5/11-223
	County employees	40-5/9-228
	Disabled firefighters; widows & children of firefighters	40-5/22-230
	IRAs and ERISA-qualified benefits	735-5/12-1006
	Firefighters	40-5/4-135; 40-5/6-213
	General Assembly members	40-5/2-154
	House of correction employees	40-5/19-117
	Judges	40-5/18-161
	Municipal employees	40-5/7-217(a); 40-5/8-244
	Park employees	40-5/12-190
	Police officers	40-5/3-144.1; 40-5/5-218
	Public employees	735-5/12-1006
	Public library employees	40-5/19-218
	Sanitation district employees	40-5/13-805
	State employees	40-5/14-147
	State university employees	40-5/15-185
	Teachers	40-5/16-190; 40-5/17-151
personal property	Bible, family pictures, schoolbooks, & clothing	735-5/12-1001(a)
	Health aids	735-5/12-1001(e)
	Motor vehicle to $2,400	735-5/12-1001(c)
	Personal injury recoveries to $15,000	735-5/12-1001(h)(4)
	Pre-need cemetery sales funds, care funds, & trust funds	235-5/6-1; 760-100/4; 815-390/16
	Prepaid tuition trust fund	110-979/45(g)
	Proceeds of sold exempt property	735-5/12-1001
	Wrongful death recoveries	735-5/12-1001(h)(2)
public benefits	Aid to aged, blind, disabled; public assistance	305-5/11-3
	Crime victims' compensation	735-5/12-1001(h)(1)
	Restitution payments on account of WWII relocation of Aleuts & Japanese Americans	735-5/12-1001(12)(h)(5)
	Social Security	735-5/12-1001(g)(1)
	Unemployment compensation	735-5/12-1001(g)(1),(3)
	Veterans' benefits	735-5/12-1001(g)(2)
	Workers' compensation	820-305/21
	Workers' occupational disease compensation	820-310/21
tools of trade	Implements, books, & tools of trade to $1,500	735-5/12-1001(d)
wages	Minimum 85% of earned but unpaid weekly wages or 45 times the federal minimum hourly wage (or state minimum hourly wage, if higher); bankruptcy judge may authorize more for low-income debtors	740-170/4
wildcard	$4,000 of any personal property (does not include wages)	735-5/12-1001(b)

Indiana

Federal bankruptcy exemptions not available. All law references are to Indiana Statutes Annotated unless otherwise noted.

ASSET	EXEMPTION	LAW
homestead *see also wildcard*	Real or personal property used as residence to $15,000	34-55-10-2(c)(1)
	Property held as tenancy by the entirety may be exempt against debts incurred by only one spouse	34-55-10-2(c)(5); 32-17-3-1
insurance	Employer's life insurance policy on employee	27-1-12-17.1
	Fraternal benefit society benefits	27-11-6-3
	Group life insurance policy	27-1-12-29
	Life insurance policy, proceeds, cash value, or avails if beneficiary is insured's spouse or dependent	27-1-12-14
	Life insurance proceeds if clause prohibits proceeds to be used to pay beneficiary's creditors	27-2-5-1
	Mutual life or accident proceeds needed for support	27-8-3-23; *In re Stinnet*, 321 B.R. 477 (SD. Ind. 2005)
miscellaneous	Property of business partnership	23-4-1-25
pensions	Tax-exempt retirement accounts, including 401(k)s, 403(b)s, profit-sharing and money purchase plans, SEP and SIMPLE IRAs, and defined-benefit plans	11 U.S.C. § 522(b) (3)(C)
	Traditional and Roth IRAs to $1,095,000 per person	11 U.S.C. § 522(b) (3)(C); (n)
	Firefighters	36-8-7-22 36-8-8-17
	Police officers	36-8-8-17; 10-12-2-10
	Public employees	5-10.3-8-9
	Public or private retirement benefits & contributions	34-55-10-2(c)(6)
	Sheriffs	36-8-10-19
	State teachers	5-10.4-5-14
personal property	Health aids	34-55-10-2(c)(4)
	Money in medical care savings account	34-55-10-2(c)(7)
	Spendthrift trusts	30-4-3-2
	$300 of any intangible personal property, except money owed to you	34-55-10-2(c)(3)
public benefits	Crime victims' compensation, unless seeking to discharge the debts for which the victim was compensated	5-2-6.1-38
	Unemployment compensation	22-4-33-3
	Workers' compensation	22-3-2-17
tools of trade	National Guard uniforms, arms, & equipment	10-16-10-3
wages	Minimum 75% of earned but unpaid weekly disposable earnings, or 30 times the federal hourly minimum wage; bankruptcy judge may authorize more for low-income debtors	24-4.5-5-105
wildcard	$8,000 of any real estate or tangible personal property	34-55-10-2(c)(2)

Iowa

Federal bankruptcy exemptions not available. All law references are to Iowa Code Annotated unless otherwise noted.

ASSET	EXEMPTION	LAW
homestead	May record homestead declaration	561.4
	Real property or an apartment to an unlimited value; property cannot exceed ½ acre in town or city, 40 acres elsewhere (husband & wife may not double)	499A.18; 561.2; 561.16
insurance	Accident, disability, health, illness, or life proceeds or avails	627.6(6)
	Disability or illness benefit	627.6(8)(c)
	Employee group insurance policy or proceeds	509.12
	Fraternal benefit society benefits	512B.18
	Life insurance proceeds if clause prohibits proceeds from being used to pay beneficiary's creditors	508.32
	Life insurance proceeds paid to spouse, child, or other dependent (limited to $10,000 if acquired within 2 years of filing for bankruptcy)	627.6(6)
	Upon death of insured, up to $15,000 total proceeds from all matured life, accident, health, or disability policies exempt from beneficiary's debts contracted before insured's death	627.6(6)
miscellaneous	Alimony, child support needed for support	627.6(8)(d)
	Liquor licenses	123.38
pensions *see also wages*	Tax-exempt retirement accounts, including 401(k)s, 403(b)s, profit-sharing and money purchase plans, SEP and SIMPLE IRAs, and defined-benefit plans	11 U.S.C. § 522(b)(3)(C)
	Traditional and Roth IRAs to $1,095,000 per person	11 U.S.C. § 522(b)(3)(C); (n)
	Disabled firefighters, police officers (only payments being received)	410.11
	Federal government pension	627.8
	Firefighters	411.13
	Other pensions, annuities, & contracts fully exempt; however, contributions made within 1 year prior to filing for bankruptcy not exempt to the extent they exceed normal & customary amounts	627.6(8)(e)
	Peace officers	97A.12
	Police officers	411.13
	Public employees	97B.39
	Retirement plans, Keoghs, IRAs, Roth IRAs, ERISA-qualified benefits	627.6(8)(f)
personal property	Bibles, books, portraits, pictures, & paintings to $1,000 total	627.6(3)
	Burial plot to 1 acre	627.6(4)
	Clothing & its storage containers, household furnishings, appliances, musical instruments, and other personal property to $7,000	627.6(5)
	Health aids	627.6(7)
	Jewelry to $2,000	627.6(1)(6)
	Residential security or utility deposit, or advance rent, to $500	627.6(14)
	Rifle or musket; shotgun	627.6(2)

ASSET	EXEMPTION	LAW
personal property (continued)	One motor vehicle to $7,000	627.6(9)
	Wedding or engagement rings, limited to $7,000 if purchased after marriage and within last two years	627.6(1)(a)
	Wrongful death proceeds and awards needed for support of debtor and dependants	627/6(15)
public benefits	Adopted child assistance	627.19
	Aid to dependent children	239B.6
	Any public assistance benefit	627.6(8)(a)
	Social Security	627.6(8)(a)
	Unemployment compensation	627.6(8)(a)
	Veterans' benefits	627.6(8)(b)
	Workers' compensation	627.13
tools of trade	Farming equipment; includes livestock, feed to $10,000	627.6(11)
	Nonfarming equipment to $10,000	627.6(10)

wages	Expected annual earnings	Amount NOT exempt per year	642.21
	$0 to $12,000	$250	
	$12,000 to $16,000	$400	
	$16,000 to $24,000	$800	
	$24,000 to $35,000	$1,000	
	$35,000 to $50,000	$2,000	
	More than $50,000	10%	
	Not exempt from spousal or child support		
	Wages or salary of a prisoner		356.29
wildcard	$1,000 of any personal property, including cash		627.6(14)

Kansas

Federal bankruptcy exemptions not available. All law references are to Kansas Statutes Annotated unless otherwise noted.

ASSET	EXEMPTION	LAW
homestead	Real property or mobile home you occupy or intend to occupy to unlimited value; property cannot exceed 1 acre in town or city, 160 acres on farm	60-2301; Constitution 15-9
insurance	Cash value of life insurance; not exempt if obtained within 1 year prior to bankruptcy with fraudulent intent	60-2313(a)(7); 40-414(b)
	Disability & illness benefits	60-2313(a)(1)
	Fraternal life insurance benefits	60-2313(a)(8)
	Life insurance proceeds	40-414(a)
miscellaneous	Alimony, maintenance, & support	60-2312(b)
	Liquor licenses	60-2313(a)(6); 41-326
pensions	Tax-exempt retirement accounts, including 401(k)s, 403(b)s, profit-sharing and money purchase plans, SEP and SIMPLE IRAs, and defined-benefit plans	11 U.S.C. § 522(b)(3)(C)
	Traditional and Roth IRAs to $1,095,000 per person	11 U.S.C. § 522(b)(3)(C); (n)
	Elected & appointed officials in cities with populations between 120,000 & 200,000	13-14a10
	ERISA-qualified benefits	60-2308(b)
	Federal government pension needed for support & paid within 3 months of filing for bankruptcy (only payments being received)	60-2308(a)

ASSET	EXEMPTION	LAW
pensions (continued)	Firefighters	12-5005(e); 14-10a10
	Judges	20-2618
	Police officers	12-5005(e); 13-14a10
	Public employees	74-4923; 74-49,105
	State highway patrol officers	74-4978g
	State school employees	72-5526
	Payment under a stock bonus, pension, profit-sharing, annuity, or similar plan or contract on account of illness, disability, death, age, or length of service, to the extent reasonably necessary for support	60-2312(b)
personal property	Burial plot or crypt	60-2304(d)
	Clothing to last 1 year	60-2304(a)
	Food & fuel to last 1 year	60-2304(a)
	Funeral plan prepayments	60-2313(a)(10); 16-310(d)
	Furnishings & household equipment	60-2304(a)
	Jewelry & articles of adornment to $1,000	60-2304(b)
	Motor vehicle to $20,000; if designed or equipped for disabled person, no limit	60-2304(c)
public benefits	Crime victims' compensation	60-2313(a)(7); 74-7313(d)
	General assistance	39-717(c)
	Social Security	60-2312(b)
	Unemployment compensation	60-2313(a)(4); 44-718(c)
	Veterans' benefits	60-2312(b)
	Workers' compensation	60-2313(a)(3); 44-514
tools of trade	Books, documents, furniture, instruments, equipment, breeding stock, seed, grain, & stock to $7,500 total	60-2304(e)
	National Guard uniforms, arms, & equipment	48-245
wages	Minimum 75% of disposable weekly wages or 30 times the federal minimum hourly wage per week, whichever is greater; bankruptcy judge may authorize more for low-income debtors	60-2310
wildcard	None	

Kentucky

Federal bankruptcy exemptions not available. All law references are to Kentucky Revised Statutes unless otherwise noted.

ASSET	EXEMPTION	LAW
homestead	Real or personal property used as residence to $5,000; sale proceeds exempt	427.060; 427.090
insurance	Annuity contract proceeds to $350 per month	304.14-330
	Cooperative life or casualty insurance benefits	427.110(1)
	Fraternal benefit society benefits	427.110(2)
	Group life insurance proceeds	304.14-320
	Health or disability benefits	304.14-310
	Life insurance policy if beneficiary is a married woman	304.14-340
insurance (continued)	Life insurance proceeds if clause prohibits proceeds from being used to pay beneficiary's creditors	304.14-350
	Life insurance proceeds or cash value if beneficiary is someone other than insured	304.14-300
miscellaneous	Alimony, child support needed for support	427.150(1)
pensions	Tax-exempt retirement accounts, including 401(k)s, 403(b)s, profit-sharing and money purchase plans, SEP and SIMPLE IRAs, and defined-benefit plans	11 U.S.C. § 522(b)(3)(C)
	Traditional and Roth IRAs to $1,095,000 per person	11 U.S.C. § 522(b)(3)(C); (n)
	ERISA-qualified benefits, including IRAs, SEPs, & Keoghs deposited more than 120 days before filing	427.150
	Firefighters	67A.620; 95.878
	Police officers	427.120; 427.125
	State employees	61.690
	Teachers	161.700
	Urban county government employees	67A.350
personal property	Burial plot to $5,000, in lieu of homestead	427.060
	Clothing, jewelry, articles of adornment, & furnishings to $3,000 total	427.010(1)
	Health aids	427.010(1)
	Lost earnings payments needed for support	427.150(2)(d)
	Medical expenses paid & reparation benefits received under motor vehicle reparation law	304.39-260
	Motor vehicle to $2,500	427.010(1)
	Personal injury recoveries to $7,500 (not to include pain & suffering or pecuniary loss)	427.150(2)(c)
	Prepaid tuition payment fund account	164A.707(3)
	Wrongful death recoveries for person you depended on, needed for support	427.150(2)(b)
public benefits	Aid to blind, aged, disabled; public assistance	205.220(c)
	Crime victims' compensation	427.150(2)(a)
	Unemployment compensation	341.470(4)
	Workers' compensation	342.180
tools of trade	Library, office equipment, instruments, & furnishings of minister, attorney, physician, surgeon, chiropractor, veterinarian, or dentist to $1,000	427.040
	Motor vehicle of auto mechanic, mechanical, or electrical equipment servicer, minister, attorney, physician, surgeon, chiropractor, veterinarian, or dentist to $2,500	427.030
	Tools, equipment, livestock, & poultry of farmer to $3,000	427.010(1)
	Tools of nonfarmer to $300	427.030
wages	Minimum 75% of disposable weekly earnings or 30 times the federal minimum hourly wage per week, whichever is greater; bankruptcy judge may authorize more for low-income debtors	427.010(2),(3)
wildcard	$1,000 of any property	427.160

Louisiana

Federal bankruptcy exemptions not available. All law references are to Louisiana Revised Statutes Annotated unless otherwise noted.

ASSET	EXEMPTION	LAW
homestead	Property you occupy to $25,000 (if debt is result of catastrophic or terminal illness or injury, limit is full value of property as of 1 year before filing); cannot exceed 5 acres in city or town, 200 acres elsewhere (husband & wife may not double)	20:1(A)(1),(2),(3)
	Spouse or child of deceased owner may claim homestead exemption; spouse given home in divorce gets homestead	20:1(B)
insurance	Annuity contract proceeds & avails	22:647
	Fraternal benefit society benefits	22:558
	Group insurance policies or proceeds	22:649
	Health, accident, or disability proceeds or avails	22:646
	Life insurance proceeds or avails; if policy issued within 9 months of filing, exempt only to $35,000	22:647
miscellaneous	Property of minor child	13:3881(A)(3); Civil Code Art. 223
pensions	Tax-exempt retirement accounts, including 401(k)s, 403(b)s, profit-sharing and money purchase plans, SEP and SIMPLE IRAs, and defined-benefit plans	11 U.S.C. § 522(b) (3)(C)
	Traditional and Roth IRAs to $1,095,000 per person	11 U.S.C. § 522(b) (3)(C); (n)
	Assessors	11:1403
	Court clerks	11:1526
	District attorneys	11:1583
	ERISA-qualified benefits, including IRAs, Roth IRAs, & Keoghs, if contributions made over 1 year before filing for bankruptcy	13:3881; 20:33(1)
	Firefighters	11:2263
	Gift or bonus payments from employer to employee or heirs whenever paid	20:33(2)
	Judges	11:1378
	Louisiana University employees	11:952.3
	Municipal employees	11:1735
	Parochial employees	11:1905
	Police officers	11:3513
	School employees	11:1003
	Sheriffs	11:2182
	State employees	11:405
	Teachers	11:704
	Voting registrars	11:2033
personal property	Arms, military accoutrements; bedding; dishes, glassware, utensils, silverware (nonsterling); clothing, family portraits, musical instruments; bedroom, living room, & dining room furniture; poultry, 1 cow, household pets; heating & cooling equipment, refrigerator, freezer, stove, washer & dryer, iron, sewing machine	13:3881(A)(4)
	Cemetery plot, monuments	8:313

personal property (continued)	Disaster relief insurance proceeds	13:3881(A)(7)
	Engagement & wedding rings to $5,000	13:3881(A)(5)
	Motor vehicle to $7,500	13:3881(A)(7)
	Motor vehicle modified for disability to $7,500	13:3881(A)(8)
	Spendthrift trusts	9:2004
public benefits	Aid to blind, aged, disabled; public assistance	46:111
	Crime victims' compensation	46:1811
	Earned income tax credit	13:3881 (A)(6)
	Unemployment compensation	23:1693
	Workers' compensation	23:1205
tools of trade	Tools, instruments, books, $7,500 of equity in a motor vehicle, one firearm to $500, needed to work	13:3881(A)(2)
wages	Minimum 75% of disposable weekly earnings or 30 times the federal minimum hourly wage per week, whichever is greater; bankruptcy judge may authorize more for low-income debtors	13:3881(A)(1)
wildcard	None	

Maine

Federal bankruptcy exemptions not available. All law references are to Maine Revised Statutes Annotated, in the form title number-section number, unless otherwise noted.

ASSET	EXEMPTION	LAW
homestead	Real or personal property (including cooperative) used as residence to $35,000; if debtor has minor dependents in residence, to $70,000; if debtor over age 60 or physically or mentally disabled, $70,000; proceeds of sale exempt for six months	14-4422(1)
insurance	Annuity proceeds to $450 per month	24-A-2431
	Death benefit for police, fire, or emergency medical personnel who die in the line of duty	25-1612
	Disability or health proceeds, benefits, or avails	14-4422(13) (A),(C); 24-A-2429
	Fraternal benefit society benefits	24-A-4118
	Group health or life policy or proceeds	24-A-2430
	Life, endowment, annuity, or accident policy, proceeds or avails	14-4422(14)(C); 24-A-2428
	Life insurance policy, interest, loan value, or accrued dividends for policy from person you depended on, to $4,000	14-4422(11)
	Unmatured life insurance policy, except credit insurance policy	14-4422(10)
miscellaneous	Alimony & child support needed for support	14-4422(13)(D)
pensions	Tax-exempt retirement accounts, including 401(k)s, 403(b)s, profit-sharing and money purchase plans, SEP and SIMPLE IRAs, and defined-benefit plans	11 U.S.C. § 522(b) (3)(C)
	Traditional and Roth IRAs to $1,095,000 per person	11 U.S.C. § 522(b) (3)(C); (n)
	ERISA-qualified benefits	14-4422(13)(E)
	Judges	4-1203
	Legislators	3-703
	State employees	5-17054

personal property	Animals, crops, musical instruments, books, clothing, furnishings, household goods, appliances to $200 per item	14-4422(3)
	Balance due on repossessed goods; total amount financed can't exceed $2,000	9-A-5-103
	Burial plot in lieu of homestead exemption	14-4422(1)
	Cooking stove; furnaces & stoves for heat	14-4422(6)(A),(B)
	Food to last 6 months	14-4422(7)(A)
	Fuel not to exceed 10 cords of wood, 5 tons of coal, or 1,000 gal. of heating oil	14-4422(6)(C)
	Health aids	14-4422(12)
	Jewelry to $750; no limit for one wedding & one engagement ring	14-4422(4)
	Lost earnings payments needed for support	14-4422(14)(E)
	Military clothes, arms, & equipment	37-B-262
	Motor vehicle to $5,000	14-4422(2)
	Personal injury recoveries to $12,500	14-4422(14)(D)
	Seeds, fertilizers, & feed to raise & harvest food for 1 season	14-4422(7)(B)
	Tools & equipment to raise & harvest food	14-4422(7)(C)
	Wrongful death recoveries needed for support	14-4422(14)(B)
public benefits	Maintenance under the Rehabilitation Act	26-1411-H
	Crime victims' compensation	14-4422(14)(A)
	Federal, state, or local public assistance benefits; earned income and child tax credits	14-4422(13)(A); 22-3180, 22-3766
	Social Security	14-4422(13)(A)
	Unemployment compensation	14-4422(13)(A),(C)
	Veterans' benefits	14-4422(13)(B)
	Workers' compensation	39-A-106
tools of trade	Books, materials, & stock to $5,000	14-4422(5)
	Commercial fishing boat, 5-ton limit	14-4422(9)
	One of each farm implement (& its maintenance equipment needed to harvest & raise crops)	14-4422(8)
wages	None (use federal nonbankruptcy wage exemption)	
wildcard	Unused portion of exemption in homestead to $6,000; or unused exemption in animals, crops, musical instruments, books, clothing, furnishings, household goods, appliances, tools of the trade, & personal injury recoveries	14-4422(15)
	$400 of any property	14-4422(15)

insurance (continued)	Life insurance or annuity contract proceeds or avails if beneficiary is insured's dependent, child, or spouse	Ins. 16-111(a); Estates & Trusts 8-115
	Medical insurance benefits deducted from wages plus medical insurance payments to $145 per week or 75% of disposable wages	Commercial Law 15-601.1(3)
miscellaneous	Child support	11-504(b)(6)
	Alimony to same extent wages are exempt	11-504(b)(7)
pensions	Tax-exempt retirement accounts, including 401(k)s, 403(b)s, profit-sharing and money purchase plans, SEP and SIMPLE IRAs, and defined-benefit plans	11 U.S.C. § 522(b)(3)(C)
	Traditional and Roth IRAs to $1,095,000 per person	11 U.S.C. § 522(b)(3)(C); (n)
	ERISA-qualified benefits, including IRAs, Roth IRAs, & Keoghs	11-504(h)(1), (4)
	State employees	State Pers. & Pen. 21-502
personal property	Appliances, furnishings, household goods, books, pets, & clothing to $1,000 total	11-504(b)(4)
	Burial plot	Bus. Reg. 5-503
	Health aids	11-504(b)(3)
	Perpetual care trust funds	Bus. Reg. 5-603
	Prepaid college trust funds	Educ. 18-1913
	Lost future earnings recoveries	11-504(b)(2)
public benefits	Baltimore Police death benefits	Code of 1957 art. 24, 16-103
	Crime victims' compensation	Crim. Proc. 11-816(b)
	Unemployment compensation	Labor & Employment 8-106
	Workers' compensation	Labor & Employment 9-732
tools of trade	Clothing, books, tools, instruments, & appliances to $5,000	11-504(b)(1)
wages	Earned but unpaid wages, the greater of 75% or $145 per week; in Kent, Caroline, & Queen Anne's of Worcester Counties, the greater of 75% or 30 times federal minimum hourly wage	Commercial Law 15-601.1
wildcard	$6,000 in cash or any property, if claimed within 30 days of attachment or levy	11-504(b)(5)
	An additional $5,000 in real or personal property	11-504(f)

Maryland

Federal bankruptcy exemptions not available. All law references are to Maryland Code of Courts & Judicial Proceedings unless otherwise noted.

ASSET	EXEMPTION	LAW
homestead	None; however, property held as tenancy by the entirety is exempt against debts owed by only one spouse	*In re Birney*, 200 F.3d 225 (4th Cir. 1999)
insurance	Disability or health benefits, including court awards, arbitrations, & settlements	11-504(b)(2)
	Fraternal benefit society benefits	Ins. 8-431; Estates & Trusts 8-115

Massachusetts

Federal bankruptcy exemptions available. All law references are to Massachusetts General Laws Annotated, in the form title number-section number, unless otherwise noted.

ASSET	EXEMPTION	LAW
homestead	If statement of homestead is not in title to property, must record homestead declaration before filing bankruptcy	188-2
	Property held as tenancy by the entirety may be exempt against debt for nonnecessity owed by only one spouse	209-1

homestead (continued)	Property you occupy or intend to occupy (including mobile home) to $500,000 (special rules if over 65 or disabled)	188-1; 188-1A
	Spouse or children of deceased owner may claim homestead exemption	188-4
insurance	Disability benefits to $400 per week	175-110A
	Fraternal benefit society benefits	176-22
	Group annuity policy or proceeds	175-132C
	Group life insurance policy	175-135
	Life insurance or annuity contract proceeds if clause prohibits proceeds from being used to pay beneficiary's creditors	175-119A
	Life insurance policy if beneficiary is married woman	175-126
	Life or endowment policy, proceeds, or cash value	175-125
	Medical malpractice self-insurance	175F-15
miscellaneous	Property of business partnership	108A-25
pensions *see also wages*	Tax-exempt retirement accounts, including 401(k)s, 403(b)s, profit-sharing and money purchase plans, SEP and SIMPLE IRAs, and defined-benefit plans	11 U.S.C. § 522(b)(3)(C)
	Traditional and Roth IRAs to $1,095,000 per person	11 U.S.C. § 522(b)(3)(C); (n)
	Credit union employees	171-84
	ERISA-qualified benefits, including IRAs & Keoghs to specified limits.	235-34A; 246-28
	Private retirement benefits	32-41
	Public employees	32-19
	Savings bank employees	168-41; 168-44
personal property	Bank deposits to $125	235-34
	Beds & bedding; heating unit; clothing	235-34
	Bibles & books to $200 total; sewing machine to $200	235-34
	Burial plots, tombs, & church pew	235-34
	Cash for fuel, heat, water, or light to $75 per month	235-34
	Cash to $200/month for rent, in lieu of homestead	235-34
	Cooperative association shares to $100	235-34
	Food or cash for food to $300	235-34
	Furniture to $3,000; motor vehicle to $700	235-34
	Moving expenses for eminent domain	79-6A
	Trust company, bank, or credit union deposits to $500	246-28A
	2 cows, 12 sheep, 2 swine, 4 tons of hay	235-34
public benefits	Aid to families with dependent children	118-10
	Public assistance	235-34
	Unemployment compensation	151A-36
	Veterans' benefits	115-5
	Workers' compensation	152-47
tools of trade	Arms, accoutrements, & uniforms required	235-34
	Fishing boats, tackle, & nets to $500	235-34
	Materials you designed & procured to $500	235-34
	Tools, implements, & fixtures to $500 total	235-34
wages	Earned but unpaid wages to $125 per week	246-28
wildcard	None	

Michigan

Federal bankruptcy exemptions available. All law references are to Michigan Compiled Laws Annotated unless otherwise noted.

Under Michigan law, bankruptcy exemption amounts are adjusted for inflation every three years (starting in 2005) by the Michigan Department of Treasury. These amounts have already been adjusted, so the amounts listed in the statutes are not current. You can find the current amounts at www.michigan.gov/documents/BankruptcyExemptions2005_141050_7.pdf or by going to www.michigan.gov/treasury and typing "bankruptcy exemptions" in the search box.

ASSET	EXEMPTION	LAW
homestead	Property held as tenancy by the entirety may be exempt against debts owed by only one spouse	600.5451(1)(o)
	Real property including condo to $31,900 ($47,825 if over 65 or disabled); property cannot exceed 1 lot in town, village, city, or 40 acres elsewhere; spouse or children of deceased owner may claim homestead exemption	600.5451(1)(n); (5)(d)
insurance	Disability, mutual life, or health benefits	600.5451(1)(j)
	Employer-sponsored life insurance policy or trust fund	500.2210
	Fraternal benefit society benefits	500.8181
	Life, endowment, or annuity proceeds if clause prohibits proceeds from being used to pay beneficiary's creditors	500.4054
	Life insurance	500.2207
miscellaneous	Property of business partnership	449.25
pensions	Tax-exempt retirement accounts, including 401(k)s, 403(b)s, profit-sharing and money purchase plans, SEP and SIMPLE IRAs, and defined-benefit plans	11 U.S.C. § 522(b)(3)(C)
	Traditional and Roth IRAs to $1,095,000 per person	11 U.S.C. § 522(b)(3)(C); (n)
	ERISA-qualified benefits, except contributions within last 120 days	600.5451(1)(m)
	Firefighters, police officers	38.559(6); 38.1683
	IRAs & Roth IRAs, except contributions within last 120 days	600.5451(1)(l)
	Judges	38.2308; 38.1683
	Legislators	38.1057; 38.1683
	Probate judges	38.2308; 38.1683
	Public school employees	38.1346; 38.1683
	State employees	38.40; 38.1683
personal property	Appliances, utensils, books, furniture, & household goods to $475 each, $3,200 total	600.5451(1)(c)
	Building & loan association shares to $1,075 par value, in lieu of homestead	600.5451(1)(k)
	Burial plots, cemeteries	600.5451(1)(a)
	Church pew, slip, seat for entire family to $525	600.5451(1)(d)
	Clothing; family pictures	600.5451(1)(a)
	Food & fuel to last family for 6 months	600.5451(1)(b)
	Crops, animals, and feed to $2,125	600.5451(1)(d)
	1 motor vehicle to $2,950	600.5451(1)(g)
	Computer & accessories to $525	600.5451(1)(h)
	Household pets to $525	600.5451(1)(f)
	Professionally prescribed health aids	600.5451(a)

public benefits	Crime victims' compensation	18.362
	Social welfare benefits	400.63
	Unemployment compensation	421.30
	Veterans' benefits for Korean War veterans	35.977
	Veterans' benefits for Vietnam veterans	35.1027
	Veterans' benefits for WWII veterans	35.926
	Workers' compensation	418.821
tools of trade	Arms & accoutrements required	600.6023(1)(a)
	Tools, implements, materials, stock, apparatus, team, motor vehicle, horse, & harness to $1,000 total	600.6023(1)(e)
wages	Head of household may keep 60% of earned but unpaid wages (no less than $15/week), plus $2/week per nonspouse dependent; if not head of household may keep 40% (no less than $10/week)	600.5311
wildcard	None	

Minnesota

Federal bankruptcy exemptions available. All law references are to Minnesota Statutes Annotated, unless otherwise noted.

NOTE: Section 550.37(4)(a) requires certain exemptions to be adjusted for inflation on July 1 of even-numbered years; this table includes all changes made through July 1, 2006. Exemptions are published on or before the May 1 issue of the Minnesota State Register, *www.comm.media.state.mn.us/bookstore/stateregister.asp*, or call the Minnesota Dept. of Commerce at 651-296-7977.

ASSET	EXEMPTION	LAW
homestead	Home & land on which it is situated to $300,000; if homestead is used for agricultural purposes, $750,000; cannot exceed ½ acre in city, 160 acres elsewhere (husband & wife may not double)	510.01; 510.02
	Manufactured home to an unlimited value	550.37 subd. 12
insurance	Accident or disability proceeds	550.39
	Fraternal benefit society benefits	64B.18
	Life insurance proceeds to $40,000, if beneficiary is spouse or child of insured, plus $10,000 per dependent	550.37 subd. 10
	Police, fire, or beneficiary association benefits	550.37 subd. 11
	Unmatured life insurance contract dividends, interest, or loan value to $8,000 if insured is debtor or person debtor depends on	550.37 subd. 23
miscellaneous	Earnings of minor child	550.37 subd. 15
pensions	Tax-exempt retirement accounts, including 401(k)s, 403(b)s, profit-sharing and money purchase plans, SEP and SIMPLE IRAs, and defined-benefit plans	11 U.S.C. § 522(b)(3)(C)
	Traditional and Roth IRAs to $1,095,000 per person	11 U.S.C. § 522(b)(3)(C); (n)
	ERISA-qualified benefits or needed for support, up to $60,000 in present value	550.37 subd. 24
	IRAs or Roth IRAs needed for support, up to $60,000 in present value	550.37 subd. 24
	Public employees	353.15; 356.401
	State employees	352.96 subd. 6; 356.401
	State troopers	352B.071; 356.401

personal property	Appliances, furniture, jewelry, radio, phonographs, & TV to $9,000 total	550.37 subd. 4(b)
	Bible & books	550.37 subd. 2
	Burial plot; church pew or seat	550.37 subd. 3
	Clothing, one watch, food, & utensils for family	550.37 subd. 4(a)
	Motor vehicle to $4,000 (up to $40,000 if vehicle has been modified for disability)	550.37 subd. 12(a)
	Personal injury recoveries	550.37 subd. 22
	Proceeds for damaged exempt property	550.37 subds. 9, 16
	Wedding rings to $2,250	550.37 subd. 4(c)
	Wrongful death recoveries	550.37 subd. 22
public benefits	Crime victims' compensation	611A.60
	Public benefits	550.37 subd. 14
	Unemployment compensation	268.192 subd. 2
	Veterans' benefits	550.38
	Workers' compensation	176.175
tools of trade total (except teaching materials) can't exceed $13,000	Farm machines, implements, livestock, produce, & crops	550.37 subd. 5
	Teaching materials of college, university, public school, or public institution teacher	550.37 subd. 8
	Tools, machines, instruments, stock in trade, furniture, & library to $10,000 total	550.37 subd. 6
wages	Minimum 75% of weekly disposable earnings or 40 times federal minimum hourly wage, whichever is greater	571.922
	Wages deposited into bank accounts for 20 days after depositing	550.37 subd. 13
	Wages, paid within 6 mos. of returning to work, after receiving welfare or after incarceration; includes earnings deposited in a financial institution in the last 60 days	550.37 subd. 14
wildcard	None	

NOTE: In cases of suspected fraud, the Minnesota constitution permits courts to cap exemptions that would otherwise be unlimited. *In re Tveten*, 402 N.W.2d 551 (Minn. 1987); *In re Medill*, 119 B.R. 685 (Bankr. D. Minn. 1990); *In re Sholdan*, 217 F.3d 1006 (8th Cir. 2000).

Mississippi

Federal bankruptcy exemptions not available. All law references are to Mississippi Code unless otherwise noted.

ASSET	EXEMPTION	LAW
homestead	May file homestead declaration	85-3-27; 85-3-31
	Mobile home does not qualify as homestead unless you own land on which it is located (*see personal property*)	*In re Cobbins*, 234 B.R. 882 (S.D. Miss. 1999)
	Property you own & occupy to $75,000; if over 60 & married or widowed may claim a former residence; property cannot exceed 160 acres; sale proceeds exempt	85-3-1(b)(i); 85-3-21; 85-3-23
insurance	Disability benefits	85-3-1(b)(ii)
	Fraternal benefit society benefits	83-29-39
	Homeowners' insurance proceeds to $75,000	85-3-23
	Life insurance proceeds if clause prohibits proceeds from being used to pay beneficiary's creditors	83-7-5; 85-3-11

pensions	Tax-exempt retirement accounts, including 401(k)s, 403(b)s, profit-sharing and money purchase plans, SEP and SIMPLE IRAs, and defined-benefit plans	11 U.S.C. § 522(b)(3)(C)
	Traditional and Roth IRAs to $1,095,000 per person	11 U.S.C. § 522(b)(3) (C); (n)
	ERISA-qualified benefits, IRAs, Keoghs deposited over 1 yr. before filing bankruptcy	85-3-1(e)
	Firefighters (includes death benefits)	21-29-257; 45-2-1
	Highway patrol officers	25-13-31
	Law enforcement officers' death benefits	45-2-1
	Police officers (includes death benefits)	21-29-257; 45-2-1
	Private retirement benefits to extent tax-deferred	71-1-43
	Public employees retirement & disability benefits	25-11-129
	State employees	25-14-5
	Teachers	25-11-201(1)(d)
	Volunteer firefighters' death benefits	45-2-1
personal property	Mobile home to $30,000	85-3-1(d)
	Personal injury judgments to $10,000	85-3-17
	Sale or insurance proceeds for exempt property	85-3-1(b)(i)
	State health savings accounts	85-3-1(f)
	Tangible personal property to $10,000: any items worth less than $200 each; furniture, dishes, kitchenware, household goods, appliances, 1 radio & 1 TV, 1 firearm, 1 lawn-mower, clothing, wedding rings, motor vehicles, tools of the trade, books, crops, health aids, domestic animals (does not include works of art, antiques, jewelry, or electronic entertainment equipment)	85-3-1(a)
public benefits	Assistance to aged	43-9-19
	Assistance to blind	43-3-71
	Assistance to disabled	43-29-15
	Crime victims' compensation	99-41-23(7)
	Federal income tax refund to $5,000; earned income tax credit to $5,000; state tax refunds to $5,000	85-3-1(h); (i); (j)
	Social Security	25-11-129
	Unemployment compensation	71-5-539
	Workers' compensation	71-3-43
tools of trade	*See personal property*	
wages	Earned but unpaid wages owed for 30 days; after 30 days, minimum 75% of earned but unpaid weekly disposable earnings, or 30 times the federal hourly minimum wage, whichever is greater (bankruptcy judge may authorize more for low-income debtors)	85-3-4
wildcard	$50,000 of any property, including deposits of money, available to Mississippi resident who is at least 70 years old; *also see personal property*	85-3-1(g)

Missouri

Federal bankruptcy exemptions not available. All law references are to Annotated Missouri Statutes unless otherwise noted.

ASSET	EXEMPTION	LAW
homestead	Property held as tenancy by the entirety may be exempt against debts owed by only one spouse	*In re Eads*, 271 B.R. 371 (Bankr. W.D. Mo. 2002).
	Real property to $15,000 or mobile home to $5,000 (joint owners may not double)	513.430(6); 513.475 *In re Smith*, 254 B.R. 751 (Bank. W.D. Mo. 2000)
insurance	Assessment plan or life insurance proceeds	377.090
	Disability or illness benefits	513.430(10)(c)
	Fraternal benefit society benefits to $5,000, bought over 6 months before filing	513.430(8)
	Life insurance dividends, loan value, or interest to $150,000, bought over 6 months before filing	513.430(8)
	Life insurance proceeds if policy owned by unmarried woman & insures her father or brother	376.550
	Stipulated insurance premiums	377.330
	Unmatured life insurance policy	513.430(7)
miscellaneous	Alimony, child support to $750 per month	513.430(10)(d)
	Property of business partnership	358.250
pensions	Tax-exempt retirement accounts, including 401(k)s, 403(b)s, profit-sharing and money purchase plans, SEP and SIMPLE IRAs, and defined-benefit plans	11 U.S.C. § 522(b)(3)(C)
	Traditional and Roth IRAs to $1,095,000 per person	11 U.S.C. § 522(b)(3)(C); (n)
	Employee benefit spendthrift trust	456.014
	Employees of cities with 100,000 or more people	71.207
	ERISA-qualified benefits, IRAs, Roth IRAs, & other retirement accounts needed for support	513.430(10)(e), (f)
	Firefighters	87.090; 87.365; 87.485
	Highway & transportation employees	104.250
	Police department employees	86.190; 86.353; 86.1430
	Public officers & employees	70.695; 70.755
	State employees	104.540
	Teachers	169.090
personal property	Appliances, household goods, furnishings, clothing, books, crops, animals, & musical instruments to $3,000 total	513.430(1)
	Burial grounds to 1 acre or $100	214.190
	Health aids	513.430(9)
	Motor vehicle to $3,000	513.430(5)
	Wedding ring to $1,500, & other jewelry to $500	513.430(2)
	Wrongful death recoveries for person you depended on	513.430(11)

public benefits	Crime victim's compensation	595.025
	Public assistance	513.430(10)(a)
	Social Security	513.430(10)(a)
	Unemployment compensation	288.380(10)(l); 513.430(10)(c)
	Veterans' benefits	513.430(10)b
	Workers' compensation	287.260
tools of trade	Implements, books, & tools of trade to $3,000	513.430(4)
wages	Minimum 75% of weekly earnings (90% of weekly earnings for head of family), or 30 times the federal minimum hourly wage, whichever is more; bankruptcy judge may authorize more for low-income debtors	525.030
	Wages of servant or common laborer to $90	513.470
wildcard	$1,250 of any property if head of family, else $600; head of family may claim additional $350 per child	513.430(3); 513.440

Montana

Federal bankruptcy exemptions not available. All law references are to Montana Code Annotated unless otherwise noted.

ASSET	EXEMPTION	LAW
homestead	Must record homestead declaration before filing for bankruptcy	70-32-105
	Real property or mobile home you occupy to $250,000; sale, condemnation, or insurance proceeds exempt for 18 months	70-32-104; 70-32-201; 70-32-213
insurance	Annuity contract proceeds to $350 per month	33-15-514
	Disability or illness proceeds, avails, or benefits	25-13-608(1)(d); 33-15-513
	Fraternal benefit society benefits	33-7-522
	Group life insurance policy or proceeds	33-15-512
	Hail insurance benefits	80-2-245
	Life insurance proceeds if clause prohibits proceeds from being used to pay beneficiary's creditors	33-20-120
	Medical, surgical, or hospital care benefits	25-13-608(1)(f)
	Unmatured life insurance contracts	25-13-608(1)(k)
miscellaneous	Alimony, child support	25-13-608(1)(g)
pensions	Tax-exempt retirement accounts, including 401(k)s, 403(b)s, profit-sharing and money purchase plans, SEP and SIMPLE IRAs, and defined-benefit plans	11 U.S.C. § 522(b)(3)(C)
	Traditional and Roth IRAs to $1,095,000 per person	11 U.S.C. § 522(b)(3)(C); (n)
	ERISA-qualified benefits deposited over 1 year before filing bankruptcy or up to 15% of debtor's gross annual income	31-2-106
	Firefighters	19-18-612(1)
	IRA & Roth IRA contributions & earnings made before judgment filed	25-13-608(1)(e)
	Police officers	19-19-504(1)
	Public employees	19-2-1004; 25-13-608(i)
	Teachers	19-20-706(2); 25-13-608(j)
	University system employees	19-21-212

personal property	Appliances, household furnishings, goods, animals with feed, crops, musical instruments, books, firearms, sporting goods, clothing, & jewelry to $600 per item, $4,500 total	25-13-609(1)
	Burial plot	25-13-608(1)(h)
	Cooperative association shares to $500 value	35-15-404
	Health aids	25-13-608(1)(a)
	Motor vehicle to $2,500	25-13-609(2)
	Proceeds from sale or for damage or loss of exempt property for 6 mos. after received	25-13-610
public benefits	Aid to aged, disabled needy persons	53-2-607
	Crime victims' compensation	53-9-129
	Local public assistance	25-13-608(1)(b)
	Silicosis benefits	39-73-110
	Social Security	25-13-608(1)(b)
	Subsidized adoption payments to needy persons	53-2-607
	Unemployment compensation	31-2-106(2); 39-51-3105
	Veterans' benefits	25-13-608(1)(c)
	Vocational rehabilitation to blind needy persons	53-2-607
	Workers' compensation	39-71-743
tools of trade	Implements, books, & tools of trade to $3,000	25-13-609(3)
	Uniforms, arms, accoutrements needed to carry out government functions	25-13-613(b)
wages	Minimum 75% of earned but unpaid weekly disposable earnings, or 30 times the federal hourly minimum wage, whichever is greater; bankruptcy judge may authorize more for low-income debtors	25-13-614
wildcard	None	

Nebraska

Federal bankruptcy exemptions not available. All law references are to Revised Statutes of Nebraska unless otherwise noted.

ASSET	EXEMPTION	LAW
homestead	$60,000 for married debtor or head of household; cannot exceed 2 lots in city or village, 160 acres elsewhere; sale proceeds exempt 6 months after sale (husband & wife may not double)	40-101; 40-111; 40-113
	May record homestead declaration	40-105
insurance	Fraternal benefit society benefits to $100,000 loan value unless beneficiary convicted of a crime related to benefits	44-1089
	Life insurance proceeds and avails to $100,000	44-371
pensions *see also wages*	Tax-exempt retirement accounts, including 401(k)s, 403(b)s, profit-sharing and money purchase plans, SEP and SIMPLE IRAs, and defined-benefit plans	11 U.S.C. § 522(b)(3)(C)
	Traditional and Roth IRAs to $1,095,000 per person	11 U.S.C. § 522(b)(3)(C); (n)
	County employees	23-2322
	Deferred compensation of public employees	48-1401
	ERISA-qualified benefits including IRAs & Roth IRAs needed for support	25-1563.01
	Military disability benefits	25-1559
	School employees	79-948
	State employees	84-1324

personal property	Burial plot	12-517
	Clothing	25-1556(2)
	Crypts, lots, tombs, niches, vaults	12-605
	Furniture, household goods & appliances, household electronics, personal computers, books, & musical instruments to $1,500	25-1556(3)
	Health aids	25-1556(5)
	Medical or health savings accounts to $25,000	8-1, 131(2)(b)
	Perpetual care funds	12-511
	Personal injury recoveries	25-1563.02
	Personal possessions	25-1556
public benefits	Aid to disabled, blind, aged; public assistance	68-1013
	General assistance to poor persons	68-148
	Unemployment compensation	48-647
	Workers' compensation	48-149
tools of trade	Equipment or tools including a vehicle used in/or for commuting to principal place of business to $2,400 (husband & wife may double)	25-1556(4); *In re Keller*, 50 B.R. 23 (D. Neb. 1985)
wages	Minimum 85% of earned but unpaid weekly disposable earnings or pension payments for head of family; minimum 75% of earned but unpaid weekly disposable earnings, or 30 times the federal hourly minimum wage, whichever is greater, for all others; bankruptcy judge may authorize more for low-income debtors	25-1558
wildcard	$2,500 of any personal property, except wages, in lieu of homestead	25-1552

Nevada

Federal bankruptcy exemptions not available. All law references are to Nevada Revised Statutes Annotated unless otherwise noted.

ASSET	EXEMPTION	LAW
homestead	Must record homestead declaration before filing for bankruptcy	115.020
	Real property or mobile home to $350,000	115.010; 21.090(1)(m)
insurance	Annuity contract proceeds to $350 per month	687B.290
	Fraternal benefit society benefits	695A.220
	Group life or health policy or proceeds	687B.280
	Health proceeds or avails	687B.270
	Life insurance policy or proceeds if annual premiums not over $1,000	21.090(1)(k); *In re Bower*, 234 B.R. 109 (Nev. 1999)
	Life insurance proceeds if you're not the insured	687B.260
miscellaneous	Alimony & child support	21.090(1)(r)
	Property of some business partnerships	87.250
pensions	Tax-exempt retirement accounts, including 401(k)s, 403(b)s, profit-sharing and money purchase plans, SEP and SIMPLE IRAs, and defined-benefit plans	11 U.S.C. § 522(b)(3)(C)
	Traditional and Roth IRAs to $1,095,000 per person	11 U.S.C. § 522(b)(3)(C); (n)
	ERISA-qualified benefits, deferred compensation, SEP IRA, Roth IRA, or IRA to $500,000	21.090(1)(q)
	Public employees	286.670

personal property	Appliances, household goods, furniture, home & yard equipment to $12,000 total	21.090(1)(b)
	Books, works of art, musical instruments, & jewelry to $5,000	21.090(1)(a)
	Burial plot purchase money held in trust	689.700
	Funeral service contract money held in trust	689.700
	Health aids	21.090(1)(p)
	Keepsakes & pictures	21.090(1)(a)
	Metal-bearing ores, geological specimens, art curiosities, or paleontological remains; must be arranged, classified, catalogued, & numbered in reference books	21.100
	Mortgage impound accounts	645B.180
	Motor vehicle to $15,000; no limit on vehicle equipped for disabled person	21.090(1)(f),(o)
	One gun	21.090(1)(i)
	Personal injury compensation to $16,500	21.090(t)
	Restitution received for criminal act	21.090(w)
	Wrongful death awards to survivors	21.090(u)
public benefits	Aid to blind, aged, disabled; public assistance	422.291
	Crime victim's compensation	21.090
	Industrial insurance (workers' compensation)	616C.205
	Public assistance for children	432.036
	Unemployment compensation	612.710
	Vocational rehabilitation benefits	615.270
tools of trade	Arms, uniforms, & accoutrements you're required to keep	21.090(1)(j)
	Cabin or dwelling of miner or prospector; mining claim, cars, implements, & appliances to $4,500 total (for working claim only)	21.090(1)(e)
	Farm trucks, stock, tools, equipment, & seed to $4,500	21.090(1)(c)
	Library, equipment, supplies, tools, inventory, & materials to $10,000	21.090(1)(d)
wages	Minimum 75% of disposable weekly earnings or 30 times the federal minimum hourly wage per week, whichever is more; bankruptcy judge may authorize more for low-income debtors	21.090(1)(g)
wildcard	None	

New Hampshire

Federal bankruptcy exemptions available. All law references are to New Hampshire Revised Statutes Annotated unless otherwise noted.

ASSET	EXEMPTION	LAW
homestead	Real property or manufactured housing (& the land it's on if you own it) to $100,000	480:1
insurance	Firefighters' aid insurance	402:69
	Fraternal benefit society benefits	418:17
	Homeowners' insurance proceeds to $5,000	512:21(VIII)
miscellaneous	Jury, witness fees	512:21(VI)
	Property of business partnership	304-A:25
	Wages of minor child	512:21(III)

pensions	Tax-exempt retirement accounts, including 401(k)s, 403(b)s, profit-sharing and money purchase plans, SEP and SIMPLE IRAs, and defined-benefit plans	11 U.S.C. § 522(b)(3)(C)
	Traditional and Roth IRAs to $1,095,000 per person	11 U.S.C. § 522(b)(3) (C); (n)
	ERISA-qualified retirement accounts including IRAs & Roth IRAs	512:2 (XIX)
	Federally created pension (only benefits building up)	512:21(IV)
	Firefighters	102:23
	Police officers	103:18
	Public employees	100-A:26
personal property	Beds, bedding, & cooking utensils	511:2(II)
	Bibles & books to $800	511:2(VIII)
	Burial plot, lot	511:2(XIV)
	Church pew	511:2(XV)
	Clothing	511:2(I)
	Cooking & heating stoves, refrigerator	511:2(IV)
	Domestic fowl to $300	511:2(XIII)
	Food & fuel to $400	511:2(VI)
	Furniture to $3,500	511:2(III)
	Jewelry to $500	511:2(XVII)
	Motor vehicle to $4,000	511:2(XVI)
	Proceeds for lost or destroyed exempt property	512:21(VIII)
	Sewing machine	511:2(V)
	1 cow, 6 sheep & their fleece, 4 tons of hay	511:2(XI); (XII)
	1 hog or pig or its meat (if slaughtered)	511:2(X)
public benefits	Aid to blind, aged, disabled; public assistance	167:25
	Unemployment compensation	282-A:159
	Workers' compensation	281-A:52
tools of trade	Tools of your occupation to $5,000	511:2(IX)
	Uniforms, arms, & equipment of military member	511:2(VII)
	Yoke of oxen or horse needed for farming or teaming	511:2(XII)
wages	50 times the federal minimum hourly wage per week	512:21(II)
	Deposits in any account designated a payroll account.	512:21(XI)
	Earned but unpaid wages of spouse	512:21(III)
wildcard	$1,000 of any property	511:2(XVIII)
	Unused portion of bibles & books, food & fuel, furniture, jewelry, motor vehicle, & tools of trade exemptions to $7,000	511:2(XVIII)

New Jersey

Federal bankruptcy exemptions available. All law references are to New Jersey Statutes Annotated unless otherwise noted.

ASSET	EXEMPTION	LAW
homestead	None, but survivorship interest of a spouse in property held as tenancy by the entirety is exempt from creditors of a single spouse	*Freda v. Commercial Trust Co. of New Jersey,* 570 A.2d 409 (N.J.,1990)

insurance	Annuity contract proceeds to $500 per month	17B:24-7
	Disability benefits	17:18-12
	Disability, death, medical, or hospital benefits for civil defense workers	App. A:9-57.6
	Disability or death benefits for military member	38A:4-8
	Group life or health policy or proceeds	17B:24-9
	Health or disability benefits	17:18-12; 17B:24-8
	Life insurance proceeds if clause prohibits proceeds from being used to pay beneficiary's creditors	17B:24-10
	Life insurance proceeds or avails if you're not the insured	17B:24-6b
pensions	Tax-exempt retirement accounts, including 401(k)s, 403(b)s, profit-sharing and money purchase plans, SEP and SIMPLE IRAs, and defined-benefit plans	11 U.S.C. § 522(b)(3)(C)
	Traditional and Roth IRAs to $1,095,000 per person	11 U.S.C. § 522(b)(3)(C); (n)
	Alcohol beverage control officers	43:8A-20
	City boards of health employees	43:18-12
	Civil defense workers	App. A:9-57.6
	County employees	43:10-57; 43:10-105
	ERISA-qualified benefits for city employees	43:13-9
	Firefighters, police officers, traffic officers	43:16-7; 43:16A-17
	IRAs	*In re Yuhas,* 104 F.3d 612 (3d Cir. 1997)
	Judges	43:6A-41
	Municipal employees	43:13-44
	Prison employees	43:7-13
	Public employees	43:15A-53
	School district employees	18A:66-116
	State police	53:5A-45
	Street & water department employees	43:19-17
	Teachers	18A:66-51
	Trust containing personal property created pursuant to federal tax law, including 401(k) plans, IRAs, Roth IRAs, & higher education (529) savings plans	25:2-1; *In re Yuhas,* 104 F.3d 612 (3d Cir. 1997)
personal property	Burial plots	45:27-21
	Clothing	2A:17-19
	Furniture & household goods to $1,000	2A:26-4
	Personal property & possessions of any kind, stock or interest in corporations to $1,000 total	2A:17-19
public benefits	Old age, permanent disability assistance	44:7-35
	Unemployment compensation	43:21-53
	Workers' compensation	34:15-29
tools of trade	None	
wages	90% of earned but unpaid wages if annual income is less than 250% of federal poverty level; 75% if annual income is higher	2A:17-56
	Wages or allowances received by military personnel	38A:4-8
wildcard	None	

New Mexico

Federal bankruptcy exemptions available. All law references are to New Mexico Statutes Annotated unless otherwise noted.

ASSET	EXEMPTION	LAW
homestead	$60,000	42-10-9
insurance	Benevolent association benefits to $5,000	42-10-4
	Fraternal benefit society benefits	59A-44-18
	Life, accident, health, or annuity benefits, withdrawal or cash value, if beneficiary is a New Mexico resident	42-10-3
	Life insurance proceeds	42-10-5
miscellaneous	Ownership interest in unincorporated association	53-10-2
	Property of business partnership	54-1A-501
pensions	Tax-exempt retirement accounts, including 401(k)s, 403(b)s, profit-sharing and money purchase plans, SEP and SIMPLE IRAs, and defined-benefit plans	11 U.S.C. § 522(b)(3)(C)
	Traditional and Roth IRAs to $1,095,000 per person	11 U.S.C. § 522(b)(3)(C); (n)
	Pension or retirement benefits	42-10-1; 42-10-2
	Public school employees	22-11-42A
personal property	Books & furniture	42-10-1; 42-10-2
	Building materials	48-2-15
	Clothing	42-10-1; 42-10-2
	Cooperative association shares, minimum amount needed to be member	53-4-28
	Health aids	42-10-1; 42-10-2
	Jewelry to $2,500	42-10-1; 42-10-2
	Materials, tools, & machinery to dig, drill, complete, operate, or repair oil line, gas well, or pipeline	70-4-12
	Motor vehicle to $4,000	42-10-1; 42-10-2
public benefits	Crime victims' compensation	31-22-15
	General assistance	27-2-21
	Occupational disease disablement benefits	52-3-37
	Unemployment compensation	51-1-37
	Workers' compensation	52-1-52
tools of trade	$1,500	42-10-1; 42-10-2
wages	Minimum 75% of disposable earnings or 40 times the federal hourly minimum wage, whichever is more; bankruptcy judge may authorize more for low-income debtors	35-12-7
wildcard	$500 of any personal property	42-10-1
	$5,000 of any real or personal property, in lieu of homestead	42-10-10

New York

Federal bankruptcy exemptions not available. All references are to Consolidated Laws of New York unless otherwise noted; Civil Practice Law & Rules are abbreviated C.P.L.R.

ASSET	EXEMPTION	LAW
homestead	Real property including co-op, condo, or mobile home, to $50,000	C.P.L.R. 5206(a); *In re Pearl*, 723 F.2d 193 (2nd Cir. 1983)
insurance	Annuity contract benefits due the debtor, if debtor paid for the contract; $5,000 limit if purchased within 6 mos. prior to filing & not tax-deferred	Ins. 3212(d); Debt. & Cred. 283(1)
	Disability or illness benefits to $400/month	Ins. 3212(c)
	Life insurance proceeds & avails if the beneficiary is not the debtor, or if debtor's spouse has taken out policy	Ins. 3212(b)
	Life insurance proceeds left at death with the insurance company, if clause prohibits proceeds from being used to pay beneficiary's creditors	Est. Powers & Trusts 7-1.5(a)(2)
miscellaneous	Alimony, child support	C.P.L.R. 5205 (d)(3); Debt. & Cred. 282(2)(d)
	Property of business partnership	Partnership 51
pensions	Tax-exempt retirement accounts, including 401(k)s, 403(b)s, profit-sharing and money purchase plans, SEP and SIMPLE IRAs, and defined-benefit plans	11 U.S.C. § 522(b)(3)(C)
	Traditional and Roth IRAs to $1,095,000 per person	11 U.S.C. § 522(b)(3)(C); (n)
	ERISA-qualified benefits, IRAs, Roth IRAs, & Keoghs & income needed for support	C.P.L.R. 5205(c); Debt. & Cred. 282(2)(e)
	Public retirement benefits	Ins. 4607
	State employees	Ret. & Soc. Sec. 10
	Teachers	Educ. 524
	Village police officers	Unconsolidated 5711-o
	Volunteer ambulance workers' benefits	Vol. Amb. Wkr. Ben. 23
	Volunteer firefighters' benefits	Vol. Firefighter Ben. 23
personal property	Bible, schoolbooks, other books to $50; pictures; clothing; church pew or seat; sewing machine, refrigerator, TV, radio; furniture, cooking utensils & tableware, dishes; food to last 60 days; stoves with fuel to last 60 days; domestic animal with food to last 60 days, to $450; wedding ring; watch to $35; exemptions may not exceed $5,000 total (including tools of trade & limited annuity)	C.P.L.R. 5205(a)(1)-(6); Debt. & Cred. 283(1)
	Burial plot without structure to ¼ acre	C.P.L.R. 5206(f)
	Cash (including savings bonds, tax refunds, bank & credit union deposits) to $2,500, or to $5,000 after exemptions for personal property taken, whichever amount is less (for debtors who do not claim homestead)	Debt. & Cred. 283(2)
	College tuition savings program trust fund	C.P.L.R. 5205(j)
	Health aids, including service animals with food	C.P.L.R. 5205(h)

personal property (continued)	Lost future earnings recoveries needed for support	Debt. & Cred. 282(3)(iv)
	Motor vehicle to $2,400	Debt. & Cred. 282(1); *In re Miller*, 167 B.R. 782 (S.D. N.Y. 1994)
	Personal injury recoveries up to 1 year after receiving	Debt. & Cred. 282(3)(iii)
	Recovery for injury to exempt property up to 1 year after receiving	C.P.L.R. 5205(b)
	Savings & loan savings to $600	Banking 407
	Security deposit to landlord, utility company	C.P.L.R. 5205(g)
	Spendthrift trust fund principal, 90% of income if not created by debtor	C.P.L.R. 5205(c),(d)
	Wrongful death recoveries for person you depended on	Debt. & Cred. 282(3)(ii)
public benefits	Aid to blind, aged, disabled	Debt. & Cred. 282(2)(c)
	Crime victims' compensation	Debt. & Cred. 282(3)(i)
	Home relief, local public assistance	Debt. & Cred. 282(2)(a)
	Public assistance	Soc. Serv. 137
	Social Security	Debt. & Cred. 282(2)(a)
	Unemployment compensation	Debt. & Cred. 282(2)(a)
	Veterans' benefits	Debt. & Cred. 282(2)(b)
	Workers' compensation	Debt. & Cred. 282(2)(c); Work. Comp. 33, 218
tools of trade	Farm machinery, team, & food for 60 days; professional furniture, books, & instruments to $600 total	C.P.L.R. 5205(a),(b)
	Uniforms, medal, emblem, equipment, horse, arms, & sword of member of military	C.P.L.R. 5205(e)
wages	90% of earned but unpaid wages received within 60 days before & anytime after filing	C.P.L.R. 5205(d)
	90% of earnings from dairy farmer's sales to milk dealers	C.P.L.R. 5205(f)
	100% of pay of noncommissioned officer, private, or musician in U.S. or N.Y. state armed forces	C.P.L.R. 5205(e)
wildcard	None	

North Carolina

Federal bankruptcy exemptions not available. All law references are to General Statutes of North Carolina unless otherwise noted.

ASSET	EXEMPTION	LAW
homestead	Property held as tenancy by the entirety may be exempt against debts owed by only one spouse	*In re Chandler*, 148 B.R. 13 (E.D. N.C., 1992)
	Real or personal property, including co-op, used as residence to $18,500; up to $5,000 of unused portion of homestead may be applied to any property	1C-1601(a)(1),(2)
insurance	Employee group life policy or proceeds	58-58-165
	Fraternal benefit society benefits	58-24-85
	Life insurance on spouse or children	1C-1601(a)(6); Const. Art. X § 5
miscellaneous	Alimony, support, separate maintenance, and child support necessary for support of debtor and dependents	1C-1601(a)(12)

miscellaneous (continued)	Property of business partnership	59-55
	Support received by a surviving spouse for 1 year, up to $10,000	30-15
pensions	Tax-exempt retirement accounts, including 401(k)s, 403(b)s, profit-sharing and money purchase plans, SEP and SIMPLE IRAs, and defined-benefit plans	11 U.S.C. § 522(b)(3)(C)
	Traditional and Roth IRAs to $1,095,000 per person	11 U.S.C. § 522(b)(3)(C); (n)
	Firefighters & rescue squad workers	58-86-90
	IRAs & Roth IRAs	1C-1601(a)(9)
	Law enforcement officers	143-166.30(g)
	Legislators	120-4.29
	Municipal, city, & county employees	128-31
	Retirement benefits from another state to extent exempt in that state	1C-1601(a)(11)
	Teachers & state employees	135-9; 135-95
personal property	Animals, crops, musical instruments, books, clothing, appliances, household goods & furnishings to $5,000 total; may add $1,000 per dependent, up to $4,000 total additional (all property must have been purchased at least 90 days before filing)	1C-1601(a)(4),(d)
	Burial plot to $18,500, in lieu of homestead	1C-1601(a)(1)
	College savings account established under 26 U.S.C. § 529 to $25,000, excluding certain contributions within prior year	1C-1601(a)(10)
	Health aids	1C-1601(a)(7)
	Motor vehicle to $3,500	1C-1601(a)(3)
	Personal injury & wrongful death recoveries for person you depended on	1C-1601(a)(8)
public benefits	Aid to blind	111-18
	Crime victims' compensation	15B-17
	Public adult assistance under work first program	108A-36
	Unemployment compensation	96-17
	Workers' compensation	97-21
tools of trade	Implements, books, & tools of trade to $2,000	1C-1601(a)(5)
wages	Earned but unpaid wages received 60 days before filing for bankruptcy, needed for support	1-362
wildcard	$5,000 of unused homestead or burial exemption	1C-1601(a)(2)
	$500 of any personal property	Constitution Art. X § 1

North Dakota

Federal bankruptcy exemptions not available. All law references are to North Dakota Century Code unless otherwise noted.

ASSET	EXEMPTION	LAW
homestead	Real property, house trailer, or mobile home to $80,000 (husband & wife may not double)	28-22-02(10); 47-18-01
insurance	Fraternal benefit society benefits	26.1-15.1-18; 26.1-33-40
	Life insurance proceeds payable to deceased's estate, not to a specific beneficiary	26.1-33-40

insurance (continued)	Life insurance surrender value to $100,000 per policy, if beneficiary is insured's dependent & policy was owned over 1 year before filing for bankruptcy; limit does not apply if more needed for support	28-22-03.1(3)
miscellaneous	Child support payments	14-09-09.31
pensions	Tax-exempt retirement accounts, including 401(k)s, 403(b)s, profit-sharing and money purchase plans, SEP and SIMPLE IRAs, and defined-benefit plans	11 U.S.C. § 522(b)(3)(C)
	Traditional and Roth IRAs to $1,095,000 per person	11 U.S.C. § 522(b)(3)(C); (n)
	Disabled veterans' benefits, except military retirement pay	28-22-03.1(4)(d)
	ERISA-qualified benefits, IRAs, Roth IRAs, & Keoghs to $100,000 per plan; no limit if more needed for support; total exemption (with life insurance surrender value) cannot exceed $200,000	28-22-03.1(3)
	Public employees deferred compensation	54-52.2-06
	Public employees pensions	28-22-19(1)
personal property	1. All debtors may exempt:	
	Bible, schoolbooks; other books to $100	28-22-02(4)
	Burial plots, church pew	28-22-02(2),(3)
	Clothing & family pictures	28-22-02(1),(5)
	Crops or grain raised by debtor on 160 acres where debtor resides	28-22-02(8)
	Food & fuel to last 1 year	28-22-02(6)
	Insurance proceeds for exempt property	28-22-02(9)
	Motor vehicle to $1,200 (or $32,000 for vehicle that has been modified to accommodate owner's disability)	28-22-03.1(2)
	Personal injury recoveries to $15,000	28-22-03.1(4)(b)
	Wrongful death recoveries to $15,000	28-22-03.1(4)(a)
	2. Head of household not claiming crops or grain may claim $5,000 of any personal property or:	28-22-03
	Books & musical instruments to $1,500	28-22-04(1)
	Household & kitchen furniture, beds & bedding, to $1,000	28-22-04(2)
	Library & tools of professional, tools of mechanic, & stock in trade, to $1,000	28-22-04(4)
	Livestock & farm implements to $4,500	28-22-04(3)
	3. Nonhead of household not claiming crops or grain may claim $2,500 of any personal property	28-22-05
public benefits	Crime victims' compensation	28-22-19(2)
	Old age & survivor insurance program benefits	52-09-22
	Public assistance	28-22-19(3)
	Social Security	28-22-03.1(4)(c)
	Unemployment compensation	52-06-30
	Workers' compensation	65-05-29
tools of trade	*See personal property, Option 2*	
wages	Minimum 75% of disposable weekly earnings or 40 times the federal minimum wage, whichever is more; bankruptcy judge may authorize more for low-income debtors	32-09.1-03
wildcard	$7,500 of any property in lieu of homestead	28-22-03.1(1)

Ohio

Federal bankruptcy exemptions not available. All law references are to Ohio Revised Code unless otherwise noted.

ASSET	EXEMPTION	LAW
homestead	Property held as tenancy by the entirety may be exempt against debts owed by only one spouse	*In re Pernus*, 143 B.R. 856 (N.D. Ohio, 1992)
	Real or personal property used as residence to $5,000	2329.66(A)(1)(b)
insurance	Benevolent society benefits to $5,000	2329.63; 2329.66(A)(6)(a)
	Disability benefits to $600 per month	2329.66(A)(6)(e); 3923.19
	Fraternal benefit society benefits	2329.66(A)(6)(d); 3921.18
	Group life insurance policy or proceeds	2329.66(A)(6)(c); 3917.05
	Life, endowment, or annuity contract avails for your spouse, child, or dependent	2329.66(A)(6)(b); 3911.10
	Life insurance proceeds for a spouse	3911.12
	Life insurance proceeds if clause prohibits proceeds from being used to pay beneficiary's creditors	3911.14
miscellaneous	Alimony, child support needed for support	2329.66(A)(11)
	Property of business partnership	1775.24; 2329.66(A)(14)
pensions	Tax-exempt retirement accounts, including 401(k)s, 403(b)s, profit-sharing and money purchase plans, SEP and SIMPLE IRAs, and defined-benefit plans	11 U.S.C. § 522(b)(3)(C)
	Traditional and Roth IRAs to $1,095,000 per person	11 U.S.C. § 522(b)(3)(C); (n)
	ERISA-qualified benefits needed for support	2329.66(A)(10)(b)
	Firefighters, police officers	742.47
	IRAs, Roth IRAs, & Keoghs needed for support	2329.66(A)(10)(c), (a)
	Public employees	145.56
	Public safety officers' death benefit	2329.66(A)(10)(a)
	Public school employees	3309.66
	State highway patrol employees	5505.22
	Volunteer firefighters' dependents	146.13
personal property	Animals, crops, books, musical instruments, appliances, household goods, furnishings, firearms, hunting & fishing equipment to $200 per item; jewelry to $400 for 1 item, $200 for all others; $1,500 total ($2,000 if no homestead exemption claimed)	2329.66(A)(4)(b),(c),(d); *In re Szydlowski*, 186 B.R. 907 (N.D. Ohio 1995)
	Beds, bedding, clothing to $200 per item	2329.66(A)(3)
	Burial plot	517.09; 2329.66(A)(8)
	Cash, money due within 90 days, tax refund, bank, security, & utility deposits to $400 total	2329.66(A)(4)(a); *In re Szydlowski*, 186 B.R. 907 (N.D. Ohio 1995)
	Compensation for lost future earnings needed for support, received during 12 months before filing	2329.66(A)(12)(d)

personal property (continued)	Cooking unit & refrigerator to $300 each	2329.66(A)(3)
	Health aids (professionally prescribed)	2329.66(A)(7)
	Motor vehicle to $1,000	2329.66(A)(2)(b)
	Personal injury recoveries to $5,000, received during 12 months before filing	2329.66(A)(12)(c)
	Tuition credit or payment	2329.66(A)(16)
	Wrongful death recoveries for person debtor depended on, needed for support, received during 12 months before filing	2329.66(A)(12)(b)
public benefits	Crime victim's compensation, received during 12 months before filing	2329.66(A)(12)(a); 2743.66(D)
	Disability assistance payments	2329.66(A)(9)(f); 5115.07
	Public assistance	2329.66(A)(9)(d); (e); 5107.75; 5108.08
	Unemployment compensation	2329.66(A)(9)(c); 4141.32
	Vocational rehabilitation benefits	2329.66(A)(9)(a); 3304.19
	Workers' compensation	2329.66(A)(9)(b); 4123.67
tools of trade	Implements, books, & tools of trade to $750	2329.66(A)(5)
wages	Minimum 75% of disposable weekly earnings or 30 times the federal hourly minimum wage, whichever is higher; bankruptcy judge may authorize more for low-income debtors	2329.66(A)(13)
wildcard	$400 of any property	2329.66(A)(18)

Oklahoma

Federal bankruptcy exemptions not available. All law references are to Oklahoma Statutes Annotated (in the form title number-section number), unless otherwise noted.

ASSET	EXEMPTION	LAW
homestead	Real property or manufactured home to unlimited value; property cannot exceed 1 acre in city, town, or village, or 160 acres elsewhere; $5,000 limit if more than 25% of total sq. ft. area used for business purposes; okay to rent homestead as long as no other residence is acquired	31-1(A)(1); 31-1(A)(2); 31-2
insurance	Annuity benefits & cash value	36-3631.1
	Assessment or mutual benefits	36-2410
	Fraternal benefit society benefits	36-2718.1
	Funeral benefits prepaid & placed in trust	36-6125
	Group life policy or proceeds	36-3632
	Life, health, accident, & mutual benefit insurance proceeds & cash value, if clause prohibits proceeds from being used to pay beneficiary's creditors	36-3631.1
	Limited stock insurance benefits	36-2510
miscellaneous	Alimony, child support	31-1(A)(19)
	Beneficiary's interest in a statutory support trust	6-3010
	Liquor license	37-532
	Property of business partnership	54-1-504

pensions	Tax-exempt retirement accounts, including 401(k)s, 403(b)s, profit-sharing and money purchase plans, SEP and SIMPLE IRAs, and defined-benefit plans	11 U.S.C. § 522(b)(3)(C)
	Traditional and Roth IRAs to $1,095,000 per person	11 U.S.C. § 522(b)(3)(C); (n)
	County employees	19-959
	Disabled veterans	31-7
	ERISA-qualified benefits, IRAs, Roth IRAs, Education IRAs, & Keoghs	31-1(A)(20), (24)
	Firefighters	11-49-126
	Judges	20-1111
	Law enforcement employees	47-2-303.3
	Police officers	11-50-124
	Public employees	74-923
	Tax-exempt benefits	60-328
	Teachers	70-17-109
personal property	Books, portraits, & pictures	31-1(A)(6)
	Burial plots	31-1(A)(4); 8-7
	Clothing to $4,000	31-1(A)(7)
	College savings plan interest	31-1A(24)
	Deposits in an IDA (Individual Development Account)	31-1A(22)
	Federal earned income tax credit	31-1(A)(23)
	Food & seed for growing to last 1 year	31-1(A)(17)
	Guns for household use to $2,000	31-1A(14)
	Health aids (professionally prescribed)	31-1(A)(9)
	Household & kitchen furniture; personal computer and related equipment	31-1(A)(3)
	Livestock for personal or family use: 5 dairy cows & calves under 6 months; 100 chickens; 20 sheep; 10 hogs; 2 horses, bridles, & saddles; forage & feed to last 1 year	31-1(A)(10),(11), (12),(15),(16),(17)
	Motor vehicle to $7,500	31-1(A)(13)
	Personal injury & wrongful death recoveries to $50,000	31-1(A)(21)
	Prepaid funeral benefits	36-6125(H)
	War bond payroll savings account	51-42
	Wedding and anniversary rings to $3,000	31-1(A)(8)
public benefits	Crime victims' compensation	21-142.13
	Public assistance	56-173
	Social Security	56-173
	Unemployment compensation	40-2-303
	Workers' compensation	85-48
tools of trade	Implements needed to farm homestead, tools, books, & apparatus to $10,000 total	31-1(A)(5); 31-1(C)
wages	75% of wages earned in 90 days before filing bankruptcy; bankruptcy judge may allow more if you show hardship	12-1171.1; 31-1(A)(18); 31-1.1
wildcard	None	

Oregon

Federal bankruptcy exemptions not available. All law references are to Oregon Revised Statutes unless otherwise noted.

ASSET	EXEMPTION	LAW
homestead	Prepaid rent & security deposit for renter's dwelling	*In re Casserino*, 379 F.3d 1069 (9th cir. 2004)
	Real property of a soldier or sailor during time of war	408.440
	Real property you occupy or intend to occupy to $30,000 ($39,600 for joint owners); mobile home on property you own or houseboat to $23,000 ($30,000 for joint owners); mobile home not on your land to $20,000 ($27,000 for joint owners); property cannot exceed 1 block in town or city or 160 acres elsewhere; sale proceeds exempt 1 year from sale, if you intend to purchase another home or use sale proceeds for rent	18.428; 18.395; 18.402; *In re Wynn*, 369 B.R. 605 (D. Or. 2007)
	Tenancy by entirety not exempt, but subject to survivorship rights of nondebtor spouse	*In re Pletz*, 225 B.R. 206 (D. Or., 1997)
insurance	Annuity contract benefits to $500 per month	743.049
	Fraternal benefit society benefits to $7,500	748.207; 18.348
	Group life policy or proceeds not payable to insured	743.047
	Health or disability proceeds or avails	743.050
	Life insurance proceeds or cash value if you are not the insured	743.046; 743.047
miscellaneous	Alimony, child support needed for support	18.345(1)(i)
	Liquor licenses	471.292 (1)
pensions	Tax-exempt retirement accounts, including 401(k)s, 403(b)s, profit-sharing and money purchase plans, SEP and SIMPLE IRAs, and defined-benefit plans	11 U.S.C. § 522(b)(3)(C)
	Traditional and Roth IRAs to $1,095,000 per person	11 U.S.C. § 522(b)(3)(C); (n)
	ERISA-qualified benefits, including IRAs & SEPs; & payments to $7,500	18.358; 18.348
	Public officers', employees' pension payments to $7,500	237.980; 238.445; 18.348 (2)
personal property	Bank deposits to $7,500; cash for sold exempt property	18.348; 18.345(2)
	Books, pictures, & musical instruments to $600 total	18.345(1)(a)
	Building materials for construction of an improvement	87.075
	Burial plot	65.870
	Clothing, jewelry, & other personal items to $1,800 total	18.345(1)(b)
	Compensation for lost earnings payments for debtor or someone debtor depended on, to extent needed	18.345(1)(L),(3)
	Domestic animals, poultry, & pets to $1,000 plus food to last 60 days	18.345(1)(e)
	Federal earned income tax credit	18.345(1)(n)
	Food & fuel to last 60 days if debtor is householder	18.345(1)(f)

ASSET	EXEMPTION	LAW
personal property (continued)	Furniture, household items, utensils, radios, & TVs to $3,000 total	18.345(1)(f)
	Health aids	18.345(1)(h)
	Higher education savings account to $7,500	348.863; 18.348(1)
	Motor vehicle to $2,150	18.345(1)(d),(3)
	Personal injury recoveries to $10,000	18.345(1)(k),(3)
	Pistol; rifle or shotgun (owned by person over 16) to $1,000	18.362
public benefits	Aid to blind to $7,500	411.706; 411.760; 18.348
	Aid to disabled to $7,500	411.706; 411.760; 18.348
	Civil defense & disaster relief to $7,500	401.405; 18.348
	Crime victims' compensation	18.345(1)(j)(A),(3); 147.325
	General assistance to $7,500	411.760; 18.348
	Injured inmates' benefits to $7,500	655.530; 18.348
	Medical assistance to $7,500	414.095; 18.348
	Old-age assistance to $7,500	411.706; 411.760; 18.348
	Unemployment compensation to $7,500	657.855; 18.348
	Veterans' benefits & proceeds of Veterans loans	407.125; 407.595; 18.348(m)
	Vocational rehabilitation to $7,500	344.580; 18.348
	Workers' compensation to $7,500	656.234; 18.348
tools of trade	Tools, library, team with food to last 60 days, to $3,000	18.345(1)(c),(3)
wages	75% of disposable wages or $170 per week, whichever is greater; bankruptcy judge may authorize more for low-income debtors	18.385
	Wages withheld in state employee's bond savings accounts	292.070
wildcard	$400 of any personal property not already covered by existing exemption	18.348(1)(o)

Pennsylvania

Federal bankruptcy exemptions available. All law references are to Pennsylvania Consolidated Statutes Annotated unless otherwise noted.

ASSET	EXEMPTION	LAW
homestead	None; however, property held as tenancy by the entirety may be exempt against debts owed by only one spouse	*In re Martin*, 269 B.R. 119 (M.D. Pa. 2001)
insurance	Accident or disability benefits	42-8124(c)(7)
	Fraternal benefit society benefits	42-8124(c)(1),(8)
	Group life policy or proceeds	42-8124(c)(5)
	Insurance policy or annuity contract payments, where insured is the beneficiary, cash value or proceeds to $100 per month	42-8124(c)(3)
	Life insurance & annuity proceeds if clause prohibits proceeds from being used to pay beneficiary's creditors	42-8214(c)(4)
	Life insurance annuity policy cash value or proceeds if beneficiary is insured's dependent, child or spouse	42-8124(c)(6)
	No-fault automobile insurance proceeds	42-8124(c)(9)
miscellaneous	Property of business partnership	15-8342

pensions	Tax-exempt retirement accounts, including 401(k)s, 403(b)s, profit-sharing and money purchase plans, SEP and SIMPLE IRAs, and defined-benefit plans	11 U.S.C. § 522(b)(3)(C)
	Traditional and Roth IRAs to $1,095,000 per person	11 U.S.C. § 522(b)(3)(C); (n)
	City employees	53-13445; 53-23572; 53-39383; 42-8124(b)(1)(iv)
	County employees	16-4716
	Municipal employees	53-881.115; 42-8124(b)(1)(vi)
	Police officers	53-764; 53-776; 53-23666; 42-8124(b)(1)(iii)
	Private retirement benefits to extent tax-deferred, if clause prohibits proceeds from being used to pay beneficiary's creditors; exemption limited to deposits of $15,000 per year made at least 1 year before filing (limit does not apply to rollovers from other exempt funds or accounts)	42-8124(b)(1)(vii), (viii),(ix)
	Public school employees	24-8533; 42-8124(b)(1)(i)
	State employees	71-5953; 42-8124(b)(1)(ii)
personal property	Bibles & schoolbooks	42-8124(a)(2)
	Clothing	42-8124(a)(1)
	Military uniforms & accoutrements	42-8124(a)(4); 51-4103
	Sewing machines	42-8124(a)(3)
public benefits	Crime victims' compensation	18-11.708
	Korean conflict veterans' benefits	51-20098
	Unemployment compensation	42-8124(a)(10); 43-863
	Veterans' benefits	51-20012; 20048; 20098; 20127
	Workers' compensation	42-8124(c)(2)
tools of trade	Seamstress's sewing machine	42-8124(a)(3)
wages	Earned but unpaid wages	42-8127
	Prison inmate's wages	61-1054
	Wages of victims of abuse	42-8127(f)
wildcard	$300 of any property, including cash, real property, securities, or proceeds from sale of exempt property	42-8123

Rhode Island

Federal bankruptcy exemptions available. All law references are to General Laws of Rhode Island unless otherwise noted.

ASSET	EXEMPTION	LAW
homestead	$300,000 in land & buildings you occupy or intend to occupy as a principal residence (husband & wife may not double)	9-26-4.1
insurance	Accident or sickness proceeds, avails, or benefits	27-18-24
insurance (continued)	Fraternal benefit society benefits	27-25-18
	Life insurance proceeds if clause prohibits proceeds from being used to pay beneficiary's creditors	27-4-12
	Temporary disability insurance	28-41-32
miscellaneous	Earnings of a minor child	9-26-4(9)
	Property of business partnership	7-12-36
pensions	Tax-exempt retirement accounts, including 401(k)s, 403(b)s, profit-sharing and money purchase plans, SEP and SIMPLE IRAs, and defined-benefit plans	11 U.S.C. § 522(b)(3)(C)
	Traditional and Roth IRAs to $1,095,000 per person	11 U.S.C. § 522(b)(3)(C); (n)
	ERISA-qualified benefits	9-26-4(12)
	Firefighters	9-26-5
	IRAs & Roth IRAs	9-26-4(11)
	Police officers	9-26-5
	Private employees	28-17-4
	State & municipal employees	36-10-34
personal property	Beds, bedding, furniture, household goods, & supplies, to $8,600 total (husband & wife may not double)	9-26-4(3); *In re Petrozella*, 247 B.R. 591 (R.I. 2000)
	Bibles & books to $300	9-26-4(4)
	Burial plot	9-26-4(5)
	Clothing	9-26-4(1)
	Consumer cooperative association holdings to $50	7-8-25
	Debt secured by promissory note or bill of exchange	9-26-4(7)
	Jewelry to $1,000	9-26-4 (14)
	Motor vehicles to $10,000	9-26-4 (13)
	Prepaid tuition program or tuition savings account	9-26-4 (15)
public benefits	Aid to blind, aged, disabled; general assistance	40-6-14
	Crime victims' compensation	12-25.1-3(b)(2)
	Family assistance benefits	40-5.1-15
	State disability benefits	28-41-32
	Unemployment compensation	28-44-58
	Veterans' disability or survivors' death benefits	30-7-9
	Workers' compensation	28-33-27
tools of trade	Library of practicing professional	9-26-4(2)
	Working tools to $1,200	9-26-4(2)
wages	Earned but unpaid wages due military member on active duty	30-7-9
	Earned but unpaid wages due seaman	9-26-4(6)
	Earned but unpaid wages to $50	9-26-4(8)(iii)
	Wages of any person who had been receiving public assistance are exempt for 1 year after going off of relief	9-26-4(8)(ii)
	Wages of spouse & minor children	9-26-4(9)
	Wages paid by charitable organization or fund providing relief to the poor	9-26-4(8)(i)
wildcard	None	

South Carolina

Federal bankruptcy exemptions not available. All law references are to Code of Laws of South Carolina unless otherwise noted.

ASSET	EXEMPTION	LAW
homestead	Real property, including co-op, to $50,000	15-41-30(1)
insurance	Accident & disability benefits	38-63-40(D)
	Benefits accruing under life insurance policy after death of insured, where proceeds left with insurance company pursuant to agreement; benefits not exempt from action to recover necessaries if parties agree	38-63-50
	Disability or illness benefits	15-41-30(10)(C)
	Fraternal benefit society benefits	38-38-330
	Group life insurance proceeds; cash value to $50,000	38-63-40(C); 38-65-90
	Life insurance avails from policy for person you depended on to $4,000	15-41-30(8)
	Life insurance proceeds from policy for person you depended on, needed for support	15-41-30(11)(C)
	Proceeds & cash surrender value of life insurance payable to beneficiary other than insured's estate & for the express benefit of insured's spouse, children, or dependents (must be purchased 2 years before filing)	38-63-40(A)
	Proceeds of life insurance or annuity contract	38-63-40(B)
	Unmatured life insurance contract, except credit insurance policy	15-41-30(7)
miscellaneous	Alimony, child support	15-41-30(10)(D)
	Property of business partnership	33-41-720
pensions	Tax-exempt retirement accounts, including 401(k)s, 403(b)s, profit-sharing and money purchase plans, SEP and SIMPLE IRAs, and defined-benefit plans	11 U.S.C. § 522(b)(3)(C)
	Traditional and Roth IRAs to $1,095,000 per person	11 U.S.C. § 522(b)(3)(C); (n)
	ERISA-qualified benefits; your share of the pension plan fund	15-41-30(10)(E),(13)
	Firefighters	9-13-230
	General assembly members	9-9-180
	IRAs & Roth IRAs needed for support	15-41-30(12)
	Judges, solicitors	9-8-190
	Police officers	9-11-270
	Public employees	9-1-1680
personal property	Animals, crops, appliances, books, clothing, household goods, furnishings, musical instruments to $2,500 total	15-41-30(3)
	Burial plot to $50,000, in lieu of homestead	15-41-30(1)
	Cash & other liquid assets to $1,000, in lieu of burial or homestead exemption	15-41-30(5)
	College investment program trust fund	59-2-140
	Health aids	15-41-30(9)
	Jewelry to $500	15-41-30(4)
	Motor vehicle to $1,200	15-41-30(2)
	Personal injury & wrongful death recoveries for person you depended on for support	15-41-30(11)(B)

ASSET	EXEMPTION	LAW
public benefits	Crime victims' compensation	15-41-30(11)(A); 16-3-1300
	General relief; aid to aged, blind, disabled	43-5-190
	Local public assistance	15-41-30(10)(A)
	Social Security	15-41-30(10)(A)
	Unemployment compensation	15-41-30(10)(A)
	Veterans' benefits	15-41-30(10)(B)
	Workers' compensation	42-9-360
tools of trade	Implements, books, & tools of trade to $750	15-41-30(6)
wages	None (use federal nonbankruptcy wage exemption)	
wildcard	None	

South Dakota

Federal bankruptcy exemptions not available. All law references are to South Dakota Codified Law unless otherwise noted.

ASSET	EXEMPTION	LAW
homestead	Gold or silver mine, mill, or smelter not exempt	43-31-5
	May file homestead declaration	43-31-6
	Real property to unlimited value or mobile home (larger than 240 sq. ft. at its base & registered in state at least 6 months before filing) to unlimited value; property cannot exceed 1 acre in town or 160 acres elsewhere; sale proceeds to $30,000 ($170,000 if over age 70 or widow or widower who hasn't remarried) exempt for 1 year after sale (husband & wife may not double)	43-31-1; 43-31-2; 43-31-3; 43-31-4; 43-45-3
	Spouse or child of deceased owner may claim homestead exemption	43-31-13
insurance	Annuity contract proceeds to $250 per month	58-12-6; 58-12-8
	Endowment, life insurance, policy proceeds to $20,000; if policy issued by mutual aid or benevolent society, cash value to $20,000	58-12-4
	Fraternal benefit society benefits	58-37A-18
	Health benefits to $20,000	58-12-4
	Life insurance proceeds, if clause prohibits proceeds from being used to pay beneficiary's creditors	58-15-70
	Life insurance proceeds to $10,000, if beneficiary is surviving spouse or child	43-45-6
pensions	Tax-exempt retirement accounts, including 401(k)s, 403(b)s, profit-sharing and money purchase plans, SEP and SIMPLE IRAs, and defined-benefit plans	11 U.S.C. § 522(b)(3)(C)
	Traditional and Roth IRAs to $1,095,000 per person	11 U.S.C. § 522(b)(3)(C); (n)
	City employees	9-16-47
	ERISA-qualified benefits, limited to income & distribution on $1,000,000	43-45-16
	Public employees	3-12-115
personal property	Bible, schoolbooks; other books to $200	43-45-2(4)
	Burial plots, church pew	43-45-2(2),(3)
	Cemetery association property	47-29-25
	Clothing	43-45-2(5)
	Family pictures	43-45-2(1)
	Food & fuel to last 1 year	43-45-2(6)

public benefits	Crime victim's compensation	23A-28B-24
	Public assistance	28-7A-18
	Unemployment compensation	61-6-28
	Workers' compensation	62-4-42
tools of trade	None	
wages	Earned wages owed 60 days before filing bankruptcy, needed for support of family	15-20-12
	Wages of prisoners in work programs	24-8-10
wildcard	Head of family may claim $6,000, or nonhead of family may claim $4,000 of any personal property	43-45-4

Tennessee

Federal bankruptcy exemptions not available. All law references are to Tennessee Code Annotated unless otherwise noted.

ASSET	EXEMPTION	LAW
homestead	$5,000; $7,500 for joint owners; $25,000 if at least one dependent is a minor child (if 62 or older, $12,500 if single; $20,000 if married; $25,000 if spouse is also 62 or older)	26-2-301
	2–15-year lease	26-2-303
	Life estate	26-2-302
	Property held as tenancy by the entirety may be exempt against debts owed by only one spouse, but survivorship right is not exempt	*In re Arango*, 136 B.R. 740 aff'd, 992 F.2d 611 (6th Cir. 1993); *In re Arwood*, 289 B.R. 889 (Bankr. E.D. Tenn. 2003)
	Spouse or child of deceased owner may claim homestead exemption	26-2-301
insurance	Accident, health, or disability benefits for resident & citizen of Tennessee	26-2-110
	Disability or illness benefits	26-2-111(1)(C)
	Fraternal benefit society benefits	56-25-1403
	Life insurance or annuity	56-7-203
miscellaneous	Alimony, child support owed for 30 days before filing for bankruptcy	26-2-111(1)(E)
	Educational scholarship trust funds & prepayment plans	49-4-108; 49-7-822
pensions	Tax-exempt retirement accounts, including 401(k)s, 403(b)s, profit-sharing and money purchase plans, SEP and SIMPLE IRAs, and defined-benefit plans	11 U.S.C. § 522(b)(3)(C)
	Traditional and Roth IRAs to $1,095,000 per person	11 U.S.C. § 522(b)(3)(C); (n)
	ERISA-qualified benefits, IRAs, & Roth IRAs	26-2-111(1)(D)
	Public employees	8-36-111
	State & local government employees	26-2-105
	Teachers	49-5-909
personal property	Bible, schoolbooks, family pictures, & portraits	26-2-104
	Burial plot to 1 acre	26-2-305; 46-2-102
	Clothing & storage containers	26-2-104
	Health aids	26-2-111(5)
	Health savings accounts	26-2-105

personal property (continued)	Lost future earnings payments for you or person you depended on	26-2-111(3)
	Personal injury recoveries to $7,500; wrongful death recoveries to $10,000 ($15,000 total for personal injury, wrongful death, & crime victims' compensation)	26-2-111(2)(B),(C)
	Wages of debtor deserting family, in hands of family	26-2-109
public benefits	Aid to blind	71-4-117
	Aid to disabled	71-4-1112
	Crime victims' compensation to $5,000 (*see personal property*)	26-2-111(2)(A); 29-13-111
	Local public assistance	26-2-111(1)(A)
	Old-age assistance	71-2-216
	Relocation assistance payments	13-11-115
	Social Security	26-2-111(1)(A)
	Unemployment compensation	26-2-111(1)(A)
	Veterans' benefits	26-2-111(1)(B)
	Workers' compensation	50-6-223
tools of trade	Implements, books, & tools of trade to $1,900	26-2-111(4)
wages	Minimum 75% of disposable weekly earnings or 30 times the federal minimum hourly wage, whichever is more, plus $2.50 per week per child; bankruptcy judge may authorize more for low-income debtors	26-2-106,107
wildcard	$4,000 of any personal property including deposits on account with any bank or financial institution	26-2-103

Texas

Federal bankruptcy exemptions available. All law references are to Texas Revised Civil Statutes Annotated unless otherwise noted.

ASSET	EXEMPTION	LAW
homestead	Unlimited; property cannot exceed 10 acres in town, village, city or 100 acres (200 for families) elsewhere; sale proceeds exempt for 6 months after sale (renting okay if another home not acquired, Prop. 41.003)	Prop. 41.001; 41.002; Const. Art. 16 §§ 50, 51
	Must file homestead declaration, or court will file it for you & charge you for doing so	Prop. 41.005(f); 41.021 to 41.023
insurance	Church benefit plan benefits	1407a (6)
	Fraternal benefit society benefits	Ins. 885.316
	Life, health, accident, or annuity benefits, monies, policy proceeds, & cash values due or paid to beneficiary or insured	Ins. 1108.051
	Texas employee uniform group insurance	Ins. 1551.011
	Texas public school employees group insurance	Ins. 1575.006
	Texas state college or university employee benefits	Ins. 1601.008
miscellaneous	Alimony & child support	Prop. 42.001(b)(3)
	Higher education savings plan trust account	Educ. 54.709(e)
	Liquor licenses & permits	Alco.Bev.Code 11.03

miscellaneous (continued)	Prepaid tuition plans	Educ. 54.639
	Property of business partnership	6132b-5.01
pensions	Tax-exempt retirement accounts, including 401(k)s, 403(b)s, profit-sharing and money purchase plans, SEP and SIMPLE IRAs, and defined-benefit plans	11 U.S.C. § 522(b)(3)(C)
	Traditional and Roth IRAs to $1,095,000 per person	11 U.S.C. § 522(b)(3)(C); (n)
	County & district employees	Gov't. 811.006
	ERISA-qualified government or church benefits, including Keoghs & IRAs	Prop. 42.0021
	Firefighters	6243e(5); 6243a-1(8.03); 6243b(15); 6243e(5); 6243e.1(1.04)
	Judges	Gov't. 831.004
	Law enforcement officers, firefighters, emergency medical personnel survivors	Gov't. 615.005
	Municipal employees & elected officials, state employees	6243h(22); Gov't. 811.005
	Police officers	6243d-1(17); 6243j(20); 6243a-1(8.03); 6243b(15); 6243d-1(17)
	Retirement benefits to extent tax-deferred	Prop. 42.0021
	Teachers	Gov't. 821.005
personal property *to $60,000 total for family, $30,000 for single adult (see also tools of trade)*	Athletic & sporting equipment, including bicycles	Prop. 42.002(a)(8)
	Bible or other book containing sacred writings of a religion (doesn't count toward $30,000 or $60,000 total)	Prop. 42.001(b)(4)
	Burial plots (exempt from total)	Prop. 41.001
	Clothing & food	Prop. 42.002(a)(2),(5)
	Health aids (exempt from total)	Prop. 42.001(b)(2)
	Health savings accounts	Prop. 42.0021
	Home furnishings including family heirlooms	Prop. 42.002(a)(1)
	Jewelry (limited to 25% of total exemption)	Prop. 42.002(a)(6)
	Pets & domestic animals plus their food: 2 horses, mules, or donkeys & tack; 12 head of cattle; 60 head of other livestock; 120 fowl	Prop. 42.002(a)(10),(11)
	1 two-, three- or four-wheeled motor vehicle per family member or per single adult who holds a driver's license; or, if not licensed, who relies on someone else to operate vehicle	Prop. 42.002(a)(9)
	2 firearms	Prop. 42.002(a)(7)
public benefits	Crime victims' compensation	Crim. Proc. 56.49
	Medical assistance	Hum. Res. 32.036
	Public assistance	Hum. Res. 31.040
	Unemployment compensation	Labor 207.075
	Workers' compensation	Labor 408.201
tools of trade *included in aggregate dollar limits for personal property*	Farming or ranching vehicles & implements	Prop. 42.002(a)(3)
	Tools, equipment (includes boat & motor vehicles used in trade), & books	Prop. 42.002(a)(4)

wages	Earned but unpaid wages	Prop. 42.001(b)(1)
	Unpaid commissions not to exceed 25% of total personal property exemptions	Prop. 42.001(d)
wildcard	None	

Utah

Federal bankruptcy exemptions not available. All law references are to Utah Code unless otherwise noted.

ASSET	EXEMPTION	LAW
homestead	Must file homestead declaration before attempted sale of home	78-23-4
	Real property, mobile home, or water rights to $20,000 if primary residence; $5,000 if not primary residence	78-23-3(1),(2),(4)
	Sale proceeds exempt for 1 year	78-23-3(5)(b)
insurance	Disability, illness, medical, or hospital benefits	78-23-5(1)(a)(iii)
	Fraternal benefit society benefits	31A-9-603
	Life insurance policy cash surrender value, excluding payments made on the contract within the prior year	78-23-5(a)(xiii)
	Life insurance proceeds if beneficiary is insured's spouse or dependent, as needed for support	78-23-5(a)(xi)
	Medical, surgical, & hospital benefits	78-23-5(1)(a)(iv)
miscellaneous	Alimony needed for support	78-23-5(1)(a)(vi)
	Child support	78-23-5(1)(a)(vi), (f),(k)
	Property of business partnership	48-1-22
pensions	Tax-exempt retirement accounts, including 401(k)s, 403(b)s, profit-sharing and money purchase plans, SEP and SIMPLE IRAs, and defined-benefit plans	11 U.S.C. § 522(b)(3)(C)
	Traditional and Roth IRAs to $1,095,000 per person	11 U.S.C. § 522(b)(3)(C); (n)
	ERISA-qualified benefits, IRAs, Roth IRAs, & Keoghs (benefits that have accrued & contributions that have been made at least 1 year prior to filing)	78-23-5(1)(a)(xiv)
	Other pensions & annuities needed for support	78-23-6(3)
	Public employees	49-11-612
personal property	Animals, books, & musical instruments to $500	78-23-8(1)(c)
	Artwork depicting, or done by, a family member	78-23-5(1)(a)(ix)
	Bed, bedding, carpets	78-23-5(1)(a)(viii)
	Burial plot	78-23-5(1)(a)(i)
	Clothing (cannot claim furs or jewelry)	78-23-5(1)(a)(viii)
	Dining & kitchen tables & chairs to $500	78-23-8(1)(b)
	Food to last 12 months	78-23-5(1)(a)(viii)
	Health aids	78-23-5(1)(a)(ii)
	Heirlooms to $500	78-23-8(1)(d)
	Motor vehicle to $2,500	78-23-8(3)
	Personal injury, wrongful death recoveries for you or person you depended on	78-23-5(1)(a)(x)
	Proceeds for sold, lost, or damaged exempt property	78-23-9

personal property (continued)	Refrigerator, freezer, microwave, stove, sewing machine, washer & dryer	78-23-5(1)(a)(viii)
	Sofas, chairs, & related furnishings to $500	78-23-8(1)(a)
public benefits	Crime victims' compensation	63-25a-421(4)
	General assistance	35A-3-112
	Occupational disease disability benefits	34A-3-107
	Unemployment compensation	35A-4-103(4)(b)
	Veterans' benefits	78-23-5(1)(a)(v)
	Workers' compensation	34A-2-422
tools of trade	Implements, books, & tools of trade to $3,500	78-23-8(2)
	Military property of National Guard member	39-1-47
wages	Minimum 75% of disposable weekly earnings or 30 times the federal hourly minimum wage, whichever is more; bankruptcy judge may authorize more for low-income debtors	70C-7-103
wildcard	None	

Vermont

Federal bankruptcy exemptions available. All law references are to Vermont Statutes Annotated unless otherwise noted.

ASSET	EXEMPTION	LAW
homestead	Property held as tenancy by the entirety may be exempt against debts owed by only one spouse	*In re McQueen*, 21 B.R. 736 (D. Ver. 1982)
	Real property or mobile home to $75,000; may also claim rents, issues, profits, & outbuildings	27-101
	Spouse of deceased owner may claim homestead exemption	27-105
insurance	Annuity contract benefits to $350 per month	8-3709
	Disability benefits that supplement life insurance or annuity contract	8-3707
	Disability or illness benefits needed for support	12-2740(19)(C)
	Fraternal benefit society benefits	8-4478
	Group life or health benefits	8-3708
	Health benefits to $200 per month	8-4086
	Life insurance proceeds for person you depended on	12-2740(19)(H)
	Life insurance proceeds if clause prohibits proceeds from being used to pay beneficiary's creditors	8-3705
	Life insurance proceeds if beneficiary is not the insured	8-3706
	Unmatured life insurance contract other than credit	12-2740(18)
miscellaneous	Alimony, child support	12-2740(19)(D)
pensions	Tax-exempt retirement accounts, including 401(k)s, 403(b)s, profit-sharing and money purchase plans, SEP and SIMPLE IRAs, and defined-benefit plans	11 U.S.C. § 522(b)(3)(C)
	Traditional and Roth IRAs to $1,095,000 per person	11 U.S.C. § 522(b)(3)(C); (n)
	Municipal employees	24-5066
	Other pensions	12-2740(19)(J)
	Self-directed accounts (IRAs, Roth IRAs, Keoghs); contributions must be made 1 year before filing	12-2740(16)

pensions (continued)	State employees	3-476
	Teachers	16-1946
personal property	Appliances, furnishings, goods, clothing, books, crops, animals, musical instruments to $2,500 total	12-2740(5)
	Bank deposits to $700	12-2740(15)
	Cow, 2 goats, 10 sheep, 10 chickens, & feed to last 1 winter; 3 swarms of bees plus honey; 5 tons coal or 500 gal. heating oil, 10 cords of firewood; 500 gal. bottled gas; growing crops to $5,000; yoke of oxen or steers, plow & ox yoke; 2 horses with harnesses, halters, & chains	12-2740(6),(9)-(14)
	Health aids	12-2740(17)
	Jewelry to $500; wedding ring unlimited	12-2740(3),(4)
	Motor vehicles to $2,500	12-2740(1)
	Personal injury, lost future earnings, wrongful death recoveries for you or person you depended on	12-2740(19)(F), (G),(I)
	Stove, heating unit, refrigerator, freezer, water heater, & sewing machines	12-2740(8)
public benefits	Aid to blind, aged, disabled; general assistance	33-124
	Crime victims' compensation needed for support	12-2740(19)(E)
	Social Security needed for support	12-2740(19)(A)
	Unemployment compensation	21-1367
	Veterans' benefits needed for support	12-2740(19)(B)
	Workers' compensation	21-681
tools of trade	Books & tools of trade to $5,000	12-2740(2)
wages	Entire wages, if you received welfare during 2 months before filing	12-3170
	Minimum 75% of weekly disposable earnings or 30 times the federal minimum hourly wage, whichever is greater; bankruptcy judge may authorize more for low-income debtors	12-3170
wildcard	Unused exemptions for motor vehicle, tools of trade, jewelry, household furniture, appliances, clothing, & crops to $7,000	12-2740(7)
	$400 of any property	12-2740(7)

Virginia

Federal bankruptcy exemptions not available. All law references are to Code of Virginia unless otherwise noted.

ASSET	EXEMPTION	LAW
homestead	$5,000 plus $500 per dependent; rents & profits; sale proceeds exempt to $5,000 (unused portion of homestead may be applied to any personal property)	*Cheeseman v. Nachman*, 656 F.2d 60 (4th Cir. 1981); 34-4; 34-18; 34-20
	May include mobile home	*In re Goad*, 161 B.R. 161 (W.D. Va. 1993)
	Must file homestead declaration before filing for bankruptcy	34-6
	Property held as tenancy by the entirety may be exempt against debts owed by only one spouse	*In re Bunker*, 312 F.3d 145 (4th Cir., 2002)
	Surviving spouse may claim $15,000; if no surviving spouse, minor children may claim exemption	64.1-151.3

insurance	Accident or sickness benefits	38.2-3406
	Burial society benefits	38.2-4021
	Cooperative life insurance benefits	38.2-3811
	Fraternal benefit society benefits	38.2-4118
	Group life or accident insurance for government officials	51.1-510
	Group life insurance policy or proceeds	38.2-3339
	Industrial sick benefits	38.2-3549
	Life insurance proceeds	38.2-3122
miscellaneous	Property of business partnership	50-73.108
pensions *see also wages*	Tax-exempt retirement accounts, including 401(k)s, 403(b)s, profit-sharing and money purchase plans, SEP and SIMPLE IRAs, and defined-benefit plans	11 U.S.C. § 522(b)(3)(C)
	Traditional and Roth IRAs to $1,095,000 per person	11 U.S.C. § 522(b)(3)(C); (n)
	City, town, & county employees	51.1-802
	ERISA-qualified benefits to same extent permitted by federal bankruptcy law	34-34
	Judges	51.1-300
	State employees	51.1-124.4(A)
	State police officers	51.1-200
personal property	Bible	34-26(1)
	Burial plot	34-26(3)
	Clothing to $1,000	34-26(4)
	Family portraits & heirlooms to $5,000 total	34-26(2)
	Health aids	34-26(6)
	Household furnishings to $5,000	34-26(4a)
	Motor vehicle to $2,000	34-26(8)
	Personal injury causes of action & recoveries	34-28.1
	Pets	34-26(5)
	Prepaid tuition contracts	23-38.81(E)
	Wedding & engagement rings	34-26(1a)
public benefits	Aid to blind, aged, disabled; general relief	63.2-506
	Crime victims' compensation unless seeking to discharge debt for treatment of injury incurred during crime	19.2-368.12
	Payments to tobacco farmers	3.1-1111.1
	Unemployment compensation	60.2-600
	Workers' compensation	65.2-531
tools of trade	For farmer, pair of horses, or mules with gear; one wagon or cart, one tractor to $3,000; 2 plows & wedges; one drag, harvest cradle, pitchfork, rake; fertilizer to $1,000	34-27
	Tools, books, & instruments of trade, including motor vehicles, to $10,000, needed in your occupation or education	34-26(7)
	Uniforms, arms, equipment of military member	44-96
wages	Minimum 75% of weekly disposable earnings or 40 times the federal minimum hourly wage, whichever is greater; bankruptcy judge may authorize more for low-income debtors	34-29
wildcard	Unused portion of homestead or personal property exemption	34-13
	$2,000 of any property for disabled veterans	34-4.1

Washington

Federal bankruptcy exemptions available. All law references are to Revised Code of Washington Annotated unless otherwise noted.

ASSET	EXEMPTION	LAW
homestead	Must record homestead declaration before sale of home if property unimproved or home unoccupied	6.15.040
	Real property or manufactured home to $125,000; unimproved property intended for residence to $15,000 (husband & wife may not double)	6.13.010; 6.13.030
insurance	Annuity contract proceeds to $2,500 per month	48.18.430
	Disability proceeds, avails, or benefits	48.36A.180
	Fraternal benefit society benefits	48.18.400
	Group life insurance policy or proceeds	48.18.420
	Life insurance proceeds or avails if beneficiary is not the insured	48.18.410
miscellaneous	Child support payments	6.15.010(3)(d)
pensions	Tax-exempt retirement accounts, including 401(k)s, 403(b)s, profit-sharing and money purchase plans, SEP and SIMPLE IRAs, and defined-benefit plans	11 U.S.C. § 522(b)(3)(C)
	Traditional and Roth IRAs to $1,095,000 per person	11 U.S.C. § 522(b)(3)(C); (n)
	City employees	41.28.200; 41.44.240
	ERISA-qualified benefits, IRAs, Roth IRAs, & Keoghs	6.15.020
	Judges	2.10.180; 2.12.090
	Law enforcement officials & firefighters	41.26.053
	Police officers	41.20.180
	Public & state employees	41.40.052
	State patrol officers	43.43.310
	Teachers	41.32.052
	Volunteer firefighters	41.24.240
personal property	Appliances, furniture, household goods, home & yard equipment to $2,700 total for individual ($5,400 for community)	6.15.010(3)(a)
	Books to $1,500	6.15.010(2)
	Burial ground	68.24.220
	Burial plots sold by nonprofit cemetery association	68.20.120
	Clothing, no more than $1,000 in furs, jewelry, ornaments	6.15.010(1)
	Fire insurance proceeds for lost, stolen, or destroyed exempt property	6.15.030
	Food & fuel for comfortable maintenance	6.15.010(3)(a)
	Health aids prescribed	6.15.010(3)(e)
	Keepsakes & family pictures	6.15.010(2)
	Motor vehicle to $2,500 total for individual (two vehicles to $5,000 for community)	6.15.010(3)(c)
	Personal injury recoveries to $16,150	6.15.010(3)(f)

public benefits	Child welfare	74.13.070
	Crime victims' compensation	7.68.070(10)
	General assistance	74.04.280
	Industrial insurance (workers' compensation)	51.32.040
	Old-age assistance	74.08.210
	Unemployment compensation	50.40.020
tools of trade	Farmer's trucks, stock, tools, seed, equipment, & supplies to $5,000 total	6.15.010(4)(a)
	Library, office furniture, office equipment, & supplies of physician, surgeon, attorney, clergy, or other professional to $5,000 total	6.15.010(4)(b)
	Tools & materials used in any other trade to $5,000	6.15.010(4)(c)
wages	Minimum 75% of weekly disposable earnings or 30 times the federal minimum hourly wage, whichever is greater; bankruptcy judge may authorize more for low-income debtors	6.27.150
wildcard	$2,000 of any personal property (no more than $200 in cash, bank deposits, bonds, stocks, & securities)	6.15.010(3)(b)

West Virginia

Federal bankruptcy exemptions not available. All law references are to West Virginia Code unless otherwise noted.

ASSET	EXEMPTION	LAW
homestead	Real or personal property used as residence to $25,000; unused portion of homestead may be applied to any property	38-10-4(a)
insurance	Fraternal benefit society benefits	33-23-21
	Group life insurance policy or proceeds	33-6-28
	Health or disability benefits	38-10-4(j)(3)
	Life insurance payments from policy for person you depended on, needed for support	38-10-4(k)(3)
	Unmatured life insurance contract, except credit insurance policy	38-10-4(g)
	Unmatured life insurance contract's accrued dividend, interest, or loan value to $8,000, if debtor owns contract & insured is either debtor or a person on whom debtor is dependent	38-10-4(h)
miscellaneous	Alimony, child support needed for support	38-10-4(j)(4)
pensions	Tax-exempt retirement accounts, including 401(k)s, 403(b)s, profit-sharing and money purchase plans, SEP and SIMPLE IRAs, and defined-benefit plans	11 U.S.C. § 522(b)(3)(C)
	Traditional and Roth IRAs to $1,095,000 per person	11 U.S.C. § 522(b)(3)(C); (n)
	ERISA-qualified benefits, IRAs needed for support	38-10-4(j)(5)
	Public employees	5-10-46
	Teachers	18-7A-30
personal property	Animals, crops, clothing, appliances, books, household goods, furnishings, musical instruments to $400 per item, $8,000 total	38-10-4(c)
	Burial plot to $25,000, in lieu of homestead	38-10-4(a)

personal property (continued)	Health aids	38-10-4(i)
	Jewelry to $1,000	38-10-4(d)
	Lost earnings payments needed for support	38-10-4(k)(5)
	Motor vehicle to $2,400	38-10-4(b)
	Personal injury recoveries to $15,000	38-10-4(k)(4)
	Prepaid higher education tuition trust fund & savings plan payments	38-10-4(k)(6)
	Wrongful death recoveries for person you depended on, needed for support	38-10-4(k)(2)
public benefits	Aid to blind, aged, disabled; general assistance	9-5-1
	Crime victims' compensation	38-10-4(k)(1)
	Social Security	38-10-4(j)(1)
	Unemployment compensation	38-10-4(j)(1)
	Veterans' benefits	38-10-4(j)(2)
	Workers' compensation	23-4-18
tools of trade	Implements, books, & tools of trade to $1,500	38-10-4(f)
wages	Minimum 30 times the federal minimum hourly wage per week; bankruptcy judge may authorize more for low-income debtors	38-5A-3
wildcard	$800 plus unused portion of homestead or burial exemption, of any property	38-10-4(e)

Wisconsin

Federal bankruptcy exemptions available. All law references are to Wisconsin Statutes Annotated unless otherwise noted.

ASSET	EXEMPTION	LAW
homestead	Property you occupy or intend to occupy to $40,000; sale proceeds exempt for 2 years if you intend to purchase another home (husband & wife may not double)	815.20
insurance	Federal disability insurance benefits	815.18(3)(ds)
	Fraternal benefit society benefits	614.96
	Life insurance proceeds for someone debtor depended on, needed for support	815.18(3)(i)(a)
	Life insurance proceeds held in trust by insurer, if clause prohibits proceeds from being used to pay beneficiary's creditors	632.42
	Unmatured life insurance contract (except credit insurance contract) if debtor owns contract & insured is debtor or dependents, or someone debtor is dependent on	815.18(3)(f)
	Unmatured life insurance contract's accrued dividends, interest, or loan value to $4,000 total, if debtor owns contract & insured is debtor or dependents, or someone debtor is dependent on	815.18(3)(f)
miscellaneous	Alimony, child support needed for support	815.18(3)(c)
	Property of business partnership	178.21(3)(c)
pensions	Tax-exempt retirement accounts, including 401(k)s, 403(b)s, profit-sharing and money purchase plans, SEP and SIMPLE IRAs, and defined-benefit plans	11 U.S.C. § 522(b)(3)(C)
	Traditional and Roth IRAs to $1,095,000 per person	11 U.S.C. § 522(b)(3)(C); (n)

pensions (continued)	Certain municipal employees	62.63(4)
	Firefighters, police officers who worked in city with population over 100,000	815.18(3)(ef)
	Military pensions	815.18(3)(n)
	Private or public retirement benefits	815.18(3)(j)
	Public employees	40.08(1)
personal property	Burial plot, tombstone, coffin	815.18(3)(a)
	College savings account or tuition trust fund	14.64(7); 14.63(8)
	Deposit accounts to $1,000	815.18(3)(k)
	Fire & casualty proceeds for destroyed exempt property for 2 years from receiving	815.18(3)(e)
	Household goods & furnishings, clothing, keepsakes, jewelry, appliances, books, musical instruments, firearms, sporting goods, animals, & other tangible personal property to $5,000 total	815.18(3)(d)
	Lost future earnings recoveries, needed for support	815.18(3)(i)(d)
	Motor vehicles to $1,200; unused portion of $5,000 personal property exemption may be added	815.18(3)(g)
	Personal injury recoveries to $25,000	815.18(3)(i)(c)
	Tenant's lease or stock interest in housing co-op, to homestead amount	182.004(6)
	Wages used to purchase savings bonds	20.921(1)(e)
	Wrongful death recoveries, needed for support	815.18(3)(i)(b)
public benefits	Crime victims' compensation	949.07
	Social services payments	49.96
	Unemployment compensation	108.13
	Veterans' benefits	45.03(8)(b)
	Workers' compensation	102.27
tools of trade	Equipment, inventory, farm products, books, & tools of trade to $7,500 total	815.18(3)(b)
wages	75% of weekly net income or 30 times the greater of the federal or state minimum hourly wage; bankruptcy judge may authorize more for low-income debtors	815.18(3)(h)
	Wages of county jail prisoners	303.08(3)
	Wages of county work camp prisoners	303.10(7)
	Wages of inmates under work-release plan	303.065(4)(b)
wildcard	None	

Wyoming

Federal bankruptcy exemptions not available. All law references are to Wyoming Statutes Annotated unless otherwise noted.

ASSET	EXEMPTION	LAW
homestead	Property held as tenancy by the entirety may be exempt against debts owed by only one spouse	In re Anselmi, 52 B.R. 479 (D. Wy. 1985)
	Real property you occupy to $10,000 or house trailer you occupy to $6,000	1-20-101; 102; 104
	Spouse or child of deceased owner may claim homestead exemption	1-20-103

insurance	Annuity contract proceeds to $350 per month	26-15-132
	Disability benefits if clause prohibits proceeds from being used to pay beneficiary's creditors	26-15-130
	Fraternal benefit society benefits	26-29-218
	Group life or disability policy or proceeds, cash surrender & loan values, premiums waived, & dividends	26-15-131
	Individual life insurance policy proceeds, cash surrender & loan values, premiums waived, & dividends	26-15-129
	Life insurance proceeds held by insurer, if clause prohibits proceeds from being used to pay beneficiary's creditors	26-15-133
miscellaneous	Liquor licenses & malt beverage permits	12-4-604
pensions	Tax-exempt retirement accounts, including 401(k)s, 403(b)s, profit-sharing and money purchase plans, SEP and SIMPLE IRAs, and defined-benefit plans	11 U.S.C. § 522(b)(3)(C)
	Traditional and Roth IRAs to $1,095,000 per person	11 U.S.C. § 522(b)(3)(C); (n)
	Criminal investigators, highway officers	9-3-620
	Firefighters' death benefits	15-5-209
	Game & fish wardens	9-3-620
	Police officers	15-5-313(c)
	Private or public retirement funds & accounts	1-20-110
	Public employees	9-3-426
personal property	Bedding, furniture, household articles, & food to $2,000 per person in the home	1-20-106(a)(iii)
	Bible, schoolbooks, & pictures	1-20-106(a)(i)
	Burial plot	1-20-106(a)(ii)
	Clothing & wedding rings to $1,000	1-20-105
	Medical savings account contributions	1-20-111
	Motor vehicle to $2,400	1-20-106(a)(iv)
	Prepaid funeral contracts	26-32-102
public benefits	Crime victims' compensation	1-40-113
	General assistance	42-2-113(b)
	Unemployment compensation	27-3-319
	Workers' compensation	27-14-702
tools of trade	Library & implements of profession to $2,000 or tools, motor vehicle, implements, team & stock in trade to $2,000	1-20-106(b)
wages	Earnings of National Guard members	19-9-401
	Minimum 75% of disposable weekly earnings or 30 times the federal hourly minimum wage, whichever is more	1-15-511
	Wages of inmates in adult community corrections program	7-18-114
	Wages of inmates in correctional industries program	25-13-107
	Wages of inmates on work release	7-16-308
wildcard	None	

Federal Bankruptcy Exemptions

Married couples filing jointly may double all exemptions. All references are to 11 U.S.C. § 522. These exemptions were last adjusted in 2007. Every three years ending on April 1, these amounts will be adjusted to reflect changes in the Consumer Price Index. Debtors in the following states may select the federal bankruptcy exemptions:

Arkansas	Massachusetts	New Jersey	Texas
Connecticut	Michigan	New Mexico	Vermont
District of Columbia	Minnesota	Pennsylvania	Washington
Hawaii	New Hampshire	Rhode Island	Wisconsin

ASSET	EXEMPTION	SUBSECTION
homestead	Real property, including co-op or mobile home, or burial plot to $20,200; unused portion of homestead to $10,125 may be applied to any property	(d)(1); (d)(5)
insurance	Disability, illness, or unemployment benefits	(d)(10)(C)
	Life insurance payments from policy for person you depended on, needed for support	(d)(11)(C)
	Life insurance policy with loan value, in accrued dividends or interest, to $10,775	(d)(8)
	Unmatured life insurance contract, except credit insurance policy	(d)(7)
miscellaneous	Alimony, child support needed for support	(d)(10)(D)
pensions	Tax exempt retirement accounts (including 401(k)s, 403(b)s, profit-sharing and money purchase plans, SEP and SIMPLE IRAs, and defined-benefit plans	(b)(3)(C)
	IRAs and Roth IRAs to $1,095,000 per person	(b)(3)(C)(n)
personal property	Animals, crops, clothing, appliances, books, furnishings, household goods, musical instruments to $525 per item, $10,775 total	(d)(3)
	Health aids	(d)(9)
	Jewelry to $1,350	(d)(4)
	Lost earnings payments	(d)(11)(E)
	Motor vehicle to $3,225	(d)(2)
	Personal injury recoveries to $20,200 (not to include pain & suffering or pecuniary loss)	(d)(11)(D)
	Wrongful death recoveries for person you depended on	(d)(11)(B)
public benefits	Crime victims' compensation	(d)(11)(A)
	Public assistance	(d)(10)(A)
	Social Security	(d)(10)(A)
	Unemployment compensation	(d)(10)(A)
	Veterans' benefits	(d)(10)(A)
tools of trade	Implements, books, & tools of trade to $2,025	(d)(6)
wages	None	
wildcard	$1,075 of any property	(d)(5)
	Up to $10,125 of unused homestead exemption amount, for any property	(d)(5)

Federal Nonbankruptcy Exemptions

These exemptions are available only if you select your state exemptions. You may use them for any exemptions in addition to those allowed by your state, but they cannot be claimed if you file using federal bankruptcy exemptions. All law references are to the United States Code.

ASSET	EXEMPTION	LAW
death & disability benefits	Government employees	5 § 8130
	Longshoremen & harbor workers	33 § 916
	War risk, hazard, death, or injury compensation	42 § 1717
retirement	Civil service employees	5 § 8346
	Foreign Service employees	22 § 4060
	Military Medal of Honor roll pensions	38 § 1562(c)
	Military service employees	10 § 1440
	Railroad workers	45 § 231m
	Social Security	42 § 407
	Veterans' benefits	38 § 5301
survivor's benefits	Judges, U.S. court & judicial center directors, administrative assistants to U.S. Supreme Court Chief Justice	28 § 376
	Lighthouse workers	33 § 775
	Military service	10 § 1450
miscellaneous	Indian lands or homestead sales or lease proceeds	25 § 410
	Klamath Indian tribe benefits for Indians residing in Oregon	25 § 543; 545
	Military deposits in savings accounts while on permanent duty outside U.S.	10 § 1035
	Military group life insurance	38 § 1970(g)
	Railroad workers' unemployment insurance	45 § 352(e)
	Seamen's clothing	46 § 11110
	Seamen's wages (while on a voyage) pursuant to a written contract	46 § 11109
	Minimum 75% of disposable weekly earnings or 30 times the federal minimum hourly wage, whichever is more; bankruptcy judge may authorize more for low-income debtors	15 § 1673

Tear-Out Forms

Voluntary Petition

Exhibit C to Voluntary Petition

Exhibit D to Voluntary Petition

Schedule A—Real Property

Schedule B—Personal Property

Schedule C—Property Claimed as Exempt

Schedule D—Creditors Holding Secured Claims

Schedule E—Creditors Holding Unsecured Priority Claims

Schedule F—Creditors Holding Unsecured Nonpriority Claims

Schedule G—Executory Contracts and Unexpired Leases

Schedule H—Codebtors

Schedule I—Current Income of Individual Debtor(s)

Schedule J—Current Expenditures of Individual Debtor(s)

Declaration Concerning Debtor's Schedules

Summary of Schedules and Statistical Summary of Certain Liabilities, and Related Data

Form 3A—Application and Order to Pay Filing Fee in Installments

Form 7—Statement of Financial Affairs

Form 10—Proof of Claim

Form 20A—Notice of Motion or Objection

Form 21—Statement of Social Security Number(s)

Form 22A—Statement of Current Monthly Income and Means-Test Calculation

Form 22C—Statement of Current Monthly Income and Calculation of Commitment Period and Disposable Income

Form 23—Debtor's Certification of Completion of Postpetition Instructional Course Concerning Personal Financial Management

Form 201—Notice to Individual Consumer Debtor Under § 342(b) of the Bankruptcy Code

Amendment Cover Sheet

Daily Expenses

Notice of Plan Amendment and Confirmation Hearing Date

Proof of Service by Mail

Chapter 13 Repayment Plan

United States Bankruptcy Court	Voluntary Petition

Name of Debtor (if individual, enter Last, First, Middle):	Name of Joint Debtor (Spouse) (Last, First, Middle):
All Other Names used by the Debtor in the last 8 years (include married, maiden, and trade names):	All Other Names used by the Joint Debtor in the last 8 years (include married, maiden, and trade names):
Last four digits of Soc. Sec. or Indvidual-Taxpayer I.D. (ITIN) No./Complete EIN (if more than one, state all):	Last four digits of Soc. Sec. or Indvidual-Taxpayer I.D. (ITIN) No./Complete EIN (if more than one, state all):
Street Address of Debtor (No. and Street, City, and State): ZIP CODE	Street Address of Joint Debtor (No. and Street, City, and State): ZIP CODE
County of Residence or of the Principal Place of Business:	County of Residence or of the Principal Place of Business:
Mailing Address of Debtor (if different from street address): ZIP CODE	Mailing Address of Joint Debtor (if different from street address): ZIP CODE
Location of Principal Assets of Business Debtor (if different from street address above):	ZIP CODE

Type of Debtor
(Form of Organization)
(Check **one** box.)

☐ Individual (includes Joint Debtors)
See Exhibit D on page 2 of this form.
☐ Corporation (includes LLC and LLP)
☐ Partnership
☐ Other (If debtor is not one of the above entities, check this box and state type of entity below.)

_____

Nature of Business
(Check **one** box.)

☐ Health Care Business
☐ Single Asset Real Estate as defined in 11 U.S.C. § 101(51B)
☐ Railroad
☐ Stockbroker
☐ Commodity Broker
☐ Clearing Bank
☐ Other

Tax-Exempt Entity
(Check box, if applicable.)

☐ Debtor is a tax-exempt organization under Title 26 of the United States Code (the Internal Revenue Code).

Chapter of Bankruptcy Code Under Which the Petition is Filed (Check **one** box.)

☐ Chapter 7
☐ Chapter 9
☐ Chapter 11
☐ Chapter 12
☐ Chapter 13

☐ Chapter 15 Petition for Recognition of a Foreign Main Proceeding
☐ Chapter 15 Petition for Recognition of a Foreign Nonmain Proceeding

Nature of Debts
(Check one box.)

☐ Debts are primarily consumer debts, defined in 11 U.S.C. § 101(8) as "incurred by an individual primarily for a personal, family, or household purpose."
☐ Debts are primarily business debts.

Filing Fee (Check one box.)

☐ Full Filing Fee attached.

☐ Filing Fee to be paid in installments (applicable to individuals only). Must attach signed application for the court's consideration certifying that the debtor is unable to pay fee except in installments. Rule 1006(b). See Official Form 3A.

☐ Filing Fee waiver requested (applicable to chapter 7 individuals only). Must attach signed application for the court's consideration. See Official Form 3B.

Chapter 11 Debtors

Check one box:
☐ Debtor is a small business debtor as defined in 11 U.S.C. § 101(51D).

☐ Debtor is not a small business debtor as defined in 11 U.S.C. § 101(51D).

Check if:
☐ Debtor's aggregate noncontingent liquidated debts (excluding debts owed to insiders or affiliates) are less than $2,190,000.
- -
Check all applicable boxes:
☐ A plan is being filed with this petition.
☐ Acceptances of the plan were solicited prepetition from one or more classes of creditors, in accordance with 11 U.S.C. § 1126(b).

Statistical/Administrative Information

☐ Debtor estimates that funds will be available for distribution to unsecured creditors.
☐ Debtor estimates that, after any exempt property is excluded and administrative expenses paid, there will be no funds available for distribution to unsecured creditors.

THIS SPACE IS FOR COURT USE ONLY

Estimated Number of Creditors

☐	☐	☐	☐	☐	☐	☐	☐	☐	☐
1-49	50-99	100-199	200-999	1,000-5,000	5,001-10,000	10,001-25,000	25,001-50,000	50,001-100,000	Over 100,000

Estimated Assets

☐	☐	☐	☐	☐	☐	☐	☐	☐	☐
$0 to $50,000	$50,001 to $100,000	$100,001 to $500,000	$500,001 to $1 million	$1,000,001 to $10 million	$10,000,001 to $50 million	$50,000,001 to $100 million	$100,000,001 to $500 million	$500,000,001 to $1 billion	More than $1 billion

Estimated Liabilities

☐	☐	☐	☐	☐	☐	☐	☐	☐	☐
$0 to $50,000	$50,001 to $100,000	$100,001 to $500,000	$500,001 to $1 million	$1,000,001 to $10 million	$10,000,001 to $50 million	$50,000,001 to $100 million	$100,000,001 to $500 million	$500,000,001 to $1 billion	More than $1 billion

Voluntary Petition *(This page must be completed and filed in every case.)*	Name of Debtor(s):

All Prior Bankruptcy Cases Filed Within Last 8 Years (If more than two, attach additional sheet.)		
Location Where Filed:	Case Number:	Date Filed:
Location Where Filed:	Case Number:	Date Filed:

Pending Bankruptcy Case Filed by any Spouse, Partner, or Affiliate of this Debtor (If more than one, attach additional sheet.)		
Name of Debtor:	Case Number:	Date Filed:
District:	Relationship:	Judge:

Exhibit A	**Exhibit B**
(To be completed if debtor is required to file periodic reports (e.g., forms 10K and 10Q) with the Securities and Exchange Commission pursuant to Section 13 or 15(d) of the Securities Exchange Act of 1934 and is requesting relief under chapter 11.)	(To be completed if debtor is an individual whose debts are primarily consumer debts.) I, the attorney for the petitioner named in the foregoing petition, declare that I have informed the petitioner that [he or she] may proceed under chapter 7, 11, 12, or 13 of title 11, United States Code, and have explained the relief available under each such chapter. I further certify that I have delivered to the debtor the notice required by 11 U.S.C. § 342(b).
☐ Exhibit A is attached and made a part of this petition.	X _____ Signature of Attorney for Debtor(s) (Date)

Exhibit C

Does the debtor own or have possession of any property that poses or is alleged to pose a threat of imminent and identifiable harm to public health or safety?

☐   Yes, and Exhibit C is attached and made a part of this petition.

☐   No.

Exhibit D

(To be completed by every individual debtor. If a joint petition is filed, each spouse must complete and attach a separate Exhibit D.)

☐   Exhibit D completed and signed by the debtor is attached and made a part of this petition.

If this is a joint petition:

☐   Exhibit D also completed and signed by the joint debtor is attached and made a part of this petition.

Information Regarding the Debtor - Venue
(Check any applicable box.)

☐   Debtor has been domiciled or has had a residence, principal place of business, or principal assets in this District for 180 days immediately preceding the date of this petition or for a longer part of such 180 days than in any other District.

☐   There is a bankruptcy case concerning debtor's affiliate, general partner, or partnership pending in this District.

☐   Debtor is a debtor in a foreign proceeding and has its principal place of business or principal assets in the United States in this District, or has no principal place of business or assets in the United States but is a defendant in an action or proceeding [in a federal or state court] in this District, or the interests of the parties will be served in regard to the relief sought in this District.

Certification by a Debtor Who Resides as a Tenant of Residential Property
(Check all applicable boxes.)

☐   Landlord has a judgment against the debtor for possession of debtor's residence. (If box checked, complete the following.)

_____
(Name of landlord that obtained judgment)

_____
(Address of landlord)

☐   Debtor claims that under applicable nonbankruptcy law, there are circumstances under which the debtor would be permitted to cure the entire monetary default that gave rise to the judgment for possession, after the judgment for possession was entered, and

☐   Debtor has included with this petition the deposit with the court of any rent that would become due during the 30-day period after the filing of the petition.

☐   Debtor certifies that he/she has served the Landlord with this certification. (11 U.S.C. § 362(l)).

Voluntary Petition *(This page must be completed and filed in every case.)*	Name of Debtor(s):

Signatures

Signature(s) of Debtor(s) (Individual/Joint)	**Signature of a Foreign Representative**

Signature(s) of Debtor(s) (Individual/Joint)

I declare under penalty of perjury that the information provided in this petition is true and correct.

[If petitioner is an individual whose debts are primarily consumer debts and has chosen to file under chapter 7] I am aware that I may proceed under chapter 7, 11, 12 or 13 of title 11, United States Code, understand the relief available under each such chapter, and choose to proceed under chapter 7.

[If no attorney represents me and no bankruptcy petition preparer signs the petition] I have obtained and read the notice required by 11 U.S.C. § 342(b).

I request relief in accordance with the chapter of title 11, United States Code, specified in this petition.

X _____
   Signature of Debtor

X _____
   Signature of Joint Debtor

   _____
   Telephone Number (if not represented by attorney)

   _____
   Date

Signature of a Foreign Representative

I declare under penalty of perjury that the information provided in this petition is true and correct, that I am the foreign representative of a debtor in a foreign proceeding, and that I am authorized to file this petition.

(Check only **one** box.)

☐ I request relief in accordance with chapter 15 of title 11, United States Code. Certified copies of the documents required by 11 U.S.C. § 1515 are attached.

☐ Pursuant to 11 U.S.C. § 1511, I request relief in accordance with the chapter of title 11 specified in this petition. A certified copy of the order granting recognition of the foreign main proceeding is attached.

X _____
   (Signature of Foreign Representative)

   _____
   (Printed Name of Foreign Representative)

   _____
   Date

Signature of Attorney*

X _____
   Signature of Attorney for Debtor(s)

   _____
   Printed Name of Attorney for Debtor(s)

   _____
   Firm Name

   _____
   Address

   _____

   _____

   _____
   Telephone Number

   _____
   Date

*In a case in which § 707(b)(4)(D) applies, this signature also constitutes a certification that the attorney has no knowledge after an inquiry that the information in the schedules is incorrect.

Signature of Debtor (Corporation/Partnership)

I declare under penalty of perjury that the information provided in this petition is true and correct, and that I have been authorized to file this petition on behalf of the debtor.

The debtor requests the relief in accordance with the chapter of title 11, United States Code, specified in this petition.

X _____
   Signature of Authorized Individual

   _____
   Printed Name of Authorized Individual

   _____
   Title of Authorized Individual

   _____
   Date

Signature of Non-Attorney Bankruptcy Petition Preparer

I declare under penalty of perjury that: (1) I am a bankruptcy petition preparer as defined in 11 U.S.C. § 110; (2) I prepared this document for compensation and have provided the debtor with a copy of this document and the notices and information required under 11 U.S.C. §§ 110(b), 110(h), and 342(b); and, (3) if rules or guidelines have been promulgated pursuant to 11 U.S.C. § 110(h) setting a maximum fee for services chargeable by bankruptcy petition preparers, I have given the debtor notice of the maximum amount before preparing any document for filing for a debtor or accepting any fee from the debtor, as required in that section. Official Form 19 is attached.

_____
Printed Name and title, if any, of Bankruptcy Petition Preparer

_____
Social-Security number (If the bankruptcy petition preparer is not an individual, state the Social-Security number of the officer, principal, responsible person or partner of the bankruptcy petition preparer.) (Required by 11 U.S.C. § 110.)

_____
Address

_____

X _____

_____
Date

Signature of bankruptcy petition preparer or officer, principal, responsible person, or partner whose Social-Security number is provided above.

Names and Social-Security numbers of all other individuals who prepared or assisted in preparing this document unless the bankruptcy petition preparer is not an individual.

If more than one person prepared this document, attach additional sheets conforming to the appropriate official form for each person.

A bankruptcy petition preparer's failure to comply with the provisions of title 11 and the Federal Rules of Bankruptcy Procedure may result in fines or imprisonment or both. 11 U.S.C. § 110; 18 U.S.C. § 156.

Exhibit "C"

[If, to the best of the debtor's knowledge, the debtor owns or has possession of property that poses or is alleged to pose a threat of imminent and identifiable harm to the public health or safety, attach this Exhibit "C" to the petition.]

[Caption as in Form 16B]

Exhibit "C" to Voluntary Petition

1. Identify and briefly describe all real or personal property owned by or in possession of the debtor that, to the best of the debtor's knowledge, poses or is alleged to pose a threat of imminent and identifiable harm to the public health or safety (attach additional sheets if necessary):

....
....
....
....

2. With respect to each parcel of real property or item of personal property identified in question 1, describe the nature and location of the dangerous condition, whether environmental or otherwise, that poses or is alleged to pose a threat of imminent and identifiable harm to the public health or safety (attach additional sheets if necessary):

....
....
....
....

UNITED STATES BANKRUPTCY COURT

_____District of_____

In re_____   Case No._____
         Debtor(s)   (if known)

EXHIBIT D - INDIVIDUAL DEBTOR'S STATEMENT OF COMPLIANCE WITH CREDIT COUNSELING REQUIREMENT

Warning: You must be able to check truthfully one of the five statements regarding credit counseling listed below. If you cannot do so, you are not eligible to file a bankruptcy case, and the court can dismiss any case you do file. If that happens, you will lose whatever filing fee you paid, and your creditors will be able to resume collection activities against you. If your case is dismissed and you file another bankruptcy case later, you may be required to pay a second filing fee and you may have to take extra steps to stop creditors' collection activities.

Every individual debtor must file this Exhibit D. If a joint petition is filed, each spouse must complete and file a separate Exhibit D. Check one of the five statements below and attach any documents as directed.

□ 1. Within the 180 days **before the filing of my bankruptcy case**, I received a briefing from a credit counseling agency approved by the United States trustee or bankruptcy administrator that outlined the opportunities for available credit counseling and assisted me in performing a related budget analysis, and I have a certificate from the agency describing the services provided to me. *Attach a copy of the certificate and a copy of any debt repayment plan developed through the agency.*

□ 2. Within the 180 days **before the filing of my bankruptcy case**, I received a briefing from a credit counseling agency approved by the United States trustee or bankruptcy administrator that outlined the opportunities for available credit counseling and assisted me in performing a related budget analysis, but I do not have a certificate from the agency describing the services provided to me. *You must file a copy of a certificate from the agency describing the services provided to you and a copy of any debt repayment plan developed through the agency no later than 15 days after your bankruptcy case is filed.*

☐ 3. I certify that I requested credit counseling services from an approved agency but was unable to obtain the services during the five days from the time I made my request, and the following exigent circumstances merit a temporary waiver of the credit counseling requirement so I can file my bankruptcy case now. *[Must be accompanied by a motion for determination by the court.] [Summarize exigent circumstances here.]* _____
_____.

If the court is satisfied with the reasons stated in your motion, it will send you an order approving your request. You must still obtain the credit counseling briefing within the first 30 days after you file your bankruptcy case and promptly file a certificate from the agency that provided the briefing, together with a copy of any debt management plan developed through the agency. Any extension of the 30-day deadline can be granted only for cause and is limited to a maximum of 15 days. A motion for extension must be filed within the 30-day period. Failure to fulfill these requirements may result in dismissal of your case. If the court is not satisfied with your reasons for filing your bankruptcy case without first receiving a credit counseling briefing, your case may be dismissed.

☐ 4. I am not required to receive a credit counseling briefing because of: *[Check the applicable statement.]* *[Must be accompanied by a motion for determination by the court.]*
☐ Incapacity. (Defined in 11 U.S.C. § 109(h)(4) as impaired by reason of mental illness or mental deficiency so as to be incapable of realizing and making rational decisions with respect to financial responsibilities.);
☐ Disability. (Defined in 11 U.S.C. § 109(h)(4) as physically impaired to the extent of being unable, after reasonable effort, to participate in a credit counseling briefing in person, by telephone, or through the Internet.);
☐ Active military duty in a military combat zone.

☐ 5. The United States trustee or bankruptcy administrator has determined that the credit counseling requirement of 11 U.S.C. § 109(h) does not apply in this district.

I certify under penalty of perjury that the information provided above is true and correct.

Signature of Debtor: _____

Date: _____

In re _____,   Case No. _____
                        Debtor   **(If known)**

SCHEDULE A - REAL PROPERTY

Except as directed below, list all real property in which the debtor has any legal, equitable, or future interest, including all property owned as a co-tenant, community property, or in which the debtor has a life estate. Include any property in which the debtor holds rights and powers exercisable for the debtor's own benefit. If the debtor is married, state whether the husband, wife, both, or the marital community own the property by placing an "H," "W," "J," or "C" in the column labeled "Husband, Wife, Joint, or Community." If the debtor holds no interest in real property, write "None" under "Description and Location of Property."

Do not include interests in executory contracts and unexpired leases on this schedule. List them in Schedule G - Executory Contracts and Unexpired Leases.

If an entity claims to have a lien or hold a secured interest in any property, state the amount of the secured claim. See Schedule D. If no entity claims to hold a secured interest in the property, write "None" in the column labeled "Amount of Secured Claim."

If the debtor is an individual or if a joint petition is filed, state the amount of any exemption claimed in the property only in Schedule C - Property Claimed as Exempt.

DESCRIPTION AND LOCATION OF PROPERTY	NATURE OF DEBTOR'S INTEREST IN PROPERTY	HUSBAND, WIFE, JOINT OR COMMUNITY	CURRENT VALUE OF DEBTOR'S INTEREST IN PROPERTY, WITHOUT DEDUCTING ANY SECURED CLAIM OR EXEMPTION	AMOUNT OF SECURED CLAIM

Total► | |
(Report also on Summary of Schedules.)

In re _____ ,   Case No. _____
                      Debtor   **(If known)**

SCHEDULE B - PERSONAL PROPERTY

Except as directed below, list all personal property of the debtor of whatever kind. If the debtor has no property in one or more of the categories, place an "x" in the appropriate position in the column labeled "None." If additional space is needed in any category, attach a separate sheet properly identified with the case name, case number, and the number of the category. If the debtor is married, state whether the husband, wife, both, or the marital community own the property by placing an "H," "W," "J," or "C" in the column labeled "Husband, Wife, Joint, or Community." If the debtor is an individual or a joint petition is filed, state the amount of any exemptions claimed only in Schedule C - Property Claimed as Exempt.

Do not list interests in executory contracts and unexpired leases on this schedule. List them in Schedule G - Executory Contracts and Unexpired Leases.

If the property is being held for the debtor by someone else, state that person's name and address under "Description and Location of Property."
If the property is being held for a minor child, simply state the child's initials and the name and address of the child's parent or guardian, such as "A.B., a minor child, by John Doe, guardian." Do not disclose the child's name. See, 11 U.S.C. §112 and Fed. R. Bankr. P. 1007(m).

TYPE OF PROPERTY	N O N E	DESCRIPTION AND LOCATION OF PROPERTY	HUSBAND, WIFE, JOINT, OR COMMUNITY	CURRENT VALUE OF DEBTOR'S INTEREST IN PROPERTY, WITH-OUT DEDUCTING ANY SECURED CLAIM OR EXEMPTION
1. Cash on hand.				
2. Checking, savings or other financial accounts, certificates of deposit or shares in banks, savings and loan, thrift, building and loan, and homestead associations, or credit unions, brokerage houses, or cooperatives.				
3. Security deposits with public utilities, telephone companies, landlords, and others.				
4. Household goods and furnishings, including audio, video, and computer equipment.				
5. Books; pictures and other art objects; antiques; stamp, coin, record, tape, compact disc, and other collections or collectibles.				
6. Wearing apparel.				
7. Furs and jewelry.				
8. Firearms and sports, photographic, and other hobby equipment.				
9. Interests in insurance policies. Name insurance company of each policy and itemize surrender or refund value of each.				
10. Annuities. Itemize and name each issuer.				
11. Interests in an education IRA as defined in 26 U.S.C. § 530(b)(1) or under a qualified State tuition plan as defined in 26 U.S.C. § 529(b)(1). Give particulars. (File separately the record(s) of any such interest(s). 11 U.S.C. § 521(c).)				

In re _____,   Case No. _____
               Debtor   **(If known)**

SCHEDULE B - PERSONAL PROPERTY
(Continuation Sheet)

TYPE OF PROPERTY	N O N E	DESCRIPTION AND LOCATION OF PROPERTY	HUSBAND, WIFE, JOINT, OR COMMUNITY	CURRENT VALUE OF DEBTOR'S INTEREST IN PROPERTY, WITH-OUT DEDUCTING ANY SECURED CLAIM OR EXEMPTION
12. Interests in IRA, ERISA, Keogh, or other pension or profit sharing plans. Give particulars.				
13. Stock and interests in incorporated and unincorporated businesses. Itemize.				
14. Interests in partnerships or joint ventures. Itemize.				
15. Government and corporate bonds and other negotiable and non-negotiable instruments.				
16. Accounts receivable.				
17. Alimony, maintenance, support, and property settlements to which the debtor is or may be entitled. Give particulars.				
18. Other liquidated debts owed to debtor including tax refunds. Give particulars.				
19. Equitable or future interests, life estates, and rights or powers exercisable for the benefit of the debtor other than those listed in Schedule A – Real Property.				
20. Contingent and noncontingent interests in estate of a decedent, death benefit plan, life insurance policy, or trust.				
21. Other contingent and unliquidated claims of every nature, including tax refunds, counterclaims of the debtor, and rights to setoff claims. Give estimated value of each.				

B 6B (Official Form 6B) (12/07) -- Cont.

In re _____ , Case No. _____
         Debtor   **(If known)**

SCHEDULE B - PERSONAL PROPERTY
(Continuation Sheet)

TYPE OF PROPERTY	NONE	DESCRIPTION AND LOCATION OF PROPERTY	HUSBAND, WIFE, JOINT, OR COMMUNITY	CURRENT VALUE OF DEBTOR'S INTEREST IN PROPERTY, WITHOUT DEDUCTING ANY SECURED CLAIM OR EXEMPTION
22. Patents, copyrights, and other intellectual property. Give particulars.				
23. Licenses, franchises, and other general intangibles. Give particulars.				
24. Customer lists or other compilations containing personally identifiable information (as defined in 11 U.S.C. § 101(41A)) provided to the debtor by individuals in connection with obtaining a product or service from the debtor primarily for personal, family, or household purposes.				
25. Automobiles, trucks, trailers, and other vehicles and accessories.				
26. Boats, motors, and accessories.				
27. Aircraft and accessories.				
28. Office equipment, furnishings, and supplies.				
29. Machinery, fixtures, equipment, and supplies used in business.				
30. Inventory.				
31. Animals.				
32. Crops - growing or harvested. Give particulars.				
33. Farming equipment and implements.				
34. Farm supplies, chemicals, and feed.				
35. Other personal property of any kind not already listed. Itemize.				

_____continuation sheets attached   Total▶ $ _____

(Include amounts from any continuation sheets attached. Report total also on Summary of Schedules.)

In re _____,   Case No. _____
                    Debtor   **(If known)**

SCHEDULE C - PROPERTY CLAIMED AS EXEMPT

Debtor claims the exemptions to which debtor is entitled under: ☐   Check if debtor claims a homestead exemption that exceeds
(Check one box) $136,875.
☐   11 U.S.C. § 522(b)(2)
☐   11 U.S.C. § 522(b)(3)

DESCRIPTION OF PROPERTY	SPECIFY LAW PROVIDING EACH EXEMPTION	VALUE OF CLAIMED EXEMPTION	CURRENT VALUE OF PROPERTY WITHOUT DEDUCTING EXEMPTION

In re _____,   Case No. _____
              Debtor   **(If known)**

SCHEDULE D - CREDITORS HOLDING SECURED CLAIMS

State the name, mailing address, including zip code, and last four digits of any account number of all entities holding claims secured by property of the debtor as of the date of filing of the petition. The complete account number of any account the debtor has with the creditor is useful to the trustee and the creditor and may be provided if the debtor chooses to do so. List creditors holding all types of secured interests such as judgment liens, garnishments, statutory liens, mortgages, deeds of trust, and other security interests.

List creditors in alphabetical order to the extent practicable. If a minor child is the creditor, state the child's initials and the name and address of the child's parent or guardian, such as "A.B., a minor child, by John Doe, guardian." Do not disclose the child's name. See, 11 U.S.C. §112 and Fed. R. Bankr. P. 1007(m). If all secured creditors will not fit on this page, use the continuation sheet provided.

If any entity other than a spouse in a joint case may be jointly liable on a claim, place an "X" in the column labeled "Codebtor," include the entity on the appropriate schedule of creditors, and complete Schedule H – Codebtors. If a joint petition is filed, state whether the husband, wife, both of them, or the marital community may be liable on each claim by placing an "H," "W," "J," or "C" in the column labeled "Husband, Wife, Joint, or Community."

If the claim is contingent, place an "X" in the column labeled "Contingent." If the claim is unliquidated, place an "X" in the column labeled "Unliquidated." If the claim is disputed, place an "X" in the column labeled "Disputed." (You may need to place an "X" in more than one of these three columns.)

Total the columns labeled "Amount of Claim Without Deducting Value of Collateral" and "Unsecured Portion, if Any" in the boxes labeled "Total(s)" on the last sheet of the completed schedule. Report the total from the column labeled "Amount of Claim Without Deducting Value of Collateral" also on the Summary of Schedules and, if the debtor is an individual with primarily consumer debts, report the total from the column labeled "Unsecured Portion, if Any" on the Statistical Summary of Certain Liabilities and Related Data.

☐   Check this box if debtor has no creditors holding secured claims to report on this Schedule D.

CREDITOR'S NAME AND MAILING ADDRESS INCLUDING ZIP CODE AND AN ACCOUNT NUMBER (*See Instructions Above.*)	CODEBTOR	HUSBAND, WIFE, JOINT, OR COMMUNITY	DATE CLAIM WAS INCURRED, NATURE OF LIEN , AND DESCRIPTION AND VALUE OF PROPERTY SUBJECT TO LIEN	CONTINGENT	UNLIQUIDATED	DISPUTED	AMOUNT OF CLAIM WITHOUT DEDUCTING VALUE OF COLLATERAL	UNSECURED PORTION, IF ANY
ACCOUNT NO.								
			VALUE $					
ACCOUNT NO.								
			VALUE $					
ACCOUNT NO.								
			VALUE $					
_____ continuation sheets attached			Subtotal ▶ (Total of this page)				$	$
			Total ▶ (Use only on last page)				$	$
							(Report also on Summary of Schedules.)	(If applicable, report also on Statistical Summary of Certain Liabilities and Related Data.)

In re _____,　　Case No. _____
　　　　　　　Debtor　　　　　　　　　　　　　　　　　　　**(if known)**

SCHEDULE D - CREDITORS HOLDING SECURED CLAIMS
(Continuation Sheet)

CREDITOR'S NAME AND MAILING ADDRESS INCLUDING ZIP CODE AND AN ACCOUNT NUMBER (*See Instructions Above.*)	CODEBTOR	HUSBAND, WIFE, JOINT, OR COMMUNITY	DATE CLAIM WAS INCURRED, NATURE OF LIEN , AND DESCRIPTION AND VALUE OF PROPERTY SUBJECT TO LIEN	CONTINGENT	UNLIQUIDATED	DISPUTED	AMOUNT OF CLAIM WITHOUT DEDUCTING VALUE OF COLLATERAL	UNSECURED PORTION, IF ANY
ACCOUNT NO.								
			VALUE $					
ACCOUNT NO.								
			VALUE $					
ACCOUNT NO.								
			VALUE $					
ACCOUNT NO.								
			VALUE $					
ACCOUNT NO.								
			VALUE $					

Sheet no._____of_____continuation sheets attached to Schedule of Creditors Holding Secured Claims

Subtotal (s)▶ (Total(s) of this page)　$　　$

Total(s) ▶ (Use only on last page)　$　　$

(Report also on Summary of Schedules.)　(If applicable, report also on Statistical Summary of Certain Liabilities and Related Data.)

In re _____,   Case No._____
                 Debtor   **(if known)**

SCHEDULE E - CREDITORS HOLDING UNSECURED PRIORITY CLAIMS

A complete list of claims entitled to priority, listed separately by type of priority, is to be set forth on the sheets provided. Only holders of unsecured claims entitled to priority should be listed in this schedule. In the boxes provided on the attached sheets, state the name, mailing address, including zip code, and last four digits of the account number, if any, of all entities holding priority claims against the debtor or the property of the debtor, as of the date of the filing of the petition. Use a separate continuation sheet for each type of priority and label each with the type of priority.

The complete account number of any account the debtor has with the creditor is useful to the trustee and the creditor and may be provided if the debtor chooses to do so. If a minor child is a creditor, state the child's initials and the name and address of the child's parent or guardian, such as "A.B., a minor child, by John Doe, guardian." Do not disclose the child's name. See, 11 U.S.C. §112 and Fed. R. Bankr. P. 1007(m).

If any entity other than a spouse in a joint case may be jointly liable on a claim, place an "X" in the column labeled "Codebtor," include the entity on the appropriate schedule of creditors, and complete Schedule H-Codebtors. If a joint petition is filed, state whether the husband, wife, both of them, or the marital community may be liable on each claim by placing an "H," "W," "J," or "C" in the column labeled "Husband, Wife, Joint, or Community."   If the claim is contingent, place an "X" in the column labeled "Contingent." If the claim is unliquidated, place an "X" in the column labeled "Unliquidated." If the claim is disputed, place an "X" in the column labeled "Disputed." (You may need to place an "X" in more than one of these three columns.)

Report the total of claims listed on each sheet in the box labeled "Subtotals" on each sheet. Report the total of all claims listed on this Schedule E in the box labeled "Total" on the last sheet of the completed schedule. Report this total also on the Summary of Schedules.

Report the total of amounts entitled to priority listed on each sheet in the box labeled "Subtotals" on each sheet. Report the total of all amounts entitled to priority listed on this Schedule E in the box labeled "Totals" on the last sheet of the completed schedule. Individual debtors with primarily consumer debts report this total also on the Statistical Summary of Certain Liabilities and Related Data.

Report the total of amounts <u>not</u> entitled to priority listed on each sheet in the box labeled "Subtotals" on each sheet. Report the total of all amounts not entitled to priority listed on this Schedule E in the box labeled "Totals" on the last sheet of the completed schedule. Individual debtors with primarily consumer debts report this total also on the Statistical Summary of Certain Liabilities and Related Data.

☐ Check this box if debtor has no creditors holding unsecured priority claims to report on this Schedule E.

TYPES OF PRIORITY CLAIMS (Check the appropriate box(es) below if claims in that category are listed on the attached sheets.)

☐ **Domestic Support Obligations**

Claims for domestic support that are owed to or recoverable by a spouse, former spouse, or child of the debtor, or the parent, legal guardian, or responsible relative of such a child, or a governmental unit to whom such a domestic support claim has been assigned to the extent provided in 11 U.S.C. § 507(a)(1).

☐ **Extensions of credit in an involuntary case**

Claims arising in the ordinary course of the debtor's business or financial affairs after the commencement of the case but before the earlier of the appointment of a trustee or the order for relief. 11 U.S.C. § 507(a)(3).

☐ **Wages, salaries, and commissions**

Wages, salaries, and commissions, including vacation, severance, and sick leave pay owing to employees and commissions owing to qualifying independent sales representatives up to $10,950* per person earned within 180 days immediately preceding the filing of the original petition, or the cessation of business, whichever occurred first, to the extent provided in 11 U.S.C. § 507(a)(4).

☐ **Contributions to employee benefit plans**

Money owed to employee benefit plans for services rendered within 180 days immediately preceding the filing of the original petition, or the cessation of business, whichever occurred first, to the extent provided in 11 U.S.C. § 507(a)(5).

In re _____ ,   Case No._____
                          Debtor   **(if known)**

☐ **Certain farmers and fishermen**

Claims of certain farmers and fishermen, up to $5,400* per farmer or fisherman, against the debtor, as provided in 11 U.S.C. § 507(a)(6).

☐ **Deposits by individuals**

Claims of individuals up to $2,425* for deposits for the purchase, lease, or rental of property or services for personal, family, or household use, that were not delivered or provided. 11 U.S.C. § 507(a)(7).

☐ **Taxes and Certain Other Debts Owed to Governmental Units**

Taxes, customs duties, and penalties owing to federal, state, and local governmental units as set forth in 11 U.S.C. § 507(a)(8).

☐ **Commitments to Maintain the Capital of an Insured Depository Institution**

Claims based on commitments to the FDIC, RTC, Director of the Office of Thrift Supervision, Comptroller of the Currency, or Board of Governors of the Federal Reserve System, or their predecessors or successors, to maintain the capital of an insured depository institution. 11 U.S.C. § 507 (a)(9).

☐ **Claims for Death or Personal Injury While Debtor Was Intoxicated**

Claims for death or personal injury resulting from the operation of a motor vehicle or vessel while the debtor was intoxicated from using alcohol, a drug, or another substance. 11 U.S.C. § 507(a)(10).

* Amounts are subject to adjustment on April 1, 2010, and every three years thereafter with respect to cases commenced on or after the date of adjustment.

____ continuation sheets attached

B 6E (Official Form 6E) (12/07) – Cont.

In re _____,   Case No. _____
                    Debtor   **(if known)**

SCHEDULE E - CREDITORS HOLDING UNSECURED PRIORITY CLAIMS
(Continuation Sheet)

Type of Priority for Claims Listed on This Sheet

CREDITOR'S NAME, MAILING ADDRESS INCLUDING ZIP CODE, AND ACCOUNT NUMBER (*See instructions above.*)	CODEBTOR	HUSBAND, WIFE, JOINT, OR COMMUNITY	DATE CLAIM WAS INCURRED AND CONSIDERATION FOR CLAIM	CONTINGENT	UNLIQUIDATED	DISPUTED	AMOUNT OF CLAIM	AMOUNT ENTITLED TO PRIORITY	AMOUNT NOT ENTITLED TO PRIORITY, IF ANY
Account No.									
Account No.									
Account No.									
Account No.									

Sheet no. _____ of _____ continuation sheets attached to Schedule of Creditors Holding Priority Claims

Subtotals➤ (Totals of this page) $ _____ | $ _____

Total➤ (Use only on last page of the completed Schedule E. Report also on the Summary of Schedules.) $ _____

Totals➤ (Use only on last page of the completed Schedule E. If applicable, report also on the Statistical Summary of Certain Liabilities and Related Data.) $ _____ | $ _____

In re _____, Case No. _____
                     Debtor   **(if known)**

SCHEDULE F - CREDITORS HOLDING UNSECURED NONPRIORITY CLAIMS

State the name, mailing address, including zip code, and last four digits of any account number, of all entities holding unsecured claims without priority against the debtor or the property of the debtor, as of the date of filing of the petition. The complete account number of any account the debtor has with the creditor is useful to the trustee and the creditor and may be provided if the debtor chooses to do so. If a minor child is a creditor, state the child's initials and the name and address of the child's parent or guardian, such as "A.B., a minor child, by John Doe, guardian." Do not disclose the child's name. See, 11 U.S.C. §112 and Fed. R. Bankr. P. 1007(m). Do not include claims listed in Schedules D and E. If all creditors will not fit on this page, use the continuation sheet provided.

If any entity other than a spouse in a joint case may be jointly liable on a claim, place an "X" in the column labeled "Codebtor," include the entity on the appropriate schedule of creditors, and complete Schedule H - Codebtors. If a joint petition is filed, state whether the husband, wife, both of them, or the marital community may be liable on each claim by placing an "H," "W," "J," or "C" in the column labeled "Husband, Wife, Joint, or Community."

If the claim is contingent, place an "X" in the column labeled "Contingent." If the claim is unliquidated, place an "X" in the column labeled "Unliquidated." If the claim is disputed, place an "X" in the column labeled "Disputed." (You may need to place an "X" in more than one of these three columns.)

Report the total of all claims listed on this schedule in the box labeled "Total" on the last sheet of the completed schedule. Report this total also on the Summary of Schedules and, if the debtor is an individual with primarily consumer debts, report this total also on the Statistical Summary of Certain Liabilities and Related Data..

☐ Check this box if debtor has no creditors holding unsecured claims to report on this Schedule F.

CREDITOR'S NAME, MAILING ADDRESS INCLUDING ZIP CODE, AND ACCOUNT NUMBER (See instructions above.)	CODEBTOR	HUSBAND, WIFE, JOINT, OR COMMUNITY	DATE CLAIM WAS INCURRED AND CONSIDERATION FOR CLAIM. IF CLAIM IS SUBJECT TO SETOFF, SO STATE.	CONTINGENT	UNLIQUIDATED	DISPUTED	AMOUNT OF CLAIM
ACCOUNT NO.							
ACCOUNT NO.							
ACCOUNT NO.							
ACCOUNT NO.							

Subtotal▶ $ _____

___continuation sheets attached   Total▶ $ _____
(Use only on last page of the completed Schedule F.)
(Report also on Summary of Schedules and, if applicable, on the Statistical Summary of Certain Liabilities and Related Data.)

In re _____ ,   Case No. _____
          Debtor   **(if known)**

SCHEDULE F - CREDITORS HOLDING UNSECURED NONPRIORITY CLAIMS
(Continuation Sheet)

CREDITOR'S NAME, MAILING ADDRESS INCLUDING ZIP CODE, AND ACCOUNT NUMBER (See instructions above.)	CODEBTOR	HUSBAND, WIFE, JOINT, OR COMMUNITY	DATE CLAIM WAS INCURRED AND CONSIDERATION FOR CLAIM. IF CLAIM IS SUBJECT TO SETOFF, SO STATE.	CONTINGENT	UNLIQUIDATED	DISPUTED	AMOUNT OF CLAIM
ACCOUNT NO.							
ACCOUNT NO.							
ACCOUNT NO.							
ACCOUNT NO.							
ACCOUNT NO.							

Sheet no._____ of_____ continuation sheets attached   Subtotal➤ $
to Schedule of Creditors Holding Unsecured
Nonpriority Claims

Total➤ $
(Use only on last page of the completed Schedule F.)
(Report also on Summary of Schedules and, if applicable on the Statistical
Summary of Certain Liabilities and Related Data.)

In re _____ ,   Case No._____
         Debtor   **(if known)**

SCHEDULE G - EXECUTORY CONTRACTS AND UNEXPIRED LEASES

　　　Describe all executory contracts of any nature and all unexpired leases of real or personal property. Include any timeshare interests. State nature of debtor's interest in contract, i.e., "Purchaser," "Agent," etc. State whether debtor is the lessor or lessee of a lease. Provide the names and complete mailing addresses of all other parties to each lease or contract described. If a minor child is a party to one of the leases or contracts, state the child's initials and the name and address of the child's parent or guardian, such as "A.B., a minor child, by John Doe, guardian." Do not disclose the child's name. See, 11 U.S.C. §112 and Fed. R. Bankr. P. 1007(m).

☐ Check this box if debtor has no executory contracts or unexpired leases.

NAME AND MAILING ADDRESS, INCLUDING ZIP CODE, OF OTHER PARTIES TO LEASE OR CONTRACT.	DESCRIPTION OF CONTRACT OR LEASE AND NATURE OF DEBTOR'S INTEREST. STATE WHETHER LEASE IS FOR NONRESIDENTIAL REAL PROPERTY. STATE CONTRACT NUMBER OF ANY GOVERNMENT CONTRACT.

In re _____ ,　　　　　Case No. _____
　　　　　　　　　Debtor　　　　　　　　　　　　　　　　　　　　　　　**(if known)**

SCHEDULE H - CODEBTORS

　　　　Provide the information requested concerning any person or entity, other than a spouse in a joint case, that is also liable on any debts listed by the debtor in the schedules of creditors. Include all guarantors and co-signers. If the debtor resides or resided in a community property state, commonwealth, or territory (including Alaska, Arizona, California, Idaho, Louisiana, Nevada, New Mexico, Puerto Rico, Texas, Washington, or Wisconsin) within the eight-year period immediately preceding the commencement of the case, identify the name of the debtor's spouse and of any former spouse who resides or resided with the debtor in the community property state, commonwealth, or territory. Include all names used by the nondebtor spouse during the eight years immediately preceding the commencement of this case. If a minor child is a codebtor or a creditor, state the child's initials and the name and address of the child's parent or guardian, such as "A.B., a minor child, by John Doe, guardian." Do not disclose the child's name. See, 11 U.S.C. §112 and Fed. R. Bankr. P. 1007(m).

☐　Check this box if debtor has no codebtors.

NAME AND ADDRESS OF CODEBTOR	NAME AND ADDRESS OF CREDITOR

In re _____ ,   Case No. _____
       Debtor   **(if known)**

SCHEDULE I - CURRENT INCOME OF INDIVIDUAL DEBTOR(S)

The column labeled "Spouse" must be completed in all cases filed by joint debtors and by every married debtor, whether or not a joint petition is filed, unless the spouses are separated and a joint petition is not filed. Do not state the name of any minor child. The average monthly income calculated on this form may differ from the current monthly income calculated on Form 22A, 22B, or 22C.

Debtor's Marital Status:	DEPENDENTS OF DEBTOR AND SPOUSE	
	RELATIONSHIP(S):	AGE(S):

Employment:	DEBTOR	SPOUSE
Occupation		
Name of Employer		
How long employed		
Address of Employer		

INCOME: (Estimate of average or projected monthly income at time case filed)

	DEBTOR	SPOUSE
	$_____	$_____
1. Monthly gross wages, salary, and commissions (Prorate if not paid monthly)	$_____	$_____
2. Estimate monthly overtime		
3. SUBTOTAL	$_____	$_____
4. LESS PAYROLL DEDUCTIONS		
a. Payroll taxes and social security	$_____	$_____
b. Insurance	$_____	$_____
c. Union dues	$_____	$_____
d. Other (Specify): _____	$_____	$_____
5. SUBTOTAL OF PAYROLL DEDUCTIONS	$_____	$_____
6. TOTAL NET MONTHLY TAKE HOME PAY	$_____	$_____
7. Regular income from operation of business or profession or farm (Attach detailed statement)	$_____	$_____
8. Income from real property	$_____	$_____
9. Interest and dividends	$_____	$_____
10. Alimony, maintenance or support payments payable to the debtor for the debtor's use or that of dependents listed above	$_____	$_____
11. Social security or government assistance (Specify):_____	$_____	$_____
12. Pension or retirement income	$_____	$_____
13. Other monthly income (Specify):_____	$_____	$_____
14. SUBTOTAL OF LINES 7 THROUGH 13	$_____	$_____
15. AVERAGE MONTHLY INCOME (Add amounts on lines 6 and 14)	$_____	$_____
16. COMBINED AVERAGE MONTHLY INCOME: (Combine column totals from line 15)	$_____	

(Report also on Summary of Schedules and, if applicable, on Statistical Summary of Certain Liabilities and Related Data)

17. Describe any increase or decrease in income reasonably anticipated to occur within the year following the filing of this document:

_____

In re _____ ,   **Case No.** _____
　　　　　　　Debtor　　　　　　　　　　　　　　　　　　　　　　　**(if known)**

SCHEDULE J - CURRENT EXPENDITURES OF INDIVIDUAL DEBTOR(S)

　　　Complete this schedule by estimating the average or projected monthly expenses of the debtor and the debtor's family at time case filed. Prorate any payments made bi-weekly, quarterly, semi-annually, or annually to show monthly rate. The average monthly expenses calculated on this form may differ from the deductions from income allowed on Form 22A or 22C.

☐　　Check this box if a joint petition is filed and debtor's spouse maintains a separate household. Complete a separate schedule of expenditures labeled "Spouse."

1. Rent or home mortgage payment (include lot rented for mobile home)　　　　　　　　　　　$ _____
　　a. Are real estate taxes included?　　　Yes _____　　No _____
　　b. Is property insurance included?　　　Yes _____　　No _____

2. Utilities:　a. Electricity and heating fuel　　　　　　　　　　　　　　　　　　　　$ _____
　　　　　　b. Water and sewer　　　　　　　　　　　　　　　　　　　　　　　　$ _____
　　　　　　c. Telephone　　　　　　　　　　　　　　　　　　　　　　　　　　$ _____
　　　　　　d. Other _____　$ _____

3. Home maintenance (repairs and upkeep)　　　　　　　　　　　　　　　　　　　　$ _____
4. Food　　　　　　　　　　　　　　　　　　　　　　　　　　　　　　　　　$ _____
5. Clothing　　　　　　　　　　　　　　　　　　　　　　　　　　　　　　　$ _____
6. Laundry and dry cleaning　　　　　　　　　　　　　　　　　　　　　　　　$ _____
7. Medical and dental expenses　　　　　　　　　　　　　　　　　　　　　　　$ _____
8. Transportation (not including car payments)　　　　　　　　　　　　　　　　　$ _____
9. Recreation, clubs and entertainment, newspapers, magazines, etc.　　　　　　　　　$ _____
10. Charitable contributions　　　　　　　　　　　　　　　　　　　　　　　　$ _____
11. Insurance (not deducted from wages or included in home mortgage payments)
　　　a. Homeowner's or renter's　　　　　　　　　　　　　　　　　　　　　$ _____
　　　b. Life　　　　　　　　　　　　　　　　　　　　　　　　　　　　　$ _____
　　　c. Health　　　　　　　　　　　　　　　　　　　　　　　　　　　　$ _____
　　　d. Auto　　　　　　　　　　　　　　　　　　　　　　　　　　　　　$ _____
　　　e. Other _____　$ _____

12. Taxes (not deducted from wages or included in home mortgage payments)
(Specify) _____　　　　$ _____

13. Installment payments: (In chapter 11, 12, and 13 cases, do not list payments to be included in the plan)
　　　a. Auto　　　　　　　　　　　　　　　　　　　　　　　　　　　　　$ _____
　　　b. Other _____　　　　　　　$ _____
　　　c. Other _____　　　　　　　$ _____

14. Alimony, maintenance, and support paid to others　　　　　　　　　　　　　　$ _____
15. Payments for support of additional dependents not living at your home　　　　　　$ _____
16. Regular expenses from operation of business, profession, or farm (attach detailed statement)　$ _____
17. Other _____　　　　$ _____

18. AVERAGE MONTHLY EXPENSES (Total lines 1-17. Report also on Summary of Schedules and,
　　if applicable, on the Statistical Summary of Certain Liabilities and Related Data.)　$ _____

19. Describe any increase or decrease in expenditures reasonably anticipated to occur within the year following the filing of this document:

20. STATEMENT OF MONTHLY NET INCOME
　　a. Average monthly income from Line 15 of Schedule I　　　　　　　　　　　$ _____
　　b. Average monthly expenses from Line 18 above　　　　　　　　　　　　　$ _____
　　c. Monthly net income (a. minus b.)　　　　　　　　　　　　　　　　　　$ _____

B6 Declaration (Official Form 6 - Declaration) (12/07)

In re _____ ,   **Case No.** _____
          Debtor   **(if known)**

DECLARATION CONCERNING DEBTOR'S SCHEDULES

DECLARATION UNDER PENALTY OF PERJURY BY INDIVIDUAL DEBTOR

I declare under penalty of perjury that I have read the foregoing summary and schedules, consisting of _____ sheets, and that they are true and correct to the best of my knowledge, information, and belief.

Date _____   Signature: _____
                                                                Debtor

Date _____   Signature: _____
                                                          (Joint Debtor, if any)

[If joint case, both spouses must sign.]

DECLARATION AND SIGNATURE OF NON-ATTORNEY BANKRUPTCY PETITION PREPARER (See 11 U.S.C. § 110)

I declare under penalty of perjury that: (1) I am a bankruptcy petition preparer as defined in 11 U.S.C. § 110; (2) I prepared this document for compensation and have provided the debtor with a copy of this document and the notices and information required under 11 U.S.C. §§ 110(b), 110(h) and 342(b); and, (3) if rules or guidelines have been promulgated pursuant to 11 U.S.C. § 110(h) setting a maximum fee for services chargeable by bankruptcy petition preparers, I have given the debtor notice of the maximum amount before preparing any document for filing for a debtor or accepting any fee from the debtor, as required by that section.

_____   _____
Printed or Typed Name and Title, if any,   Social Security No.
of Bankruptcy Petition Preparer   *(Required by 11 U.S.C. § 110.)*

If the bankruptcy petition preparer is not an individual, state the name, title (if any), address, and social security number of the officer, principal, responsible person, or partner who signs this document.

_____
_____
_____
Address

X _____   _____
Signature of Bankruptcy Petition Preparer   Date

Names and Social Security numbers of all other individuals who prepared or assisted in preparing this document, unless the bankruptcy petition preparer is not an individual:

If more than one person prepared this document, attach additional signed sheets conforming to the appropriate Official Form for each person.

A bankruptcy petition preparer's failure to comply with the provisions of title 11 and the Federal Rules of Bankruptcy Procedure may result in fines or imprisonment or both. 11 U.S.C. § 110; 18 U.S.C. § 156.

DECLARATION UNDER PENALTY OF PERJURY ON BEHALF OF A CORPORATION OR PARTNERSHIP

I, the _____ [the president or other officer or an authorized agent of the corporation or a member or an authorized agent of the partnership] of the _____ [corporation or partnership] named as debtor in this case, declare under penalty of perjury that I have read the foregoing summary and schedules, consisting of _____ sheets (*Total shown on summary page plus 1*), and that they are true and correct to the best of my knowledge, information, and belief.

Date _____

                    Signature: _____

                                   _____
                                   [Print or type name of individual signing on behalf of debtor.]

[An individual signing on behalf of a partnership or corporation must indicate position or relationship to debtor.]

Penalty for making a false statement or concealing property: Fine of up to $500,000 or imprisonment for up to 5 years or both. 18 U.S.C. §§ 152 and 3571.

United States Bankruptcy Court

In re _____,　　　　Case No. _____
　　　　　　　Debtor

　　　　　　　　　　　　　　　　　　　　　　　Chapter _____

SUMMARY OF SCHEDULES

Indicate as to each schedule whether that schedule is attached and state the number of pages in each. Report the totals from Schedules A, B, D, E, F, I, and J in the boxes provided. Add the amounts from Schedules A and B to determine the total amount of the debtor's assets. Add the amounts of all claims from Schedules D, E, and F to determine the total amount of the debtor's liabilities. Individual debtors also must complete the "Statistical Summary of Certain Liabilities and Related Data" if they file a case under chapter 7, 11, or 13.

NAME OF SCHEDULE	ATTACHED (YES/NO)	NO. OF SHEETS	ASSETS	LIABILITIES	OTHER
A - Real Property			$		
B - Personal Property			$		
C - Property Claimed as Exempt					
D - Creditors Holding Secured Claims				$	
E - Creditors Holding Unsecured Priority Claims (Total of Claims on Schedule E)				$	
F - Creditors Holding Unsecured Nonpriority Claims				$	
G - Executory Contracts and Unexpired Leases					
H - Codebtors					
I - Current Income of Individual Debtor(s)					$
J - Current Expenditures of Individual Debtors(s)					$
TOTAL			$	$	

United States Bankruptcy Court

In re _____,
        Debtor

Case No. _____

Chapter _____

STATISTICAL SUMMARY OF CERTAIN LIABILITIES AND RELATED DATA (28 U.S.C. § 159)

If you are an individual debtor whose debts are primarily consumer debts, as defined in § 101(8) of the Bankruptcy Code (11 U.S.C. § 101(8)), filing a case under chapter 7, 11 or 13, you must report all information requested below.

□ Check this box if you are an individual debtor whose debts are NOT primarily consumer debts. You are not required to report any information here.

This information is for statistical purposes only under 28 U.S.C. § 159.

Summarize the following types of liabilities, as reported in the Schedules, and total them.

Type of Liability	Amount
Domestic Support Obligations (from Schedule E)	$
Taxes and Certain Other Debts Owed to Governmental Units (from Schedule E)	$
Claims for Death or Personal Injury While Debtor Was Intoxicated (from Schedule E) (whether disputed or undisputed)	$
Student Loan Obligations (from Schedule F)	$
Domestic Support, Separation Agreement, and Divorce Decree Obligations Not Reported on Schedule E	$
Obligations to Pension or Profit-Sharing, and Other Similar Obligations (from Schedule F)	$
TOTAL	$

State the following:

Average Income (from Schedule I, Line 16)	$
Average Expenses (from Schedule J, Line 18)	$
Current Monthly Income (from Form 22A Line 12; **OR**, Form 22B Line 11; **OR**, Form 22C Line 20)	$

State the following:

1. Total from Schedule D, "UNSECURED PORTION, IF ANY" column		$
2. Total from Schedule E, "AMOUNT ENTITLED TO PRIORITY" column.	$	
3. Total from Schedule E, "AMOUNT NOT ENTITLED TO PRIORITY, IF ANY" column		$
4. Total from Schedule F		$
5. Total of non-priority unsecured debt (sum of 1, 3, and 4)		$

UNITED STATES BANKRUPTCY COURT

In re _____,   Case No. _____
                    Debtor

                                                 Chapter _____

APPLICATION TO PAY FILING FEE IN INSTALLMENTS

1.   In accordance with Fed. R. Bankr. P. 1006, I apply for permission to pay the filing fee amounting to $_____ in installments.

2.   I am unable to pay the filing fee except in installments.

3.   Until the filing fee is paid in full, I will not make any additional payment or transfer any additional property to an attorney or any other person for services in connection with this case.

4.   I propose the following terms for the payment of the Filing Fee.*

      $ _____   Check one ☐   With the filing of the petition, or
                                        ☐   On or before _____

      $ _____   on or before _____

      $ _____   on or before _____

      $ _____   on or before _____

*   The number of installments proposed shall not exceed four (4), and the final installment shall be payable not later than 120 days after filing the petition. For cause shown, the court may extend the time of any installment, provided the last installment is paid not later than 180 days after filing the petition. Fed. R. Bankr. P. 1006(b)(2).

5.   I understand that if I fail to pay any installment when due, my bankruptcy case may be dismissed and I may not receive a discharge of my debts.

_____   _____
Signature of Attorney   Date   Signature of Debtor   Date
                                              (In a joint case, both spouses must sign.)

_____
Name of Attorney   _____
                                              Signature of Joint Debtor (if any)   Date

----

DECLARATION AND SIGNATURE OF NON-ATTORNEY BANKRUPTCY PETITION PREPARER (See 11 U.S.C. § 110)

   I declare under penalty of perjury that: (1) I am a bankruptcy petition preparer as defined in 11 U.S.C. § 110; (2) I prepared this document for compensation and have provided the debtor with a copy of this document and the notices and information required under 11 U.S.C. §§ 110(b), 110(h), and 342(b); (3) if rules or guidelines have been promulgated pursuant to 11 U.S.C. § 110(h) setting a maximum fee for services chargeable by bankruptcy petition preparers, I have given the debtor notice of the maximum amount before preparing any document for filing for a debtor or accepting any fee from the debtor, as required under that section; and (4) I will not accept any additional money or other property from the debtor before the filing fee is paid in full.

_____   _____
Printed or Typed Name and Title, if any, of Bankruptcy Petition Preparer   Social-Security No. (Required by 11 U.S.C. § 110.)
If the bankruptcy petition preparer is not an individual, state the name, title (if any), address, and social-security number of the officer, principal, responsible person, or partner who signs the document.

_____

_____
Address

x_____   _____
Signature of Bankruptcy Petition Preparer   Date

Names and Social-Security numbers of all other individuals who prepared or assisted in preparing this document, unless the bankruptcy petition preparer is not an individual:

If more than one person prepared this document, attach additional signed sheets conforming to the appropriate Official Form for each person.
A bankruptcy petition preparer's failure to comply with the provisions of title 11 and the Federal Rules of Bankruptcy Procedure may result in fines or imprisonment or both. 11 U.S.C. § 110; 18 U.S.C. § 156.

UNITED STATES BANKRUPTCY COURT

In re _____,
　　　　　　　　　　Debtor

Case No. _____

Chapter _____

ORDER APPROVING PAYMENT OF FILING FEE IN INSTALLMENTS

☐　　　IT IS ORDERED that the debtor(s) may pay the filing fee in installments on the terms proposed in the foregoing application.

☐　　　IT IS ORDERED that the debtor(s) shall pay the filing fee according to the following terms:

$ _____　　　Check one　☐　With the filing of the petition, or
　　　　　　　　　　　　　　　　　　☐　On or before _____

$ _____ on or before _____

$ _____ on or before _____

$ _____ on or before _____

☐　　　IT IS FURTHER ORDERED that until the filing fee is paid in full the debtor(s) shall not make any additional payment or transfer any additional property to an attorney or any other person for services in connection with this case.

BY THE COURT

Date: _____

_____
United States Bankruptcy Judge

UNITED STATES BANKRUPTCY COURT

In re:_____ _____,   Case No. _____

                    Debtor   (if known)

STATEMENT OF FINANCIAL AFFAIRS

This statement is to be completed by every debtor. Spouses filing a joint petition may file a single statement on which the information for both spouses is combined. If the case is filed under chapter 12 or chapter 13, a married debtor must furnish information for both spouses whether or not a joint petition is filed, unless the spouses are separated and a joint petition is not filed. An individual debtor engaged in business as a sole proprietor, partner, family farmer, or self-employed professional, should provide the information requested on this statement concerning all such activities as well as the individual's personal affairs. To indicate payments, transfers and the like to minor children, state the child's initials and the name and address of the child's parent or guardian, such as "A.B., a minor child, by John Doe, guardian." Do not disclose the child's name. See, 11 U.S.C. §112 and Fed. R. Bankr. P. 1007(m).

Questions 1 - 18 are to be completed by all debtors. Debtors that are or have been in business, as defined below, also must complete Questions 19 - 25. **If the answer to an applicable question is "None," mark the box labeled "None."** If additional space is needed for the answer to any question, use and attach a separate sheet properly identified with the case name, case number (if known), and the number of the question.

DEFINITIONS

"In business." A debtor is "in business" for the purpose of this form if the debtor is a corporation or partnership. An individual debtor is "in business" for the purpose of this form if the debtor is or has been, within six years immediately preceding the filing of this bankruptcy case, any of the following: an officer, director, managing executive, or owner of 5 percent or more of the voting or equity securities of a corporation; a partner, other than a limited partner, of a partnership; a sole proprietor or self-employed full-time or part-time. An individual debtor also may be "in business" for the purpose of this form if the debtor engages in a trade, business, or other activity, other than as an employee, to supplement income from the debtor's primary employment.

"Insider." The term "insider" includes but is not limited to: relatives of the debtor; general partners of the debtor and their relatives; corporations of which the debtor is an officer, director, or person in control; officers, directors, and any owner of 5 percent or more of the voting or equity securities of a corporate debtor and their relatives; affiliates of the debtor and insiders of such affiliates; any managing agent of the debtor. 11 U.S.C. § 101.

---

1. **Income from employment or operation of business**

None
☐

State the gross amount of income the debtor has received from employment, trade, or profession, or from operation of the debtor's business, including part-time activities either as an employee or in independent trade or business, from the beginning of this calendar year to the date this case was commenced. State also the gross amounts received during the **two years** immediately preceding this calendar year. (A debtor that maintains, or has maintained, financial records on the basis of a fiscal rather than a calendar year may report fiscal year income. Identify the beginning and ending dates of the debtor's fiscal year.) If a joint petition is filed, state income for each spouse separately. (Married debtors filing under chapter 12 or chapter 13 must state income of both spouses whether or not a joint petition is filed, unless the spouses are separated and a joint petition is not filed.)

AMOUNT   SOURCE

2. Income other than from employment or operation of business

None
☐

State the amount of income received by the debtor other than from employment, trade, profession, operation of the debtor's business during the **two years** immediately preceding the commencement of this case. Give particulars. If a joint petition is filed, state income for each spouse separately. (Married debtors filing under chapter 12 or chapter 13 must state income for each spouse whether or not a joint petition is filed, unless the spouses are separated and a joint petition is not filed.)

AMOUNT   SOURCE

---

3. Payments to creditors

Complete a. or b., as appropriate, and c.

None
☐

a. *Individual or joint debtor(s) with primarily consumer debts:* List all payments on loans, installment purchases of goods or services, and other debts to any creditor made within **90 days** immediately preceding the commencement of this case unless the aggregate value of all property that constitutes or is affected by such transfer is less than $600. Indicate with an asterisk (*) any payments that were made to a creditor on account of a domestic support obligation or as part of an alternative repayment schedule under a plan by an approved nonprofit budgeting and credit counseling agency. (Married debtors filing under chapter 12 or chapter 13 must include payments by either or both spouses whether or not a joint petition is filed, unless the spouses are separated and a joint petition is not filed.)

NAME AND ADDRESS OF CREDITOR   DATES OF PAYMENTS   AMOUNT PAID   AMOUNT STILL OWING

None
☐

b. *Debtor whose debts are not primarily consumer debts: List each payment or other transfer to any creditor made* within **90 days** immediately preceding the commencement of the case unless the aggregate value of all property that constitutes or is affected by such transfer is less than $5,475. If the debtor is an individual, indicate with an asterisk (*) any payments that were made to a creditor on account of a domestic support obligation or as part of an alternative repayment schedule under a plan by an approved nonprofit budgeting and credit counseling agency. (Married debtors filing under chapter 12 or chapter 13 must include payments and other transfers by either or both spouses whether or not a joint petition is filed, unless the spouses are separated and a joint petition is not filed.)

NAME AND ADDRESS OF CREDITOR   DATES OF PAYMENTS/ TRANSFERS   AMOUNT PAID OR VALUE OF TRANSFERS   AMOUNT STILL OWING

None
☐

c. *All debtors:* List all payments made within **one year** immediately preceding the commencement of this case to or for the benefit of creditors who are or were insiders. (Married debtors filing under chapter 12 or chapter 13 must include payments by either or both spouses whether or not a joint petition is filed, unless the spouses are separated and a joint petition is not filed.)

NAME AND ADDRESS OF CREDITOR AND RELATIONSHIP TO DEBTOR	DATE OF PAYMENT	AMOUNT PAID	AMOUNT STILL OWING

4. Suits and administrative proceedings, executions, garnishments and attachments

None
☐

a. List all suits and administrative proceedings to which the debtor is or was a party within **one year** immediately preceding the filing of this bankruptcy case. (Married debtors filing under chapter 12 or chapter 13 must include information concerning either or both spouses whether or not a joint petition is filed, unless the spouses are separated and a joint petition is not filed.)

CAPTION OF SUIT AND CASE NUMBER	NATURE OF PROCEEDING	COURT OR AGENCY AND LOCATION	STATUS OR DISPOSITION

None
☐

b. Describe all property that has been attached, garnished or seized under any legal or equitable process within **one year** immediately preceding the commencement of this case. (Married debtors filing under chapter 12 or chapter 13 must include information concerning property of either or both spouses whether or not a joint petition is filed, unless the spouses are separated and a joint petition is not filed.)

NAME AND ADDRESS OF PERSON FOR WHOSE BENEFIT PROPERTY WAS SEIZED	DATE OF SEIZURE	DESCRIPTION AND VALUE OF PROPERTY

5. Repossessions, foreclosures and returns

None
☐

List all property that has been repossessed by a creditor, sold at a foreclosure sale, transferred through a deed in lieu of foreclosure or returned to the seller, within **one year** immediately preceding the commencement of this case. (Married debtors filing under chapter 12 or chapter 13 must include information concerning property of either or both spouses whether or not a joint petition is filed, unless the spouses are separated and a joint petition is not filed.)

NAME AND ADDRESS OF CREDITOR OR SELLER	DATE OF REPOSSESSION, FORECLOSURE SALE, TRANSFER OR RETURN	DESCRIPTION AND VALUE OF PROPERTY

6. Assignments and receiverships

None ☐ a. Describe any assignment of property for the benefit of creditors made within **120 days** immediately preceding the commencement of this case. (Married debtors filing under chapter 12 or chapter 13 must include any assignment by either or both spouses whether or not a joint petition is filed, unless the spouses are separated and a joint petition is not filed.)

NAME AND ADDRESS OF ASSIGNEE	DATE OF ASSIGNMENT	TERMS OF ASSIGNMENT OR SETTLEMENT

None ☐ b. List all property which has been in the hands of a custodian, receiver, or court-appointed official within **one year** immediately preceding the commencement of this case. (Married debtors filing under chapter 12 or chapter 13 must include information concerning property of either or both spouses whether or not a joint petition is filed, unless the spouses are separated and a joint petition is not filed.)

NAME AND ADDRESS OF CUSTODIAN	NAME AND LOCATION OF COURT CASE TITLE & NUMBER	DATE OF ORDER	DESCRIPTION AND VALUE Of PROPERTY

7. Gifts

None ☐ List all gifts or charitable contributions made within **one year** immediately preceding the commencement of this case except ordinary and usual gifts to family members aggregating less than $200 in value per individual family member and charitable contributions aggregating less than $100 per recipient. (Married debtors filing under chapter 12 or chapter 13 must include gifts or contributions by either or both spouses whether or not a joint petition is filed, unless the spouses are separated and a joint petition is not filed.)

NAME AND ADDRESS OF PERSON OR ORGANIZATION	RELATIONSHIP TO DEBTOR, IF ANY	DATE OF GIFT	DESCRIPTION AND VALUE OF GIFT

8. Losses

None ☐ List all losses from fire, theft, other casualty or gambling within **one year** immediately preceding the commencement of this case **or since the commencement of this case**. (Married debtors filing under chapter 12 or chapter 13 must include losses by either or both spouses whether or not a joint petition is filed, unless the spouses are separated and a joint petition is not filed.)

DESCRIPTION AND VALUE OF PROPERTY	DESCRIPTION OF CIRCUMSTANCES AND, IF LOSS WAS COVERED IN WHOLE OR IN PART BY INSURANCE, GIVE PARTICULARS	DATE OF LOSS

9. Payments related to debt counseling or bankruptcy

None
☐

List all payments made or property transferred by or on behalf of the debtor to any persons, including attorneys, for consultation concerning debt consolidation, relief under the bankruptcy law or preparation of a petition in bankruptcy within **one year** immediately preceding the commencement of this case.

NAME AND ADDRESS OF PAYEE	DATE OF PAYMENT, NAME OF PAYER IF OTHER THAN DEBTOR	AMOUNT OF MONEY OR DESCRIPTION AND VALUE OF PROPERTY

---

10. Other transfers

None
☐

a. List all other property, other than property transferred in the ordinary course of the business or financial affairs of the debtor, transferred either absolutely or as security within **two years** immediately preceding the commencement of this case. (Married debtors filing under chapter 12 or chapter 13 must include transfers by either or both spouses whether or not a joint petition is filed, unless the spouses are separated and a joint petition is not filed.)

NAME AND ADDRESS OF TRANSFEREE, RELATIONSHIP TO DEBTOR	DATE	DESCRIBE PROPERTY TRANSFERRED AND VALUE RECEIVED

None
☐

b. List all property transferred by the debtor within **ten years** immediately preceding the commencement of this case to a self-settled trust or similar device of which the debtor is a beneficiary.

NAME OF TRUST OR OTHER DEVICE	DATE(S) OF TRANSFER(S)	AMOUNT OF MONEY OR DESCRIPTION AND VALUE OF PROPERTY OR DEBTOR'S INTEREST IN PROPERTY

---

11. Closed financial accounts

None
☐

List all financial accounts and instruments held in the name of the debtor or for the benefit of the debtor which were closed, sold, or otherwise transferred within **one year** immediately preceding the commencement of this case. Include checking, savings, or other financial accounts, certificates of deposit, or other instruments; shares and share accounts held in banks, credit unions, pension funds, cooperatives, associations, brokerage houses and other financial institutions. (Married debtors filing under chapter 12 or chapter 13 must include information concerning accounts or instruments held by or for either or both spouses whether or not a joint petition is filed, unless the spouses are separated and a joint petition is not filed.)

NAME AND ADDRESS OF INSTITUTION	TYPE OF ACCOUNT, LAST FOUR DIGITS OF ACCOUNT NUMBER, AND AMOUNT OF FINAL BALANCE	AMOUNT AND DATE OF SALE OR CLOSING

12. Safe deposit boxes

None ☐

List each safe deposit or other box or depository in which the debtor has or had securities, cash, or other valuables within **one year** immediately preceding the commencement of this case. (Married debtors filing under chapter 12 or chapter 13 must include boxes or depositories of either or both spouses whether or not a joint petition is filed, unless the spouses are separated and a joint petition is not filed.)

NAME AND ADDRESS OF BANK OR OTHER DEPOSITORY	NAMES AND ADDRESSES OF THOSE WITH ACCESS TO BOX OR DEPOSITORY	DESCRIPTION OF CONTENTS	DATE OF TRANSFER OR SURRENDER, IF ANY

13. Setoffs

None ☐

List all setoffs made by any creditor, including a bank, against a debt or deposit of the debtor within **90 days** preceding the commencement of this case. (Married debtors filing under chapter 12 or chapter 13 must include information concerning either or both spouses whether or not a joint petition is filed, unless the spouses are separated and a joint petition is not filed.)

NAME AND ADDRESS OF CREDITOR	DATE OF SETOFF	AMOUNT OF SETOFF

14. Property held for another person

None ☐

List all property owned by another person that the debtor holds or controls.

NAME AND ADDRESS OF OWNER	DESCRIPTION AND VALUE OF PROPERTY	LOCATION OF PROPERTY

15. Prior address of debtor

None ☐

If debtor has moved within **three years** immediately preceding the commencement of this case, list all premises which the debtor occupied during that period and vacated prior to the commencement of this case. If a joint petition is filed, report also any separate address of either spouse.

ADDRESS	NAME USED	DATES OF OCCUPANCY

16. Spouses and Former Spouses

None
☐
If the debtor resides or resided in a community property state, commonwealth, or territory (including Alaska, Arizona, California, Idaho, Louisiana, Nevada, New Mexico, Puerto Rico, Texas, Washington, or Wisconsin) within **eight years** immediately preceding the commencement of the case, identify the name of the debtor's spouse and of any former spouse who resides or resided with the debtor in the community property state.

NAME

---

17. Environmental Information.

For the purpose of this question, the following definitions apply:

"Environmental Law" means any federal, state, or local statute or regulation regulating pollution, contamination, releases of hazardous or toxic substances, wastes or material into the air, land, soil, surface water, groundwater, or other medium, including, but not limited to, statutes or regulations regulating the cleanup of these substances, wastes, or material.

"Site" means any location, facility, or property as defined under any Environmental Law, whether or not presently or formerly owned or operated by the debtor, including, but not limited to, disposal sites.

"Hazardous Material" means anything defined as a hazardous waste, hazardous substance, toxic substance, hazardous material, pollutant, or contaminant or similar term under an Environmental Law.

None
☐
a. List the name and address of every site for which the debtor has received notice in writing by a governmental unit that it may be liable or potentially liable under or in violation of an Environmental Law. Indicate the governmental unit, the date of the notice, and, if known, the Environmental Law:

SITE NAME AND ADDRESS	NAME AND ADDRESS OF GOVERNMENTAL UNIT	DATE OF NOTICE	ENVIRONMENTAL LAW

None
☐
b. List the name and address of every site for which the debtor provided notice to a governmental unit of a release of Hazardous Material. Indicate the governmental unit to which the notice was sent and the date of the notice.

SITE NAME AND ADDRESS	NAME AND ADDRESS OF GOVERNMENTAL UNIT	DATE OF NOTICE	ENVIRONMENTAL LAW

None
☐
c. List all judicial or administrative proceedings, including settlements or orders, under any Environmental Law with respect to which the debtor is or was a party. Indicate the name and address of the governmental unit that is or was a party to the proceeding, and the docket number.

NAME AND ADDRESS OF GOVERNMENTAL UNIT	DOCKET NUMBER	STATUS OR DISPOSITION

---

18 . Nature, location and name of business

None
☐
a. *If the debtor is an individual*, list the names, addresses, taxpayer-identification numbers, nature of the businesses, and beginning and ending dates of all businesses in which the debtor was an officer, director, partner, or managing

executive of a corporation, partner in a partnership, sole proprietor, or was self-employed in a trade, profession, or other activity either full- or part-time within **six years** immediately preceding the commencement of this case, or in which the debtor owned 5 percent or more of the voting or equity securities within **six years** immediately preceding the commencement of this case.

If the debtor is a partnership, list the names, addresses, taxpayer-identification numbers, nature of the businesses, and beginning and ending dates of all businesses in which the debtor was a partner or owned 5 percent or more of the voting or equity securities, within **six years** immediately preceding the commencement of this case.

If the debtor is a corporation, list the names, addresses, taxpayer-identification numbers, nature of the businesses, and beginning and ending dates of all businesses in which the debtor was a partner or owned 5 percent or more of the voting or equity securities within **six years** immediately preceding the commencement of this case.

NAME	LAST FOUR DIGITS OF SOCIAL-SECURITY OR OTHER INDIVIDUAL TAXPAYER-I.D. NO. (ITIN)/ COMPLETE EIN	ADDRESS	NATURE OF BUSINESS	BEGINNING AND ENDING DATES

None

☐

b. Identify any business listed in response to subdivision a., above, that is "single asset real estate" as defined in 11 U.S.C. § 101.

NAME	ADDRESS

The following questions are to be completed by every debtor that is a corporation or partnership and by any individual debtor who is or has been, within **six years** immediately preceding the commencement of this case, any of the following: an officer, director, managing executive, or owner of more than 5 percent of the voting or equity securities of a corporation; a partner, other than a limited partner, of a partnership, a sole proprietor, or self-employed in a trade, profession, or other activity, either full- or part-time.

*(An individual or joint debtor should complete this portion of the statement **only** if the debtor is or has been in business, as defined above, within six years immediately preceding the commencement of this case. A debtor who has not been in business within those six years should go directly to the signature page.)*

---

19. Books, records and financial statements

None

☐

a. List all bookkeepers and accountants who within **two years** immediately preceding the filing of this bankruptcy case kept or supervised the keeping of books of account and records of the debtor.

NAME AND ADDRESS	DATES SERVICES RENDERED

None

☐

b. List all firms or individuals who within **two years** immediately preceding the filing of this bankruptcy case have audited the books of account and records, or prepared a financial statement of the debtor.

NAME	ADDRESS	DATES SERVICES RENDERED

None ☐ c. List all firms or individuals who at the time of the commencement of this case were in possession of the books of account and records of the debtor. If any of the books of account and records are not available, explain.

NAME   ADDRESS

None ☐ d. List all financial institutions, creditors and other parties, including mercantile and trade agencies, to whom a financial statement was issued by the debtor within **two years** immediately preceding the commencement of this case.

NAME AND ADDRESS   DATE ISSUED

---

20. Inventories

None ☐ a. List the dates of the last two inventories taken of your property, the name of the person who supervised the taking of each inventory, and the dollar amount and basis of each inventory.

		DOLLAR AMOUNT OF INVENTORY
DATE OF INVENTORY	INVENTORY SUPERVISOR	(Specify cost, market or other basis)

None ☐ b. List the name and address of the person having possession of the records of each of the inventories reported in a., above.

DATE OF INVENTORY	NAME AND ADDRESSES OF CUSTODIAN OF INVENTORY RECORDS

---

21 . Current Partners, Officers, Directors and Shareholders

None ☐ a. If the debtor is a partnership, list the nature and percentage of partnership interest of each member of the partnership.

NAME AND ADDRESS	NATURE OF INTEREST	PERCENTAGE OF INTEREST

None ☐ b. If the debtor is a corporation, list all officers and directors of the corporation, and each stockholder who directly or indirectly owns, controls, or holds 5 percent or more of the voting or equity securities of the corporation.

NAME AND ADDRESS	TITLE	NATURE AND PERCENTAGE OF STOCK OWNERSHIP

22 . Former partners, officers, directors and shareholders

None
☐

a.   If the debtor is a partnership, list each member who withdrew from the partnership within **one year** immediately preceding the commencement of this case.

NAME	ADDRESS	DATE OF WITHDRAWAL

None
☐

b.   If the debtor is a corporation, list all officers or directors whose relationship with the corporation terminated within **one year** immediately preceding the commencement of this case.

NAME AND ADDRESS	TITLE	DATE OF TERMINATION

---

23 . Withdrawals from a partnership or distributions by a corporation

None
☐

If the debtor is a partnership or corporation, list all withdrawals or distributions credited or given to an insider, including compensation in any form, bonuses, loans, stock redemptions, options exercised and any other perquisite during **one year** immediately preceding the commencement of this case.

NAME & ADDRESS OF RECIPIENT, RELATIONSHIP TO DEBTOR	DATE AND PURPOSE OF WITHDRAWAL	AMOUNT OF MONEY OR DESCRIPTION AND VALUE OF PROPERTY

---

24. Tax Consolidation Group.

None
☐

If the debtor is a corporation, list the name and federal taxpayer-identification number of the parent corporation of any consolidated group for tax purposes of which the debtor has been a member at any time within **six years** immediately preceding the commencement of the case.

NAME OF PARENT CORPORATION	TAXPAYER-IDENTIFICATION NUMBER (EIN)

---

25. Pension Funds.

None
☐

If the debtor is not an individual, list the name and federal taxpayer-identification number of any pension fund to which the debtor, as an employer, has been responsible for contributing at any time within **six years** immediately preceding the commencement of the case.

NAME OF PENSION FUND	TAXPAYER-IDENTIFICATION NUMBER (EIN)

*   *   *   *   *   *

[If completed by an individual or individual and spouse]

I declare under penalty of perjury that I have read the answers contained in the foregoing statement of financial affairs and any attachments thereto and that they are true and correct.

Date _____ Signature
of Debtor _____

Date _____ Signature of
Joint Debtor
(if any) _____

[If completed on behalf of a partnership or corporation]

I declare under penalty of perjury that I have read the answers contained in the foregoing statement of financial affairs and any attachments thereto and that they are true and correct to the best of my knowledge, information and belief.

Date _____ Signature _____

Print Name and
Title _____

[An individual signing on behalf of a partnership or corporation must indicate position or relationship to debtor.]

_____continuation sheets attached

Penalty for making a false statement: Fine of up to $500,000 or imprisonment for up to 5 years, or both. 18 U.S.C. §§ 152 and 3571

DECLARATION AND SIGNATURE OF NON-ATTORNEY BANKRUPTCY PETITION PREPARER (See 11 U.S.C. § 110)

I declare under penalty of perjury that: (1) I am a bankruptcy petition preparer as defined in 11 U.S.C. § 110; (2) I prepared this document for compensation and have provided the debtor with a copy of this document and the notices and information required under 11 U.S.C. §§ 110(b), 110(h), and 342(b); and, (3) if rules or guidelines have been promulgated pursuant to 11 U.S.C. § 110(h) setting a maximum fee for services chargeable by bankruptcy petition preparers, I have given the debtor notice of the maximum amount before preparing any document for filing for a debtor or accepting any fee from the debtor, as required by that section.

_____ _____
Printed or Typed Name and Title, if any, of Bankruptcy Petition Preparer   Social-Security No. (Required by 11 U.S.C. § 110.)

If the bankruptcy petition preparer is not an individual, state the name, title (if any), address, and social-security number of the officer, principal, responsible person, or partner who signs this document.

_____
Address

_____ _____
Signature of Bankruptcy Petition Preparer   Date

Names and Social-Security numbers of all other individuals who prepared or assisted in preparing this document unless the bankruptcy petition preparer is not an individual:

If more than one person prepared this document, attach additional signed sheets conforming to the appropriate Official Form for each person

A bankruptcy petition preparer's failure to comply with the provisions of title 11 and the Federal Rules of Bankruptcy Procedure may result in fines or imprisonment or both. 18 U.S.C. § 156.

UNITED STATES BANKRUPTCY COURT	PROOF OF CLAIM

Name of Debtor:	Case Number:

NOTE: *This form should not be used to make a claim for an administrative expense arising after the commencement of the case. A request for payment of an administrative expense may be filed pursuant to 11 U.S.C. § 503.*

Name of Creditor (the person or other entity to whom the debtor owes money or property):

Name and address where notices should be sent:

Telephone number:

☐ Check this box to indicate that this claim amends a previously filed claim.

Court Claim Number: _____
(*If known*)

Filed on: _____

Name and address where payment should be sent (if different from above):

Telephone number:

☐ Check this box if you are aware that anyone else has filed a proof of claim relating to your claim. Attach copy of statement giving particulars.

☐ Check this box if you are the debtor or trustee in this case.

---

1. Amount of Claim as of Date Case Filed: $_____

If all or part of your claim is secured, complete item 4 below; however, if all of your claim is unsecured, do not complete item 4.

If all or part of your claim is entitled to priority, complete item 5.

☐ Check this box if claim includes interest or other charges in addition to the principal amount of claim. Attach itemized statement of interest or charges.

2. Basis for Claim: _____
(See instruction #2 on reverse side.)

3. Last four digits of any number by which creditor identifies debtor: _____

   3a. Debtor may have scheduled account as: _____
   (See instruction #3a on reverse side.)

4. Secured Claim (See instruction #4 on reverse side.)
Check the appropriate box if your claim is secured by a lien on property or a right of setoff and provide the requested information.

Nature of property or right of setoff: ☐ Real Estate   ☐ Motor Vehicle   ☐ Other
Describe:

Value of Property: $_____   **Annual Interest Rate** ___%

Amount of arrearage and other charges as of time case filed included in secured claim,

  if any: $_____   **Basis for perfection:** _____

Amount of Secured Claim: $_____   **Amount Unsecured:** $_____

6. Credits: The amount of all payments on this claim has been credited for the purpose of making this proof of claim.

7. Documents: Attach redacted copies of any documents that support the claim, such as promissory notes, purchase orders, invoices, itemized statements of running accounts, contracts, judgments, mortgages, and security agreements. You may also attach a summary. Attach redacted copies of documents providing evidence of perfection of a security interest. You may also attach a summary. (*See definition of "redacted" on reverse side.*)

DO NOT SEND ORIGINAL DOCUMENTS. ATTACHED DOCUMENTS MAY BE DESTROYED AFTER SCANNING.

If the documents are not available, please explain:

---

5. Amount of Claim Entitled to Priority under 11 U.S.C. §507(a). If any portion of your claim falls in one of the following categories, check the box and state the amount.

Specify the priority of the claim.

☐ Domestic support obligations under 11 U.S.C. §507(a)(1)(A) or (a)(1)(B).

☐ Wages, salaries, or commissions (up to $10,950*) earned within 180 days before filing of the bankruptcy petition or cessation of the debtor's business, whichever is earlier – 11 U.S.C. §507 (a)(4).

☐ Contributions to an employee benefit plan – 11 U.S.C. §507 (a)(5).

☐ Up to $2,425* of deposits toward purchase, lease, or rental of property or services for personal, family, or household use – 11 U.S.C. §507 (a)(7).

☐ Taxes or penalties owed to governmental units – 11 U.S.C. §507 (a)(8).

☐ Other – Specify applicable paragraph of 11 U.S.C. §507 (a)(__).

Amount entitled to priority:

$_____

Amounts are subject to adjustment on 4/1/10 and every 3 years thereafter with respect to cases commenced on or after the date of adjustment.

Date:	**Signature:** The person filing this claim must sign it. Sign and print name and title, if any, of the creditor or other person authorized to file this claim and state address and telephone number if different from the notice address above. Attach copy of power of attorney, if any.	FOR COURT USE ONLY

Penalty for presenting fraudulent claim: Fine of up to $500,000 or imprisonment for up to 5 years, or both. 18 U.S.C. §§ 152 and 3571.

INSTRUCTIONS FOR PROOF OF CLAIM FORM

The instructions and definitions below are general explanations of the law. In certain circumstances, such as bankruptcy cases not filed voluntarily by the debtor, there may be exceptions to these general rules.

Items to be completed in Proof of Claim form

Court, Name of Debtor, and Case Number:
Fill in the federal judicial district where the bankruptcy case was filed (for example, Central District of California), the bankruptcy debtor's name, and the bankruptcy case number. If the creditor received a notice of the case from the bankruptcy court, all of this information is located at the top of the notice.

Creditor's Name and Address:
Fill in the name of the person or entity asserting a claim and the name and address of the person who should receive notices issued during the bankruptcy case. A separate space is provided for the payment address if it differs from the notice address. The creditor has a continuing obligation to keep the court informed of its current address. See Federal Rule of Bankruptcy Procedure (FRBP) 2002(g).

1. Amount of Claim as of Date Case Filed:
State the total amount owed to the creditor on the date of the Bankruptcy filing. Follow the instructions concerning whether to complete items 4 and 5. Check the box if interest or other charges are included in the claim.

2. Basis for Claim:
State the type of debt or how it was incurred. Examples include goods sold, money loaned, services performed, personal injury/wrongful death, car loan, mortgage note, and credit card.

3. Last Four Digits of Any Number by Which Creditor Identifies Debtor:
State only the last four digits of the debtor's account or other number used by the creditor to identify the debtor.

3a. Debtor May Have Scheduled Account As:
Use this space to report a change in the creditor's name, a transferred claim, or any other information that clarifies a difference between this proof of claim and the claim as scheduled by the debtor.

4. Secured Claim:
Check the appropriate box and provide the requested information if the claim is fully or partially secured. Skip this section if the claim is entirely unsecured. (See DEFINITIONS, below.) State the type and the value of property that secures the claim, attach copies of lien documentation, and state annual interest rate and the amount past due on the claim as of the date of the bankruptcy filing.

5. Amount of Claim Entitled to Priority Under 11 U.S.C. §507(a).
If any portion of your claim falls in one or more of the listed categories, check the appropriate box(es) and state the amount entitled to priority. (See DEFINITIONS, below.) A claim may be partly priority and partly non-priority. For example, in some of the categories, the law limits the amount entitled to priority.

6. Credits:
An authorized signature on this proof of claim serves as an acknowledgment that when calculating the amount of the claim, the creditor gave the debtor credit for any payments received toward the debt.

7. Documents:
Attach to this proof of claim form redacted copies documenting the existence of the debt and of any lien securing the debt. You may also attach a summary. You must also attach copies of documents that evidence perfection of any security interest. You may also attach a summary. FRBP 3001(c) and (d). Do not send original documents, as attachments may be destroyed after scanning.

Date and Signature:
The person filing this proof of claim must sign and date it. FRBP 9011. If the claim is filed electronically, FRBP 5005(a)(2), authorizes courts to establish local rules specifying what constitutes a signature. Print the name and title, if any, of the creditor or other person authorized to file this claim. State the filer's address and telephone number if it differs from the address given on the top of the form for purposes of receiving notices. Attach a complete copy of any power of attorney. Criminal penalties apply for making a false statement on a proof of claim.

_____DEFINITIONS_____

Debtor
A debtor is the person, corporation, or other entity that has filed a bankruptcy case.

Creditor
A creditor is the person, corporation, or other entity owed a debt by the debtor on the date of the bankruptcy filing.

Claim
A claim is the creditor's right to receive payment on a debt that was owed by the debtor on the date of the bankruptcy filing. See 11 U.S.C. §101 (5). A claim may be secured or unsecured.

Proof of Claim
A proof of claim is a form used by the creditor to indicate the amount of the debt owed by the debtor on the date of the bankruptcy filing. The creditor must file the form with the clerk of the same bankruptcy court in which the bankruptcy case was filed.

Secured Claim Under 11 U.S.C. §506(a)
A secured claim is one backed by a lien on property of the debtor. The claim is secured so long as the creditor has the right to be paid from the property prior to other creditors. The amount of the secured claim cannot exceed the value of the property. Any amount owed to the creditor in excess of the value of the property is an unsecured claim. Examples of liens on property include a mortgage on real estate or a security interest in a car.

A lien may be voluntarily granted by a debtor or may be obtained through a court proceeding. In some states, a court judgment is a lien. A claim also may be secured if the creditor owes the debtor money (has a right to setoff).

Unsecured Claim
An unsecured claim is one that does not meet the requirements of a secured claim. A claim may be partly unsecured if the amount of the claim exceeds the value of the property on which the creditor has a lien.

Claim Entitled to Priority Under 11 U.S.C. §507(a)
Priority claims are certain categories of unsecured claims that are paid from the available money or property in a bankruptcy case before other unsecured claims.

Redacted
A document has been redacted when the person filing it has masked, edited out, or otherwise deleted, certain information. A creditor should redact and use only the last four digits of any social-security, individual's tax-identification, or financial-account number, all but the initials of a minor's name and only the year of any person's date of birth.

Evidence of Perfection
Evidence of perfection may include a mortgage, lien, certificate of title, financing statement, or other document showing that the lien has been filed or recorded.

_____INFORMATION_____

Acknowledgment of Filing of Claim
To receive acknowledgment of your filing, you may either enclose a stamped self-addressed envelope and a copy of this proof of claim or you may access the court's PACER system (www.pacer.psc.uscourts.gov) for a small fee to view your filed proof of claim.

Offers to Purchase a Claim
Certain entities are in the business of purchasing claims for an amount less than the face value of the claims. One or more of these entities may contact the creditor and offer to purchase the claim. Some of the written communications from these entities may easily be confused with official court documentation or communications from the debtor. These entities do not represent the bankruptcy court or the debtor. The creditor has no obligation to sell its claim. However, if the creditor decides to sell its claim, any transfer of such claim is subject to FRBP 3001(e), any applicable provisions of the Bankruptcy Code (11 U.S.C. § 101 *et seq.*), and any applicable orders of the bankruptcy court.

Official Form 20A
(12/03)

United States Bankruptcy Court

_____ District Of _____

In re _____,)
                Set forth here all names including married,)
                maiden, and trade names used by debtor within)
                last 6 years.])
                       Debtor)   Case No. _____
)

Address _____)
)

        _____)   Chapter _____

Employer's Tax Identification (EIN) No(s). *[if any]:* _____)
_____)
Last four digits of Social Security No(s).: _____)

NOTICE OF [MOTION TO   ] [OBJECTION TO   ]

_____has filed papers with the court to [relief sought in motion or objection].

<u>Your rights may be affected.</u> You should read these papers carefully and discuss them with your attorney, if you have one in this bankruptcy case. (If you do not have an attorney, you may wish to consult one.)

       If you do not want the court to [relief sought in motion or objection], or if you want the court to consider your views on the [motion] [objection], then on or before <u>(date)</u>, you or your attorney must:

[File with the court a written request for a hearing {*or, if the court requires a written response*, an answer, explaining your position} at:

       {address of the bankruptcy clerk's office}

If you mail your {request}{response} to the court for filing, you must mail it early enough so the court will **receive** it on or before the date stated above.

You must also mail a copy to:

       {movant's attorney's name and address}

       {names and addresses of others to be served}]

[Attend the hearing scheduled to be held on <u>(date)</u>, <u>(year)</u>, at ____a.m./p.m. in Courtroom ____, United States Bankruptcy Court, {address}.]

[Other steps required to oppose a motion or objection under local rule or court order.]

       If you or your attorney do not take these steps, the court may decide that you do not oppose the relief sought in the motion or objection and may enter an order granting that relief.

Date: _____   Signature: _____
                                           Name:
                                           Address:

UNITED STATES BANKRUPTCY COURT

In re _____,

    [Set forth here all names including married, maiden, and trade names used by debtor within last 8 years]

                Debtor

Address

Last four digits of Social-Security or Individual Taxpayer-Identification (ITIN) No(s).,(if any): _____

Employer Tax-Identification (EIN) No(s).(if any):

)
)
)
)
)
)
)
)
)
)
)
)
)
)

Case No. _____

Chapter _____

STATEMENT OF SOCIAL-SECURITY NUMBER(S)
(or other Individual Taxpayer-Identification Number(s) (ITIN(s)))*

1. Name of Debtor (Last, First, Middle):_____
(Check the appropriate box and, if applicable, provide the required information.)

    ☐ Debtor has a Social-Security Number and it is: _____
           (If more than one, state all.)
    ☐ Debtor does not have a Social-Security Number but has an Individual Taxpayer-Identification Number (ITIN), and it is: _____
           (If more than one, state all.)
    ☐ Debtor does not have either a Social-Security Number or an Individual Taxpayer-Identification Number (ITIN).

2. Name of Joint Debtor (Last, First, Middle):_____
(Check the appropriate box and, if applicable, provide the required information.)

    ☐ Joint Debtor has a Social-Security Number and it is: _____
           (If more than one, state all.)
    ☐ Joint Debtor does not have a Social-Security Number but has an Individual Taxpayer-Identification Number (ITIN) and it is: _____
           (If more than one, state all.)
    ☐ Joint Debtor does not have either a Social-Security Number or an Individual Taxpayer-Identification Number (ITIN).

I declare under penalty of perjury that the foregoing is true and correct.

X _____
       Signature of Debtor   Date
X _____
       Signature of Joint Debtor   Date

---

* *Joint debtors must provide information for both spouses.*

Penalty for making a false statement: Fine of up to $250,000 or up to 5 years imprisonment or both. 18 U.S.C. §§ 152 and 3571.

In re _____
　　　　　　　Debtor(s)

Case Number: _____
　　　　　　　(If known)

According to the calculations required by this statement:

☐ **The presumption arises.**
☐ **The presumption does not arise.**

(Check the box as directed in Parts I, III, and VI of this statement)

CHAPTER 7 STATEMENT OF CURRENT MONTHLY INCOME AND MEANS-TEST CALCULATION

In addition to Schedules I and J, this statement must be completed by every individual chapter 7 debtor, whether or not filing jointly. Joint debtors may complete one statement only.

Part I. EXCLUSION FOR DISABLED VETERANS AND NON-CONSUMER DEBTORS

1A	If you are a disabled veteran described in the Veteran's Declaration in this Part I, (1) check the box at the beginning of the Veteran's Declaration, (2) check the box for "The presumption does not arise" at the top of this statement, and (3) complete the verification in Part VIII. Do not complete any of the remaining parts of this statement. ☐ **Veteran's Declaration.** By checking this box, I declare under penalty of perjury that I am a disabled veteran (as defined in 38 U.S.C. § 3741(1)) whose indebtedness occurred primarily during a period in which I was on active duty (as defined in 10 U.S.C. § 101(d)(1)) or while I was performing a homeland defense activity (as defined in 32 U.S.C. §901(1)).
1B	If your debts are not primarily consumer debts, check the box below and complete the verification in Part VIII. Do not complete any of the remaining parts of this statement. ☐ **Declaration of non-consumer debts.** By checking this box, I declare that my debts are not primarily consumer debts.

Part II. CALCULATION OF MONTHLY INCOME FOR § 707(b)(7) EXCLUSION

2	**Marital/filing status.** Check the box that applies and complete the balance of this part of this statement as directed. a. ☐ Unmarried. **Complete only Column A ("Debtor's Income") for Lines 3-11.** b. ☐ Married, not filing jointly, with declaration of separate households. By checking this box, debtor declares under penalty of perjury: "My spouse and I are legally separated under applicable non-bankruptcy law or my spouse and I are living apart other than for the purpose of evading the requirements of § 707(b)(2)(A) of the Bankruptcy Code." **Complete only Column A ("Debtor's Income") for Lines 3-11.** c. ☐ Married, not filing jointly, without the declaration of separate households set out in Line 2.b above. **Complete both Column A ("Debtor's Income") and Column B ("Spouse's Income") for Lines 3-11.** d. ☐ Married, filing jointly. **Complete both Column A ("Debtor's Income") and Column B ("Spouse's Income") for Lines 3-11.**		

	All figures must reflect average monthly income received from all sources, derived during the six calendar months prior to filing the bankruptcy case, ending on the last day of the month before the filing. If the amount of monthly income varied during the six months, you must divide the six-month total by six, and enter the result on the appropriate line.	Column A Debtor's Income	Column B Spouse's Income
3	**Gross wages, salary, tips, bonuses, overtime, commissions.**	$	$

4	**Income from the operation of a business, profession or farm.** Subtract Line b from Line a and enter the difference in the appropriate column(s) of Line 4. If you operate more than one business, profession or farm, enter aggregate numbers and provide details on an attachment. Do not enter a number less than zero. **Do not include any part of the business expenses entered on Line b as a deduction in Part V.**			
	a.	Gross receipts	$	
	b.	Ordinary and necessary business expenses	$	
	c.	Business income	Subtract Line b from Line a	$
5	**Rent and other real property income.** Subtract Line b from Line a and enter the difference in the appropriate column(s) of Line 5. Do not enter a number less than zero. **Do not include any part of the operating expenses entered on Line b as a deduction in Part V.**			
	a.	Gross receipts	$	
	b.	Ordinary and necessary operating expenses	$	
	c.	Rent and other real property income	Subtract Line b from Line a	$
6	**Interest, dividends and royalties.**		$	$
7	**Pension and retirement income.**		$	$
8	**Any amounts paid by another person or entity, on a regular basis, for the household expenses of the debtor or the debtor's dependents, including child support paid for that purpose.** Do not include alimony or separate maintenance payments or amounts paid by your spouse if Column B is completed.		$	$
9	**Unemployment compensation.** Enter the amount in the appropriate column(s) of Line 9. However, if you contend that unemployment compensation received by you or your spouse was a benefit under the Social Security Act, do not list the amount of such compensation in Column A or B, but instead state the amount in the space below: Unemployment compensation claimed to be a benefit under the Social Security Act Debtor $ _____ Spouse $ _____		$	$
10	**Income from all other sources.** Specify source and amount. If necessary, list additional sources on a separate page. **Do not include alimony or separate maintenance payments paid by your spouse if Column B is completed, but include all other payments of alimony or separate maintenance.** Do not include any benefits received under the Social Security Act or payments received as a victim of a war crime, crime against humanity, or as a victim of international or domestic terrorism. a. _____ $ b. _____ $ Total and enter on Line 10		$	$
11	**Subtotal of Current Monthly Income for § 707(b)(7).** Add Lines 3 thru 10 in Column A, and, if Column B is completed, add Lines 3 through 10 in Column B. Enter the total(s).		$	$
12	**Total Current Monthly Income for § 707(b)(7).** If Column B has been completed, add Line 11, Column A to Line 11, Column B, and enter the total. If Column B has not been completed, enter the amount from Line 11, Column A.	$		

Part III. APPLICATION OF § 707(b)(7) EXCLUSION

13	**Annualized Current Monthly Income for § 707(b)(7).** Multiply the amount from Line 12 by the number 12 and enter the result.	$

14	**Applicable median family income.** Enter the median family income for the applicable state and household size. (This information is available by family size at www.usdoj.gov/ust/ or from the clerk of the bankruptcy court.) a. Enter debtor's state of residence: _____ b. Enter debtor's household size: _____	$
15	**Application of Section 707(b)(7).** Check the applicable box and proceed as directed. ☐ **The amount on Line 13 is less than or equal to the amount on Line 14.** Check the box for "The presumption does not arise" at the top of page 1 of this statement, and complete Part VIII; do not complete Parts IV, V, VI or VII. ☐ **The amount on Line 13 is more than the amount on Line 14.** Complete the remaining parts of this statement.	

Complete Parts IV, V, VI, and VII of this statement only if required. (See Line 15.)

	Part IV. CALCULATION OF CURRENT MONTHLY INCOME FOR § 707(b)(2)	
16	**Enter the amount from Line 12.**	$
17	**Marital adjustment.** If you checked the box at Line 2.c, enter on Line 17 the total of any income listed in Line 11, Column B that was NOT paid on a regular basis for the household expenses of the debtor or the debtor's dependents. Specify in the lines below the basis for excluding the Column B income (such as payment of the spouse's tax liability or the spouse's support of persons other than the debtor or the debtor's dependents) and the amount of income devoted to each purpose. If necessary, list additional adjustments on a separate page. If you did not check box at Line 2.c, enter zero.	

a.		$
b.		$
c.		$

Total and enter on Line 17. $

18	**Current monthly income for § 707(b)(2).** Subtract Line 17 from Line 16 and enter the result.	$

	Part V. CALCULATION OF DEDUCTIONS FROM INCOME	

	Subpart A: Deductions under Standards of the Internal Revenue Service (IRS)	
19A	**National Standards: food, clothing and other items.** Enter in Line 19A the "Total" amount from IRS National Standards for Food, Clothing and Other Items for the applicable household size. (This information is available at www.usdoj.gov/ust/ or from the clerk of the bankruptcy court.)	$
19B	**National Standards: health care.** Enter in Line a1 below the amount from IRS National Standards for Out-of-Pocket Health Care for persons under 65 years of age, and in Line a2 the IRS National Standards for Out-of-Pocket Health Care for persons 65 years of age or older. (This information is available at www.usdoj.gov/ust/ or from the clerk of the bankruptcy court.) Enter in Line b1 the number of members of your household who are under 65 years of age, and enter in Line b2 the number of members of your household who are 65 years of age or older. (The total number of household members must be the same as the number stated in Line 14b.) Multiply Line a1 by Line b1 to obtain a total amount for household members under 65, and enter the result in Line c1. Multiply Line a2 by Line b2 to obtain a total amount for household members 65 and older, and enter the result in Line c2. Add Lines c1 and c2 to obtain a total health care amount, and enter the result in Line 19B.	

Household members under 65 years of age			Household members 65 years of age or older			
a1.	Allowance per member		a2.	Allowance per member		
b1.	Number of members		b2.	Number of members		
c1.	Subtotal		c2.	Subtotal		$

20A	**Local Standards: housing and utilities; non-mortgage expenses.** Enter the amount of the IRS Housing and Utilities Standards; non-mortgage expenses for the applicable county and household size. (This information is available at www.usdoj.gov/ust/ or from the clerk of the bankruptcy court).	$

20B	**Local Standards: housing and utilities; mortgage/rent expense.** Enter, in Line a below, the amount of the IRS Housing and Utilities Standards; mortgage/rent expense for your county and household size (this information is available at www.usdoj.gov/ust/ or from the clerk of the bankruptcy court); enter on Line b the total of the Average Monthly Payments for any debts secured by your home, as stated in Line 42; subtract Line b from Line a and enter the result in Line 20B. **Do not enter an amount less than zero.**	

	a.	IRS Housing and Utilities Standards; mortgage/rental expense	$	
	b.	Average Monthly Payment for any debts secured by your home, if any, as stated in Line 42	$	
	c.	Net mortgage/rental expense	Subtract Line b from Line a.	$

21	**Local Standards: housing and utilities; adjustment.** If you contend that the process set out in Lines 20A and 20B does not accurately compute the allowance to which you are entitled under the IRS Housing and Utilities Standards, enter any additional amount to which you contend you are entitled, and state the basis for your contention in the space below: _____ _____ _____	$

22A	**Local Standards: transportation; vehicle operation/public transportation expense.** You are entitled to an expense allowance in this category regardless of whether you pay the expenses of operating a vehicle and regardless of whether you use public transportation. Check the number of vehicles for which you pay the operating expenses or for which the operating expenses are included as a contribution to your household expenses in Line 8. ☐ 0 ☐ 1 ☐ 2 or more. If you checked 0, enter on Line 22A the "Public Transportation" amount from IRS Local Standards: Transportation. If you checked 1 or 2 or more, enter on Line 22A the "Operating Costs" amount from IRS Local Standards: Transportation for the applicable number of vehicles in the applicable Metropolitan Statistical Area or Census Region. (These amounts are available at www.usdoj.gov/ust/ or from the clerk of the bankruptcy court.)	$

22B	**Local Standards: transportation; additional public transportation expense.** If you pay the operating expenses for a vehicle and also use public transportation, and you contend that you are entitled to an additional deduction for your public transportation expenses, enter on Line 22B the "Public Transportation" amount from IRS Local Standards: Transportation. (This amount is available at www.usdoj.gov/ust/ or from the clerk of the bankruptcy court.)	$

23	**Local Standards: transportation ownership/lease expense; Vehicle 1.** Check the number of vehicles for which you claim an ownership/lease expense. (You may not claim an ownership/lease expense for more than two vehicles.) ☐ 1 ☐ 2 or more. Enter, in Line a below, the "Ownership Costs" for "One Car" from the IRS Local Standards: Transportation (available at www.usdoj.gov/ust/ or from the clerk of the bankruptcy court); enter in Line b the total of the Average Monthly Payments for any debts secured by Vehicle 1, as stated in Line 42; subtract Line b from Line a and enter the result in Line 23. **Do not enter an amount less than zero.**	

	a.	IRS Transportation Standards, Ownership Costs	$	
	b.	Average Monthly Payment for any debts secured by Vehicle 1, as stated in Line 42	$	
	c.	Net ownership/lease expense for Vehicle 1	Subtract Line b from Line a.	$

24	**Local Standards: transportation ownership/lease expense; Vehicle 2.** Complete this Line only if you checked the "2 or more" Box in Line 23. Enter, in Line a below, the "Ownership Costs" for "One Car" from the IRS Local Standards: Transportation (available at www.usdoj.gov/ust/ or from the clerk of the bankruptcy court); enter in Line b the total of the Average Monthly Payments for any debts secured by Vehicle 2, as stated in Line 42; subtract Line b from Line a and enter the result in Line 24. **Do not enter an amount less than zero.**			

	a.	IRS Transportation Standards, Ownership Costs	$	
	b.	Average Monthly Payment for any debts secured by Vehicle 2, as stated in Line 42	$	
	c.	Net ownership/lease expense for Vehicle 2	Subtract Line b from Line a.	$

25	**Other Necessary Expenses: taxes.** Enter the total average monthly expense that you actually incur for all federal, state and local taxes, other than real estate and sales taxes, such as income taxes, self-employment taxes, social-security taxes, and Medicare taxes. **Do not include real estate or sales taxes.**	$
26	**Other Necessary Expenses: involuntary deductions for employment.** Enter the total average monthly payroll deductions that are required for your employment, such as retirement contributions, union dues, and uniform costs. **Do not include discretionary amounts, such as voluntary 401(k) contributions.**	$
27	**Other Necessary Expenses: life insurance.** Enter total average monthly premiums that you actually pay for term life insurance for yourself. **Do not include premiums for insurance on your dependents, for whole life or for any other form of insurance.**	$
28	**Other Necessary Expenses: court-ordered payments.** Enter the total monthly amount that you are required to pay pursuant to the order of a court or administrative agency, such as spousal or child support payments. **Do not include payments on past due obligations included in Line 44.**	$
29	**Other Necessary Expenses: education for employment or for a physically or mentally challenged child.** Enter the total average monthly amount that you actually expend for education that is a condition of employment and for education that is required for a physically or mentally challenged dependent child for whom no public education providing similar services is available.	$
30	**Other Necessary Expenses: childcare.** Enter the total average monthly amount that you actually expend on childcare—such as baby-sitting, day care, nursery and preschool. **Do not include other educational payments.**	$
31	**Other Necessary Expenses: health care.** Enter the total average monthly amount that you actually expend on health care that is required for the health and welfare of yourself or your dependents, that is not reimbursed by insurance or paid by a health savings account, and that is in excess of the amount entered in Line 19B. **Do not include payments for health insurance or health savings accounts listed in Line 34.**	$
32	**Other Necessary Expenses: telecommunication services.** Enter the total average monthly amount that you actually pay for telecommunication services other than your basic home telephone and cell phone service—such as pagers, call waiting, caller id, special long distance, or internet service—to the extent necessary for your health and welfare or that of your dependents. **Do not include any amount previously deducted.**	$
33	**Total Expenses Allowed under IRS Standards.** Enter the total of Lines 19 through 32.	$

Subpart B: Additional Living Expense Deductions
Note: Do not include any expenses that you have listed in Lines 19-32

34	**Health Insurance, Disability Insurance, and Health Savings Account Expenses.** List the monthly expenses in the categories set out in lines a-c below that are reasonably necessary for yourself, your spouse, or your dependents.	
	a. Health Insurance $	
	b. Disability Insurance $	
	c. Health Savings Account $	
	Total and enter on Line 34	$
	If you do not actually expend this total amount, state your actual total average monthly expenditures in the space below: $ _____	
35	**Continued contributions to the care of household or family members.** Enter the total average actual monthly expenses that you will continue to pay for the reasonable and necessary care and support of an elderly, chronically ill, or disabled member of your household or member of your immediate family who is unable to pay for such expenses.	$
36	**Protection against family violence.** Enter the total average reasonably necessary monthly expenses that you actually incurred to maintain the safety of your family under the Family Violence Prevention and Services Act or other applicable federal law. The nature of these expenses is required to be kept confidential by the court.	$
37	**Home energy costs.** Enter the total average monthly amount, in excess of the allowance specified by IRS Local Standards for Housing and Utilities, that you actually expend for home energy costs. **You must provide your case trustee with documentation of your actual expenses, and you must demonstrate that the additional amount claimed is reasonable and necessary.**	$
38	**Education expenses for dependent children less than 18.** Enter the total average monthly expenses that you actually incur, not to exceed $137.50 per child, for attendance at a private or public elementary or secondary school by your dependent children less than 18 years of age. **You must provide your case trustee with documentation of your actual expenses, and you must explain why the amount claimed is reasonable and necessary and not already accounted for in the IRS Standards.**	$
39	**Additional food and clothing expense.** Enter the total average monthly amount by which your food and clothing expenses exceed the combined allowances for food and clothing (apparel and services) in the IRS National Standards, not to exceed 5% of those combined allowances. (This information is available at www.usdoj.gov/ust/ or from the clerk of the bankruptcy court.) **You must demonstrate that the additional amount claimed is reasonable and necessary.**	$
40	**Continued charitable contributions.** Enter the amount that you will continue to contribute in the form of cash or financial instruments to a charitable organization as defined in 26 U.S.C. § 170(c)(1)-(2).	$
41	**Total Additional Expense Deductions under § 707(b).** Enter the total of Lines 34 through 40	$

Subpart C: Deductions for Debt Payment

42	**Future payments on secured claims.** For each of your debts that is secured by an interest in property that you own, list the name of the creditor, identify the property securing the debt, state the Average Monthly Payment, and check whether the payment includes taxes or insurance. The Average Monthly Payment is the total of all amounts scheduled as contractually due to each Secured Creditor in the 60 months following the filing of the bankruptcy case, divided by 60. If necessary, list additional entries on a separate page. Enter the total of the Average Monthly Payments on Line 42.				
		Name of Creditor	Property Securing the Debt	Average Monthly Payment	Does payment include taxes or insurance?
	a.			$	☐ yes ☐ no
	b.			$	☐ yes ☐ no
	c.			$	☐ yes ☐ no
				Total: Add Lines a, b and c.	$

43	**Other payments on secured claims.** If any of debts listed in Line 42 are secured by your primary residence, a motor vehicle, or other property necessary for your support or the support of your dependents, you may include in your deduction 1/60th of any amount (the "cure amount") that you must pay the creditor in addition to the payments listed in Line 42, in order to maintain possession of the property. The cure amount would include any sums in default that must be paid in order to avoid repossession or foreclosure. List and total any such amounts in the following chart. If necessary, list additional entries on a separate page.			
		Name of Creditor	Property Securing the Debt	1/60th of the Cure Amount
	a.			$
	b.			$
	c.			$
				Total: Add Lines a, b and c	$

44	**Payments on prepetition priority claims.** Enter the total amount, divided by 60, of all priority claims, such as priority tax, child support and alimony claims, for which you were liable at the time of your bankruptcy filing. **Do not include current obligations, such as those set out in Line 28.**	$

45	**Chapter 13 administrative expenses.** If you are eligible to file a case under chapter 13, complete the following chart, multiply the amount in line a by the amount in line b, and enter the resulting administrative expense.		
	a.	Projected average monthly chapter 13 plan payment.	$
	b.	Current multiplier for your district as determined under schedules issued by the Executive Office for United States Trustees. (This information is available at www.usdoj.gov/ust/ or from the clerk of the bankruptcy court.)	x
	c.	Average monthly administrative expense of chapter 13 case	Total: Multiply Lines a and b	$

46	**Total Deductions for Debt Payment.** Enter the total of Lines 42 through 45.	$

	Subpart D: Total Deductions from Income	
47	**Total of all deductions allowed under § 707(b)(2).** Enter the total of Lines 33, 41, and 46.	$

Part VI. DETERMINATION OF § 707(b)(2) PRESUMPTION

48	**Enter the amount from Line 18 (Current monthly income for § 707(b)(2))**	$
49	**Enter the amount from Line 47 (Total of all deductions allowed under § 707(b)(2))**	$
50	**Monthly disposable income under § 707(b)(2).** Subtract Line 49 from Line 48 and enter the result	$
51	**60-month disposable income under § 707(b)(2).** Multiply the amount in Line 50 by the number 60 and enter the result.	$

Initial presumption determination. Check the applicable box and proceed as directed.

| 52 | ☐ **The amount on Line 51 is less than $6,575** Check the box for "The presumption does not arise" at the top of page 1 of this statement, and complete the verification in Part VIII. Do not complete the remainder of Part VI.

☐ **The amount set forth on Line 51 is more than $10,950.** Check the box for "The presumption arises" at the top of page 1 of this statement, and complete the verification in Part VIII. You may also complete Part VII. Do not complete the remainder of Part VI.

☐ **The amount on Line 51 is at least $6,575, but not more than $10,950.** Complete the remainder of Part VI (Lines 53 through 55). |

53	**Enter the amount of your total non-priority unsecured debt**	$
54	**Threshold debt payment amount.** Multiply the amount in Line 53 by the number 0.25 and enter the result.	$

Secondary presumption determination. Check the applicable box and proceed as directed.

| 55 | ☐ **The amount on Line 51 is less than the amount on Line 54.** Check the box for "The presumption does not arise" at the top of page 1 of this statement, and complete the verification in Part VIII.

☐ **The amount on Line 51 is equal to or greater than the amount on Line 54.** Check the box for "The presumption arises" at the top of page 1 of this statement, and complete the verification in Part VIII. You may also complete Part VII. |

Part VII: ADDITIONAL EXPENSE CLAIMS

| 56 | **Other Expenses.** List and describe any monthly expenses, not otherwise stated in this form, that are required for the health and welfare of you and your family and that you contend should be an additional deduction from your current monthly income under § 707(b)(2)(A)(ii)(I). If necessary, list additional sources on a separate page. All figures should reflect your average monthly expense for each item. Total the expenses. |

	Expense Description	Monthly Amount
a.		$
b.		$
c.		$
	Total: Add Lines a, b and c	$

Part VIII: VERIFICATION

| 57 | I declare under penalty of perjury that the information provided in this statement is true and correct. *(If this is a joint case, both debtors must sign.)*

Date: _____   Signature: _____
                                                    (Debtor)

Date: _____   Signature: _____
                                                    (Joint Debtor, if any) |

In re _____
　　　　　　　Debtor(s)

Case Number: _____
　　　　　　(If known)

According to the calculations required by this statement:
☐ **The applicable commitment period is 3 years.**
☐ **The applicable commitment period is 5 years.**
☐ **Disposable income is determined under § 1325(b)(3).**
☐ **Disposable income is not determined under § 1325(b)(3).**
(Check the boxes as directed in Lines 17 and 23 of this statement.)

CHAPTER 13 STATEMENT OF CURRENT MONTHLY INCOME
AND CALCULATION OF COMMITMENT PERIOD AND DISPOSABLE INCOME

In addition to Schedules I and J, this statement must be completed by every individual chapter 13 debtor, whether or not filing jointly. Joint debtors may complete one statement only.

	Part I. REPORT OF INCOME		
1	**Marital/filing status.** Check the box that applies and complete the balance of this part of this statement as directed. a. ☐ Unmarried. **Complete only Column A ("Debtor's Income") for Lines 2-10.** b. ☐ Married. **Complete both Column A ("Debtor's Income") and Column B ("Spouse's Income") for Lines 2-10.**		
	All figures must reflect average monthly income received from all sources, derived during the six calendar months prior to filing the bankruptcy case, ending on the last day of the month before the filing. If the amount of monthly income varied during the six months, you must divide the six-month total by six, and enter the result on the appropriate line.	**Column A** **Debtor's** **Income**	**Column B** **Spouse's** **Income**
2	**Gross wages, salary, tips, bonuses, overtime, commissions.**	$	$
3	**Income from the operation of a business, profession, or farm.** Subtract Line b from Line a and enter the difference in the appropriate column(s) of Line 3. If you operate more than one business, profession or farm, enter aggregate numbers and provide details on an attachment. Do not enter a number less than zero. **Do not include any part of the business expenses entered on Line b as a deduction in Part IV.** a. Gross receipts — $ b. Ordinary and necessary business expenses — $ c. Business income — Subtract Line b from Line a	$	$
4	**Rent and other real property income.** Subtract Line b from Line a and enter the difference in the appropriate column(s) of Line 4. Do not enter a number less than zero. **Do not include any part of the operating expenses entered on Line b as a deduction in Part IV.** a. Gross receipts — $ b. Ordinary and necessary operating expenses — $ c. Rent and other real property income — Subtract Line b from Line a	$	$
5	**Interest, dividends, and royalties.**	$	$
6	**Pension and retirement income.**	$	$
7	**Any amounts paid by another person or entity, on a regular basis, for the household expenses of the debtor or the debtor's dependents, including child support paid for that purpose.** Do not include alimony or separate maintenance payments or amounts paid by the debtor's spouse.	$	$
8	**Unemployment compensation.** Enter the amount in the appropriate column(s) of Line 8. However, if you contend that unemployment compensation received by you or your spouse was a benefit under the Social Security Act, do not list the amount of such compensation in Column A or B, but instead state the amount in the space below: Unemployment compensation claimed to be a benefit under the Social Security Act — Debtor $ _____ Spouse $ _____	$	$

In re _____
                 Debtor(s)

Case Number: _____
                 (If known)

According to the calculations required by this statement:
☐ **The applicable commitment period is 3 years.**
☐ **The applicable commitment period is 5 years.**
☐ **Disposable income is determined under § 1325(b)(3).**
☐ **Disposable income is not determined under § 1325(b)(3).**
(Check the boxes as directed in Lines 17 and 23 of this statement.)

CHAPTER 13 STATEMENT OF CURRENT MONTHLY INCOME
AND CALCULATION OF COMMITMENT PERIOD AND DISPOSABLE INCOME

In addition to Schedules I and J, this statement must be completed by every individual chapter 13 debtor, whether or not filing jointly. Joint debtors may complete one statement only.

	Part I. REPORT OF INCOME		
1	**Marital/filing status.** Check the box that applies and complete the balance of this part of this statement as directed. a. ☐ Unmarried. **Complete only Column A ("Debtor's Income") for Lines 2-10.** b. ☐ Married. **Complete both Column A ("Debtor's Income") and Column B ("Spouse's Income") for Lines 2-10.**		
	All figures must reflect average monthly income received from all sources, derived during the six calendar months prior to filing the bankruptcy case, ending on the last day of the month before the filing. If the amount of monthly income varied during the six months, you must divide the six-month total by six, and enter the result on the appropriate line.	**Column A** **Debtor's** **Income**	**Column B** **Spouse's** **Income**
2	**Gross wages, salary, tips, bonuses, overtime, commissions.**	$	$
3	**Income from the operation of a business, profession, or farm.** Subtract Line b from Line a and enter the difference in the appropriate column(s) of Line 3. If you operate more than one business, profession or farm, enter aggregate numbers and provide details on an attachment. Do not enter a number less than zero. **Do not include any part of the business expenses entered on Line b as a deduction in Part IV.** a. Gross receipts $ b. Ordinary and necessary business expenses $ c. Business income Subtract Line b from Line a	$	$
4	**Rent and other real property income.** Subtract Line b from Line a and enter the difference in the appropriate column(s) of Line 4. Do not enter a number less than zero. **Do not include any part of the operating expenses entered on Line b as a deduction in Part IV.** a. Gross receipts $ b. Ordinary and necessary operating expenses $ c. Rent and other real property income Subtract Line b from Line a	$	$
5	**Interest, dividends, and royalties.**	$	$
6	**Pension and retirement income.**	$	$
7	**Any amounts paid by another person or entity, on a regular basis, for the household expenses of the debtor or the debtor's dependents, including child support paid for that purpose.** Do not include alimony or separate maintenance payments or amounts paid by the debtor's spouse.	$	$
8	**Unemployment compensation.** Enter the amount in the appropriate column(s) of Line 8. However, if you contend that unemployment compensation received by you or your spouse was a benefit under the Social Security Act, do not list the amount of such compensation in Column A or B, but instead state the amount in the space below: Unemployment compensation claimed to be a benefit under the Social Security Act Debtor $ _____ Spouse $ _____	$	$

9	**Income from all other sources.** Specify source and amount. If necessary, list additional sources on a separate page. Total and enter on Line 9. **Do not include alimony or separate maintenance payments paid by your spouse, but include all other payments of alimony or separate maintenance. Do not include** any benefits received under the Social Security Act or payments received as a victim of a war crime, crime against humanity, or as a victim of international or domestic terrorism.		
	a. $	$	$
	b. $		
10	**Subtotal.** Add Lines 2 thru 9 in Column A, and, if Column B is completed, add Lines 2 through 9 in Column B. Enter the total(s).	$	$
11	**Total.** If Column B has been completed, add Line 10, Column A to Line 10, Column B, and enter the total. If Column B has not been completed, enter the amount from Line 10, Column A.	$	

Part II. CALCULATION OF § 1325(b)(4) COMMITMENT PERIOD

12	**Enter the amount from Line 11.**	$
13	**Marital adjustment.** If you are married, but are not filing jointly with your spouse, AND if you contend that calculation of the commitment period under § 1325(b)(4) does not require inclusion of the income of your spouse, enter on Line 13 the amount of the income listed in Line 10, Column B that was NOT paid on a regular basis for the household expenses of you or your dependents and specify, in the lines below, the basis for excluding this income (such as payment of the spouse's tax liability or the spouse's support of persons other than the debtor or the debtor's dependents) and the amount of income devoted to each purpose. If necessary, list additional adjustments on a separate page. If the conditions for entering this adjustment do not apply, enter zero. a. $ b. $ c. $ Total and enter on Line 13.	$
14	**Subtract Line 13 from Line 12 and enter the result.**	$
15	**Annualized current monthly income for § 1325(b)(4).** Multiply the amount from Line 14 by the number 12 and enter the result.	$
16	**Applicable median family income.** Enter the median family income for applicable state and household size. (This information is available by family size at www.usdoj.gov/ust/ or from the clerk of the bankruptcy court.) a. Enter debtor's state of residence: _____ b. Enter debtor's household size: _____	$
17	**Application of § 1325(b)(4).** Check the applicable box and proceed as directed. ☐ **The amount on Line 15 is less than the amount on Line 16.** Check the box for "The applicable commitment period is 3 years" at the top of page 1 of this statement and continue with this statement. ☐ **The amount on Line 15 is not less than the amount on Line 16.** Check the box for "The applicable commitment period is 5 years" at the top of page 1 of this statement and continue with this statement.	

Part III. APPLICATION OF § 1325(b)(3) FOR DETERMINING DISPOSABLE INCOME

18	**Enter the amount from Line 11.**	$

19	**Marital adjustment.** If you are married, but are not filing jointly with your spouse, enter on Line 19 the total of any income listed in Line 10, Column B that was NOT paid on a regular basis for the household expenses of the debtor or the debtor's dependents. Specify in the lines below the basis for excluding the Column B income (such as payment of the spouse's tax liability or the spouse's support of persons other than the debtor or the debtor's dependents) and the amount of income devoted to each purpose. If necessary, list additional adjustments on a separate page. If the conditions for entering this adjustment do not apply, enter zero.	

	a.		$
	b.		$
	c.		$

Total and enter on Line 19. $

20	**Current monthly income for § 1325(b)(3).** Subtract Line 19 from Line 18 and enter the result.	
21	**Annualized current monthly income for § 1325(b)(3).** Multiply the amount from Line 20 by the number 12 and enter the result.	$
22	**Applicable median family income.** Enter the amount from Line 16.	$
23	**Application of § 1325(b)(3).** Check the applicable box and proceed as directed. ☐ **The amount on Line 21 is more than the amount on Line 22.** Check the box for "Disposable income is determined under § 1325(b)(3)" at the top of page 1 of this statement and complete the remaining parts of this statement. ☐ **The amount on Line 21 is not more than the amount on Line 22.** Check the box for "Disposable income is not determined under § 1325(b)(3)" at the top of page 1 of this statement and complete Part VII of this statement. **Do not complete Parts IV, V, or VI.**	

Part IV. CALCULATION OF DEDUCTIONS FROM INCOME

Subpart A: Deductions under Standards of the Internal Revenue Service (IRS)

24A	**National Standards: food, apparel and services, housekeeping supplies, personal care, and miscellaneous.** Enter in Line 24A the "Total" amount from IRS National Standards for Allowable Living Expenses for the applicable household size. (This information is available at www.usdoj.gov/ust/ or from the clerk of the bankruptcy court.)	$

24B	**National Standards: health care.** Enter in Line a1 below the amount from IRS National Standards for Out-of-Pocket Health Care for persons under 65 years of age, and in Line a2 the IRS National Standards for Out-of-Pocket Health Care for persons 65 years of age or older. (This information is available at www.usdoj.gov/ust/ or from the clerk of the bankruptcy court.) Enter in Line b1 the number of members of your household who are under 65 years of age, and enter in Line b2 the number of members of your household who are 65 years of age or older. (The total number of household members must be the same as the number stated in Line 16b.) Multiply Line a1 by Line b1 to obtain a total amount for household members under 65, and enter the result in Line c1. Multiply Line a2 by Line b2 to obtain a total amount for household members 65 and older, and enter the result in Line c2. Add Lines c1 and c2 to obtain a total health care amount, and enter the result in Line 24B.	

Household members under 65 years of age			Household members 65 years of age or older			
a1.	Allowance per member		a2.	Allowance per member		
b1.	Number of members		b2.	Number of members		
c1.	Subtotal		c2.	Subtotal		$

25A	**Local Standards: housing and utilities; non-mortgage expenses.** Enter the amount of the IRS Housing and Utilities Standards; non-mortgage expenses for the applicable county and household size. (This information is available at www.usdoj.gov/ust/ or from the clerk of the bankruptcy court).	$

25B	**Local Standards: housing and utilities; mortgage/rent expense.** Enter, in Line a below, the amount of the IRS Housing and Utilities Standards; mortgage/rent expense for your county and household size (this information is available at www.usdoj.gov/ust/ or from the clerk of the bankruptcy court); enter on Line b the total of the Average Monthly Payments for any debts secured by your home, as stated in Line 47; subtract Line b from Line a and enter the result in Line 25B. **Do not enter an amount less than zero.**			
	a.	IRS Housing and Utilities Standards; mortgage/rent expense	$	
	b.	Average Monthly Payment for any debts secured by your home, if any, as stated in Line 47	$	
	c.	Net mortgage/rental expense	Subtract Line b from Line a.	$

26	**Local Standards: housing and utilities; adjustment.** If you contend that the process set out in Lines 25A and 25B does not accurately compute the allowance to which you are entitled under the IRS Housing and Utilities Standards, enter any additional amount to which you contend you are entitled, and state the basis for your contention in the space below: _____ _____ _____	$

27A	**Local Standards: transportation; vehicle operation/public transportation expense.** You are entitled to an expense allowance in this category regardless of whether you pay the expenses of operating a vehicle and regardless of whether you use public transportation. Check the number of vehicles for which you pay the operating expenses or for which the operating expenses are included as a contribution to your household expenses in Line 7. ☐ 0 ☐ 1 ☐ 2 or more. If you checked 0, enter on Line 27A the "Public Transportation" amount from IRS Local Standards: Transportation. If you checked 1 or 2 or more, enter on Line 27A the "Operating Costs" amount from IRS Local Standards: Transportation for the applicable number of vehicles in the applicable Metropolitan Statistical Area or Census Region. (These amounts are available at www.usdoj.gov/ust/ or from the clerk of the bankruptcy court.)	$

27B	**Local Standards: transportation; additional public transportation expense.** If you pay the operating expenses for a vehicle and also use public transportation, and you contend that you are entitled to an additional deduction for your public transportation expenses, enter on Line 27B the "Public Transportation" amount from IRS Local Standards: Transportation. (This amount is available at www.usdoj.gov/ust/ or from the clerk of the bankruptcy court.)	$

28	**Local Standards: transportation ownership/lease expense; Vehicle 1.** Check the number of vehicles for which you claim an ownership/lease expense. (You may not claim an ownership/lease expense for more than two vehicles.) ☐ 1 ☐ 2 or more. Enter, in Line a below, the "Ownership Costs" for "One Car" from the IRS Local Standards: Transportation (available at www.usdoj.gov/ust/ or from the clerk of the bankruptcy court); enter in Line b the total of the Average Monthly Payments for any debts secured by Vehicle 1, as stated in Line 47; subtract Line b from Line a and enter the result in Line 28. **Do not enter an amount less than zero.**			
	a.	IRS Transportation Standards, Ownership Costs	$	
	b.	Average Monthly Payment for any debts secured by Vehicle 1, as stated in Line 47	$	
	c.	Net ownership/lease expense for Vehicle 1	Subtract Line b from Line a.	$

29	**Local Standards: transportation ownership/lease expense; Vehicle 2.** Complete this Line only if you checked the "2 or more" Box in Line 28. Enter, in Line a below, the "Ownership Costs" for "One Car" from the IRS Local Standards: Transportation (available at www.usdoj.gov/ust/ or from the clerk of the bankruptcy court); enter in Line b the total of the Average Monthly Payments for any debts secured by Vehicle 2, as stated in Line 47; subtract Line b from Line a and enter the result in Line 29. **Do not enter an amount less than zero.**	

	a.	IRS Transportation Standards, Ownership Costs	$	
	b.	Average Monthly Payment for any debts secured by Vehicle 2, as stated in Line 47	$	
	c.	Net ownership/lease expense for Vehicle 2	Subtract Line b from Line a.	$

30	**Other Necessary Expenses: taxes.** Enter the total average monthly expense that you actually incur for all federal, state, and local taxes, other than real estate and sales taxes, such as income taxes, self-employment taxes, social-security taxes, and Medicare taxes. **Do not include real estate or sales taxes.**	$
31	**Other Necessary Expenses: involuntary deductions for employment.** Enter the total average monthly deductions that are required for your employment, such as mandatory retirement contributions, union dues, and uniform costs. **Do not include discretionary amounts, such as voluntary 401(k) contributions.**	$
32	**Other Necessary Expenses: life insurance.** Enter total average monthly premiums that you actually pay for term life insurance for yourself. **Do not include premiums for insurance on your dependents, for whole life or for any other form of insurance.**	$
33	**Other Necessary Expenses: court-ordered payments.** Enter the total monthly amount that you are required to pay pursuant to the order of a court or administrative agency, such as spousal or child support payments. **Do not include payments on past due obligations included in Line 49.**	$
34	**Other Necessary Expenses: education for employment or for a physically or mentally challenged child.** Enter the total average monthly amount that you actually expend for education that is a condition of employment and for education that is required for a physically or mentally challenged dependent child for whom no public education providing similar services is available.	$
35	**Other Necessary Expenses: childcare.** Enter the total average monthly amount that you actually expend on childcare—such as baby-sitting, day care, nursery and preschool. **Do not include other educational payments.**	$
36	**Other Necessary Expenses: health care.** Enter the total average monthly amount that you actually expend on health care that is required for the health and welfare of yourself or your dependents, that is not reimbursed by insurance or paid by a health savings account, and that is in excess of the amount entered in Line 24B. **Do not include payments for health insurance or health savings accounts listed in Line 39.**	$
37	**Other Necessary Expenses: telecommunication services.** Enter the total average monthly amount that you actually pay for telecommunication services other than your basic home telephone and cell phone service—such as pagers, call waiting, caller id, special long distance, or internet service—to the extent necessary for your health and welfare or that of your dependents. **Do not include any amount previously deducted.**	$
38	**Total Expenses Allowed under IRS Standards.** Enter the total of Lines 24 through 37.	$

Subpart B: Additional Living Expense Deductions
Note: Do not include any expenses that you have listed in Lines 24-37

39	**Health Insurance, Disability Insurance, and Health Savings Account Expenses.** List the monthly expenses in the categories set out in lines a-c below that are reasonably necessary for yourself, your spouse, or your dependents.

a.	Health Insurance	$
b.	Disability Insurance	$
c.	Health Savings Account	$

Total and enter on Line 39 $

If you do not actually expend this total amount, state your actual total average monthly expenditures in the space below:

$ _____

40	**Continued contributions to the care of household or family members.** Enter the total average actual monthly expenses that you will continue to pay for the reasonable and necessary care and support of an elderly, chronically ill, or disabled member of your household or member of your immediate family who is unable to pay for such expenses. **Do not include payments listed in Line 34.**	$
41	**Protection against family violence.** Enter the total average reasonably necessary monthly expenses that you actually incur to maintain the safety of your family under the Family Violence Prevention and Services Act or other applicable federal law. The nature of these expenses is required to be kept confidential by the court.	$
42	**Home energy costs.** Enter the total average monthly amount, in excess of the allowance specified by IRS Local Standards for Housing and Utilities, that you actually expend for home energy costs. **You must provide your case trustee with documentation of your actual expenses, and you must demonstrate that the additional amount claimed is reasonable and necessary.**	$
43	**Education expenses for dependent children under 18.** Enter the total average monthly expenses that you actually incur, not to exceed $137.50 per child, for attendance at a private or public elementary or secondary school by your dependent children less than 18 years of age. **You must provide your case trustee with documentation of your actual expenses, and you must explain why the amount claimed is reasonable and necessary and not already accounted for in the IRS Standards.**	$
44	**Additional food and clothing expense.** Enter the total average monthly amount by which your food and clothing expenses exceed the combined allowances for food and clothing (apparel and services) in the IRS National Standards, not to exceed 5% of those combined allowances. (This information is available at www.usdoj.gov/ust/ or from the clerk of the bankruptcy court.) **You must demonstrate that the additional amount claimed is reasonable and necessary.**	$
45	**Charitable contributions.** Enter the amount reasonably necessary for you to expend each month on charitable contributions in the form of cash or financial instruments to a charitable organization as defined in 26 U.S.C. § 170(c)(1)-(2). **Do not include any amount in excess of 15% of your gross monthly income.**	$
46	**Total Additional Expense Deductions under § 707(b).** Enter the total of Lines 39 through 45.	$

Subpart C: Deductions for Debt Payment

47	**Future payments on secured claims.** For each of your debts that is secured by an interest in property that you own, list the name of the creditor, identify the property securing the debt, state the Average Monthly Payment, and check whether the payment includes taxes or insurance. The Average Monthly Payment is the total of all amounts scheduled as contractually due to each Secured Creditor in the 60 months following the filing of the bankruptcy case, divided by 60. If necessary, list additional entries on a separate page. Enter the total of the Average Monthly Payments on Line 47.

	Name of Creditor	Property Securing the Debt	Average Monthly Payment	Does payment include taxes or insurance?
a.			$	☐ yes ☐ no
b.			$	☐ yes ☐ no
c.			$	☐ yes ☐ no
			Total: Add Lines a, b, and c	$

48	**Other payments on secured claims.** If any of debts listed in Line 47 are secured by your primary residence, a motor vehicle, or other property necessary for your support or the support of your dependents, you may include in your deduction 1/60th of any amount (the "cure amount") that you must pay the creditor in addition to the payments listed in Line 47, in order to maintain possession of the property. The cure amount would include any sums in default that must be paid in order to avoid repossession or foreclosure. List and total any such amounts in the following chart. If necessary, list additional entries on a separate page.	

	Name of Creditor	Property Securing the Debt	1/60th of the Cure Amount
a.			$
b.			$
c.			$
			Total: Add Lines a, b, and c

		$
49	**Payments on prepetition priority claims.** Enter the total amount, divided by 60, of all priority claims, such as priority tax, child support and alimony claims, for which you were liable at the time of your bankruptcy filing. **Do not include current obligations, such as those set out in Line 33.**	$
50	**Chapter 13 administrative expenses.** Multiply the amount in Line a by the amount in Line b, and enter the resulting administrative expense.	

a.	Projected average monthly chapter 13 plan payment.	$
b.	Current multiplier for your district as determined under schedules issued by the Executive Office for United States Trustees. (This information is available at www.usdoj.gov/ust/ or from the clerk of the bankruptcy court.)	x
c.	Average monthly administrative expense of chapter 13 case	Total: Multiply Lines a and b

		$
51	**Total Deductions for Debt Payment.** Enter the total of Lines 47 through 50.	$

Subpart D: Total Deductions from Income

52	**Total of all deductions from income.** Enter the total of Lines 38, 46, and 51.	$

Part V. DETERMINATION OF DISPOSABLE INCOME UNDER § 1325(b)(2)

53	**Total current monthly income.** Enter the amount from Line 20.	$
54	**Support income.** Enter the monthly average of any child support payments, foster care payments, or disability payments for a dependent child, reported in Part I, that you received in accordance with applicable nonbankruptcy law, to the extent reasonably necessary to be expended for such child.	$
55	**Qualified retirement deductions.** Enter the monthly total of (a) all amounts withheld by your employer from wages as contributions for qualified retirement plans, as specified in § 541(b)(7) and (b) all required repayments of loans from retirement plans, as specified in § 362(b)(19).	$
56	**Total of all deductions allowed under § 707(b)(2).** Enter the amount from Line 52.	$

57	**Deduction for special circumstances.** If there are special circumstances that justify additional expenses for which there is no reasonable alternative, describe the special circumstances and the resulting expenses in lines a-c below. If necessary, list additional entries on a separate page. Total the expenses and enter the total in Line 57. **You must provide your case trustee with documentation of these expenses and you must provide a detailed explanation of the special circumstances that make such expenses necessary and reasonable.**	

	Nature of special circumstances	Amount of expense
a.		$
b.		$
c.		$
		Total: Add Lines a, b, and c	$

58	**Total adjustments to determine disposable income.** Add the amounts on Lines 54, 55, 56, and 57 and enter the result.	$

59	**Monthly Disposable Income Under § 1325(b)(2).** Subtract Line 58 from Line 53 and enter the result.	$

Part VI: ADDITIONAL EXPENSE CLAIMS

60	**Other Expenses.** List and describe any monthly expenses, not otherwise stated in this form, that are required for the health and welfare of you and your family and that you contend should be an additional deduction from your current monthly income under § 707(b)(2)(A)(ii)(I). If necessary, list additional sources on a separate page. All figures should reflect your average monthly expense for each item. Total the expenses.

	Expense Description	Monthly Amount
a.		$
b.		$
c.		$
	Total: Add Lines a, b, and c	$

Part VII: VERIFICATION

61	I declare under penalty of perjury that the information provided in this statement is true and correct. *(If this is a joint case, both debtors must sign.)*

Date: _____   Signature: _____
                                                                    (Debtor)

Date: _____   Signature: _____
                                                            (Joint Debtor, if any)

United States Bankruptcy Court

In re _____,   Case No. _____
                        Debtor

                                                Chapter _____

DEBTOR'S CERTIFICATION OF COMPLETION OF POSTPETITION INSTRUCTIONAL
COURSE CONCERNING PERSONAL FINANCIAL MANAGEMENT

Every individual debtor in a chapter 7, chapter 11 in which § 1141(d)(3) applies, or chapter 13 case must file this certification. If a joint petition is filed, each spouse must complete and file a separate certification. Complete one of the following statements and file by the deadline stated below:

☐ I, _____, the debtor in the above-styled case, hereby
        (Printed Name of Debtor)
certify that on _____ (Date), I completed an instructional course in personal financial management
provided by _____, an approved personal financial
                       (Name of Provider)
management provider.

Certificate No. (if any): _____.

☐ I, _____, the debtor in the above-styled case, hereby
        (Printed Name of Debtor)
certify that no personal financial management course is required because of *[Check the appropriate box.]*:
    ☐ Incapacity or disability, as defined in 11 U.S.C. § 109(h);
    ☐ Active military duty in a military combat zone; or
    ☐ Residence in a district in which the United States trustee (or bankruptcy administrator) has determined that
the approved instructional courses are not adequate at this time to serve the additional individuals who would otherwise
be required to complete such courses.

Signature of Debtor: _____

Date: _____

Instructions: Use this form only to certify whether you completed a course in personal financial management. (Fed. R. Bankr. P. 1007(b)(7).) Do NOT use this form to file the certificate given to you by your prepetition credit counseling provider and do NOT include with the petition when filing your case.

Filing Deadlines: In a chapter 7 case, file within 45 days of the first date set for the meeting of creditors under § 341 of the Bankruptcy Code. In a chapter 11 or 13 case, file no later than the last payment made by the debtor as required by the plan or the filing of a motion for entry of a discharge under § 1328(b) of the Code. (See Fed. R. Bankr. P. 1007(c).)

UNITED STATES BANKRUPTCY COURT

NOTICE TO INDIVIDUAL CONSUMER DEBTOR UNDER § 342(b)
OF THE BANKRUPTCY CODE

In accordance with § 342(b) of the Bankruptcy Code, this notice: (1) Describes briefly the services available from credit counseling services; (2) Describes briefly the purposes, benefits and costs of the four types of bankruptcy proceedings you may commence; and (3) Informs you about bankruptcy crimes and notifies you that the Attorney General may examine all information you supply in connection with a bankruptcy case. You are cautioned that bankruptcy law is complicated and not easily described. Thus, you may wish to seek the advice of an attorney to learn of your rights and responsibilities should you decide to file a petition. Court employees cannot give you legal advice.

1. Services Available from Credit Counseling Agencies

With limited exceptions, § 109(h) of the Bankruptcy Code requires that all individual debtors who file for bankruptcy relief on or after October 17, 2005, receive a briefing that outlines the available opportunities for credit counseling and provides assistance in performing a budget analysis. The briefing must be given within 180 days **before** the bankruptcy filing. The briefing may be provided individually or in a group (including briefings conducted by telephone or on the Internet) and must be provided by a nonprofit budget and credit counseling agency approved by the United States trustee or bankruptcy administrator. The clerk of the bankruptcy court has a list that you may consult of the approved budget and credit counseling agencies.

In addition, after filing a bankruptcy case, an individual debtor generally must complete a financial management instructional course before he or she can receive a discharge. The clerk also has a list of approved financial management instructional courses.

2. The Four Chapters of the Bankruptcy Code Available to Individual Consumer Debtors

Chapter 7: Liquidation ($245 filing fee, $39 administrative fee, $15 trustee surcharge: Total fee $299)
1. Chapter 7 is designed for debtors in financial difficulty who do not have the ability to pay their existing debts. Debtors whose debts are primarily consumer debts are subject to a "means test" designed to determine whether the case should be permitted to proceed under chapter 7. If your income is greater than the median income for your state of residence and family size, in some cases, creditors have the right to file a motion requesting that the court dismiss your case under § 707(b) of the Code. It is up to the court to decide whether the case should be dismissed.
2. Under chapter 7, you may claim certain of your property as exempt under governing law. A trustee may have the right to take possession of and sell the remaining property that is not exempt and use the sale proceeds to pay your creditors.
3. The purpose of filing a chapter 7 case is to obtain a discharge of your existing debts. If, however, you are found to have committed certain kinds of improper conduct described in the Bankruptcy Code, the court may deny your discharge and, if it does, the purpose for which you filed the bankruptcy petition will be defeated.
4. Even if you receive a general discharge, some particular debts are not discharged under the law. Therefore, you may still be responsible for most taxes and student loans; debts incurred to pay nondischargeable taxes; domestic support and property settlement obligations; most fines, penalties, forfeitures, and criminal restitution obligations; certain debts which are not properly listed in your bankruptcy papers; and debts for death or personal injury caused by operating a motor vehicle, vessel, or aircraft while intoxicated from alcohol or drugs. Also, if a creditor can prove that a debt arose from fraud, breach of fiduciary duty, or theft, or from a willful and malicious injury, the bankruptcy court may determine that the debt is not discharged.

Chapter 13: Repayment of All or Part of the Debts of an Individual with Regular Income ($235 filing fee, $39 administrative fee: Total fee $274)
1. Chapter 13 is designed for individuals with regular income who would like to pay all or part of their debts in installments over a period of time. You are only eligible for chapter 13 if your debts do not exceed certain dollar amounts set forth in the Bankruptcy Code.

2. Under chapter 13, you must file with the court a plan to repay your creditors all or part of the money that you owe them, using your future earnings. The period allowed by the court to repay your debts may be three years or five years, depending upon your income and other factors. The court must approve your plan before it can take effect.

3. After completing the payments under your plan, your debts are generally discharged except for domestic support obligations; most student loans; certain taxes; most criminal fines and restitution obligations; certain debts which are not properly listed in your bankruptcy papers; certain debts for acts that caused death or personal injury; and certain long term secured obligations.

Chapter 11: Reorganization ($1000 filing fee, $39 administrative fee: Total fee $1039)

Chapter 11 is designed for the reorganization of a business but is also available to consumer debtors. Its provisions are quite complicated, and any decision by an individual to file a chapter 11 petition should be reviewed with an attorney.

Chapter 12: Family Farmer or Fisherman ($200 filing fee, $39 administrative fee: Total fee $239)

Chapter 12 is designed to permit family farmers and fishermen to repay their debts over a period of time from future earnings and is similar to chapter 13. The eligibility requirements are restrictive, limiting its use to those whose income arises primarily from a family-owned farm or commercial fishing operation.

3. Bankruptcy Crimes and Availability of Bankruptcy Papers to Law Enforcement Officials

A person who knowingly and fraudulently conceals assets or makes a false oath or statement under penalty of perjury, either orally or in writing, in connection with a bankruptcy case is subject to a fine, imprisonment, or both. All information supplied by a debtor in connection with a bankruptcy case is subject to examination by the Attorney General acting through the Office of the United States Trustee, the Office of the United States Attorney, and other components and employees of the Department of Justice.

WARNING: Section 521(a)(1) of the Bankruptcy Code requires that you promptly file detailed information regarding your creditors, assets, liabilities, income, expenses and general financial condition. Your bankruptcy case may be dismissed if this information is not filed with the court within the time deadlines set by the Bankruptcy Code, the Bankruptcy Rules, and the local rules of the court.

Certificate of [Non-Attorney] Bankruptcy Petition Preparer

I, the [non-attorney] bankruptcy petition preparer signing the debtor's petition, hereby certify that I delivered to the debtor this notice required by § 342(b) of the Bankruptcy Code.

_____
Printed name and title, if any, of Bankruptcy Petition Preparer

Address:

_____

X_____
Signature of Bankruptcy Petition Preparer or officer, principal, responsible person, or partner whose Social Security number is provided above.

Social Security number (If the bankruptcy petition preparer is not an individual, state the Social Security number of the officer, principal, responsible person, or partner of the bankruptcy petition preparer.) (Required by 11 U.S.C. § 110.)

Certificate of the Debtor

I (We), the debtor(s), affirm that I (we) have received and read this notice.

_____
Printed Name(s) of Debtor(s)

Case No. (if known) _____

X_____
Signature of Debtor   Date

X_____
Signature of Joint Debtor (if any)   Date

UNITED STATES BANKRUPTCY COURT

_____ DISTRICT OF _____

In re _____)
    [*Set forth here all names including married,*)
    maiden, and trade names used by debtor)
    within last 8 years.])
                                   Debtor)   Case No. _____

Address _____)

_____)   Chapter 13

Last four digits of Social Security or Individual)
Tax Payer Identification (ITIN) No(s). (if any):_____)

Employer's Tax Identification (EIN) No(s). (if any):)

_____)

AMENDMENT COVER SHEET

Presented herewith are the original and one copy of the following:

☐ Voluntary Petition (Note: Spouse may not be added or deleted subsequent to initial filing.)

☐ Schedule A—Real Property

☐ Schedule B—Personal Property

☐ Schedule C—Property Claimed as Exempt

☐ Schedule D—Creditors Holding Secured Claims

☐ Schedule E—Creditors Holding Unsecured Priority Claims

☐ Schedule F—Creditors Holding Unsecured Nonpriority Claims

☐ Schedule G—Executory Contracts and Unexpired Leases

☐ Schedule H—Codebtors

☐ Schedule I—Current Income of Individual Debtor(s)

☐ Schedule J—Current Expenditures of Individual Debtor(s)

☐ Summary of Schedules

☐ Statement of Financial Affairs

☐ I have enclosed a $26 fee because I am adding new creditors or changing addresses after the original Meeting of Creditors Notice has been sent.

_____   _____
Signature of Debtor   Signature of Debtor's Spouse

I (we) _____ and

_____ ,

the debtor(s) in this case, declare under penalty of perjury that the information set forth in the amendment attached hereto

consisting of _____ pages

is true and correct to the best of my (our) information and belief.

Dated: _____, 20_____

_____   _____
Signature of Debtor   Signature of Debtor's Spouse

Daily Expenses

Date: _____

Item	Cost
Daily Total	

Date: _____

Item	Cost
Daily Total	

Date: _____

Item	Cost
Daily Total	

Date: _____

Item	Cost
Daily Total	

UNITED STATES BANKRUPTCY COURT

_____DISTRICT OF _____

In re _____)
     [*Set forth here all names including married,*)
     maiden, and trade names used by debtor)
     within last 8 years.])
                            Debtor) Case No. _____
)
Address _____)
) Chapter 13
_____)
) Date: _____
Last four digits of Social Security or Individual)
Tax Payer Identification (ITIN) No(s). (if any):_____) Time: _____
)
Employer's Tax Identification (EIN) No(s). (if any):) Court Address: _____
_____)

NOTICE OF PLAN AMENDMENT AND CONFIRMATION HEARING DATE

TO THE HONORABLE JUDGE, THE CHAPTER 13 TRUSTEE, ALL INTERESTED PARTIES AND THEIR ATTORNEYS OF RECORD, AND THE U.S. TRUSTEE:

    PLEASE TAKE NOTICE that on the above noticed date and time, Debtor [YOUR NAME] will seek to have the amended plan attached to this notice confirmed by the honorable court. The reasons why debtor seeks modification of the previous plan filed with the court are:

☐ extension of the plan from _____ months to _____ months.

☐ acceleration of payment of secured debt arrearage owed to _____

    from _____ months to _____ months.

☐ adjustment of interest rate on secured debt or secured debt arrears owed to _____

_____ from _____ % to _____ %.

☐ adjustment in the secured portion of a debt owed to _____

_____ that is partially secured and partially unsecured.

☐ adjustment in the interest rate owed on the secured portion of a debt owed _____

_____ that is partially secured and partially unsecured.

☐ create   ☐ eliminate a subclass of unsecured creditors

☐ increase the amount creditor class(es) _____ will receive under the plan.

☐ decrease the amount creditor class(es) _____ will receive under the plan.

☐ increase the amount of adequate assurance payable to _____
_____ under the plan.

☐ other reasons: _____
_____
_____

Dated: _____

Respectfully Submitted,

_____

Signature of Debtor

UNITED STATES BANKRUPTCY COURT

_____ DISTRICT OF _____

In re _____)
     [_Set forth here all names including married,_)
     maiden, and trade names used by debtor)
     within last 8 years.])
                             Debtor)   Case No. _____
)
Address _____)
)
_____)   Chapter 13
)
Last four digits of Social Security or Individual)
Tax Payer Identification (ITIN) No(s). (if any):_____)
)
Employer's Tax Identification (EIN) No(s). (if any):)
_____)

PROOF OF SERVICE BY MAIL

I, _____ , declare that: I am a

resident or employed in the County of _____ , State of _____ .

My residence/business address is_____

_____ . I am over the age of eighteen years and not a party to this case.

On _____ , 20___ , I served the enclosed _____

_____

on the following parties by placing true and correct copies thereof enclosed in a sealed envelope with postage thereon fully

prepaid in the United States Mail at _____ , addressed as follows:

I declare under penalty of perjury that the foregoing is true and correct, and that this declaration was executed on

Date: _____ , 20___ at _____
                                           City and State

_____
Signature

UNITED STATES BANKRUPTCY COURT

_____ *[Name of district]* _____ DISTRICT OF _____ *[Your state]* _____

In re _____)
      [Set forth here all names including married,)
      maiden, and trade names used by debtor)
      within last 8 years.])
                                Debtor)   Case No. _____
)
Address _____)
)
_____)   Chapter 13
)
Last four digits of Social Security or Individual)
Tax Payer Identification (ITIN) No(s). (if any):_____)
)
Employer's Tax Identification (EIN) No(s). (if any):)
_____)

Chapter 13 Repayment Plan

Notice

This plan is proposed by the above debtor under penalty of perjury. Any creditor can object to this plan being confirmed by written notice filed with the court and served upon the debtor, the trustee, and other parties in interest not less than 8 days before the date set for the meeting of creditors. Absent a timely objection, the court may confirm this plan as drafted. The plan, and payments under the plan, will be subject to all relevant Bankruptcy Code provisions.

With certain exceptions, a confirmed plan holds the debtor and creditors to the treatment provided in the plan—even if the plan modifies rights and duties held by the debtor and creditor. The exceptions are:

a. Each creditor will retain its lien until the earlier of payment of the underlying debt determined under nonbankruptcy law or discharge under Section 1328. If the case under this chapter is dismissed or converted without completion of the plan, the holder of such lien shall retain it to the extent recognized by applicable nonbankruptcy law.

b. Defaults will be cured using the interest rate set forth below in the plan. Any ongoing obligation will be paid according to the terms of the plan.

c. Holders of secured claims and Class 1 claimants will be paid according to the plan after confirmation unless the secured creditor or Class 1 claimant files a proof of claim in a different amount than that provided in the plan.

d. If a secured creditor files a proof of claim, that creditor will be paid according to that creditor's proof of claim, unless the court orders otherwise. Holders of all other claims must timely file proofs of claims, if the code so requires, or they will not be paid any amount. A debtor who confirms a Chapter 13 plan may be eligible thereafter to receive a discharge of debts to the extent specified in 11 U.S.C. Section 1328.

Plan Payments

The debtor proposes the following Chapter 13 plan and makes the following declarations:

Monthly Amounts Paid to Trustee Under the Plan

The debtor submits the following to the supervision and control of the trustee:

A. Payments by debtor of $_____ per month for sixty (60) months. The monthly payment will begin within 30 days of the date the petition was filed.

B. The base plan amount is $_____ , which will pay _____% of the allowed claims of nonpriority unsecured creditors. If that percentage is less than 100%, the debtor will pay the plan payment stated in this plan for the full term of the plan.

C. Amounts necessary for the payment of postpetition claims allowed under 11 U.S.C. Section 1305.

D. If the plan provides for less than 100% payment of nonpriority unsecured claims, all postpetition tax refunds received by the debtor during the plan term.

E. Preconfirmation Adequate Protection Payments for any creditor who holds an allowed claim secured by personal property:

_____ .

F. Other property: _____ .

Classification and Treatment of Claims

Class 1: Allowed unsecured claims entitled to priority under 11 U.S.C. 507

The debtor will pay Class 1 allowed claims in full; except the debtor may provide for less than full payment of domestic support obligations assigned to a government agency.

Category	1. Amount of Priority Claim	2. Interest Rate If Any	3. Monthly Payment	4. Number of Months	5. Total Payment
Administrative					
1. Trustee's fee					
2. Attorney fees					
3. Ch. 7 trustee fees					
4. Other Admin.					
5. IRS					
6. State Tax					
7. Support					
8. Other					
9. Support not to be paid in full					
Totals					

Class 2: Claims secured solely by real property that is the debtor's principal residence

☐ 1. The postconfirmation monthly mortgage payment will be made by the trustee from the plan payment to: _____

_____ .

☐ 1.2. The postconfirmation monthly mortgage payment will be made by the debtor directly to: _____ .

The debtor will cure all prepetition arrearages for the primary residence through the plan payment as set forth below. If the debtor pays the cure amount while timely making all required postpetition payments, the mortgage will be reinstated according to its original terms, extinguishing any right of the mortgagee to recover any amount alleged to have arisen prior to the filing of the petition.

1. Name of Creditor	2. Last Four Digits of Loan #	3. Amount of Arrearage	4. Interest Rate	5. Monthly Payment	6. Number of Months	7. Total Payment

Class 3: Secured claims to be paid in full through the plan

1. Name of Creditor	2. Last Four Digits of Loan #	3. Amount of Claim	4. Interest Rate	5. Monthly Payment	6. Number of Months	7. Total Payment

The debtor will cure all prepetition arrearages on these claims through the plan payment as set forth below:

1. Name of Creditor	2. Last Four Digits of Loan #	3. Amount of Arrearage	4. Interest Rate	5. Monthly Payment	6. Number of Months	7. Total Payment

Class 4: Secured claims to be bifurcated under the plan

1. Name of Creditor	2. Last Four Digits of Loan #	3. Claim Total	4. Secured Claim	5. Unsecured Claim	6. Interest Rate	7. Equal Monthly Payments	8. Number of Months	9. Total Payment	10. Purchase for Debtor's Personal Use?	11. Date of Purchase	12. Purchase Money Loan?
									Y ☐ N ☐		Y ☐ N ☐

The debtor will cure all prepetition arrearages on these claims through the plan payment as set forth below:

1. Name of Creditor	2. Last Four Digits of Loan #	3. Amount of Arrearage	4. Interest Rate	5. Monthly Payment	6. Number of Months	7. Total Payment

Class 5: Secured or unsecured claims other than residential mortgages on which the last payment is due after date on which final payment under the plan is due

☐ 3. The postconfirmation monthly payment pursuant to the promissory note will be made by the trustee from the plan payment to: _____ .

☐ 3.4. The postconfirmation monthly payment pursuant to the promissory note will be made by the debtor directly to:

_____ .

The debtor will cure all prepetition arrearages on these claims through the plan payment as set forth below:

1. Name of Creditor	2. Last Four Digits of Loan #	3. Amount of Arrearage	4. Interest Rate	5. Monthly Payment	6. Number of Months	7. Total Payment

Class 6: Nonpriority unsecured claims

The debtor estimates that allowed nonpriority unsecured claims will be the sum of $_____ .

Class 6 claims will be paid as follows:

Check one box only

☐ Class 6 claims (including the unsecured claims in Class 4) are of one class and will be paid pro rata.

☐ Class 6 claims will be divided into subclasses as shown below and the creditors in each class will be paid pro rata.

Claim	Reason for Subclass	Amount

Comparison With Chapter 7

The value as of the effective date of the plan of property to be distributed under the plan on account of each allowed claim is not less than the amount that would be paid on such claim if the estate of the debtor were liquidated under Chapter 7 of the Bankruptcy Code on such date. The amount distributed to nonpriority unsecured creditors in Chapter 7 would be $_____, which is estimated to pay _____% of the scheduled nonpriority debt. The plan proposes to pay _____% of the debtor's nonpriority unsecured debt.

Plan Analysis

Total Payments Provided for Under the Plan	
Class 1 (Priority Claims)	
Class 2 Residence (current and arrearage)	
Class 3 (Secured claims paid in full)	
Class 4 (Secured claims bifurcated)	
Class 5 (Claims due beyond final payment)	
Class 6 (Nonpriority unsecured)	
Subtotal	
Trustee's Fee (10% unless otherwise)	
Total Payment	

Order of Payment

Except as otherwise provided in the plan or by court order, the Chapter 13 trustee shall disburse all available funds for the payment of claims in the following order:

First: The Chapter 13 trustee's fee up to but not more than the amount accrued on payments made to date.

Second: Any domestic support orders.

Third: Administrative expenses (including, but not limited to, attorneys' fees) in an amount up to but not more than 10% of each plan payment until paid in full.

Fourth: Ongoing payments on secured debts that are to be made by the trustee from the plan payment.

Fifth: Pro rata to all other claims except as otherwise provided in the plan.

Sixth: No payment shall be made on general unsecured claims until all secured and priority claims have been paid in full.

Other Plan Provisions

A. The debtor rejects the following executory contracts and unexpired leases: _____ .

B. The debtor assumes the executory contracts or unexpired leases set forth in this section. The debtor has a leasehold interest in personal property and will make all postpetition payments directly to the lessor(s): _____

C. In addition to the payments specified in Class _____ and Class _____, the debtor will make regular payments directly to the following: _____

D. The debtor hereby surrenders the following personal or real property (identify property and creditor to which it is surrendered):

Property	Creditor

E. Preconfirmation Adequate Protection Payments will be paid to the trustee for the following creditor(s) in the following amounts:

Creditor Name	Amount

Each adequate protection payment will commence on the 30th day from the date of filing of the case. The trustee shall deduct the foregoing adequate protection payment(s) from the debtor's plan payment and disburse the adequate protection payment to the secured creditor(s) at the next available disbursement or as soon as practicable after the payment is received and posted to the trustee's account. The trustee will take his or her statutory fee on all disbursements made for preconfirmation adequate protection payments.

F. The debtor shall incur no debt greater than $_____ unless the debt is incurred in the ordinary course of business pursuant to 11 U.S.C. Section 1304(b) or for medical emergencies.

G. The debtor will pay timely all postconfirmation tax liabilities directly to the appropriate taxing authorities as they come due.

H. The trustee is authorized to disburse funds after the date of confirmation in open court.

I. The debtor will pay all amounts required to be paid under a domestic support obligation that first became payable after the date of the filing of the petition.

Revestment of Property

Property of the estate shall not revest in the debtor until such time as a discharge is granted or the case is dismissed or closed without discharge. Revestment shall be subject to all liens and encumbrances in existence when the case was filed, except those liens avoided by court order extinguished by operation of law. In the event the case is converted to a case under Chapter 7, 11, or 12 of the Bankruptcy Code, the property of the estate shall vest in accordance with applicable law. After confirmation of the plan, the Chapter 13 trustee shall have no further authority or fiduciary duty regarding use, sale, or refinance of property of the estate except to respond to any motion for proposed use, sale, or refinance as required by the Local Bankruptcy Rules. Prior to any discharge or dismissal, the debtor must seek approval of the court to purchase, sell, or refinance real property .

Charts

Median Family Income Chart

State	Family Size				State	Family Size			
	1 Earner	2 People	3 People	4 People *		1 Earner	2 People	3 People	4 People *
Alabama	$35,190	$43,674	$49,688	$60,298	Montana	$37,889	$46,748	$52,111	$60,576
Alaska	$43,766	$66,125	$70,378	$71,781	Nebraska	$36,179	$51,231	$58,055	$68,917
Arizona	$39,811	$51,681	$58,127	$65,050	Nevada	$44,378	$56,258	$63,231	$66,095
Arkansas	$31,633	$40,604	$47,588	$52,185	New Hampshire	$50,086	$61,746	$70,722	$87,396
California	$45,518	$60,032	$64,766	$74,801	New Jersey	$54,596	$63,026	$80,999	$94,441
Colorado	$42,979	$60,577	$64,883	$75,775	New Mexico	$34,703	$47,517	$47,517	$52,034
Connecticut	$53,876	$66,972	$76,786	$93,821	New York	$43,352	$52,891	$62,882	$75,513
Delaware	$43,149	$54,105	$64,840	$78,321	North Carolina	$35,267	$47,895	$53,961	$61,420
D.C.	$38,410	$65,913	$65,913	$71,571	North Dakota	$35,718	$48,511	$59,607	$67,560
Florida	$38,927	$49,234	$55,347	$65,024	Ohio	$39,056	$48,332	$58,130	$68,579
Georgia	$38,086	$50,001	$57,254	$66,711	Oklahoma	$33,597	$44,942	$47,381	$55,031
Hawaii	$45,947	$58,555	$69,572	$84,472	Oregon	$41,284	$51,762	$58,033	$64,832
Idaho	$36,313	$46,876	$53,194	$58,066	Pennsylvania	$41,971	$49,226	$61,733	$74,072
Illinois	$43,436	$54,979	$64,763	$75,484	Rhode Island	$45,776	$58,108	$63,135	$78,189
Indiana	$38,293	$49,642	$55,917	$67,787	South Carolina	$34,211	$45,233	$51,525	$59,663
Iowa	$36,713	$49,180	$57,688	$67,792	South Dakota	$31,944	$48,051	$60,170	$63,508
Kansas	$37,525	$51,522	$56,467	$67,897	Tennessee	$35,373	$44,764	$51,860	$60,143
Kentucky	$36,070	$42,278	$50,663	$60,202	Texas	$35,280	$49,933	$52,313	$59,808
Louisiana	$33,391	$41,500	$50,785	$60,161	Utah	$44,458	$50,155	$56,671	$63,586
Maine	$37,035	$46,378	$58,225	$63,501	Vermont	$41,171	$52,137	$60,113	$67,884
Maryland	$51,141	$66,190	$78,119	$94,017	Virginia	$44,780	$59,423	$67,788	$78,413
Massachusetts	$51,176	$61,293	$75,801	$89,347	Washington	$46,700	$58,584	$66,252	$75,140
Michigan	$41,929	$50,441	$60,085	$72,591	West Virginia	$36,135	$38,505	$49,043	$55,920
Minnesota	$43,965	$58,705	$68,737	$81,477	Wisconsin	$40,378	$52,793	$63,628	$72,495
Mississippi	$29,582	$37,841	$42,380	$52,992	Wyoming	$34,946	$51,853	$58,620	$71,559
Missouri	$36,702	$47,589	$54,914	$63,274	* Add $6,900 for each individual in excess of 4.				

Bankruptcy Forms Checklist

☐ Form 1—Voluntary Petition

☐ Form 3A—(only if you are paying your filing fee in installments)

☐ Form 6, which consists of:

    ☐ Schedule A—Real Property

    ☐ Schedule B—Personal Property

    ☐ Schedule C—Property Claimed as Exempt

    ☐ Schedule D—Creditors Holding Secured Claims

    ☐ Schedule E—Creditors Holding Unsecured Priority Claims

    ☐ Schedule F—Creditors Holding Unsecured Nonpriority Claims

    ☐ Schedule G—Executory Contracts and Unexpired Leases

    ☐ Schedule H—Codebtors

    ☐ Schedule I—Current Income

    ☐ Schedule J—Current Expenditures

    ☐ Summary of Schedules A through J

    ☐ Declaration Concerning Debtor's Schedules

☐ Form 7—Statement of Financial Affairs

☐ Form 21—Full Social Security Number Disclosure

☐ Form 22C—Statement of Current Monthly Income and Disposable Income Calculation

☐ Form 201—Notice to Individual Consumer Debtor Under § 342 of the Bankruptcy Code

☐ Mailing Matrix

Bankruptcy Documents Checklist

- ☐ Your Chapter 13 repayment plan
- ☐ Required local forms, if any
- ☐ Your most recent federal tax return (or a transcript of the return obtained from the IRS)
- ☐ Proof that you've filed your tax returns for the last four years with the IRS
- ☐ Your credit counseling certificate
- ☐ Any repayment plan that was developed during your credit counseling session
- ☐ Your pay stubs for the previous 60 days (along with any accompanying local form your local court requires)

Index

CATALOG
...more from Nolo

BUSINESS	PRICE	CODE
Business Buyout Agreements (Book w/CD)	$49.99	BSAG
The California Nonprofit Corporation Kit (Binder w/CD)	$69.99	CNP
California Workers' Comp: How to Take Charge When You're Injured on the Job	$34.99	WORK
The Complete Guide to Buying a Business (Book w/CD)	$24.99	BUYBU
The Complete Guide to Selling a Business (Book w/CD)	$34.99	SELBU
Consultant & Independent Contractor Agreements (Book w/CD)	$29.99	CICA
The Corporate Records Handbook (Book w/CD)	$69.99	CORMI
Create Your Own Employee Handbook (Book w/CD)	$49.99	EMHA
Dealing With Problem Employees	$44.99	PROBM
Deduct It! Lower Your Small Business Taxes	$34.99	DEDU
Effective Fundraising for Nonprofits	$24.99	EFFN
The Employer's Legal Handbook	$39.99	EMPL
The Essential Guide to Family & Medical Leave (Book w/CD)	$39.99	FMLA
The Essential Guide to Federal Employment Laws	$39.99	FEMP
The Essential Guide to Workplace Investigations (Book w/CD)	$39.99	NVST
Every Nonprofit's Guide to Publishing (Book w/CD)	$29.99	EPNO
Form a Partnership (Book w/CD)	$39.99	PART
Form Your Own Limited Liability Company (Book w/CD)	$44.99	LIAB
Home Business Tax Deductions: Keep What You Earn	$34.99	DEHB
How to Form a Nonprofit Corporation (Book w/CD)—National Edition	$49.99	NNP
How to Form a Nonprofit Corporation in California (Book w/CD)	$49.99	NON
How to Form Your Own California Corporation (Binder w/CD)	$59.99	CACI
How to Form Your Own California Corporation (Book w/CD)	$39.99	CCOR
How to Run a Thriving Business	$19.99	THRV
How to Write a Business Plan (Book w/CD)	$34.99	SBS
Incorporate Your Business (Book w/CD)—National Edition	$49.99	NIBS
Investors in Your Backyard (Book w/CD)	$24.99	FINBUS
The Job Description Handbook (Book w/CD)	$29.99	JOB
Legal Guide for Starting & Running a Small Business	$34.99	RUNS
Legal Forms for Starting & Running a Small Business (Book w/CD)	$29.99	RUNSF
LLC or Corporation?	$24.99	CHENT
The Manager's Legal Handbook	$39.99	ELBA
Marketing Without Advertising	$20.00	MWAD
Music Law: How to Run Your Band's Business (Book w/CD)	$39.99	ML
Negotiate the Best Lease for Your Business	$24.99	LESP
Nolo's Quick LLC	$29.99	LLCQ
Patent Savvy for Managers: Spot & Protect Valuable Innovations in Your Company	$29.99	PATM
The Performance Appraisal Handbook (Book w/CD)	$29.99	PERF
The Progressive Discipline Handbook (Book w/CD)	$34.99	SDHB
Small Business in Paradise: Working for Yourself in a Place You Love	$19.99	SPAR
The Small Business Start-up Kit (Book w/CD)—National Edition	$29.99	SMBU
The Small Business Start-up Kit for California (Book w/CD)	$29.99	OPEN
Starting & Building a Nonprofit: A Practical Guide (Book w/CD)	$29.99	SNON
Starting & Running a Successful Newsletter or Magazine	$29.99	MAG
Tax Deductions for Professionals	$34.99	DEPO
Tax Savvy for Small Business	$36.99	SAVVY
The Work from Home Handbook	$19.99	US-HOM
Wow! I'm in Business	$19.99	WHOO
Working for Yourself: Law & Taxes for Independent Contractors, Freelancers & Consultants	$39.99	WAGE
Working With Independent Contractors (Book w/CD)	$29.99	HICI
Your Limited Liability Company: An Operating Manual (Book w/CD)	$49.99	LOP
Your Rights in the Workplace	$29.99	YRW

Prices subject to change.

CONSUMER

ESTATE PLANNING & PROBATE

FAMILY MATTERS

GOING TO COURT

HOMEOWNERS, LANDLORDS & TENANTS

HOMEOWNERS, LANDLORDS & TENANTS (CONTINUED)

	PRICE	CODE
Neighbor Law: Fences, Trees, Boundaries & Noise	$29.99	NEI
Nolo's Essential Guide to Buying Your First Home (Book w/CD)	$24.99	HTBH
Renters' Rights: The Basics	$24.99	RENT

IMMIGRATION

Becoming A U.S. Citizen: A Guide to the Law, Exam & Interview	$24.99	USCIT
Fiancé & Marriage Visas	$34.99	IMAR
How to Get a Green Card	$29.99	GRN
U.S. Immigration Made Easy	$39.99	IMEZ

MONEY MATTERS

101 Law Forms for Personal Use (Book w/CD)	$29.99	SPOT
The Busy Family's Guide to Money	$19.99	US-MONY
Chapter 13 Bankruptcy: Repay Your Debts	$39.99	CHB
Credit Repair (Book w/CD)	$24.99	CREP
How to File for Chapter 7 Bankruptcy	$29.99	HFB
IRAs, 401(k)s & Other Retirement Plans: Taking Your Money Out	$34.99	RET
Lower Taxes in 7 Easy Steps	$16.99	LTAX
The New Bankruptcy: Will It Work for You?	$21.99	FIBA
Nolo's Guide to Social Security Disability (Book w/CD)	$29.99	QSS
Solve Your Money Troubles	$19.99	MT
Stand Up to the IRS	$29.99	SIRS
Surviving an IRS Tax Audit	$24.95	SAUD

PATENTS & COPYRIGHTS

All I Need Is Money: How to Finance Your Invention	$19.99	FINA
The Copyright Handbook: What Every Writer Needs to Know (Book w/CD)	$39.99	COHA
Getting Permission: How to License and Clear Copyrighted Materials (Book w/CD)	$34.99	RIPER
How to Make Patent Drawings	$29.99	DRAW
The Inventor's Notebook	$24.99	INOT
Legal Guide to Web & Software Development (Book w/CD)	$44.99	SFT
Nolo's Patents for Beginners	$24.99	QPAT
Patent, Copyright & Trademark: An Intellectual Property Desk Reference	$39.99	PCTM
Patent It Yourself	$49.99	PAT
Patent Pending in 24 Hours	$34.99	PEND
Patent Savvy for Managers: Spot & Protect Valuable Innovations in Your Company	$29.99	PATM
Profit from Your Idea (Book w/CD)	$34.99	LICE
The Public Domain	$34.99	PUBL
Trademark: Legal Care for Your Business and Product Name	$39.99	TRD
What Every Inventor Needs to Know About Business & Taxes (Book w/CD)	$21.99	ILAX

RETIREMENT & SENIORS

Get a Life: You Don't Need a Million to Retire Well	$24.99	LIFE
Long-Term Care: How to Plan & Pay for It	$19.99	ELD
Retire Happy	$19.99	US-RICH
Social Security, Medicare & Goverment Pensions	$29.99	SOA
Work Less, Live More: The Way to Semi-Retirement	$17.99	RECL
The Work Less, Live More Workbook (Book w/CD)	$19.99	RECW

SOFTWARE Call or check our website at www.nolo.com for special discounts on Software!

Leasewriter Plus 2.0—Windows	$49.99	LWD2
LLC Maker—Windows	$69.99	LLP1
Patent Pending Now!—Windows	$89.99	PP1
PatentEase 6.0—Windows	$259.00	PEAS
Personal RecordKeeper 5.0—Windows	$39.99	RKD5
Quicken Legal Business Pro 2008—Windows	$79.99	SBQB8
Quicken WillMaker Plus 2008—Windows	$49.99	WQP8

Order Form

Name	
Address	
City	
State, Zip	
Daytime Phone	
E-mail	

Our "No-Hassle" Guarantee

Return anything you buy directly from Nolo for any reason and we'll cheerfully refund your purchase price. No ifs, ands or buts.

☐ Check here if you do not wish to receive mailings from other companies

Item Code	Quantity	Item	Unit Price	Total Price

Method of payment

☐ Check ☐ VISA
☐ American Express
☐ MasterCard
☐ Discover Card

Subtotal	
Add your local sales tax (California only)	
Shipping: RUSH $12, Basic $6 (See below)	
I bought 2, ship it to me FREE! (Ground shipping only)	
TOTAL	

Account Number	
Expiration Date	
Signature	

Shipping and Handling

Rush Delivery—Only $12

We'll ship any order to any street address in the U.S. by UPS 2nd Day Air* for only $12!

* Order by 9:30 AM Pacific Time and get your order in 2 business days. Orders placed after 9:30 AM Pacific Time will arrive in 3 business days. P.O. boxes and S.F. Bay Area use basic shipping. Alaska and Hawaii use 2nd Day Air or Priority Mail.

Basic Shipping—$6

Use for P.O. Boxes, Northern California and Ground Service.

Allow 1-2 weeks for delivery.

U.S. addresses only.

For faster service, use your credit card and our toll-free numbers

Call our customer service group Monday thru Friday 7am to 6 pm PST

 Phone
1-800-728-3555

 Fax
1-800-645-0895

 Mail
Nolo
950 Parker St.
Berkeley, CA 94710

Order 24 hours a day @ www.nolo.com

Get the Latest in the Law

Nolo's Legal Updater
We'll send you an email whenever a new edition of your book is published!
Sign up at **www.nolo.com/legalupdater**.

Updates at Nolo.com
Check **www.nolo.com/update** to find recent changes in the law that
affect the current edition of your book.

Nolo Customer Service
To make sure that this edition of the book is the most recent one, call us at
800-728-3555 and ask one of our friendly customer service representatives
(7:00 am to 6:00 pm PST, weekdays only). Or find out at **www.nolo.com**.

Complete the Registration & Comment Card ...
... and we'll do the work for you! Just indicate your preferences below:

Registration & Comment Card

NAME _____ DATE _____

ADDRESS _____

CITY _____ STATE _____ ZIP _____

PHONE _____ EMAIL _____

COMMENTS _____

WAS THIS BOOK EASY TO USE?   (VERY EASY)   5   4   3   2   1   (VERY DIFFICULT)

☐ Yes, you can quote me in future Nolo promotional materials. *Please include phone number above.*

☐ Yes, send me **Nolo's Legal Updater** via email when a new edition of this book is available.

Yes, I want to sign up for the following email newsletters:

    ☐ **NoloBriefs** (monthly)
    ☐ **Nolo's Special Offer** (monthly)
    ☐ **Nolo's BizBriefs** (monthly)
    ☐ **Every Landlord's Quarterly** (four times a year)

☐ Yes, you can give my contact info to carefully selected
partners whose products may be of interest to me.

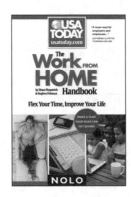